APPLIED BUSINESS LAW

13th Ed.

Norbert J. Mietus
Professor of Law and Management
College of Business
California State University
Sacramento, California

John E. Adamson
Assistant Professor of Business and Law
Finance and General Business Department
Southwest Missouri State University
Springfield, Missouri

Edward J. Conry
Associate Professor
College of Business and Administration
University of Colorado
Denver, Colorado

L87

Published by
SOUTH-WESTERN PUBLISHING CO.

CINCINNATI WEST CHICAGO, IL DALLAS LIVERMORE, CA

South-Western Publishing Co.
Cincinnati, Ohio

ISBN: 0-538-12870-4

Library of Congress Catalog Card Number: 86-62458

1 2 3 4 5 6 7 8 9 10 11 12 K 5 4 3 2 1 0 9 8 7

Printed in the United States of America

Photo Credits: Cover, © Barry Kaplan; p. 1, H. G. Ross/H. Armstrong Roberts; p. 3, © John Bird; p. 21, Glenn Cruickshank/West Stock; p. 35, H. Armstrong Roberts; p. 61, Jon L. Barkan/The Picture Cube; p. 82, © John Bird; p. 99, © John Bird; p. 101, © John Bird; p. 141, © John Bird; p. 159, Tim Carlson/Stock, Boston; p. 161, J. R. Holland/Stock, Boston; p. 180, Campbell & Boulanger/West Light; p. 197, © John Bird, p. 211, © John Bird; p. 231, Pierre Kopp/West Light; p. 252, Keith Gunnar/West Stock; p. 269, Donald Dietz/Stock, Boston; p. 285, © John Bird; p. 287, David Falconer/West Stock; p. 377, © Mark Stephenson/West Light; p. 399, © Chuck O'Rear/West Light; p. 418, © John Bird; p. 433, Jeffry Myers/West Stock; p. 451, Martin Rogers/Stock, Boston; p. 469, Cindy McIntyre/West Stock; p. 485, Paul Kotz/West Stock; p. 537, © John Bird; p. 569, Alan Carey/The Image Works; p. 585, Cary Wolinsky/Stock, Boston; p. 587, © John Bird; p. 603, © Chuck O'Rear/West Light; p. 627, Comstock, Inc./ Tom Musto; p. 642, © John Bird; p. 671, Bob Peterson/West Stock; p. 693, Courtesy of the Proctor & Gamble Company

PREFACE TO TEACHERS

We are confident that you will find this thirteenth edition of APPLIED BUSINESS LAW, with its supplementary teaching aids, to be the most comprehensive and most effective instructional package in the field. Because of its profound impact on how people live, and on how business produces and distributes goods and services, the law has a fascination that few subjects approach. We know that you will be pleased by the genuine enjoyment of your students as they learn about concepts and rules that will be useful to them for the rest of their lives.

Various principles of the science and art of pedagogy have been carefully incorporated here in a comprehensive learning system. The textbook is printed in full color for added appeal and heightened realism: interest and concentration are enhanced when reading materials are visually attractive. As with earlier editions, the workbook is geared to the chapters, with questions and exercises that facilitate retention. Summary and review exercises are included in the workbook at appropriate intervals. Transparency masters which highlight key points are available in the teacher's manual, for use at your discretion during regular classes or for reviewing. Tests can be obtained from the publisher. The total effect is a powerful supplement and support for your classroom presentations. And your students will have a sense of accomplishment as they progress through the course.

Those of you who have used earlier editions of APPLIED BUSINESS LAW will note that time-tested learning aids remain although many factual situations are changed to inject immediacy and relevance to the students' daily lives. At the beginning of every chapter the "teasers" instantly capture reader interest, stimulate curiosity, and encourage the quest for answers through careful reading of the chapter. In a variation of the Socratic method of teaching, every section begins with a question, followed by an authentic legal problem phrased in understandable language. Again, the student is challenged to think analytically and then to check the conclusion reached in the text before the next problem is presented. Thus students form the "connection of interest with materials" so important for durable learning. Condensed definitions of key legal terms appear in the margins to provide variety in visual appeal, as well as a quick source of information for preview and review. At the end of each chapter, the very popular (for students and their parents!) "Preventing Legal Difficulties" feature remains, along with "Strengthening Your Legal Vocabulary," "Reviewing Important Points," the fascinating hypotheticals of "Applying Law to Everyday Life," and carefully selected actual appellate cases in "Solving Case Problems." The cases include short versions of old classics used in the nation's leading law schools, as well as recently decided cases which demonstrate the continuing evolution of the common law.

This edition presents, for the first time, specific materials on ethics. In a secularized society the law is an official statement of what is right conduct and what is wrong conduct. Ethics is the science or discipline of moral duty, a study of what is right and wrong. Accordingly, the study of law can be seen as a way to study and to apply ethics. Certainly in this course it is appropriate for teachers to raise questions about what is right and wrong conduct in business and society, in the light of applicable law. To help you do this we have included chapter-end questions which specifically introduce ethical issues. The teacher's manual also contains some exercises designed to explore ethical issues.

An innovation which should be well-received by many students is the occasional one-page essay on law-related topics such as careers in law. These essays provide the opportunity to explore facets of the law and the legal profession not specifically covered elsewhere in the text.

Experienced teachers know that because our laws are made by 50 different sovereign states as well as by the federal government, because every law is subject to judicial interpretation which may vary with changing facts, and because human beings engage in an infinite variety of activities under the law, it is impossible to cover every possibility with precision. Exceptions, distinctions, and variations exist in the seemingly most simple rules. Where important differences exist, an attempt has been made to present the generally prevailing or preferred view, including noteworthy exceptions. But a textbook of this nature is intended neither to be definitive nor to take the place of professional legal counsel for the resolution of specific legal problems.

Nevertheless, students who conscientiously read this book and successfully do the assigned work will better understand the world in which they live. They will expand their vocabularies and sharpen their abilities to think analytically and systematically. They will be better equipped than most citizens to recognize legal problems and to utilize professional counsel.

To those many dedicated teachers who have worked with our book in the past and to those teachers and other friends who have been so generous with suggestions for its continued improvement, we express our sincere gratitude.

Norbert J. Mietus • John E. Adamson • Edward J. Conry

CONTENTS

INTRODUCTION TO STUDENTS

You will soon find that business law is one of your most interesting subjects. The problems you will study reflect true situations where business law has a major impact on the lives of young persons such as you and your friends, as well as on adults and on business firms, large and small. The learning materials will help you to achieve an understanding of legal principles which will be useful throughout your life.

Below is a plan for effectively studying the text material.

HOW TO STUDY BUSINESS LAW

1. Each chapter is introduced by three questions that you should be able to answer from what you already know or what you think is fair or reasonable. Answer each question before you read the chapter.

2. After you have answered the three introductory questions, scan the topic headings to get a general idea of what is included in the chapter.

3. After you have scanned the chapter, read it more slowly and carefully; make notes of the important points. Topic headings are stated in the form of a question; try to answer each question before you study the next topic. Be sure that you understand its meaning before you continue. If in doubt, read the topic again and, if necessary, ask someone to help you with it. If you do not know the meaning of a legal word, look it up in the glossary.

4. As you read, try to apply the rules to yourself or to your family and friends. Think about situations within your own experience to which the rules apply.

5. After you have carefully studied the chapter, complete the section entitled "Strengthening Your Legal Vocabulary" and read "Reviewing Important Points" to refresh your memory.

6. Examples of legal problems from real life ("Applying Law to Everyday Life") and actual case problems ("Solving Case Problems") appear at the end of each chapter. Each case or problem relates the law discussed in the body of the text. You can sharpen your wits by being the judge and solving them. Make a note of the page on which you think the answer to each is found.

HOW YOU CAN SOLVE LEGAL PROBLEMS

Following each chapter, you will find a number of real-life problems under the heading "Applying Law to Everyday Life." You will also find actual cases that have been decided by courts, headed "Solving Case Problems." The method of solving is essentially the same in both problems and cases.

To answer the question raised in a problem or case, first read it carefully. Be sure you understand the question. Then analyze the situation, determine the rule of law involved, and reach a decision. You will find it helpful to answer these five questions:

1. What are the facts?
2. What is the disputed point?
3. What rule of law is involved?
4. How does this rule apply to the facts?
5. What is the answer or decision?

Your teacher may prefer that you use the steps below, in this order:

1. State your answer or decision.
2. Give the rule of law that supports your answer.
3. Explain how the rule of law applies to the facts.

LEGAL ADVICE

1. Choose a family lawyer.
2. Consult your lawyer if you have any doubts about your rights or duties when your property, life, or liberty is endangered or if significant changes occur in your circumstances.
3. Familiarize yourself with local, state, and federal laws to help avoid violations. Ignorance of the law is normally no excuse.
4. Remember that a minor is generally liable for crimes and torts and may also be bound by contracts.
5. If you are involved in a legal dispute, try to learn the other person's version and honestly seek a friendly solution out of court. In every court action at least one person loses—and often both find the costs burdensome.
6. If someone injures you or your property, do not rush to sign a statement releasing the person from liability in exchange for some payment of money. The damages may be greater than first determined. On the other hand, do not delay in consulting your attorney and in taking action if appropriate.
7. Although oral agreements can be legally binding, it is prudent to write all contracts which involve significant time, money, or detail and to have both parties sign and receive copies.

Unit One
UNDERSTANDING THE LAW

UNIT OBJECTIVES

UPON COMPLETION OF THIS UNIT, you should be able to

1. describe the historical development of the law.
2. state the benefits, rights, and duties of citizenship.
3. define civil disobedience and contrast it with the conduct of a scofflaw.
4. name the main governmental sources of law and describe the types of law each source creates.
5. explain the differences between civil and criminal laws and between civil and criminal trials.
6. distinguish among the processes of litigation, mediation, and arbitration, as well as describe the roles of trial, juvenile, small claims, and appellate courts.
7. describe the trial process.
8 name and state the elements of business-related crimes. Identify infractions, felonies, and misdemeanors.
9. describe the rights of persons accused of crimes and identify *defenses* to charges of criminal conduct.
10. list the types of penalties for crimes.
11. contrast the elements of tort law with the elements of criminal law.
12. describe the elements of several intentional torts.
13. explain the tort concepts of *negligence* and *strict liability*.

1

Law and the Individual

1. Sharon is knowledgeable about tax laws and the way the government audits tax returns. She knows a way to cheat on her tax return which would save her almost $2,000. She thinks the chance of being caught is about 1 in 100. Would it be ethical for Sharon to prepare her tax return in this way?

2. James owns four dry cleaning stores employing 22 people. He needs a bookkeeper and advertises for one in the local newspaper. Twelve persons respond, and Joni is clearly the best qualified. However, James prefers to hire a man. If the law requires James to hire Joni, but he thinks he would not be caught if he hires a less qualified male instead, whom should he hire?

3. Several parents complained to the city council about a local record shop which also sold adult magazines. In response, the city council passed an ordinance making illegal the sale of such materials by businesses which sell other products to persons under 18. The ordinance was passed during an evening session at 7:30 p.m. At 8:00 p.m. the police arrived at the record store and arrested the owner. Do you think the arrest was fair and in accord with the U.S. Constitution?

WHAT PROBLEMS MAKE LAWS NECESSARY?

PROBLEM: Alden and Tabbart were neighbors. Tabbart had built a toolshed in his backyard between his house and the border with Alden's property. Later, when he decided to build a fence on the property line, he discovered that the shed was so close to the border that he would not be able to drive between the border and the shed to park his boat in the backyard. So, he built the fence one foot onto Alden's property. Alden did not discover this until six months later. Is Tabbart's conduct justified?

laws: rules of conduct made by the lawmaking authorities

Laws are the rules of conduct established by the lawmaking authorities of a society. In our country, lawmaking authorities exist on the federal, state, and local levels of government.

1. Private Conflicts Make Laws Necessary

Individuals frequently have interests which conflict. Often they are unable to resolve these conflicts reasonably by themselves. Sometimes people resort to harassment, threats, or physical violence. When this happens, the most powerful or strongest person usually wins. This is unfair; the person who is right should win. Therefore in a civilized society such as our own, a legal system has been created to help resolve conflicts peacefully, fairly, and impartially. Thus, in the problem, Alden could sue Tabbart and the judge would probably order Tabbart to remove the fence.

civil conflict: private dispute

When conflicts arise strictly between private parties (that is, when society in general does not have a large stake in the resolution of the conflict), the encounters are called **civil conflicts**. Another way to think of a civil conflict is as a private offense. In the problem, Tabbart and Alden had a civil conflict.

2. Public Problems Make Laws Necessary

criminal conduct: conflict between an individual and society

Often conflicts arise between individuals and society as a whole. For example, when an individual uses violence in trying to resolve a conflict, the violence may be directed only at another individual; however, it is so disruptive of the public peace that it is viewed by the law as an offense against the whole of society. Similarly, someone driving 90 miles per hour down a freeway imposes the risk of death or injury on all others in the vicinity. When an individual's behavior creates a conflict with society as a whole, it is called **criminal conduct**.

3. Human Weaknesses Make Laws Necessary

One of the reasons conflicts arise between individuals or between an individual and society as a whole is that people are subject to psychological (mental) processes which may make it difficult for them to know what is right or fair. **Selective perception** is one of these processes. This causes us to see or hear only those things which our existing attitudes or our self-interest allows us to see or hear. In the problem, Tabbart might, after a long period of time, through selective perception, come to believe that the true boundary is beneath the fence. A similar psychological process is **rationalization**. This causes us to try to justify an action or belief by inventing reasons which seem reasonable to us, but are not to others. Thus, Tabbart might rationalize his conduct by saying that a foot of land is not enough to squabble over or that Alden is unreasonable and overly sensitive because he does not use that small strip of land or that he will not notice it or care once the fence is in place.

selective perception: distortion of reality caused by attitudes or self-interest

rationalization: using obviously invalid reasoning to justify an action or belief

Self-interest often causes conflicts which make laws necessary. The law seeks to reconcile individual self-interest with society's need for conduct which respects the interests of others. If there were no laws and everyone acted only in self-interest, many people would be unfairly injured.

self-interest: action or thinking which advances self over others

The legal system uses two basic concepts to *balance* self-interest with the interests of others. These are the concepts of rights and duties. **Legal rights** are those things to which a person is entitled by law. For example, high-school-aged persons have a legal right to a public school education paid for by the government and financed by taxation. The other side of the coin is the legal duty. A **legal duty** is an obligation enforced by law upon certain parties. Thus, citizens are under a legal duty to pay property taxes and other taxes so that young persons can be educated. For every right in our society, there is a corresponding duty. To illustrate, if you obtained a part-time job paying $5.25 per hour, this job would create both legal rights and duties. Your duty is to do the assigned work; your right is to receive wages. The employer's duty is to pay your wages; the employer's right is to receive your services.

legal rights: something to which one is legally entitled

legal duty: something one is legally obligated to do

WHAT BASIC GOALS DOES SOCIETY SEEK TO ACHIEVE THROUGH THE USE OF LAWS?

PROBLEM: Corky owned a parcel of land in the middle of the business district in Toledo, Ohio. He planned to build a dry cleaning store on the land. Ted, who owned a dry cleaning store three blocks away, was a member of the city council. Ted proposed to the council a law which would prohibit the use of Corky's property for any business use. Would Ted's proposed law promote a goal of society?

There are certain fundamental goals which all legal systems seek. Sometimes a law seeks to advance only a single goal. In other instances, a law attempts to advance multiple goals or to balance conflicting goals.

1. To Enforce the Will of the People

In our country, most laws reflect the desires of those subject to the laws. That is, the people, directly or indirectly, determine the laws which will bind them. They do this by electing representatives to lawmaking bodies such as city councils, state legislatures, or the Congress of the United States. To be reelected, these representatives are under pressure to vote for and to support laws acceptable to their constituents. **Constituents** are the persons who elect the representatives.

constituents: those who elect someone to represent them

In the example, Ted might get his law passed because of his personal influence. This law probably would not reflect the will of those governed because the competition provided by another dry cleaning business would benefit the neighborhood. Rather, the law would reflect Ted's desire to restrict competition with his own business. Thus, Ted's conduct would not promote a goal of society.

The Constitution of the United States seeks to ensure that our federal lawmaking system reflects the desires of our citizens. It does this by creating a national legislature composed of two bodies—the House of Representatives and the Senate. Together, these bodies are called Congress. The Constitution provides for the election of the members of Congress by the citizenry. States have similar legislative structures.

2. To Ensure Just Treatment for All

While many laws reflect the desires of those governed, the laws desired by the majority may not promote justice. **Justice** means treating everyone fairly and impartially. The majority may benefit from unjust laws. For example, it might increase the wealth of the majority of persons in this country if we were to confiscate the property of the 10 percent of our citizens with red hair and distribute it to

justice: treating everyone fairly and impartially

the other 90 percent of the population. While a law designed to bring this about might reflect the will of the majority, it would violate a fundamental principle of justice. Such a law would treat redheads unfairly. Under the Constitution of the United States, such a law would be declared invalid because it denies "equal protection of the law" to redheads.

Other principles of justice are used to protect political minorities from exploitation by those who make up the political majority. For example, the Fifth Amendment to the Constitution of the United States declares that "No person shall be . . . deprived of life, liberty, or property, without due process of law."

Justice also seeks to protect basic natural rights. **Natural rights** are those rights to which individuals are entitled because of their status as members of the human race. Our Declaration of Independence recognized these rights when it stated:

natural rights: rights to which all persons are entitled because they are human beings

> We hold these truths to be self-evident, that all men are created equal, that they are endowed by their Creator with certain inalienable Rights, that among these are Life, Liberty, and the pursuit of Happiness.

The United States of America is a country which recognizes and supports natural rights. Other countries of the world vary dramatically in the extent to which they do so.

Civil rights (or civil liberties) generally are personal, natural rights recognized and guaranteed by our Constitution. Among the civil rights so recognized are:

civil rights: personal, natural rights guaranteed by our Constitution

1. In Article IV, the Constitution provides that "The Citizens of each State shall be entitled to all Privileges . . . of Citizens in [other] States."
2. The First Amendment of the Constitution provides that "Congress shall make no law respecting an establishment of religion . . . or abridging the freedom of speech, or of the press . . ."
3. The Fourth Amendment provides that "The right of the people to be secure in their persons, houses, papers, and effects, against unreasonable searches and seizures, shall not be violated, and no Warrants shall issue, but upon probable cause . . ."
4. The Fifth Amendment provides that "No person . . . shall be compelled in any criminal case to be a witness against himself . . ."

5. The Sixth Amendment provides that "In all criminal prosecutions, the accused shall enjoy the right to a speedy and public trial, by an impartial jury . . . and to have the Assistance of Counsel . . ."
6. The Eighth Amendment provides that "Excessive bail shall not be required, nor excessive fines imposed, nor cruel and unusual punishments inflicted."
7. The Fourteenth Amendment states, "No state shall . . . deny to any person . . . the equal protection of the laws."
8. The Fifteenth Amendment states, "The right of citizens of the United States to vote shall not be denied or abridged . . . on account of race [or] color . . ."

ethical principles: basic conclusions about what is right and wrong

Laws which seek justice are generally based on ethical principals. **Ethical principles** are *basic* philosophical conclusions about what is right and wrong conduct. We call laws which are based on ethical principles **natural law.**

natural laws: laws which reflect ethical principles

3. To Maintain Order

Often, matters simply need a consistent rule for order and predictability. The rule need not be based on consent of the majority or on a principle of justice. Sometimes this means that the rule or law is arbitrary. For example, teachers are required to award grades on exams and for courses. Assume that the cut-off between an *A* and a *B* at one school is a 90-percent average. A student who has an 89-percent average and therefore receives a *B* may argue that this grade is unfair because it is arbitrary; a student who receives a 90-percent average has not done substantially better work. Yet the letter grades do indicate a substantial difference. If the grade for the 89-percent student is changed to an *A*, then the argument for the student with the 88-percent average must be addressed and resolved the same way. A rule is needed, and it is perhaps more important that the rule exist than it is that the rule be completely fair.

To be fair, it is essential to communicate rules or laws to those affected *before* they engage in prohibited conduct. Also, rules must be applied consistently. To some degree, laws derive their legitimacy from the process by which they are created rather than from the consent of those governed or from the fairness of the rule. The Constitution of the United States requires advance notice, consistent application, and proper legal procedures in the Fourteenth Amendment where it states, "No state shall . . . deprive any person of life, liberty, or property, without due process of law."

Reflecting the will of the governed and providing justice and order are the basic legal goals of society. Subordinate goals include protection of the state, of persons, and of property, and enhancement of the general welfare.

WHY ARE WE OBLIGATED TO OBEY LAWS?

> **PROBLEM:** During Christmas vacation, Clementine worked part-time as a salesclerk in the jewelry department of a large department store. Because it was a busy time of the year, there were many occasions when she thought that she could put a certain watch in her purse without being detected. Clementine felt that the store had not treated her fairly. Also, the watch was one which she wanted very much but could not afford. Should she take the watch if she thinks there is no chance of being caught?

In general, we should obey the law because we thereby do what society, acting through the government of the people, properly tells us to do or not to do because it is right and good to so behave. More specifically, we obey the law because we have consented to obey, by obeying we help others, and by obeying we avoid punishment.

1. We Consent to be Governed by Laws

Socrates was a philosopher who lived in Athens, Greece during 470–399 B.C. Socrates believed that he had consented to be governed by the laws of Athens by living in Athens and accepting the benefits of that society. He believed that he should leave the country, or not accept the benefits which the country conferred on citizens, if he was not willing to obey all of the country's laws. Through this type of reasoning, Socrates concluded that it would be ethically wrong for him to violate the law of Athens. Socrates was willing to die rather than violate his belief about each citizen's duty to obey the laws of his or her country.

Socrates is widely regarded as a person of great integrity. **Integrity** is the capacity to do what is right even in the face of temptation or pressure to do otherwise.

integrity: the capacity to do what is right even under pressure

In the problem, Clementine would, according to Socrates, be required to obey the law because she has accepted the benefits of the society which made the law. Free schooling is only one of the dozens of benefits this society has provided Clementine. Examples of other benefits include protection from criminal acts, support for safe roads, unemployment compensation, welfare systems, social security, and protection from foreign enemies in times of war.

2. We Help Society by Obeying Laws

When you read the goals of society, you saw that laws help society in at least three ways. Laws help by reflecting the will of the majority, by promoting justice, and by creating order. For persons who embrace formal religious views (for example, Buddhists, Christians, Hindus, Jews, or Muslims), there is a requirement to live one's life so that it helps others. Hence, many persons feel obligated to obey the law in order to help others as well as for the reason identified by Socrates.

3. We Want to Avoid Punishment

Some persons comply with the law primarily to avoid punishment. A person convicted of a crime may be fined, jailed, or, in some instances, put to death. While these penalties are widely known, there are a great many other penalties imposed upon criminals. For instance, persons convicted of serious crimes may be barred from jobs that require a security clearance. In many companies and government agencies, a security clearance is required for every employee. Also, some industries automatically exclude persons with criminal records from employment consideration. Banks, savings and loan associations, credit unions, and finance companies are examples. Similarly, many jobs require a **fidelity bond**. This is an insurance policy which pays the employer money in the case of theft by employees. Generally those convicted of a serious crime cannot qualify for a fidelity bond. Fidelity bonds would be required for persons who handle large sums of money, such as cashiers, managers of movie theaters, or shift supervisors of fast-food restaurants.

fidelity bond: an insurance policy which pays the employer in case of theft by an employee

Also, many professions are closed to those convicted as adults of serious crimes. For example, prospective lawyers, public accountants, and medical doctors are subjected to a background check which includes a check for criminal convictions before they are licensed to practice their professions. In the problem, if Clementine were caught and convicted, the biggest penalty would be the one she would "pay" outside the judicial system: the probable loss of many future job opportunities.

In civil conflicts, the penalties for violating the law are not as severe. However, in addition to paying for the injury you cause another person, involvement in a serious civil lawsuit may injure your ability to borrow money and to buy goods on credit if the lawsuit is recorded as a part of your credit history.

Andy borrowed money from a local bank and bought a three-year-old Corvette. After losing his job, he was able to make only two more payments. Instead of discussing his financial difficulty with the bank, he moved to Florida. Eventually the bank sued Andy and recovered the money it was owed. A credit reporting agency checked the court records and included a statement about the lawsuit in Andy's credit history. Four years later, Andy applied for another bank loan and was turned down because of this prior lawsuit.

ARE WE EVER JUSTIFIED IN VIOLATING THE LAW?

PROBLEM: Donna worked as a waitress. She earned the minimum wage from her employer but also earned approximately $2.50 per hour in tips. On her annual income tax return she disclosed her wages but not the tips. She knew she was violating the law. When asked why she cheated on her tax return, Donna said she thought the law was unfair, that tips were really gifts to her from customers, and that she should not have to pay taxes on them. Is Donna's conduct justifiable?

Some persons are **scofflaws**. These are persons who do not respect or comply with certain laws. They assess the risk of being caught against the benefits obtained by breaking the law. They think they are smart because they frequently violate laws without being caught. A scofflaw is never justified in violating the law.

scofflaw: a person who does not respect nor comply with certain laws

In contrast, some persons care passionately about justice. Unlike Socrates, their concern for justice sometimes compels them to violate a clearly unjust law. While such persons do violate the law, they are not scofflaws. They sometimes engage in acts of **civil disobedience**. Civil disobedience is openly, but peacefully, disobeying a law to protest its alleged injustice or unfairness. The goal of those who engage in civil disobedience is not to advance their self-interest but, rather, to make the legal system more just.

civil disobedience: peaceful violation of a law thought to be unjust

Dr. Martin Luther King, Jr. said, "How does one determine when a law is just or unjust? A just law is a man-made code that squares with the moral law or the law of God. An unjust law is a code that is out of harmony with the moral law. To put it in the terms of Saint Thomas Aquinas, an unjust law is a human law that is not rooted in eternal and natural law. Any law that uplifts human personality is just. Any law that degrades human personality is unjust. . . .

"An unjust law is a code that a majority inflicts on a minority that is not binding on itself. This is *difference* made legal. On the other hand, a just law is a code that a majority compels a minority to follow that it is willing to follow itself. This is *sameness* made legal."

Like others, Dr. King believed that civil disobedience is justified only in extremely limited circumstances. He and others conclude that civil disobedience is ethical only when:

1. a written law is in conflict with natural law,
2. there are no political methods available to change the law,
3. the civil disobedience is nonviolent,
4. it does not advance one's immediate self-interest, and
5. the civil disobedience is public and one willingly accepts the punishment for violating the law.

In the problem, Donna would not be justified in failing to report her tips as income. She seeks to violate the law for her self-interest. In addition, she plans to do it in secret and hopes to avoid punishment for the violation. Her failure to pay just taxes unfairly shifts that much of the burden to all other taxpayers who do pay their taxes.

WHAT ARE REASONS FOR STUDYING THE LAW?

PROBLEM: Jordan operated a drugstore and employed about ten people full-time. His neighbor's daughter, Sara, wanted a part-time job and asked if she could work for Jordan. Jordan agreed and, since Sara worked only part-time, he paid her in cash and did not make the usual payroll deductions for unemployment compensation, workers' compensation, or social security. Jordan thought he handled the situation appropriately. But when Sara was injured on the job, Jordan learned that he had violated the law by not making the deductions. One consequence of this was that Sara sued Jordan and collected $26,000. What was Jordan's most basic mistake?

Most basically, we study the law so we will understand it and be better able to obey it. The reasons for studying law are similar to the reasons for obeying the law. Thus, some people view the study of law as necessary because they believe they have consented to obey society's laws by accepting its benefits. Others study the law so they can obey it and thereby help society. Still others study the law to avoid being punished for violations. In the problem, Jordan violated the law by not making the proper payroll deductions. As a result, Jordan became personally liable for on-the-job injuries to Sara. If Jordan had studied the law, he could have obeyed it and saved $26,000.

A significantly different type of desire motivates a few people. They study the law out of a desire for integrity. Before being able to exhibit integrity, a person must have a belief about what is right or wrong. For example, Socrates had to possess his belief about complying with the law before he could "act with integrity." If there is no real belief, there can be no integrity.

Collectively, the law is similar to society's ethical code. Therefore some persons may study the law to help them better understand what is right and wrong conduct. The critical study of law is one of the best ways to clarify one's own ethical beliefs.

WHAT IS CITIZENSHIP?

> **PROBLEM:** Boone objects to government spending for welfare and for free public education. Dalton objects to government spending for defense and for regulation of business. Both citizens refuse to pay their state and federal income taxes. "Too darn high. And the money is wasted!" they say. Can they be *compelled* (forced) to pay?

Citizenship is membership in the civil and political community—the nation and the state of one's residence. Citizenship is a give-and-take relationship between individuals and their government. The citizens give allegiance and support to the government. In return, the government provides the citizens, individually and collectively, with protection and numerous other benefits.

citizenship: membership in a civil and political community

Allegiance is the bond of loyalty of citizens to their government and their obedience to its laws, in exchange for protection and other benefits. When citizens are called upon to serve in the armed forces or as members of a jury, allegiance requires them to cooperate. When the law requires certain acts, such as the payment of legally levied taxes, citizens have a duty to pay. Thus, in the problem, the government can compel both Boone and Dalton to pay their income taxes.

allegiance: loyalty and obedience of citizens to their government

One must be a citizen to enjoy the right to vote or to hold public offices. Other fundamental rights and related duties are extended to all persons living in this country. For example, *aliens* (foreigners) enjoy the right of freedom of speech, and they have the duty to pay taxes.

HOW DOES ONE GAIN OR LOSE CITIZENSHIP?

PROBLEM: The Tsushiba twins were born in New York City while their parents, Japanese citizens, were students at Columbia University. Are the twins American citizens?

U.S. citizen: person born or naturalized in the United States and subject to its jurisdiction

Most of us take our citizenship for granted. Have you ever considered what makes you a **U.S. citizen**? The Fourteenth Amendment to the U.S. Constitution states: "All persons born or naturalized in the United States, and subject to the jurisdiction thereof, are citizens of the United States and of the State wherein they reside." Thus, by virtue of being born in the United States, one is a citizen. In the problem, the twins are United States citizens and citizens of the state where they reside, even though their parents are not. At the same time, the twins may also be citizens of Japan under Japanese law.

Congress has provided that certain other persons are citizens of this country by virtue of their parentage. This group includes those born in a foreign land while one or both parents are U.S. citizens.

Thompson was born in Rio de Janeiro while her parents, who were United States citizens, were working there. Thompson was a Brazilian citizen by birth. Because of her parents' United States citizenship, she was also a citizen of the United States.

naturalized persons: aliens who have become citizens

Naturalized persons are former aliens who have been granted all the rights and privileges of native-born citizens except the right to become president of the United States. People of the United States have come from all over the world. All Americans are either immigrants or descendants of immigrants. Even the first Americans, American Indians, can trace their origins to immigrants who came from Asia across the Bering Strait north of Alaska.

United States citizens are subject to the jurisdiction of both the United States and the state in which they live. Thus, one holds a *dual* (double) citizenship. This means that a person is a citizen of the United States and of the state of residence. Furthermore, the U.S. Constitution provides that a state may not discriminate against the citizens of another state in favor of its own citizens.

By statute, a person may voluntarily *renounce* (give up) citizenship and allegiance to the United States. This act of abandoning one's country and citizenship is known as **expatriation**. It may be done in one of several ways, but only after the citizen has actually moved from the United States and has reached 18 years of age.

expatriation: act of voluntarily giving up citizenship

Hartman, a native-born United States citizen, voluntarily enlisted in the French Foreign Legion. He did so without prior approval of the U.S. Secretary of State, as required by statute. After returning to this country, Hartman ran for an important public office. His opponent challenged his right to do so. The court held that Hartman had voluntarily given up his citizenship by joining the army of another nation, and thus could not run for the public office. However, Hartman could regain his citizenship through the process of naturalization.

HOW DOES THE CITIZEN SHOW ALLEGIANCE?

PROBLEM: An ordinance of the city of Sacramento prohibited backyard burning of trash. The Duffers were cited for violating the ordinance. They claimed they were not aware of the law and, therefore, should not have to pay the fine. Do you agree?

Allegiance is the primary obligation of citizenship. In addition to loyalty and obedience to the law, allegiance implies a duty to keep oneself informed of the law. Ignorance of the law is no excuse for violating it. Of course, no one knows all laws. But every person, before beginning a new experience with legal implications—driving a car, getting married, buying a house, starting a business—should investigate the applicable laws or should consult a lawyer. Therefore, in the problem, the Duffers will have to pay the fine.

One is not punished for failure to vote, yet voting is an important right and privilege of citizenship. Before voting, a good citizen becomes informed of election issues, qualifications of candidates for office, and government operations in general.

Being a good citizen could also mean expressing one's opinion on controversial current public problems. An important obligation of citizenship is the duty to accept decisions of the majority even when one disagrees and then to work peacefully for the change desired. Reciprocally, a member of the majority should be tolerant of opinions of those who disagree and must permit them to speak out. Indeed, as a court stated, one purpose of protecting speech is to invite dispute in the quest for truth.

> I disapprove of what you say, but I will defend to the death your right to say it.
>
> —*Attributed to Voltaire*

PREVENTING LEGAL DIFFICULTIES

As a Citizen . . .

You have certain rights set forth in the Constitution and protected by laws. These individual rights distinguish our free society from totalitarian systems.

Your rights under the law include:

1. the right to equal protection of laws and equal justice in the courts,
2. the right to be free from arbitrary search or arrest,
3. the right to equal educational and economic opportunity,
4. the right to choose public officers in free elections,
5. the right to own, use, and dispose of property,
6. the right of free speech, press, and assembly,
7. the right to attend the church of your choice, and
8. the right to have legal counsel of your choice and a prompt trial if accused of a crime.

With your rights as a citizen go individual responsibilities. Every American shares them. Only by fulfilling our duties are we able to maintain our rights.

Your duties as a citizen include:

1. the duty to obey the law,
2. the duty to respect the rights of others,
3. the duty to inform yourself on issues of government and community welfare,
4. the duty to vote in elections,
5. the duty to serve on juries if called,

6. the duty to serve and defend your country,
7. the duty to assist agencies of law enforcement, and
8. the duty to practice and teach the principles of good citizenship in your home.

—Adapted from *Law Day USA*
American Bar Association

Strengthening Your Legal Vocabulary

allegiance
citizenship
civil conflict
civil disobedience
civil rights
constituents
criminal conduct
ethical principles
expatriation
fidelity bond
integrity
justice
laws
legal duty
legal rights
natural laws
natural rights
naturalized persons
rationalization
scofflaw
selective perception
self-interest
U.S. citizen

1. A private dispute.
2. A conflict between an individual and society.
3. Something one is legally obligated to do.
4. Treating everyone fairly and impartially.
5. Something to which one is legally entitled.
6. Laws which reflect ethical principles.
7. Membership in a civil and political community.
8. The capacity to do what is right even under pressure.
9. A person who does not respect nor comply with certain laws.
10. A distortion of reality caused by existing attitudes or self-interest.

Reviewing Important Points

1. Laws are necessary because there are conflicts among individuals and between certain individuals and society. Individuals sometimes have difficulty acting fairly because of selective perception or rationalization.
2. The law tries to advance the goals of:
   a. reflecting the will of those governed
   b. justice
   c. order
3. We should obey the law as socially responsible citizens, complying with rules defined by the government of the people as to what is right conduct.

4. We are obligated to obey the law because we have consented to be bound by accepting society's benefits.
5. We are obligated to obey the law if we believe in helping others.
6. We should obey the law if we desire to avoid punishment.
7. Integrity is the capacity to do what is right even in the face of temptation or pressure.
8. Civil disobedience is the open, peaceful violation of a law to protest its alleged injustice or unfairness.
9. We can study the law to better understand what is right and wrong conduct, and thus to clarify our own ethical beliefs.
10. All persons born or naturalized in the United States are citizens.

Applying Law to Everyday Life

1. Timmin was arrested for reckless driving which had caused a serious accident. She was found guilty, fined, and sentenced to six months in jail. Labelle, who had been injured in the accident, sued Timmin for $100,000 in damages. Do these facts describe civil or criminal matters or both?

2. The Liquor Control Board revoked the license of the Frisco-Disco Dance Club. This caused the club to go bankrupt. This action was taken after proper notice and a public hearing. At the hearing, the owners were represented by legal counsel and had full opportunity to defend their right to the license. How can the legal action be justified?

3. An ordinance of Walker County provided that all automobiles had to pass a smog emissions test once a year. Ross was ticketed because his car had not been inspected and approved at an emissions testing center. Ross claimed to be a skilled mechanic who kept his car well tuned and "cleaner" than the law required. According to Ross, the law violated his natural rights. Do you agree?

4. Staub, Conte and Winfield were employees of the Quick Burger Restaurant.They were aware that the owner never checked the totals on the sales checks against the cash in the register. Therefore it would be very easy to steal from the cash register. However, no one did steal. When asked why, the three gave the following reasons. Staub said he did not take the money because he was afraid of being caught. Conte said she did not take the money because she felt obligated to obey the law. Winfield said he did not take the money because of his religious beliefs. To which person do you best relate?

5. Crawford was caught shoplifting by a store detective. The police were called, and he was arrested. When his parents came to bail him out of jail, they asked him why he did it. Crawford responded that he had applied for a summer job at the store and was not hired. He thought he was treated unfairly, and this justified the shoplifting. What do you think of Crawford's justification?

6. The Seymours wanted their 15-year-old daughter, Anna, to help out in the family business. The business was a convenience grocery store which was open 24 hours every day. The Seymours thought Anna could learn the business best this way. They insisted that state school attendance rules interfered both with parental rights to educate their children and with the child's right to get ahead faster. Could the Seymours ethically refuse to send their daughter to school? What action could the Seymours ethically take in response to the situation?

7. Adam's parents were citizens of the United States. When his mother was pregnant with Adam, she traveled to Cairo, Egypt. While there she gave birth to Adam. He was raised in Egypt, did not learn to speak English, and never visited the United States. Is Adam a citizen of the United States?

Solving Case Problems

1. Poppy Construction Company was engaged in the business of developing, building, and selling a tract of houses in San Francisco. Mr. and Mrs. Burks, who were black, offered to purchase one of the houses. Poppy had a policy and practice of refusing to sell housing in the tract to blacks on the same conditions as to others. When their offer was rejected, Mr. and Mrs. Burks sued on the grounds of racial discrimination. Racial discrimination was contrary to the law of California as well as to the Constitution of the United States. Poppy was required to accept their offer to purchase the house. Is this law best justified by ethical principles, as seeking to create order, or as reflecting the will of those governed? (*Burks v. Poppy Construction Company*, 307 P.2d 313, Cal.)

2. The City of Chicago sued to stop operation of the Commonwealth Edison Company's coal-burning, electricity-generating plant in nearby Hammond, Indiana. The City of Chicago claimed that the plant emitted too much smoke, sulfur dioxide, and other harmful substances. The city also claimed that the plant was a common law public nuisance because it caused "an unreasonable interference with a right common to the general public" to clean, unpolluted air. Edison argued that it had spent much money to reduce harmful emissions and that the emissions were now well below the levels prescribed by federal clean air regulations and by the City of Hammond. Edison also claimed that the plant was located in a highly industrialized area necessitating "unpleasant odors, smoke, and film." The trial court refused to issue an injunction. Therefore the City of Chicago appealed to a higher court which *affirmed* (upheld) the trial court. How can this legal action be justified? (*City of Chicago v. Commonwealth Edison Co.*, 321 N.E. 2d 412, Ill.)

3. Briney owned an old farm house in Iowa, which had been unoccupied for years. He had posted "No Trespassing" signs outside. Nevertheless, there were intruders. So, Briney set a loaded shotgun inside the building and

rigged it to fire when the bedroom door was opened. Soon after, Katko and a companion burglar broke into the house to steal old bottles they considered antiques. As Katko started to open the bedroom door, the shotgun blasted him, blowing off much of one leg. Katko sued Briney for damages and won. How can the legal action be justified? (*Katko v. Briney*, 183 N.W. 2d 657, Iowa)

4. Reader's Digest Association, Inc. promoted magazine subscriptions in 1970 by sending materials which included "simulated checks" to potential subscribers. The government concluded that use of the simulated checks was, for some consumers, unfair and deceptive and thus illegal. Therefore the government ordered the Digest to stop using "similar checks or any confusingly simulated item of value." The Digest agreed to be bound to this government order. Later the Digest mailed promotional material which used misleading "travel checks." After the government notified the Digest that these "travel checks" were illegal, the Digest mailed millions of additional checks to consumers. Was the conduct of the Digest that of a scofflaw or was the Digest engaged in civil disobedience? (*United States v. Reader's Digest Association, Inc.*, 662 F.2d 955)

5. In 1968, Ford Motor Company designed and decided to manufacture a car to be called the Pinto which weighed less than 2,000 pounds and cost less than $2,000. The fuel tank was designed to be between the rear bumper and the rear axle. In crash tests, Ford learned that rear-end collisions could cause the fuel tank to rupture, spilling gas. The spillage could be prevented by spending between $4.00 and $8.00 to cover the fuel tank with a protective device. Total cost for the devices on all the vehicles manufactured would amount to $20.9 million. Ford declined to spend the money. In 1982, Richard Grimshaw, age 13, was riding in a new Pinto when it was struck in the rear by a car traveling at 28- to 37-miles per hour. The impact ruptured the fuel tank, causing gasoline to spill into the passenger compartment. When Richard emerged from the car, his clothing was almost completely burned off. He had to undergo numerous and extensive surgeries and skin grafts. The driver suffered severe burns and died a few days after the accident. Discuss the ethical aspects of the decision not to cover the fuel tanks with the protective devices. (*Grimshaw v. Ford Motor Co.*, 174 Cal. Rptr. 348, Cal.)

2

Nature and Kinds of Law

1. You are planning to start a small business and need to know what laws affect your business. What levels of government enact laws that regulate business activities?

2. Spirry rented an apartment from Yun. When Spirry fell behind in her monthly rental payments, Yun threatened to call the police and have Spirry arrested. Can Spirry be arrested for failing to pay her rent?

3. While driving toward an intersection, Landrum sees the traffic light change from green to yellow. Attempting to "beat the signal," Landrum suddenly accelerates. The car roars ahead, racing well above the posted speed limit. However, the light turns red seconds before the car reaches the corner. Brakes screech, and a deafening crash follows as the car smashes into the side of a sedan which is moving across the intersection. Landrum is knocked unconscious and partially paralyzed. The other driver is killed, and two passengers are seriously injured. What kinds of law have been violated?

HOW DID OUR LAW DEVELOP?

PROBLEM: The labor strike was in its fifth bitter week. The atmosphere was tense. The strikers were restless and angry as were those workers who had remained on the job. For several days, about a thousand picketers and sympathizers had gathered at the main gate, chanting slogans and jeering at "scabs" (replacement workers) who entered the plant. Then a company truck was overturned and burned by the disorderly crowd. Top management went to court for protection. What could the court do?

Since the time when people first began living together, rules have been adopted to protect individuals and groups and to govern their relationships. In early medieval England, there was no formal body of written law. Each feudal lord or baron administered law personally. Although these baronial courts had similarities, the laws tended to differ by locality or region. Disputes were settled on the basis of local customs and the baron's judgment. In time, the king was able to establish a system of courts which enforced a common law throughout England. The rules of law, which were stated in these early cases, became *precedents* (examples) for settling future, similar cases. In the beginning, few decisions were recorded, and so the early common law was sometimes known as "unwritten law." Eventually, the principles and rules announced by the courts were preserved in writing. The particular rules thus became fixed, and people knew what to expect if similar problems arose in the future. This resulted in what has come to be known as the **common law**—judge-made case law which has its origin in the traditions, customs, and trade practices of the people.

common law: case law, reflecting customs of the people

In medieval England, sometimes there was no remedy available from a common law court to enforce certain rights or to correct certain wrongs. This was because in civil cases the court could give only monetary damages. A person who wanted any other kind of relief would appeal directly to the king. The king would refer the person to his chancellor, who was usually a clergyman of good conscience and fairness. The chancellor would hear the case without a jury and would then give appropriate relief. Such hearings developed into what came to be known as a separate system of courts of **equity**.

equity: form of justice administered when there is no suitable remedy available in common law courts

For example, suppose that Citizen A promised to sell a parcel of land to Citizen B and then refused to complete the deal. Citizen B could have then bought a similar, but possibly more expensive, parcel of land and sued in a common law court for money damages to cover the extra cost. But every piece of land is *unique* (one of a kind) in location. Therefore if the original parcel was desired, Citizen B could have gone to the chancellor for equitable relief. The chancellor would have ordered **specific performance** of the agreement. Thus, the seller would have had to deliver the land as promised.

specific performance: completion of an agreement as promised

In the United States today, the same court can give both the common law relief of dollar damages and equitable relief. Thus, in the problem at the beginning of this section, a court can grant equitable relief in the form of an order called an **injunction**, limiting the number of picketers and sympathizers at the plant entrance to perhaps ten. Violators would then be jailed for contempt of court. Note that a remedy at law—such as a judgment for monetary damages—would be worthless in this case. That is because it would be impossible to identify in a large mob the actual offenders—those who threw rocks or otherwise hurt persons or damaged property.

injunction: order of a court to do or not to do a specified thing

In 1215, the English barons forced the adoption of the **Magna Carta**, which provided in writing certain guarantees and protection against unreasonable acts of the king. Later, the Magna Carta was revised, and other documents, such as the English Bill of Rights (1689), were adopted. When the thirteen American colonies broke away from Great Britain after the Revolutionary War, the colonists adopted the principles of the Magna Carta and the common law. These principles became the foundation of the legal system of our federal government and of all the states except Louisiana, where French influence and Roman civil law prevailed.

Magna Carta: great charter of liberties for English people

Today, the two great systems of law in the Western world are the common law of the English-speaking world and the Roman civil law found on the continent of Europe. Both systems have the same objectives, but they differ in origins and methods. The **Roman civil law** originated in *codes* (systematic collections of written rules of law) imposed on the people by the emperors of ancient Rome. In contrast, the English common law originated in decisions of judges based on widely held customs of the people. Also, English common law uniquely provided for trial by a jury of one's *peers* (equals).

Roman civil law: body of regulations imposed by emperors of ancient Rome

WHAT KINDS OF LAW DO WE HAVE TODAY?

PROBLEM: Congress has enacted a law that requires cigarette makers to print these words on every cigarette package: "Warning: the Surgeon General has determined that cigarette smoking is dangerous to your health." What kind of law is this?

There are 51 basic legal systems in the United States: the federal system and a separate system in each of the 50 states. Although these systems are similar in many ways, they also have important differences. For example, laws governing marriage and divorce are not the same in all states.

The differences among our legal systems exist because each of the original 13 states was theoretically *sovereign* (independent). After the American Revolution in 1776, the states became loosely allied in a "league of friendship" under the Articles of Confederation. The United States Constitution, which was adopted in 1789, thirteen years after the revolution, created a strong central government. However, the Tenth Amendment states: "The powers not delegated to the United States by the Constitution, nor prohibited by it to the States, are reserved to the States respectively, or to the people." Thus, our current law consists of the following:

1. the constitutions of the United States and of the 50 states and charters or constitutions for cities or counties,
2. the statutes enacted by our elected representatives, as in the problem,
3. administrative law, and
4. case law, as expressed in court decisions.

These four types of laws—constitutional, statutory, administrative, and case—are each created by federal and state governments. Thus, there are two levels of government which create four types of laws. Local governments generally create only statutory and administrative laws.

1. Constitutional Law

Law is created when people adopt constitutions or amend existing constitutions. You are governed by both the Constitution of the United States and the constitution of the state where you live.

constitution: a supreme source of law for a government

Constitutions are the supreme sources of law. Thus, no New York statute, administrative regulation, or court decision is valid if it conflicts with the constitution of the State of New York. Similarly, no federal legislation, regulation, or court decision is valid if it conflicts with the Constitution of the United States. In addition, the federal Constitution is said to be "the supreme law of the land." This means that any state law—including a part of a state constitution—is void to the extent that it conflicts with the federal Constitution.

The Supreme Court of the United States is the final interpreter of the federal Constitution and each state supreme court is the final authority on the meaning of its state constitution.

The federal and state constitutions are concerned primarily with allocating certain powers in our society. Our constitutions allocate powers:

1. between the people and their governments,
2. between state governments and the federal government, and
3. among the branches of the governments.

The federal Constitution is the main instrument for allocating powers between persons and their governments. It does this with its first ten amendments, called the **Bill of Rights**, which protect citizens from certain acts of their governments. Some of these limitations on governmental power apply only to the federal government while others apply to both state and federal governments. Included in the Bill of Rights are important rights which many of us take for granted yet which people of many nations do not enjoy. For example:

Bill of Rights: the first ten amendments to the federal Constitution

1. freedom of religion,
2. freedom of speech, press, and peaceable assembly,
3. security in person and property against unreasonable searches and seizures,
4. right to remain silent if accused of a crime and to enjoy a speedy and public trial by an impartial jury,
5. protection from any cruel or unusual punishment if convicted of a crime,
6. right to fair compensation for private property taken by the government for any public purpose, and
7. protection from deprivation of life, liberty, or property without due process of law.

interstate commerce: commerce between two or more states which can be regulated by the federal government

The federal Constitution allocates certain governmental powers to the federal government and certain other powers to the state governments. For example, many governmental powers over business are divided between state governments and the federal government on the basis of interstate commerce. In general, the federal Constitution gives the federal government exclusive power to regulate **interstate** (between two or more states) **commerce**. Regulation of **intrastate** (occurring within one state) **commerce** is left to the states.

intrastate commerce: commerce occurring within one state which cannot be regulated by the federal government

State and federal constitutions allocate governmental powers among the three branches of government: the executive, the legislative, and the judicial. Constitutions do this to create a system of checks and balances among the branches so that no branch of government becomes too powerful.

Suppose Congress held hearings and determined that a certain person was a member of the Mafia. If Congress passed a statute sentencing that person to prison, the courts would declare the statute invalid and unenforceable. The courts, not Congress, have the constitutional authority to sentence criminals. Congress, on the other hand, could pass a statute defining actions which would subject violators to sentencing by federal courts.

2. Statutory Law

The federal and state constitutions created respectively the Congress of the United States and the state legislatures. These state and federal legislatures are composed of elected representatives of the people. Acting on behalf of their citizens, these legislatures may enact new **statutes**.

statute: law enacted by a state or federal legislature

All state legislatures have delegated some of their legislative authority to local governments. Thus, towns, cities, and counties can legislate in their own geographic areas on matters over which the state has given them authority. This legislation is created by a town or city council or by a county board or county commission. Legislation of this type is usually called an **ordinance** rather than a statute.

ordinance: statutory law created by a town, city, or county

To be valid, the statute or ordinance must be **constitutional**. This means that it must not conflict with the provisions of the federal Constitution or of the applicable state constitution. In addition, ordinances must not exceed the powers delegated to local governments by the state legislature. The courts will determine the constitutionality of statutes and ordinances and whether they exceed the scope of powers delegated by the legislature.

constitutional: conforming with the applicable constitution

The City of Sparrow enacted a law which made it illegal to sell gasoline for more than $1.00 per gallon and another law which made the death penalty mandatory for persons who commit murder within the city limits. Both ordinances were challenged in court. The first was declared invalid because it conflicted with the federal Constitution, which gives the power to regulate interstate commerce to the federal government. The second was invalidated because it was outside the authority delegated by the state legislature.

3. Administrative Law

The federal, state, and local legislatures all create administrative agencies. **Administrative agencies** are governmental bodies formed to supervise the carrying out of particular laws. For example, the National Labor Relations Board (NLRB) administers the National Labor Relations Act governing union-management relations. The federal Social Security Administration, your state's division of motor vehicles, and your county's zoning commission are other examples of administrative agencies.

administrative agencies: governmental bodies which administer certain statutes

Although they are created by legislatures, administrative agencies are usually operated by the executive branch of the government. Thus, the President, governor, or mayor will supervise the agency's activities. For example, the United States Congress created the Internal Revenue Service (an agency) and directed that the President appoint and supervise the staff of the agency.

Legislatures sometimes create independent administrative agencies which possess legislative and executive powers to govern, as well as limited judicial powers to hold hearings and to make decisions in particular cases. An example is the National Labor Relations Board. Such agencies are authorized to create **administrative laws** which are usually called **rules** and **regulations**.

administrative laws: laws created by an administrative agency

rules and regulations: the names given to laws created by an administrative agency

The rules and regulations established by an administrative agency generally have the force of law. Like statutes, the regulations can be reviewed by courts to determine whether they are constitutional. In addition, the courts may invalidate a rule or regulation if it is outside the scope of powers delegated by the legislature.

4. Case Law

Case law is created by the judicial branches of our governments. Each state creates case law through its state courts. Similarly, federal courts establish federal case law. Case law is usually made after a trial has concluded and one of the parties has appealed the case. This may result in a review of parts of the trial by a higher court—a process called **appellate review**. When the appellate court publishes its opinion on a case, that opinion may state, and thereby create, new **case law**.

appellate review: a review of a trial by an appellate court

case law: law created by appellate courts

Carol borrowed her stepfather's car without his express permission. The police stopped her, discovered the car was not registered in her name, then phoned the stepfather. When he said he did not know where his car was, Carol was arrested. At her trial, Carol and her stepfather testified that she had permission to use the car without asking each time. The trial judge nevertheless found Carol guilty of auto theft which, the judge stated, occurs when one person takes the car of another without express permission. Carol appealed to the state supreme court. That appellate court ruled that implied permission is enough and therefore Carol was innocent. This rule becomes case law.

doctrine of stare decisis: the principle that new cases must be decided in ways consistent with prior case law

The effectiveness of case law arises out of the **doctrine of stare decisis** (Latin for "to abide by, or adhere to decided cases"). This doctrine requires that once case law is established, it must be followed by lower courts in other similar cases. Thus, in the illustration about auto theft, all the trial courts in that state would be required to follow as case law the rule that one is not guilty of auto theft if she or he has implied permission to use the car. Stare decisis generally does not strictly bind appellate courts; they can overturn their own case law when justified by new conditions or better understanding of the issues.

While courts are the final authority on the interpretation of constitutions and the constitutionality of statutes, rules, and ordinances, they are not the final authority on the content and meaning of such legislation. Legislative bodies can, in effect, nullify a court decision interpreting its statute, ordinance, or rule by abolishing or rewriting the statute or amending the constitution.

HOW DO CRIMINAL AND CIVIL LAWS DIFFER?

PROBLEM: Worthington went to the grocery store four days before the end of the month. Although he knew his checking account was overdrawn, he wrote a check for $111.21 for supplies for a party he was planning. Because he was ill on payday, and therefore did not deposit his paycheck soon enough, the check to the grocery store bounced. Has Worthington violated the law?

When the private legal rights of an individual are violated, the matter is governed by **civil law**. Civil law in this sense differs from the comprehensive system of Roman civil law discussed earlier in this chapter and refers instead to the branch of common law concerned with wrongs against individuals. It applies whenever one person has a right to sue another person. An example of such a situation is when a tenant fails to pay the rent. The police will not investigate civil conflicts.

civil law: law concerned with private wrongs against individuals

When a person violates certain duties to society and disturbs public peace and order, the violation is governed by **criminal law**. The government, acting in the name of all the people, investigates, prosecutes, and tries to fine or imprison the alleged wrongdoer.

criminal law: law concerned with public wrongs against society

Generally, when a crime occurs, private rights of the individual victim are violated at the same time. Thus, the civil law may also apply. The victim of the crime may, therefore, sue the wrongdoer but seldom does because it is usually difficult to collect damages from criminals.

In the problem, Worthington committed a civil offense. Therefore the grocery store could sue and recover the $111.21 from him. In addition, intentionally writing a check without sufficient funds in the account and with no intention to deposit the required funds before the check is presented to the bank is a crime. Had Worthington been guilty of such conduct, he could have been arrested and prosecuted for the crime.

WHAT IS BUSINESS LAW?

PROBLEM: Royale, a teacher, agreed to buy a new subcompact automobile from Morgan Motors, on a time payment plan. Royale signed a lengthy printed form with specific terms of the transaction typed in. However, he was uncertain about the full meaning of the contents. How would a knowledge of business law have helped?

Business law (also known as *commercial law*) covers rules that apply to business situations and transactions. A look at the table of contents of this book will show that the scope of business law is very broad.

business law: rules that apply to business situations

While you may think that business law should interest only those planning to go into business, this is not so. The majority of business transactions involve both a merchant and a consumer. Thus, as you are studying business law, you are gaining knowledge of law which will make you a much more competent consumer.

Business law is largely concerned with civil law, especially contracts. Some business law applies to *torts* (private wrongs against individuals, distinct from breaches of contracts). For example, a tort may occur when a manufacturer makes a defective product that injures a user. Criminal law sometimes governs business-related activities, too. For example, criminal law would punish a firm that conspires with competitors to fix prices or an employee who steals company tools.

As noted earlier, each state has its own laws. Although the laws are similar, there are many state-to-state differences. With the growth of interstate commerce and large business firms, and with the speed of modern transportation and communication, greater uniformity of laws governing business and commercial transactions became a necessity. All states have adopted all or at least parts of the **Uniform Commercial Code (UCC)**, a major step toward achieving that uniformity. The UCC has simplified, clarified, and modernized many laws relating to commercial transactions such as sales. It has made the laws more flexible and responsive to modern conditions. Thus, between merchants, the UCC will enforce certain reasonable agreements even if such agreements do not conform precisely to generally accepted legal principles. The UCC also applies a higher standard of conduct to merchants than to those not regularly engaged in business.

Uniform Commercial Code (UCC): uniform business rules adopted by all but one state

PREVENTING LEGAL DIFFICULTIES

As a Citizen . . .

1. recognize that if you make a promise and break it you may be liable for money damages *or* specific performance,
2. when moving to a new location, find out which county and/or city makes laws which affect you,
3. before beginning a new business, consult an attorney to learn which city, county, state, and federal laws may affect you,
4. never *intentionally* do something unlawful which may injure others—such conduct might violate the criminal or tort law, and
5. study business law diligently so you can become a consumer who is knowledgeable of legal matters.

Strengthening Your Legal Vocabulary

administrative agencies
administrative laws
appellate review
Bill of Rights
business law
case law
civil law
common law
constitution
constitutional
criminal law
doctrine of stare decisis
equity
injunction
interstate commerce
intrastate commerce
Magna Carta
ordinance
Roman civil law
rules or regulations
specific performance
statute
Uniform Commercial Code (UCC)

1. Term describing statutes which conform with the federal Constitution or a state constitution.
2. Principle under which new cases are treated in ways consistent with prior case law.
3. Enactment of Congress or state legislature.
4. Commerce between two or more states.
5. Enactment of a local governmental body.
6. Case decisions and opinions reflecting customs and practices of the people.
7. Rules of law that apply to business situations and transactions.
8. Name of a code of laws that simplifies, clarifies, and modernizes the law of commercial transactions.
9. First ten amendments to the U.S. Constitution.
10. Rulings and regulations of government administrative agencies.

Reviewing Important Points

1. The two great systems of law in the Western world are the English common law and the Roman civil law. All states but Louisiana follow the common law.
2. The common law arose from the customs and practices of the people. It operates through the doctrine of stare decisis.
3. When no adequate remedy is available through the common law, a person may often obtain relief through a supplementary system of justice known as equity.
4. Law is found in constitutions, statutes, cases decided by courts, and regulations and rulings of administrative agencies.
5. Civil law governs relations between individuals. Criminal law governs violations of public duties owed to society as a whole.
6. Business law is concerned with the rules that apply to business situations and transactions. The UCC is an important part of business law.

Applying Law to Everyday Life

1. Jose promised his brother Juan that he would sell to him the wedding ring of their deceased father for $250. Juan agreed and paid the money. Later Jose refused to deliver the ring. Can Juan get back either the ring or the money?

2. The City of Oakland needed land to widen an important road. Without prior notice, or a public hearing, or payment of compensation, it notified Slovin that a four-foot-wide strip of his land had been seized by the city for the road. Is the city's conduct legal?

3. A statute of a certain state limited freight trains to 75 cars. The federal government had no such limitation. Northern Atlantic Railways was running a 100-car train from Chicago to Los Angeles. Did Northern Atlantic have to stop the train at the border of the state that had the limitations and divide the train into two sections?

4. Sonoma County passed a law making it legal to drive 65 mph on freeways inside the county. A state law limited all vehicles anywhere in the state to 55 mph. What is the legal speed limit on freeways inside Sonoma County?

5. A defect in the fuel line caused a fire which destroyed Jiminez's automobile when it was beyond the one-year warranty period. Although Jiminez was not the original owner of the car, she sued and obtained a judgment against the manufacturer. The case was not appealed. May owners of the same model of car in the same state rely on the rule of strict liability declared by the trial court in this case and collect damages if they have similar trouble?

6. A group of people cruising in a car intentionally threw empty pop bottles in front of a group of bicyclists who were moving fast down a hill behind the car. The glass shattered, and almost every bike tire was cut beyond repair. One rider was badly injured after skidding and falling. Were the car occupants guilty of violating the civil or the criminal law?

7. In what ways would the following people find the study of business law helpful:

   (a) Architect
   (b) Farmer
   (c) Motel owner
   (d) Taxicab driver
   (e) Consumer

Solving Case Problems

1. Andrews was stopped by a police officer on the street in an area where a murder had been committed a few hours earlier. The officer had no search warrant but arrested Andrews for carrying a concealed weapon—a .38 caliber Cobra revolver. The officer relied on a clause in the Michigan Constitution concerning the use of search warrants. The clause exempted from the

requirement of a search warrant in "any criminal proceeding, any. . . firearm. . . seized by a peace officer outside the curtilage (yard) of any dwelling house in this state." However, the U.S. Supreme Court had earlier held that the Fourth Amendment to the U.S. Constitution, which prohibited unreasonable search and seizure, applied to the states through the Fourteenth Amendment. Also, a United States court of appeals had previously held in another case that the clause in the Michigan Constitution relied on by the officer was in conflict with the U.S. Constitution. Must the Michigan courts recognize the superior authority of the United States Supreme Court and the Constitution of the United States? (*People v. Andrews*, 21 Mich. App. 731, 176 N.W. 2d 460)

2. Alaska enacted a statute known as "Alaska Hire." It required employers in the state to hire qualified Alaskan residents in preference to nonresidents. Hicklin, a nonresident, sued Orbeck, the state official charged with enforcing the statute. After the Supreme Court of Alaska found the statute constitutional, Hicklin appealed to the United States Supreme Court which found the statute unconstitutional. Which supreme court is the final authority in this case? (*Hicklin v. Orbeck*, 437 U.S. 518)

3. The statute enacted by the United States Congress which created the Selective Service authorized it to register and classify draft-age men. It also authorized the Service to reclassify persons who fail to appear before the Service or who fail to provide it with certain information. Peter Wolff was registered with the Selective Service. During the Vietnam War, he received a deferment for being a student at the University of Michigan. When Wolff participated in a demonstration protesting American involvement in the war, the Service eliminated his deferment. Is it legal for the Selective Service to do this? (*Wolff v. Selective Service*, 372 F.2d 817)

4. In 1896, the U.S. Supreme Court held (*Plessy v. Ferguson*, 163 U.S. 537) that equality of treatment of different races in our country is provided when public and semipublic facilities, even though separate, are substantially equal in quality. For years, railroad cars, buses, restaurants, schools, and other facilities in many states had separate and presumably equal facilities for blacks. In 1954, fifty-eight years later, black plaintiffs in Kansas, South Carolina, Virginia, and Delaware sought admission for their children to public schools on a nonsegregated basis. Does the doctrine of stare decisis bar the U.S. Supreme Court from granting the relief requested? (*Brown v. Board of Education*, 347 U.S. 483)

5. Seneca reported to the police that his Corvette had disappeared. A few weeks later, a police officer saw a Corvette with an expired inspection sticker. When the car was stopped, the officer asked the driver for his driver's license and certificate of registration. The driver could produce neither. A serial number check indicated that the Corvette was Seneca's stolen car. The driver was charged with receiving stolen property and with unauthorized use of an automobile. Does this case come under civil or criminal law? (*Commonwealth of Pennsylvania v. Belcher*, 335 A.2d 505, Pa.)

SPECIAL SECTION:
History of the Law

The earliest generally recognized systematic approach to the law was the law code of Hammurabi, a King of Babylon around 2000 B.C. Hammurabi s Code dealt with many of the same subjects as our legal system today. Business law, real and personal property law, family law, and criminal law were all covered.

The laws set forth in Hammurabi's Code were derived from the King, allegedly a divinely-inspired authority. Only the King could change such laws. This absolutism of power in the monarch was typical of legal systems until the time of the Greeks around 300 B.C.

The Greek system emphasized that law was made by man, for man, and was changeable by man. Rather than being an instrument of overt social control of the general population by a monarch, the law was to serve to enhance the peace and prosperity of the people.

The Greek ideals were carried over into the Roman system of laws. As the Roman Empire increased, a set of laws was codified to handle the more sophisticated legal questions of the day. This compilation of laws was called the Justinian Code, and, with some modification by Napoleon at the beginning of the nineteenth century, it still is the model for the legal codes governing most of the modern nation-states of Europe today. It is also reflected in the common law.

The English common law began to develop in the century following the conquest of England by William the Conqueror in 1066. To keep order and peace, the Kings of England tried to create a uniform or "common" law to govern the different regions of the British Isles. Circuit-riding judges and the use of the jury aided the Norman Kings in the consolidation of their realm.

The English colonies in America recognized the English common law as governing until July 4, 1776. After that date, existing rules were retained, but further changes in the law had to be made in the courts of the newly formed American country, not in England. The common law, with its emphasis on judges making rules of law based on real controversies in cases brought before them, has declined in importance in America since the Great Depression. The Depression brought on the "New Deal" and a flood of new laws providing for social and economic reform. The modern tendency is to rely more on statutes and codification of the law. As thus augmented, the common law system continues to serve us well.

3

Law Enforcement and the Courts

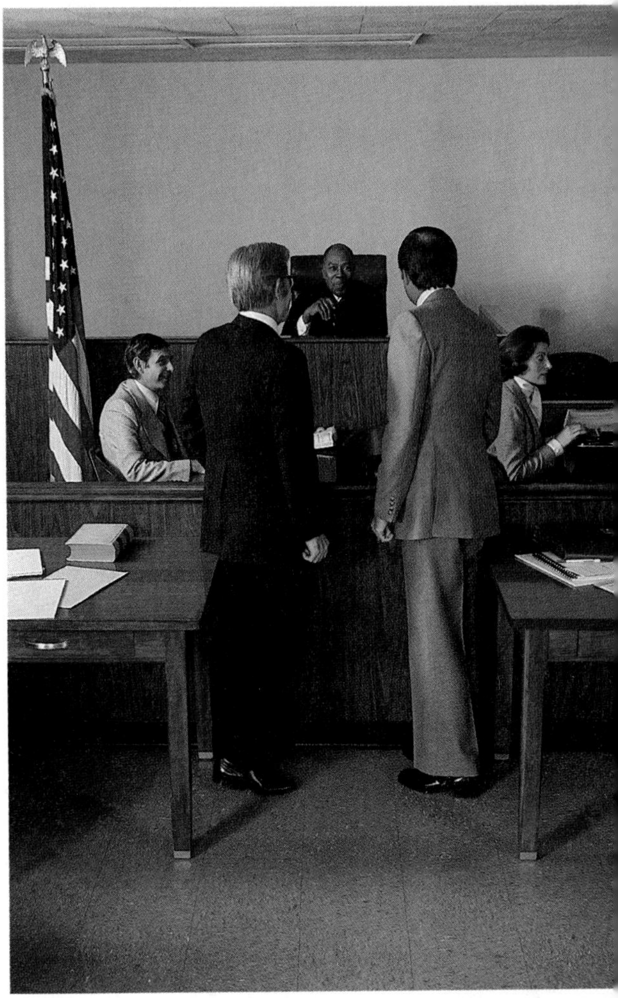

1. Woody sold Ed a used car for $1,500. Two days after the sale, the engine failed and needed to be rebuilt. Ed felt Woody had misrepresented the car's mechanical condition and should pay for the necessary repairs. After arguing about the situation, they decided to let an independent third party, Dennis, decide how to resolve their dispute. Dennis decided that they should split the cost of a new engine. Ed did not like the decision. Is he nevertheless bound by Dennis's decision?

2. Woodstock was found guilty of evading federal income taxes and was sentenced to prison. Woodstock's attorney insisted that the judge was biased and had erred in instructions to the jury. The attorney claimed that, as a result, Woodstock had not received a fair trial. Does Woodstock have any recourse?

3. Whipple had sued her employer for discriminating against her as a woman by paying higher wages to male employees who did identical work. The judge found for Whipple and ruled that she was entitled to receive $15,000 from her employer. Six months after the trial Whipple still had not been paid the $15,000. What can she do to get the money?

HOW CAN DISPUTES BE RESOLVED PRIVATELY?

PROBLEM: Seven-Eleven sold franchises for stores bearing its name. The franchise agreement required that disputes between Seven-Eleven and the franchises be settled by arbitration rather than by a trial in court. Can Seven-Eleven require its franchises to use arbitration instead of litigation?

litigate: to take a dispute to court

Many persons decide too quickly to **litigate** their disputes—to take their disputes to court. When someone injures another person or fails to keep a binding agreement, it usually makes sense to first try to settle by direct negotiation. The injured person should discuss the problem with the wrongdoer as calmly as posible. The two of them can often reach a mutually acceptable solution. If there has been an automobile accident and the prospective defendent is injured, the insurance company will sometimes send an adjuster to the injured prospective plaintiff. The adjuster tries to learn the facts about the accident and may suggest a mutually acceptable settlement.

mediator: one who tries to get parties to settle their dispute voluntarily

arbitrator: one who makes a decision that is binding on parties in a dispute

In some cases, an independent third party may be called in to act as **mediator** (also known as a *conciliator*). The mediator talks to both parties and tries to develop a solution acceptable to both parties.

In other cases, an independent third party known as an **arbitrator** may be brought in by agreement of the parties. Sometimes a provision for arbitration of disputes is included in the original agreement between the parties. In the problem, Seven-Eleven could require its franchisees to use arbitration. The arbitrator holds an informal hearing and listens to the parties and witnesses explain what happened. The arbitrator's decision, unlike that of a mediator, is binding on both parties. By using negotiation, mediation, or arbitration, the disputing parties may avoid the heavy costs and delays and difficulties of *litigation* (court trial). Moreover, the *arbitrator's decision* (award) can be enforced by court order if necessary.

When no provision has been made for arbitration, and if the parties cannot reach an agreement by any other method, either party may go to court. However, courts generally treat the decisions of arbitrators as final; the matter cannot be reheard by a trial court.

HOW IS THE LAW ENFORCED?

PROBLEM: Roberts, a builder, contracted with McGee to construct a building to be occupied by one of McGee's Hamburger Havens. A short time later, the state revealed plans to build a super highway nearby. The proposed highway would isolate the site and make access to it difficult. Therefore McGee canceled the construction contract. Roberts had already bought some materials for the job, but they were usable elsewhere. However, Roberts lost the hoped-for profit. McGee refused to pay anything, but she indicated that Roberts would be consulted for a future job. What can Roberts do to recover the loss of profit?

Governments create laws. They are also very involved in enforcing the law. In our country, we have three levels of government—federal, state, and local. All three levels create laws and all three levels enforce laws. Each level of government usually uses police, public prosecutors, and courts to enforce the law. Table 3-1 lists examples of common names used for police, public prosecutors, and courts of the three levels of government.

Level of Government	Police	Prosecutors	Courts
Federal	FBI Agent Federal Marshal Customs Inspector Internal Revenue Agent	U.S. Attorney General	U.S. Supreme Court Circuit Court of Appeals District Court Tax Court Bankruptcy Court
State	Highway Patrol State Trooper	Attorney General State Prosecutor	Supreme Court Court of Appeals Superior Court
Local (City and County)	Police Officer or Detective Sheriff	District Attorney County Attorney City Attorney Public Prosecutor	City Court Municipal Court Traffic Court Small Claims Court Divorce Court Juvenile Court Justice Court

Table 3-1. Police, Prosecuter, and Court Names by Level of Government

In general, each level of government is most concerned with its own laws. Thus, agents of the Federal Bureau of Investigation (FBI) investigate only violations of federal laws. However, all police and judges take oaths to uphold the Constitution of the United States in so far as it applies to their work.

procedural law: rules for enforcement of legal rights and duties

substantive law: rules that define legal rights and duties

Procedural law deals with methods of enforcing legal rights and duties. Laws which specify how and when police can make arrests and what procedures can be used in a trial are procedural laws. In contrast, **substantive law** defines rights and duties; it is concerned with all rules of conduct except those involved in enforcement.

There are two types of procedural law—civil procedure and criminal procedure. Criminal procedure defines the process for enforcing the law when someone is charged with a crime. A crime is an offense against society, as well as a violation of the rights of the victim. Because a crime is an offense against society, representatives of society such as city police, the state highway patrol, or FBI agents investigate the alleged criminal conduct and try to arrest and imprison those who commit criminal acts. Other representatives of society—city prosecutors, state attorneys general, or U.S. attorneys try to convict the alleged criminal during a criminal trial. The law of criminal procedure controls each of these activities.

Civil procedure is used when a civil law has been violated. Civil law is concerned only with private offenses. These are offenses against a particular person who has been injured. When a civil law is violated, the injured party uses civil procedure to protect his or her rights, primarily through a civil trial. Since civil matters involve a private offense, police and public prosecutors generally do not involve themselves in the dispute.

One act may be both a crime and a civil offense. That is, one act may violate the criminal laws and at the same time violate the civil laws by causing a private injury.

Wilson was driving 47 miles per hour in a 25 mile-per-hour zone when he ran into the rear of Gibson's car. The cost to repair Gibson's car was $4,200. Wilson committed a crime by speeding. Police will investigate the speeding; a city prosecutor will represent society in the criminal trial which may result in a fine or imprisonment for Wilson. In a second, separate trial, Gibson can sue and win an award for the cost of her repairs. Speeding was an offense against society. Hitting the car was a civil offense against Gibson.

In the earlier problem, Roberts's claim against McGee is a civil matter. Therefore police and prosecutors will not become involved. If Roberts initiates a lawsuit to recover lost profits, the rules of civil procedure will govern the trial.

WHAT IS A COURT?

PROBLEM: Doyle was *cited* (ordered to appear in court) by a police officer for making an illegal U-turn at a street intersection. Doyle claimed that the sign forbidding a U-turn at that intersection was obstructed by a tree branch. The officer replied, "Sorry, you can tell it to the judge in court." Why is a court necessary in this situation?

A **court** is a tribunal established to administer justice under the law. It may decide civil disputes or criminal cases brought properly before it. A court may award damages, impose punishment for crimes, or grant other appropriate relief. In the problem, a court was necessary to decide whether Doyle had a good excuse for not seeing the sign. This is because courts use impartial and thorough procedures to make decisions. For example, witnesses can be compelled to give testimony and an accused party is allowed equal opportunity to argue her or his side of the case.

court: tribunal established to administer justice

There are two different levels of courts: trial courts and appellate courts. A **trial court** is the first court to hear a dispute. Witnesses testify and other information is also presented to prove the alleged facts. An **appellate court** sometimes reviews decisions of a trial court when a party claims an error of law was made at the trial level.

trial court: court where a dispute is first heard

appellate court: court that reviews trial court decisions

An action is filed and tried in the appropriate trial court. In most cases, the decision may be appealed to the next higher court, including the state supreme court. The decision of the supreme court of a state is final in all cases which do not involve the federal Constitution, federal laws, or treaties. Cases decided by state supreme courts may be reviewed by the Supreme Court of the United States if a federal Constitutional question is involved.

Comparatively few cases are appealed since the parties "have had their day in court" with a fair trial and, therefore, accept the judgment. Usually there have not been significant errors of law, and the appellate court normally is not concerned with questions of fact.

A trial court consists not only of a judge but also of lawyers, who are officers of the court, and others who are necessary for the court's operation. The words *court* and *judge* are often used to mean the same thing. While presiding over a legal action, the judge may be referred to as "The Court" or "Your Honor."

Courts vary in authority (or jurisdiction) from justice of the peace and small claims courts to the supreme courts of various states and the Supreme Court of the United States. State courts have power to decide cases involving state and local laws. Federal courts have power to decide cases involving federal law.

transcript: copy of the written record of a trial

Unlike trial courts, appellate courts do not hear witnesses or accept new evidence. They examine the **transcript**—the word-for-word written record of what was said at the trial. They also read *appellate briefs* (written arguments on the issues submitted by the opposing attorneys). Then the appellate courts listen to oral arguments of the attorneys and may question them about the case. Finally, the appellate courts decide whether, as a matter of law, the decision below should be *affirmed* (upheld), *reversed* (overturned), *amended* (changed), or *remanded* (sent back to the trial court for corrective action, including possibly a new trial).

WHAT IS OUR SYSTEM OF COURTS?

PROBLEM: During a trip to Europe, Wold purchased several clocks. When she returned with the clocks, she claimed that they were more than 100 years old. If true, this would qualify the clocks as antiques and exempt them from import *duties* (taxes). The collector of customs disagreed and demanded payment of the assessed tax. Did Wold have any recourse from the collector's ruling?

As stated earlier, in this country courts exist on the federal, state, and local levels.

1. Federal Courts

The United States Constitution provides that "The judicial power of the United States, shall be vested in one Supreme Court, and in such inferior courts as the Congress may from time to time ordain and establish." The Supreme Court's decisions about federal Constitutional law are final, and such decisions may affect the powers of government and rights of the people. This Court consists of nine judges, called justices of the Supreme Court. The presiding judge is the chief justice. All of the justices are appointed for life by the President, with the advice and consent of the Senate.

From time to time, Congress has created other federal courts below the Supreme Court. The present federal court system includes 13 intermediate U.S. courts of appeals. Most are located in *circuits* (assigned areas) in different sections of the country. They receive most of the appeals from the federal trial courts. Most federal cases are tried in a U.S. district court. There are district courts in all states, as well as in the District of Columbia and in U.S. overseas territories. In general, federal courts hear cases which involve rights created by the Constitution or by other federal laws. As indicated in Figure 3-1, there are other federal courts with specialized powers. For example, the bankruptcy courts hear all requests for discharge in bankruptcy.

In the problem, Wold could appeal the ruling of the collector of customs to the Customs Court. If dissatisfied with the decision of the Customs Court, she could appeal to the Court of Appeals for the Federal Circuit, and ultimately to the U.S. Supreme Court.

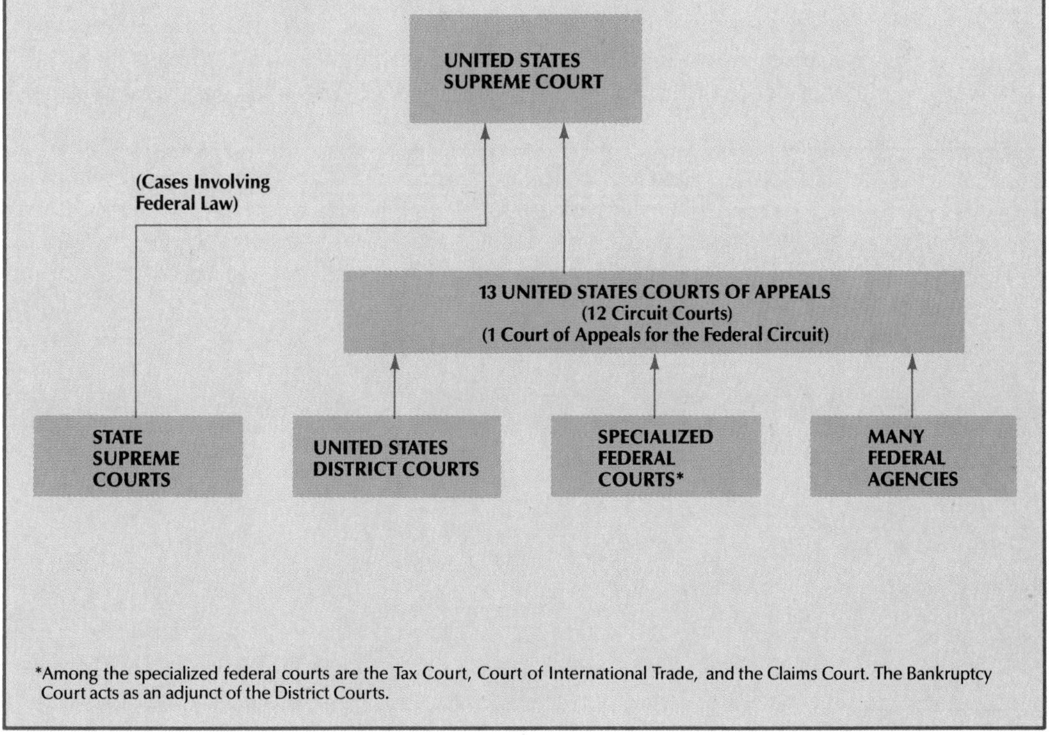

*Among the specialized federal courts are the Tax Court, Court of International Trade, and the Claims Court. The Bankruptcy Court acts as an adjunct of the District Courts.

Figure 3-1. A Simplified Diagram of the Federal Court System

2. State and Local Courts

The systems of courts in the different states are organized along similar lines. Each state ordinarily has (1) a supreme court; (2) trial courts—they are variously named county, circuit, superior, or district courts and have original, general jurisdiction over important cases; and (3) courts of limited jurisdiction—other courts with original jurisdiction over specialized cases. Most of the populous states also have intermediate courts of appeals, which ease the supreme court's load. (See Figure 3-2).

States use different names for their courts. For example, in New York the court of final authority is the court of appeals. The principal original trial court, which is the county, circuit, or district court in other states, is called the supreme court. In some states, the trial court or the court of original general jurisdiction is called the court of common pleas.

Many cities have police, traffic, or municipal courts for minor criminal offenses and for civil actions involving small sums. Some states also have other courts with limited jurisdiction. These courts include criminal courts, probate or surrogate courts, juvenile or children's courts, family courts or courts of domestic relations, and the

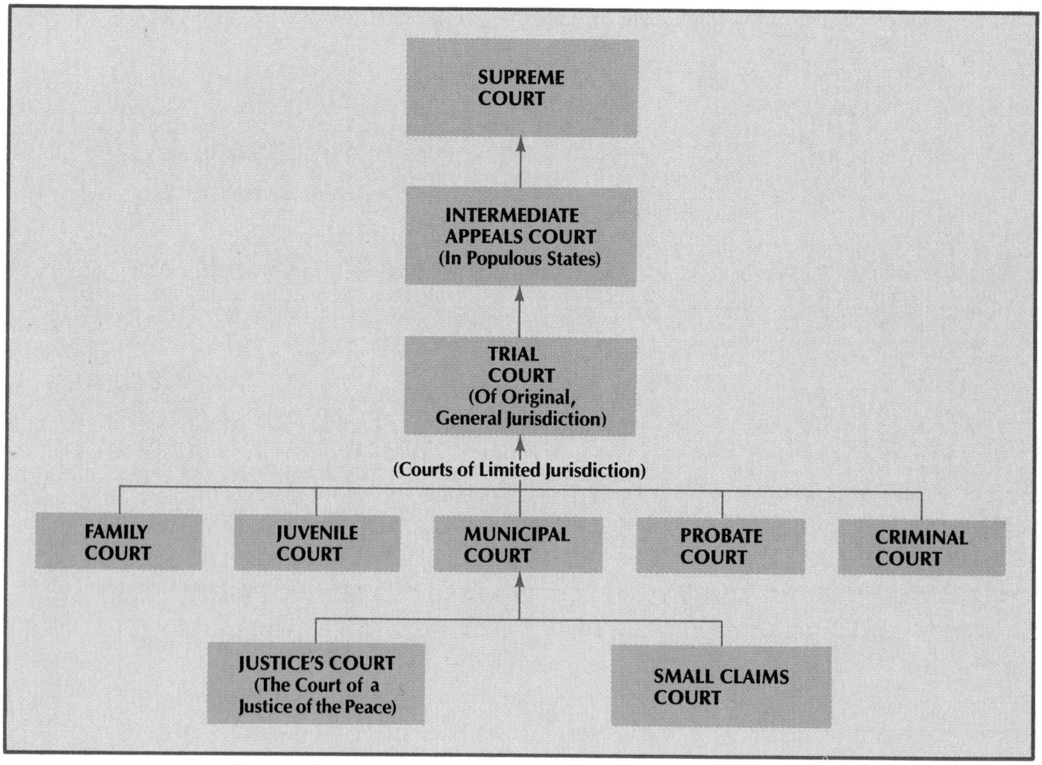

Figure 3-2. A Typical State Court System

courts of justices of the peace. These courts may simply be specialized departments of the trial court of original jurisdiction. There is a national trend to abolish the courts of justices of the peace, which often have nonlawyers as judges. The function of this court is then transferred to a municipal court or other tribunal presided over by a judge who is a lawyer.

Many states or cities have small claims courts. In a **small claims court**, a civil action for a small amount, up to $1,000 or more in some states, can be filed. The cost of filing is nominal, and each party may represent himself or herself. (In some states, attorneys are not permitted unless they are acting on their own behalf or for an employer, such as a corporation which employs them as full-time staff members.) The proceedings of such courts are conducted informally, quickly, and economically.

small claims court: court in which a person may sue on a small claim

Arnote owed Bruce $150 for some bricks Bruce had sold and delivered. The state where Bruce lived has a small claims court. Therefore Bruce filed his suit against Arnote in the small claims court. Bruce received a judgment for $150 plus $11.50 in court costs.

HOW DOES A JUVENILE COURT DIFFER FROM OTHERS?

PROBLEM: Reid, age 15, was detained by the police for shoplifting and was referred to the juvenile court. Would Reid be treated differently there than in a criminal court for adults?

All states have special courts with exclusive jurisdiction over **juveniles** (also known as *minors*)—persons under the age of majority. In most states, these tribunals (which are called juvenile, children's, or family courts) have jurisdiction over persons under 18. All states provide that for certain crimes, notably murder, and under certain conditions, the juvenile court may transfer a minor of specified age to a regular criminal court to be tried as an adult. Depending on the state, the minimum age for such a transfer may be as low as 13 or as high as 16. The transfer is made when it has been determined that the minor had the maturity and moral perception (1) to distinguish between right and wrong and (2) to understand the legal consequences of the acts sufficiently to be prosecuted and, if convicted, punished as an adult.

juveniles: persons under the age of majority

When a minor sues or is sued for damages for a tort or for breach of contract, the action is brought into a regular court. This is because there is no compelling reason to have a separate juvenile court for civil damage claims. A parent or other person is named by the court as a special guardian to prosecute or defend the suit on behalf of the minor.

The juvenile court is a court of special and limited jurisdiction, designed to look after the interests of minors who get into trouble or who do not have parents or *guardians* (those appointed to substitute for parents) to take care of them. Generally the court protects minors from the results of their own immaturity. The court may serve as the guardian of children who are abandoned, orphaned, or incapable of self-support.

juvenile delinquents: minors who violate any law

incorrigible: uncontrollable by parents or guardians

Minors who commit crimes are treated not as criminals but as **juvenile delinquents**. The definition of juvenile delinquent varies by state statute. However, in general, the term means a child under a specified age who violates any law, is **incorrigible** (ungovernable or uncontrollable), is immoral, repeatedly runs away from home, is truant from school, violates curfews, or is growing up in idleness and crime.

status offenses: acts which are wrongful because of the offender's age

The juvenile court seeks to provide guidance, rehabilitation, and reform rather than to fix criminal responsibility and to impose punishment. Accordingly, in the problem, Reid would not be treated as an adult. Instead, he would be entitled to a hearing that would take age and level of maturity into consideration. Some offenses of minors are **status offenses**, which are based on the minority status of the offenders. The acts, such as violating a curfew or being a truant, would not be crimes if committed by adults.

A juvenile court decided that a 13-year-old girl was a delinquent because she was repeatedly absent from school without excuse and had run away from home numerous times. In accordance with the law governing status offenses, she was placed in a foster home after a hearing in a juvenile court.

For a minor who is in trouble for violating the law, there are advantages in being under the jurisdiction of a juvenile court rather than a regular criminal court. The juvenile normally is not "arrested," "booked," and "jailed" but is "detained" or "taken into custody" and "confined." Under the laws of most states, juveniles are taken to a detention facility rather than an adult jail. Some states provide that juveniles 16 to 18 years of age taken into custody are not to be confined with persons convicted of a crime or awaiting trial on criminal charges. If the juvenile is declared delinquent, the record is not open to the public, although outsiders do learn of these facts sometimes.

Hearings in juvenile courts are much different from those in other courts. There is no "trial" in the usual sense. The proceedings are very informal, are not open to the public, and are usually held in the office of the judge or in a conference room. The parents or guardians are required to be present along with any witnesses. The juvenile, as an accused person, is entitled to an attorney and all the other constitutional rights discussed earlier, except that of a trial by jury. The U.S. Supreme Court has said that a jury trial would inject into juvenile court proceedings the traditional delay, formality, and clamor of the adversary system.

The purpose of the juvenile court hearing is first to determine whether the juvenile committed the offense as charged. If it is found that the juvenile did so, then those at the hearing consider what should be done to rehabilitate the juvenile and, if possible, to prevent a similar occurrence in the future. Accordingly, professional specialists such as psychologists, social workers, and physicians may be present as consultants.

The hearing includes presentation of the evidence and discussion with the accused minor, the parents, and others concerned. If the minor is found guilty of the offense, the judge will decide what should be done. Statutes give the court wide discretion in making its decisions. If found to be delinquent, the juvenile may be placed on probation or committed to a detention home or some other facility, such as a medical or psychiatric hospital. A minor may be released to the parents, especially if it is a first offense, or may be placed either under the supervision of a probation officer or in the care of a social agency. Often the child is placed in the home of a relative, in a youth hostel, or in a foster family home. If the offense is serious or if the offender has been in trouble before or is incorrigible, the court may order different treatment. In such a case, the court may order confinement in a local detention home.

WHAT IS THE PROCEDURE IN A CRIMINAL ACTION?

PROBLEM: Walden was suspected of deliberately failing to file and pay his income tax—a criminal offense. What steps must be taken to determine whether Walden committed a crime?

criminal action: lawsuit brought against a person accused of a crime

A **criminal action** is a lawsuit brought by the state (also known as the *people*) against a person accused of a crime. If found innocent, the person is released; if found guilty, he or she is sentenced by the judge. Under our system of law, a person is presumed to be innocent until (1) guilt is admitted or (2) guilt is proven beyond a reasonable doubt in a competent court. Thus, in the problem, if Walden does not admit that he deliberately failed to file and pay his income tax, the government must prove these facts. The government must do this through evidence submitted in a trial in open court before a judge. There may be a jury if either the state prosecutor or Walden asks for one. Walden is entitled to all rights of an accused person, as guaranteed by the U.S. Constitution. Thus, he may be represented by a lawyer. Also, he is presumed innocent and need not testify or say anything in his own defense because it might *incriminate* him (make him appear to be involved in the crime).

Codes of procedure specify in detail the conduct of a trial. This is done to assure *due process* (fairness and the protection of the rights of the accused person). Each state has its own system, and the procedures vary in details, but Figure 3-3 on page 47 shows the usual steps involved.

The first step is usually an investigation by the proper authorities to determine who may have committed a reported crime. The investigators seek evidence to present in court. Usually an *arrest warrant* (written court order) must be issued by a court for the suspect to be arrested. Upon arrest, the suspect must be advised of his or her constitutional rights and *booked* (fingerprinted and photographed). After the booking, a judge, in a preliminary hearing, determines whether the suspect shall be kept in jail or released on bail. **Bail** is a sum of money or property deposited or pledged to guarantee that the arrested person will appear for a preliminary hearing or trial. The amount in each case is set by the judge.

bail: deposit of money to guarantee appearance at one's trial

In some cases, the accused person may be released on his or her own **recognizance**. This means that the suspect promises to appear as scheduled without putting up bail. This usually happens if the accused is a reputable citizen with substantial assets.

recognizance: promise of the accused person to appear in court, without posting bail

For some minor offenses, including most traffic violations, the arresting officer may give the offending person a **citation**. This is a notice that identifies the offense and directs the person to (1) appear in court at a specified time if he or she wants to dispute the charge or (2) pay a prescribed amount without appearing in court. The amount is a standardized fine for the offense.

citation: order requiring a defendant to appear in court

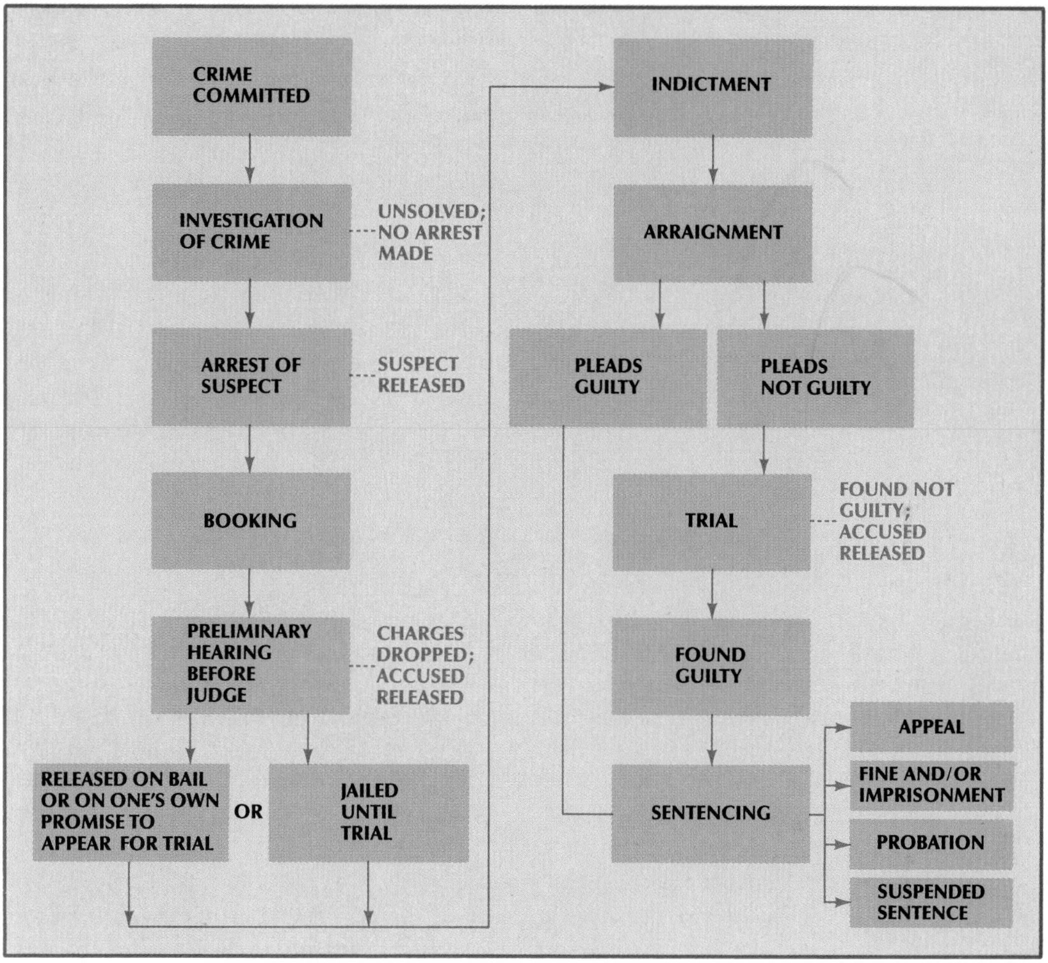

Figure 3-3. Criminal Action Procedure

In some states and at the federal level, an indictment by a grand jury is required before a person can be brought to trial for a *felony* (serious crime punishable either by death or by imprisonment for more than one year). An **indictment** is a written accusation which declares that there is sufficient evidence to try the identified individual for a specified crime. A **grand jury** is a group of citizens selected to hear, in secret, the evidence of alleged crimes submitted by the prosecutor.

One who has not been indicted by a grand jury is given a preliminary hearing before a judge. The purpose of the hearing is to determine from the evidence whether the accused person should be

indictment: accusation by a grand jury declaring there is reason to try a person for a crime

grand jury: group of citizens selected to hear evidence of alleged felonies

defendant: person against whom a criminal (or civil) action is brought

prosecution: state as the party bringing a legal action against a person accused of a crime

arraignment: court proceeding where the defendant pleads guilty or not guilty to the formal charge of a crime

released or held (also referred to as "bound over") for trial as charged. After the filing of the formal charge, the accused person is called the defendant. A **defendant** is the person against whom a criminal (or civil) action is brought. In a criminal action, the state—the party bringing suit against the defendant—is known as the **prosecution**.

Before the criminal trial, the defendant is brought before the court to hear the formal charges. The defendant is also required to plead guilty or not guilty. This court proceeding is known as **arraignment**. If the defendant pleads guilty, the defendant is sentenced. If the plea is not guilty, the defendant must stand trial.

WHAT IS THE PROCEDURE IN A CIVIL ACTION?

PROBLEM: Knox owed Dodge $15,000, which he did not pay when it came due. How could Dodge compel Knox to pay?

A person injured by the wrongful conduct of another may be able to obtain relief by having a lawyer bring a civil action against the wrongdoer. Thus, in the problem, Dodge could bring a civil suit against Knox.

plaintiff: one who brings a civil action

A civil action involves two parties. Each of these parties may consist of one or more persons. The party who brings a civil action in order to enforce a private right is the **plaintiff**. The party against whom the civil action is brought is the defendant.

Shade and Bailey negligently ran their motorboat near a beach area and injured Knudsen, who was swimming. Knudsen sued to collect for doctor and hospital bills and for pain and suffering. Knudsen was the plaintiff. Shade and Bailey were the defendants.

complaint: first paper in a civil action, filed by the plaintiff, stating the claim for judgment

summons: court order directing the defendant to answer the plaintiff's complaint

In state courts, a civil action is begun by the filing of the plaintiff's **complaint** with the clerk of the court. (See Figure 3-4 on page 49.) This step is usually done by the attorney for the plaintiff. The complaint states the plaintiff's claims, which allegedly justify the relief demanded.

Next, the defendant must be properly served with a copy of the complaint and with a summons. The **summons** is a court order,

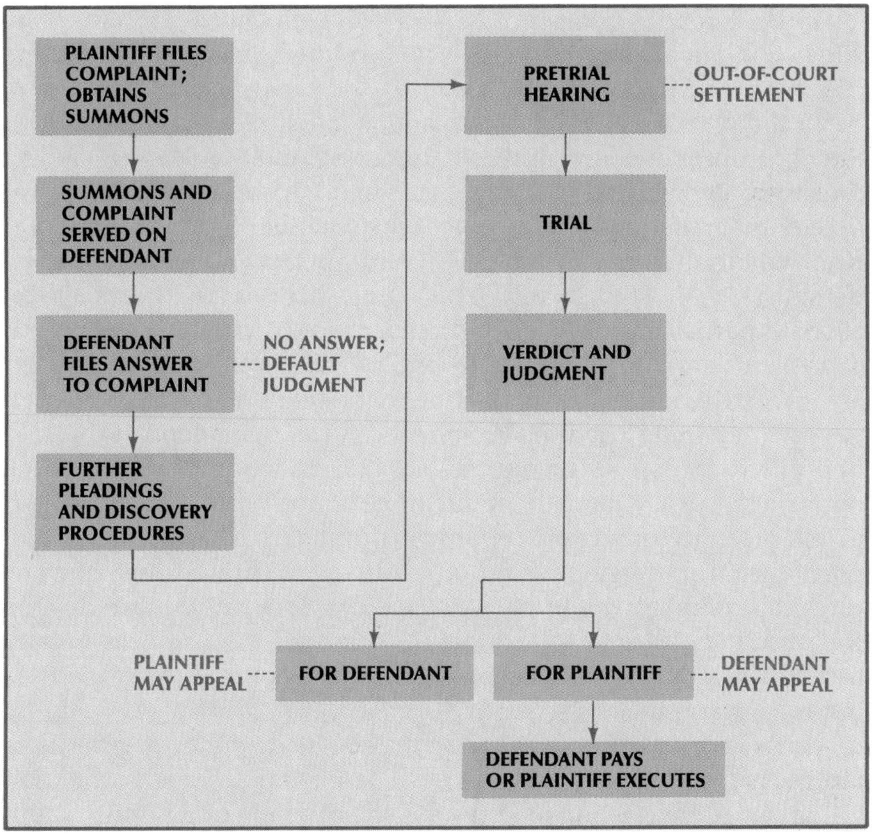

Figure 3-4. Civil Action Procedure

obtained by the plaintiff, which directs the defendant to answer the complaint. The defendant, who also usually acts through an attorney, normally files an **answer** (statement in reply). In the answer, the defendant may do any one of the following:

answer: defendant's statement in reply to the plaintiff's complaint

1. Declare that even if the facts alleged in the complaint are true, they do not constitute a wrong for which the defendant has any duty to pay or otherwise act. This is an issue of law which is decided by the judge in a hearing.
2. Deny the truth of the facts alleged in the complaint. This raises an issue of fact. The dispute can then proceed to trial.
3. Admit the facts alleged but introduce other facts that excuse the defendant from liability. The dispute can then proceed to trial.

default judgment: judgment given (without a trial) to the plaintiff when the defendant fails to answer the complaint

If the defendant does not answer the complaint within the time allowed (generally not more than 20 days), the plaintiff may win the case by **default judgment**.

In the problem, Dodge, the plaintiff, must file a complaint with the appropriate court and obtain a summons from the court directing Knox to answer. Dodge would have a process server deliver the summons and a copy of the complaint to the defendant. Knox would then have to answer the complaint or he would lose by default.

discovery procedures: court-ordered means of getting facts about the dispute from the opposing party and witnesses before the trial

deposition: pretrial questioning of the opposing party and witnesses under oath

Both parties may engage in **discovery procedures**. These pretrial procedures are done under court order to obtain facts about the case and to identify the issues in dispute that require decision at the trial. A very frequently used discovery procedure is the **deposition**. In a deposition, parties and witnesses are questioned under oath by the opposing attorney, usually in the office of one of the attorneys, and in the presence of a court reporter, who makes a written record of what is said. Depositions and other discovery procedures, such as physical examinations of persons claiming they were injured, help the attorneys learn the facts before the trial. The process greatly assists both attorneys in preparing for the trial and often leads to out-of-court settlements.

pretrial hearing: conference of the judge with the opposing attorneys before the trial

At this point, a **pretrial hearing** may be held by the judge and the attorneys to specify what issues of fact must be decided at the trial. Often, an attempt is made to resolve the differences without trial. If the attorneys cannot compromise and agree on some settlement, either party may ask the court to set a date for the trial.

HOW IS A CASE TRIED?

PROBLEM: Claxon collided with Da Lucia in an intersection which had four-way stop signs. Claxon, whose car was badly damaged by Da Lucia's truck, sued for damages. She claimed he was going at least 20 mph and had not stopped for the sign but had merely slowed down. Da Lucia claimed he had stopped and could not have reached the alleged speed. He said that he had entered the intersection first and that Claxon had tried to swing around his front end but had failed. Two witnesses saw the accident and could testify. How can the court determine what really happened?

In a trial, issues of *fact* are determined by a jury if one is used. The jurors listen to the witnesses and decide who and what to believe. Both the plaintiff and the defendant may voluntarily *waive* (give up) the right to trial by jury. If they do so, the judge alone listens to the testimony and decides the facts.

Issues of *law*, however, are always decided by the judge. The judge explains to the jury what rules of law to apply to the facts.

A **trial jury** is a body of impartial citizens (usually 12) selected to determine questions of fact. The method of jury selection varies from state to state.

The procedure followed in a jury trial is shown in Figure 3-5. After the jury for a specific case has been selected and sworn, the attorney for each side may give an opening statement. These statements briefly outline what will be proved and may indicate the highlights of the evidence to be offered. The evidence is then presented to the jury, first by the plaintiff and then by the defendant. **Evidence**

trial jury: body of citizens selected to determine questions of fact

evidence: anything that provides information used to prove or disprove alleged facts

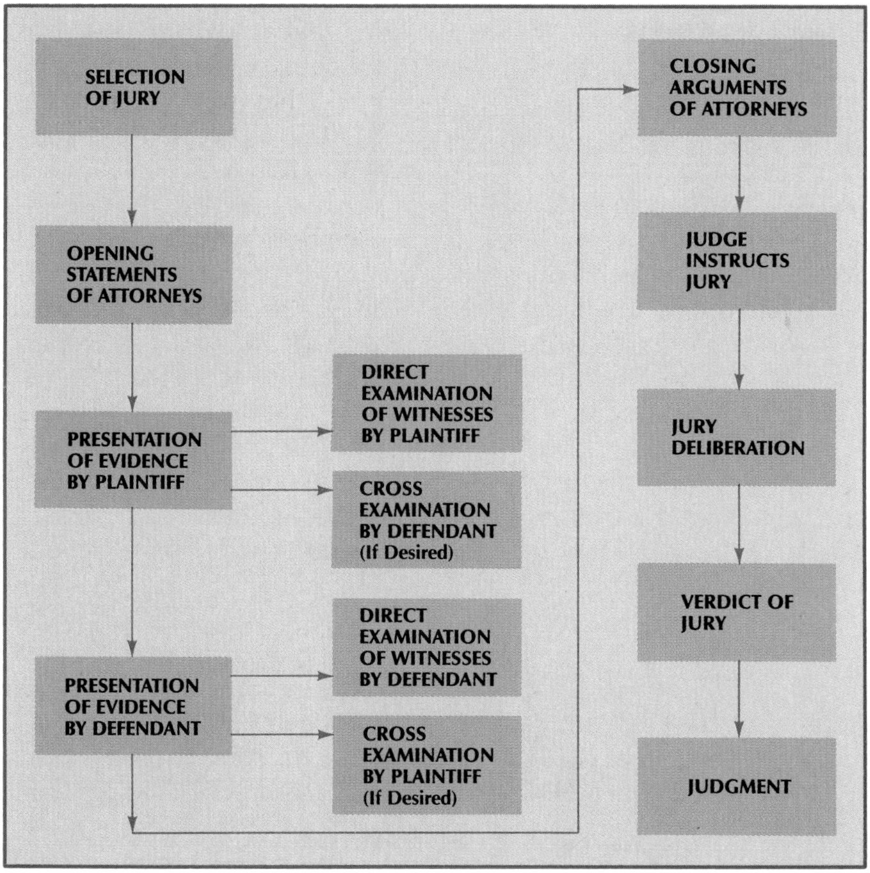

Figure 3-5. Jury Trial Procedure

testimony: oral statements given as evidence by witnesses under oath

witness: person who has personal knowledge of the facts

subpoena: written order commanding a person to appear in court as a witness

contempt of court: willful disrespect to a court or disobedience of its orders

includes anything that provides information used to prove or disprove the alleged facts. Evidence may consist of written documents, records, charts, weapons, photographs, and other objects. Usually it is the testimony of witnesses. **Testimony** consists of statements made by witnesses in court under oath. A **witness** is someone who was present during the incident and has personal knowledge of the facts. Sometimes *expert witnesses* (witnesses who possess superior knowledge about a subject in dispute) are called upon to give opinions. For example, an expert witness may be an engineer who could testify that certain skid marks left by braking tires indicate that the vehicle was moving at approximately 70 mph before a collision.

The attendance of a witness in the court is brought about by means of a subpoena. A **subpoena** is a written order by the judge commanding the named person to appear in court at a given time and place to give testimony. Willful, unexcused failure to appear is a type of **contempt of court** and can be punished by the judge, without a trial.

> While waiting for a bus, Charlesworth observed a collision in which Phillips made a left turn without signaling and was struck by a pickup truck driven by Thornburgh. If there should be a legal action as a result of this accident, Charlesworth could be subpoenaed as a witness by either side. Charlesworth would be required to tell, under oath, the truth as to what she observed.

verdict: decision of a jury

Following the presentation of the evidence, the attorney for each side gives closing remarks. During those remarks, each attorney summarizes the case, trying to persuade the judge (and jury if there is one) to favor his or her side. After consultation with the attorneys, the judge then instructs the jury as to the rules of law governing the issues of fact they must decide. For example, in a civil case involving an auto accident, the judge will define the technical terms of *negligence* and *contributory negligence*. In a criminal case, the judge will specify the required elements of the alleged crime. The jury then retires to the jury room for secret discussion and deliberation in order to reach a **verdict**. The verdict is the decision of the jury. In a civil case, the verdict will be for either the plaintiff or the defendant. In a criminal case, the verdict will be for either the prosecution or the defendant.

For conviction of a crime, a unanimous verdict of guilty is usually required. This means that every juror must vote the same way. A jury which cannot reach an agreement is called a **hung jury**. In this event, the case may be retried by another jury. Or it may be dropped if the prosecuting attorney so chooses.

hung jury: jury unable to agree unanimously upon a verdict

In a civil action, a majority or three-fourths majority is usually required for a verdict. In the problem, the jury, after considering all the evidence, would determine what had really happened in the accident. By a vote, the jury would decide whether Claxon was entitled to damages and, if so, how much she should get.

WHO RENDERS THE JUDGMENT?

PROBLEM: Ladega was tried on a charge of possession and sale of heroin. He was found guilty by a jury and was sentenced to prison by the judge. Through his attorney, Ladega argued that the judge had erred in admitting certain evidence. The evidence had been obtained by police through secret surveillance of Ladega's home. The police watched Ladega with powerful binoculars over a period of several weeks. Ladega claimed this procedure was an unconstitutional invasion of his right to privacy. What recourse does he have?

After the verdict of a jury has been returned, the judge, in accordance with the verdict, renders a judgment. The **judgment** is the final result of the trial. In a criminal action, as in the problem, the judgment is the sentencing of the defendant to jail or prison, or it is the imposition of other punishment, such as a fine. The judge may use discretion in determining the punishment and may consider recommendations made by the jury. In a few states, the jury determines the punishment.

judgment: final result of a trial

In a civil action, the judgment will normally be for a sum of money if the plaintiff wins. If the defendant wins, the judgment will merely be "judgment for the defendant." The loser is sometimes required to pay the court costs of the trial, but ordinarily each party pays his or her own attorney's fees. As a consequence, even the winning defendant may incur heavy costs in money, as well as in time, energy, and peace of mind.

Generally a judgment of a lower court is not final in regard to the rights of the parties. Either of the parties is ordinarily entitled to have the case reviewed for errors by a higher court. As was explained earlier, issues of law are decided by the judge. If either party believes the judge did not rule properly on any such issue, an appeal claiming error may be made to a higher court. Thus, in the problem, Ladega may appeal the decision to a higher court.

When an appeal is taken, the higher court may find that an important error was made during the trial in the lower court. Examples of errors would include incorrect instructions to the jury, admission of evidence that should have been rejected, or exclusion of evidence that should have been admitted. In such an event, the court may modify or reverse the judgment of the lower court or order a new trial. If there is no error in the record, the reviewing court will affirm the judgment of the lower court.

HOW IS A JUDGMENT SATISFIED?

PROBLEM: Stevens brought a civil suit against Alvarez for breach of contract in building a warehouse. Judgment for $35,000 was awarded to Stevens. Alvarez objected to the decision. However, he didn't appeal because his lawyer told him that there was no basis for appeal. Nevertheless, Alvarez stubbornly refused to pay Stevens. What steps could Stevens take to collect the judgment?

execution: process by which a judgment for money is enforced by court order

Ordinarily, when a civil judgment for the plaintiff becomes final, the defendant will pay or arrange to pay the amount or perform any other requirements of the judgment. If the defendant does not pay, the plaintiff may obtain a *writ* (court order) of execution. **Execution** is the process by which a judgment for money is enforced. The court directs the sheriff, or other officer, to seize and sell specific property of the defendant identified by the plaintiff. The proceeds, after deduction of the costs of seizure and sale, are applied to the payment of the judgment. Certain items, such as essential clothes, household goods, and tools of trade are exempt from execution. In the problem, Stevens could get a writ of execution, since Alvarez refused to pay voluntarily.

If the defendant has no property over the amount that is exempt, nothing can be obtained by execution. The judgment will remain unsatisfied because the defendant is "judgment proof." Sometimes the plaintiff or the plaintiff's attorney will determine this status before any action and will therefore refrain from filing suit.

PREVENTING LEGAL DIFFICULTIES

If You Are Involved in a Court Action . . .

As a party to the action:

1. get a lawyer who is competent and experienced for the kind of case in which you are involved. It helps if you already have a family lawyer whom you can call in the case of any emergency or legal difficulty;
2. keep accurate records of all events related to the case. While the details are still fresh in your memory, put in writing your recollection of the event, be it an accident or contract dispute. If there are witnesses, ask them to do the same. Give these records to your attorney if requested to do so;
3. try to become familiar with the terminology and legal procedure of the case;
4. if you disagree with your lawyer about a legal matter, realize that the lawyer is probably right. If you are in serious doubt, you can consult another lawyer. You can change lawyers, but you must pay for services previously received;
5. if you are a plaintiff, don't delay in consulting a lawyer. This is because evidence may be lost. Also, you may forfeit your right to sue because of a statute of limitations (see pages 277-278). If you win a judgment, press promptly for payment, through execution by court order if necessary; and
6. if you are a prospective defendant, promptly consult a lawyer when you get into legal difficulty. If served with *process* (summons and a copy of the complaint), immediately give the papers to your lawyer. Your lawyer can then file a timely answer so that you will not lose your case by default. Be guided by Items 1 through 4 above.

As a witness:

1. if you are subpoenaed, be sure to appear. Failure to appear may result in punishment for contempt of court, which could be a jail sentence or fine;
2. on the witness stand, always tell the truth to the best of your recollection. To do otherwise is *perjury*, which is a serious crime; and
3. if you do not know or cannot remember the answer to a question, say so.

As a juror:

1. if you are called for jury duty, report as directed unless you are excused in advance;
2. if you are selected as a juror for a particular case, listen attentively. Follow the judge's instructions and vote as objectively and fairly as possible. Do

not agree with other jurors out of fear, tiredness, or indifference. Likewise, do not disagree out of stubbornness or pride. Keep an open mind during the discussion and exchange of viewpoints. Remember that a verdict is often the result of compromise among honest, intelligent, and well-intentioned jurors; and

3. do not discuss the case with anyone. During the trial, such discussion could result in a mistrial. After the trial, such discussion could result in misunderstanding and embarrassment.

Strengthening Your Legal Vocabulary

answer
appellate court
arbitrator
arraignment
bail
citation
complaint
contempt of court
court
criminal action
default judgment
defendant
deposition
discovery procedures
evidence
execution
grand jury
hung jury
incorrigible
indictment
judgment
juvenile delinquents
juveniles
litigate
mediator
plaintiff
pretrial hearing
procedural law
prosecution
recognizance
small claims court
status offenses
subpoena
substantive law
summons
testimony
transcript
trial court
trial jury
verdict
witness

1. Promise of an accused person to appear in court, without posting bail.
2. Decision of a jury.
3. Acts which are wrongful because of the offender's age.
4. The body of law concerned with *enforcement* of legal rights and duties.
5. Written order commanding a person to appear in court as a witness and to give testimony.
6. Oral statements given as evidence by witnesses under oath.
7. Party who brings a civil action against another.
8. One, other than a judge, who can make a decision that is binding on the parties to a dispute.

9. Process by which a judgment for money is enforced.
10. Person who was present during an incident and has personal knowledge of the facts.

Reviewing Important Points

1. Law includes not only the rules of conduct but also the means for enforcing those rules. Any set of rules would be futile without machinery for enforcement.
2. Civil law is enforced through the courts at the request of the injured party, who is assisted by a private lawyer. Criminal law is enforced through the courts by the prosecuting attorney, who is aided by the police.
3. The federal government and each state, and some cities or counties, have separate court systems.
4. In civil actions, the plaintiff brings suit against the defendant. In criminal actions, the prosecution (the state) brings action against the defendant (the accused).
5. In every state there are juvenile courts with special jurisdiction limited to persons under the age of majority. These courts are conducted with less formality than adult courts and emphasize rehabilitation of offenders.
6. Juvenile courts treat as delinquents those minors who commit offenses that would be crimes if the offenders were adults. Juvenile courts also treat as delinquents those minors who commit status offenses—actions which would be legal if committed by adults. (An example of a status offense is staying out all night.) Delinquency is not a crime. Delinquent children are deemed to be in need of rehabilitation and guidance rather than punishment.
7. A criminal action usually begins with an arraignment. The defendant must plead guilty or not guilty to the charges.
8. A civil action is generally begun by the plaintiff filing a complaint. A process server then delivers a summons and copy of the complaint to the defendant. The defendant must answer the complaint or lose the case by default.
9. Members of a trial jury should be impartial, should not be biased or prejudiced, and should vote honestly and fairly in reaching a verdict.
10. Evidence usually consists of testimony, but it may include documents, objects, pictures, etc.
11. Persons who have knowledge of the facts in a case may be ordered by subpoena to appear in court as witnesses and to give testimony.
12. Most trials are concluded with judgment by the trial court. However, a judgment may ordinarily be appealed to a higher court. The higher court will either affirm or (if there was a serious error of law in the trial) reverse the decision or send the case back to the court from which it came to have further action taken on it there.

13. Judgment in a criminal action consists of sentencing by the judge. Judgment in a civil action normally consists of either (*a*) a judgment for money for the plaintiff or (*b*) a judgment for the defendant. If a judgment for money is not paid by the defendant, his or her nonexempt property may be seized and sold under court order to satisfy the claim.

Applying Law to Everyday Life

1. Gomez wanted to sue Shapiro for breach of contract but could not afford the expenses and time delays associated with litigation. What other alternatives are available to resolve this matter?

2. A warrant was issued by a judge in Muncie, Indiana, for the arrest of the notorious "Gun Clip" Carden. Carden was wanted for armed robbery of a federally licensed bank and for murder. He was placed on the FBI's Most Wanted List. A reward was offered for his arrest, and an all-points bulletin (APB) was issued to police departments throughout the country. Shortly after the warrant was issued, Carden was apprehended in an all-night cocktail bar in Carson City, Nevada. Why was it proper for FBI agents to assist in his capture?

3. Able and Beta were neighbors who did not like each other. One day as Beta was driving to work on his motorcycle, Able tried to run him down in his pickup truck. After three tries, Able was successful and caused serious personal and property damage. Is this a civil or criminal matter—or both?

4. Glootin was an alcoholic and the town's penniless ne'er-do-well. One night while drunk, he stole Buchanan's pickup truck and crashed into Goldman's Old-Fashioned Pharmacy. When police arrived, Glootin resisted arrest. Which of Glootin's acts are civil offenses and which are criminal offenses? Is anyone likely to collect damages?

5. The High Spirit Club of Central High contracted with Martinez and her rock band to play at the homecoming dance. The price agreed upon was $750. One week before the event, Martinez notified the club president that the band members were ill and could not play. In reality, they appeared at another event. The club hastily got a replacement band, but the replacement cost $1,000. Is the club justified in suing Martinez? If so, in what court would the club probably sue and how much could it sue for? What would happen if the club did file suit and Martinez ignored the summons and the complaint filed by the club?

6. Wilson, age 12, was habitually running away from home and was repeatedly truant from school. Can he be placed under the jurisdiction of a juvenile court as a delinquent child and be confined in a special institution until he becomes an adult?

7. Mike ran into the rear of Sharon's new car causing $32,000 in personal and property damage. Sharon won a civil judgment for the amount of the damages but Mike still has not paid anything. What can Sharon do?

Solving Case Problems

1. Taylor and Fitz Coal Company had a dispute over the amount of money due under a mineral lease. They submitted the dispute to arbitration according to the provisions of the lease. The arbitrators awarded the lessor, Taylor, $37,214.67. Taylor did not like the amount awarded and filed suit in court. Can this matter be tried in court? (*Taylor v. Fitz Coal Company*, 618 S.W.2d 432, Ky.)

2. Kent, a 16-year-old boy, was taken into custody by the police of Washington, D.C. He was held and questioned about breaking into an apartment, raping the occupant, and stealing a wallet. He admitted the offenses and volunteered information on several similar offenses. At the time, Kent was on probation for housebreaking and attempted purse snatching. Under the Juvenile Court Act, the case of any child 16 years of age or older who is charged with an offense which in the case of an adult would be a felony may be transferred by the juvenile court to the district court after full investigation by the juvenile court judge. The juvenile court waived its jurisdiction in the case of Kent, and he was properly tried and found guilty by a jury in the district court. Kent, admitting through his attorney that the court had the right to waive its jurisdiction after a full investigation, claimed nevertheless that the juvenile court had acted in an arbitrary manner and denied him due process by transferring him to the jurisdiction of the district court without a hearing at which he was present and without stating its reasons for so doing. Was the court within its rights in waiving jurisdiction after full investigation without a hearing? (*Kent v. United States,* 383 U.S. 541)

3. Bruce Mincey was killed by the explosion of a steel drum which he was cutting with a power saw. His wife, Pearl, filed suit against his employer, Dorsey Trailers, alleging Dorsey was responsible for the death. Dorsey initiated discovery procedures, but Pearl did not respond to them. Dorsey asked for a court order instructing Pearl to respond. Is Dorsey entitled to this? (*Mincey v. Dorsey Trailers, Inc.*, 397 So. 2d 98, Ala.)

4. A government-owned P-51 fighter plane landed at a Los Angeles airport and, on instructions from the tower, waited on a runway for a tow truck. Shortly thereafter, a plane owned by Douglas Aircraft Co. began approaching the airfield to land. The Douglas aircraft struck the P-51, which was parked on the runway. The U.S. brought suit against Douglas claiming that the Douglas pilot was negligent. During the trial, evidence was introduced which indicated that the Douglas pilot was careless in not seeing the parked P-51, but that the airport was covered with a haze and the P-51 was painted in camouflage colors. Also, the Douglas pilot had "zigzagged" his plane while taxiing in order to improve his forward vision. The trial was conducted before a jury. The government claimed that the issue of whether the Douglas pilot was negligent was an issue of law for the judge to decide. Douglas claimed that it was an issue of fact for the jury to decide. Who is correct? (*United States v. Douglas Aircraft Company*, 169 F.2d 755, 9th Cir.)

5. A judgment of $79.13 was entered against Sprecker for failure to pay a debt to Roper. Unable to collect the amount awarded, Roper had the sheriff seize three improved lots (with buildings) owned by Sprecker. At the execution sale, Roper stood by while each lot was separately offered unsuccessfully for sale. When the three lots were offered as a unit, Roper then bid $162.62, which was the amount of the judgment plus interest and costs. The minimum value of the property was between $53,000 and $59,000 (300 times the amount bid). There were no other bidders, so the sheriff sold the property to Roper and issued a deed to him. Roper collected rents on the property and used part of the property as a warehouse. Sprecker filed an action against Roper and the sheriff. Sprecker sought to set aside the sale as being unconscionable, or unfairly one-sided, and also asked for damages. Should Sprecker succeed? (*Sprecker v. Roper*, 529 P.2d 1367, Colo.)

4
Crimes

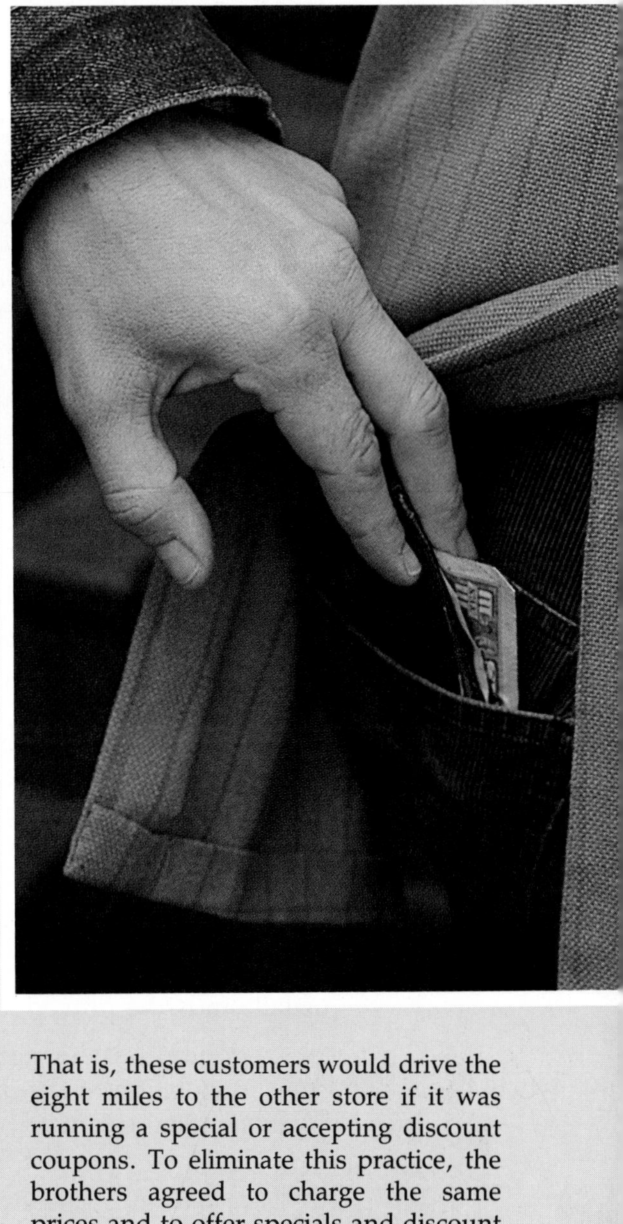

1. A woman was shopping in the local grocery store with her four-year-old daughter. When they walked past the candy display the daughter took $4.00 worth of candy and put it in the mother's purse which was in the shopping cart. The mother did not see what the daughter had done. When they left the store the mother was arrested for shoplifting. Has either the mother or daughter committed a crime?
2. Two students, 13 and 14 years old, broke into their school building one weekend and vandalized it. They smashed equipment, sprayed paint on walls, broke furniture, and started fires in trash cans. The total amount of the damage was $2,700. Did the students commit a crime?
3. Two brothers opened separate video rental stores in towns located eight miles apart. Each owned one of the stores. After two years of successful operation, they discovered that about 15 percent of their customers were "price shopping." That is, these customers would drive the eight miles to the other store if it was running a special or accepting discount coupons. To eliminate this practice, the brothers agreed to charge the same prices and to offer specials and discount coupons only at the same time. Have the brothers committed a crime?

WHAT ARE CRIMES?

PROBLEM: Davis, the chief accountant of the Del Norte Credit Union, cleverly juggled the company records over a period of years. During that time, he took at least $35,000 belonging to the union. When the theft was discovered by outside auditors, Davis repaid the money with interest. Is he still guilty of any crime?

Because criminal conduct creates a risk of severe punishment, it is very important for every individual to know which acts are criminal.

1. Offenses Against Society

crime: a punishable offense against society

The most fundamental characteristic of a **crime** is that it is a *punishable offense against society*. Consequently, when a crime occurs, society, acting through such employees as the police and prosecutors, attempts to identify, arrest, prosecute, and punish the criminal. These efforts are designed to protect society rather than to aid the victim of the crime. Victims of almost all crimes can sue identified criminals for civil damages, but seldom do because it is costly and difficult to collect from such defendants.

2. Elements of Crimes

Before anyone can be convicted of a crime, three elements usually must be proved at the trial. They are:

1. a duty to do or not to do a certain thing,
2. a violation of the duty, and
3. criminal intent.

Duty. The *duty* usually is described by state statutes which prohibit certain conduct. Less frequently, federal statutes or city ordinances identify criminal behavior. Generally only conduct that is serious—involving violence or theft of property—is classified as an offense against society and therefore criminal.

criminal battery: intentional causing of bodily harm

Violation of the Duty. The *breach* of duty must also be proved in a criminal trial. This is the specific conduct by the defendant which violates the duty. For example, all states have statutes which make battery a crime. **Criminal battery** is often defined in statutes as "the intentional causing of corporal harm." Corporal harm means bodily harm. A breach of this duty could be established in a trial by the testimony of a witness who swore that she saw the defendant deliberately punch the victim.

Criminal Intent. The third element, *criminal intent*, must be proved in most cases. Criminal intent generally means that the defendant intended to commit the act and intended to do evil. For example, if you lost your balance and began flailing your arms to regain your balance, and as a result your fist hit the nose of a bystander, there would be no criminal intent. You did not intend the act or intend to do evil. Another example can be taken from the common crime of assault. Statutes often define **criminal assault** as "a threat which creates a well-founded fear of immediate bodily harm." Suppose you are attending a football game with a friend from another school and you shake your fist and say, "If your team scores another touchdown, I'm going to punch you in the nose." Clearly you intend the statement. If, however, you mean the statement as a joke, you lack the intent to do evil and therefore lack criminal intent.

criminal assault: a threat which causes a well-founded fear of immediate bodily harm

A few crimes do not require criminal intent. These are generally less serious crimes, for which a jail sentence is very unlikely. Traffic offenses fall within this classification. You may not have intended to speed or have intended evil but you have still committed this crime.

The age of the person who engages in criminal conduct raises the issue of criminal intent. Under early common law, children less than 7 years of age were considered to be below the age of reason and, therefore, not capable of having the criminal intent necessary for crimes. Those over 14 years old were presumed to know the difference between right and wrong and, therefore, were accountable as adults for their acts. For children 7 through 14, such knowledge had to be proved.

Today, statutes of most states fix the age of criminal liability at 18, but the figure ranges from 16 to 19. As you learned in Chapter 3, statutes often provide that minors as young as 13 or 16 may be tried and punished as adults if they are accused of serious crimes such as murder. Generally, however, what is a crime for adults is **juvenile delinquency** for minors.

juvenile delinquency: violation by minors of criminal and other laws

Ignorance or mistake is generally no excuse for violating a law. A person is presumed to know what the law is. To have criminal intent, one must have sufficient mental capacity at the time one commits a crime to know the difference between right and wrong and to be capable of deciding what to do. Accordingly, insane persons are not held liable for their criminal acts.

Normally neither voluntary intoxication nor use of drugs is a good defense against a criminal charge. However, intoxication may be a good defense against a charge of certain crimes, such as first-degree murder. This is because first-degree murder requires a specific intent or state of mind; namely, the predetermined intent to take willfully the life of another. Intoxication may prevent one from having such intent.

In the problem, Davis owed a duty, defined by state statute, not to take from others money or other property which had been entrusted to his care. Violation of this duty is known as the crime of **embezzlement**. Violation of this duty could be proved by establishing the juggling of the books and the taking of the money. Davis's criminal intent can be established by his conduct; the acts were intentional and he intended to do the evil. If Davis were very young or insane, he might escape criminal liability.

embezzlement: fraudulent taking of money or other property entrusted to one's care

HOW ARE CRIMES CLASSIFIED?

PROBLEM: Munroo was a witness at a civil trial for damages. As all witnesses do before testifying, she took an oath "to tell the truth, the whole truth, and nothing but the truth." Nevertheless, while being questioned by one of the attorneys, Munroo deliberately lied, hoping to help the defendant. If this could be proved, could she be punished for a crime?

Crimes are classified in terms of their seriousness as (1) felonies or (2) misdemeanors. Each state has its own criminal law, which distinguishes between felonies and misdemeanors and states the applicable punishments. In addition, the federal government identifies a special category of crime known as *treason*. This crime consists of levying war against the United States or giving aid and comfort to enemies of the United States.

1. Felonies

felony: serious crime punishable by death or imprisonment for more than one year

A **felony** is a crime of a serious nature. It exists when the act (1) is labeled so by law or (2) is punishable by death or confinement for more than one year in a state prison. Murder, kidnapping, arson, rape, robbery, burglary, embezzlement, forgery, larceny (also called theft) of large sums, and perjury are examples of felonies. A person who lies when under oath, as Munroo did in the problem, commits **perjury**.

perjury: lying under oath

2. Misdemeanors

A **misdemeanor** is a crime of a less serious nature. It is usually punishable (1) by confinement in a county or city jail for less than one year, (2) by fine, or (3) by both confinement and fine. Crimes such as drunkenness in public, driving an automobile at an illegal speed, shoplifting, and larceny of small sums are usually misdemeanors. Some states have adopted a new classification of lesser misdemeanors. Such a lesser misdemeanor is known as an **infraction.** Parking overtime, failing to clear snow from sidewalks, and littering are examples of infractions. Ordinarily, no jury is allowed in cases involving infractions because the punishment is no more than a fine.

misdemeanor: crime of a less serious nature punishable by fine and/or jail up to one year

infraction: minor misdemeanor punishable by a fine

WHAT ARE BUSINESS-RELATED CRIMES?

PROBLEM: Officers of six competing manufacturers of a widely used cosmetic met at a trade convention. All of the officers agreed to use the same wholesale price for the cosmetic. They also agreed to follow the lead of the biggest company in making future price changes. Each officer agreed to promote sales by advertising only within an assigned geographical region. Were the officers and their companies guilty of any crime?

A business, like any person, is subject to general criminal law. Some crimes, however, are found more frequently in the business world than elsewhere. Business firms are frequently the victims of crimes such as robbery, burglary, shoplifting, employee pilferage, passing bad checks, vandalism, receiving stolen property, and embezzlement. Less frequently, but often with much larger sums of money involved, business persons and firms may commit crimes. Because such criminals are generally well-educated, respected members of the community, the offenses are called **white-collar crimes**. These criminals exploit their victims through concealment and deceit. Common examples of white-collar crimes are income tax evasion, consumer fraud, cheating with false weighing machines, conspiring to fix prices, making false fire insurance and auto insurance

white-collar crimes: nonviolent crimes committed by respected persons or corporations

claims, false advertising, bribery, political corruption, and embezzlement. Normally no physical violence is involved in crimes of this nature. Thus, courts tend to be more lenient with the criminals, punishing them with fines or short prison sentences. In the problem, the six manufacturers and their involved officers were guilty of violating certain laws. These laws state that competing companies may not cooperate in fixing prices or in dividing sales regions. Business firms should compete freely and fairly with one another.

victimless crimes: crimes for which there may be no real victim

Some critics claim that too much time and money are spent in vain attempts by police to suppress what are often called **victimless crimes.** Included in this category are commercial gambling, illegal drug trafficking and use, *loan sharking* (charging excessive, illegal interest on loans of money), and prostitution. All of these activities are conducted as profitable businesses by criminals. Most states insist that there are victims in such crimes even though such persons may become involved voluntarily.

Violations of administrative regulations may also be crimes even though they are not usually thought of as such. For example, a company may commit a crime by violating pure food and drug regulations or by violating occupational health and safety rules.

Crimes may be classified in various ways. One type of classification is given below. As you read the following list, however, keep in mind that human beings are the ultimate victims in all crimes:

1. crimes against a person (murder, assault and battery, kidnapping, rape),
2. crimes against property (larceny, robbery, hijacking loaded trucks, embezzlement, receiving stolen property),
3. crimes against the government and the administration of justice (treason, tax evasion, bribery, counterfeiting, perjury),
4. crimes against public peace and order (rioting, carrying concealed weapons, drunk and disorderly conduct, illegal speeding),
5. crimes against buildings (burglary, arson, criminal trespass),
6. crimes against consumers (fraudulent sale of worthless securities, violation of pure food and drug laws), or
7. crimes against decency (bigamy, obscenity, prostitution, contributing to the delinquency of a minor).

Some of the more common business-related crimes are discussed on the following pages.

1. Larceny

Larceny (commonly known as *theft*) is the wrongful taking of money or personal property belonging to someone else, with intent to deprive the owner of possession. Variations of larceny include **robbery** (taking property from another's person or immediate presence, against the victim's will, and by force or by causing fear) and **burglary** (entering a building or occupied structure with the intent to commit a crime, unless the premises were open to the public at the time or the person had a right to enter). Other types of larceny include shoplifting, pickpocketing, and purse snatching. A growing form of crime is larceny by computer. In this type of crime, a skilled operator of a computer manipulates the computer to divert funds to himself or herself.

larceny: wrongful taking of money or other personal property

robbery: taking of property by force from the person or presence of another

burglary: illegally entering a building with the intent to commit a crime

Larceny may be either a felony or a misdemeanor. The classification is determined by the value of the property stolen and the circumstances surrounding the act. However, burglary is always a felony. In addition, if the burglar sells the stolen goods, he or she is guilty of two crimes—burglary and selling stolen property. As explained below, this double crime frequently involves another criminal.

2. Receiving Stolen Property

Knowingly **receiving stolen property** is an offense separate from larceny. It consists of receiving, concealing, or buying property known to be stolen, with intent to deprive the rightful owner of the property. One who receives stolen property is known as a fence. Special statutes in most states deal with the fencing of types of property that are commonly stolen, such as motor vehicles and valuable airplane, ship, or truck cargoes.

receiving stolen property: buying known stolen property with the intent to deprive the rightful owner

Police throughout the country have used federal grants successfully to set up phony storefronts where they pose as criminal fences. For months they buy stolen goods from unsuspecting thieves, paying the customary small fraction of the true value. These transactions are filmed by video equipment without the thieves' knowledge. The police then close the particular sting operation and arrest the criminals. Because the evidence of guilt is so clear when these methods are used, there is a high rate of conviction for the crimes. The high rate helps to discourage both thieves and fences.

3. False Pretenses

false pretenses: obtaining property by lying

One who obtains money or other property from another person by lying about a past or existing fact is guilty of **false pretenses** (also known as *false representation).* This crime differs from larceny because the victim parts with the property voluntarily. False pretenses is a type of fraud (see page 89).

> Allen went to a credit union and filled out a credit application. Although he was unemployed, he indicated a salary of $1200 per month on the application. By error, the credit union did not verify his employment. Allen was thereby allowed to borrow $6,000 which he was unable to repay. Allen was guilty of obtaining the money under false pretenses.

4. Forgery

forgery: making or materially altering any writing, with intent to defraud

Forgery is falsely making or *materially* (in some important detail) altering any writing which, if it were genuine, might have legal value. An example of such a writing would be the signature of another person. In forgery there must be intent to defraud either the person whose name is signed or someone else. The most common forgeries are found on checks when one has signed another's name without permission to do so. Forgery also includes altering a check, such as when one changes "$7" to "$70" and "Seven" to "Seventy." False pretense enters into forgery because the signer pretends to be someone else. Forgery is usually a felony. Of course, if someone authorizes you to sign his or her name and you do so, there is no forgery because there is no intent to defraud.

bribery: offering, giving, or receiving money to influence official action

5. Bribery

Bribery is offering or giving to a government official money or anything of value which the official was not authorized to receive in order to influence performance of an official duty. Accepting the money or offer is also bribery.

Bribery became so common in international trade that Congress enacted the Foreign Corrupt Practices Act of 1977. This act forbids such conduct by American companies overseas. Unfortunately foreign countries and salespeople are not bound by these rules. This situation sometimes places American exporters at a competitive disadvantage.

Crimes similar to bribing a government official include bribing a private company's purchasing agent to obtain a sale. Another example is when professional gamblers pay an athlete to lose a game intentionally.

6. Extortion

Extortion (commonly known as *blackmail*) is obtaining money or other property from a person by wrongful use of force, fear, or the power of office. The extortionist (*blackmailer*) may threaten to inflict bodily injury on the victim or a close relative of the victim. Sometimes the extortionist threatens to expose a secret crime or some embarrassing fact if payment is not made. Kidnapping is a related crime.

extortion: obtaining property wrongfully by force, fear, or the power of office

> The head of a labor union threatened to call a costly strike among the employees of a company unless he was paid $10,000 by the employer. This was extortion.

7. Conspiracy

Conspiracy is an agreement between two or more persons to do an unlawful criminal act, or to do a lawful act by unlawful means. Usually the agreement is secret. Depending on the circumstances, the crime may be either a felony or a misdemeanor. Business executives of competing corporations sometimes conspire to fix prices or to divide markets.

conspiracy: agreement to commit a crime

> Thompson and two others were convicted of conspiring to smuggle heroin into the United States, to rent boats for this purpose in Mexico, and to distribute the drug. Thompson appealed the conviction. She claimed that no heroin was introduced as evidence to prove that the conspiracy was carried out; therefore, the accused persons were not guilty. The court held that the crime of conspiracy is not dependent upon the success or failure of the planned scheme.

8. Arson

Arson is the willful and illegal burning of a building. Under early common law, the courts sought primarily to protect human life. Therefore, arson was limited to the malicious burning of another's home. This definition has since been extended to include other structures. Arson has been committed when someone intentionally starts a fire or causes an explosion that results in any burning or

arson: intentional, illegal burning of a building

even charring of wood or other materials. In most states, a special offense has been created by statute that covers fraudulently destroying or damaging any property, whether one's own or another's, to collect insurance for the loss. One may, of course, destroy one's own building or other property when there is no intent to defraud, no risk to others, and no violation of statute.

9. Selling and Buying Narcotic Drugs

Narcotics, when abused, can cause serious mental and physical harm. Therefore, all states have passed laws which make certain narcotic-related activities criminal offenses. The activities include selling or offering to sell, possessing, transporting, administering, or giving narcotics without a license, except by medical prescription. Drugs classified as narcotics are usually specified by statute, as in the Uniform Narcotic Drug Act, which is in force with modifications in most states. The federal government also regulates the manufacture and distribution of narcotics for legitimate medical purposes.

Violations of narcotic laws are usually felonies but can be misdemeanors. Adults who supply others with narcotic drugs are usually dealt with harshly. Some states make prison sentences mandatory for one convicted of distributing narcotics. Also, in some states, increased punishment is required by statute if one has a prior narcotic conviction. Life imprisonment is prescribed in some cases.

It is reported that most burglaries and other crimes against property are drug related. That is because the habitual drug user may commit other crimes to raise money to support the costly practice. Government authorities around the world refuse to legalize production and sale of these drugs. They fear that legalization would result in an increase in the number of users. These users could constitute a large group of unproductive citizens, dependent on others for support.

10. Computer Crime

Society has only recently addressed the problems of crimes made possible by the computer revolution, a development of major economic proportions.

One problem involves the stealing of valuable information expressed as electrical impulses from computers owned by other persons. Recall that larceny is "the wrongful taking of the personal property of others." This traditional definition of the crime made it difficult to prosecute those who steal computer data for two reasons.

First, many courts concluded that there was not a "taking" if an intruder merely *copied* the information in the computer. Second, even if an intruder copied and erased computer information, some courts concluded that there was no taking of "personal property" but only the loss of electrical impulses which no one really owns. The response of some states has been to create new criminal laws. For example, Arizona enacted a statute which states that "accessing, altering, damaging, or destroying without authorization any computer . . . [is criminal conduct]. . ." Notice that under this statute merely "accessing" another's computer without authorization is a crime.

WHAT RIGHTS DOES ONE HAVE WHEN ARRESTED?

PROBLEM: A state law provides that "hit-and-run" driving is a crime. The law requires the driver of a motor vehicle involved in an accident to stay at the scene, give name and address, and show driver's license. Barlow, who was arrested for violating this law, claimed that the law was unconstitutional. He said that the law violated the right against self-incrimination, as provided in the Fifth Amendment to the United States Constitution. Is he correct?

One of the major objectives of the Constitution of the United States is to protect individuals from certain governmental actions. That document contains many clauses which specifically limit the power of the federal government in the criminal law area. These limitations now also apply to state and local governments. The framers of the Constitution believed it was better for our society to give individuals too much liberty than to allow the government too much power. Thus, in this country, persons suspected or accused of criminal conduct have rights which are not available to people in many other countries.

However, the rights of accused persons are subject to reasonable limitations. In the problem, Barlow's right against self-incrimination was not violated by the law which requires one to remain at the scene of the accident and identify oneself. It is true that such actions would indicate involvement and could lead to criminal prosecution if a crime has been committed. However, the constitutional prohibition against self-incrimination excludes only statements which would implicate the person in a crime. Merely identifying oneself as a party to an accident does not in itself show guilt or innocence.

In recent years, the United States Supreme Court's interpretation of the Constitutional rights of persons accused of committing crimes has focused on due process. Due process is a concept embodied in the Fifth and Fourteenth Amendments of the U.S. Constitution. In general, **due process** requires fundamental fairness and compliance with the basic rules for a fair and orderly trial.

due process: the constitutional requirement that investigations and trials be conducted in fair and orderly ways

The list of specific due process rights is extensive. Some of these important rights are listed in Figure 4-1. Due process also refers to procedures followed during an investigation before one is arrested, as well as procedures after arrest and in court. The thorough, detailed steps in a criminal trial are designed to determine the facts and to assure fairness, justice, and equal treatment. Because of the complex procedures involved in a criminal proceeding, probably the most important right of the accused is the right to be represented by a lawyer. For a person who cannot afford to hire a lawyer, a public defender or private lawyer is provided by the state, if requested, to help the defendant establish a good defense. Even if the defendant is guilty, a lawyer is needed to help determine the proper degree of crime, to protect the defendant's rights, to try to persuade the court to be lenient in punishment, and perhaps to obtain release on probation. Sometimes the lawyer may advise the client to waive certain rights, such as the right to a trial, by pleading guilty to a lesser offense with a lighter punishment. **Waiver** is the voluntary, intentional relinquishment of a legal right.

waiver: voluntarily giving up a legal right

WHEN IS ONE PARTY RESPONSIBLE FOR THE CRIMINAL CONDUCT OF ANOTHER?

PROBLEM: Musk, a career criminal, planned a bank robbery. Spiro and Adann were sent to do the "job." Greene, driving a stolen car, served as chauffeur and lookout. Spiro killed a bank guard during the getaway. Who is guilty of what crimes?

A person who aids another in the commission of a crime is also guilty of criminal wrongdoing. For example, one who acts as a lookout to warn a robber of the approach of police is an accomplice in the robbery. Similarly, one who plans the crime, or otherwise aids the actual perpetrators, is guilty of the same crime. In many jurisdictions, if someone is killed during a felony which in itself endangers lives, all accomplices are guilty of murder. Thus, in the problem, all four persons were guilty of car theft and armed bank robbery. All

- No illegal search of suspects or seizure of evidence. Normally police must have a warrant from a judge for search and seizure unless they are "in hot pursuit" after witnessing a crime.

- No arrest without *probable cause* (reasonable grounds to believe the accused committed the crime).

- Due process upon being arrested, which includes the following rights:

  –To be advised of the right to remain silent and to be told that anything said may be held against the accused.
  –To be advised that the accused may have a lawyer present during the questioning and to be told that a lawyer will be provided if the accused cannot afford to hire one and so requests.
  –To be able to make a limited number of telephone calls.
  –No forced confession.

- Due process after being arrested and booked, which includes the following rights:

  –To be treated reasonably and protected from harm while in custody.
  –To be informed of the charges.
  –To be represented by a lawyer (personal or court-appointed) at all stages in the proceeding, or to be one's own lawyer if one is able and so desires.
  –To be released on reasonable bail, or on recognizance, in most cases.
  –To have a fair preliminary hearing, with a lawyer present, in order to determine whether there is enough evidence for a trial.
  –To be informed of the time and place of the trial.

- A fair, speedy, and public trial which includes the following rights:

  –To be tried by a just and unbiased judge.
  –To appear in person.
  –To have an impartial jury.
  –To require witnesses to appear and testify.
  –To confront adverse witnesses and to cross-examine them.
  –To be heard in person if desired, but otherwise to refrain from being a witness against oneself.
  –No conviction by use of illegally obtained evidence.
  –No double jeopardy.
  –No cruel or unusual punishment if convicted.
  –To appeal conviction to a higher court to correct any alleged errors in the arrest or trial.

Figure 4-1. Rights of an Accused Person

four might also be guilty of murder. Anyone who later knowingly helped to conceal and shield the four criminals from arrest would be guilty, as an accessory after the fact, of a separate crime—that of harboring a criminal.

In many states, an employer can be criminally liable for certain crimes committed by employees in the course of business. For example, many states make the employer criminally liable if an employee sells goods that are short weighted. Furthermore, corporations are now being charged with crimes if the crime advances the interest of the corporation and was known to officers or members of the board of directors. In these cases, where one party is liable for the criminal conduct of another, lack of criminal intent is sometimes not a defense.

WHAT ARE SOME DEFENSES TO CRIMINAL CHARGES?

> **PROBLEM:** Wark and Zanch, who were arrested for possession of cocaine, signed confessions at the police station. At their trial, they claimed that their right of due process had been violated. They said they had not been advised of their right to remain silent and to have a lawyer present when questioned. If true, is that a good defense?

To discourage harassment by police and to prevent conviction of innocent persons charged with crimes, the law provides many defenses. Some defenses seek to justify or excuse the alleged crime. Other defenses relate to the way evidence is obtained and the way the accused person is arrested, questioned, tried, and punished. In the problem, Wark and Zanch should have been advised of their rights at the time of the arrest. If they were not so advised, their procedural rights under the U. S. Constitution were violated. Such a violation would be a good defense.

Four common defenses, other than procedural ones, are alibi, criminal insanity, self-defense, and immunity. The defendant has the burden of proving any defense. Although technically not a defense, **alibi** is a claim of innocence based on the assertion that the accused was somewhere other than at the scene of the crime when it was committed. Accordingly, the accused could not have committed the crime.

alibi: claim that the accused was elsewhere at the time of the crime

Even **criminal insanity**, which is a good defense, must be proved because an accused person who stands trial is presumed to be sane.

criminal insanity: lack of prescribed mental capacity to appreciate the wrongfulness of certain conduct or to comply with the law

Self-defense against attack is legal *only* if it is reasonable under the circumstances. An innocent victim may use that force which appears to be reasonably necessary for self-protection against the threat of death, serious bodily harm, kidnapping, or rape. (The privilege of self-defense extends to members of one's family and household and to others whom one has a legal duty to protect.)

self-defense: reasonable and lawful resistance to attack

One may not use deadly force if nondeadly force appears reasonably sufficient. Moreover, only nondeadly force may be used to protect or recover property alone, and it may be used only when it appears reasonably necessary. Thus, one may not set deadly traps or spring guns to protect unoccupied buildings. In addition, a civilian may not shoot a thief who is escaping with stolen property.

Another type of defense in criminal proceedings is **immunity** (freedom from prosecution). A witness in a criminal investigation or trial who is granted immunity is then required to testify. Normally such a requirement would violate the constitutional privilege against self-incrimination. However, the state agrees not to prosecute the witness on the basis of any facts disclosed by the testimony. Removal of the danger of prosecution removes the privilege of withholding self-incriminating statements. Continued refusal to testify is punishable as contempt of court.

immunity: freedom from prosecution

Sometimes an accused person will be granted immunity or a lesser sentence for giving *state's evidence* (becoming a witness for the state), thus providing testimony which could lead to conviction of an accomplice in a crime.

The fact that others may have committed the same offense but were not arrested or prosecuted is no defense. For example, the police cannot arrest all motorists who speed on busy stretches of highway. Therefore, a person who is arrested for speeding cannot use the speeding habits of others as a defense. Having no prior record of arrests or offering to pay back what was stolen are not defenses but may serve to reduce the punishment.

Often, an accused person will agree to plead guilty to a less serious crime in exchange for having a more serious charge dropped. This is called **plea bargaining.** The accused voluntarily gives up the right to a public trial and the possibility of being found not guilty but avoids the risk of a heavier penalty if convicted. Consequently, the prosecutor need not prove that the accused is guilty beyond a reasonable doubt, which is difficult to do even with strong evidence.

plea bargaining: pleading guilty to a less serious crime

Pipereno was cited for drunk driving. Mitsui, the prosecuting attorney, knew the evidence was weak. Therefore, she offered to drop the charge if the defendant would plead guilty to the lesser charge of reckless driving. The judge agreed. Pipereno pleaded guilty to reckless driving and was punished accordingly.

WHAT IS THE PUNISHMENT FOR CRIMES?

PROBLEM: A city ordinance required that water not be wasted by being allowed to run into the street and sewers. Gilland turned the sprinklers on in his garden but forgot to turn the water off later. The water ran into the street all night, making a considerable stream. Gilland was cited for wasting water. What was his liability for violating this law?

punishment: penalty imposed for committing a crime

"Let the punishment fit the crime" is more easily said than done. **Punishment** is any fine, confinement in jail or prison, or other penalty provided by law and imposed by the court. The purpose of punishment is not to remedy the wrong but rather to discipline the wrongdoer. If reasonably swift and certain, punishment should deter the wrongdoer, and hopefully others as well, from similar behavior in the future. The fact that many "career criminals" are arrested repeatedly indicates that our penal system is far from perfect.

In the problem, Gilland was guilty of a misdemeanor, which did not require criminal intent. It was, nevertheless, prohibited as a matter of public policy, and so he would probably be fined. Criminal statutes ordinarily set maximum limits for punishment but allow a judge freedom in determining the appropriate punishment within those limits.

probation: punishment allowing liberty under court-ordered supervision

A court may impose and then suspend punishment, subject to the good behavior of the guilty party, who may be placed on probation for a prescribed period of time. **Probation** is a type of punishment which allows the convicted person to avoid confinement and to remain at liberty for a prescribed time under the supervision of a probation officer. Sometimes a fine is also imposed, or *restitution* (returning what was stolen) is required. Specific conditions are usually attached to the probation. These conditions may include keeping a job, avoiding certain companions and meeting places, and not leaving the area. A defendant who violates the probation terms may have the probation and suspended sentence revoked at a court hearing and then be sent to jail or prison.

Sometimes a convict serving in prison may be released early on **parole** because of good behavior and evidence of rehabilitation. The decision is made by a parole board and may be revoked if specified conditions are violated. These conditions generally include periodically reporting to a parole officer and avoiding any criminal activity. **Pardon**, by the governor or president, releases the convict from the entire punishment, including future disabilities such as the ban on holding public office.

parole: early release of a prisoner with suspension of the remainder of the prisoner's sentence

pardon: release from all punishment

PREVENTING LEGAL DIFFICULTIES

As a Business Person . . .

1. study business law carefully, particularly when an activity is identified as criminal in nature,
2. never intentionally do something illegal,
3. never misrepresent a fact to obtain the goods or services of others, or to sell your goods or services,
4. never threaten others with an illegal act to compel them to do something, and
5. if arrested, immediately contact a lawyer.

Strengthening Your Legal Vocabulary

alibi
arson
bribery
burglary
conspiracy
crime
criminal assault
criminal battery
criminal insanity
due process
embezzlement
extortion
false pretenses
felony
forgery
immunity
infraction
juvenile delinquency
larceny
misdemeanor
pardon
parole
perjury
plea bargaining
probation
punishment
receiving stolen property
robbery
self-defense
victimless crimes
waiver
white-collar crimes

1. Wrongful taking of another's personal property with intent to deprive the owner of possession.
2. Breach of duty to society for which punishment may be imposed.
3. Violation by minors of laws.
4. Nonviolent crimes committed by generally respected persons.
5. Fine, confinement, or other penalty imposed for committing a crime.
6. Crime of giving or receiving money with the intention of illegally influencing one in the discharge of his or her governmental duty.
7. Making or materially altering a legal document, with intent to defraud.
8. Serious crime punishable by death or imprisonment in a state prison for more than one year.
9. Agreement, usually secret, between two or more people to do an unlawful act or to do a lawful act by unlawful means.
10. Freedom from prosecution.

Reviewing Important Points

1. A crime is an offense against society. In order to convict, the prosecution must establish a duty to do or not to do a certain thing, a violation of the duty, and, in most cases, criminal intent.
2. A crime is punishable by the appropriate government—federal, state, or local.
3. Crimes are generally divided into (a) felonies and (b) misdemeanors.
4. Some crimes in which a business may be the victim are robbery, burglary, shoplifting, employee pilferage, passing bad checks, vandalism, receiving stolen property, and embezzlement.
5. Some crimes in which a business person or firm may be the perpetrator are income tax evasion, consumer fraud, conspiring to fix prices, violating antitrust laws, making false insurance claims, false advertising, embezzlement, and bribery. The offenses are often termed white-collar crimes because of the respected status of the criminals.
6. Victimless crimes include commercial gambling, illegal drug trafficking and use, loan sharking, and prostitution. Despite the label and the voluntary involvement of the parties, there are often victims in such crimes.
7. Generally any adult capable of knowing the difference between right and wrong is responsible for his or her crimes.
8. Generally what would be criminal conduct for an adult is juvenile delinquency for a minor, with lighter penalties and an emphasis on reform and rehabilitation.
9. Anyone accused of committing a crime has certain constitutional rights including (*a*) no arrest without probable cause, (*b*) equal protection of the law, (*c*) due process, and (*d*) a speedy, public, fair trial.
10. In the interests of providing justice and protecting innocent persons from improper prosecution, the law recognizes certain defenses. Common defenses are (*a*) alibi, (*b*) criminal insanity, (*c*) self-defense, and (*d*) immunity.

11. Crimes are punished by fine, imprisonment, or both. Probation and parole are mild punishments because the criminals remain at liberty, subject to limited restraints on their actions.

Applying Law to Everyday Life

1. Suarez started a trash collection business. After two successful years, he purchased a personal computer to handle his billing and other accounting functions. Later he used the computer to prepare and mail letters soliciting new customers. By mistake he merged the mailing lists of existing customers and prospective customers. As a result, 195 prospective customers received bills for trash collection services which were never provided. Twenty-seven of these people paid these bills. One person called the police. Has Suarez committed a crime? Why or why not?

2. Phillips developed a scheme to generate funds by sending bogus bills for relatively small amounts for "District Sanitation Services" to residents of certain affluent neighborhoods. Enough people paid these bills to make the practice quite profitable. Has Phillips committed a crime? If so, what crime? How does the law distinguish between Suarez in Question 1 and Phillips?

3. A corporation was cited and charged with illegal pollution as a result of their dumping chemical wastes into a river. The dumping had occurred when an employee had mistakenly opened the wrong valve. The company pleaded not guilty because the dumping was not intentional. Moreover, neither the company nor the employee knew of the ban on dumping this particular chemical. Is either argument a good defense?

4. Baxter became intoxicated while celebrating on New Year's Eve. He drove his car the wrong way on a one-way street, struck another car head on, and killed the other driver. Was Baxter's intoxication a good defense against a criminal charge?

5. There was nothing Lovette wanted more than a stereo sound system. When Harper, an older student, offered to sell him a practically new deluxe system for just $100, Lovette agreed to buy. But then Lovette said, "Hey, Man, how come so cheap?" Harper replied, "Had some happy hunting, and now I've got surplus stock." Later that day, the deal was completed. Has any crime been committed?

6. Buttler, a contractor, ordered $24,600 worth of plywood from K. C. Lumber Company without intending to pay for it. Buttler told the company it was to be used in building houses in a subdivision. When Buttler failed to pay for the plywood, the lumber company investigated. Their investigation revealed that after the plywood was delivered to the building site, Buttler had it transported across the state line, hidden, and resold for cash. A criminal complaint was then filed against Buttler. With what crime or crimes could he be charged?

7. Sharon spent the weekend with her friend Amelia. Amelia proposed a plan for shoplifting records from a local record store. Sharon was to go to the store clerk, say she felt very ill, then pretend to faint and fall on the floor. This distraction would allow Amelia—at the other end of the store—to place record albums in her shopping bag without risk of being spotted. Sharon at first said she could not do something like that because it is against the law. Amelia argued that Sharon would not be breaking the law, only Amelia would. Is Amelia right? If a person can think of a way to profit by violating the law without risk, what reasons are there for not breaking the law?

Solving Case Problems

1. The Royal Scotsman Inn had constructed a motel that did not comply with the building code. Therefore, Scotsman was refused both a certificate of final inspection and an occupancy permit. The defendant, chairperson of the county council, approached a representative of the motel and offered to have "everything taken care of" in exchange for the payment of $12,000. Scotsman was faced with the possibility of a large loss from both the need for substantial reconstruction and the delay in commencing operations. Therefore, Scotsman agreed to pay the defendant the money. Having been notified by Scotsman, the FBI arrested the defendant after hearing the discussion and seeing the exchange of the money. What kind of a crime did the defendant commit? (*United States v. Price*, 507 F.2d 1349)

2. The defendant was charged with burglary. The evidence showed that a drive-in restaurant had been broken into sometime between 10 p.m., March 16, and 7 a.m., March 17. Vending machines were damaged, and the contents were taken. The defendant's fingerprints were found on one of the vending machines, and it was shown that he was not employed by the drive-in nor had he serviced the machines. The defendant had an alibi. His mother testified that he was at her home on the night of March 16 from 8:45 until about 11 p.m. She said that when he left her home, he said he was going to the home of a friend. An acquaintance of the defendant, Carter, testified that the defendant came to his home about 11:30 p.m., March 16, and remained until about 5:45 the next morning. Carter's home was about three blocks from the drive-in. In view of this evidence, should the jury accept the alibi and find the defendant not guilty? (*Johnson v. Commonwealth of Virginia*, 168 S.E.2d 97, Va.)

3. Pack was the president of Acme Markets, Inc., a large national retail food chain. Both Pack and Acme were charged with violating criminal provisions of the federal Food, Drug and Cosmetics Act for allowing interstate shipments of food which had been contaminated by rodents in one of Acme's warehouses. Pack defended by stating that although he was aware of the problem, he had delegated responsibility for the sanitary conditions of food

storage to responsible subordinates. Can Pack be criminally liable in these circumstances? (*United States v. Pack*, 95 S. Ct. 1903)

4. Shortly before 2 a.m., two young men entered a restaurant in New York City. They had handkerchiefs covering their faces and were armed with pistols. One of the criminals stole money from the cash register. The other criminal, Roper, forced the customers to go to the rear of the restaurant. There he robbed them of money and shot and killed one of them. Roper was convicted of first-degree murder because the killing had taken place during the commission of a felony, robbery. Roper appealed the decision because at the trial it was established that he had been under 16 years of age at the time of the crime. Under the state statutes, proof of participation in what would be a felony if committed by an adult shows only juvenile delinquency if committed by a person under 16. Decide. (*People v. Roper*, 181 N.E.88, N.Y.)

5. Feinberg owned a cigar store in a very poor part of Philadelphia. He sold cans of Sterno, which contains about 4 percent alcohol, to area people who mixed it with water and drank it. After conducting this business for some time, Feinberg purchased and resold "Institutional Sterno" which contains 54 percent alcohol. While the cans were marked "Danger," "Poison" and displayed a picture of a skull and crossbones, Feinburg did not warn his customers of the difference between the old Sterno and the Institutional Sterno. As a result, 33 persons died from alcohol poisoning. Did Feinberg commit a crime? (*Commonwealth v. Feinberg*, 234 A.2d 913, Pa.)

5

Torts

1. A motorcyclist roars his engine and deliberately rides at high speed toward a group of young people standing on a sidewalk, intending to scare them. As the youngsters scatter, a girl is struck and injured. What kind of wrong has the motorcyclist committed?

2. Your best friend is very interested in computers. He learns the password required to gain access to your school's computer. Out of curiosity, he attempts to look at the grades of his friends. In doing this, he accidentally erases the computer records for 74 students. When the school discovers the problem, it spends $6,800 in overtime pay to reconstruct the records. Is your best friend liable for the $6,800 even though he did not intend to erase the records?

3. Your neighbor is using a multipurpose woodcutting machine in his basement hobby shop. Suddenly, a metal clamp from the machine breaks and strikes his left eye, injuring it badly. The defective machine is beyond the manufacturer's one-year warranty period. Is your neighbor barred from recovering any sum for his injury?

HOW DO CRIMES AND TORTS DIFFER?

PROBLEM: After a long day of skiing, Josephina was driving home after sunset. As she dozed off momentarily, her car crossed the dividing lane on the highway. It then crashed head-on into John's approaching panel truck. Both drivers were seriously injured, and their vehicles were "totaled." Although Josephina was asleep at the time, has she violated any rights of the other driver?

In Chapter 4, you learned that a crime is an offense against society. It is a public wrong. A **tort**, in contrast, is a private or civil wrong—an offense against an individual. If a tort occurs, the person injured can sue and obtain a judgment for money damages from the person who committed the tort. The money is intended to compensate for the injury.

tort: an offense against an individual

One act can be both a tort and a crime. In the problem, Josephina committed an offense against society—the crime of "reckless driving." Police will investigate the crime, then give her a ticket or possibly arrest her. A county or district attorney will prosecute her in a criminal trial. If convicted, she may be fined or jailed. But Josephina also committed a tort by injuring John and his property. John may bring a civil suit against Josephina. If John wins, he can obtain a judgment against her as compensation for his injuries. Thus, Josephina's one act caused her to be criminally liable (for a fine and/or a jail sentence) and civilly liable (for monetary damages).

WHAT ARE THE ELEMENTS OF A TORT?

PROBLEM: On a windy autumn day, Mason was burning dry leaves in the backyard. Mason went inside to answer a telephone call, leaving the fire unattended. Within minutes the flames leaped to the next-door neighbor's fence and then to a toolshed where a small can of gasoline exploded. Soon the neighbor's house was ablaze, and it burned to the ground. Was a tort committed by Mason?

Like criminal law, tort law is a broad legal category. Just as there are many specific crimes, such as murder and shoplifting, there are many specific torts. There are, however, certain elements which are common to all torts. In a trial, these elements must be proved to establish liability (legal responsibility) for any specific tort. The elements of a tort are:

1. a *duty* owed by one person to another to do or not to do a certain thing,
2. *violation* or *breach* of the duty,
3. *injury* recognized by the law, and
4. *proximate causation* of the injury by the breach.

Thus, in the problem, Mason owed a duty to the neighbors not to injure their property. That duty was violated when Mason left the fire unattended and it spread to one neighbor's property. The unattended fire caused the neighbor's house to be burned to the ground. Destruction of a home is an injury recognized by tort law. Therefore the neighbor can obtain a judgment against Mason for the value of the fence, the tool shed, and the house.

1. The Duty

By law everyone has certain rights. Since everyone has the duty to respect the rights of others, everyone therefore has certain resultant duties. The following are the principal duties created by tort law:

1. the duty not to injure the *person* of another: this includes bodily injury, injury to someone's reputation, or invasion of someone's privacy,
2. the duty not to interfere with the property rights of others, such as by trespassing on their land, and
3. the duty not to interfere with the economic rights of others, such as the right to contract.

These duties are most often expressed in the case and statutory law of the 50 states. Whether or not a duty exists under given circumstances of a case is a question of law for the judges to decide.

2. Violation of the Duty

A breach, or violation of the duty, must be proved before the injured party can collect damages for a tort. Whether there has been a breach of a tort duty is almost always a question of fact for a jury to decide.

Some torts require that the breach be intentional. In other torts, intent is not required; it is enough if the breach occurred because someone was careless or negligent. In still other torts, even carelessness is not required. Liability is imposed simply because a duty was violated and this caused injury. Torts are often classified on the basis of their requirements for intent or carelessness. One group of torts is called intentional torts. Another tort is called negligence. The last group, where neither intent nor carelessness is required, is strict liability.

3. Injury

Generally injury resulting from the breach of duty is required before the courts will hold a person liable in tort. For example, if you act very recklessly, but no one is injured, there is usually no tort.

4. Proximate Causation

Causation is simply the idea that the breach of the duty caused the injury. There are degrees of causation. For example, one can argue that the first people on earth are the ultimate causes of every injury which occurs in the world today. When the amount of causation is great enough for it to be recognized by the law, it is called **proximate cause**. Generally proximate cause exists when it is reasonably foreseeable that a particular breach of duty will result in a particular injury.

proximate cause: reasonably foreseeable cause of injury

WHAT ARE SOME COMMON INTENTIONAL TORTS?

PROBLEM: During deer-hunting season, Rinehart drove miles out in the country in search of game. He parked his pickup truck alongside a dirt road, climbed a nearby fence, and hiked into the woods. Rinehart thought the land was part of a national forest. However, it actually belonged to Quincy, who had posted "No Trespassing" signs. Confronted by Quincy, Rinehart apologized for his mistake and left. Was Rinehart guilty of a tort?

1. Assault

A person has the right to be free from reasonable fear of personal injury from others. An intentional failure to respect this right is an **assault**. This tort consists of placing another person in *fear* of an immediate harmful or offensive touching. (Note that there need be no actual physical contact.) There must be a threat of injury, coupled with an *apparent ability* to carry it into effect.

assault: placing another in fear of harmful or offensive touching

> Spencer, elderly and totally blind, thought Wills had swindled him. Spencer told Wills that he was going to "beat your face to a pulp." Because it was obvious that Spencer could not carry out his threat, there was no assault.

2. Battery

battery: harmful or offensive touching of another

A person has the right to be free from unlawful harmful or offensive touching. An intentional breach of the duty to observe this right is a **battery**. Shooting, pushing in anger, spitting at, or throwing a pie in the face of another are all batteries. A battery is frequently the follow-through of an assault, and so one frequently reads about "an assault and battery." When the victim is hit without warning from behind, there is a battery without assault.

Even though there is harmful or offensive touching, there may be no battery. If the contact is not intentional there is no battery. Also, the contact may be justified. For example, when you act in self-defense, you have not committed a battery. Further, there may be consent to the contact. Thus a boxer does not commit battery because the opponent consents to the contact.

3. Defamation

defamation: injury of a person's reputation by false statements, oral or written

slander: oral defamation

libel: written defamation

A person has the right to be free from false reports about his or her character or conduct which lead to ridicule, contempt, or hatred by others. The victim's reputation is undermined by such reports, and goodwill previously enjoyed is destroyed. The tort described is **defamation**. If the defamation is spoken, it is **slander**. If the defamation is written or printed, it is **libel**. To be legally defamatory, the material must (1) be false (truth is a complete defense), (2) be communicated to a third person (one's reputation with others is not harmed if no other person hears or reads the lie), and (3) bring the victim into disrepute, contempt, or ridicule by others.

> A news commentator reported on a radio program that an officer of a local corporation had a conflict of interest. The commentator said that a small company secretly owned by the officer was selling goods to the corporation at a high profit to the officer. This was true. Therefore the news commentator was not guilty of defamation.

An exception to the requirements for defamation is made for defamatory comments about public officers or other prominent public personalities. There is no liability in such cases unless the defamer acted with actual malice; that is, if he or she knew the words were false when they were said. This exception is intended to encourage free discussion of issues of public concern. For the same reason, legislators' statements made in the course of their official duties are absolutely privileged. They may say anything, even with malice. Thus, the lawmakers are immune from liability for defamation for anything said during legislative meetings. Judges, lawyers, jurors, witnesses, and other parties in judicial proceedings are also immune from liability for statements made during the actual trial or hearing.

4. Invasion of Privacy

In recent years, the right of privacy has concerned many persons. This concern is largely traceable to the growth of the population of our nation and related extensive record keeping about people through the use of computers that collect, store, and report personal data. Therefore Congress enacted the Privacy Act of 1974, which deals with the collection and use of personal information by government agencies. In enacting this legislation, Congress stated that "the right of privacy is a personal, and fundamental right protected by the Constitution of the United States." Invasion of this right is the tort of **invasion of privacy**. This tort is defined as the unwelcome and unlawful intrusion into one's private life so as to cause outrage, mental suffering, or humiliation.

invasion of privacy: unlawful intrusion into another's private life causing mental or emotional injury

In general, privacy is the right to be left alone if one so wishes. Specifically, it includes freedom from unnecessary publicity regarding personal matters. It also includes freedom from commercial exploitation of one's name, picture, or endorsement without permission. The right to privacy bans illegal eavesdropping by listening and electronic devices, interference with telephone calls, and unauthorized opening of letters and telegrams.

However, the right of privacy is not unlimited. For example, the FBI is permitted to tap telephone lines secretly, under limited circumstances, when such action is necessary for the national defense. Also, public figures, such as politicians, actors and actresses, and people in the news, have limited rights of privacy.

Even ordinary citizens may not complain if they are included in pictures taken at public events, such as games and rallies, which are later printed in newspapers. However, in a public place such as a fun house at a carnival, one may not take and later publish a photo of a woman whose dress is unexpectedly blown up by compressed air.

5. Trespass

trespass: wrongful interference with the use of another's property

A person has the right to the possession of land and buildings (real property) without unlawful interference by others. Failure to observe this property right is **trespass**. This tort is usually thought of as wrongful entry onto the property of another. However, trespass may consist of other forms of interference with the possession of property. Dumping rubbish on the land of another or breaking the windows of a neighbor's house are trespasses.

Of course, intent is required to commit the tort of trespass. However, the only requirement is that the intruder intended to be on the particular property. If a person was thrown onto another's land there would be no intent and no trespass. If a person thought she was walking on her own property, but was mistaken, there would be a trespass because she intended to be on that particular property. Thus, in the problem, Rinehart was guilty of trespass, even though he thought he was in a national forest.

6. Conversion

conversion: wrongfully depriving another of possession of personal property

When the right to possession of *personal* property, such as a diamond ring, is violated by another who steals, uses, or destroys the property in a manner inconsistent with the owner's rights, the wrongdoer is guilty of **conversion**. A thief is always a converter. So, too, is the buyer of stolen goods even if the buyer acts in good faith and does not know that the goods are stolen. Conversion does not depend on the intent to do a wrongful act. Intent to do the act is enough. Thus, even an innocent converter is liable for damages.

> Sanchez bought a car from Wirtz without knowing that the car had been stolen from Wilson. Although Sanchez innocently purchased the car, he is guilty of conversion and is liable to Wilson for either its return or the fair market value and for damages.

7. Wrongful Interference with Business Relations

wrongful interference with business relations: invasion of right to conduct a business

Every individual has the legal right to enter any business, trade, or profession. When minimum standards are set by law, as for professions and many licensed trades, no one may be barred from qualifying. If the right to establish and conduct a lawful business is violated, the tort of **wrongful interference with business** is committed. Interference with the right to contract is a tort, also.

A brilliant scientist had a long-term contract with Laboratory A to do genetic research. Laboratory B unlawfully persuaded the scientist to breach the agreement and come to work for Laboratory B. As a result, Laboratory A could sue both the scientist and the competitor for damages. In addition, Laboratory A could probably get an injunction barring the scientist from working on genetic research for anyone else until the original contract term expired.

The mere fact that a person has injured another's business does not give rise to a tort action. Fair competition through better service and reduced prices, even though this causes injury to a competitor, is legal. However, if there is dishonest dealing and malicious action which intentionally injures another, the victim may sue the wrongdoer.

8. Fraud

Fraud involves interference with the economic rights of others. This tort occurs when someone makes an intentional misrepresentation of fact and thereby causes financial injury to a person who relies on the misrepresentation.

fraud: intentional misrepresentation of fact, relied upon by another to her or his injury

Smith is trying to sell her home. While showing the property to Hernandez, Smith said, "This roof is in very good repair and has never leaked." Hernandez buys the house and later learns that the roof leaks and is in need of repairs costing $8,500. Hernandez also learns that Smith was given an estimate for similar repairs before the sale occurred. Smith committed fraud.

WHAT IS NEGLIGENCE?

PROBLEM: Biff was driving home late one night after much drinking. Traveling down residential streets at speeds up to 50 mph, he raced through the rain with only one operating headlight. Meanwhile Yee was slowly backing her station wagon out of her driveway, but she failed to look both ways when she should have. Biff rammed into the right rear end of her vehicle. Her wagon was badly damaged, and she was injured. Can Yee collect from Biff?

negligence: causing injury by failing to act as a reasonable person

Negligence is a specific tort. In fact, it is the most common tort. Intent is not required for this tort, only carelessness. Like the other torts, negligence involves the elements of a duty, breach of the duty, causation, and injury.

1. The Duty in Negligence

reasonable man standard: the duty to act with the care, prudence, and good judgment of a reasonable person

The duty imposed by negligence law is called the **reasonable man standard**. This duty requires that we act with the care, prudence, and good judgment of a reasonable person so as not to cause injury to others. In general, by this test, everyone is subject to the same objective duty of care.

There are, however, some individuals for whom a different degree of care is applied. Generally children under seven years of age are presumed incapable of negligence. Older children are only required to act with that care which a reasonable child of like age, intelligence, and experience would act. If, however, a child undertakes an adult activity, such as driving a boat or car, the child is held to the adult standard.

Professionals and persons skilled in a trade are also held to a different degree of care—in this case a higher one. These persons are required to act in their work with that degree of care and skill which is normally possessed by members of the profession or trade. Thus, an attorney must act with the care and skill normally possessed by attorneys in that community. Similarly, a plumber must perform work with the care and skill normally exercised by plumbers in that community.

2. The Breach of Duty in Negligence

The reasonable man standard defines the duty. A defendant's conduct, such as that of Biff in the problem, is compared with the reasonable man standard to determine whether a violation of the duty has occurred. We could conclude that a reasonable person would drive a car only at a safe speed and only when sober. Since Biff engaged in speeding and driving after much drinking, he clearly violated the reasonable man standard.

3. Causation and Injury in Negligence

As with other torts, the violation of the duty must be the proximate cause of an injury, such as personal injury and property damage, recognized by negligence law.

In most states, for many years, a plaintiff could not recover for loss caused by another's negligence if the plaintiff's own negligence contributed along with the negligence of the defendant in causing the injury. Every person was supposed to use proper care to avoid injury. Failure to do so was **contributory negligence**. Thus, in the problem, if Yee lived in a state which still recognizes contributory negligence she could recover nothing from Biff because she was contributorily negligent. Under this legal rule, it does not matter that one party, like Biff, was grossly negligent and primarily responsible for causing the collision while the other, like Yee, was only slightly negligent.

contributory negligence: system in which recovery is barred if the injury is partly the result of carelessness by the plaintiff

Many injustices have arisen because of the harshness of the contributory negligence rule. The rule sometimes results in the plaintiff's recovering nothing even when the plaintiff's own negligence was minimal. Most states have substituted **comparative negligence** for contributory negligence. Comparative negligence applies when a plaintiff in a negligence action is partially at fault. Instead of being able to recover nothing, the plaintiff is awarded damages that are reduced in proportion to the extent of the plaintiff's negligence.

comparative negligence: system in which damages are awarded in proportion to the plaintiff's negligence

Curtis tripped over an electric cord in Emerson's Electric Shop and suffered a broken hip. The cord was visible, and Curtis would have noticed it if she had been more careful. In a legal action, the jury found her damages to be $50,000. But the jury concluded that she contributed 20 percent of the total negligence. Therefore the judge deducted $10,000 and gave Curtis judgment for $40,000.

WHAT IS STRICT LIABILITY?

PROBLEM: Mrs. Embs went to a grocery store and placed a carton of a carbonated soft drink in her shopping cart. One of the bottles exploded and the broken glass cut her leg. Can she collect in tort from the grocery store or the bottler?

strict liability: responsibility for injury regardless of negligence or intent

Sometimes the law holds one guilty of tort on the basis of absolute or **strict liability**—liability that exists even though the defendant meant or intended no harm and was not negligent. *Public policy* (body of principles developed to promote the welfare of society) dictates that absolute liability be imposed under certain circumstances.

In essence, strict liability makes the defendant liable, not on the basis of provable fault, but rather on the basis that the defendant engaged in a particular activity which resulted in injury. In strict liability, proof of both the activity and the injury substitutes for proof of a violation of a duty.

Engaging in abnormally dangerous activities, such as blasting, or crop burning, or storing flammable liquids in large quantities, gives rise to strict liability. If you engage in activities of this type and someone is injured as a result, you will be liable.

Another strict-liability activity is ownership of dangerous animals. Domesticated animals are not considered dangerous unless the owner knows that a particular animal is vicious. Dogs, cats, cows, and horses are domesticated animals. Bears, tigers, snakes, elephants, and monkeys are wild or dangerous animals. If the dangerous animal causes injury, the owner is strictly liable.

A third strict-liability activity is the sale of goods which are unreasonably dangerous. If the goods are defective, and the defect makes them dangerous, and this causes an injury, any merchant who sold those goods is strictly liable, as is the manufacturer.

Under strict liability, the manufacturer and any seller in the chain of distribution are liable to any buyer or user of the defective product who is injured by it. However, the manufacturer is usually the party that is sued because it usually has the best ability to pay. Sometimes liability insurance helps to cushion the blow, but the cost to the manufacturer still can be enormous. Despite this fact, public policy says it is better that the manufacturer pay under the doctrine of strict liability and then spread the cost through a higher price to all consumers of the product. Otherwise, the individual victim might suffer without compensation because negligence or intent to injure may be difficult to prove. Ideally, the manufacturer is expected to avoid such lawsuits through certain preventative measures. These measures include (1) better product design, (2) better quality control through inspection in manufacture, (3) more careful testing, (4) more complete instructions or training on use, and (5) recall for repair if defects are discovered after sale. In the problem, Mrs. Embs could collect from either the store or the bottler. The bottle was defective. This defect made the product unreasonably dangerous.

WHEN IS A PERSON RESPONSIBLE FOR THE TORTS OF ANOTHER?

PROBLEM: Huntgate was taking riding lessons from Saddleback Stables. Patterson, the Saddleback instructor, was a skilled rider although only 17 years old. Nevertheless, Patterson negligently lost control of the horse that Huntgate was riding. As a result, Huntgate was thrown to the ground and injured. Who was liable for Huntgate's injuries?

In general, all persons, including minors, are responsible for their conduct and are therefore liable for their torts. Thus, even children or insane persons may be held liable for negligently or intentionally injuring others.

With some exceptions, parents are not liable for the torts of their children. In some states, by statute, parents are liable up to a specified amount of money for property damage by their minor children. This is usually designed to cover vandalism and malicious destruction of school property. Most states also provide that parents are liable, up to the limits of financial responsibility laws, for damages negligently caused by their children while operating motor vehicles. Parents may also be liable if they give their children "dangerous instrumentalities," such as guns, without proper instructions. Similarly, parents may be liable for their children's dangerous habits, such as throwing rocks at trains and vehicles.

When one person is liable for the torts of another, the liability is called **vicarious liability**. The most common example of this is the liability of an employer for the acts of employees committed within the scope of the employment. To prevent such liability, the employer should select, train, and supervise employees carefully. The employer should also carry adequate liability insurance.

vicarious liability: responsibility of one person for the torts of another

In the problem, Saddleback Stables was liable for the negligence of its employee. The employee, Patterson, although a minor, was also liable because an employer's responsibility does not relieve the employee of liability. In such a situation, the injured party may sue both the employer and the employee. Although the plaintiff may then get a judgment against both, he or she can collect only one full recovery. Usually it is the employer, or the employer's insurance company, who pays.

WHAT CAN THE VICTIM OF A TORT COLLECT?

PROBLEM: Horsley, the owner of a dry cleaning store, lived next door to Early, who was the editor of a small newspaper in their town. The two quarreled frequently and became enemies. As a consequence, when Early published a story on the drug problem in the town, he identified Horsley as "a drug dealer." This statement was untrue. What can Horsley collect from Early?

damages: monetary compensation for loss or injury

punitive or exemplary damages: added damages intended to punish and make an example of the defendant

Damages are awarded to the injured party to compensate for loss caused by tort. The purpose of the award is to place the injured party in the same position as if the tort had not occurred. In many cases, the loss may be difficult to measure. An example would be where negligence causes bodily injury with ongoing pain and suffering or even death. However, the dollar value of the injury or loss must be set. The value is usually decided by a jury.

In the problem, if Horsley could prove that Early's defamation injured his business, he could probably get damages as compensation. If Horsley could prove that Early acted with *malice* (deliberate intention to cause injury), the jury might award her additional **punitive or exemplary damages**. These damages would be awarded as punishment for Early's intentional tort and as an example to deter others. Punitive damages are never awarded for ordinary negligence.

PREVENTING LEGAL DIFFICULTIES

In the World of Torts, Remember. . .

1. avoid legal liability for torts by consistently respecting other persons and their property;
2. ignorance of the law is no excuse for any violation of the law;
3. If you commit a tort or are the victim of a tort which may lead to a lawsuit, promptly consult a lawyer. Critical evidence may be lost if you delay;
4. in some states, your own negligence—however slight—may bar any recovery under the doctrine of contributory negligence. However, in many states, the doctrine of comparative negligence may permit recovery. Check with your lawyer;
5. if you injure a third party while on the job, both you and your employer are

liable. The employer, or an insurer, would probably pay, but the incident could cost you your job;
6. minors are generally liable for their torts;
7. the automobile is the principal source of tort liability for most persons, young and old. Drive carefully; and
8. if you are injured by a tort, don't be rushed by insurance adjusters or others into signing a statement releasing the other party from liability. Let your doctor decide if you are well. Let your lawyer decide if the settlement offer is fair.

Strengthening Your Legal Vocabulary

assault
battery
comparative negligence
contributory negligence
conversion
damages
defamation
fraud
invasion of privacy
libel
negligence
proximate cause
punitive or exemplary damages
reasonable man standard
slander
strict liability
tort
trespass
vicarious liability
wrongful interference with business relations

1. System of awarding damages in proportion to the plaintiff's negligence.
2. Responsibility for injury even if the defendant was not negligent and had no intent to harm.
3. Injury of a person's reputation by false oral or written statements.
4. Failure to use reasonable care.
5. Temporary or partial interference with the right to possession and use of one's property.
6. Plaintiff's failure to exercise reasonable care to avoid injury, which bars recovery of any damages.
7. Natural and foreseeable cause of injury.
8. Compensation for injury.
9. Harmful or offensive personal touching without consent or legal justification.
10. Responsibility of one person for the torts of another.

Reviewing Important Points

1. A tort is an unlawful act which causes private injury to the person or property of another.
2. Most crimes are also torts, but not all torts are crimes.

3. Torts may be broadly classified as intentional torts, negligence, or strict liability.
4. The most common tort is negligence, which is the failure to act with reasonable care, thus causing a foreseeable injury to another.
5. In a tort caused by negligence, the negligent act (or failure to act) must be the proximate cause of the injury. That is, the injury must follow as a natural and reasonably forseeable effect of the act (or failure to act).
6. Generally every individual is personally responsible for damage resulting from any torts committed by that individual. Employers are also liable for the torts of employees if the torts are committed within the scope of their employment.
7. In some states, if the injured person was also negligent and the negligence contributed to the injury, the injured person may be barred from recovering damages. In many states today, however, some recovery may be obtained under the doctrine of comparative negligence.
8. A person injured by a tort is entitled to damages—monetary compensation for the loss or injury suffered. The amount of damages is determined by the jury.

Applying Law To Everyday Life

1. Filepe drove a tractor-trailer rig onto a ferry boat and left the rig in gear because of a failure in the braking system. Filepe wanted to be able to move as quickly as possible once the ferry landed. Therefore, when the ferry was about 50 feet from the dock, he cranked the engine of the rig to get it started. He did this despite regulations forbidding the starting of engines before docking. The tractor-trailer jumped forward and struck Herrick's car, which in turn hit Patton's car. Patton's car, at the head of the line, crashed through the ferry's barricades and plunged into the water. What was the proximate cause of this accident?

2. Betty was at a baseball game seated one row behind a famous movie star. When she stood up to cheer, she was bumped by the person beside her. She lost her balance and fell into the lap of the movie star. He sued her for the tort of assault. Who prevails?

3. McDonald and Smyth were sitting in a bar watching a professional football game. When they discovered they were rooting for opposing teams, Smyth hit McDonald in the face, breaking McDonald's glasses and nose. McDonald called the police, who arrested Smyth. Does McDonald have any legal claims against Smyth?

4. Every morning on the way to work, Sharon rode an elevator up 14 floors. Sometimes, when it was crowded, the elevator operator would intentionally touch her in an offensive way. What can Sharon do besides making a scene in the elevator?

5. Jackson was a lawyer, respected by his peers. He successfully represented several persons who were charged with income tax evasion. All three defendants were reputed to be leaders of an organized crime syndicate. The local newspaper then printed an editorial calling for the tightening of tax laws "to protect society against mobsters and shyster lawyers—we think of Jackson—who would sell their souls to the devil for 30 pieces of silver." Was this an actionable tort?

6. Ham was a guest in Leidecker's home. While leaving the house, Ham was injured when she slipped on some ice that had formed on the steps leading from the door. Leidecker had cautioned Ham about the possibility of the steps being slippery, and Ham admitted seeing the ice. In a legal action claiming negligence, would Leidecker be liable?

7. Yardly and Whiple, ages 12 and 13, intentionally threw stones which smashed 57 windows in an old warehouse. The warehouse had been standing vacant for the past nine months. Yardly and Whiple were caught and disciplined by the juvenile court. Then the owner of the warehouse sued them and their parents for damages. The girls said they were "just having fun and not hurting anyone because the place was empty." Who, if anyone, is liable and why?

Solving Case Problems

1. A train stopped at the defendant's railroad platform. As it started up again, a man carrying a small package jumped aboard. He appeared unsteady and about to fall. Therefore a guard on the train, holding the door open, reached out to help him. Another guard, standing on the platform, pushed the man from behind. The man made it onto the train, but he dropped the package, which was about 15 inches in length. The package was wrapped in newspaper and contained fireworks that exploded when the package hit the rails. The shock of the explosion caused some scales at the other end of the platform, many feet away, to fall down. As they fell, they struck the plaintiff, injuring her. She sued the railroad, claiming the guards were negligent. Is the railroad liable? (*Palsgraf v. Long Island R. Co.*, 162 N.E. 99, N.Y.)

2. Town Finance Corporation (TFC) foreclosed a mortgage following a dispute with Hughes as to whether a loan had been repaid. TFC had a locksmith remove the locks of the dwelling of Hughes. TFC personnel then entered the house, seized household goods, and left the inside of the house in disarray. No one was home when this was done. Hughes filed suit over the debt. The court held that the finance company had been paid and thus had no further right of action against Hughes. Hughes thereupon filed this action which claimed malicious and willful trespass and asked both actual (compensatory) and punitive damages. Was Hughes entitled to judgment? (*Town Finance Corporation v. Hughes*, 214 S.E. 2d 387)

3. The Chicago Medical School distributed a bulletin and brochure which invited persons to apply for admission. The bulletin stated that applicants

would be selected on the basis of academic criteria such as test scores, grades, and personal interviews. After reading the bulletin, Steinberg paid a $15 application fee but was rejected. Later, he learned that the school used nonacademic criteria in admissions. These included the applicant's ability to contribute large sums of money to the school. Steinberg sued on behalf of all rejected applicants claiming that the defendant was guilty of fraud. Should he prevail? (*Steinberg v. Chicago Medical School*, 371 N.E. 2d 634)

4. An operator of an earth-moving vehicle was severely injured when the pants on his left leg caught between the rotating drums of the clutch, pulling his leg through the drums. The operator and his wife sued the manufacturer, claiming there was a defect in the design of the vehicle. They also claimed that the manufacturer knew of this defect. The evidence showed that a perforated guard was installed on the right side but not on the left. The evidence also showed that if there had been a guard on the left side, the accident would not have occurred. Should the operator be awarded damages? (*Carpenter v. Koehring Company*, 391 F.Supp. 206)

5. David Allen, age two, was attacked and severely bitten in the face and ear by a dog owned by Joseph Whitehead. Whitehead admitted that the dog barked frequently, was large, looked mean, and chased cars. On the other hand, no one had ever complained about the dog, it had never bitten anyone before, and it frequently played with other children. Is Whitehead liable for the injuries to David? (*Allen v. Whitehead*, 423 So.2d 835, Ala.)

Unit Two
UNDERSTANDING SPECIAL LAWS

UNIT OBJECTIVES

UPON COMPLETION OF THIS UNIT, you should be able to

1. discuss the rights and duties of minors as individuals, students, and drivers.
2. discuss the rights and duties of parents.
3. explain the importance and function of the juvenile court system.
4. understand why the government had to intervene to protect the consumer.
5. identify the situations in which consumer protection laws may apply.
6. recall the specific protection afforded by consumer protection laws.
7. assist federal, state, and local governments in consumer protection by notifying the proper authorities of violations.
8. explain why we use the law to regulate business.
9. identify the specific objectives of governmental regulation of business.
10. describe how the need for administrative agencies developed.
11. explain the procedure and sanctions used to regulate business.
12. identify the areas regulated by at least ten administrative agencies.

6

Law for the Minor

1. You become carried away with the spirit of Halloween and intentionally destroy a neighbor's $650 lawn statue. When the neighbor threatens to sue you for the damage, a friend tells you not to worry because, being a minor, you would not be held liable. Is your friend correct?
2. The driver of a van negligently makes a left turn in front of a motorcycle, causing it to crash. The motorcycle rider, Eric, suffers severe head and back injuries. Must Eric, a minor, have an adult act on his behalf to bring suit against the van driver?
3. You are a minor skilled in computer programming and video games. You have written and sold a game program to a major software manufacturer. Could your parents legally claim as their own the $12,725 you received for the program?

WHAT ARE THE LEGAL RIGHTS AND DUTIES OF MINORS?

PROBLEM: Janson, age 17, maintains that as a minor she has more rights in certain areas of the law than her adult friend, Boyer, age 22. Is she correct?

Our legal system withholds full adult rights and duties from persons until they reach a certain age. This occurs in areas such as being held responsible for criminal acts; being bound to contracts; or being able to vote, get married, drink alcoholic beverages, and bring lawsuits. Persons who are under the age at which they have full adult rights and duties are known as **minors**.

minor: person who is under the age to have full adult rights and duties

Different states prescribe different minimum ages for the same activity. Statutes within states prescribe different minimum ages for different activities. For example, the age for voting may differ from the ages for liability for crimes or torts, for holding public office, for making a will, or for buying cigarettes. In a few states, minors are deemed to be adults upon marriage. In most states, minors who are veterans or who are in the armed forces are given adult rights, such as the power to buy and sell real estate. In some states, a minor may be given certain adult rights by court order. In some instances, rights may be given to minors and then be taken away. For example, with reference to purchase and public use of alcoholic beverages, some states lowered the drinking age from 21 to 18, but then raised it back.

In the area of contracts, society has long believed that minors need to be protected against harming themselves and against being harmed by adults and other minors who might take advantage of them. Therefore minors are permitted to avoid (block the enforcement of) their contracts. Once individuals reach the age of **majority**, however, they can be legally bound to their contracts.

majority: age at which one is legally bound to contracts

Similarly, minors are treated differently from adults in the area of criminal law. In most states, a minor who is arrested is kept apart from adult inmates to avoid bad influences or other abuses. Minors who commit acts that would be crimes for adults are generally regarded as juvenile delinquents and specially handled by the juvenile court system. Runaways (minors who leave home without parental consent), if found by the police, may also be placed under the control of a juvenile court. The emphasis in juvenile delinquency proceedings is on helping and reforming, rather than on punishing, the offenders. The right of a minor to such preferential treatment in the areas of contracts and criminal law proves Janson correct in the problem.

Most states permit transfer of a minor from a juvenile court to an adult criminal court when the offense is a particularly serious one, such as murder. In some states, the transfer takes place if the minor is a repeat offender or if the offense would be a felony if committed by an adult. Depending on the state, the minor could be as young as 13. However, 16 is the usual minimum age for transfer.

A group of students, all 16 and 17 years of age, were arrested for rioting, for seriously injuring a teacher, and for destroying school property. The state law provided that minors 16 years of age and older charged with felonies could be tried as adults in criminal court rather than as juveniles in juvenile court. The students were tried, convicted, and punished as adults.

Minors who commit torts and thereby injure the person or property of another are usually liable for the loss. This could happen, for example, if a minor negligently drives an automobile. Sometimes the parents of the minor are also liable. A judgment against a minor with no assets might not be immediately collectible. But it could be imposed and remain in effect as a claim against future earnings.

For many purposes, an adult must represent or act for a minor. Minors who have no living parents, and in some cases even those who do, have a guardian appointed for them by a court. The **guardian** acts in place of the parents or may perform some special service, such as suing on behalf of the minor.

guardian: person who acts in place of parents

The parents of Flood, age 15, were killed in a two-car accident. A court appointed her grandparents as her guardians. Thus, it became their duty to take care of her, to act in the capacity of parents, and to be responsible for her estate. This guardianship will last until Flood reaches adulthood. The court also named her adult uncle, White, **guardian ad litem**—Latin words meaning "for the suit." This gave the uncle the power to sue, on behalf of Flood, the driver of the other car who had allegedly been negligent in causing the accident.

guardian ad litem: adult named to sue or defend on behalf of a minor

To marry, a minor under 18 generally must have parental consent. Only two states permit a minor under 14 to marry, even with parental consent. Some states require authorization of a court as well as the consent of the parents for the marriage of minors.

annulment: judicial declaration that a marriage never existed

McCarver and Gibson, both minors, eloped to a neighboring state and were married without their parents' consent. Either spouse, or their parents, could probably obtain an **annulment** (judicial declaration that a marriage never existed) of the marriage in court, if the application was made before the couple became adults.

Although they are often given special treatment under our laws, it is important to remember that minors, like other citizens, retain their constitutional rights. When arrested, for example, minors have basically the same rights as adults. They are presumed to be innocent unless proved guilty beyond a reasonable doubt. They, and their parents, are entitled to adequate notice of charges, so that they can prepare a defense. They also have the right to be represented by qualified lawyers, who will be provided without charge if the minors (or their parents) cannot afford to hire counsel. Minors have a right to confront adverse witnesses in court. In addition, minors need not testify in their own defense because such testimony could lead to self-incrimination.

Minors have other rights upon attaining ages specified by statute. For example, usually at age 16, minors may be employed full-time (see Chapter 22), although there may be restrictions as to hours and kinds of work. Minors under 16 may be employed part-time when the work does not interfere with required attendance at school. However, a work permit is often required. Minors also have the right to obtain a motor vehicle operator's license upon meeting statutory age and other requirements.

Generally the laws giving special treatment to minors were made with the best interest of minors in mind. While some of these laws might appear to be too restrictive, their intent is to steer minors through a difficult transition period and to allow everyone to begin life as an adult free from legal burdens that might have been unwisely incurred as a youth.

WHAT ARE THE RIGHTS AND DUTIES OF PARENTS?

PROBLEM: Groat receives a promotion to vice-president and her employer plans to transfer her to company headquarters in Houston. Her twin children, age 16, prefer to remain in Oregon with their friends and to finish high school there rather than to move. Can the parents legally compel the twins to move and to live with them?

By statute, all states routinely allow qualified parents to have custody and control of their natural and adopted children. Accordingly, the parents have authority to restrain their children and to administer reasonable punishment if necessary. They also have authority to compel obedience to reasonable directions. These rights continue until the children reach the age of majority or until the parents give up or are denied their rights by court order. Parents also have the right to determine the residence of their minor children. Thus, in the problem, the elder Groats have the legal right to require the twins to move to Houston. Parents, of course, have obligations to their children. Included are the duties to protect and to care for them, to provide food, clothing, and shelter according to the parents' financial means, and to see that the children are educated. Less tangible and not legally enforceable are the mutual obligations of affection and moral support.

Penalties may be imposed on parents who fail in any of these duties. Willful failure by parents to care for their children, as through neglect, desertion, or child abuse, subjects the parents to legal punishment and possible loss of custody. Parents who do not require their children to attend school during the years prescribed by statute are subject to fine or imprisonment.

As previously mentioned, under certain circumstances, parents are liable for damages to others caused by their minor children. This is because parents are supposed to exercise proper control. This liability is usually limited in dollar amount. However, it may be unlimited if a child is entrusted with a dangerous instrument, such as a gun, without instruction as to its proper operation and use.

Parents are entitled to the services of their children. This means children who live at home are expected to assist their parents as requested and to do so without payment. By agreement, of course, children may be paid by parents for work performed, but this is usually done on a voluntary basis. Normally, minor children working for their parents are exempt from most child labor laws (see Chapter 22). If a child earns wages, the wages legally belong to the parents. Statutes usually provide that employers must pay the child's wages to the parents, if parents request employers to do so. However, many parents allow their children to keep their earnings in order to develop habits of industry and thrift in the children. The right to the services of children makes it possible for parents to claim damages when they are wrongfully deprived of the child's services due to a third party's tort.

> Keane was 17 years old. He had been helping with heavy chores on the family farm for the past five years. One rainy day while Keane was driving to town, his pickup truck was rammed in the side by Brock, who had negligently run a red light. The resulting injuries kept Keane hospitalized for six months during the planting and harvesting seasons. His parents were forced to hire another worker to take his place. Keane's parents are legally entitled to collect from Brock the cost of such services.

Normally the rights and duties of the parents are shared by the mother and father. However, these responsibilities may be given up or lost in a number of ways. For example, should either parent die, the survivor receives all the rights and duties previously shared with the deceased. Also, children who are abused or treated unreasonably by their parents may, by juvenile court order, be taken away and placed in foster homes or in other protective custody. In the event of divorce or legal separation of the parents, the custody of each child is awarded to the parent best qualified to fulfill the child's needs. The spouse without custody generally retains the right to visit and to spend time with the children. The timing and duration of such visits are usually set by court order. In most cases, the spouse without custody is also ordered to help pay for the children's support. A deliberate failure to comply with a court order for child support may be held to be contempt of court, which can be punished by fine or imprisonment. Even if the parent who is required to make the support payments flees to another state, a newly enacted federal law compels payment. The law allows the government to withhold the amount due from the wages and the federal tax refund of the delinquent parent.

Parents also may relinquish all rights and free themselves from all duties by giving their children to other adults. This is usually done through the legal process of **adoption**. This procedure is fairly common when the mother is very young and unmarried. Even if the mother is a minor, her consent must be given or the adoption process cannot occur. Likewise, the child may not be taken from the mother without her consent just because she is a minor and the father is not providing support.

adoption: legally taking another's child as one's own

Parents may voluntarily surrender responsibility for the care, custody, and control of a minor child as well as claims for the child's earnings by **emancipation**. A minor naturally becomes emancipated upon reaching the age of majority. But a minor may also be emancipated before that time if that person is legally married or, with parental consent, is independent and self-supporting. Some states recognize partial emancipation, which may consist of allowing minors to retain any earnings and to spend them as they please. This is because "at some point," as stated in a court decision, "minors must have some right to their own views and needs for their independent and painful transition from minority to adulthood."

emancipation: release by parents of their parental rights

WHAT ARE THE RIGHTS AND DUTIES OF STUDENTS?

PROBLEM: The Shannon children, ages 13 and 15, were frequently absent from school. This was because their parents kept them at home to work as office help in the family business. The children enjoyed the work and preferred it to school. Were the children truants?

One of the most important rights of a young citizen of the United States is the guarantee of a free education, generally through the high-school level. Consequently, courts have held that it is one of the most important obligations of parents to see that their children receive that education whether in a public school system or through qualified private schools or tutors.

Minors who do not attend school when lawfully required to do so are **truants**, and their parents are held responsible. Accordingly, in the problem, the Shannon children are truants. Their parents can be fined or jailed for failing to see that the children attend school. If truancy is habitual, the parents can be charged with child neglect. The child can then be declared delinquent and placed under the jurisdiction of the juvenile court. School authorities and the courts are usually lenient in enforcing these statutes unless the breach of duty is willful and repeated. In some states, before a truant can be referred to a juvenile court, a school attendance review board must consider the problem. The truant and the truant's parents have the right to be present at the hearing.

truants: minors who do not attend school when lawfully required to do so

Within the school, students age 18 and over have the right to inspect, challenge, and, to some extent, control the release of information about them which appears in school records. For students under 18, this right is given to the parents. Also, teachers and administrators are required to protect the rights of students to study, learn, and participate in the various activities of the school. School personnel must provide reasonable supervision to ensure the physical safety of students. Such personnel and their employers may be liable if a student is injured.

In addition to the rights that minors have as students, they also have duties to fulfill to ensure a successful educational experience for themselves and their classmates. These duties center on the rules that need to be followed for the orderly and efficient functioning of the school. School authorities are authorized by statute to make such rules. However, the rules must be reasonable. Under the due process clause of the Fourteenth Amendment to the U. S. Constitution, regulations may not be arbitrary or capricious. This means that the regulations must not simply reflect the personal prejudices, likes, or dislikes of those who make them. For example, students are entitled to the right of free speech. However, the Supreme Court has held that free speech is subject to reasonable restrictions as to time, place, manner, and duration in the light of the special environment of the school. Therefore regulations may not deprive students of this right unless it is evident that a particular incident will cause "a material and substantial disruption" and will interfere with the work of the school. Likewise, there must be good reason for adopting a rule prohibiting extreme styles of dress or personal grooming—something more than the fact that those who make the rules do not like the styles.

Legally, students have no right to determine the curriculum or school regulations or to control school property. As a practical procedure and as a learning experience, however, many schools provide for student government and for student participation in other activities. From these experiences, students learn the importance of the ability to tolerate others' opinions. Students also learn the wisdom and need for compromise in resolving different points of view. Students in these activities gain an understanding of the necessity of obeying rules and regulations adopted by majority vote or prescribed by authorized school officials even when they may disagree with some of those rules. Schools may thus permit students to establish rules for their own conduct, including the use of student courts to discipline violators.

School authorities are authorized by statute to provide penalties for disobedience. Even though some of this authority may be delegated to a school's student government, the responsibility for its just and reasonable use remains with the school officials. Therefore the most serious penalties are administered by the school officials themselves. These penalties may include reasonable physical punishment, suspension (temporary exclusion from school), or expulsion (permanent dismissal from school).

Students may not be suspended or expelled without due process in the school system, and then they may seek review by the courts. Thus, such drastic disciplinary action may not be taken without advance notice informing the student of the nature of the alleged offense. This must be followed by a conference or hearing where the student has an opportunity to explain and to justify the conduct. For example, a student involved in a fight may have been acting in reasonable self-defense against unprovoked attack. The student has the right to explain this at a hearing.

Although expulsion usually requires a review of the facts and a decision by the school board, a trouble-making student may be temporarily barred from classes and sent home with little delay or formality. This can happen when the student's continued presence poses a danger to persons or property or when it threatens to disrupt the academic process.

WHAT ARE A MINOR'S RIGHTS AND DUTIES AS A DRIVER?

PROBLEM: During an extremely heavy rainstorm, Buchek was stopped by the highway patrol and ticketed for reckless driving. At the time, Buchek had been driving steadily and at the posted speed limit of 55 miles per hour. Most other cars had pulled off onto the shoulder of the road. Buchek maintains that she was not driving recklessly. Is she correct?

In owning and driving a motor vehicle, a minor is generally treated as an adult. There are no legal restrictions to simply owning an automobile, truck, motorcyle, snowmobile, or any other type of transport that the various states may consider a motor vehicle. However, a document of title showing such ownership is usually required. In addition, all states require annual registration of motor vehicles. The purpose of this requirement is to exercise control over the use of the highways and to identify vehicles and their owners. License plates or tabs showing the year of registration are issued to be attached to the vehicle.

The law may also require periodic inspection of vehicles for correction of defects and for maintenance of safety and pollution-control devices. Most states do not require car owners to carry liability insurance (see Chapter 27). However, drivers who injure others must generally demonstrate **financial responsibility.** This may be done by carrying a certain minimum amount of liability insurance or by posting an equivalent amount of cash or bond in the event of an accident. Otherwise the driver's license may be revoked and the car *impounded* (seized and held), pending settlement with the other driver.

financial responsibility: ability to pay damages

Every state requires the operator of a motor vehicle to hold a valid driver's license and, usually, to have it in possession while driving the vehicle. A **driver's license** is a permit issued by a state to operate a motor vehicle on the public highways. To obtain a driver's license, an applicant in any state is required to (1) be a certain age (generally 16), (2) pass one or more examinations, and (3) pay a prescribed fee. The examinations usually include a driving test, a test of vision, and a written exam on motor vehicle laws and road sign recognition. Some states require a photograph or fingerprints.

driver's license: permit to operate a motor vehicle on public highways

To prepare high school students to pass driving tests, most schools offer driver education courses. Some states require such courses for high school graduation. In a few states, special temporary licenses are issued to students enrolled in driver training. In other states, students who successfully complete approved courses in driver training receive their licenses without further testing. Several states issue a provisional license or a probationary license to a minor to be a sole operator. These licenses usually must be renewed each year, whereas regular licenses may need to be renewed less often. Some states issue permanent licenses or licenses "good until revoked." A driver's license may be revoked following a vehicle code violation.

Restricted, junior, or learner's licenses may be issued to younger and inexperienced drivers. A fully licensed driver must be present when such persons are driving. Some states also issue restricted licenses to elderly persons or those with physical handicaps. The holder may be limited in driving. For example, that person may be allowed to drive only to and from school or work by the most direct route. Also, a fully licensed person may have to accompany the driver. Many states require the signature of one or both parents, or a guardian, before issuing a license to a minor. In many states, the parents must agree to be responsible—through insurance—for damage, up to specified limits, caused by the minor's negligence while driving.

Most states require special licenses for persons who operate motorcycles or who are employed to drive trucks, buses, or cars for others as chauffeurs. Often, stricter standards are demanded of such drivers than are demanded of ordinary drivers.

Great responsibilities accompany driving privileges. Unfortunately, statistics indicate that drivers who are minors have a higher accident rate than do older drivers. Because of this, insurance companies charge substantially higher rates for minors. However, some insurance companies offer lower automobile insurance rates for licensed students who maintain excellent cumulative grade point averages.

The driver of a motor vehicle is required to exercise reasonable care to avoid injury both to persons and to the property of others. What constitutes reasonable care depends upon the circumstances, such as speed, visibility, amount of traffic, weather, road condition, as well as presence and type of pedestrian. For example, reasonable care requires of the driver greater alertness and thoughtful consideration for others when children or when persons obviously under a physical disability are on the road. Failure to exercise reasonable care renders the driver liable in a civil action for damages resulting from the driver's negligence. It may also make the driver liable in a criminal action for violation of one or more traffic laws.

Anyone who (1) does not exercise reasonable care, (2) unreasonably interferes with the use of a public road by others, or (3) deliberately disregards the safety of self or of others may be prosecuted for **reckless driving**. In the problem, Buchek was not correct. She was driving too fast considering the poor weather conditions and thereby showed a lack of reasonable care.

reckless driving: deliberately driving without reasonable care

Reckless driving, along with certain other offenses and circumstances, may result in the suspension or revocation of a driver's license. In most states, a person's driver's license may be taken away if that person:

1. is convicted of reckless driving three times within 12 or 18 months,
2. kills someone while driving negligently,
3. drives a car while intoxicated or while under the influence of drugs,
4. commits a felony while using a car,
5. makes false statements under oath involving the registration or operation of an automobile,
6. habitually or persistently violates traffic ordinances or regulations, or

7. is involved in an accident that results in death or injury to another person and fails to report it.

Responsible driving practices are required of everyone. Proper care and understanding by any competent individual can ensure that the privilege of operating a motor vehicle on our highways is never lost.

PREVENTING LEGAL DIFFICULTIES

1. Since the age of majority varies from state to state for drinking alcoholic beverages, mandatory education, responsibility for contracts, emancipation, and for other rights and duties, minors should become familiar with the applicable laws in each state they enter.

If you become involved in an automobile accident:

2. stop your car and assess the damage. If no one is present and you have damaged another's property, leave a note with your name, address, and telephone number or some other means by which you may be contacted. If the accident is serious, see that the police are called and a report made of the occurrence;
3. exchange identifications with any other involved drivers and obtain the names and addresses of all witnesses. In addition, write down the license number and description of each car involved and its part in the accident;
4. if required by your state's financial responsibility law, report the accident to the proper authorities promptly. If you have insurance, report the accident to your insurance company as soon as possible; and
5. do not say anything or sign any statement regarding responsibility for the accident until you have talked with your attorney. Do not admit fault to the other driver, to any witness, to an insurance adjuster, or even to the police. You may not know or understand all the facts, and such admission could later be held against you in court.

Strengthening Your Legal Vocabulary

adoption
annulment
driver's license
emancipation
financial responsibility
guardian
guardian ad litem
majority
minor
reckless driving
truants

1. Minors who fail to attend school when legally required to do so.
2. Person who has not yet reached majority.
3. Adult appointed to sue or defend on behalf of a minor.
4. Age at which one is legally bound to contracts.
5. Voluntary surrender by the parents of the rights to care, custody, control, and earnings of a minor child.
6. Adult appointed to have custody and care of a child during minority.
7. Deliberately driving a vehicle without reasonable care, thus disregarding one's own safety and that of others.
8. Legally taking another's child as one's own.
9. Court declaration that a marriage never existed.
10. Ability to pay damages.

Reviewing Important Points

1. Minors are persons who are under the age at which they have full adult legal rights and duties.
2. Minors and adults alike are required to obey the law and generally are held responsible for their failure to do so.
3. Upon arrest and thereafter, minors, although often subject to the control of a juvenile court system, have constitutional rights similar to those of adults.
4. Parents have custody and control of their children and the right to their services and earnings until the children are emancipated.
5. Emancipation occurs when a minor reaches the age of majority, is legally married, or is self-supporting. It also occurs when the parents voluntarily surrender parental rights.
6. One of the basic rights of a minor is a free education through high school or, in some states, through age 14. Schools have special legal rights to control the conduct of students, but students may not be denied their constitutional rights.
7. In owning and driving a car, minors are subject to the same duty of obeying traffic regulations as are adults. Like adults, minors' drivers' licenses may be suspended or revoked if they repeatedly fail to comply with traffic regulations or if they drive recklessly.

Applying Law to Everyday Life

1. Shultz, age 17, found and kept a wallet. It contained a credit card, which he used by forging the owner's signature. With the credit card, Shultz bought a camera for $475, a video recorder for $1,100, stereo equipment for $565, and a round-trip airline ticket to Hawaii for $750. When Shultz got to Hawaii, the Honolulu police found him and placed him under arrest for obtaining property under false pretenses. Shultz was extradited to his home state. Will he be prosecuted as a delinquent in juvenile court or as an adult in criminal court?

2. Craig, 16 years old, has worked as a clerk in a legal clinic for several months. She earns $100 a week and saves it for her college education. Her father needs money to pay an overdue debt. He claims that all of her wages belong to her parents. Is he correct?

3. Betsy Ann and Fred were both 16. One night they slipped away, were married, then returned to their respective homes. Their parents did not find out about the marriage until a year later. Can the parents still annul the marriage?

4. Sadeck, a high school senior, was suspended from school and not allowed to graduate with her class because she was caught trying to disable one of her teacher's cars. She insisted that she was just turning off the headlights, which the teacher had inadvertently left on. Prior to imposing the suspension, the school principal failed to give Sadeck the opportunity to tell her version of what had happened. Were her constitutional rights violated?

5. Yecker, Warwick, and Washburn, student activists, published an underground newspaper, which they distributed at their high school. A series of caustic articles criticized the school board for eliminating most interscholastic sports, as well as music and art classes, in order to balance the budget. School officials prohibited further distribution of the newspaper on or off the school grounds. They told the student activists that the school board's decisions were "none of your business. We design the program, and you study what's offered." Was the ban a valid and proper exercise of the school officials' authority?

6. Simmons and some other students came to school wearing buttons proclaiming "No Busing!" The students did so despite a school regulation prohibiting the wearing of buttons and other insignias of a controversial nature. The regulation had been adopted as a result of many school disturbances, including fights, sit-ins, and destruction of property, which had occurred at various times and on various issues. After a proper hearing, the students were suspended. They claimed that they had been denied their right to freedom of speech. Do you agree?

7. Spears, age 17, had an unblemished safety record for the year that he had been a licensed driver. To reward him, his parents bought him a new sports car. Late one evening, on a nearly deserted interstate highway, Spears was stopped by the highway patrol, who had clocked him at speeds in excess of 115 mph. With what should he be charged?

Solving Case Problems

1. Ohio statutes provide for free education for all children from ages 6 to 21. The statutes also empower the principal of a public school to suspend for up to ten days or to expel a pupil who misbehaves. In either case, the student's

parents must be notified within 24 hours, and the reason for the action must be stated. The suspended or expelled pupil, or the parents, may appeal the decision to the board of education. Nine suspended students of high schools in Columbus sued to have the statute declared unconstitutional. They claimed that the statute permitted public school administrators to deprive, without a hearing, the students of their rights to an education, a violation of due process. The nine students' alleged offenses varied from physical attack on a police officer to being bystanders, according to their claims, at disturbances. None of the students were told the reasons for suspension. A three-judge district court held that the students had been denied due process. The court held that in connection with a suspension of up to ten days, students must be given oral or written notice of the charges against them. If the students deny the charges, they must be given a hearing of the evidence and an opportunity to present statements in defense. The decision of the district court was appealed. Should the Supreme Court uphold the decision of the lower court? (*Goss* v. *Lopez*, 419 U.S. 565)

2. On the complaint of Cook, Gault, age 15, was taken to the Children's Detention Home. Cook claimed that Gault had telephoned her and made obscene remarks—a violation of Arizona law. Gault's parents were not notified of the arrest but learned of it through a friend. At the time, Gault was on probation as a result of being in the company of another boy who, four months earlier, had stolen a wallet from a woman. A hearing date was set, but Gault's parents were not notified of the hearing until two or three days before it took place. At the informal hearing, Gault was found to be delinquent even though he did not admit to the charges. He was committed to the State Industrial School "for the period of his minority" unless discharged sooner. No attorney was present to represent Gault. Nor was Cook, the complaining witness, present. The judge found Gault delinquent because he was "habitually involved in immoral matters." Under Arizona law, there is no appeal from the decisions of a juvenile court. Gault claimed that he had been denied due process of law. He claimed that he was entitled to the same constitutional rights as adults even though hearings for juvenile offenders are more informal than are criminal trials. Is he right? (*Application of Gault,* 187 S.Ct. 1428)

3. Kallio, age 18, had purchased a car out of his part-time earnings and was paying for its operation and maintenance, including insurance. About 4:00 one morning, Kallio crashed into the rear of Foran's car while Foran, who had run out of gas, was refueling it. Foran sued Kallio for damages and included Kallio's parents as defendants. Foran claimed that because Kallio was living at home while attending college, Kallio was under the control of the parents. Thus, Foran claimed, the parents were entitled to Kallio's earnings and were liable for his acts. The senior Kallio claimed that his son was at least partially emancipated. He presented evidence that his son had been allowed to keep his earnings and that the son had not only purchased and maintained the car out of those earnings but also was paying for his college education. Do you agree with the claim of partial emancipation? (*Foran v. Kallio*, 56 Wash.2d 769, 355 P.2d 544)

4. Moshe Menora and other basketball players at two orthodox Jewish high schools in Chicago brought suit challenging a rule of the Illinois High School Association. The rule prohibited the wearing of any headgear during interscholastic basketball competition except for glasses and headbands no wider than two inches. Under the rule the plaintiffs could not wear their yarmulkes (small skull caps) as required by their religion. Previously the players had tried to comply with the rule by affixing their yarmulkes with bobby pins, but the caps fell off nonetheless, thereby creating the safety hazard the rule was designed to avoid. The District Court struck down the rule, and the Association appealed. Decide. (*Menora v. Illinois High School Association*, 683 F.2d 1030, 7th Cir.)

5. In 1966 Catherine and William Franz were married. In the ensuing years, the couple had three children. Then, in 1976, they were divorced. Catherine retained custody of the children, and William was awarded visitation rights which he exercised regularly. Prior to the divorce, Catherine developed a "personal relationship" with one Charles Allen. Allen later confessed to authorities that he was involved with Philadelphia's organized crime leaders. In return for the relocation and protection of himself, Catherine, and the three children under the Federal Witness Protection Program, Allen testified in an important criminal trial. Therefore, in early 1978, federal marshals moved Allen, Catherine, and the three children to a new, undisclosed location and provided them with new identities. This was allegedly accomplished without the participation or consent of William Franz or the children. Thereafter, Franz brought suit against the United States, the Attorney General of the United States, and the Department of Justice to be allowed to exercise his court-granted right to visit his children. Franz also sued for money damages. The District Court dismissed the case. Franz has appealed. How should the appellate court rule? (*Franz v. United States*, 707 F.2d 582, D.C. Cir.)

7

Law for the Consumer

1. A newspaper ad for a large computer store promises a portable computer at $750 off its regular price to the first ten customers through the store's doors on Saturday. On that day you are second in line as the store opens, but the store employee informs you the store is sold out of the computer promised in the ad. Can you legally force the store to obtain and sell you that model of computer at the promised price?
2. You receive a "chain letter" in the mail. The letter promises that you will make thousands of dollars if you send $10 to the name at the top of an enclosed list of five names and addresses. You are then to put your name and address at the bottom of the list, delete the name you sent money to, and send the new list and a copy of the letter to ten of your friends. Has the sender violated the law? Will you violate the law if you comply with the letter?
3. A door-to-door salesperson persuades your parents to buy a vacuum cleaner. But the next day, your parents decide that the family does not really need a new machine. Can they cancel the contract?

WHY DOES THE LAW PROTECT THE CONSUMER?

> **PROBLEM:** Simmons wanted his car painted. He saw a newspaper advertisement for "car painting, $99.99 complete." He went to the shop, contracted for the service, and selected a dark blue metallic finish. When the car was finished, the color looked light blue. Simmons complained, but the manager claimed the color was close enough and refused to make any correction. The color difference is obvious. What should Simmons do?

consumer: a buyer of goods primarily intended for personal, family, or household use

caveat emptor: maxim which means "let the buyer beware"

A **consumer** is a person who acquires goods that are primarily intended for personal, family, or household use as opposed to business use. The relationship between sellers and consumers has been governed primarily by the legal maxim **caveat emptor**—Latin words meaning "let the buyer beware." It was once thought that consumers would be adequately protected by their own ability to judge a product's safety and utility. In addition, it was presumed that the economic forces of supply and demand in a competitive marketplace would induce producers and sellers to make and to sell good products at fair prices to maintain their reputations with customers.

Unfortunately these safeguards proved inadequate. In a modern, affluent, technology-oriented society such as ours, the complexity and sheer abundance of products sometimes leaves the consumer unable to judge quality or comparative advantage. Some products are so sophisticated that the average person cannot determine if they are substandard and could not repair them if they were to break down.

In addition, the products are often offered by distant giant corporations which, by their size alone, find themselves capable of controlling the market. As a consequence, these corporations may not be responsive to consumer dissatisfaction. The volume of their sales is not as dependent on their reputation with consumers as it once was. Instead, such sellers find themselves relying heavily on intensive advertising campaigns costing millions of dollars. Such advertising can be even more effective in shaping consumer attitudes toward the product than actual first-hand experience.

In response to the failure of some of the traditional consumer defenses, local, state, and federal governments have passed legislation to help restore balance in the marketplace. Some of the federal statutes are listed in Figure 7-1. In addition, numerous administrative agencies, such as the federal Office of Consumer Affairs, have

Federal Statute	Basic Objective
Consumer Credit Protection Act	Full disclosure of cost of credit and loans.
Consumer Product Safety Act	Safety of consumer products.
Equal Credit Opportunity Act	Equal access to credit regardless of sex or marital status.
Fair Credit Billing Act	Accuracy and fairness in billing credit accounts.
Fair Credit Reporting Act	Accuracy and fairness in credit agency records.
Fair Debt Collection Practices Act	Elimination of unfair harassment of debtors.
Fair Packaging and Labeling Act	Accuracy and fairness in labels and containers.
Federal Trade Commission Act (as amended)	Fairness in product promotion.
Magnuson-Moss Warranty Act	Clarity of rights under full and limited warranties in sales.
Motor Vehicle Information and Cost Saving Act	Disclosure of factory-recommended prices of various components of new cars.
National Traffic and Motor Vehicle Safety Act	Higher safety standards for automobiles and tires.
Wholesome Meat Act	Upgrading of state inspection standards to federal level.

Figure 7-1. Important Federal Consumer Legislation

been created or have had their powers strengthened to aid consumers. Some of the more important of these agencies are listed in Figure 7-2.

Of course, the basic law of contracts, torts, and crimes continues to provide protection against certain kinds of violations. For example, anyone intentionally deceived while contracting may sue the wrongdoer for fraud. However, court action is costly and time consuming. It is often not worth the effort for a single customer. To overcome this problem, **class actions** have been authorized by court rules. Such lawsuits permit one or several persons to sue on behalf of themselves and possibly on behalf of thousands of similarly affected persons who need not participate in the suit.

class actions: legal suits brought on behalf of large groups

In addition, at certain times the government, in the form of an administrative agency such as one of those listed, can act on behalf of the injured consumer. For example, the administrative agency

Agency	Area of Action
Consumer Product Safety Commission	Assurance of safety of consumer products.
Department of Agriculture	Assurance of wholesomeness of fish, meat, and poultry.
Department of Housing and Urban Development	Establishment of minimum building standards for mobile homes.
Department of Justice—Antitrust Division	Prevention of monopolies.
Department of Labor	Assurance of payment of private pensions.
Environmental Protection Agency	Control over pollution of air and water.
Federal Deposit Insurance Corporation	Control over insurance of bank deposits.
Federal Reserve Board	Control over money supply and inflation.
Federal Savings and Loan Insurance Corporation	Control over insurance of savings accounts.
Federal Trade Commission	Restraint of unfair practices and monopolies.
Food and Drug Administration	Assurance of purity of foods, drugs, and cosmetics.
National Highway Traffic Safety Administration	Assurance of safety of motor vehicles and tires.
Securities and Exchange Commission	Regulation of stock and bond sales.
U. S. Postal Service	Control over mail fraud.

Figure 7-2. Federal Agencies Providing Consumer Protection

cease and desist order: order requiring a firm to stop an illegal practice

consent order: voluntary agreement to stop an illegal practice

restitution: repayment of money illegally obtained

may issue a **cease and desist order** to a company. This is an order requiring a company to stop certain conduct. If the company disagrees with the agency's issuance of the order, the order may be appealed to the federal district court. If the defendant violates the final order, heavy civil penalties may be imposed. Often, a defendant will voluntarily sign a **consent order** rather then resist a charge in a long and costly battle with the administrative agency. The agency may also require **restitution**—the return to customers of money wrongfully obtained.

Many of the consumer-oriented laws and agencies will be discussed in the remainder of this chapter. However, it should be noted that, in addition to government action, a number of private organizations are active in the field of consumerism. Consumers Union, a nonprofit organization, studies consumer services and scientifically tests consumer goods. It publishes helpful information and comparative product ratings in its monthly magazine, *Consumer Reports*. Better Business Bureaus (BBB) are nonprofit corporations made up of local business firms. BBBs are located in more than 100 cities. BBBs warn consumers of fraudulent schemes. They sometimes provide arbitrators to decide disputes between customers and member firms. Because of their low budgets, BBBs have no enforcement powers and do little investigative work. Critics of the Better Business Bureau say there is a conflict of interest because member companies may themselves be guilty of unfair practices.

Many leading corporations have customer service departments which handle inquiries and complaints. Smart consumers with honest complaints have learned that a direct phone call or letter addressed to the head of the manufacturing company involved will often get action when local dealers stubbornly refuse to do anything.

In any case, consumers seeking help should report violations to the proper authorities. Thus, in the problem, Simmons should take such an action. For example, he might complain to a consumer affairs office listed in the telephone directory. Or he could complain to the local district attorney. He could notify the newspaper, which might stop using that business's advertisements. He might notify the local Better Business Bureau, which would warn future prospective buyers if they inquired. As a last resort, Simmons might take his problem to the local small claims court (see page 43).

HOW DO THE CONSUMER LAWS PROVIDE PROTECTION?

PROBLEM: The LaSalles agreed to allow a contractor to install aluminum siding on their home. The materials and service were to be free if the LaSalles would allow their home to be used as a "model." They also would receive $200 commission for every person to whom they showed the siding, provided the person also purchased such siding. The LaSalles had to sign a contract obligating them to pay $5,000 even though under ordinary circumstances similar siding and installation cost about $3,400. The contractor said the $5,000 would be made up "in no time" when their commission checks came in. In fact, although the LaSalles showed the siding to many friends, not one of them purchased similar siding. Is there anything the LaSalles can do?

Consumer laws provide protection in four basic ways. They may:

1. help protect against the sale of substandard consumer goods;
2. prohibit unfair, deceptive, or unreasonable trade practices;

3. establish procedures, such as licensing and inspection, to ensure compliance with applicable laws; and
4. provide remedies for injuries suffered.

Some cities have established independent offices of consumer protection. Some states have consumer specialists within the office of the attorney general. Thus, in the problem, the LaSalles could report their experience to the proper authority if their state or city has such a service. They would probably obtain some assistance, such as a reduction in the contract price. Moreover, they might be able to protect others by forcing the contractor out of business through loss of license.

HOW DOES THE LAW PROTECT AGAINST SUBSTANDARD CONSUMER GOODS?

PROBLEM: The MightyMo Lawn Mower Company sold thousands of a new type of robot lawn mower with special sensors and a microprocessor memory. The human user of the mower simply would guide it around the perimeter of the area to be mowed. The robot would then take control and cut all the grass within the area. Unfortunately, recently received consumer reports have shown that the integrated circuit chip in the robot is too sensitive to vibration which causes the lawn mower to go out of control. What is MightyMo required to do?

Although the basic responsibility for protection against substandard consumer goods still rests with the user, the law helps in a number of ways.

1. By Making and Enforcing Safety Standards

Each year millions of people are injured and thousands killed by products in use around the home. As a consequence, in 1972, the Consumer Product Safety Act was passed. The Consumer Product Safety Commission (CPSC) was thereby created and charged with responsibility for carrying out the Act's provisions. To do so, the CPSC was given authority to issue and enforce safety standards for most consumer products. However, drugs, foods, cosmetics, motor vehicles, airplanes, boats, and firearms are exempt from the CPSC's supervision because other agencies are responsible for their regulation.

The CPSC now requires that any manufacturer, distributor, or retailer that discovers that a product fails to comply with safety regulations must report it to the Commission. If the CPSC then finds that the product is substantially hazardous, the manufacturer, distributor, or retailer must notify purchasers of the product by public or individual notice.

The seller must then take one of the following actions:

1. recall and repair the product,
2. replace it with a product that is not defective, or
3. refund the purchase price.

If the product has been in use for more than one year, a reasonable allowance for such use may be deducted from any cash refund made by the seller. Thus, in the problem, MightyMo must notify the CPSC and the retailers and consumers to whom the defective product had been sold. The company may then repair or replace the defective mowers or refund the purchase price. Failure to comply could lead to fine or imprisonment. If necessary, the CPSC has the power to seize the hazardous product and ban it from the marketplace.

2. By Regulating the Development, Production, and Sale of Drugs, Food, and Cosmetics

To protect consumers using these products, the Food and Drug Administration was created. Its regulatory powers are extensive. Under its rules and regulations, foods, drugs, and cosmetics must be prepared under sanitary conditions. Factories or laboratories used for production must be clean. Ingredients must not be filthy, decomposed, or otherwise unfit for use, and they may not come from diseased animals. Substandard products may be *confiscated* (seized) under the government's police power. Such products may be destroyed without payment to owners.

Congress has passed several laws authorizing the use of quality and quantity **standards** (prescribed measures) for various products. For the most part, use of these standards is not required. However, if the terms found in standards are used on labels for goods in interstate or foreign commerce, the goods must conform to the government definitions. For example, if beef has been labeled U.S. Choice, it must conform to U.S. standards for that grade. If, however, it is labeled only with the name of the meat packer and is not sold in interstate commerce, beef is not required to meet U.S. Choice standards. Federal standards have been set up not only for meats

standards: prescribed measures

but also for poultry, eggs, dairy products, fruits, and many other foods. (Many states also prescribe quality standards for meat, poultry, and seafoods.)

Another source of legal protection of consumers is the United States Department of Agriculture, which inspects canners, packers, and processors. A seal is placed on the product to indicate that it was inspected. In most cases, the inspection is voluntary and paid for by the processor. In other cases, as for poultry and meat entering interstate commerce, the inspection is required by law. The seal verifies that the product was disease free and was processed under clean and sanitary conditions.

adulterated: does not meet minimum standards of purity and quality

In addition, an **adulterated** product is one that does not meet minimum standards of purity and quality as set by the FDA. If a product is adulterated, it may be confiscated. In general, a food, drug, or cosmetic is adulterated if any substance has been mixed or packed with it so as to reduce its quality or strength below the prescribed standards. A product is also adulterated if it contains harmful foreign matter.

A meat packer made hot dogs that contained 30 percent cereal. The hot dogs were adulterated because they did not meet standards set by the FDA.

The FDA also requires that all foods, drugs, and cosmetics have labels which identify the product. The labels must state (1) the name and address of the manufacturer, packager, or distributor and (2) the quantity, such as the weight of the contents. In addition, certain special items of information must be included on labels for packaged food products, drugs, and cosmetics. Standardized information regarding the nutritional value of food is encouraged for all foods. Such information is required on the labels of any food to which another nutrient (for example, sugar) has been added. If the number of servings is stated, the size of each must be disclosed. The label on a packaged food product must include any directions that are necessary if the food is for special dietary use. A label on a drug or cosmetic product must warn against use that may be dangerous to health. Proper labeling of products is required for the physical well-being of consumers. It is also required for their economic well-being. Consumers should not be required to pay for something expected but not received. Failure to state required facts on the label is **misbranding**.

misbranding: failure to state required facts on a label

To help ensure that drugs are safe and effective, new ones may not be sold in interstate commerce without approval of the FDA. A new drug receives approval for marketing only after careful testing. Unfortunately, qualified scientists cannot predict with certainty all long-term side effects of what initially appears to be a wonderfully useful new drug. Therefore the law requires continued observation and reporting of adverse effects. If added field experience shows the drug to be unsafe, marketing approval must be withdrawn. Injuries cannot be undone, and drug companies have been successfully sued for damages in some cases. Prior government clearance of a product for sale does not eliminate the manufacturer's ultimate responsibility for its safety.

The FDA also regulates drug advertising and blood banks.

3. By Standardizing Weights and Measures

The Constitution of the United States gave to Congress the power to fix standards of weights and measures. Accordingly, Congress created the National Bureau of Standards which provides uniform sets of actual weights and measures to state and local governments. Due to national standards and proper inspection, testing, and enforcement at these levels, you can be sure that the gallon of gas, pound of bacon, or foot of rope that you buy while on an interstate vacation is quantitatively the same as that which you would buy at home.

Most states inspect and test weighing and measuring devices at least once a year. Seals certifying the accuracy of the devices, such as gasoline pumps, supermarket scales, and taxicab meters, are then placed on them. Violations of the weights and measures laws are punishable by fine, imprisonment, or both. In addition, the goods involved may be confiscated.

WHAT TRADE PRACTICES ARE PROHIBITED BY CONSUMER LAW?

PROBLEM: All the real estate brokers in a certain heavily populated county informally agreed to charge a 6 percent commission on all sales of residential property. In the same county, the lawyers' professional association published a schedule of recommended fees for a long list of common legal services. Are these unfair trade practices?

unfair trade practice: dishonest or illegal method of business competition

The federal and state governments have enacted numerous laws to protect the consumer against unfair trade practices. Generally, an **unfair trade practice** is any method of business that is dishonest or fraudulent or that illegally limits free competition. Such practices are prohibited because they violate good business conduct and fair dealing, or they tend to boost prices or reduce supply.

Chief among the federal laws prohibiting unfair trade practices are the antitrust laws (to prevent monopolies and other illegal means of concentrating economic power) and the Federal Trade Commission Act (to create an agency, the Federal Trade Commission or FTC, to regulate unfair trade practices and to administer portions of the antitrust acts). These are intended to prevent unfair trade practices in interstate commerce. States have similar laws for intrastate commerce (business conducted wholly within one state).

1. Agreements to Control or Fix Prices

Unfair trade practices take many forms. One of the more serious involves competitors who enter into agreements to control or fix prices. Such agreements, like the agreements of the real estate brokers and the lawyers mentioned in the previous problem, are illegal and unenforceable. These agreements eliminate price competition and tend to keep prices to consumers unnecessarily high. Those who form such pricing agreements would be subject to criminal penalties.

2. Using False and Misleading Advertising

PROBLEM: The Smolenskis needed a new washing machine. One day they read a newspaper ad telling of "famous washing machines for sale for a limited time. Fully automatic. We can't name the standard brand because the price is so low: only $159!" When the Smolenskis went to the store, they discovered that the advertised machines were not a famous national brand and were not fully automatic. The Smolenskis also discovered that the sale had been going on for six months. A salesperson tried to sell them a genuinely famous brand, truly automatic machine. But the price of the machine was over $400. "Get the best!" the salesperson urged. "It's cheaper in the long run. And we'll keep the payments within your budget." Was the ad false and misleading?

The federal government and most states have banned false and misleading advertising. The ban applies to newspapers, magazines, and other printed matter. It also applies to radio, television, and other media. A type of false and misleading advertising would be a TV commercial which misuses optical illusions. For example, a commercial for a razor might show it shaving coarse sandpaper—but the sandpaper would actually be loose sand on glass that, on television, gave the appearance of sandpaper. This would be misleading. **False and misleading advertising** is advertising which deceives, makes untrue claims of quality or effectiveness, or fails to reveal critically important facts. In the problem, the store was guilty of false and misleading advertising. Moreover, it was guilty of an illegal practice called **bait and switch advertising.** This is a "come-on" to lure prospective buyers into the store. Once they are there, they are deftly redirected to a better, but more expensive, product.

false and misleading advertising: untrue claims of quality or effectiveness about goods or services offered for sale

bait and switch advertising: illegal "come-on" advertising to induce customers to buy costlier goods

Two regulations strengthen government authority over advertising. One is known as **affirmative disclosure**. This means that an advertiser may be required to include certain information in an ad if leaving the information out would mislead. The theory is that what is *not* said may deceive the consumer even if what *is* said is the truth. For example, the Food and Drug Administration (FDA) may order disclosure of possible harmful side effects of an advertised drug. Or the FTC may require disclosure of the true odds in a national promotion of magazine subscriptions where millions of addressees may participate, free of charge, but each has a very remote chance of winning a prize.

affirmative disclosure: inclusion of information which would mislead if left out

The other effective regulation is known as **corrective advertising**. This regulation requires an advertiser who has created a false impression to admit and correct the wrongdoing in a prescribed number of future ads.

corrective advertising: advertising which corrects a false prior impression

The Clean and Pure Company advertised that its popular mouthwash Clearbreath would prevent and cure colds and sore throats. The FTC proved that this claim was false. Accordingly, Clean and Pure had to include in future ads (for up to $10 million in cost) these words: "Contrary to prior advertising, Clearbreath will not help prevent colds or sore throats or lessen their severity."

It is also an unfair trade practice for stores to advertise sale items that are not in stock or that are not available in adequate quantities unless the ad states the quantity available or that quantities are limited. Even when reasonable stocks are exhausted, consumer-conscious retailers will give "rain checks." These tickets permit later purchase at the advertised price.

3. Conducting Illegal Lotteries or Confidence Games

PROBLEM: The *Weekly Sports Digest*, a national magazine, planned to boost its subscriptions by giving away prizes up to $1,000,000 in a drawing. People contacted in a huge mail campaign could enter the contest by return mail whether or not they actually subscribed to the magazine. However, instructions on how to enter would be placed in the text of the promotional material so a contacted person would have to read about the magazine to find out how to enter the drawing. A senior officer of the magazine canceled the plans because he thought it was an illegal lottery. Was he correct?

lottery: gamble involving a payment to play, a winner determined by luck, and a prize to some participants

A **lottery** is any gambling scheme or game which has the following three elements:

1. a payment of money or something of value by each player,
2. a winner determined by luck rather than skill, and
3. a prize awarded to one or more, but not all, participants.

Holding or participating in such a gambling scheme is illegal and violators are subject to fine and imprisonment. Regardless, many states by statute have exempted certain religious and benevolent groups from the lottery prohibition. These groups are allowed to run bingo and other games to produce revenue for their activities. Also, some states hold their own lotteries to generate revenue for state projects, most notably educational programs.

Nonetheless, the statute still applies to businesses where the use of lotteries to promote sales remains an unfair method of competition. This is because the customer is induced to purchase not by the quality of the goods but rather by the remote chance of winning a prize. The cost of the chance would almost always be better applied to the purchase of goods or services. In the problem, the *Weekly Sports Digest* promotion was legal because no payment was required to participate. Nevertheless, the FTC regulates such programs by requiring that all promised prizes be awarded.

Postal laws prohibit the sending of any matter that is a lottery or a confidence game through the United States mail. A *confidence game* is a fraudulent money-making scheme in which the victim is persuaded to trust the swindler. An example of the confidence game is the chain letter, whereby the sender swindles the recipient into sending money to the person whose name appears at the top of an enclosed list. After sending the money, the recipient is to place his or her name on the list and mail copies of the letter and the list to friends. The swindler's name and aliases will comprise the first two or three names on the initial list. Initiating or participating in such a scheme is a felony under the laws of most states.

4. Using Unfair Pricing Methods

PROBLEM: Uplet advertised a set of nonstick cookware at "fabulous savings, regularly $39.95, now $19.95." In fact, these sets were marked at the factory with the inflated price of $39.95. Uplet paid only $12.50 for each set and regularly sold them for $19.95. Is this an unfair pricing method?

The following are some of the more common unfair trade practices that exist in the pricing and sale of goods:

Representing goods or services as being sold at a considerable discount when that is not true. This type of unfair trade practice is illustrated in the problem.

Representing goods or services as being "free" provided a customer buys something else, when in fact the price is higher than it would be without the "free" item. Of course, reputable manufacturers often honestly introduce new products by giving away free samples. Merchants also may legitimately have "2 for 1" sales—sales in which two items are offered for the price of one. Merchants may also have "one-cent sales"—sales in which one item of a kind is sold at the regular price and a second really costs only 1 cent.

Representing prices to be wholesale prices when they are actually retail prices.

A luggage dealer marked merchandise with what were claimed to be regular retail prices. Prospective buyers were given cards enabling them to purchase luggage at the "wholesale price," which was stated to be $33\frac{1}{3}$ percent off the marked price. In fact, the marked price less the discount was the same as the retail price for identical luggage in other stores. This is an unfair trade practice.

Cutting prices below cost. Many states have enacted "unfair sales acts." These acts forbid retailers to sell goods at prices less than the cost to themselves plus some minimum markup if the intent is to harm competition. These acts thus prohibit the use of well-known brands as loss leaders. **Loss leaders** are "bait" used to attract customers who then pay regular or inflated prices for other goods in the store.

loss leaders: selected items sold at a loss to attract customers to buy costlier goods

5. Misbranding and Mislabeling Goods

PROBLEM: The three gasoline pumps at Lomy's Service Station were labeled "Premium," "Regular," and "Unleaded." The prices varied by 3 to 5 cents per gallon between grades. An investigation revealed that the gasoline from the three pumps had identical octane ratings and that it came from the same underground tank. Was this illegal mislabeling?

Misbranding and mislabeling occur frequently. For example, the initials "M and J" were used on a cheap coffee that was not a blend of mocha and java coffee. This was held to be unfair competition. The use of "super" in the brand names of second-line tires was held to mislead the public into thinking these tires were superior to the first-line tires, named "deluxe." Similarly, in the problem, the different labeling of the gasoline pumps when there was no difference in the product was fraudulent representation.

Laws require certain products to carry specific labeling. Poisons and insecticides must have appropriate warnings. Cigarette packages and advertisements must include these words: "Warning: the Surgeon General has determined that cigarette smoking is dangerous to your health."

Acts also regulate labels of textile and fur products. Such acts require that any garment containing a textile, wool, or fur and sold in interstate commerce must be marked to show the kind and proportion of each fiber used.

The federal Hazardous Substances Labeling Act provides that labels must warn of the hazards of using products which may cause illness or death if improperly used. These products include furniture polish, cleaning fluids, and other substances. Enforcement of the Flammable Fabrics Act is a responsibility of the CPSC. This act is designed to prevent the sale of wearing apparel that is easily set on fire.

Finally, containers must not mislead as a result of either their shape or the manner in which they are filled. When the container is much too large for the contents, giving the impression that the container holds much more than it does, it is said to be "slack-filled." However, some empty space may be necessary to prevent breakage or may legitimately result from the settling of the contents after filling.

6. Selling Used Articles as New

PROBLEM: Reliable Typewriter Sales Company advertised and labeled used electric typewriters as "completely rebuilt at the factory." In fact, the machines had simply been cleaned and carefully serviced in the retail store's own repair shop. Was this unfair competition?

Many misrepresentations involve selling used, secondhand, or rebuilt articles as if they were new or in a better condition than they are. The most common misrepresentation occurs when no indication is given that the goods are secondhand. Others falsely refer to the condition or quality of secondhand or rebuilt articles, as in the problem. In used cars, for example, odometers, which show total miles traveled, may be turned back. This is illegal.

7. Other Unfair Trade Practices

PROBLEM: Superior Cars, Inc., had been selling different models of its luxury limousine called the "Excelsior" to the very wealthy for more than half a century. Therefore when it discovered that a nearby company was making and selling "Excelsior" brand dog food, Superior sued and asked the court to prohibit such use of the Excelsior trademark. Superior claimed that such use was unfair competition as it misused the good name of Excelsior and destroyed the car's reputation as a luxury item. Is Superior correct?

There are numerous other forms of unfair trade practices and unfair competition. One is the use of a brand name or trademark so similar to a competitor's that it confuses or deceives the public. In the problem, however, the court held that no confusion or deception resulted. That is because the products involved were completely different and were not in competition with each other. The decision would have gone the other way, however, if both companies had made the same product for sale in the same market area.

The FTC has adopted many guidelines and regulations that require manufacturers and distributors to act in certain ways. These include the following:

1. explaining to credit customers the methods of figuring finance charges (see page 349);
2. under certain circumstances, providing written warranties (Chapter 18); and
3. in the case of door-to-door selling, giving the buyer three days in which to "cool off" and cancel the contract.

Another unfair practice is *commercial bribery*. This may involve buying secret information from the employee of some other firm. It also arises when a corrupt supplier gives a purchasing agent money "under the counter" in exchange for a purchase order. A variation of commercial bribery is *industrial espionage*. This activity involves getting a spy employed by a competitor to learn and report trade secrets, such as product formulas, cost information, and customer lists.

Another unfair trade practice is when a manufacturer pays a retailer's salesperson "push money" for greater effort in promoting the manufacturer's product. Sending unordered merchandise and demanding either payment for it or its return is an unfair trade practice. Indeed, according to federal law, when someone deliberately sends unordered merchandise through the mail, the recipient is under no obligation to return it or to pay for it. This is true even if the merchandise is consumed.

HOW DO STATE AND LOCAL LAWS PROTECT CONSUMERS?

PROBLEM: The Auxarcs were having difficulty starting their car so they took it to Vladamir's Garage for adjustment or repair. After examining the engine, a mechanic said the repairs would cost $239. The price included new parts, which he listed. The Auxarcs had the work done. Later, however, they learned that all the car had needed was a minor adjustment. It had not needed any new parts. A fair price would have been less than $50. What rights, if any, do the Auxarcs have against the garage owners?

A great variety of state laws protect consumers. Many are discussed later. Some, such as those dealing with unfair sales practices, credit, and product safety, are similar to federal laws. For example, door-to-door sales are often made by high-pressure sales agents. Therefore many states permit the buyer to cancel the contract within three days, either with no liability or upon payment of a modest charge. The FTC has a similar regulation. This right to cancel applies only to door-to-door sales, not sales made in stores or other places outside the home.

Also, most states and many large cities have various kinds of laws that supplement the federal protection of consumers. For example, some states have enacted the **Uniform Consumer Credit Code (UCCC).** This code contains a variety of measures for the protection of consumers who buy on credit. Critics object because the UCCC permits an annual effective carrying charge or interest rate which they think is excessive. The charge is 36 percent for amounts of $300 or less. It is 21 percent for amounts between $300 and $1000 and 15 percent for amounts over $1000. As another example, all states except Louisiana have adopted the Uniform Commercial Code (UCC). This code permits a court to give relief from an *unconscionable* sales contract. Such a contract is one that is oppressive or causes the consumer unfair surprise as to the nature of the agreement.

Uniform Consumer Credit Code (UCCC): organized collection of consumer credit protection laws

Other state and local support for the consumer includes:

1. Laws That Increase the Remedies Available to Injured Consumers

Instead of leaving consumers to rely on state officials taking the appropriate legal step to prevent or remedy harm, many states now give consumers, individually or in class actions, rights against those who take unfair advantage or cause injury. The victimized consumer may sue for damages and get a court order preventing future repetition of the act. Thus, in the problem, if the Auxarcs lived in a state with such a law, they could sue for damages and possibly get an injunction protecting others. The Auxarcs might also get punitive damages to penalize the garage owners and set an example for other shops.

2. Licensing Laws

Consumer protection often begins with legal standards and licensing for specified practitioners and establishments. This is particularly true for those who render personal service related to health. Such persons include physicians, dentists, nurses, psychologists, laboratory technicians, and pharmacists. Licenses may also be required of others. Some include teachers, beauticians, barbers, lawyers, morticians, accountants, contractors, plumbers, electricians, realtors, and insurance agents.

Certain institutions and business establishments may also be required to meet minimum standards before they are licensed. Examples include hospitals, rest homes, private schools, check-cashing agencies, banks, savings and loan associations, credit unions, and insurance companies. Failure to maintain minimum standards may cause suspension or even *revocation* (permanent cancellation) of the license.

In addition, some states license garages. Such states also require both written estimates in advance and detailed bills for all work performed. The states also require return of all replaced parts if such return is requested when the work order is given. Similar laws govern television and radio repair shops, where dishonesty has been a common complaint.

Finally, most states regulate going-out-of-business sales and bankruptcy sales. Often, a special license is required, and the business must shut down after the sale. Fraud occurs when customers are induced to believe they are getting close-out bargains when, in fact, the merchant is selling merchandise that was bought especially for the sale.

3. Sanitation and Safety Regulations

Statutes generally provide for inspection of businesses where food is handled. Such businesses include meat markets, bakeries, hotels, camps, and restaurants. Some states and cities rate the cleanliness of restaurants and other businesses selling food. They then often require public display of the ratings. Standards of cleanliness and sanitation are prescribed, and periodic health examinations may be required for food handlers. Establishments not meeting the standards may be closed.

Bedding and upholstery laws are in force in most states. These laws regulate the use of secondhand or *shoddy* (reclaimed) material in the manufacture of mattresses, comforters, quilts, cushions, pillows, and upholstered furniture. However, most states will permit the use of such materials if they have been sterilized and correctly labeled.

Safety laws apply to buildings and places used for public gatherings. These laws govern type of construction, location, and use. Detailed regulations apply to sanitary facilities, fire escapes, and sprinkler systems. Detailed regulations also apply to the maximum number of persons allowed in the place and the location, marking, and lighting of exits.

4. Food Adulteration Laws

Laws prohibiting the sale of tainted meat and unclean milk have been on the statute books of some states and cities since 1850. Now all states regulate the purity and quality of these products. Some states require that milk, when served in a public eating place, be opened and poured from an individual carton or bottle in front of the customer. This requirement helps to ensure cleanliness and wholesomeness.

Some states regulate the kinds and amounts of insecticides and herbicides that may be applied to growing fruit, vegetables, and other crops. For ecological reasons, the very effective insecticide DDT, which was once widely used, has been generally outlawed in this country.

PREVENTING LEGAL DIFFICULTIES

To Avoid Being Victimized. . .

1. remember that self-protection through prior knowledge of the good or service is the consumer's best protection. Therefore engage in comparison shopping for value and price and never purchase on impulse, in haste, or in frustration;
2. be cautious of "bargains." Usually they are genuine, but occasionally they are a part of a bait-and-switch scheme or are loss leaders surrounded by overpriced goods or are of substandard quality;
3. do not be misled into trying to make money by gambling. Even in free and honest sweepstakes, most participants receive nothing;
4. never sign any important agreement or receipt you have not read or do not understand. When in doubt, first consult a trustworthy friend or a lawyer;
5. read labels, warranties, ingredient lists, and other product information carefully; and
6. if you have a valid complaint about a fraudulent or unfair business practice, first try to negotiate in a friendly manner with the seller. If you are not

satisfied with the result, do not hesitate to write or telephone the manufacturer. Also, do not hesitate to contact the Better Business Bureau, the appropriate consumer affairs office, or the local district attorney. Check your telephone directory or call information for addresses and numbers. As a last resort, you could take legal action.

Strengthening Your Legal Vocabulary

adulterated
affirmative disclosure
bait and switch advertising
caveat emptor
cease and desist order
class actions
consent order
consumer
corrective advertising
false and misleading advertising
loss leaders
lottery
misbranding
restitution
standards
unfair trade practice
Uniform Consumer Credit Code (UCCC)

1. Game that involves a payment to play, a winner determined by luck, and a prize to some, but not all, participants.
2. Maxim meaning "let the buyer beware."
3. Repayment of money obtained by illegal means.
4. Goods, usually well-known brands, sold below cost to attract buyers into a store.
5. Quality and purity below minimum standards generally because of the addition of another substance.
6. Legal suits brought by one or several persons on behalf of themselves and other similarly affected persons.
7. Voluntary agreement to stop an illegal practice.
8. Untrue or deceptive claims of quality or effectiveness concerning goods or services offered for sale.
9. Illegal "come-on" advertising to lure prospective customers into a store in order to persuade them to buy costlier goods.
10. Dishonest or illegal method of competition in business.

Reviewing Important Points

1. Buyers have long been urged to beware by the Latin phrase "caveat emptor." Now the complexity of today's products and the inaccessibility of their makers require consumers not only to beware but to be aware of the various federal, state, and local laws designed to inform and protect them.
2. The federal government has authorized the Federal Trade Commission to prohibit certain unfair and deceptive trade practices in interstate commerce. Many states have similar laws for intrastate commerce.

3. The federal Food, Drug, and Cosmetic Act prohibits the manufacture or the introduction into interstate commerce of any food, drug, medical device, or cosmetic that is unsanitary, adulterated, or misbranded. Certain information must be given on the labels of all foods, drugs, medical devices, and cosmetics. Most states have similar laws for intrastate commerce.

4. The Consumer Product Safety Commission sets and enforces safety standards for most consumer products. Manufacturers, distributors, and retailers who do not comply with these standards are required to take one of three actions. They must recall and repair the defective product, replace the product, or refund the purchase price.
5. The National Bureau of Standards and assisting state agencies set and enforce regulations governing weights and measures.

Applying Law to Everyday Life

1. The Kiddy Kewpie Krib was banned as a hazardous product by the CPSC. The crib was banned because of its sharp hardware, lead-containing enamel, and improperly spaced slats. The Sabatinas bought one of the cribs and then learned of the ban. What should they do now?

2. A coffee manufacturer incorrectly stated the volume of coffee contained in one of its packages. Thousands of these packages are on the market. If necessary, can the packages be confiscated by the government to remedy the situation?

3. Packages of crackers were prominently labeled "Diet Thin Matzo Crackers." Other wording on the label indicated the vitamin content of a cracker. The FDA held that the package was misbranded. The FDA said that the label implied that Diet Thins were lower in caloric content than other matzos and, thus, were useful in weight-control diets. In fact, the crackers had the same caloric content as did plain matzos made by the same company. The FDA filed suit in a federal district court to confiscate 423 cases of Diet Thin Matzos. Should the court uphold the FDA?

4. In a national television advertising campaign, "FunTime" fruit drink was said to contain "natural food energy." The Federal Trade Commission discovered that the "natural food" providing the energy was sugar and held that the ad therefore created a false impression. What remedy would you recommend that the FTC use to correct the situation?

5. The manufacturer of Sweet-Tooth candy bars printed a number on the inside of each wrapper. Buyers who sent in 25 clipped-off numbers received a free ball-point pen. Those who returned a number ending in two 2s received a full carton of candy bars. Is this promotional scheme a lottery?

6. Noritaki joined a digital audio disc club. It operated in the same way as a traditional record club with monthly selections that the club member must reject or, failing that, have to buy. After a year in the club, she legally

terminated her contract. Subsequently the club mailed her a new disc and offered her a special discount if she would renew the contract. She did nothing. The club then billed her for the disc. Must she pay for it?

7. Late one evening, the Arnos signed a contract to buy magazine subscriptions. The contract was for one-year subscriptions to ten different magazines to be purchased "at the bargain price of only $4.95 a week." The Arnos signed the contract after an hour of persistent persuasion by a door-to-door salesperson. The next morning, the Arnos did some quick calculating and were appalled to discover that they had agreed to spend $257.40—a sum they could not afford—for magazines. Moreover, they had been buying only one of the magazines at their supermarket. Can the Arnos cancel the contract without being liable for damages?

Solving Case Problems

1. The FTC ordered Firestone Tire and Rubber Company to cease and desist from certain advertising. Firestone appealed to the Federal Court of Appeals to have the order set aside. Firestone had advertised "The Safe Tire, Firestone." It also advertised that its Wide Oval Tire "Stops 25% Quicker." The FTC claimed that the "Safe Tire" ad implied that the tires would be safe under all conditions without regard to conditions of use. The FTC said the "advertisement gives no indication that there is any limit to the safety of this tire or what such limits might be." Firestone emphasized that a large majority of persons interviewed concerning the "Safe Tire" ad thought it meant something less than a guarantee of absolute safety. The FTC also claimed that the "Stops 25% Quicker" ad was unfair and deceptive to consumers because it was "without substantial scientific test data to support it." Firestone, thus, submitted evidence of ten tests. The tests showed an average stopping distance on a wet smooth concrete surface to be 29.8 percent less for the Wide Oval tire than that for a Firestone Super Sports tire of standard tread width. Should the court uphold the FTC? (*Firestone Tire and Rubber Company v. FTC,* 481 F.2d 246).

2. Through radio and television, the defendant stores advertised a "top quality. . .Queen Anne Console Magic Stitcher" sewing machine, along with a sewing chair, for the "close-out price of just $29.50." Under the sales plan, a "lead person" would accept the customer's order, taking a deposit as small as 25 cents. After that, a demonstrator would visit the customer and "kill the sale" by having the machine jam in use. The demonstrator would tell the customer that the customer's TV set would be damaged if it was left on during the demonstration and that the machine would have to be oiled every few minutes. The demonstrator would also say that a five-pound can of grease would be needed to pack the bearings and that the customer could lose an eye if the machine jammed. Then the demonstrator would attempt to "step-up" the sale and persuade the customer to buy a higher-priced

machine. In about 19 months, only 26 of the advertised machines were sold, although 10,951 customers entered into conditional sales contracts for such machines. The 26 advertised machines were sold at a time when the defendants had received complaints from the television station and the Better Business Bureau. The defendants were prosecuted for conspiring to sell merchandise by means of deceptive and misleading advertising. The prosecutor gave evidence that the defendants never intended to sell the advertised machines, which actually cost them $45 each. Are the defendants guilty as charged? (*People v. Glubo, Exelbert, Epstein, and Atlantic Sewing Stores, Inc.*, 158 N.E.2d 699, N.Y.)

3. Registration of a trademark called "MONOPOLY" for use on men's, women's, and children's wearing apparel was sought by a New York-based corporation, Tuxedo Monopoly, Inc. The makers of the "MONOPOLY" board game, General Mills Fun Group, opposed the application. The Patent and Trademark Office Trademark Trial and Appeal Board sustained the opposition and would not allow the registration. On appeal to the U.S. Court of Customs and Patent Appeals, Tuxedo's attorneys argued that monopoly was a common term and that, regardless, there was very little likelihood of confusion between a mark used on a game and one used on clothing. They also pointed out that the court had previously allowed the registration of the famous "DIXIE" cup mark by a company using it as its mark on waxed paper. If the court finds a likelihood of confusion exists, they should affirm the Board's decision. How did they rule? (*Tuxedo Monopoly, Inc. v. General Mills Fun Group, Inc.*, 648 F.2d 1335, C.C.P.A.)

4. When Brenda Lee Suits bought a used car from the Little Motor Co., the company provided her with a mileage disclosure form. The form stated that the mileage reading on the vehicle she was buying was unknown as the actual mileage varied from the odometer reading for reasons "other than odometer calibration error." The odometer of the ten-year-old car showed 73 miles at the time of purchase by Suits. In fact, when Donald Little, Little Motor's owner, had purchased the car ten days earlier from Leiphart Chevrolet, he had received a mileage disclosure form warranting the mileage at 100,073. However, as was common practice, Little had asked Leiphart Chevrolet to mail the form to him so that he could sell the car prior to receiving the mailed form and thus be able to indicate that the vehicle's true mileage was unknown. The success of Brenda Suits' lawsuit for damages under the Motor Vehicle Information and Cost Savings Act hinges on whether or not an intent to defraud can be inferred from Little's actions. Little has stated that his reason for failing to disclose the 100,073 mileage was that the buyer of a ten-year-old car with an odometer reading 73 miles knows that it has turned over. Will Suits recover? (*Suits v. Little Motor Company*, 642 F.2d 883, 5th Cir.)

5. Best paid $5,000 in advance for 200 hours of dancing lessons from an Arthur Murray franchised dancing studio. After using a few hours of instruction, Best sued for the return of her money. She claimed that the contract

was in violation of a certain state law. The law required that all contracts for dancing instruction for more than $500 be for "a precisely measured period of years or part thereof." Best said that the 200 hours of instruction did not meet that requirement. Should Best recover the amount owed for the unused dancing lessons? (*Best v. Arthur Murray Town & Country Dance Club*, 60 Misc.2d 66, 303 N.Y.S.2d 546, N.Y.)

8

Law for the Business Firm

1. You and two other workers try to organize a union in the plumbing fixture factory where you work. Your employer, therefore, fires all three of you as troublemakers. Can the employer be forced to rehire you and to pay you lost income?
2. A friend at the fast-food restaurant where you work advises you to buy stock in a new robotics corporation with the money you are saving for college. Your friend says, "Uncle Sam has to approve every stock issue that's sold, so you can't lose your money. Plus the prices go up and down frequently—just hold on until the price is high and then sell. You'll make a killing." Is this good advice?
3. You and your cousin are getting ready to open a small business to repair personal computers. You will both contribute funds to get it started, and both of you will help manage it. Your employees will be doing extensive amounts of driving and intricate electronic repairs in customer's homes and places of business. What legal form of business should you use?

WHY DO WE USE THE LAW TO REGULATE BUSINESS?

PROBLEM: Silicon City has an ordinance requiring that all outdoor signs on business establishments be first approved by the Silicon City Planning Commission. The commission checks the design, size, and location of each sign. Thompson's Toggery, a clothing store, wished simply to replace its present sign with a new one. Must the store obtain approval from the planning commission?

business: production or sale of goods or services for a profit

Business is defined as the production or distribution of goods or services with the intention of earning a profit. For centuries during the Middle Ages, monarchs and the church tightly controlled certain businesses, if they allowed them to exist at all. The kings and queens frequently granted monopolies for the production and distribution or sale of certain products to court favorites. The quality and quantity of goods provided was low and the price paid for them very high. Then, in the late 18th century, competition between businesses that were allowed to market similar products came to be recognized as a means to lower prices and to improve the quality of the goods sold, increasing the living standard of the people as a whole. Many governments, seeing the value of this, then moved to support a policy of uncontrolled competition.

A lack of regulation, however, also brought with it many problems. Business owners tended to band together in agreements to restrain the effects of competition and thereby create their own monopolies. In certain industries economic power became concentrated in the hands of a few. Manufacture of shoddy and dangerous products, exploitation of workers through low pay and unsafe working conditions, and a near collapse of the world's market systems during the Depression of the 1930s caused government to regulate business more closely for the good of all.

Perhaps in overreaction to the bitter experience of the Depression, the regulation that resulted became so detailed it began to stifle business rather than merely purify it of unwanted and anticompetitive behavior. Consequently, various laws and regulations concerning business behavior are being reevaluated to produce a more balanced legal environment for business and the people it serves. However, even laws which some may consider objectionable are binding on all so long as the laws are constitutional. Thus, in the problem, Thompson's Toggery must receive approval for the new sign and must get a permit to put it up. This action must be taken even though the new sign is a replacement for another sign.

At present, governments at all levels regulate business. Local, state, and federal governments do so either directly or through administrative agencies.

You have already learned about special laws designed to protect consumers (see Chapter 7). Later you shall see how business must, by law, deal with borrowers (Unit 5), employees (Unit 6), and insureds (Unit 7).

Each state may use its police power to make laws which regulate intrastate commerce. Interstate commerce is regulated by the federal government under powers granted it by the federal Constitution. Business between individuals in the United States and those in foreign countries is called **foreign commerce** and is also regulated by the federal government.

foreign commerce: business between persons in the United States and persons in any foreign country

WHAT ARE THE SPECIFIC OBJECTIVES OF GOVERNMENTAL REGULATION OF BUSINESS?

PROBLEM: The Discount Buyer's Group, Inc., is a small corporation owned by shareholders who have purchased the firm's stock. The company has 37 employees who develop and manufacture role-playing games which are sold nationwide through large chain stores and by direct-mail. How does governmental regulation affect this business?

In general, all governmental regulation of business should be intended to produce a situation where the rights and needs of individuals are fairly balanced against the rights and needs of businesses. Such a situation is most likely to ensure happiness and prosperity for all concerned. Improperly placing the interests of one group ahead of another can only result in problems. Therefore, as discussed in Chapter 7, businesses such as the Discount Buyer's Group in the problem have to obey any applicable consumer laws. In addition, businesses and consumers would have to obey any and all laws designed to control their activities in ways likely to help achieve the following purposes:

1. To Maintain Free and Fair Competition

As mentioned earlier, the great importance of competition in ensuring that businesses are producing and marketing quality products at reasonable prices is well established. Our laws attempt to achieve a healthy competitive environment for business by banning illegal monopolies, price fixing, and other restraints on trade.

illegal monopoly: situation where one company, or a small group, controls supply of goods, excludes competitors, and sets prices

An **illegal monopoly** is where one company, or a small group, has the policies and the power to control the supply of goods, to exclude competitors, and to fix prices. Note that large size alone is not illegal. A company may legally become an industry leader by making better products and by selling them at lower prices than do its competitors.

Sherman Antitrust Act: act which outlaws monopolies

Clayton Act: act which outlaws mergers and forbids unfair trade practices

Robinson-Patman Act: act which outlaws price discrimination

Three federal laws governing competition are especially noteworthy. The **Sherman Antitrust Act** makes it illegal to conspire or combine with others to restrain free, competitive trade or to fix prices. The **Clayton Act** goes further and outlaws *mergers* (businesses absorbed into other businesses) and other joint behaviors which merely tend to create monopolies. This act also forbids unfair trade practices, including false and misleading advertising. The **Robinson-Patman Act** strengthens the Clayton Act by making it illegal for sellers to favor one customer over another in prices charged, such as by giving special discounts.

As far as the Discount Buyer's Group in the problem is concerned, these laws would prevent them from joining with competing companies when such action might lead to the creation of a monopoly. On the other hand, the Group would be protected by these laws because its suppliers could not conspire to raise prices charged or to withhold goods from the Group.

2. To Guarantee the Rights of Labor

collective bargaining: negotiations between representatives of employees and employers

Workers are protected by laws ensuring their rights to organize into unions and to bargain collectively with their employers. **Collective bargaining** requires the employer, or the employer's representative, to negotiate (discuss in good faith) with representatives of the workers' union. The two sides discuss wages, hours, and conditions of employment. There must be an honest effort by both sides to reach a binding agreement.

When bargaining fails to produce a satisfactory result, federal labor laws ensure workers in private industry the right to strike. These same laws give employers the right to lock out (bar) workers from their jobs in such disputes. The Discount Buyer's Group's employees are subject to these laws.

Other laws protecting workers:

a. promote the democratic operation of labor unions,
b. set minimum wages, maximum hours, and other proper work conditions, and
c. provide compensation from various sources for income loss due to disability or retirement or both.

For example, the Occupational Safety and Health Act (OSHA) empowers the U.S. Secretary of Labor to make rules and to conduct inspections of businesses to protect workers from unsafe working conditions. Programs of the Social Security Administration require employers and employees to pay special taxes to qualify for retirement plans, survivors' insurance, disability benefits, and health insurance. Most businesses find themselves subject to detailed and stringent requirements of these and many other employment laws.

3. To Assist Business Where Necessary

Often, government is called upon to aid business in performing services that the market mechanism, individual businesses, or associated businesses cannot perform. These services include:

a. the maintenance of public trust in business investments. Sales of stocks and bonds to the general public must be accompanied by extensive information about the companies offering them. Deceptive or fraudulent statements or material omissions in such information are illegal. Of course, having accurate information available about stock or bond issues does not mean that they are good investments. It is still the responsibility of the would-be investor to evaluate the information and act accordingly. The laws act to ensure that all investors have the same data at their disposal;
b. the maintenance of free and fair competition as discussed earlier;
c. the legalizing of the various alternative organizational forms that a business may use.

   These forms include the **sole proprietorship** (an unincorporated business owned by one person), the **partnership** (an unincorporated business owned by two or more persons bound by a partnership agreement), and the **corporation** (an artificial legal person, incorporated under the appropriate state or federal statutes, that is separate and distinct from its owners). The most widely used of these forms is the sole proprietorship. It requires no legal formalities to create but is restricted in practical ways because it has only one owner. As a consequence, it cannot grow as quickly nor as large as other forms of business because it can draw only on what capital (money) the owner has, can borrow, or can generate through the operation of the business. In addition, the duration of the business is generally limited to the lifetime of the owner;

sole proprietorship: unincorporated business owned by one person

partnership: unincorporated business owned by two or more persons bound by an agreement

corporation: artificial legal person, separate and distinct from its owners, created under the laws of a state or the nation

therefore, it is difficult to attract professional managers looking for career positions.

The partnership form improves on this situation by allowing the resources and energies of two or more persons to be combined in the business. However, a partnership requires a formal or informal partnership agreement which can become extremely complex, and members are liable without limit for debts of the business.

The corporate form requires the most complex legal steps to create. One appeal of the corporate form of organization is that it can attract capital quite efficiently by selling stock. Therefore its possible growth rate far exceeds that of the sole proprietorship or partnership. Also, if a corporation gets into too much debt, its owners stand to lose only the amount they have invested in the business. In contrast, the owners of a partnership and the owner of a sole proprietorship may lose both their business investments and their nonbusiness assets, such as their homes. Finally, a corporation does not end with the death or withdrawal of an owner.

Beyond providing these legal forms that business may assume, government may also inspect and license certain businesses (such as banks) to enhance public trust; protect a business' trade name; and provide for protection of trade secrets, patented products and processes, and copyrighted publications; and

d. the providing of direct aid to special types of businesses. Government agencies provide direct and indirect financial assistance to business. Such assistance is termed a **subsidy**. Most government subsidies to business, such as consulting services, publications, guarantees of the repayment of private loans of money to companies, and certain tax advantages, are indirect.

subsidy: financial assistance

State and local governments also sometimes give business firms, especially manufacturing companies, free land, tax relief, or other help. Such action is taken to induce the firms to locate in a certain community.

Agriculture is promoted by government through subsidies, crop purchases, and farm loans secured by surpluses of major crops. This action attempts to maintain a prescribed **parity price ratio** (fair balance between the prices farmers get for their crops and what they must pay for manufactured goods). In addition, agriculture is promoted by government through:

parity price ratio: balance between the prices farmers pay and receive

1. output controls to prevent surpluses,
2. price controls on milk and other products,
3. research on crops, animals, fertilizers, insecticides, and land use,
4. cooperatives, which are exempt from antitrust laws yet permit farmers to join together in storing and marketing their crops,
5. standardization of fruits, vegetables, and grains, and
6. control of injurious insects, plant diseases, weeds, and rodents.

The Discount Buyer's Group, a corporation with an important trade name and a public stock offering outstanding, would be a grateful recipient of these various types of government assistance.

4. To Promote Economic Well Being

Generally businesses and consumers alike are served by government's regulation of the economy to achieve controlled growth and the creation of more jobs. This economic development of the country is promoted by governmental involvement in:

a. taxes,
b. money,
c. credit,
d. price-wage-interest-profit relationships in time of economic distress,
e. employment levels,
f. **tariffs** (taxes on imports),
g. **embargoes** (laws banning export or import trade with specified countries),
h. the volume of government purchases of business products (note that government collectively is the largest customer of American industry), and
i. governmental spending for research and development, defense, space programs, highways, and education.

tariffs: taxes on imports

embargoes: laws banning export or import trade with specified countries

Like other businesses, the Discount Buyer's Group benefits from a stable, growing, economic environment that provides it with customers better able to afford its products today and in the future.

5. To Provide Essential Goods and Services

At times, it is economically inefficient to have competing companies providing the same good or service. Electric power, water, and gas could be provided competitively only by duplicating very expensive delivery systems. Such duplication would waste resources and cause higher prices. As a consequence, governments grant monopolies and then regulate the private businesses that provide these goods or services. Such businesses are called **public utilities** and are treated in a different manner than other businesses.

public utilities: private businesses, strictly regulated by government, which sell essential goods or services

The government grants each public utility a *franchise* (exclusive right to operate a certain business in a certain geographic location). This franchise ensures a monopoly.

Public utilities may use **eminent domain**. This is the traditional government power to take private property for public use upon payment of the fair market price. In exchange for the use of this power, public utilities agree to maintain prescribed levels of services at government-controlled prices. Moreover, the utilities must offer the service without discrimination to anyone able to pay the price.

eminent domain: government power to take private property for public use

In certain instances, the government may own the provider of the good or service, for example, a city power plant. The Discount Buyer's Group is greatly dependent on the goods and services provided at reasonable costs by the public utilities.

6. To Produce a Stable Social Environment

Businesses and consumers are best served by laws that, taken as a whole, efficiently seek to develop the potential of all citizens and, at the same time, protect the interests of the disadvantaged.

Examples of such laws include those that:

a. cultivate human talents by providing public schools, colleges, libraries, and museums. Generally the result is an individual better able to vote wisely, to understand directions, to communicate, and to be more productive in society.
b. eliminate improper discrimination based on race, color, sex, religion, national origin, or advanced age. We are all injured by the higher prices and lower production that result from the waste incurred when a worker is hired or promoted based on criteria other than how well he or she does the job at hand. Federal and state Equal Employment Opportunity Commissions (EEOC) seek to prevent such improper discrimination between employees and to punish violators.

   Sometimes employers are required to take **affirmative action** to overcome the bad effects of former discrimination. The aim is to achieve proportional representation of women and minorities in the work force. Such representation is

affirmative action: positive efforts to end discrimination

based upon the groups' numbers as percentages of the local area's population.

c. protect health by controlling pollution, requiring inspection of food producers and sellers, and regulating drug availability and usage. In addition, government supports Medicare, Medicaid, free or low-cost school lunch programs, and other efforts to help remove cost barriers that would prevent the disadvantaged from maintaining their health or preventing or curing their afflictions.
d. aid the needy with unemployment compensation, welfare grants, food stamps, free legal service in selected matters, diminished income taxes, as well as in many other ways.
e. protect persons and their property by the maintenance of police, fire, and military services.
f. provide transportation systems such as buses, airlines, subways, interstate highways, and waterways.
g. provide adequate housing through rent controls and assistance payments for apartment dwellers, guaranteed-loan programs for the purchase of homes, **zoning laws** (which allow only certain uses of land or buildings within a designated area), and **building codes** (which set standards of materials and methods used in construction).

zoning law: law which limits the use of property

building code: code which prescribes construction standards and acceptable building materials

Certainly the Discount Buyer's Group benefits indirectly from each one of these services as well as from the overall environment of stability and confidence that generally results from appropriate government regulation of business.

HOW DOES THE GOVERNMENT REGULATE BUSINESS?

> **PROBLEM:** The electric company in your area plans to raise the rates. Can its management make the change by simply notifying all customers of the new rates?

The mechanism by which most governmental regulation of business is conducted was developed over years of trial and error. At first, because the growth and diversity of business was not as great as it is today, regulation was carried out by the legislative, executive, and judicial branches of the federal and state governments. However, as time went on and the pace of business increased, it became obvious that the traditional branches of government could not respond quickly enough to the problems that resulted. As a consequence of this lack of reasonable control over undesirable practices, businesses were able to join with competitors in forming large and powerful companies that acted very much like monopolies. In addition, underhanded dealings by some led to a loss of faith in business by the public. The Wall Street crash occurred in 1929 and the Great Depression followed.

Thereafter, in order to restore confidence and stability to the economy and to ensure a quicker and better informed response to problems, the government turned to the use of administrative agencies to regulate business activity. Administrative agencies commonly combine the traditionally separated functions of the legislative, executive, and judicial branches. Administrative agencies exist at the local level as city planning or zoning commissions, transit authorities, and school boards. They are to be found at the state level in professional licensing boards and public utility commissions. But they are most prominent and powerful at the federal level.

Agencies may be independent, as is the Federal Trade Commission (FTC), or they may exist within an executive department, as does the Food and Drug Administration (FDA) or the Internal Revenue Service (IRS). In either case, the chief executive officer (the president or governor) usually appoints the members. Sometimes the chief executive officer also names the chairperson of the board or commission subject to confirmation by the appropriate legislative body. At the county and city levels, the legislative body (supervisors or council) frequently makes the appointments. In some instances, the members are elected, as is usually the case with school boards.

Figures 8-1 and 8-2 list some of the major administrative agencies at the federal, state, and local levels. (Important federal agencies dealing with consumer protection were discussed in Chapter 7.) All of these agencies supplement the work of regular government executive departments. They also relieve the courts and legislative bodies of much detailed work. Their duties and powers vary widely, but the figures suggest their scope.

Note also that agency functions are similar among the states, but the names of agencies differ. Problems sometimes arise when both federal and state agencies are concerned with the same action area. Because the U.S. Constitution is "the supreme law of the land," valid federal law prevails over conflicting state law. This is called **preemption**. In the problem, the electric company would have to obtain permission from the public utility commission of the state before rates could be increased.

preemption: when federal law takes the place of conflicting state law

Federal Agency	Area of Action
Equal Employment Opportunity Commission (EEOC)	Employment rights regardless of race, color, sex, religion, national origin, or age
Federal Aviation Administration (FAA)	Airplane and airport safety
Federal Communications Commission (FCC)	Radio, television, interstate telephone, and telegraph communication
Federal Energy Regulatory Commission (FERC)	Energy research, production, and distribution
Federal Trade Commission (FTC)	Unfair trade practices and monopolies
Internal Revenue Service (IRS)	Income tax collection
Interstate Commerce Commission (ICC)	Railroad, truck, bus, and inland waterway transportation
National Labor Relations Board (NLRB)	Labor-management relations
Nuclear Regulatory Commission (NRC)	Nuclear power plant safety
Occupational Safety and Health Administration (OSHA)	Employees' on-the-job protection
Securities and Exchange Commission (SEC)	Stocks and bonds sales
Small Business Administration (SBA)	Aid to small business
Social Security Administration (SSA)	Retirement, survivors', disability, and health insurance

Figure 8-1. Federal Administrative Agencies

Each administrative agency is created and given powers by the appropriate legislative body at the local, state, or federal level. Once staffed and in operation, the agency will notify interested parties and hold hearings to determine what rules and regulations are necessary to properly administer the assigned area of responsibility. After the hearings, the agency will pass rules and supervise those who must comply with them. Upon discovering an alleged violation of the rules, the agency will notify the accused violator and then conduct a hearing or trial to determine if the accusation was correct.

The courts may be asked to review decisions of the agency. However, judges are reluctant to upset agency rulings if the agencies acted within the powers authorized by the legislative body that created them. Judges also do not like to upset agency rulings if the rulings were not arbitrary and the party or parties concerned have been given a fair opportunity to present their side of the case. The

State Agency	Area of Action
Agricultural Price Stabilization Board	Food production quotas and prices
Alcoholic Beverage Control Board	Liquor licenses and sales in some states
Public Utilities Commission	Electricity, gas, and telephone rates and service
Workers' Compensation Board	Damages for work-related injuries and deaths

County and City Agencies	Area of Action
Air Pollution Control Board	Air purity
Airport Board	Construction and operation of airports
Library Board	Operation of libraries
Parks and Recreation Board	Operation of parks and playgrounds
Planning Commission	Land use and development
Public Housing Authority	Construction and operation of public housing projects
Redevelopment Agency	Clearance and redevelopment of slum areas
School Board	Operation of local public schools
Transit Authority	Operation of local mass transit systems

Figure 8-2. State and Local Administrative Agencies

reason is that the agency members are experts in the technical fields they regulate.

sanctions: penalties for violations of legal orders

Administrative agencies may enforce compliance with their orders and rulings by using **sanctions** (penalties for violations of legal orders). For example, usually before or after a hearing, the agency will seek voluntary compliance with any order it issues. Frequently the defendant willingly agrees to consent to the order, without admitting any guilt. If the defendant refuses, the agency may issue a type of sanction called a cease and desist order. Such an order requires the offender to stop the forbidden practice.

Agencies may use other types of sanctions. For example, various other orders may be issued. Fines and penalties may be imposed. Property may be seized or withheld. Licenses may be suspended or revoked. Damages may be assessed. If the defendant fails to comply with the sanctions, the agency must normally seek enforcement by a regular court. If the court approves the sanction, continued failure by the defendant to comply is contempt of court, which is punishable by court-ordered fine and imprisonment.

PREVENTING LEGAL DIFFICULTIES

Government—Servant, Not Ruler . . .

1. in the capacity of private individual or business manager, the wise citizen takes full advantage of government services. The just and prudent citizen obeys all government laws and regulations. The good citizen participates in government—as voter, observer, and constructive critic. Moreover, the citizen may serve as a hired civil service employee or as an elected or appointed official;
2. for business manager and private individual alike, the administrative agency is often the most important arm of government. Whenever appropriate, learn what such agencies require of you and can do for you;
3. if dissatisfied or aggrieved by action of an administrative agency, you must generally first "exhaust" (use) any available administrative remedies. If still unsatisfied, you can appeal to the regular courts for review. However, regular courts seldom overrule the administrative rulings because the agency staffs are experts in their field. As such, they are authorized to make the decisions; and
4. if dissatisfied with specific practices of a business firm which is regulated by an administrative agency, you may ask the agency to investigate and possibly provide assistance or relief.

Strengthening Your Legal Vocabulary

affirmative action
building code
business
Clayton Act
collective bargaining
corporation
embargoes
eminent domain
foreign commerce
illegal monopoly
parity price ratio
partnership
preemption
public utilities
Robinson-Patman Act
sanctions
Sherman Antitrust Act
sole proprietorship
subsidy
tariffs
zoning law

1. Act which outlaws price discrimination.
2. Financial assistance.
3. Businesses that are given monopolistic franchises but are subject to control over their rates and services.
4. Artificial legal person created under state or federal law.
5. When federal law takes the place of conflicting state law.
6. Situation where one group has the policies and power to control the supply of goods, exclude competitors, and set prices.
7. Penalties for violations of legal orders.
8. Laws banning trade with specified countries.
9. Law which specifies what use (residential, commercial, industrial) may be made of land.
10. Government power to take private property for public use.

Reviewing Important Points

1. A proper balance between free enterprise and governmental regulation of business is necessary for the well-being of all.
2. Business is supported in many ways, both directly and indirectly, by government. From acting to maintain competition to providing the free public schools necessary to ensure a better educated, more productive worker, government strives to provide the optimal environment for business.
3. The most common business regulator is the administrative agency. To be effective in the rapidly changing and complex world of business, most administrative agencies combine the traditionally separated legislative, executive, and judicial functions of government.
4. Agencies enforce compliance with their decisions by using different types of sanctions. For example, agencies can issue cease and desist orders, deny licenses, or impose fines. They can also file an action in court against one who violates a regulation and refuses to obey an administrative order.

Applying Law to Everyday Life

1. A group of survivalists and tax protesters moved into a remote valley in the wilderness of Missouri's Ozark Mountains. Their nearest neighbor was four miles away and the nearest town was 33 miles away. They made or grew all of the products to fill their needs, and their only contact with civilization came when they sold some of their produce at a nearby farmer's market. Are they still subject to governmental regulation of business?

2. Clemore owned an old riverside paper mill which used large quantities of water. In the manufacturing process, much waste was dumped into the river. A new state law required filtration of the waste water to reduce pollution. Clemore objected. She said papermakers in other states were not

required to install the expensive filtration equipment. She also said that this requirement would place the mill at a competitive disadvantage because the price of the product would have to be increased. Must Clemore either comply with the law or close down the plant?

3. By aggressive sales tactics, excellent products, and an ability to predict market needs, the Videodiske Supply Company captured over 90 percent of the market for products of the type it carried. Has it violated the antitrust acts by becoming an illegal monopoly?

4. After repeated attempts at a solution, the Electronic Storage Workers Union could not agree on contract terms with the management of the Videodiske Supply Company. Therefore, the day after the current contract expired, the management of the company locked the workers out of the plant. Is this action illegal?

5. Bill and John had been friends since childhood. Bill had worked for a defense contractor for many years when, on his own time, he developed a design for a revolutionary new radar. His friend, John, had considerable experience in management. They sat down together and worked out an agreement to form and own jointly a small business to market the radar. The agreement contained terms determining what part of the profits each was to receive and what the duties of each would be. What form of business have they created?

6. The Securities and Exchange Commission ruled that the new type of timesharing, group-ownership plan that developer Bob Rinder offered to sell for Suntan Heights, his mid-Florida condominium project, was a stock. This meant that Rinder would have to go to great expense to register this "stock" with the SEC. He wanted to appeal to the Federal Court of Appeals, but Tom Soto, his attorney, said that an appeal on such a complex matter was rarely successful. Why is this?

7. Cardinez bought a house previously identified as a historical site by the city's historical site preservation commission. The commission was authorized to identify and preserve such sites for future generations. Cardinez proposed to tear down or move the building to make room for a ten-story office building. He argued that such "higher economic use" would create jobs and benefit the community. May he go ahead with his plan?

Solving Case Problems

1. One morning an OSHA inspector entered the customer service area of Barlow's, Inc., an electrical and plumbing installation business. After showing the president of the company, Bill Barlow, the appropriate credentials, the inspector requested entry into the nonpublic area of the business. Barlow then inquired if there had been an OSHA complaint about the business or if

the inspector had a search warrant. When the inspector answered no to both questions, Barlow refused to allow the inspector into the requested area. Barlow said he was relying on his right to be protected from warrantless searches under the Fourth Amendment to the U. S. Constitution. In a later trial of the matter before the U. S. Supreme Court, the Secretary of Labor pointed out that the OSHA clearly read that "upon presenting appropriate credentials to the owner" an inspector was authorized "to enter without delay and at reasonable times any factory, plant, establishment . . . where work is performed by an employee of the employer." The Secretary also argued that the delay involved in getting a warrant would cause the loss of surprise and allow the employer to cover up violations. Should the warrantless searches be allowed? (*Marshall v. Barlow's, Inc.*, 436 U.S. 311)

2. Pollard bought a single-family residence for $12,000. The sale was secured by a mortgage of $9,200. The mortgage was insured by the Department of Housing and Urban Development (HUD). Pollard claims that before signing the contract, she had been led to believe that the house had been inspected by HUD and found to comply with the local building code. However, soon after moving in she learned that there were several defects. Pollard asked HUD for financial assistance in making repairs. HUD offered to make certain repairs, but Pollard insisted on other repairs as well. When HUD refused to finance the proposed improvements, Pollard filed suit to compel them to do so. The Housing Act provided that the decisions of the secretary of HUD regarding such disbursements "shall be final and conclusive and shall not be subject to judicial review." Under these circumstances, should the court order HUD to comply with the Housing Act as Pollard asked? (*Pollard v. Romney*, 512 F.2d 295)

3. A Burbank city ordinance made it unlawful for any jet aircraft to take off from Hollywood-Burbank Airport between 11 p.m. one day and 7 a.m. the next day. This did not apply to emergency flights. The only flight scheduled during these hours was an intrastate flight. The flight originated in Oakland and terminated in San Diego. Lockheed Air Terminal sought a court order against enforcement of the ordinance. Lockheed claimed that the Federal Noise Control Act of 1972 preempted the Burbank ordinance. This act provided that the FAA and EPA provide "for control and *abatement* (reduction) of aircraft noise" and set up certain noise standards. The act did not include any express provision for federal preemption. The city claimed that it had authority under its police power to regulate such matters as abatement of nuisances and land usage inasmuch as they do not affect interstate commerce. Is that correct? (*Burbank v. Lockheed Air Terminal, Inc.*, 411 U.S. 624)

4. Jones Beach State Parkway Authority was created by the New York State Legislature. The Authority was authorized to construct, maintain, improve and operate a portion of the Southern State Parkway. The Authority was empowered to charge a toll of 10¢ for the use of the parkway under its control. The Authority was also empowered to use the funds for improving the parkway unless the revenues "are insufficient to meet all obligations . . . and pay the costs of operating" the facilities. The Authority decided that the toll should be raised to 25¢ in order to meet increased costs. A user of the parkway filed suit to prevent the Authority from raising the toll. The petition claimed that the Authority had no such power because such power was not specifically included in the legislation. Can the petitioner stop the Authority from raising the toll? (*Russell v. Jones Beach State Parkway Authority*, 80 Misc. 2d 698, 363 N.Y.S. 2d 448, N.Y.)

5. The City of St. Louis passed an ordinance that declared walking on lawns, instead of using existing sidewalks, a trespass. Later a uniformed letter carrier was cited by a St. Louis police officer for a violation of the ordinance. The United States of America and the United States Postal Service then sued the city. The federal government argued that an existing postal service regulation allowing carriers to cross lawns while making deliveries, if patrons do not object, preempted the ordinance. The City of St. Louis argued that a letter carrier beating a daily pathway across a householder's lawn was a violation of the homeowner's Fifth Amendment right prohibiting the taking of private property for public use without just compensation. Decide. (*U.S. v. City of St. Louis*, 452 F.Supp. 1147)

SPECIAL SECTION:
Careers in Law

One can pursue a variety of careers in the field of law. Generally these can be divided into careers involving the direct practice of law and careers involving the support of that practice.

POSITIONS IN THE DIRECT PRACTICE OF LAW

Opportunities in direct practice of law include independent general practice, specialized practice, practice as legal counsel for a corporation, and practice for the government or quasi-public sector.

General Practice. For many persons the first mental image of an attorney is in a court scene, usually in a dramatic criminal trial. In fact, many lawyers seldom, if ever, appear in court. The general practitioner works to keep clients out of the courtroom by providing accurate and timely advice. A general practitioner counsels clients, prepares legal documents, does research, and appears in court or before administrative agencies when required.

Specialized Practice. The complexity of the law requires that some lawyers concentrate on a specific area of law. Specialists work almost exclusively in a particular area such as patent law, antitrust law, copyright law, tax law, labor law, criminal law, or domestic relations (family) law.

Corporate Counsel. Large corporations or other organizations typically have their own "in-house" attorneys who are salaried employees. Such counsel handle the day-to-day legal problems of the corporation, labor union, university, or other organization and provide legal advice to its executives. A career as a corporate counsel is usually more stable than that of the general practitioner, but the income may be more limited.

Government and Quasi-Public Sector Lawyers. Most legislative and executive levels of government and most administrative agencies employ full-time services of prosecutors, legal aid attorneys, judges, and public defenders. In the quasi-public sector, attorneys represent special-interest groups in areas such as business, the environment, civil rights, and consumer rights.

LAW-RELATED POSITIONS

Many careers that involve the support of the practice of law are available to persons who need not be trained as attorneys. Court reporter, legal secretary, trust officer, escrow officer, law office manager, paralegal, and court administrator are typical positions that offer challenge and involvement in the law.

Regardless of what specific career path a person follows, law—dynamic and demanding—is a fascinating, absorbing, and rewarding field.

Unit Three
CONTRACTS: MAKING BINDING AGREEMENTS

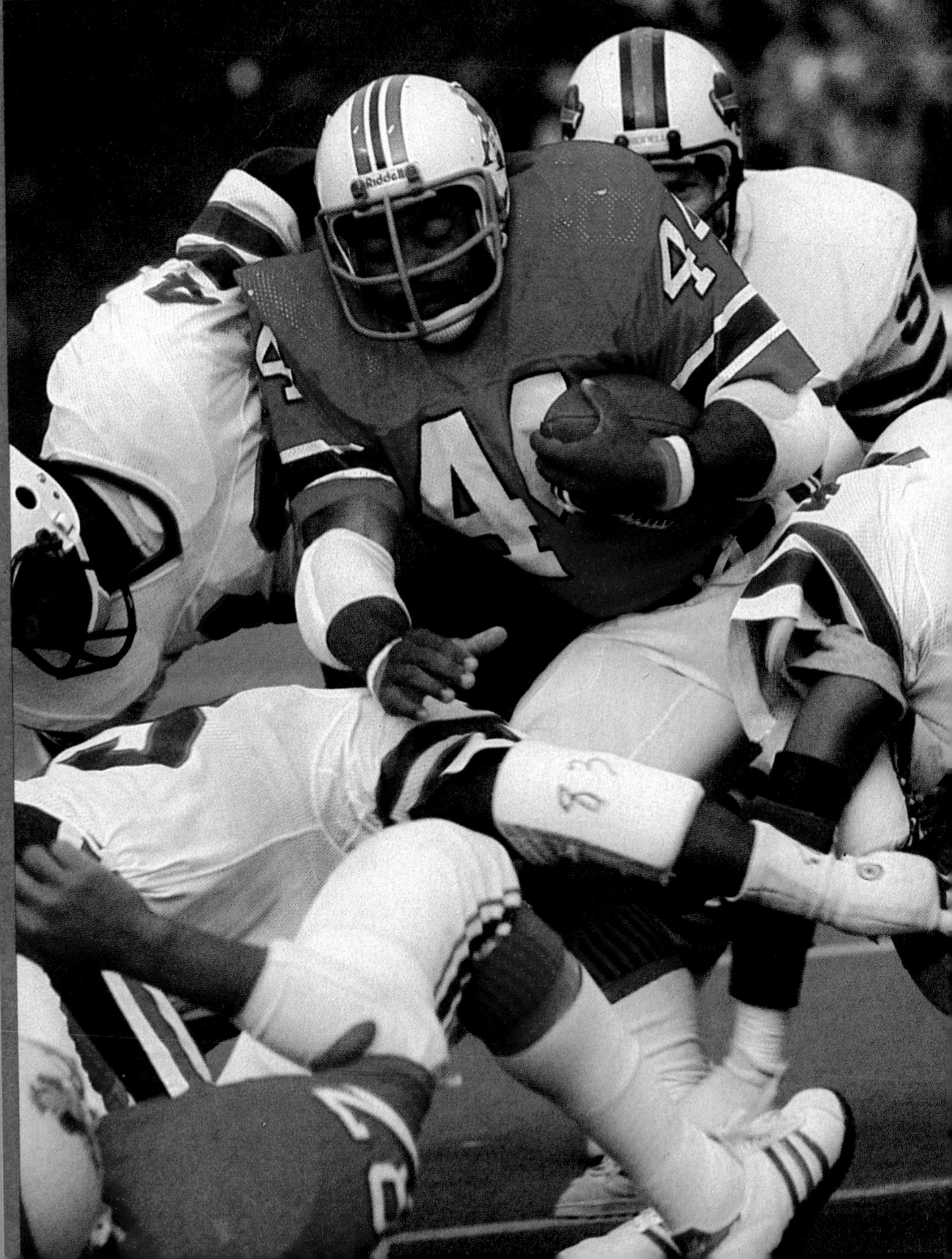

UNIT OBJECTIVES

UPON COMPLETION OF THIS UNIT, you should be able to

1. discuss the nature of contracts.
2. list the elements of an offer, and ways an offer may be ended, as well as the elements of an acceptance.
3. define valid, voidable, and unenforceable contracts, and distinguish contracts from social agreements and void agreements.
4. explain circumstances in which courts will enforce illegal agreements.
5. identify the consideration exchanged in each contract.
6. name exceptions to the requirement of consideration for a binding contract.
7. explain when and why a minor can disaffirm a contract, and also when and why a minor cannot do so.
8. discuss why fraud, duress, undue influence, and mutual mistake permit one party, and sometimes both parties, to disaffirm a contract.
9. list important types of contracts which must be in writing and signed by the party against whom enforcement is sought.
10. describe how contracts can be discharged.
11. suggest remedies which are available if a contract is breached.

9

Offer and Acceptance

1. After lunch, Rick and Mary stretched out in the sun on their high school lawn. "It's an adult world," Rick said. "Contracts—stuff like that—have nothing to do with guys like us." Mary answered, "Your first comment is true, but not your second; even little babies are affected by contracts." Who is right?

2. The owner of a small, color TV set offers to sell it to a neighbor for $75. As the neighbor rubs his jaw, thinking, a bystander says, "That's a bargain. I'll take it!" Is there a contract between the bystander and the owner?

3. You see a notice on a supermarket bulletin board offering a reward for a lost dog. That afternoon you start to look for the dog. Does your action mean that you have accepted the offer, thus binding you to continue looking until you find the dog? Would the dog's owner have to give you the reward if you had not seen the ad but found and returned the dog?

WHAT IS A CONTRACT?

PROBLEM: Moreland phoned Eagan, saying, "I'll let you have my videocassette of *Star Wars* for $15. Is it a deal?" Eagan answered, "Sounds fair; sure. Bring it to school tomorrow." Was a contract made?

Have you ever wondered how it is possible that you can eat a variety of foods produced in different parts of the world? That your TV—a very complex machine—brings you news and entertainment at the flick of a finger? That the streets are paved and crowded with vehicles? That you and others are comfortably dressed? That there is fresh running water in the kitchen tap? The list could go on and on.

These and all other marvels of modern civilization are the output of work by millions of persons. People have produced and exchanged these goods and services over the years in an intricate cooperative effort. The key or link among the people who produce and consume these many goods and services is: the contract.

contract: legally binding agreement

A **contract** is an agreement which is enforced by law. This agreement normally results from an exchange of promises.

offeror: one who makes a definite offer

offeree: one to whom a definite offer is made

For example, a husband and wife want their house painted. A painter examines the building and *offers* (promises) to do the job for $1,500 during the next month. The owners could accept the offer by promising to pay the price. For a contract to arise, the painter as **offeror** (one who makes the offer) must make a definite offer, and generally the **offeree** (one to whom the offer is made) must accept the offer exactly as presented. Of course, the parties may negotiate additional details. The homeowners could reject the offer by demanding a lower price or earlier completion. The painter, in turn, could accept or reject such a counteroffer. Without both offer and acceptance, there is no agreement. No particular language need be used. The intent of the parties is the important thing. In the problem, there was a contract even though payment and delivery were to be made later.

Over several months, Ryan had assembled a personal computer. Foley had visited Ryan several times and admired the machine. Finally, Foley wrote and asked, "How much would you take for your PC?" Ryan replied by letter, "Including my labor figured at the minimum wage, I'd say I have $2,000 in it. I'd expect at least that much." Foley immediately wrote back, "Your price of $2,000 is reasonable. I accept. When can I pay you and pick it up?" Here, no contract was formed. Ryan had stated his estimate of the cost but had made no offer to sell. Thus, Foley could not accept. However, Foley's statement could be interpreted as an offer to buy the computer for $2,000. Acting as an offeree now, Ryan could accept Foley's offer. If he did, a contract would result.

WHO MAY ENTER INTO CONTRACTS?

PROBLEM: Purcell developed a taste for fast cars and alcoholic beverages. Over the years, drinking to excess became an uncontrollable habit. Eventually, a guardian was appointed to take care of Purcell and his estate. One weekend, Purcell signed a contract to buy a new car. Is he bound by this agreement?

capacity: ability to understand the nature and effects of one's actions

legally competent: having the capacity to contract

For an agreement to be a valid contract, enforceable in court, the persons who make it must have the capacity to contract. **Capacity** means the ability to understand one's actions and the effects of those actions. Persons with the capacity to contract are said to be **legally competent**. Adults are presumed to be legally competent. Minors, intoxicated persons, insane persons, convicts, and enemy aliens are considered to lack capacity, at least to some degree.

Young people have limited experience and are more vulnerable to exploitation than are adults. Therefore, although minors are free to make contracts, the law gives minors the right to *disaffirm* (or set aside) most of them. For example, they can return unwanted purchases and demand a full refund. Even when goods which are the subject matter of the contract have been consumed or destroyed, most states permit the minor to disaffirm. However, minors seldom disaffirm their contracts. Their business agreements are usually fair and the minors want to keep what has been received. Also, minors may sense that although disaffirmance may be legally permitted, it is not necessarily right and may be difficult to accomplish.

If the minor lied about his or her age when making a contract, many states do require the minor to pay for the use of or damage to returned property. Some states flatly deny the right to disaffirm in such situations and require full payment.

If a contract is made between a minor and an adult, only the minor may disaffirm the contract; the adult is bound. A minor who wants to disaffirm a contract must do so while still a minor or within a reasonable time after becoming an adult. Otherwise the agreement is binding.

A business firm wishing to make an important contract with a minor should insist that an adult also sign the agreement. The adult may then be held liable for damages if the minor disaffirms or fails to pay. Thus, parents are frequently asked to join in signing their children's contracts. Otherwise parents are not liable for the contracts of their children, unless as explained later, the contracts are for certain necessaries.

Bailey wished to buy a motor scooter. The dealer refused to sell because Bailey was a minor. When Bailey persuaded his father to sign as a co-buyer on the contract, the dealer gladly made the sale. The dealer could now hold the father liable if Bailey does not pay for the motor scooter.

Two other important types of legally incompetent persons are (1) those who are intoxicated by alcohol or other drugs and (2) those who are insane or seriously deranged mentally. In both categories, if guardians have been appointed, then only those contracts made by the guardians are binding. Contracts of the wards are void. In the problem, Purcell's purchase was void. This is because the contract was made by Purcell, not by his guardian, and it was not for a necessary item.

Guardians seldom are appointed for persons who drink too much; they are not always appointed for persons who are insane. When such persons without guardians make contracts, their agreements can be set aside by them if, at the time of contracting, the incompetent could not understand the nature and results of the contract. If the contracts are disaffirmed, any consideration received must be returned.

Persons who are being "wined and dined" may sign agreements they would not have signed if totally sober. Nevertheless, they are bound if they understood the nature and general effects of their agreement.

For their own protection, minors, intoxicated persons, and insane persons are restricted in their freedom to contract. Some states limit the right of those convicted of major crimes to contract. In most states, aliens from countries at war with the United States lack capacity to contract. These restrictions are respectively intended as punishment, and as a means of supporting the nation's war effort.

WHAT ARE THE REQUIREMENTS OF AN OFFER?

PROBLEM: Anchors Aweigh, a boat retailer, advertised a one-day sale of cabin cruisers for the "bargain price" of $12,500 each. The dealer had five cruisers in stock, but they were sold within one hour. During the rest of the day, seven other potential buyers came in and sought to purchase a bargain cruiser. Is Anchors Aweigh bound by contract to each of them?

An **offer** is a proposal by an offeror to do or not to do some specified thing in the future, provided the offeree complies with stated conditions. If the offeree accepts the proposal, a contract arises. Generally, to be an offer, a proposal must be:

offer: proposal to enter into a legal agreement

1. intended to create a legal obligation,
2. definite, and
3. communicated to the offeree.

1. An Offer Must Be Intended to Create a Legal Obligation

The offeror must intend, or must appear to a reasonable person to intend, to create a legal obligation if the proposal is accepted. People often make agreements that no one considers legally enforceable. For example, if two friends make a date to go to the movies, no contract is intended or formed. If either breaks the date, the other may be offended but cannot sue. There is no *legal remedy* (legal means to enforce a right). That is because social invitations are not intended to create legal obligations.

Certain words which may seem to create offers really do not. Before making a contract, parties will often discuss it. The parties often bargain back and forth to reach mutually acceptable terms. Sometimes one party may state tentative terms, inviting other parties to make offers. Advertisements in newspapers and magazines, on radio or TV, or in catalogs or direct mailings are generally invitations to others to make offers. They are not offers themselves. A person who advertises something for sale cannot be expected to sell to the thousands who theoretically might reply to the advertisement. Perhaps the seller has only a limited number of items or wants to check the credit of all who want to buy on credit.

In the problem, in answering the advertisement and in *tendering* (presenting for acceptance) the purchase price of the cabin cruiser, the customers and potential customers were the offerors. Thus, Anchors Aweigh was bound by contract only to the five whose offers it accepted. However, to promote good customer relations, most business firms attempt to deliver merchandise as advertised to all who seek to buy. Note, also, that statutes forbid false and misleading advertising.

Sometimes an advertisement is worded to give a reader reasonable cause to believe it is an offer rather than an invitation to make an offer. This is true in ads which promise to pay a reward for a lost pet or jewel. It is also true in direct-mail advertisements sent to one or just a few prospects. For example, someone trying to sell a very expensive yacht mails a promotional letter to ten prospects. The letter describes the yacht and offers it for a stated price to the first person whose acceptance is received on or before a stated date. This letter would be an offer.

If a statement sounds like an offer but is made in obvious jest or in frenzied terror, the words cannot be transformed into a contract by acceptance. The person to whom the statement was made should realize that no offer was intended. The person making the statement clearly did not intend to be bound by it.

Along a beach in Hawaii, a toddler is swept out to sea by a sudden wave and undertow. The terrified mother screams out, "Save Timmy! I'll give you anything if you'll save him!" You rush in and rescue Timmy. Then you ask for $10,000. There is no legal basis for collecting.

2. An Offer Must Be Definite

PROBLEM: Arbus agreed to buy, and Oaknoll, Inc., agreed to sell, one lot from among the 200 in a large suburban subdivision. Arbus paid $1,000 as a down payment and was given a receipt. The lots shown on the preliminary plan were of various sizes, shapes, and prices, and no particular lot was specified in the agreement of Arbus and Oaknoll. Was either party bound by the agreement?

If a proposal is vague or incomplete, a court will not enforce it. The terms must be definite enough to allow the court (1) to determine what was intended by the parties and (2) to fix their legal rights and duties. Thus, there is no contract in the problem. Neither party is bound because important terms have not been agreed upon.

There are, however, some important exceptions to the requirement of definiteness. For example, medical, dental, and legal fees are often set after the work is completed. Many workers are employed on a payday-to-payday basis; the actual length of employment remains uncertain. In contracts between merchants, when either the price or the credit and delivery terms are not specified, current market prices and trade customs may be used to provide such details.

In business, producers sometimes agree to sell their entire output to a single buyer during a specified period. Sometimes buyers agree to purchase all of certain materials they may need during a given period from a single supplier. In both cases, the actual amounts remain uncertain until the contracts are performed. The parties must act in good faith as to quantities delivered or demanded.

3. An Offer Must Be Communicated to the Offeree

PROBLEM: Kommon was engaged in animated conversation with four other students on the steps of their high school. When a bell called them to class, Kommon absentmindedly left a bag behind. The bag contained a pocket computer and other valuables. After class she posted an ad on three bulletin boards, offering $15 to anyone who would return her bag. Ms. Lehman, one of Kommon's teachers, who had not seen the ad, found the bag and returned it. Is she entitled to the reward?

A person cannot accept an offer without knowing about it. That is because any action taken would not have been a response to the offer. Thus, an offer of a reward that is made to certain persons or even to the general public cannot be accepted by someone who has never seen or heard of the offer. In such cases, the offeror may get what was sought, but most courts require that anyone who claims the prize must have known of the offer and acted in response to it when performing the requested act. Therefore, in the problem, Ms. Lehman was not entitled to the reward.

HOW IS AN OFFER ENDED?

PROBLEM: On October 10, the Macro-Mercantile Bank sent a letter to Boggs, who had applied for a loan. In the letter, Macro-Mercantile offered to lend $50,000 on specified terms and stated that the acceptance had to be received no later than October 18. Boggs posted an acceptance on

October 17, but the letter was delayed and did not arrive until October 20. Was there a contract?

Once made, an offer does not last forever. If it is not accepted, it ends without any contract arising:

1. at a prescribed time, if so stated in the offer,
2. at the end of a reasonable length of time if the offer does not state how long it will remain open,
3. by rejection of the offer by the offeree,
4. if the offeree makes a counteroffer,
5. if it is *revoked* (withdrawn) or modified by the offeror before the offeree accepts, or
6. by the death or insanity of the offeror or offeree.

1. An Offer Ends at the Time Stated in the Offer

In making an offer, the offeror may state how and when the offer must be accepted. In the problem, Macro-Mercantile did not receive Bogg's reply by the time specified. Therefore there was no contract.

2. If the Offer Does Not State How Long It Will Remain Open, It Terminates at the End of a Reasonable Length of Time

PROBLEM: Farman, a produce broker in New Jersey, telephoned Dandelo in Florida one morning and offered to sell a truckload of blueberries. Farman then phoned his next-door neighbor, Sheldon, and made an offer to sell a used truck and trailer. Both Dandelo and Sheldon told Farman they would "think about it" and "get back later." How long would these offers remain open?

What is a reasonable length of time depends upon all the surrounding circumstances. In the problem, if the offer to sell the blueberries was not accepted within an hour and possibly within minutes, it probably would terminate automatically. That is because blueberries are perishable produce, which must be marketed quickly. The seller may be in touch with many prospective buyers throughout the United States and Canada.

In contrast, the offer to sell the truck and trailer, expensive, durable equipment, would not terminate until a longer time had elapsed, at least several days. Purchase of the truck and trailer would involve a long-term investment of funds. There would be only a limited number of prospective buyers in the immediate local market.

3. An Offer Ends If It Is Rejected by the Offeree

> **PROBLEM:** Kempsky offered to sell Del Rey a bicycle for $60, but Del Rey replied, "No, too much." The next day, Del Rey called Kempsky and said, "I've changed my mind. I'll take your bike for $60." Was a contract formed?

If the offeree clearly rejects the offer, the offer is terminated. This occurs even if a time limit set by the offeror has not expired. In the problem, if Del Rey had said, "That is too much. Would you take less?" he would still be negotiating on the original terms. But he flatly said "No." This refusal was a rejection, which killed the offer.

4. An Offer Ends if the Offeree Makes a Counteroffer

> **PROBLEM:** Haviland wrote to Suber offering a 40-unit apartment building for sale for $1,300,000. By telegram, Suber replied, offering to pay $1,200,000. Haviland rejected this offer. Suber then wrote a letter saying, "O.K. It's daylight robbery, but you have a deal. I will pay $1,300,000 as you demand." Was there a contract?

Generally an offeree who accepts an offer must accept it exactly as made. If the offeree changes the offeror's terms in any important way, the result is a **counteroffer**. In making a counteroffer, as in the problem, the offeree says in legal effect, "I refuse your offer; here is my counteroffer." Thus, a counteroffer not only terminates the original offer, but also immediately becomes a new offer. The original offer cannot be accepted by the offeree after a counteroffer has been made unless the original offer is renewed by the offeror. Thus, no contract was made in the problem.

counteroffer: reply to an offer, with new terms; ends the original offer

5. An Offer Is Usually Ended If It Is Revoked or Modified by the Offeror Before the Offeree Has Accepted

> **PROBLEM:** Perez offered to build 20 concrete mini-storage warehouses on Vento's land, at a fixed price of $7,770 each. Two weeks later, and

before Vento had accepted the offer, the price of concrete mix and steel bars had gone up by 10 percent. Perez telephoned Vento and said he would have to boost the price of each unit by $500. Can Perez change his offer without liability?

revocation: withdrawal of an offer before acceptance

Ordinarily, an offer can be revoked or modified by the offeror at any time before it has been accepted. This is true even if the offeror said the offer would remain open for a definite longer time. Thus, in the problem, Perez could modify his offer to Vento. The right to withdraw an offer before it is accepted is known as the right of **revocation**. A modification or revocation is not effective until it is communicated to the offeree or received at the offeree's mailing address. Until then, the offeree is free to accept the offer as originally made.

6. An Offer Is Terminated by the Death or Insanity of the Offeror or Offeree

Contracts are agreements voluntarily entered into by the parties and subject to their control. Death or insanity obviously eliminates such control. Therefore the law acts for these parties when they can no longer act and terminates their offers.

In a telegram to the New York theater star Gilda Grabow, Hollywood producer Zauder offered her the lead in his new musical. When he received no answer, Zauder left Los Angeles for New York in his private jet. He hoped to persuade Grabow in person. The plane crashed in a storm over Arizona. Zauder's death ended the offer.

HOW CAN AN OFFER BE KEPT OPEN?

PROBLEM: The Downings were offering their factory building for sale for $950,000. Robinson, a developer, was interested in buying. She needed time to persuade a group of investors to join her in a syndicate to purchase the building. Robinson offered $10,000 to the Downings to keep the offer open to her alone for 60 days. The Downings accepted the money. Are they now legally bound to keep the offer open?

Generally an offeror is not obliged to keep an offer open for a specified time even if such a promise is made. The offeree has given nothing in exchange for the promise. However, if the offeree gives the offeror something of value in return for a promise to keep the offer open, this underlying agreement itself is a binding contract. It is called an **option**. The offer may not be withdrawn during the period of the option. In the problem, Robinson held an option to buy the factory building. Thus, the Downings could not withdraw the offer nor sell to anyone else during the 60-day period without becoming liable to Robinson. The offeror keeps the amount paid for an option. Usually, if the offer is accepted within the time allowed, the money paid for the option is applied to the purchase price. However, this must be agreed to in advance.

option: underlying contract to keep an offer open

In a few states, statutes provide that a *firm offer* cannot be revoked within the stated period. A **firm offer** is a binding offer stating in writing how long it is to be held open. The UCC applies this rule to merchants selling or buying goods who agree in a signed writing to keep an offer open for a definite time (not more than three months).

firm offer: a binding offer stating in writing how long it is to be held open

On April 10, Gaspard, a supplier, offered to sell to DiSavo a year's supply of pesticide at a certain price. The offer stated in writing, "Quoted price is firm for one week." Two days later, before DiSavo had accepted, the general market price went up sharply. Gaspard immediately telephoned DiSavo and said, "The deal is off. I'd lose my shirt if I sold at the quoted price." If DiSavo nevertheless accepts, Gaspard is bound. He may not legally revoke because he is a merchant and his offer was made in writing, effective until April 17.

WHAT ARE THE REQUIREMENTS OF AN ACCEPTANCE?

PROBLEM: Darrow offered to trade his single-lens reflex camera to Monette in exchange for her videocassette recorder. Schorling, who had a recorder of the same make and model, overheard the offer and said she would make the swap. Did a contract result from Schorling's acceptance?

Acceptance occurs when a party to whom an offer has been made agrees to the proposal or does what is proposed. To create an enforceable agreement, acceptance must be:

acceptance: affirmative response to an offer

1. made only by the person or persons to whom the offer was made,

2. unconditional, and identical in terms with the offer, and
3. communicated to the offeror.

1. An Acceptance Can Be Made Only by the Person(s) to Whom the Offer Was Made

An offer made to one person cannot be accepted by another. Accordingly, no contract was made in the problem. Only Monette, or her authorized agent, could have accepted Darrow's offer.

Sometimes, however, an offer is made to a particular group or to the public and not to an individual. For example, an offer of a reward may be made to the general public. Any member of the general public who knows of the offer may accept it by doing whatever the offer requires.

RING LOST at Zuma Beach in front of beach house. Lady's yellow-gold band with 12 small diamonds. Inside inscribed: "Like diamonds. Forever. Yours, J.R.J." $1,000 reward. Call 555-8142.

Dowell saw this newspaper ad and rushed to the beach with a homemade sand sifter. About ten others were also searching, using various sifting devices. After four hours, Dowell shouted, "Eureka! I've found it!" Dowell promptly returned the ring to its owner and received the reward.

2. The Acceptance Must Be Unconditional and Identical with the Offer

PROBLEM: Schneider offered to sell his motor home to Nunzio for $28,000, but specified that the entire amount was to be paid within 30 days. Nunzio accepted the offer but changed the terms to $8,000 down and the balance in 20 equal monthly payments with interest at 10 percent a year on the unpaid balance. Did these changes affect the acceptance?

The offeror may specify precisely when and how the acceptance is to be made. To complete the agreement, the offeree must then comply with such terms. Any change by the offeree in important terms of the offer, as in the problem, results in a counteroffer. This is so even if the result would be more advantageous to the offeror. A counteroffer terminates the original offer. Suggestions as to routine details of carrying out the contract, or other unimportant matters, do not kill the offer.

On Thursday, the manager of Volume Value Furniture offered to sell a sofa to Susan at the bargain price of $399, on a cash-and-carry basis. Susan accepted, but then she added, "I'll have to pay you with a traveler's check. And my husband won't be able to pick up the sofa until Saturday when he's off from work." A contract resulted because Susan's changes were unimportant.

3. The Acceptance Must Be Communicated

PROBLEM: Kulich, an art dealer, wrote Walcott, "I understand you are interested in selling your four-panel Chinese lacquer screen. I sold it to you in 1970 for $500 and said it would go up in value. Now I offer to buy it back for $2,000. Unless I hear from you to the contrary, I'll send my truck to pick it up next Monday morning. The driver will bring my certified check for the full amount." Walcott did not reply. Is he bound by a contract?

An acceptance must be more than a mental decision. It must be communicated. Moreover, one is not obliged to reply to offers made by others. The offeror generally may not express an offer so that silence would appear to be acceptance. Thus, in the problem, Walcott would not be bound to sell the screen in accordance with Kulich's offer.

Sometimes, in a continuing relationship, the parties may agree that silence is to be regarded as acceptance. For example, in a monthly book or record sales club, it may be agreed that failure to say *no* to a proposed shipment is to be regarded as *yes*. Or a food market may have a standing order to have a wholesaler ship a certain amount of fresh produce every day unless the retailer breaks the silence with some notice.

In certain transactions, only one of the parties makes a promise. Such a transaction is called a **unilateral contract**. The offeror promises something in return for the performance of a certain act by the offeree. For example, the offeror may publicly promise to pay a $100 reward to anyone who returns a lost dog. Many persons learn of the offer; all may join the search. But no one promises to look, and no one is required to look. Only one person may find and return the dog, thus performing the act required to earn the reward. When

unilateral contract: agreement in which only one of the parties makes a promise

the act requires substantial time and resources, sometimes the offer cannot be revoked until an offeree who has begun performance has had a reasonable amount of time to complete it.

bilateral contract: agreement in which both parties make promises

In most cases, the agreement is a **bilateral contract** where both parties make promises. For example, a seller promises to deliver a load of topsoil in exchange for a homeowner's promise to pay $35. Or a dog owner promises to pay someone $10 an hour to look for a lost dog. The fee is due for the time spent looking for the dog even if it is not found. Bilateral contracts require that the offeree make and communicate the requested promise to the offeror. Until this is done, there is no agreement.

An acceptance may be communicated orally, in person or by telephone. Or it may be communicated in writing and sent by mail or telegraph. The offeror may state which method the offeree is to use. If not stated, and if business custom does not govern, the modern trend is to regard acceptance as valid if it is made in any reasonable manner. Indeed, the UCC provides that an acceptance of an offer to buy or sell *goods* (tangible personal property) may be made "in any manner and by any medium reasonable in the circumstances" unless otherwise clearly "indicated by the language or circumstances."

It sometimes becomes important to determine exactly when acceptance is made and the contract arises. Oral acceptances are effective at the moment the words are spoken to the offeror. Acceptances sent by mail generally take effect when properly posted (placed under the control of the U.S. Postal Service, with correct address and sufficient postage). A telegram takes effect as an acceptance when it is handed to the clerk at the telegraph office or telephoned to the telegraph office. The offeror may specify that an acceptance will not be binding until it is actually received. This avoids the confusion that arises when an acceptance is mailed yet never reaches the offeror because it is lost in the mail. Legally, such acceptance would otherwise be effective. Mailing could be proved by testimony of the offeree and by other evidence.

WHAT IS THE EFFECT OF ACCEPTANCE?

PROBLEM: Whitaker offered to buy the Melody Music Shop for $52,000. She gave Melody a check for $2,000 as a down payment, with the balance to be paid in ten monthly installments of $5,000 each starting July 1. The agreement provided that if the offer was not accepted by June

> 1, the check "shall be returned." Melody cashed the check before June 1, but did not notify Whitaker. What effect did cashing the check have on the offer?

A valid acceptance of a valid offer results in a contract—an agreement enforceable at law. A **valid contract** is legally effective and enforceable in court. Thus, in the problem, cashing the check indicated assent, so there was a valid acceptance.

valid contract: agreement that is legally effective

A **void** (also called *invalid*) **agreement** cannot be enforced in court by either party. It has no legal force or effect.

void agreement: agreement that is not enforceable by either party

Under certain circumstances, only one of the parties has the power to compel legal enforcement. If that party chooses otherwise, or decides to withdraw from the transaction, then the contract will not be enforced. Such an agreement is a **voidable contract**. For example, when one party persuades the other to contract by means of fraud, as by saying a used car is new, the contract is voidable by the buyer.

voidable contract: contract that can be nullified by one of the parties

The difference between a void agreement and a voidable contract is important. A voidable contract can be enforced or avoided by the injured party or by a legally incompetent party, such as a minor. A void agreement, on the other hand, cannot be enforced by either party. A valid contract sometimes becomes an **unenforceable contract** because the time limit for filing suit to enforce it has passed or because the defendant has gone bankrupt and a judgment against the person cannot be collected.

unenforceable contract: valid contract that cannot be enforced

PREVENTING LEGAL DIFFICULTIES

When You Enter into a Contract . . .

1. assume the worst possible developments in the performance of a prospective important contract. Then solve the problems in advance by using language in the contract that is clear and fair to both parties;
2. for important contracts, put offers and acceptances in writing. If either is made orally, promptly confirm in writing;
3. obtain and keep copies of all important documents you sign;
4. express your intentions in offers and acceptances in clear, complete, and understandable language. Vague and incomplete terms cause confusion and may lead to disagreements and costly litigation;
5. remember that the offeror may specify how and when the offer must be

accepted. Otherwise, the offer may usually be accepted in any reasonable manner;

6. when appropriate, buy an option, if one is available, to keep the offer open as long as you need;
7. for an offeror to withdraw or revoke an offer, almost all states require that the offeree must receive the notice. For speed, use the telephone or telegraph to withdraw or revoke an offer. If appropriate, confirm by mail. Likewise, promptly accept by phone, but confirm your acceptance by mail; and
8. to facilitate proof of your acceptance by mail, use certified mail with return receipt requested. Also, keep a copy of your acceptance letter and other documents, including the offer.

Strengthening Your Legal Vocabulary

acceptance
bilateral contract
capacity
contract
counteroffer
firm offer
legally competent
offer
offeree
offeror
option
revocation
unenforceable contract
unilateral contract
valid contract
void agreement
voidable contract

1. Party who makes an offer.
2. Agreement that is not enforceable by either party.
3. Party to whom an offer is made.
4. Contract that may be avoided by only one of the parties.
5. Response, with new terms, by offeree, which ends the original offer.
6. Contract to keep an offer open a specified length of time.
7. Affirmative response necessary to transform an offer into a contract.
8. Ability to understand the nature and effects of one's actions.
9. Agreement that is legally effective and enforceable in court.
10. Proposal that expresses willingness of the offeror to enter into a legally binding agreement.

Reviewing Important Points

1. Contracts are the promises we live by in civilized society. Our interdependent world economy is built on a foundation of contracts—past, present, and future.
2. There can be no contract without a mutual agreement.
3. A contract is a legally enforceable agreement between two or more parties. It results from a valid offer and acceptance.

4. Generally all persons who can understand the nature of a contract and its consequences have the capacity to contract. Such persons are said to be legally competent.
5. Minors, insane persons, seriously intoxicated persons, convicts, and aliens lack full capacity to contract.
6. An offer must be (a) made with the offeror's apparent intention to be bound by it, (*b*) definite, and (c) communicated to the offeree.
7. If not accepted, an offer is ended (a) at the time stated, (*b*) at the end of a reasonable time if no time is stated, (c) by rejection, (*d*) by counteroffer, (e) by the offeror's revocation or modification, or (*f*) by death or insanity of either of the parties.
8. Generally the offeree must accept the offer unconditionally and in the exact form and manner indicated by the offeror.
9. An acceptance must be communicated to the offeror. If it is sent by mail or wire, it is effective at the time it is properly sent unless the offeror specified that it had to be received to be effective.
10. Agreements that are enforceable by the courts are valid contracts. Those that are not enforceable by either party are void agreements. Contracts enforceable only by the injured or specially protected incompetent party are voidable at such party's option. Unenforceable contracts are those that are valid but cannot be enforced.
11. Freedom of contract is basic to life in a democracy. Our economy is built on contracts.

Applying Law to Everyday Life

1. Jim and Gary, both minors, were members of an American Legion-sponsored baseball team. When Jim was shifted to the outfield he bought Gary's fielder's mitt for $25. Later, when Jim was moved back to first base, he told Gary that he wanted his money back and offered to return the glove. Can Jim disaffirm the contract?

2. For months Bovard had tried to persuade Black to purchase a computerized system for all accounting records of Black's plastic manufacturing company in New Hampshire. Finally, he persuaded Black to visit New York in order to inspect a similar installation already in use. That night Bovard took Black and his wife to dinner at an exclusive restaurant and then to a Broadway play. After the play they went to a night club and had several drinks. Before the party ended, Black had signed the contract saying, "Let me sign that contract and let's get on with the fun." Is he legally bound?

3. Bill spent most of his month's allowance for expensive tickets to a rock concert after Lorene said she would go with him. On the morning of the event, Lorene phoned and said she was terribly sorry, but Tony, the high school's star fullback, had also asked her to go and she "just couldn't say no." (a) Did she breach a contract? (*b*) Could Tony be held legally liable if he knew Lorene had already promised to go with Bill?

4. When Wood was at Prescott's garage sale, he noticed a large, metal tool chest in the corner, complete with about 400 standard and metric tools. Wood offered to buy it for $1,250 and said "You can take a week to think about it before you decide to accept." Four days later, and before Prescott had responded, Wood told Prescott that he had found another set for less money and withdrew his offer. Can he legally do this?

5. On Monday, June 1, Alber sent Bryant an offer by mail to sell his graphite and fiberglass tennis racket for $50. He said, "Take a few days to think about it." The letter arrived on Wednesday, June 3. On Thursday, June 4, Alber wrote again saying, "My offer is canceled." Bryant received this letter on Saturday, June 6. Bryant had properly posted his letter of acceptance on Friday, June 5. Alber received Bryant's letter of acceptance on Monday, June 8. (*a*) Is there a contract? (*b*) What if Bryant had used the wrong address or insufficient postage on his letter of June 5?

6. Mid-East Traders, Inc., sent a telegram to Starr offering her a job as a translator in Istanbul for three years. The salary of $3,000 a month was specified and other details were given. A reply was requested. Starr immediately delivered her acceptance to the telegraph office. Was this a valid acceptance?

7. Colton, an elderly widower, wrote his daughter Janine, saying that if she and her husband would leave their home in Missouri and come to Massachusetts to care for him, they would have the use of his house for the rest of his life. Also, he said that he would will the house to them. Therefore Janine and her husband moved to Massachusetts and began taking care of her father. Was this a binding contract?

Solving Case Problems

1. In February, Crouch asked the Purex Corporation for its lowest selling price on an old mining building and its equipment in Meade, Kansas. Purex replied that the lowest price would be $500. On March 19, Crouch countered with an offer of $300 but received no reply. On April 16, Crouch wrote to Purex, agreeing to buy the building and equipment for $500 and enclosing his check for that amount. The check was cashed by Purex on April 23. However, on April 17, Purex had offered to sell the building and equipment to Asche. On April 24, Asche accepted the offer, enclosing a check for $500. On April 27, Purex telegraphed Crouch that his offer was "unacceptable." Purex stated that his check had been "mistakenly deposited." On May 6, Purex returned the $500 to Crouch in a letter. The letter explained that the reason his offer could not be accepted was that the corporation had received and accepted another offer "prior to receipt of yours on April 23." In the meantime, Asche had contracted to sell the building to Marrs for $500 and the equipment to another party for $800. Crouch claimed that cashing his check constituted acceptance of his second

offer and formed a contract. Do you agree? (*Crouch v. Marrs*, 199 Kan. 387, 430 P.2d 204)

2. Epton orally bargained for an option to buy a 54 percent share of the ownership of the Chicago White Sox baseball club for $4,800,000 from the defendant, CBC Corporation. The option, which was to have been reduced to writing, was to last one week in exchange for the payment of $1,000 by Epton. To exercise the option within the week, Epton was supposed to give CBC a certified or cashier's check for $99,000 as a down payment. Epton also was to notify the corporation in writing that he was exercising his option. Twice during the week, Epton orally assured CBC of his intent to exercise the option and he also offered to pay the $99,000 as soon as the option was signed by CBC. After the week had passed, CBC refused to sell, and Epton sued. He claimed that his oral notice of intent to exercise the option was sufficient. He said that failure of CBC to sign a written option agreement excused both the requirement of a written exercise of the option by him, and the necessity of the $99,000 deposit. Who should win? (*Epton v. CBC Corp.*, 48 Ill. App. 2d 274, 197 N.E.2d 727)

3. Scheck wanted to sell a parcel of his real property. He agreed to pay a commission to Marchiondo, a real estate broker, if Marchiondo obtained acceptance from a prospective buyer within six days of Scheck's written sales offer. However, Scheck revoked his offer on the morning of the sixth day. Later that day, Marchiondo obtained the prospect's acceptance, but Scheck refused to pay the commission. Marchiondo sued, claiming breach of contract. The trial court dismissed the complaint. The court stated that a unilateral contract had been formed and that Scheck could revoke his offer at any time before performance of the requested act. Marchiondo appealed. Decide. (*Marchiondo v. Scheck*, 78 N.M. 440, 432 P.2d 405)

4. In newspaper ads for two successive Saturdays, the defendant, Great Minneapolis Surplus Store, Inc., offered a fur stole for sale. The ads said, "1 Black Lapin Stole, Beautiful, Worth $139.50 . . . $1.00 FIRST COME FIRST SERVED." Leftkowitz was first in line on both Saturdays. The first time, the defendant said "a house rule" limited the offer to women exclusively. The second time the defendant refused to sell, saying Leftkowitz knew the house rule. Leftkowitz sued for damages. Decide. (*Leftkowitz v. Great Minneapolis Surplus Store*, 251 Minn. 188, 86 N.W.2d 689)

5. Lee Calan Imports, Inc., advertised a 1964 Volvo station wagon for sale in a Chicago newspaper. Because of an error by the newspaper, the price was listed at $1,095 instead of $1,795. The ad made no mention of such material matters as equipment to be furnished or warranties to be offered. Plaintiff O'Brien came in and said he wished to buy the station wagon. One of the defendant's salesmen at first agreed but, upon discovering the erroneous price, refused to sell. Was there a binding contract? (*O'Keefe—Administrator of Estate of O'Brien v. Lee Calan Imports, Inc.*, 128 Ill. App. 2d 410, 262 N.E.2d 758)

10

Legal Agreement

1. An elderly aunt has never married because she thinks the world is already overpopulated. She promises to leave her valuable estate to her niece if her niece will solemnly promise to follow her example and never marry. If the niece accepts the offer, will the courts enforce the agreement?

2. A friend offers you $100 if you will "get rid of" a neighbor's barking dog. "You'll be the hero of this whole block," your friend says. "Just take it far out of town and give it to some farmer." If you do as asked, have you a legal right to collect the money?

3. Top managers of seven leading makers of digital watches meet in New York after a trade convention. One urges all to agree to a system of setting prices "fairly, but cooperatively, to avoid the cut-throat competition that's killing all of us. We'll earn only a fair profit and the public will be ensured a steady supply." Would such an agreement be legal?

WHAT MAKES AN AGREEMENT ILLEGAL?

PROBLEM: A city ordinance requires both the sellers and buyers of handguns to obtain police department permits for all sales. Longe sold a revolver and ammunition to Skoflex. Neither party had obtained the necessary permit. If Skoflex refuses to pay for the revolver and ammunition, may Longe sue and collect?

Even when parties are competent to form a binding agreement, they are not free to make any contract they want. As in other areas of constitutional freedom, reasonable limits are imposed by law. Thus, for a contract to be valid, its formation, purpose, and performance must be legal. This means that the agreement must not be contrary to law as found in constitutions, statutes, and court decisions. Nor may the agreement violate public policy—a concept not precisely definable. Generally this concept means that no one has a right to harm the public good.

Illegal agreements, including the one in the problem, are generally unenforceable. Indeed, in some cases, one or both parties to an illegal agreement may be arrested and tried as criminals.

WHY DON'T THE COURTS ENFORCE ILLEGAL AGREEMENTS?

PROBLEM: In a major horse race, Darton, a jockey, was scheduled to ride Avanti, the favored horse. Before the race, Klippe, a professional gambler, paid Darton $10,000 to come in fourth or worse. Darton accepted the money but double-crossed Klippe by winning the race. Would a court help Klippe recover the money paid?

Illegal agreements are usually void and therefore unenforceable. In the problem, the agreement between Klippe and Darton was void because it was based on illegal activity: paying and accepting money to rig (fraudulently arrange) the outcome of a race or contest. If courts enforced such agreements, they would be encouraging dishonest activities. In dismissing an action for illegality, one court said, "The law leaves the parties to an illegal transaction where it finds them; . . . and the law cannot be invoked to enforce an agreement which such law denounces as invalid."

WHAT TYPES OF AGREEMENTS ARE ILLEGAL?

PROBLEM: Krono's son had been arrested for embezzling $89,700 from his employer, Certified Safety Loan Association. Krono repaid the stolen money and promised to pay an additional $5,000 if Certified would agree not to press criminal charges against the son. Certified agreed. Is the agreement enforceable?

Agreements which are illegal and therefore void and unenforceable include the following:

1. Agreements That Obstruct Legal Procedures

Agreements that obstruct legal procedures are those which delay or block the achievement of justice. For example, a party not involved in a lawsuit may finance it in exchange for part of the hoped-for judgment. This type of activity increases the workload of already crowded courts. Other more common examples include:

a. promises by witnesses to give false testimony or not to testify at all,
b. promises to give jurors something of value to influence their votes, or
c. payment of more than the regular fee to ordinary witnesses. (Note that expert witnesses may legally charge their customary professional fees, which are much higher.)

compounding a crime: accepting something of value for a promise not to prosecute a suspected criminal

restitution: restoring or making good a loss

An example of an agreement that obstructs justice is **compounding a crime**. It involves accepting money or property in exchange for a promise not to prosecute or not to inform on one who has committed a crime. In the problem, Certified might have independently and voluntarily decided not to press criminal charges. This sometimes happens if the criminal makes **restitution** by restoring the stolen property or its value to the owner. For Certified to agree to accept money for its decision, however, was itself a crime, and so the agreement was void.

2. Agreements That Injure Public Service

PROBLEM: Georgio was a lobbyist for Amalgamated Motors, Inc. He wrote a "position paper," arguing that quotas should be negotiated whereby Japan and Germany would voluntarily limit exports of automobiles to the United States. He then invited to dinner all members of a Congressional committee studying the problem. After the dinner, there were drinks, and each member received a copy of the report. Was this bribery? Would it make Georgio's contract with Amalgamated illegal?

It is important for people to have confidence in the integrity of government officials. Accordingly, agreements that tend to corrupt or injure the public service are void. Included are agreements that betray public trust and confidence or interfere with the proper performance of official duties. For example, a public official may not legally collect a fee for promising to do something the official is already duty-bound to do. A public official may not legally collect a fee for promising to vote in a particular way. It is illegal to agree to pay bribes to American or foreign officials to (1) obtain a sales contract, (2) obtain an appointment to public office, or (3) secure a legal pardon.

Lobbying contracts present a special problem. They are illegal if the parties agree that bribery or other corrupt means will be used to influence legislators or other officials to enact, reject, or repeal any law. On the other hand, there are many special-interest groups in our society. They vary widely—from creditors to debtors, from the National Rifle Association to antigun organizations, from teachers to students. All have a right to be heard. Legitimate lobbying contracts are therefore often made whereby attorneys, former legislators, or other experts are paid to talk to legislators, and to appear before government committees or other public bodies to present arguments for or against legislation.

illegal lobbying contract: agreement to use improper means to influence legislators

Kabazian was a nationally known expert on nuclear warfare. She was offered $5,000 to present her analysis of certain data to a joint Senate-House committee. The committee was considering a major arms appropriation bill. If Kabazian accepted the offer, the contract would be enforceable.

Proper efforts to inform and influence legislators may be accompanied by reasonable entertainment. Such efforts, as in the problem, are legal.

3. Agreements That Affect Marriage Negatively

PROBLEM: The Camacho's 18-year-old daughter was engaged to Dewpont, but the parents disapproved of the approaching marriage. Therefore they promised to lend $300,000 to Dewpont to finance a restaurant franchise in Paris if Dewpont would break the engagement. Is either party legally bound by such a promise?

The family is the basic unit in society. Therefore agreements that violate the freedom and security of marriage are illegal. Such agreements are contrary to public policy, which encourages family life. Although many persons freely and legally choose not to marry, an agreement in which one person promises not to marry is void. Likewise, an agreement in which a person promises to get a divorce is void. In the problem, the court would not require either party to perform. Nor would the court award damages for nonperformance. In the problem, the agreement was void.

4. Agreements to Commit Crimes or Torts

Any agreement to commit a crime or a tort is illegal. It would be foolish for the law to prohibit crimes and torts yet enforce agreements to commit such acts.

5. Agreements to Waive Certain Legal Rights

PROBLEM: Amora, a teenager, badly needed a job. Therefore, during the summer, he agreed to work for $2 an hour. By doing so, Amora was waiving his right to be paid the statutory minimum wage. In this permitted?

A waiver is the voluntary and intentional giving up of a legal right. Although many rights may be waived, some may not, such as the right to workers' compensation insurance (see Chapter 23). Public policy dictates that workers injured on the job must be given necessary medical care without charge, as well as financial help. Similarly, public policy forbids payment of less than legally prescribed minimum wages. A person may not waive such a right. Accordingly, in the problem, the agreement to work for less than minimum wage was void and the employer may be punished for violating the law.

6. Agreements Made Without a Required Competency License

All states require that persons in specified occupations and businesses have a license or permit. Physicians, teachers, lawyers, plumbers, electricians, pharmacists, real estate brokers, insurance agents, and building contractors are among such persons. Some critics claim that such laws are artificial barriers to admission, simply designed to limit competition. Actually, well-drafted licensing laws attempt to prevent incompetent and dishonest persons from harming the public. In any event, no agreement made by or with a person who lacks the required competency license may be enforced by the unlicensed person.

Cities and counties often require that business firms be licensed. When the purpose of the licensing is to raise revenue rather than to protect the public, contracts made with the unlicensed person are valid. Generally the only penalty for failure to get such a license is a higher fee.

7. Agreements That Are Unconscionable

PROBLEM: Frostifresh Corporation sold a refrigerator to Nuyen, a recent immigrant, who spoke, read, and wrote only Vietnamese and French. The refrigerator was sold on an installment payment contract. The negotiations and sale of the refrigerator were made in French. However, the written contract was entirely in English, although the seller knew that Nuyen could not read English. The refrigerator, which cost Frostifresh $348, was sold on the installment plan for $1,146 , plus a credit charge of $246. Was this agreement unconscionable?

The Uniform Commercial Code provides that a court may find that a contract or a clause of a contract is **unconscionable**—that is, grossly unfair and oppressive. An unconscionable contract or clause offends an honest person's conscience and sense of justice, as in the problem. The terms need not be criminal nor violate a statute, but simply unethical. **Contracts of adhesion** are more likely to be unconscionable. This is so because in such contracts one of the parties dictates all the important terms and the weaker party must take it as offered or not contract.

unconscionable contract: grossly unfair and oppressive agreement

contracts of adhesion: contract in which the more powerful party dictates all the important terms

If a court decides that a clause of a contract is unconscionable, it may:

a. refuse to enforce the contract,
b. enforce the contract without the unconscionable clause, or
c. limit the clause's application so that the contract is no longer unfair.

The law is not designed to relieve a person of a bad bargain. One may still be legally bound by the purchase of overpriced, poor quality, or unneeded goods.

8. Agreements That Involve Illegal Gambling, Wagers, and Lotteries

wager: bet which depends on chance

Every state either forbids or regulates gambling. Gambling involves an agreement with three elements: payment to participate; a chance to win, based on luck rather than on skill; and a prize for one or more winners. A **wager**, one of the most common forms of gambling, is a bet on any event which depends on chance or uncertainty.

Most states have legalized some form of gambling under regulated conditions. Pari-mutuel betting (a form of betting on races in which those who bet on the winner share the total amount bet) at race tracks is permitted in most states. State-run lotteries are becoming more common as a means of raising money. Although millions of dollars are sometimes awarded, little publicity is given to the fact that the chance to win may be one in 30 million. Even though the hopeful excitement presumably has pyschological value for participants, critics say the lottery is a tax, especially burdensome on the poor. Bingo, likewise, is permitted in some states, usually on a modest scale, for financing charitable, religious, or educational projects.

Unless specifically permitted by law, the winners in illegal gambling agreements cannot enforce payment of their winnings through court action. Nevertheless, illegal gambling evidently thrives even when state-sponsored, legal alternatives are available.

9. Agreements to Pay Usurious Interest

PROBLEM: The Woffords, who had no medical insurance, desperately needed money for surgery for their only child. They could not qualify for a bank loan, and they did not belong to a credit union. Then a friendly

> bartender referred them to a "fellow named Skye who'll lend you money on sight. No collateral; no credit report. Just prove you've got a steady job." The Woffords borrowed $2,500 from Skye and agreed to repay $3,888 (principal plus interest) in 12 monthly installments of $324 each. Later, a lawyer told them the contract was illegal. Was this true?

Almost all states provide that, with certain exceptions, lenders of money may not charge more than a specified **maximum rate of interest**. This rate varies among the states; 8 percent to 16 percent a year are common maximums. Some of these rates have been increased in recent years because of inflation.

maximum rate of interest: highest rate of interest generally permitted

The exact rate of interest agreed upon by borrower and lender in a particular loan is the **contract rate of interest**. This rate may not legally exceed the state's maximum rate. Lending money at a rate higher than the state's maximum rate is **usury**. In the problem, the agreement made between the Woffords and Skye would be usurious in most states. This is because the interest rate was more than 50 percent on the unpaid balances. The penalty for usury is generally that the lender cannot collect some or all of the interest, but the borrower must still repay the principal.

contract rate of interest: rate of interest agreed upon by parties in a contract

usury: charging a higher interest rate than that permitted by law

Sometimes a person borrows money for which interest is charged but no exact rate is stated. The rate to be paid is the **legal rate of interest**, which is specified by state statute. In more than half of the states, including the most populous ones, this rate is 7 percent or less per year. In most of the other states, the legal rate ranges between 8 and 12 percent.

legal rate of interest: rate of interest set by statute

Usury laws generally do not apply to the carrying charges added to the price of goods sold on credit. This is because the debtor is buying goods and not borrowing money. However, a minority of states regulate such charges as interest. They do this on the theory that the store—in effect—borrows money and relends it to the customer-debtor to finance the credit sale. The federal Truth in Lending Act (see Chapter 19) requires full disclosure of the terms of loans and credit sales. However, it does not limit the percentage rate of interest that may be charged.

Usually, no limit is placed on the rate of interest that banks may charge on loans to corporations (and in some states, to others as well). Such corporate borrowers are usually represented by knowledgeable business managers and are not likely to be victimized. Moreover, open competition for business tends to keep the bank rates at reasonable levels.

small loan rate of interest: higher rate of interest allowed on loans up to $300 or $500

Many states permit licensed loan companies and pawnbrokers (see Chapter 19) to charge a **small loan rate of interest**. This rate is typically 36 percent a year, usually on loans of up to $300 or $500. The overhead cost per dollar loaned is high, and presumably the risk of loss from defaults is also high on such loans. This concession by the states is made to protect people against criminal loan sharks, who illegally charge extremely high rates (often 100 percent annually, and sometimes more).

10. Agreements That Restrain Trade Unreasonably

PROBLEM: McKim and Stanley were competitors in the wholesale candy and tobacco business in a populous ten-state region. They controlled almost 90 percent of the available business. McKim and Stanley thought of merging to end their lively competition, which limited profits of both. However, they feared such action would be illegal. Therefore they agreed to divide the region approximately in half in terms of geography and population. McKim would sell only in one half, and Stanley would sell only in the other half. Have they violated any law?

Agreements that unreasonably restrain trade are void. Our economic system is based upon the concept of free and open competition which benefits consumers by rewarding efficient producers. It seeks to ensure all business firms of an equal opportunity to trade. It tends to protect consumers in their search for quality goods at fair prices. Hence, both state and federal law seek to prevent monopolies and combinations that either restrict competition unreasonably or that deprive a person of the means of earning a livelihood. There is no legal limit on growth from open and fair competition. But, as in the problem, parties may not contract to divide a market in order to limit competition. Both McKim and Stanley may be punished by fine and imprisonment.

Congress has enacted several important statutes to encourage competition. These laws prohibit unfair and deceptive trade practices and outlaw monopolies. They also forbid conspiracies to fix prices, limit production, or assign markets among competitors. States also have antitrust laws to govern trade within their states.

All ten pharmacy owners in the city of Weston met to discuss common problems. During the discussion, it was agreed that all the stores would charge no less than an agreed-upon minimum price for 28 different high-volume items. Because this agreement restrained free trade and controlled prices, it was illegal and void.

11. Miscellaneous Illegal Agreements

PROBLEM: Olson and Stallings live in a state that forbids contracts calling for the payment of money on Sundays. Olson borrowed $500 from Stallings and agreed to repay her in 90 days. The due date fell on a Sunday. Does this have any effect on the legality of the agreement?

Agreements made on or to be performed on a Sunday are regulated by many states. In some states such agreements are illegal and void. These "Sunday blue laws" generally seek to preserve that day for rest, but they vary widely in their scope. Even where strictly enforced, such laws typically exempt contracts for necessary work, such as the saving of life, preserving of health or property, or facilitating travel and recreation. Thus, for example, pharmacies and service stations remain open.

Practically all states provide that contracts calling for the payment of money on Sunday or a holiday are to be performed on the next business day after the Sunday or holiday. Thus, in the problem, Olson would be required to repay the loan on the next business day. Agreements made on a Sunday to be performed on a weekday are valid in most states, provided they are confirmed on a weekday.

Other agreements commonly deemed illegal are those for the sale of (1) certain drugs and narcotics, except by a physician's prescription; (2) firearms, except by permit; and (3) wild game, such as deer.

Sometimes one party will include in a contract a clause which relieves that party of all guilt or liability to others even if an injury occurs because of that party's fault. Such clauses are generally contrary to public policy and are not enforceable.

WHEN MAY COURTS HELP PARTIES TO ILLEGAL AGREEMENTS?

PROBLEM: A statute limited the interest rate on personal loans to 14 percent a year. When Evans borrowed $1,000 from Martin for one year,

Martin set the rate at 2 percent a month. Martin assured Evans that this was well within the legal limit. Evans believed her and after a year had repaid the $1,000 and $240 in interest (2 percent a month or 24 percent a year). If Evans now sues Martin for the excess interest paid in violation of the law, will the court give him judgment?

There are some exceptions to the rule that courts will not aid either party to an illegal agreement. These include the following:

1. When There Is a Divisible Contract

A contract may contain several provisions, some of which are legal and some of which are illegal. If the legal part can be separated from the illegal part, courts will usually enforce the legal part only. This is done only if the illegal part does not taint the entire agreement. For example, suppose a sporting goods retailer made a sale which included a forbidden sawed-off shotgun along with a variety of camping gear. The court would probably not enforce any part of the contract.

Conant's Country General Store sold some gold-mining equipment to Carver on credit for $460 together with some dynamite sticks for blasting, priced at $50. Under state law, a permit was required to buy dynamite. Carver did not have a permit. Later, when Conant tried to collect, Carver laughed and refused to pay. "I didn't strike gold and neither did you," he said. "You can't collect because I had no permit for the dynamite." In fact, however, Carver was liable for the $460 because the contract was divisible and the sale of the mining equipment was legitimate. Unlike sawed-off shotguns, dynamite has many legitimate civilian uses. For example, it is used for blasting in mining, road construction, excavating, and stump removal. Carver used the dynamite legitimately in gold mining. Dynamite is not an item so intrinsically illegal that the purchase of it would spoil the entire contract. If Carver had intended to use the dynamite for an illegal purpose (for example, to damage a competitor's mine), and if Conant had known of this intent before the sale, the entire contract would have been unenforceable. Indeed, Conant might have been criminally liable, along with Carver.

2. When the Parties Are Not Equally Guilty

Sometimes parties to an illegal contract are not equally guilty of wrongdoing. For example, one party may persuade the other to enter an illegal agreement by fraud, duress, or undue influence. In the problem, Evans was defrauded by Martin and was entitled to judgment for $100 in some states. In others the judgment would be for all interest charged, or $240. In a few states, where such contracts are void, Evans would be entitled to both interest and principal, or $1,240.

3. When the Violated Law Was Meant to Protect One Party

Many laws are designed to protect the public against white-collar criminals. For example, suppose a dishonest promoter persuades an innocent person to buy worthless stock issued without a proper permit by a platinum mining corporation. The corporation is falsely touted as owning a mountain with ores containing platinum. Fantastic profits are promised because of a predicted rise in the price of platinum. The victim may sue to avoid the contract and recover money paid. Unfortunately, however, the defendant may already be in jail, or does not have enough property to pay back the victim, or cannot be located.

4. When a Party Repents in Time

Money may be entrusted to a stakeholder for an illegal purpose, such as a wager on the outcome of a football game. If either party has a change of heart and decides not to bet, the money given may be recovered through court action. Understandably, to recover one must generally demand return of the money before the event takes place.

ARE ANY AGREEMENTS IN RESTRAINT OF TRADE VALID?

PROBLEM: Morris employed Weber as an apprentice horseshoer. As part of the bargain, Weber agreed that if he left the Morris shop after completing his apprenticeship, he would not open his own shop to compete with Morris within the county for one year. If Weber failed to keep his promise, could Morris get a court order to end the competition?

Not all agreements that restrain trade are illegal. That is because some trade practices of this nature are believed to be socially and economically desirable if they are reasonable. For example, a person who obtains a patent from the federal government has an exclusive right to make and sell the product for a period of 17 years. This encourages invention. Similar protection is given to writers, composers, and artists through copyrights, which are effective for the life of the author or artist, plus fifty years.

The government also authorizes certain monopolies by granting exclusive permits for purposes such as transportation, communication, and energy distribution. It would be economically inefficient to have two or more gas or electric companies serve the same block or town. Instead, an exclusive franchise is given to one company, and the government regulates its rates and services.

In the problem, the restraint agreed to by Weber was valid. That is because it was reasonable in terms of area and time and necessary to protect Morris's business.

Severski's company manufactured high-priced, specially designed milling machinery sold throughout the world. When Imperial Industries, Inc., bought Severski's company, Severski agreed not to compete anywhere in the world for three years. In this case, the restrictions as to geographical area and number of years were reasonable and enforceable because of the worldwide market and the special product line. However, area and possibly length of time would have to be scaled down if the business were, for example, a local barbershop.

PREVENTING LEGAL DIFFICULTIES

In Making Contracts . . .

1. when contracting for professional or skilled services, deal only with persons who are reputable and properly licensed, if a license is required;
2. most states impose penalties for charging interest in excess of statutory limits. As a lender or borrower, familiarize yourself with the maximum rates. Most states permit a wide range of rates; it pays to shop for loans as you shop for goods and services;
3. with limited exceptions, illegal agreements are void and unenforceable. Courts refuse relief to any of the parties involved. Unfortunately criminals sometimes seek to enforce such deals through violence. Clearly, illegal agreements should be avoided;
4. wagering is illegal in most states. Even where legal, most persons who wager lose in the long run. Therefore do not bet unless you can afford to lose; and

5. do not agree to waive any legal rights without fully understanding what you are giving up.

Strengthening Your Legal Vocabulary

compounding a crime
contract of adhesion
contract rate of interest
illegal lobbying contract
legal rate of interest
maximum rate of interest
restitution
small loan rate of interest
unconscionable contract
usury
wager

1. Rate of interest agreed upon by parties in a contract.
2. Contract under which bribery or other improper means are used to influence legislation.
3. Bet on any event which depends upon chance or uncertainty.
4. Grossly oppressive and unfair agreement.
5. Accepting something of value for a promise not to prosecute a suspected criminal.
6. Rate specified by statute when interest is called for but no percentage is stated in the contract.
7. Charging interest on a loan beyond the legally permitted maximum rate.
8. Restoring or making good a loss.
9. Contract in which one party has no realistic choice as to the terms.
10. Highest rate lenders of money may generally charge borrowers.

Reviewing Important Points

1. The formation, purpose, and performance of an agreement must not be contrary to statutory or case law, contrary to public policy, or unconscionable.
2. Illegal agreements are usually void and therefore not enforceable by either party.
3. In the following circumstances, exceptions are made to the court policy of not enforcing illegal agreements:
   (a) When the contract is divisible into legal and illegal parts.
   (b) When the parties are not equally guilty.
   (c) When the violated law was meant to protect one party.
   (d) When a guilty party repents in time.
4. Among agreements which violate law or public policy and are therefore void and unenforceable are those which:
   (a) Obstruct legal procedures.
   (b) Injure public service.

(c) Threaten the freedom or security of marriage.
(d) Require committing a crime or tort.
(e) Waive certain legal rights.
(f) Are made without a required competency license.
(g) Are unconscionable.
(h) Involve illegal gambling, wagers, and lotteries.
(i) Involve payment of usurious interest.
(j) Restrain trade unreasonably.

5. Some agreements which restrain trade are valid and enforceable. These include:
   (a) Agreements imposing reasonable limitations on competition in business or exercise of occupation.
   (b) Government patents and copyrights.
   (c) Government franchises for monopolistic utility, transportation, and communication services.

Applying Law to Everyday Life

1. Shapiro was the defendant in a legal action. Pierce was a key witness for the plaintiff. Shapiro told Pierce that he would pay her expenses if she would take a long cruise—from New York to San Francisco and back—while the trial was in progress. Pierce agreed to take the trip. Upon her return, she presented her expense account to Shapiro. Can she collect?

2. Crump was the owner of a restaurant. He applied to the state liquor control board for a $500 license to sell alcohol. When the application was denied, Lynch, a customer, told Crump that he knew someone on the board and could get a license for him for $7,500. Crump paid Lynch the money but never received the license. Can he recover the money?

3. Dixon, a wholesaler, was on the brink of bankruptcy. He bought fire insurance policies for more than twice the value of the building and contents from two companies. Then he arranged to pay a character known only as "Sparky" $10,000 to "torch" his business building. The property was leveled to the ground. Was the agreement with Sparky valid?

4. Simplex had read somewhere that California laws prohibiting marijuana production, possession and use were absurd. He agreed with what he had read. Accordingly, using his credit, he bought some marijuana plants and rented land in Humboldt County, telling the owner he intended to produce a crop of marijuana. Finally, he made a deal for the sale of the crop after the anticipated harvest. Were any of his contracts enforceable?

5. A remote community and the surrounding countryside had no doctor. The city council advertised for help, offering free office space, a six-bed infirmary, and a three-year contract. Glorgan applied and was accepted.

Three months later it was learned that although she had an M.D. degree, and had taken the state examination to practice medicine, she had failed to pass. No patients complained, but the council summarily discharged her. Glorgan sued for breach of contract. Will she win?

6. The *Daily Recorder*, a recently established daily afternoon newspaper, tried to increase circulation by sponsoring a contest for its readers. The newspaper printed, at various places in each Sunday issue of the paper, 20 telephone numbers chosen at random from the local directory. Each person whose telephone number was printed could claim a prize of $100. The publisher of the competing daily morning *Journal-Tribune* claimed that the contest was an illegal lottery and sought an injunction. Decide.

7. Hallman operated an income tax advisory service for ten years. Most of his clients lived within the boundaries of the county. When he retired at age 60, he sold his business to Kramer and agreed not to engage in a tax practice within the county for two calendar years. In fact, although Hallman moved to a lakeside resort outside the county, he continued to prepare tax returns for ten "loyal old clients" by using the telephone and mail. Kramer sued to require him to stop preparing the returns and to pay damages. Is she entitled to a judgment?

Solving Case Problems

1. Robinson was the assistant manager of a drugstore owned by the plaintiff. Robinson admitted to stealing cash and merchandise from the store. He signed an agreement to repay the store $2,000 and in fact did pay $741. But he then refused to make further payments. The store sued to require compliance with the contract. Robinson's defense is that he signed the agreement under *compulsion* (being kept from exercising free will) by the store. Therefore he seeks recovery of the money paid. The agreement between Robinson and the store clearly indicated that the plaintiff agreed not to prosecute the defendant. Should judgment be given to the plaintiff? (*Gallaher Drug Company v. Robinson*, 13 Ohio Misc. 216, 232 N.E.2d 668)

2. Karl Overbeck sued Sears, Roebuck and Co. in a class action (see page 119). Overbeck claimed that the Sears Revolving Charge Account imposed an effective interest charge of 18 percent a year on credit sales. The Indiana usury law at the time in question specified a maximum interest rate of 8 percent on "loans or forebearance of money, goods, or things in action." The trial court granted Sears's motion for summary judgment. Overbeck appealed. Was Sears guilty of usury? (*Overbeck v. Sears Roebuck and Co.*, 349 N.E.2d 286, Ind. App.)

3. A secret process known as TREAT-A-MATIC was developed by Water Services. The process was designed to purify water for industrial purposes. As part of their contract of employment, all employees of Water Services

were required to sign a statement. The statement said that for two years after termination of employment, the employee would not engage "in any business which reasonably (could) be considered competitive to Water Services in any territory in which he has performed services under this contract." Glad was employed by Water Services, and he learned the components, suppliers, and secret process of TREAT-A-MATIC. Two years later, he resigned. He was then employed by Tesco Chemical, a competitor of Water Services who had been unable to develop a water purification system. Using the confidential information acquired from his previous employer, Glad helped to develop a competitive system known as TESTOMATIC. Water Services sued to enforce its agreement with Glad. Tesco claimed Glad's contract with Water Services was in restraint of trade. To whom should judgment be awarded? (*Water Services, Inc. v. Tesco Chemical, Inc.*, 410 F.2d 163)

4. Henriolle leased a rent-subsidized apartment from Marin Ventures, Inc. The lease contract contained a clause which said the landlord shall not be liable for "any damage or injury to the Tenant, or any other person . . . occurring on the premises . . . no matter how caused." Henriolle fractured his wrist when he tripped over a rock on a common stairway in the apartment building. Could Marin be held liable despite the clause? (*Henriolle v. Marin Ventures Inc.*, 573 P.2d 465, 20 Cal. 3d 512)

5. Garretson, a college student and experienced ski jumper, seriouly injured his back in a jump during an amateur tournament in Washington. He had read and signed an entry blank which released the tournament sponsors from all liability for injuries he might suffer in the competition. He had signed similar releases in previous tournaments. Nevertheless, he now sued the tournament sponsors and the United States as owners of the site. He claimed they were negligent because they had permitted him to jump when the windy weather made it unsafe. Who wins? (*Garretson v. United States*, 456 F.2d 1017)

11

Consideration

1. You are a skilled amateur photographer. This summer, you and three friends plan to see America, by taking pictures during a 10,000-mile drive through forty-eight states. Upon learning of your plans, a local camera shop offers to give you, without charge, 30 rolls of 36-exposure color film for the trip—provided you let them develop and print the films. You agree. Are both of you legally bound?
2. A four-piece high school rock band practices for at least an hour most days of the week. Its studio is the garage of the drummer's home. Several neighbors offered to pay the rent of a local mini-warehouse as a practice room for a year if the group agreed to stop practicing at the home. The players agreed. Is there a binding contract?
3. You stop to help a motorist who is stranded because the battery of her car is "dead." You restart the car with a jumper cable from your battery. In gratitude, she promises to send you $25. Is she legally bound to keep her promise?

WHAT IS CONSIDERATION?

PROBLEM: The people next door plan to visit the Canadian Rockies for two weeks. They promise to pay you $60 if you will take care of their garden and pick up their mail and newspaper while they are away. You agree. Is this a contract? Do both you and your neighbors give and receive consideration?

promisor: person who makes a promise

promisee: person to whom a promise is made

consideration: what one gives and receives in a contract

forbearance: refraining from doing what one has a right to do

A contract is usually an agreement in which, in effect, one party says to another, "If you do this for me, I shall do that for you." The promise or action that one person (the **promisor**) gives in exchange for the promise or action of another person (the **promisee**) is **consideration**. In the problem, there was a contract. The promises exchanged were the consideration. In performing, the parties changed their promises into services and money. The neighbors will give the money and receive the gardening and pick-up services. You will provide the services and receive the money. Both parties give consideration; both parties receive consideration.

Consideration may consist of some right or benefit to one party—the promisor, or some duty or detriment (cost) to the other party—the promisee. Thus, consideration may consist of **forbearance**—that is, refraining from doing what one has a right to do. Frequently, in simple "fender-bender" accidents, the guilty party pays the innocent party in return for a promise not to sue. Often the payment is made by the wrongdoer's insurance company. The victim's forbearance is consideration for the wrongdoer's payment.

The consideration required to make a promise enforceable may consist of (1) a return promise, (2) an act other than a promise, (3) forbearance, (4) a change in a legal relation of the parties, (5) money, or (6) property.

WHY IS CONSIDERATION REQUIRED?

PROBLEM: For a college graduation present, an aunt promised to give Eileen two tickets for a Caribbean cruise with a friend of her choice. At the graduation exercises, however, her aunt gave her a kiss instead and said, "The stock market is down. Sorry, darling!" Although not likely to do so, could Eileen successfully sue her aunt for breach of contract?

Consideration is required to make a valid, enforceable contract. It must be *mutual* (also called *reciprocal*). This means that each party must give consideration, and each must receive consideration. The presence or absence of consideration is one test of whether a contract has been made. If no consideration is given and received by one of the parties, there may be a moral duty to keep the promise made. However, there is no legal obligation. In the problem, Eileen promised nothing of value in exchange for her aunt's promise of the tickets. (A "thank you" and continued love and affection do not suffice as consideration in most states. That is because such things lack determinable market value.) Therefore Eileen and her aunt did not make a contract. Instead, the aunt merely promised to make a gift. Such promises are not enforceable.

A **gift** is the voluntary transfer of the ownership of property without receiving consideration in return. Property actually transferred by gift cannot be recovered by the donor. The one who received the property by gift has good title or ownership. Thus, while Eileen's aunt could not be forced to keep the promise, if she had delivered the cruise tickets, she could not compel Eileen to return them.

gift: voluntary transfer of ownership without consideration

In some states, consideration is presumed to exist in contracts under seal. A **seal** may be any one of the following:

seal: impression on a legal document identifying the sealer

1. an impression on the document,
2. a paper or wax affixed to the document (perhaps inscribed with a design), or
3. the word "Seal" or the letters "L.S." (an abbreviation for the Latin words meaning "place of the seal") on the document.

Seals were used more frequently years ago when few people could read or write. Such persons who wished to bind themselves to some agreement would affix their seals to the writings. The seal was often a very elaborate wax impression. Sometimes a colorful ribbon was attached. These formalities indicated that the parties intended to be bound. Therefore the old common law courts did not demand proof that both parties had given and received consideration. In most states today, however, the seal is not a substitute for consideration. In these states, while still sometimes used, the seal neither adds to nor takes away from the validity of the contract.

In several states, consideration will be presumed if the promise is made by a merchant, is in writing, and is signed. As noted on page 171, this is called a firm offer.

WHAT IS ADEQUATE CONSIDERATION?

PROBLEM: While cleaning out his attic, Shreve found an old, glass lampshade. She showed it to Laval who thought it was an authentic Tiffany antique. Laval offered to buy it for $150 and Shreve accepted. When Shreve later learned that it was worth at least $450, she tried to cancel the contract. She claimed that the consideration of $150 was not adequate: "The shade is worth three times as much as you paid!" If Shreve sues, will she win?

The values that different persons place on the same property may vary widely. For example, one fashion-conscious person might gladly pay $50,000 for an original and exclusive "haute couture" (high-fashion) gown by a famous designer. Other persons would not be interested in owning such a gown even if they could afford the price. Also, for good reasons, a person may place a higher value on a product at one time than at another. When you have been baking for hours on the sunny side of a stadium, you willingly pay three times the grocery-store price for an ice-cold soft drink.

Generally what the parties give and get as consideration need not be of equal value. The actual value of consideration is unimportant as long as the contracting parties have voluntarily agreed. Thus, in the problem, Shreve is bound by the contract because she voluntarily agreed to the price of $150. However, a grossly inadequate consideration is regarded with suspicion by the courts. It sometimes may be used as evidence of fraud, duress, or undue influence. But only a few states require by statute that consideration for a binding contract be fair, reasonable, or adequate.

What is fair, reasonable, or adequate consideration is often difficult to determine. It depends on many variables, including market supply and demand, in addition to the individual buyer's and seller's personal needs and judgments. Therefore the courts will impose their judgment as to adequacy of consideration only if there is evidence of fraud or unconscionable dealing. They will also impose it when required to do so by statute, as in court-supervised sales.

In certain written contracts, consideration from one party may be one dollar or may be referred to as "one dollar ($1) and other good and valuable consideration." In such situations, the actual consideration may be substantially more. However, the parties either cannot state the amount precisely or do not want to publicize it. This token amount is known as **nominal consideration**. Courts enforce contracts supported by nominal consideration if circumstances indicate that, in fact, consideration was given.

nominal consideration: token consideration bearing no relation to real value

IS AN EXISTING OBLIGATION CONSIDERATION?

PROBLEM: Vork was employed under a three-year contract to manage a motel for Lemsky at $25,000 a year, in addition to receiving a free apartment. After six months, Flemming offered Vork $30,000 a year to manage a larger motel. Upon learning of the offer, Lemsky said to Vork, "You're competent. You're honest. I need you. I'll meet any offer you get from anyone else." Vork remains on the job. Must Lemsky pay him the higher salary?

If one person does or promises to do something that he or she is already bound to do by law or by prior contract, the act or promise cannot be consideration for a new promise of any other person. This rule applies in the problem. Vork was still bound to work for Lemsky for an additional 30 months under the original contract. Therefore Lemsky's promise to pay more money is unenforceable. To hold him to the new promise, Vork would have to provide new, additional consideration. Otherwise Vork is obligated to carry out the contract as he originally agreed. Realistically, of course, Lemsky might voluntarily pay the extra compensation to keep Vork on the job, content, and productive.

The same rule holds true when a person demands further compensation for carrying out a contract already made.

Overman contracted with a corporation to build a float for a nationally televised parade. Two weeks before the parade, because the cost of materials had gone up, Overman refused to complete the float unless the corporation would promise to pay an extra $7,500. The corporation made the promise. However, Overman could not collect the additional money through a lawsuit based on the contract because there was no consideration for the promise. Overman was already obligated to complete the float.

This rule is also applied when a *creditor* (a person to whom a debt is owed) agrees to accept less than the total amount due in full settlement of a debt. Thus, if one person owes another $200, and there is no dispute as to that amount, a promise by the creditor to accept $150 in full payment is not binding. The creditor may later sue for the balance of $50 because no consideration was received for the release. Some states enforce such a promise if it is made in writing or they may treat the balance as a gift. However, a *debtor* (a person who owes the debt) may pay a smaller amount before the due date. This is valid consideration because the creditor has use of the funds sooner than required by the contract. Likewise, if something extra is given by the debtor, such as a pen and pencil set, the new consideration supports the release.

Bennet owed Huffman $500 but said he could pay only $400. Huffman agreed to accept $400 and a wristwatch in payment of the entire debt. The wristwatch was consideration for Huffman's release of the remaining $100.

On the other hand, sometimes there is a genuine dispute between the parties as to how much is owed. In such a case, partial payment offered in full settlement by the debtor and accepted by a creditor settles the claim. For example, suppose that a debtor in good faith claims that a certain debt is $50. The creditor in good faith contends that it is $100. If the parties agree respectively to pay and accept $75, the agreement is binding. The consideration for the promise of each is the other's refraining or promising to refrain from taking the matter to court. This is known as **compromise of a disputed claim**. Also, the claim would be settled if the debtor paid by check and made a clear notation which read: "In full settlement of all claims outstanding." The notation should preferably be on the back where the creditor *indorses* (signs) it. The claim is settled even if the creditor disagrees with the notation and so crosses it out before cashing it.

compromise of a disputed claim: mutual promises to refrain from bringing suit

Gilbert repaired Sullivan's leaky roof and submitted a bill for $500. Sullivan claimed that the bill should be for only $300 because water still seeped through and further repairs might cost as much as $200 more. Sullivan, therefore, sent a check for $300 with a notation on the back that it was "in full settlement of all accounts due." Gilbert crossed out the words, cashed the check, and filed suit in small-claims court for $200. The judge denied the claim. Crossing out the terms did not invalidate them. If Gilbert disagreed, he should not have cashed the check.

In contrast, some states say that the debt is discharged even when the claim is not in dispute, if there is an appropriate writing on the check, and the creditor indorses. The Uniform Commercial Code (UCC) adopts this rule. However, under the UCC, if the amount of the debt is not disputed, the creditor may cash the check and still sue for the balance if the creditor adds appropriate words such as "under protest" and/or "without prejudice" before indorsing. As an alternative, the creditor could send the check back and sue for the full amount.

Occasionally a group of creditors will cooperatively agree to accept less than what they are entitled to, in full satisfaction of their claims against a debtor. This is called a **composition of creditors**. Consideration for the promise of each creditor to release the debtor from full payment is found in the reciprocal promises of the other creditors to refrain from suing for the entire amounts due them. If the creditors did not agree to this arrangement, the debtor could go bankrupt, and the creditors might receive much less (see Chapter 19).

composition of creditors: agreement of all creditors to accept a proportion of their claims as full payment

Eubank was in financial trouble. He owed Murray $15,000; Irwin $10,000; Bunker $3,000; and Grummand $2,000. To enable Eubank to stay in business, all the creditors except Grummand agreed to accept 50 percent of their claims in full settlement. The first three agreed to let Eubank pay Grummand 100 percent of his claim. Their agreement was a composition of creditors, and none of the cooperating creditors could legally demand the remaining 50 percent.

IS PAST PERFORMANCE CONSIDERATION?

PROBLEM: While the Griffins were out of the country on a combined business and pleasure trip, a fire broke out in their unoccupied home. Hiller, a neighbor who had a key to the house, called the fire department. He then risked his life to save three very valuable paintings from the living room before the building was destroyed. When the Griffins returned, they thanked Hiller profusely and promised to pay him with a valuable Japanese tea set which was being shipped. When the set arrived, they changed their minds and gave Hiller nothing. Will Hiller win if he sues to get either the tea set or damages for breach of contract?

Recall that consideration is what one person asks of another in return for a promise. The bargaining takes place in the present time, for immediate or future performance by both parties. Therefore an act that has already been performed cannot serve as consideration for a promise made in the present. Such an act is **past consideration** and legally is not consideration at all. Thus, in the problem, Hiller was being a good neighbor when he voluntarily saved the paintings. However, his deed was not consideration for any promise made by the Griffins. When they returned, their promise of the tea set was unenforceable. That is because the action of Hiller was past consideration. To be effective, consideration must be given after the promisor states to the promisee that which is demanded.

past consideration: value given before a contract is made

WHAT ARE THE EXCEPTIONS TO THE REQUIREMENT OF CONSIDERATION?

> **PROBLEM:** The Branyan family pledged $25,000 to the building fund of the community hospital. Relying on this and other pledges, the board of directors of the hospital entered into a contract for construction of a new section. Can the Branyans be held to their pledge?

The following are important exceptions to the general rule that consideration is necessary for a valid contract or binding promise:

1. Promises of Financial Support to Charitable Organizations

People often pledge or promise to give a lump sum of money or a series of future payments to charitable organizations. Because nothing of value is given to the donor in return, such a person may think the promise is unenforceable. In fact, however, courts generally enforce such promises because the charity (such as a church, a nonprofit school, a foundation, or a hospital) acted in reliance on the promises. For example, a hospital may have contracted for new facilities, as in the problem. It would be unjust to deprive the hospital of promised support it reasonably relied on. Courts sometimes hold that the promise of each donor (contributor) was given in exchange for the promises of all others. Or they point to the donor's personal pride and enjoyment of public esteem. In reality, courts enforce promises of donations to charities as a matter of public policy. This rule sometimes discourages conscientious contributors from pledging substantial sums. They fear they might not be able to pay because of unforeseen future difficulties. Accordingly, many charities simply waive their legal rights to enforce the pledges, as indicated in Figure 11-1.

OLD TOWN REHABILITATION FOUNDATION

To help restore historic, publicly-owned buildings in the Old Town section of Pioneerville, and in consideration of the gifts of others, I (we) subscribe to the OLD TOWN REHABILITATION FUND

the sum of** Five hundred **Dollars ($** 500 **)

TOTAL SUBSCRIPTION	$ 500.00
AMOUNT PAID	100.00
BALANCE	$ 400.00

Balance to be paid: $100 quarterly, beginning August 1, 19--

It is understood and agreed that if the donor's economic circumstances change, making payment impracticable in his/her sole judgment, this pledge will not be enforced. All contributions are tax deductible.*

Ellen C. Yates — 5/1/--
(Donor's Signature) ***(Date)***

OLD TOWN REHABILITATION FOUNDATION

BY: James P. Roston — 5/1/--
(Authorized Solicitor) ***(Date)***

*Note that not all pledge forms contain this waiver clause.

Figure 11-1. Pledge Card Containing Waiver Clause

2. Promissory Estoppel

If consideration is not present, a promise may still be enforced under the doctrine of promissory estoppel. It is a substitute for con-

promissory estoppel: when a promise is enforced even though no consideration is given for it

sideration. The doctrine of **promissory estoppel** is available when all of the following conditions are met:

a. the promisor should reasonably foresee that the promisee will rely on the promise,
b. the promisee does, in fact, act in reliance on the promise,
c. the promisee would suffer a substantial economic loss if the promise were not enforced, and
d. injustice can be avoided only by enforcement of the promise.

Silvertone, a wealthy financier, strongly believes that world travel is essential for a balanced education. Accordingly, he told his twin niece and nephew that if they would "cap" their college degrees with a trip around the world, he would pay all their expenses upon their return, up to $7,500 for each. Using savings and some borrowed money, the twins took off on a 90-day journey. Total expenses for each exceeded $7,500 by the time they returned home. Silvertone is legally bound to reimburse each with $7,500. Although he received no consideration for his promise, he is *estopped* (barred) from denying his liability.

3. Commercial Paper

The government tries to encourage ready acceptance of commercial paper, such as checks and notes. Therefore a person who writes commercial paper cannot, by claiming he or she received no consideration for writing the paper, refuse to pay a person who later acquires commercial paper, such as a check, honestly and for value. This is true even if the person who wrote the paper was defrauded in the original transaction and actually never received value for the commercial paper.

4. State Statutory Exceptions

A few states exclude certain contracts from the requirement of consideration. An example would be when a party, in a signed writing, expressly states the intention to be legally bound. Also, under the UCC, a new promise to pay a debt no longer enforceable because too long a time period has passed requires no consideration. Likewise, under the UCC, a good-faith agreement that modifies an existing contract for the sale of goods needs no new consideration. Also, a merchant who makes a firm offer in writing to buy or sell goods is bound for up to three months even when she or he has not given nor received payment for such a promise.

PREVENTING LEGAL DIFFICULTIES

To Prevent Misunderstandings about Contracts, Remember that . . .

1. generally both parties must give and receive consideration if their agreement is to be enforceable as a contract;
2. adequacy or equality of consideration is generally unnecessary. It is sufficient when something of value is given and received;
3. use care and good judgment in making contracts. Courts generally will not rescue you from "bad bargains" or unfavorable deals voluntarily made;
4. accepting money or other value in exchange for giving up a legal right, such as the right to sue for damages after an accident, constitutes consideration and is binding. Consult a lawyer before making such an agreement in any major dispute;
5. a pledge to a charitable institution is generally binding and should not be made unless you intend to fulfill it; and
6. promises to make gifts cannot be enforced by the intended donee (receiver). An exception is made under the unusual conditions of promissory estoppel.

Strengthening Your Legal Vocabulary

composition of creditors
compromise of a disputed claim
consideration
forbearance
gift
nominal consideration
past consideration
promisee
promisor
promissory estoppel
seal

1. An agreement by all creditors to accept something less than the total amount of their claims in full satisfaction of a debtor's obligations.
2. Token consideration, which bears no relation to the real value of the contract.
3. The promise or action of one person in exchange for the promise or the action of another person.
4. Refraining from doing what one has a right to do.
5. Voluntary transfer of ownership of property without consideration.
6. Mutual promises of a debtor and creditor not to go to court to settle a disagreement regarding the amount of a debt.
7. Act that has already been performed and thus cannot be consideration for a promise in the present.
8. When a promise is enforced to avoid injustice, even though no consideration is given for it.
9. Person who makes a promise.
10. Person to whom a promise is made.

Reviewing Important Points

1. Lawful consideration is necessary to make a promise binding. Such consideration may consist of a return promise, an act, a forbearance, a change in a legal relation of the parties, money, or property.
2. Each party to the contract gives consideration; each party receives consideration. Such exchange is a test of the existence of a contract. It is the reason for the performance of the contract.
3. The adequacy, equality, or fairness of the consideration given and received is immaterial as long as the consideration has value and is voluntarily agreed to by both parties.
4. Performing or promising to perform an existing obligation is not consideration.
5. Past performance is not consideration for a promise given in the present or the future.
6. Pledges to pay money to charitable organizations are usually enforceable even though no consideration was given for the pledges.
7. Agreements modifying contracts for the sale of goods need no consideration to be binding.
8. Under special circumstances, promises of gifts are enforceable under the doctrine of promissory estoppel.

Applying Law to Everyday Life

1. Glenn contracted to add a room to Reid's home for $10,000. When Glenn was partway through, he realized that the job was more time consuming than anticipated. Therefore he refused to continue until Reid promised to pay an additional $2,000. Is Glenn legally entitled to the extra $2,000?

2. Shea owed Barlow $1,200 that was due and payable. Shea had been furloughed (laid off temporarily) at work, so he asked Barlow to extend the due date for six months. Barlow agreed, but a month later sued Shea to collect the debt. Will she win?

3. Lemke's son bought a videocassette recorder from Dyer on an installment plan. When he was unable to keep up the payments, Dyer came to repossess the recorder. Lemke promised in writing to make the payments if Dyer would allow the son to keep the equipment. If Dyer agreed, could Lemke hold him to his promise?

4. Kamiar owed Rubio $5,000 which was due in a year. There was no dispute as to the amount. However, Rubio needed money immediately, so Kamiar offered to pay $4,000 early in full settlement of the debt. If Kamiar pays the $4,000 now, may Rubio sue and collect the remaining $1,000 later?

5. Mackey, who had no children, told Lark that if she would attend his alma mater—Ahoya College—and graduate, he would pay all expenses she

incurred. Relying on loans and some of her own funds, she financed her way through college and earned the degree. Now Mackey says Lark suffered no detriment and he got no benefit. Since there was no consideration, he need not pay as promised. Do you agree?

6. When they were both freshmen in college, Faber borrowed $200 from Steiner so he could attend the big game in Chicago. Faber never repaid the debt, and after five years it was barred by the statute of limitations. Then Steiner sent Faber a Christmas card on which he added this note: "I haven't forgotten those four 50's I borrowed from you for the big game. Now that I am working, I'll pay you. In addition, I'll take you to this year's big game at my expense." Are Steiner's promises enforceable?

7. Kari promised to deed ten acres of land to the Ezlers. In reliance on the promise, they took possession of the land, cleared it, installed an irrigation system over a one-acre section, and planted 50 young fruit trees. Then Kari, seeing the improved property, changed his mind. May the Ezlers compel the transfer even though they gave Kari no consideration?

Solving Case Problems

1. Marine Contractors Co., Inc., did various marine repair work within a 100-mile radius of Boston. The company maintained a trust fund for the benefit of retired employees. The trust agreement provided that employees who resigned could withdraw their share of the fund after waiting five years. Hurley, general manager of the company, had accumulated $12,000 in the trust fund. When Hurley resigned, the president of Marine offered to pay his $12,000 immediately if he would agree not to compete with Marine directly or indirectly within 100 miles of Boston for five years. The parties made a written contract which set forth a "consideration of One Dollar and other good and valuable consideration." It also stated that the parties have "set their hands and seals" to this contract. Within four months after leaving Marine's employ, Hurley began doing repair work similar to that of Marine. Soon after, he organized his own company, hiring two supervisors of Marine. Marine sued to stop Hurley from breaking his contract. Hurley defended with a plea of no consideration. Do you agree with Hurley? (*Marine Contractors Co., Inc. v. Hurley*, 310 N.E.2d 915)

2. Under a written contract with the Robert Chuckrow Construction Company, Gough agreed to do the carpentry work on a commercial building. Gough was to supply all necessary labor, materials, and other requirements to complete the work "in accordance with the drawings and specifications." After Gough's employees had erected 38 trusses, 32 trusses fell off the building. Gough did not claim that the plans or specifications were defective or that Chuckrow was to blame for the collapse. Gough was told by a Chuckrow representative to remove the fallen trusses and to rebuild and re-

erect them. Gough was also told to submit an additional bill for this work. He completed the job and submitted the additional bill. However, Chuckrow paid only the amount promised under the original written contract. Therefore Gough sued Chuckrow for the extra costs of reconstruction. Is he entitled to the added money? (*Robert Chuckrow Construction Company v. Gough*, 159 S.E.2d 469, Ga.)

3. Kadish supplied $681.46 worth of materials to a subcontractor who was building a property for Paul and Stella Glitsos. When he was not paid, Kadish filed a *lien* (claim) against the property. Under the lien, he could have forced a sale of the property by foreclosure to get his money out of the proceeds. Instead, he contacted Paul Glitsos, who promised to pay the money. Kadish did not promise not to foreclose the lien, so there was no bargained-for forbearance and no consideration. Paul Glitsos did not pay as he promised, and after it was too late to foreclose, the couple still refused to pay. They argued that foreclosure was his sole remedy, claiming that Paul's promise did not create a contract. Now foreclosure was barred by the statute of limitations. Although the Glitsoses received no consideration from Kadish, is there any legal basis for holding them liable? (*Glitsos v. Kadish*, 4 Ariz. App. 134, 418 P.2d 129)

4. Hoffman and his wife owned a bakery in Wautoma, Wisconsin. Lukowitz, an agent for Red Owl Stores, Inc., represented to and agreed with Hoffman that Red Owl would erect a grocery store building for them in Chilton and stock it with merchandise. In return, the Hoffmans were to invest a total of $18,000 and Hoffman was to operate the store as a Red Owl franchise. In reliance on Red Owl's assurances and advice, the Hoffmans sold their bakery, paid $1,000 down on a lot in Chilton, and rented a residence there. In negotiations over some 17 months, Red Owl boosted the required investment to $24,100; then $26,000; and finally $34,000 which was to include $13,000 from Hoffman's father-in-law. Red Owl insisted the $13,000 must either be a gift or a loan which would be inferior in claim to all general creditors. Hoffman balked and sued for damages. Should the Hoffmans win and if so, on what grounds? (*Hoffman v. Red Owl Stores*, 133 N.W. 2d 267, 26 Wis. 2d 683)

5. Petty, a general contractor, made a series of purchases from Field Lumber Company. Field's records showed a total price of $1,752.21. Petty admitted he owed $1,091.96, but denied liability for the difference of $660.25. He claimed the difference was a result of an unauthorized $292.60 purchase by an employee, plus related finance charges. Petty sent a check for $500 along with a letter stating that the check must be accepted in full settlement of the total claim or returned. Field phoned to say the lumber company required full payment, but nevertheless Field cashed the check and sued for the full balance it claimed was due. Decide. (*Field Lumber Co. v. Petty*, 512 P.2d 764, Wash. Ct. of App.)

12

Void and Voidable Agreements

1. Planning to marry, two minors pool their savings to make a down payment on a used RV (recreation vehicle) to use as their first home. Under parental pressure, they agree not to marry until both finish college. Can they return the RV and get their money back?
2. An adult friend of yours buys a single-lens reflex (SLR) camera outfit for $519.97 including a carrying case and a special lens. In her excitement, she fails to note that the case and special lens are advertised as "optional equipment." The two items cost an additional $122.94, which is listed on the contract she signs. When the bill for $642.91 plus sales tax arrives, your friend objects. Is she bound by the contract?
3. Your parents offer to sell some used camping gear for $190 to a prospective buyer. However, when the offer is typed, the figures are accidentally typed as "$109." The buyer accepts the offer, sending a check for $109. Can your parents avoid the sale?

WHAT MAKES AN AGREEMENT VOID OR VOIDABLE?

PROBLEM: Pernal, a minor, worked hard as a farmhand all summer and saved her money. In September, she bought a moped for cash from Shihara's Cycles. Pernal rode the moped home. When she got there, however, her parents said it would be too dangerous to ride the moped on downtown streets as planned. Pernal returned the moped and asked for her money. Was she entitled to a full refund?

genuine assent: consent that is not negated by fraud, duress, undue influence, or mistake

disaffirmance: refusal to carry out a voidable contract

A *valid* (legally effective) offer and acceptance generally result in an enforceable contract. However, sometimes the agreement may be void or voidable because one of the parties lacked capacity to contract or failed to give consideration. The contract also may be void or voidable because one of the parties failed to genuinely assent to the agreement. **Genuine assent** exists when consent is not clouded by fraud, duress, undue influence, or mistake. Generally, if genuine assent is lacking, the victim may cancel or disaffirm the contract.

Disaffirmance is a refusal to carry out or comply with the terms of a voidable contract, without any liability to pay damages. Disaffirmance is permitted in certain cases when the offer and acceptance were not given freely and voluntarily in a spirit of honesty and fairness. If a court decides that a person who used reasonable care and judgment was nevertheless deceived or misled about an important fact, that person may disaffirm (or avoid) the contract. A person who was compelled to enter into a contract against his or her free will may also disaffirm. Similarly, any person who lacks capacity to contract (see Chapter 9) might be able to disaffirm, as Pernal did in the problem.

WHEN CAN A MINOR DISAFFIRM A VOIDABLE CONTRACT?

PROBLEM: While still a minor, Beach bought a stereo sound system from McReam's Electronic Cloud for $675 plus a credit charge of 18 percent a year. He paid $100 down and promised to pay $50 a month on the unpaid balance until the debt was paid. After making four payments, two of which were made after he reached the age of majority, Beach decided to disaffirm the contract and return the equipment. Can he legally do this?

A minor can disaffirm a voidable contract any time while still a minor or within a reasonable time after reaching majority. As an exception, a minor who has transferred real property usually cannot disaffirm the contract until reaching majority. Likewise, a minor cannot disaffirm a contract made with court approval, nor a contract to enter the armed services, nor—in some states—insurance contracts.

If a minor decides to disaffirm a contract, the entire agreement must be disaffirmed. It does not matter whether the contract has been fully performed.

After reaching majority, a person may ratify a voidable contract made while a minor. **Ratification** is the approval of a voidable contract. Ratification may not be made while one is still under age. After reaching majority, the minor must disaffirm or ratify the entire contract. One may not disaffirm one part and ratify another, unless the other party agrees. Once properly made, ratification may not be withdrawn.

ratification: approval of a voidable contract

Ratification may consist of any of the following:

1. an express new promise to perform as agreed,
2. silence, or the failure to disaffirm, for an unreasonably long time after attaining majority, or
3. any act (such as continued use of the property) that clearly indicates the person's intention to be bound.

In the problem, Beach had ratified the contract by making payments after reaching majority. Some courts require continued use or an express promise. In neither such case can the minor then disaffirm.

Although a minor's contracts are generally voidable by the minor, the minor can enforce them against adults. However, adults generally cannot enforce the contracts against the minor. Nor can an adult avoid any part of a contract because the other party is a minor.

Kensterm, a minor, sold his used science encyclopedia set to Blumrich, age 22. Blumrich paid $125 which was about half the original price. Three months later, a new, expanded edition of the same encyclopedia set appeared on the market. Blumrich told Kensterm that he was returning the books and wanted the money back. He claimed the set was obsolete, and moreover, Kensterm—being a minor—could not make a binding contract. Blumrich was wrong. Kensterm could indeed sell his books, and he alone could disaffirm the contract.

When a minor does disaffirm, anything of value that the minor still has must be returned. The minor is then entitled to get back everything that was given to the other party. In some states, however, a minor must return everything received in as good a condition as it was when it was received. If this cannot be done, the minor must pay the difference in value. Or the minor must have the difference deducted from the amount to be refunded. In most states, a minor can legally refuse to pay for goods received or can get back all money paid. This is true even if the minor returns used or damaged goods. It is also true even if the minor returns nothing because the goods have been lost, consumed, destroyed, or sold to an innocent third party.

Lamon, a minor, bought a diamond engagement ring and a novelty necklace for his fiancée, Morgan. He paid for the items in weekly installments of $10. On the day of Lamon's majority, Lamon and Morgan quarreled. Morgan returned the ring to Lamon but refused to part with the necklace. She was legally entitled to keep the necklace because it was an ordinary gift not connected with the proposed marriage. The next day, Lamon returned the ring to the jeweler and demanded a refund of the money he had paid for both pieces of jewelry. Lamon was entitled to the money he had paid on the ring. In most states, he was even entitled to what he had paid on the necklace. That is because he returned everything that was still in his possession. In a few states, he could be held liable for the price of the necklace.

WHAT CONTRACTS OF MINORS CANNOT BE DISAFFIRMED?

PROBLEM: Upon graduation from high school, Vukovich, age 17, became a sales representative of the Muller Broom Company. She was required to buy a $375 kit of samples of household brushes, brooms, and other supplies for house-to-house selling. The venture was a disappointing failure. Discouraged after a month, Vukovich asked Muller to take back the samples and to return her $375 payment. Must Muller do so?

Some contracts of minors cannot be disaffirmed. Generally minors cannot void any contracts approved for them by a court. For example, minors who are employed as actors or actresses or as professionals in sports usually have their contracts approved by a court. Once approved, these contracts may not be disaffirmed.

A minor who owns real property may not sell it or borrow money against it without a court's approval. The minor would be bound by a court-approved contract.

In most states, minors who engage in a business or trade cannot disaffirm agreements involving their business. Accordingly, in the problem, Vukovich would not be able to avoid her contract if she lived in a state with such a law.

More than half of the states provide that minors who are over a certain age may not disaffirm certain contracts of life insurance. Minors are generally permitted to make deposits in banks and in savings and loan associations. Most states also permit minors to make withdrawals as if they were adults, without any right to disaffirm these transactions. Contracts to enlist in the armed services and contracts for educational loans cannot be disaffirmed.

CAN MINORS DISAFFIRM CONTRACTS FOR NECESSARIES?

PROBLEM: Against their parents' wishes, Mead and Hobson—both minors—left home. Together, they signed a lease to rent a nearby furnished apartment from Krohn for a year for $150 a month. Krohn thought that both teenagers looked like young adult college men, so he never asked their ages. After three months, the teenagers ran out of money and returned to their homes. Krohn could not find new tenants. Could he hold the minors or their parents liable for the rent?

Although the law permits minors to disaffirm most of their contracts, it does not allow them to avoid responsibility when they buy truly needed goods or services. If minors could disaffirm such contracts, business firms might understandably refuse to supply goods which are necessary for life. Therefore one who supplies necessaries to a minor can collect from the minor or from parents of the minor. The law says the parents—who are responsible for the care of their children—have, in effect, authorized the children to purchase necessaries which are not otherwise provided or made available. However, the goods must in fact be necessary, and the supplier is entitled only to their reasonable value, not necessarily the contract price.

necessaries: goods and services essential to maintain one's life-style

Necessaries are goods and services that are reasonably required to maintain one's life-style. In the case of a minor, these goods and services must be suitable to the minor's economic and social status. They must not already be possessed by the minor or be in the process of being supplied by parents or guardians. Courts have found such things as food, clothing, shelter, education, medical care, and tools used to earn a living to be necessaries. In contrast, jewelry, liquor, tobacco, pleasure trips, television sets, record albums, and expensive food for parties are not necessaries. Some courts hold that an automobile is a necessary when the automobile is essential for the minor to earn a living.

An article must meet all of the following four requirements for necessaries before a minor or parent can be held responsible for payment:

1. The Item Must Be Reasonably Required

Shelter is a basic human requirement. Because it fulfills this need for shelter, housing is clearly a necessary. In the problem, Krohn's claim would meet this first requirement.

2. The Item Must Be Actually Furnished

The minor who agrees to buy is not bound to pay unless the necessary is actually supplied. In the problem, the apartment was occupied for only three months. There is no liability for the remaining nine.

3. The Item Must Be Reasonably Suitable to the Age and Social and Economic Status of the Minor

What is considered a necessary for one person is not always a necessary for another. The apartment rented by Mead and Hobson would have to be in keeping with their families' life-styles to be a necessary. Here the court could require further evidence as to the families' life-styles and the type of apartment in question.

4. The Item Must Not Be Otherwise Furnished

If the parents of both Mead and Hobson provided adequate shelter, the apartment would not be a necessary. Therefore neither the minors nor their parents would be legally obliged to pay future rent. In addition, the minors have a valid claim against Krohn for a refund of the $450 already paid.

DOES MISSTATING ONE'S AGE BIND A MINOR?

PROBLEM: Rombie, a mature-looking minor, lied about his age when he bought an extensive wardrobe of summer clothing from Duds For Dolls And Dudes. As identification Rombie showed the driver's license taken from his adult brother. Rombie had also used the brother's name on the installment contract. By October, Rombie had paid $325 on the $785 contract. But he was bored with the wardrobe, and so he returned it to the store and demanded the return of all payments. Must the store comply?

In most states, minors who falsely state their age may nevertheless disaffirm their contracts. However, also in most states, a minor who gives a false age may be held liable for the false representation. This is a tort (see Chapter 5). Minors are liable for their torts and delinquent conduct, although they are usually not liable for their contracts. The other party to the contract may collect from a minor any damages suffered because of the minor's fraud even though the minor cannot be held to the agreement. Thus, Rombie is within his rights as a minor in disaffirming the contract. But in most states, Duds For Dolls And Dudes could probably hold back from the refund an amount of money sufficient to cover the decrease in value of the wardrobe as returned. Or the store could hold back the full amount if nothing was returned. Moreover, because of his tort of fraud, Rombie could be held liable in damages for deceiving the seller.

On the other hand, some states will not permit adults to collect damages from minors even if they have misrepresented their age. In protecting the minor, one court said it will not close the front door of contract liability, only to open the rear door of tort liability.

WHAT IS FRAUD?

PROBLEM: When Milliken sold a used car to Camacho, he told her that the car had been driven only 50,000 miles, had never been in an accident, and had the original paint. He said that the car had new steel-belted radial tires and that the engine had been overhauled. In fact, Milliken had stolen the car, set back the odometer from 90,000 miles, and repainted the exterior in the original color. The tires were a retreaded glass-belted type; the engine had merely been tuned and steam cleaned. Moreover, Milliken had stood between Camacho and the right rear end of the car.

He did this so that she would not see a crudely repaired fender, which had been damaged in an accident. After Camacho learns the truth and if she can find Milliken, can she avoid the contract?

fraud: deliberate misrepresentation or concealment of a material fact

The basis of **fraud** is false representation or concealment of a material fact. However, not every misrepresentation or concealment amounts to fraud. All of the following elements must be present for fraud to exist:

1. The False Representation or Concealment of a Present or Past Fact Must Be Deliberate

Fraud results from deliberate lies. It also results from deliberate concealment of unfavorable facts which otherwise could be noticed by a reasonable person. Generally neither seller nor buyer is obliged to reveal all good or bad facts about the subject matter of the contract. Courts would have trouble trying to define what must be known and disclosed in every case. Moreover, buyers are free to ask questions as they investigate before they invest. The seller who responds must answer the questions honestly. If the seller refuses to answer a question, the buyer is alerted to a possible problem and need not enter the contract.

In addition, the seller must not volunteer false information or act to prevent the other party from learning important facts. In the problem, Milliken was a criminal who acted fraudulently. He lied about the car and actively concealed the damaged rear fender. Accordingly, if Camacho could find Milliken, she could avoid the contract and sue for damages for the tort of fraud. Milliken should be prosecuted as a criminal, and the car should be returned to its true owner.

Keep in mind that to constitute fraud, the misrepresentation or concealment must be deliberate. Normally silence is not blameworthy. But sometimes fraud arises when the party has a duty to speak yet does not. For example, basic honesty requires a seller to tell about a concealed defect not readily discoverable by a reasonably alert buyer.

If a seller innocently misrepresents a material fact, the buyer may avoid the contract or collect compensatory damages for the injury suffered. However, no tort has been committed, so the buyer is not entitled to punitive damages. On the other hand, one may not claim fraud when the means were available for determining the truth, as by simply reading a paper before signing.

The Rankins bought a new house perched on a hillside, with a beautiful view over a valley. After some heavy rains, the house sagged in one corner and shifted on its foundation. Only then did they discover that the house had been built on land filled in by the developer-seller. The Rankins sued the developer for fraud. They claimed that the developer had a duty to inform them of this fact. The court agreed.

The false representation or concealment must be of a present or past fact. This does not include opinions of value or predictions. For example, if someone tells you that a certain article "will pay for itself," "is a bargain," "is the best on the market," or "is a super value," you have no legal right to rely upon such remarks. They are usually no more than statements of **personal opinion** (personal belief or judgment), not statements of fact. Opinions which prove to be wrong normally do not constitute fraud. However, if a person claims to be an expert, for example, in the valuation of Tibetan art, an innocent buyer may hold the expert liable if the opinion proves to be erroneous and a loss is suffered.

personal opinion: personal belief or judgment

Two neighbors, Edgar and Burbridge, were negotiating for the sale of an antique colonial chair. Edgar, the seller, honestly told Burbridge he had paid $450 for it 10 years ago. He also stated, "It is worth at least $1,200 now." The first statement was one of fact. The buyer could rely upon it to be true and could claim fraud if it were false. But the reference to the present value was a statement of Edgar's opinion. Because Edgar was not an expert, the reference would not be fraudulent even if it were false. Burbridge had no right to rely upon it.

2. The Misrepresented or Concealed Fact Must Be Material

To be fraudulent, a statement must be a false representation or concealment of a present or a past **material fact**. A fact is material, regardless of its apparent importance, if it influences the other person's decision to enter into the agreement. Misrepresentation or concealment of such a fact usually means that the person who was misled would not have entered into the contract if he or she had known the truth.

material fact: fact which influences a decision

3. The Person Who Makes the False Representation Must Know It to Be False or Make It Recklessly without Regard to Its Truth

PROBLEM: Dimmer was a new sales agent for Proto Metal Supply Co. Stein was the purchasing agent for Space-Age Specialties Corporation. Eager to make a sale, Dimmer told Stein that certain steel sheets and rods had a high chromium content and would not rust. Actually she did not know the chemical content but said what her prospect wanted to hear. Stein believed her and ordered a carload shipment. When the facts were discovered after many Space-Age customers had complained, Space-Age sued Proto Metal and Dimmer for fraud. Should Space-Age win the suit?

Fraud clearly exists when a person deliberately makes a false statement or conceals a material fact. Fraud also exists if a person makes a statement of fact rashly, without determining its truth or falsity. This is especially true if that person should know the facts.

In the problem, Dimmer, acting as agent for Proto Metal, made the statements about the steel products with reckless disregard of the truth. Hence, Space-Age was justified in claiming fraud and should win the suit against Proto Metal and Dimmer.

4. The Misrepresentation Must Be Made with the Intention of Influencing the Other Person to Act upon It

PROBLEM: Braak was deep in debt and needed more credit to keep his business going. He gave Central Credit Controls (CCC) false information which showed his financial condition to be good. Grant subsequently obtained a credit report on Braak from CCC. Relying on the report, Grant sold a computer and expensive software to Braak on account. Within a month, Braak became *insolvent* (unable to pay debts) and failed to make a payment. Grant then learned the truth about Braak's financial condition. Claiming fraud, Grant sued to repossess the equipment. Should he succeed?

For a statement to be fraudulent, the person making the statement must intend that it be relied upon and acted upon. Generally the false statement is made directly to the intended victim. However, this is not essential. A person may tell someone something with the intent that the statement will be passed on to another whose conduct is to be influenced. Such was the case with Braak in

the problem. Accordingly, Grant will be allowed to repossess the equipment.

5. The Misrepresentation or Concealment Must Induce Action and Cause Injury to the Other Party

> **PROBLEM:** In bargaining to sell his sailboat, Martz deliberately tried to deceive Andza by saying it was one of a limited edition of deluxe Mariners. Andza actually knew it was the cheaper Islander model, but he bought it anyway. Later, when Andza became dissatisfied with the boat, he claimed fraud and sought to disaffirm the contract. Can he do so?

A misrepresentation or concealment is not fraudulent unless it actually deceives. There is no fraud if the intended victim is not misled. Likewise, there is no fraud if the wrongful concealment or misrepresentation did not affect the buyer's decision to enter into a contract. In the problem, Martz's misrepresentation did not influence Andza's decision to buy. Therefore Andza may not disaffirm the contract. Moreover, if a defrauded party suffers no injury, there is no need to sue for damages. An example would be if the goods received were worth more than the price paid. In some states, there would be no right to sue in such cases.

WHAT ARE THE RIGHTS OF THE DEFRAUDED PARTY?

> **PROBLEM:** Salvat was fraudulently induced by Chapman to buy a painting. Chapman had described the painting as an authentic Van Gogh. Upon discovering the fraud, before payment or delivery, Salvat notified Chapman that she was canceling the contract. Was she within her rights?

Contracts entered into as a result of fraud are voidable by the injured party. Thus, a defrauded party may *repudiate* (disaffirm) the agreement. Normally when one decides to disaffirm a contract, anything that has been received must be returned. A deceived party who has performed part of the contract may recover what has been paid or given under its terms. A defrauded party who has done nothing, like Salvat, may cancel the contract and be released with no obligation to pay. If sued on the contract, the defrauded party can plead fraud as a defense. In either case, the victim may sue in tort and collect damages caused by the fraud.

A defrauded person may choose not to disaffirm but instead to ratify the agreement. Either party may then enforce it. However, a defrauded party who decides to ratify an agreement may seek *reimbursement* (financial compensation) for any loss suffered.

Winn was fraudulently induced to purchase a heating system from N. S. Klevar. Additional duct work costing $2,500 proved to be necessary to make the system perform as promised. Winn ratified the contract by demanding and receiving the corrective work from Klevar. He thus waived his right to sue Klevar for damages for fraud.

WHAT IS DURESS?

PROBLEM: Cameron owned a promising racehorse that Link had offered to buy for undisclosed parties. When Cameron refused to sell, Link lowered his voice and slowly said, "Listen, the guys I represent don't take no for an answer. If you don't sell, they'll hurt you; they'll hurt your family. Like a good friend, I'm telling you to sell. You're getting a fair price." Cameron, who had secretly recorded the conversation, sold. Then he called in the police. Can he now disaffirm the contract and get his horse back?

duress: overpowering of another's free will through coercion or by illegal imprisonment

An agreement is said to be made under **duress** if one person compels another to enter into it through *coercion* (threat of force or an act of violence) or by *illegal imprisonment* (unlawful arrest or detention). The victim in such cases has been denied the exercise of free will. Therefore he or she may disaffirm the resulting contract.

The threatened or actual violence may be to the life, liberty, or property of (1) the victim, (2) the victim's immediate family, or (3) the victim's near relatives. In the problem, Cameron acted under duress in making the contract and therefore could avoid it.

A person usually is not guilty of duress when the act or threat is to do something the person has a legal right to do. Thus, to persuade another to contract under threat of a justifiable civil lawsuit is permissible. To threaten to have another arrested if the contract is not signed would be duress and possibly criminal coercion.

Cutler owed Mason $1,000 on an unpaid account. When Mason threatened to sue, Cutler signed a note promising to pay the amount in 90 days. When Cutler failed to pay the note, Mason filed suit. Cutler's defense was that the note was signed under duress. This was rejected by the court because Mason had a legal right to threaten civil action.

WHAT IS UNDUE INFLUENCE?

PROBLEM: Shabade was an 84-year-old, somewhat senile widow lacking business experience. After investing an inheritance in a house for herself, she accepted Jane Wyles, a middle-aged stranger, as a boarder. Wyles lived there for two months. During that time, she was very attentive to Shabade, who had become bedridden. Four weeks before her death, and mistakenly believing herself to be in need of money for hospitalization, Shabade sold the house to Wyles. The price, paid in cash, was only one-third of the true market value. After Shabade died, her children sued to have the agreement nullified. They claimed that Wyles had used undue influence on their mother. Will they succeed?

undue influence: overpowering another's free will to take unfair advantage in a contract

Undue influence occurs when one party overpowers the free will of the other, taking unfair advantage to get the other to make a contract that is unfavorable.

It is more likely to be present when a relationship of trust, confidence, or authority exists between two parties. Thus, undue influence is presumed to exist in unfavorable contracts between attorney and client, husband and wife, parent and child, guardian and ward, physician and patient. When a contract is made as a result of undue influence, the contract is voidable by the victim.

A charge of undue influence can be overcome by proving that the contract is fair and benefits both parties. To forestall a claim of undue influence, the stronger party should act with scrupulous honesty, fully disclose all important facts, and insist that the other party talk to independent counsel before contracting.

Normally the relations between a landlord and a tenant would not involve undue influence. In the problem, however, undue influence did exist because of Shabade's physical and mental condition, and the gross unfairness of the sales contract.

WHAT IS THE EFFECT OF MISTAKE?

PROBLEM: Toledano wanted to have new gutters installed on his house. He signed a contract to pay $300 for labor and up to $125 for materials.

When he was later sued for $410 for labor and materials, Toledano pleaded innocent mistake. He said he thought the materials were included in the $300 bid. He admitted that he had not read the contract before he signed it. Was that a good defense?

unilateral mistake: important contractual mistake made by only one of the parties

When there is a **unilateral mistake**, one of the parties has an incorrect idea about the facts of a contract. Such a mistake generally does not affect the validity and enforceability of the contract. Thus, in the problem, mistake was not a good defense.

Frequently a party to a contract has erroneous expectations of high profits. For example, suppose a person buys some corporate stock, confidently expecting the price to go up. If the price goes down, the buyer alone suffers the loss. Or again, suppose a building contractor bids to do a job for $10,000. Actual costs run up to $12,000. The mistaken contractor alone suffers the loss. These are examples of unilateral mistakes.

Failure to read a contract before signing, or a hurried or careless reading of it, may also result in obligations that a person had no intention of assuming. In making contracts, persons are ordinarily bound by what they outwardly do and say, regardless of what they may inwardly think, understand, or intend. The resulting unilateral mistakes generally do not affect the contract. However, if the mistake was recognized but not disclosed by one party alone, who apparently hoped to gain an advantage by remaining silent, courts may grant relief by declaring the agreement void.

Galaxie Genetic Products, Inc., asked for bids (offers to build) on construction of its new office building. Eight bids were received. Seven of them were within $100,000 under or over the architect's estimate of $3 million. However, the bid from New Horizon Builders was $500,000 below the architect's estimate. New Horizon's chief estimator had made a gross error which had reduced their bid far below those of all other competitors. Galaxie recognized this, and may not seize upon New Horizon's unilateral mistake to demand performance for the erroneous bargain price.

Under some circumstances, a contractor may submit a bid and then discover an error after the bids have been opened. The bidder may still revoke the bid provided the bidder (a) had acted in good faith and without gross negligence; (b) promptly notified the other party; (c) would suffer a substantial loss if the bid were binding; and (d) the other party would not suffer significantly and unfairly.

WHAT MISTAKES MAKE AGREEMENTS VOID OR VOIDABLE?

PROBLEM: In a large metropolis in the Midwest, there were two streets with the name of "Highland." Fisher owned the lot located at 231 Highland Avenue. Neece, who lived in New York City, wanted to buy the lot located at 231 Highland Boulevard. He wrote to Fisher, offering "to buy your lot on Highland" on specified terms. Fisher promptly mailed his acceptance of the offer. Was there a contract?

When there is a **mutual mistake** (also called a *bilateral mistake*) of material fact, both parties are wrong about some important facts. In such a case, either party may disaffirm. Thus, in the problem, the parties' mutual mistake as to the identity of the subject matter made the contract void. Neece, in his offer, was referring to the lot on Highland Boulevard; Fisher, in his acceptance, was referring to the lot on Highland Avenue. Mutual mistake as to the existence of the subject matter has the same effect.

mutual mistake: important contractual mistake made by both parties

Falkhausen, who lived in Indianapolis, owned a Formula One racing car which he kept in Miami. On March 18, he sold the car to Firenzi. Unknown to either party, the car had been destroyed in an accident on March 17. Because of the mutual mistake as to the existence of the car, there was no contract.

Some states hold that when the mutual mistake was one of fact concerning applicable law, the contract is valid. This would be true, for example, if both parties to a real estate sale mistakenly believed that local zoning laws permitted construction of duplexes on a large lot that was being transferred. All persons are presumed to know the law. The buyer, at least, should have checked the statutes before signing.

PREVENTING LEGAL DIFFICULTIES

When Entering a Contract . . .

1. always carefully investigate before entering into an important transaction. When appropriate, consult trustworthy, independent experts. The other

party in a transaction is seldom primarily concerned with your best interest, and is generally not obligated to volunteer information or disclose all facts known;
2. do not rush into a decision. Take the time necessary to review and understand the advantages and disadvantages of the proposed contract. Legitimate proposals will usually survive a delay;
3. learn to distinguish between fact and opinion. Do not rely on the other party's opinion unless that party is a trustworthy expert;
4. if you suspect or know of fraud, do not enter into the contract; and
5. if you believe you have been defrauded, act promptly to disaffirm the contract and possibly take other steps (such as consulting a lawyer) to protect your rights. "Sitting on your rights" may cause you to lose them.

Strengthening Your Legal Vocabulary

disaffirmance
duress
fraud
genuine assent
material fact
mutual mistake
necessaries
personal opinion
ratification
undue influence
unilateral mistake

1. Fact which has a substantial influence on a person's decision to act.
2. Personal belief or judgment; not a fact.
3. Use of coercion or illegal imprisonment to force another party to make a contract.
4. Deliberate false representation or concealment of a material fact, which is meant to and which does induce another to make an unfavorable contract.
5. Approval of a voidable contract.
6. Overpowering of another's free will by taking unfair advantage to induce the person to make an unfavorable contract.
7. Refusal to comply with the terms of a voidable contract.
8. Mistake about an important fact believed by both parties to a contract.
9. Goods and services reasonably needed to maintain one's life-style.
10. Consent or agreement not clouded by fraud, duress, undue influence, or mistake.

Reviewing Important Points

1. An offer and its acceptance must be made with genuine assent.
2. A minor may usually disaffirm a voidable contract anytime before becoming of age or within a reasonable time thereafter. In doing so, the minor must return anything that has been received if the minor still possesses it.

3. After reaching majority, a person may ratify a contract made during minority. This can be done either by an express promise or by an act such as payment. In most states, silence or the failure to disaffirm within a reasonable time is considered ratification.
4. Fraud exists when deliberate false representation or concealment of a material fact is intended to and does influence the action of another, causing injury. Contracts induced by fraud are voidable by the victim.
5. Duress consists of either coercion or illegal imprisonment which induces the victim to make an unwanted contract. Such contracts are voidable by the victim.
6. Undue influence exists when one person, because of trust, confidence, or authority, uses an overpowering influence over another, depriving the victim of freedom of will in making a contract. The contract is voidable by the victim.
7. Generally a unilateral mistake of fact does not affect the validity of a contract.
8. Generally a mutual (bilateral) mistake of material fact (as to identity or existence of the subject matter) makes the agreement void. In some states, if the mistake concerns the applicable law, the contract may be valid.

Applying Law to Everyday Life

1. Agnes, age 16, bought a pair of tinted shoes to match her junior prom formal. She wore the shoes to the prom. Then she returned them to the store after she realized they would be of no further use to her. She demanded a refund. (a) Must the store give her the money? (b) Would your answer be the same if her mother had made the purchase?

2. Blick, a minor, bought a video musical recording from Shawn, another minor. After making a copy on his video recorder, Blick tried to return the original recording to Shawn and demanded a full refund. (a) If Shawn still has the money, must the full price be returned? (b) If Shawn does not have the money, what will happen?

3. In Western states, water rights are often critical to the use and value of rural land. They determine how much water a landowner may take from surface and underground sources. In negotiations for the purchase of a ranch, Adler, the seller, discussed water rights with Folt, the buyer. Adler never mentioned an on-going dispute he had over such rights with a neighboring rancher. After the purchase, Folt realized that he had "bought a lawsuit" when his neighbor sued him over the water rights. In turn, he therefore sued Adler for rescission of their contract. Decide.

4. During negotiations for the sale of a salt well, Hutton said the well was free of gypsum and that the brine was 90 percent in strength. In fact, the well did contain gypsum and was deficient in strength. Curry, the purchaser, refused to pay, claiming the contract was void because of fraud. Was it?

5. Ashbery, a salesperson, told Gelman that a new computer and its accounting software should do the work of at least five employees, and maybe more. Relying on this statement, Gelman bought the products. When Gelman found that he could eliminate only three employees but needed a new specialist, he claimed fraud. Was fraud committed?

6. Moser had no automobile liability insurance, although it was required by state law. He negligently collided with Arena's car. Arena threatened to sue if Moser failed to pay $1,000 for pain and suffering and $2,000 for car repairs. Moser gave Arena a check for $3,000. Then he stopped payment, claiming duress. (a) Was it duress? (b) What should your answer be if Arena threatened to file a criminal complaint unless paid?

7. Carlyle bought discontinued lines of clothing from manufacturers and sold them through "discount house" retail stores. When Lady Vogue, Ltd., offered him all the garments in a designated storeroom for $25,000, he made a quick inspection and accepted. Later, Lady Vogue discovered that a group of new designs had somehow been included by error. Carlyle had acted in good faith and had not recognized the mistake. Lady Vogue refused to release any goods unless Carlyle agreed to pay an extra $4,000. He refused and filed suit. Decide.

Solving Case Problems

1. Vaughn Turner gave his consent for his son Clifford, age 17, to marry Marcella E. Gilbert. Later, after the wedding, Vaughn filed suit to have his consent canceled and the marriage annulled. Vaughn claimed that he was induced by fraud to give his parental consent to the marriage. Clifford and Marcella had represented to him that they had already been married in Tijuana, Mexico. They had also represented that Marcella was pregnant and that Clifford was the father of the expected baby. Because of these representations, Vaughn had given his consent. (Parental consent was required by law because the son was under 18.) However, the representation that Clifford was the father was false. Marcella had been about seven months pregnant when Clifford met her. Indeed, the child's birth certificate listed the name of the mother as Marcella T. Belden and the father as James Taylor Belden. Could the consent be canceled and the marriage annulled? (*Turner v. Turner*, 167 Cal.App.2d 636, 334 P.2d 1011)

2. Richard purchased a lot and model home from the defendant, a developer of residential real estate. The sales agreement provided that the sale was subject to zoning ordinances. At the time of the sale, the defendant delivered a plot plan to Richard. The plot plan showed a 20-foot side yard, which complied with minimum requirements of the zoning regulations. After taking possession of the house, however, Richard discovered that the building was, in fact, only 18 feet from the property line. Richard claimed that he

relied on the representations of the developer, who should have known that the property did not meet the zoning requirements. Richard sought damages for the misrepresentation. Should he recover? (*Richard v. Waldman and Sons, Inc.*, 155 Conn. 343, 232 A.2d 307)

3. Defendant Darigold Farms was one of a number of dairies which submitted bids to supply 1.5 million half pints of milk to the plaintiff, Clover Park School District. Its low bid was $.07013 per half pint; the next lowest bid was $.072. A usually reliable Darigold secretary had seen pencilled figures on a bid form and had erroneously typed them in the bid. The figures were actually the previous year's low price. Because the manager was away at the time, the bid was submitted without review. When the bids were opened on May 25, Darigold's manager immediately recognized the error and on the same day notified Clover Park, asking that the bid be rejected. Nevertheless, it was accepted by the school board on June 11. Darigold's lawyer told Clover Park that Darigold could not supply the milk at the bid price, but that Foremost Dairies would. Then Foremost backed out and Darigold persuaded Sanitary Cloverleaf Dairy to take over. It supplied milk until October, when it became insolvent and went out of business. Clover Park then sued Darigold for breach of contract. Decide. (*Clover Park School District v. Consolidated Dairy Products Co.-Darigold Farms*, 550 P.2d 47, Wash.)

4. The defendant contracted to buy 125 bales of Surat cotton from the plaintiff. It was agreed by both parties that the goods were to arrive on the ship *Peerless* from Bombay, India. Unknown to either party, however, there were two ships named *Peerless* sailing from Bombay. The defendant meant the *Peerless* which sailed in October. The plaintiff meant the *Peerless* which sailed in December. When the plaintiff's *Peerless* arrived with the cotton, the defendant refused to accept it. The plaintiff sued for damages. Who should win and why? (*Raffles v. Wichelhaus*, 159 Eng. Rep. 375)

5. In 1971, using modern technology, Treasure Salvors Inc., located a Spanish ship on the ocean bottom in 55 feet of water about 46 miles off the Florida coast. The ship, the *Nuestra Senora de Atocha*, sunk in a hurricane while heading from Havana to Spain in 1622. It was carrying "a treasure worthy of Midas: 160 gold bullion pieces, 900 silver ingots, over 250,000 silver coins, 600 copper planks, 350 chests of indigo and 25 tons of tobacco." On the mistaken assumption that the seabed where the *Atocha* lay was state land, Treasure Salvors made a series of contracts with Florida whereby the state was to receive 25 percent of all items recovered. After the U.S. Supreme Court, in another case, had decided that the continental shelf where the ship rested was federal land, Treasure Salvors sued to rescind its contracts with Florida and to recover all items as the exclusive owner of the *Atocha*. Decide. (*State of Florida, Department of State v. Treasure Salvors Inc.*, 621 F.2d 1340)

SPECIAL SECTION:
How to Become an Attorney

If this course and other contacts with the law and legal professionals spark a desire in you to pursue a career as an attorney, now is a good time to start planning. While in high school, take courses in English, political science, and history. If available, take specialized courses dealing with legal issues and perspectives. Latin will improve your command of English and provide some useful understanding of legal terminology. Be aware that although a college degree is a prerequisite for admission to many law schools, some schools allow you to combine your senior year in college with your first year in law school. This reduces from seven to six the years of formal higher educational preparation necessary for entry into the profession. Being an undergraduate at a given university sometimes helps in obtaining admission to that institution's law school.

During your college years, a concentration in liberal arts and fundamental business courses will assist your future performance in law school and beyond. In addition, many undergraduate institutions offer courses which complement courses offered in most law schools. Advice on identifying such courses and other valuable assistance can be obtained through participation in any prelaw club or similar organization on campus.

Most law schools reduce the number of applicants who are acceptable candidates for admission by setting minimum standards for grade point averages and scores on the Law School Admission Test (LSAT). The LSAT is a standardized exam which tests a person's aptitude for the study of law.

In law school, a student will be required to take certain basic courses in contracts, torts, and crimes, as well as courses in property, wills, trusts and estates, legal procedure, evidence, and constitutional law. The student may also choose courses which may lead to specialization in a particular field, such as labor law, family law, or tax law.

Law school graduates cannot practice law until they pass the bar exam in the state where they intend to practice. Because most law schools do not emphasize the law of any particular state but instead concentrate on imparting general principles, most law school graduates must take a bar exam preparation course before taking the exam.

Upon passing the bar exam, each potential practitioner's record is examined by a committee of the state bar to ensure that the person is of sound character. Typically, any felony convictions will prevent the applicant from being admitted to practice.

13

Proper Contractual Form

1. A customer in a restaurant accidentally lodged a piece of food in his windpipe and became unconscious. A licensed surgeon on the scene performed an emergency tracheotomy by cutting into the windpipe to let air pass below the blockage. Although no promise to pay for this emergency operation was made, is the surgeon entitled to collect for her services?

2. A dealer tries to persuade you, a minor, to buy an electronic musical instrument with twelve instrumental voices and twelve digital rhythms. The price is $299 plus carrying charges. You finally sign the installment contract after the dealer orally promises that you can return the instrument if you cannot learn to play it. Can you hold the dealer to this promise?

3. You receive a check on which the amount is shown in figures as "$89." However, the amount is spelled out in words as "ninety-eight dollars." Which amount is payable?

MUST CONTRACTS BE IN ANY SPECIAL FORM?

PROBLEM: De Frank orally agreed to buy a mini-warehouse from Stein. Over the telephone, De Frank then persuaded Keith to promise to lend $100,000, which De Frank needed for the down payment on the purchase price. A *mortgage* (claim on the property) was to be given to Keith as security for the loan. De Frank and Stein then signed the sales contract. Early the next day, De Frank was stunned when Keith said that the loan could not be made as promised. Can De Frank force Keith to make the loan? Is the sales contract with Stein enforceable?

Unless a particular form is required by statute, contracts may be oral or written. They may even be implied from conduct. Most contracts are oral. Many of those are made by telephone. Others are made and carried out in a single face-to-face conversation. For example, in the sale of goods, payment by buyer and delivery by seller often occur when the agreement is made. A person may take a job, rent an apartment, and enter many other business agreements without the formality of a written contract. Sometimes conduct alone is sufficient. For example, a person may hail a bus, board it, deposit the proper coins, and later get off. No words are spoken or written by either passenger or driver, yet there is a valid contract.

There are, however, certain important kinds of contracts which will not be enforced in court unless some properly signed writing proves their existence. For example, contracts to transfer an interest in real property (land or objects permanently attached to the land) must be in writing. Thus, the written agreement between Stein and De Frank is enforceable. However, the oral agreement between Stein and De Frank is not enforceable. Also, the oral agreement between Keith and De Frank would not be enforceable. The two oral agreements pertained to an interest in real property—one an agreement to buy a building, the other an agreement giving a mortgage on the building. Thus, they were insufficient because they were not in writing and properly signed.

Even when a written contract is not required by law, it is often wise to put the agreement in writing and have a signed copy for each party. This is particularly true if the agreement is complex and contains many details which could lead to later misunderstandings. It also is important when large sums of money or long periods of time are involved. In such cases, it is advantageous for both parties to express their intentions with reasonable precision in written form. In this way, the agreement can be easily referred to or readily proved if necessary. The chance of later confusion or disagreement is greatly reduced. Neither party can effectively deny having agreed to particular terms. Also, the process of putting ideas into writing encourages the parties to anticipate and provide for problems that could arise later. It is usually easier to settle such matters before either party signs and while both parties are inclined to compromise in order to conclude the agreement. Later, each party tends to demand strict performance of the terms. Of course, whenever appropriate, prudent persons seek the aid of a lawyer in the preparation or review of important contracts.

HOW ARE CONTRACTS CLASSIFIED?

PROBLEM: Rissan walked into a telephone booth, dropped some coins into the telephone, and dialed a number. No words were spoken until the party answered. A conversation followed between Rissan and the party. A few minutes later Rissan hung up the receiver and left. What kind of contract had Rissan made with the telephone company?

Contracts can be classified as either unilateral or bilateral, according to whether one or both parties make a promise. Contracts also can be classified according to enforceability as valid, voidable, unenforceable, or void. The following classifications are also important:

1. Method of Creation

The way a contract comes into being gives some idea of its nature. Thus, there are express contracts, implied contracts, and quasi contracts.

express contract: contract in which the agreement is stated in written or spoken words

Express contracts. In an **express contract**, the agreement is stated in words—written or spoken. For example, upon graduation from high school, Upham agrees in a written contract to work as a carpenter's apprentice for three years.

implied contract: contract in which intent is shown by conduct and circumstances

Implied contracts. In an **implied contract**, the agreement is not stated in words. Instead, the intent of the parties is shown by their conduct and by the surrounding circumstances. For example, Prout buys some fruit juice in the high school cafeteria by inserting coins into a vending machine.

quasi contract: circumstances under which the parties are bound as in a valid contract to prevent unjust enrichment

Quasi contracts. In a **quasi contract**, the parties are bound as though there were a valid contract even though technically there is none. Thus, the law creates an obligation in the absence of an actual agreement between the parties. This is done to prevent unjust enrichment of one party. Strictly speaking, no contract exists because some essential element is missing. For example, a minor who lacks capacity to contract will be held liable for the reasonable value of necessaries purchased (see Chapter 12). Otherwise the minor would be unjustly enriched at the expense of the seller. Similarly, a doctor may voluntarily give first aid to a skier who is knocked unconscious in an accident. There is no agreement. Yet the doctor may submit a bill and collect a charge reasonable for such a professional service. Someone who is not a doctor could give similar first aid yet not be entitled to payment since the service is not done with the expectation of payment nor by a licensed specialist.

2. Formality

A few contracts must meet strict requirements as to formality. They are called formal contracts. Most need not meet such requirements. They are called simple contracts.

formal contract: written contract that must be in a special form to be enforceable

Formal contracts. A **formal contract** is a written contract that must be in some special form to be enforceable. Examples are commercial paper and contracts under seal. Commercial paper, such as an ordinary check, must meet certain requirements to be valid. A contract under seal is one with a seal attached or with a similar impression made on the paper. Seals served to validate agreements years ago, when few people could read or write. Today, in most states, the legal effect of the seal on contracts has been limited or ended.

simple contract: contract that is not formal

Simple contracts. A contract that is not formal is a **simple contract**. This is true whether the contract is oral, written, or based on conduct. Figure 13-1 is an example of a simple, written contract.

3. Extent of Performance

Contracts can be classified as either executed or executory, according to whether or not they have been completed. Many contracts are performed almost immediately; others require days, months, or years to complete. Many life insurance contracts are not completed for decades.

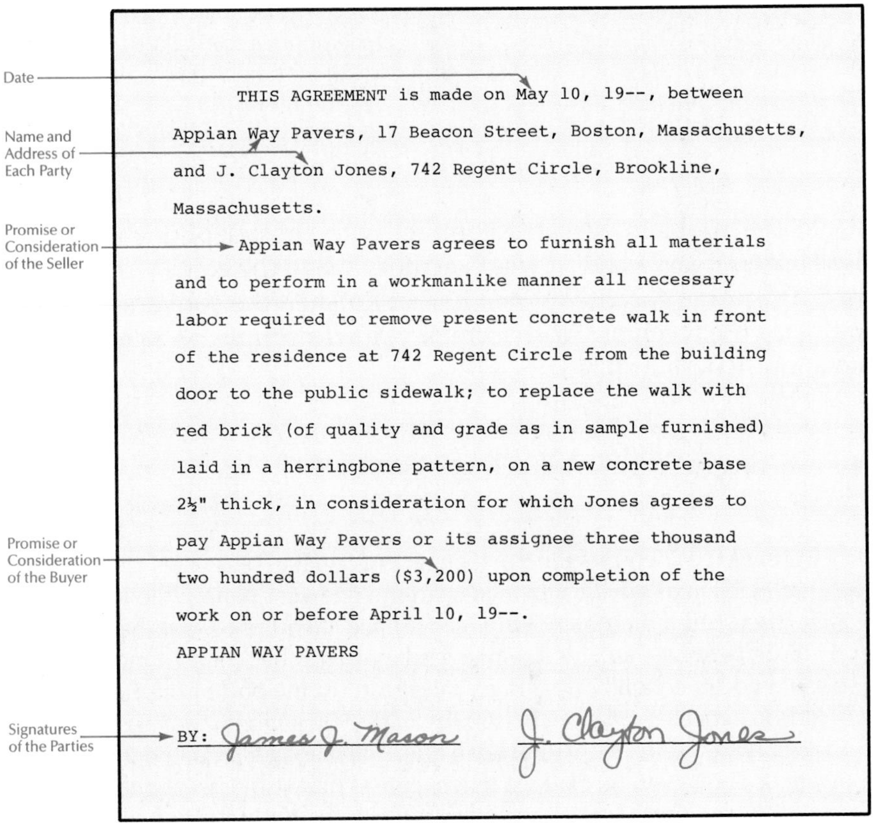
THIS AGREEMENT is made on May 10, 19--, between Appian Way Pavers, 17 Beacon Street, Boston, Massachusetts, and J. Clayton Jones, 742 Regent Circle, Brookline, Massachusetts.

Appian Way Pavers agrees to furnish all materials and to perform in a workmanlike manner all necessary labor required to remove present concrete walk in front of the residence at 742 Regent Circle from the building door to the public sidewalk; to replace the walk with red brick (of quality and grade as in sample furnished) laid in a herringbone pattern, on a new concrete base 2½" thick, in consideration for which Jones agrees to pay Appian Way Pavers or its assignee three thousand two hundred dollars ($3,200) upon completion of the work on or before April 10, 19--.

APPIAN WAY PAVERS

BY: James J. Mason   J. Clayton Jones

Figure 13-1. Simple, Written Contract

Executed contracts. An **executed contract** is one that has been fully performed. Both parties have done all they promised to do.

executed contract: contract that has been fully performed

You order a five-dish, carryout Chinese dinner at the Forbidden City Cafe. When the meal is ready, you give the cashier the purchase price and receive five cartons of food in an insulated bag. This is an executed contract because it has been fully performed by both parties.

Executory contracts. An **executory contract** is one that has not been fully performed. Something as agreed upon remains to be done by one or both of the parties.

executory contract: contract that has not been fully performed

Peg and Paul Patman ordered a "Treat of the Month" from a mail-order company in the Pacific Northwest. They paid $135 by check which the seller, World Delights, had cashed. In December, a fruitcake had been delivered. During each of the following eleven months a different "Treat" was to be delivered. The contract will be executory until all promised treats are delivered. Then it will be classified as an executed contract.

In the problem Rissan's contract with the telephone company was bilateral and valid. It was executory when the coins were deposited. It became executed when Rissan finished the conversation and hung up the receiver. As to formality, it was simple; as to method of creation, it was implied.

WHAT IS THE STATUTE OF FRAUDS?

PROBLEM: When the general manager of Special-Teas Sales Company hired Hudson as advertising manager for a five-year period, the two parties discussed the terms of employment and then they shook hands. As Hudson later recalled, his beginning salary was to be $3,000 a month but would go up annually if, and as, sales rose. At the end of the first year, Hudson expected a pay increase of at least $500 a month, but his pay did not increase at all. He threatened to quit. The manager admitted that sales were up; however, he claimed that expenses had also risen and therefore profits were down. He threatened to sue Hudson for breach of contract if he actually left. How could their misunderstanding have been avoided?

An important purpose of business law is to protect and assist persons in their business dealings. One such way is to create awareness that certain types of agreements be evidenced by a signed writing in order to be enforceable. A writing is more reliable proof of an executory agreement than is oral testimony based on memory. Also, a writing is not affected by the death or absence of witnesses. In addition, a writing helps to prevent dishonest persons from intentionally misrepresenting the facts and it prevents honest but forgetful persons from innocently doing so. Thus, the dispute between Hudson and Special-Teas could have been avoided if their contract had been in the form of a signed writing with all important terms clearly spelled out.

Years ago, injustices arising from the failure of memory or from intentional misrepresentation were frequently found in court cases involving certain kinds of important oral contracts. Sometimes parties would lie under oath—although perjury is a crime, it was difficult to prove. To help prevent such injustices, and for certain procedural reasons, England adopted a remedial statute in 1677. The statute required that certain agreements be in writing and be signed by the party against whom the contract was to be enforced in court: the defendant in the action. Because the statute was designed to prevent frauds and perjuries, it was called the Statute of Frauds and Perjuries. The name **statute of frauds** is now commonly used to designate statutes enacted by all states which require certain contracts to be evidenced by a signed writing in order to be enforceable in court.

statute of frauds: law requiring certain contracts to be in writing and signed by the defendant in order to be enforceable

Thus, you should always get the other party's signature on important contracts. Note that sometimes one party will wisely postpone signing to gain more time to think about the deal.

> Treen made an offer in writing to sell her house to Barrol. Barrol orally agreed to buy but had not yet signed; therefore, he is not bound. However, Treen would be bound if Barrol accepted the offer. Barrol could accept by signing the contract at any time before Treen revokes her offer.

The statute of frauds does not prevent the voluntary performance of oral agreements that should have been in writing. It has no effect on oral agreements which have been fully performed. After all, contracts subject to the statute are not illegal if oral; they are simply not enforceable. Courts will not enforce oral contracts when the statute of frauds requires that they be in writing.

WHAT CONTRACTS ARE SUBJECT TO THE STATUTE OF FRAUDS?

> **PROBLEM:** Parker and Ashberg were good friends. When they graduated from high school, both were eighteen. They planned to marry, but first wanted to become financially secure. So they shook hands and agreed to become partners in operating a small, fast-food stand at the county fair. "This is just the beginning," Parker said. "Till death do us part!" both said. Are they legally bound to remain partners in business until one dies?

To be enforceable under the statute of frauds, six important types of executory contracts must be in writing and signed by the party against whom the contract is to be enforced. As an alternative, the contract must be provable by some other writing, such as a letter signed by such party. Obviously, since either party might later want to sue the other in case of breach, good business practice calls for both parties to sign.

Contracts subject to the statute of frauds include those to:

1. buy and sell goods for a price of $500 or more;[1]
2. buy and sell real property or any interest in real property;
3. do something that cannot be performed within a year;
4. pay the debt or answer for a legal obligation of another person;
5. give something of value in return for a promise of marriage;
6. be personally liable for a debt of an estate of someone who has died.

1. A Contract for the Sale of Goods for $500 or More

PROBLEM: Brandon bought a new car and wanted to sell her old car. She advertised in the local paper and Smythe agreed to buy the car for $885. He promised to pay for it when he received his paycheck in two weeks and to take delivery then. Must this contract be in writing to be enforceable?

To be enforceable, a contract for the sale of goods (tangible personal property) for $500 or more would usually have to be a signed writing or a signed agreement. (Exceptions to this requirement are discussed in Chapter 16.) The writing would need to be signed by the person against whom enforcement was sought. In the problem, if Brandon refused to sell, Smythe could enforce the agreement only if Brandon had signed a written agreement. Likewise, if Smythe refused to buy, Brandon could collect damages only if Smythe had signed.

2. A Contract to Sell or a Sale of Any Interest in Real Property

PROBLEM: The Maiers orally agreed to sell their mountain cabin, and Harrell orally agreed to buy it. The price agreed upon was $8,950. Sup-

[1]All states except Louisiana have adopted the $500 figure specified by the UCC. Also, in Louisiana, there is no requirement for a writing.

pose that before the contract is executed, the Maiers get a better offer from someone else. Or suppose they simply change their minds about the sale. Could Harrell still hold them to their promise to sell for the agreed-upon price?

The transfer, or promise of transfer, of any interest in real property must be in writing to be enforceable. (Note that real property includes land, buildings, and other things permanently attached to land; personal property includes all other property.)

Thus, there should be written evidence of contracts to transfer title to the entire property. Likewise, transfers of lesser interests, such as the right to remove oil or timber from land, must be in writing. Leases also come under this classification. However, most states have special statutes which provide that oral leases for a period of one year or less are enforceable. In some states, an agreement authorizing or employing an agent (see Unit 6) to buy or sell land must also be in writing.

In the problem, unless the agreement is evidenced by a writing signed by the Maiers, Harrell cannot hold them to the oral contract. Similarly, if Harrell changes his mind, he cannot be held to the agreement unless it is in writing and he has signed it. As an exception to the general rule, a court will enforce the oral contract if the buyer has also done all of the following:

a. made partial payment,
b. occupied or possessed the land, and
c. made substantial improvements to the land.

3. A Contract That Cannot Be Performed within One Year after Being Made

PROBLEM: Late in March, Borger, personnel manager of Data Dash Data, Inc., orally promised Westerman a job in the information processing department of the company. The job was to be for a year at $1,000 a month plus benefits. It was to begin a month after Westerman received his diploma in June from the Civic Center High School. Westerman, still a minor, discussed the offer with his parents. The next day, he telephoned Borger and accepted the offer. Later, Borger refused to employ Westerman. Was the contract enforceable by either party?

A contract which cannot be performed within a year from the time it is made will not be enforced by courts unless there is a signed writing or a signed memorandum of the agreement. The year is figured from the time the contract is made, not from the time performance is to begin. Accordingly, the oral agreement in the problem was not enforceable against Data Dash Data or its agent, Borger. Nor could the company enforce it against Westerman. The fact that Westerman was a minor did not affect the outcome of this case. Had there been a written contract, however, only Westerman could have avoided it.

This time provision does not apply to agreements that can be executed within a year. This is true even if such agreements are not actually carried out within that time. The test is not whether the agreement is actually performed within a year but whether there is a possibility of performance within a year. To illustrate, two persons shake hands and orally agree to be business partners. But they don't say for how long. Because either partner may legally quit within a year, their agreement need not be in writing. On the other hand, their partnership could last indefinitely.

Thus, in the problem on page 237, the partnership agreement between Parker and Ashberg did not have to be in writing. That is because the agreement was for an indefinite time that could be less than one year. Although they said, "Till death do us part," either might die within a year. Because the agreement was for an indefinite time, either partner could withdraw at any time, "at will," without liability to the other for breach of contract. Of course, it is always wise to prepare a contract to form a partnership very carefully and to put it in writing. That is because of the complexity of a partnership as well as the amount of money and potentially long time involved.

4. A Contract to Pay a Debt or Answer for the Legal Obligation of Another Person

PROBLEM: Rinozzi wished to buy an electric guitar for $495 from the Big Bands Music Shop. He lacked cash, and his credit rating was poor. Amaro, a professional music instructor, told the music store owner, "Rinozzi has a rare talent. He will soon earn the full price. But if he doesn't pay when payments are due, I will." If Big Bands sells the guitar on credit and Rinozzi later fails to pay, is Amaro liable for the balance due?

One provision of the statute of frauds requires a writing for a promise to answer for the debt or default of another person (see Unit 5). In the problem, Amaro's promise in unenforceable. That is because it is not in writing and signed by him. On the other hand, if Amaro had said, "Sell the guitar to Rinozzi, and I will pay you," it would be a direct, primary promise to the seller. Amaro would therefore be liable even if this promise was oral.

Sometimes a third party is liable under an oral promise to pay another's debt, but only if the payment serves the promisor's own financial interest. Thus, a buyer of a house under construction is anxious to see it completed. He orally promises to pay a lumberyard for continuation of supplies when the general contractor falls behind in payments. The home buyer is legally bound, even though the contractor remains primarily liable.

5. A Contract for Which the Consideration Is Marriage

PROBLEM: Jim had a long conversation with his girlfriend, Rita, in the presence of her elderly father. Jim solemnly promised Rita and her father that if Rita would marry him, he would support the father if that ever became necessary. Rita agreed, and the couple married. Is Jim's promise enforceable?

A writing is required for agreements in which marriage is the consideration for a promise to pay money or to give valuable consideration to the offeree or to some third party if the offeree marries as requested. It is sometimes made by a parent of the woman or man contemplating marriage. It does not refer to mutual promises of persons to marry. In the problem, Jim's oral promise was not enforceable.

In some states, mutual promises to marry are enforceable, but the trend is to ban such suits for damages. Generally, however, if the man breaches his promise to marry, the woman may keep the engagement ring. If the woman breaches, the ring must be returned. Ordinary gifts from one another need not be returned.

6. A Contract by an Executor or Administrator to Be Personally Liable for Claims against the Estate of a Deceased Person

PROBLEM: Lando was executrix and principal beneficiary of her father's estate. At the time of his death, the father owed his friend Clifton $2,500.

Clifton urgently needed the money, but probate court rules would have delayed payment for at least six months. Therefore Clifton offered to accept $2,000 in full settlement if the amount would be paid immediately. Lando agreed in writing to pay Clifton immediately out of her own funds. Is this promise enforceable?

An *executor* (called *executrix* if female) is one named in a will to settle affairs of a deceased person. The executor pays the debts and distributes the rest of the estate according to the terms of the will. If there is no will, the court appoints an *administrator (administratrix)* to do the necessary work. The court also appoints someone if the will doesn't name an executor. Such personal representatives are not personally liable for debts of the deceased person unless they expressly agree in a signed writing to pay. Thus, in the problem, Lando is personally liable for payment of Clifton's claim against her father's estate, since she agreed in writing to pay.

WHAT TYPE OF WRITING IS REQUIRED?

PROBLEM: In June, Bachman orally agreed to sell to Caruso Commodities Company the entire next harvest of wheat from his 640-acre farm. He agreed to sell the wheat at the current market price. Later, he changed his mind and wrote to Caruso, "Complications force me to alter plans for the sale of my wheat crop. I will not be able to let you have my harvest at the June price as we discussed. It's a good year. Therefore I trust you'll get all the wheat you can handle from other sources." Bachman then signed his name to the writing. Was this writing sufficient to allow Caruso to enforce the oral contract against Bachman?

In most states, a memorandum satisfies the writing requirement of the statute of frauds for evidence of an agreement. Usually any words that clearly state the important terms of the agreement suffice. Note, however, that the memorandum is enforceable only against those who have signed it. Thus, in the problem, the letter Bachman wrote would actually prove the existence of the agreement to sell his wheat to Caruso. Bachman is bound.

The memorandum need not be in any special form. Nor does it have to be a single writing. A series of writings, such as an exchange of letters or telegrams, is sufficient if it includes all essential terms. Also, the later writings must refer to earlier writings in such a way that they are clearly part of the same agreement. The memorandum may be printed, typed, or written with pen or pencil. The signature may be written, stamped, engraved, or printed. It may consist of any mark that is intended as a signature. An adequate memorandum includes the following items:

1. date and place of the contract;
2. names of the parties;
3. all material terms of the agreement. These usually include the subject matter, price, and any special conditions, such as time or method of delivery or terms of payment (However, in the case of a sale of goods, the UCC provides that the memorandum need only state a quantity of described goods which are involved and indicate that there has been a related sale.); and
4. the signature of the party against whom the contract is to be enforced. This signature may be by an agent authorized to sign.

These items do not need to be in any particular order. If custom or business usage is well established, some items may be excluded. For example, such items as terms of payment and delivery, even price, are often omitted from orders for goods. The Uniform Commercial Code permits this because such items are governed by trade usage or custom.

WHAT IS THE PAROL EVIDENCE RULE?

> **PROBLEM:** Highman bought a new personal computer from Advance Electronics. She signed the store's usual contract, which stated the terms completely. Later, Highman alleged that as part of the bargain, the salesperson orally promised that if the factory list price was reduced within two months, he would refund the same amount to Highman. The factory list price was reduced, but Advance Electronics refused to pass the savings on to Highman. What were Highman's rights?

The parol evidence rule applies whenever parties put their agreement in writing, whether or not a writing is required under the statute of frauds. With certain exceptions, under the **parol evidence rule** the writing itself is the only evidence allowed in court to prove the terms of a written contract if the writing appears to be the complete agreement between the parties.

parol evidence rule: rule that bars use of prior written or spoken words to alter a written contract which appears to be complete

The parol evidence rule bars evidence of prior or contemporaneous (made at the same time) oral or written agreements related to the written contract being disputed if these agreements were not mentioned or included in the written contract. Under the rule, such evidence is generally not allowed to add to, subtract from, or otherwise change the written contract. The court presumes that when the parties reduced their agreement to writing, they included all essential terms and intended to exclude all previous agreements. Accordingly, the written contract is held to be the only evidence of their intent. In the problem, therefore, Highman loses. She probably could not prove that the salesperson's promise was ever made. All important terms of the agreement were presumably included in the written contract.

In the interests of justice, however, the trial judge will sometimes permit parol evidence to be introduced to prove certain things. These include mistake, fraud, illegality, custom and trade usage, clerical errors, and the meaning of terms. Also, when a contract is obviously ambiguous, parol evidence may be used to clarify terms to determine the true intent of the parties. Such evidence does not change the writing. Instead, it explains the meaning of the writing or shows that there never was any enforceable contract.

HOW ARE WRITTEN CONTRACTS INTERPRETED?

PROBLEM: Milo contracted with Corrigan for the installation of a complete burglar alarm system for $2,900. The printed contract provided that Milo was to pay $900 down and the balance at $100 a month for twenty months. Failure to pay any installment when due would accelerate the debt and make the entire balance due. The payments were to be made on the first day of each month. Milo explained that he did not receive his paycheck until the tenth. Therefore, he said, he would prefer to make the payments on that date. Corrigan agreed and in the margin wrote in "tenth," and initialed it on Milo's copy only. During the first month, Corrigan demanded the full balance when Milo failed to make the payment on the first day. Is Corrigan entitled to the full balance immediately?

Even when the parties put their contract in writing, something in the contract may not be quite clear or may require interpretation. This is frequently the case when standardized, printed order blanks are used. It also occurs when printed contract forms with blank spaces are used. In the completion of the forms, some contradictory terms may be added. Moreover, words do not always have the same meaning to different persons. One person may use a term that seems perfectly clear but which may mean something quite different to another party.

Annually, in millions of transactions, consumers buy, borrow, and lease goods and services. Usually the consumers are asked to accept and sign what amounts to a contract of adhesion. These are contracts, such as credit purchases and life insurance policies, prepared by the stronger party with the help of their lawyers to favor their own interests. Generally such contracts are not subject to modification; the consumer must "take it or leave it." Understandably, in disputes over the meaning of the language in such contracts, courts favor the party who did not prepare the document. Another helpful development is the requirement by statute in some states that the language of consumer contracts be clear, simple, and understandable to the average person.

Generally courts seek to determine and to enforce the intent of the parties by applying the following rules of interpretation to written contracts:

1. The Writing Is to Be Considered as a Single, Whole Document

Each clause is interpreted in the light of all other provisions of the contract. Words are interpreted as they are ordinarily used unless circumstances indicate a different meaning. Legal and other technical terms or abbreviations are given their technical meaning unless the contract as a whole shows that a different meaning is intended.

2. Where a Printed Form Is Used, Added Typewritten Provisions Will Prevail over Contradictory Printed Provisions, and Added Handwritten Ones Will Prevail over Both Printed and Typewritten Ones

An individual's typewriting *supersedes* (replaces) printing because it presumably represents that person's most recent intentions. Similarly, handwriting prevails over both printing and typewriting. Thus, in the problem, Milo's payments were not due until the tenth of the month. The handwritten change to that effect made by Corrigan on Milo's copy of the contract superseded the printed version. It was not essential that Milo add his initials because he was the party benefitted by the change. He could, and undoubtedly would, add his initials if requested or if the validity of the change were challenged. It is, nevertheless, good preventive law practice to have both parties initial all changes and to do this on all copies of the contract.

3. If Words and Figures Are Inconsistent, the Words Will Prevail

One is less likely to make a mistake in writing out a number in words than writing it in figures. Thus, words prevail over figures.

4. Where There Is a Custom or Trade Practice Which Applies, Both Parties Will Be Presumed to Know It, and the Contract Will Be Interpreted in Light of That Custom or Trade Practice

Many contracts include certain terms that are implied because of custom or as a matter of reasonableness and propriety. Thus, a clause requiring "payment in cash" usually may be satisfied by check. Services promised are to be performed with reasonable care and skill even though nothing is said about these subjects. When no time is specified for performance, a reasonable time is allowed. Parties are always expected to act legally and fairly. When securities are bought and sold by telephone, the transfers may be made almost immediately. Sometimes, appropriate certificates are supplied many days later.

By telephone, Swann ordered delivery of the *Daily Tribune* newspaper. He correctly assumed that he would be billed by mail at the end of the month. As was customary, the bill was then payable ten days after receipt.

PREVENTING LEGAL DIFFICULTIES

When You Enter a Contract. . .

1. if a contract is complex or involves much time or money, put it in writing even when not required by the statute of frauds. Be sure the words are understandable, cover all important contingencies, and clearly reflect your intentions. When appropriate, consult a qualified lawyer;
2. if a prepared contract is presented to you for signature, read it carefully, especially if it is a contract of adhesion;

3. insist on definition and explanation of any terms of the contract which you do not understand. Make necessary changes, or reject the entire contract;
4. make sure that all changes are written into the contract on all copies as well as on the original, and that all changes are initialled by both parties;
5. be sure your entire agreement is included in the writing. The parol evidence rule may bar evidence of all prior and contemporaneous oral or written agreements; and
6. when any payments have been made in cash, be sure to get a receipt if payment is not acknowledged in the contract. (If payments are made by check, indicate the purpose on the face of the check. The canceled check will serve as your receipt.)

Strengthening Your Legal Vocabulary

executed contract
executory contract
express contract
formal contract
implied contract
parol evidence rule
quasi contract
simple contract
statute of frauds

1. Rule under which a written contract cannot be changed by prior oral or written agreements.
2. Contract in which the agreement of the parties is spoken or written.
3. Written contract that must be in a special form to be enforceable.
4. Contract that has been fully performed.
5. Any contract that is not a formal contract.
6. Contract in which intent of the parties is shown by conduct or circumstances.
7. Obligation that is enforced as if it were a contract in order to prevent unjust enrichment of one party.
8. Law stating that certain agreements are not enforceable unless they are in writing and are signed by the party against whom the contract is to be enforced.
9. Contract that has not been fully performed.

Reviewing Important Points

1. Unless required by law, contracts need not be in writing.
2. An express contract is stated in words, written or spoken. An implied contract is shown by conduct of the parties and by surrounding circumstances.
3. A formal contract must be in some special, written form. All contracts which are not formal contracts are simple contracts.

4. An executory contract has not been fully performed. An executed contract has been completed by both parties.
5. A quasi contract exists when some element of a valid contract is missing, yet the arrangement is enforced as if it were a contract. This is done to prevent unjust enrichment of one party.
6. To be enforceable, the following contracts must be in writing (or evidenced by some other written proof) and signed by the party against whom enforcement is sought:
   (a) contracts to buy and sell goods for a price of $500 or more,
   (b) contracts to buy and sell real property or any interest in real property,
   (c) contracts that cannot be performed within one year after being made,
   (d) contracts to pay a debt or answer for a legal obligation of another person,
   (e) contracts having marriage as the consideration, and
   (f) contracts of an executor or administrator to be personally liable for the debts of an estate.
7. A memorandum of an agreement need not be in any special form. However, it must contain all the material facts and must be signed by the party against whom the contract is to be enforced.
8. The terms of a written contract may not be changed by parol evidence unless the writing is clearly ambiguous. Parol evidence may also be used to show that a written agreement is not binding because of mistake, fraud, or illegality.

Applying Law to Everyday Life

1. Vancura and Trickett are competent adults. Under a written contract, Vancura bought Trickett's motor scooter for $800. Vancura gave Trickett a check for $300 as a down payment and took delivery of the scooter. On the way home, Vancura bought some gas at a self-service station. She then got a soft drink from a vending machine. What kinds of contracts were these?

2. Bruno bought Hummel's condominium under a written contract. The title was to be transferred in 30 days. Bruno then orally agreed to buy most of Hummel's furniture for the lump sum of $2,800. When she took possession of the condo, Bruno told Hummel she had changed her mind about buying the furniture. Can Hummel enforce the furniture deal?

3. Central-Cal Lands Corporation orally agreed to sell a 640-acre producing ranch to Ceres, Inc., for $1,280,000. Ceres paid $25,000 and immediately took possession. (a) Can Central-Cal legally withdraw from the agreement? (b) Suppose Ceres proceeds to spend $75,000 to level part of the land for improved irrigation purposes. Can Ceres now enforce the oral contract?

4. Kelley was admitted to University Hospital as an emergency heart transplant patient. The next day, the business manager discussed the cost of the surgery

with Kelley's two sons. Both sons told the manager, "Do whatever is necessary to save his life, and we will pay you." When the hospital presented the staggering bill to the junior Kelleys, they said the contract was oral and, therefore, they were not liable. A promise to pay the debt of another (their father) had to be in writing. Is that true?

5. Robert told Barbara, "If you marry me, I can't give you a yacht or a castle in Spain, but I will deed to you a one-half interest in 75 cows, 200 hogs, 5,000 chickens, and the farm I've spent ten years improving: Meadowland Acres." Barbara was impressed and persuaded. She said "Yes" and married Robert. Is his promise legally enforceable?

6. In a detailed, written purchase contract, Trans-Continental Supply Corporation, a food distributor, agreed to buy a large quantity of beet sugar from Col-Rocky Mountaineers. Some sugar was delivered, but then Col-Rocky stopped all shipments. It claimed that Trans-Continental had breached an oral promise to make advance cash payments. Trans-Continental denied making the promise, and sued Col-Rocky for breach of contract. At the trial, Col-Rocky sought to introduce evidence of the alleged oral promise. Can it do so?

7. Silvio Development Co. bought an insurance policy to cover the risk of damage to their corporate helicopter. For coverage, the standard printed insurance policy required that every pilot of the plane be licensed by the Federal Aviation Agency (FAA) and have a minimum of 500 logged (recorded by the pilot) flying hours. A typewritten addition specified that every pilot had to have a minimum of 200 logged helicopter flying hours. When the plane crashed, the pilot had logged only 75 helicopter flying hours. However, she was FAA licensed and had logged over 2,000 flying hours in conventional planes. Must the insurance company pay?

Solving Case Problems

1. Between 1964 and 1973, Kiyosi served as a teaching associate and lecturer at Indiana University, Bloomington. Meanwhile, he continued to study and write to qualify for a Ph.D. degree. He relied on an oral promise by the defendant university that he would be appointed to a permanent position with perpetual renewals, starting at the rank of Assistant Professor upon obtaining the degree. It was customary for the university to make such appointments for terms of three years. When Kiyosi received his Ph.D. in 1973, he was appointed Assistant Professor, but was told that he would not be reappointed for the following year of 1974-75. He then sued for damages for breach of contract. The university officials claimed that his action was barred by the statute of frauds because a lifetime contract cannot be performed within one year. Decide. (*Kiyosi v. The Trustees of Indiana University*, 166 Ind. App. 34, 333 N.E.2d 886)

2. Hanan had been employed as a management consultant by Corning Glass Works for almost two years. On March 14, 1966, after two months of negotiations, Corning entered into an oral agreement to employ Hanan for a third year. The third year was to begin on May 1, 1966, at an annual salary of $25,000. Because this agreement could not be performed within a year, it was void and unenforceable under the statute of frauds. However, Hanan argued that he had already been employed for two years and had then continued on the job for twelve days into the third year. He admitted that there was only an oral contract for the third year. But he claimed that there was a contract implied in fact from the conduct of the parties, and that therefore the statute of frauds did not apply. Decide. (*Hanan v. Corning Glass Works*, 35 A.D. 2d 697, 314 N.Y.S. 2d 804)

3. Unit, Inc., was the general contractor for a real estate development owned by Sciota Park, Ltd. Unit subcontracted to plaintiff Wilson Floors Company the job of furnishing and installing flooring materials. When Unit fell behind in making promised payments for completed work, Wilson stopped work. The Pittsburgh National Bank had already loaned seven million dollars to Sciota for the project, which was now two-thirds completed. The bank representatives orally assured Wilson that if it returned to work, it would be paid. Wilson did so and finished the job. When it was not paid, it sued Unit, Sciota Park, and the Pittsburgh Bank for the $15,443.06, plus interest. It received judgment. When Sciota and Unit failed to pay, Wilson sought recovery from the bank. But the bank claimed it was not liable because a promise to pay another's debt had to be in writing. Decide. (*Wilson Floors Co. v. Sciota Park, Ltd., et al.*, 54 Ohio St. 2d 451, 377 N.E.2d 514)

4. For safekeeping, Kula deposited $18,300 with the cashier of a hotel casino and was given a receipt for the money. Kula and a friend, Goldfinger, gambled in the hotel's casino. (Casino gambling is legal in Nevada.) Kula made withdrawals and deposits from time to time with the casino cashier and at the time had a balance of $18,000. One evening Goldfinger lost $500 in gambling and was unable to pay it. He asked the shift boss, Ponto, to telephone Kula for a guarantee of the loss. Ponto did so and received Kula's authorization to give Goldfinger credit up to $1,000 but no more. Ponto confirmed this but stated that Kula had also said Goldfinger could gamble the entire deposit of $18,000. Goldfinger was permitted to gamble until he lost $18,000. The casino tried to collect the amount from Kula on his alleged oral promise to cover Goldfinger's debt to $18,000. They did this by refusing to return to Kula the amount he had on deposit. Kula was willing to honor his oral guarantee of Goldfinger's debt up to $1,000 but no more. Kula sued the hotel for return of his deposit. Should he get it? (*Kula v. Karat, Inc.*, 531 P.2d 1353)

5. Nicolella, a building contractor, was asked by Palmer to submit a bid for the construction of an addition to a food market. After reviewing the plans and specifications for the addition, Nicolella bid $57,027 for the job. Two revi-

sions of the written plans were subsequently made by Palmer. Thereafter the parties entered into a written contract. At the time of its execution, Nicolella orally asked Palmer if changes in the plans would materially affect the bid and Palmer said no. Palmer added that if there were any substantial changes, the price paid would be adjusted. After the start of construction, Nicolella discovered that 1,340 square feet had been added to the building. Palmer orally urged Nicolella to continue and said that any additional amount claimed would be paid. Upon completion of the job, Nicolella asked for an additional $10,653, based on the original price per square foot. Palmer refused to pay, so Nicolella sued, alleging that Palmer's statements had been made fraudulently. (a) Could the terms of the original written agreement be varied by any prior or contemporaneous promises made by Palmer? (b) Was Palmer bound by his later oral promise to pay any additional amount claimed by Nicolella? (*Nicolella v. Palmer*, 432 Pa. 502, 248 A.2d 20)

14

Transfer and Discharge of Contracts

1. Your parents contract to have a new house built. Shortly thereafter, your father's employer promotes him. The new position requires a move to corporate headquarters in Atlanta, Georgia, which is 2,000 miles away. Can your parents transfer their rights and duties under the building contract to someone else without becoming liable for breach of contract?

2. Your school has purchased new band uniforms. The contract states that "time is of the essence," and if the goods are not received in time for the first public performance by the band on September 1, the old uniforms will be used for another year. The manufacturer does not deliver the uniforms until October 15. Can the school cancel the contract?

3. A friend is under contract to play professional football. In an automobile accident, he suffers internal injuries and is unable to play for the remainder of the current season. Does he remain on the team payroll?
one-year warranty period. Is your neighbor barred from recovering any sum for his injury?

CAN RIGHTS UNDER A CONTRACT BE TRANSFERRED?

PROBLEM: Cooke bought a compact, Japanese-built sports sedan from Midtown Motors for $9,250. There was a small down payment, and the balance was due in installments over the next 48 months. Because Midtown wanted its money immediately to rebuild its inventory of cars, it transferred all rights to the installment payments to Freed Finance Co. Freed, in turn, gave Midtown the full amount due less a discount charge of $350. Freed then told Cooke to make future payments to Freed, the assignee. Must Cooke do so?

Persons frequently have contractual rights which they wish to transfer to others. Such a transfer of contractual rights is called an **assignment**. The party who makes the assignment is the **assignor**. The party to whom the assignment is made is the **assignee**.

assignment: transfer of contractual rights

assignor: party who makes an assignment

assignee: one to whom an assignment is made

performance: fulfillment of an agreement as promised

Generally unless prohibited by statute or by the contract creating the right, a party may assign any rights to another, provided performance will not be materially changed. **Performance** is the fulfillment or accomplishment of the agreement. Frequently assignments of future wages are prohibited or limited by statute. A right to collect a debt is assignable because performance remains the same after assignment. In the problem, when Cooke was notified of the assignment, he became obligated to pay Freed instead of Midtown. Retailers and restaurants assign to issuers of credit cards the right to collect the amounts due from customers.

Rights may not be assigned if doing so makes performance of the contract substantially more difficult. For example, A has a claim against B for $1,000. A may not assign that claim in 2,000 parts to the 2,000 students at Central High. Rights which may not be transferred include:

1. claims to damages for personal injuries,
2. claims against the United States, and
3. rights to personal services especially of a skilled nature, and when personal trust and confidence are involved.

Ford, a dentist, owed Bentin $5,000 for office furniture. Bentin agreed to accept $1,000 in cash and $4,000 in orthodontic services for his children. Soon after, Bentin needed the money so he assigned his right to receive the dental services to Lakely. Unless Ford consented, this assignment would not be valid because it included rights to personal services of a skilled, professional nature.

Assignment of contractual rights is usually made voluntarily by the assignor. Assignment may also occur automatically by operation of law, as when one of the contracting parties dies. Then the *decedent's* (deceased person's) rights are assigned to the executor or administrator of the estate. Assignment also occurs by operation of law when a trustee in bankruptcy receives title to a debtor's assets, including contractual claims against third persons.

Ordinarily, no particular form is required for an assignment. It may be oral or written. However, statutes sometimes require certain assignments to be in writing.

CAN DUTIES UNDER A CONTRACT BE DELEGATED?

PROBLEM: Larnow hired Cullen to care for her child while Larnow was at work. Could Cullen legally delegate the child-care duties to a third party?

Routine contractual duties may be *delegated* (turned over) to another party. However, a person cannot delegate to another any duty where performance requires unique personal skill or special qualifications. Thus, in the problem, Cullen cannot delegate the duties. That is because caring for children involves special qualifications of trust and skill.

delegation of duties: turning over to another party one's routine contractual duties

A **delegation of duties** is not an assignment of the contract. The original party to the contract is still obligated and liable for proper performance even though someone else may actually do the work. Thus, a general contractor who agrees to build a house is responsible for providing the finished structure as promised. However, the general contractor almost always delegates most of the work to subcontractors. Subcontractors are specialists who lay foundations and do masonry, carpentry, plumbing, electrical, painting, and other work. The general contractor makes individual contracts with them and pays them as agreed. The subcontractors are responsible to the general contractor for proper performance. But the general contractor remains responsible to the buyer for the finished job. Note that the general contractor, in a separate contract, may also assign to a bank the right to collect all or a percentage of the purchase price from the buyer. This is often done even before construction has begun so that the general contractor can buy materials and pay for labor.

> Ziegler operated a letter shop. Bassler contracted with Ziegler to duplicate 12,000 letters and to mail them to a computer-generated list of individuals. Ziegler delegated the job to Gayle for an agreed price. This was a valid delegation of duties, not an assignment. Performance of the contract did not require skill or involve any special relation of trust or confidence. Ziegler, however, remained personally liable to Bassler for proper completion of the job. Under a separate contract, Gayle was liable to Ziegler for proper performance.

Sometimes a contracting party will both assign rights and delegate duties.

> The Pyramid Builders, a ready-mix concrete company, received more orders than it could fill on schedule. Therefore it arranged to have a competitor, Gibraltar Rock and Stone, Inc., supply certain customers. Pyramid would bill the customers and turn over the proceeds to Gibraltar, after deducting a commission for Pyramid's assistance. If the concrete delivered was faulty, Pyramid remained liable to the customer for damages. In turn, Gibraltar would be liable to Pyramid if Gibraltar were at fault.

It is possible for the party entitled to receive performance under a contract to release the other party from the duty to perform and to accept a substitute party. This is neither assignment nor delegation of duties. It is referred to as a **novation**; in effect, a new contract is formed.

novation: substitution of a party, creating a new contract

> Revell had contracted to install a skylight in the roof of Sinclair's workshop. Because of difficulties on another job, Revell asked Sinclair if he would accept a qualified substitute carpenter named Lowry. Lowry was willing to do the job for the same price. All three parties were agreeable. By novation, Lowry took Revell's place in the original contract.

WHAT ARE THE RIGHTS OF AN ASSIGNEE?

PROBLEM: Ginsburg, a distinguished concert violinist, purchased "a genuine Stradivarius violin" from Krone for $150,000. Ginsburg paid $50,000 down. She agreed to pay the balance in 24 equal monthly installments along with an annual carrying charge of 18 percent. Krone knew the violin was not a Stradivarius. Therefore he immediately assigned his right to collect the balance of $100,000 to the Continental Finance Company. In return, Continental gave Krone $90,000 in cash. Krone then disappeared. Shortly thereafter, Ginsburg discovered the fraud. Can she now refuse to pay Continental if it tries to collect?

Courts sometimes say that the assignee "stands in the shoes of the assignor." This means that the assignee receives exactly the same contractual rights and duties as the assignor had—no more and no less.

obligor: debtor

To protect newly acquired rights, the assignee should promptly notify the obligor of the assignment. The **obligor** is the *debtor*—the one who owes the money or other obligation. This notification may be done orally or in writing. Until notified, the obligor has no reason to assume that the contractual obligations have been changed and may continue to pay the original creditor. After notification, however, the obligor is liable to the assignee for performance.

In making an assignment, the assignor does not promise to make good if the obligor fails to perform, unless this is specifically required by the assignment. However, the assignor does guarantee that there is a right to assign, and that the assigned right is legally enforceable. In the problem, Ginsburg can claim fraud. Because Continental now stands in the place of Krone, Ginsburg can refuse to pay Continental. This is true even though Continental is an innocent third party. Also, if Krone is located, Ginsburg can sue him for damages caused by the fraud and Continental can sue him for the $90,000. Krone may also be criminally liable.

HOW ARE CONTRACTS USUALLY DISCHARGED?

PROBLEM: Wesley loaned Hudson $900 to be repaid within three months. When the debt was due, Hudson did not have the money. But he offered to give Wesley an aquamarine ring that was worth about $1,000. Must Wesley accept the ring instead of payment, thus discharging Hudson from his contractual obligations?

When a contract is made, the parties take on certain duties or obligations. **Discharge of contract** (termination of obligations) occurs when the parties perform as promised. Or it occurs when the parties are released from their responsibilities by action of the other party or by law. Generally contracts are discharged by performance; most parties do perform as they have promised. Partial performance does not discharge the obligation.

discharge of contract: end of the obligation to perform

Frequently, complex contracts are discharged by **substantial performance**. This occurs when there is only a minor modification or failure to fulfill all terms of the contract. The performance is incomplete but substantial.

substantial performance: incomplete but acceptable performance of contractual terms

An appropriate allowance is made in the price to cover the deviation. If the deviation is deliberate, the victim may treat it as a breach.

Kitchen Konstruction Kompany, Inc., remodeled the kitchen in the Hamill's mid-Victorian house. However, the new built-in cabinets were made of top-grade plywood instead of solid wood as specified in the contract. (The mistake was due to an oversight in the contractor's purchasing department.) The substituted materials were actually more durable. The Hamills were not aware of the difference until a friend whose hobby was woodworking pointed it out. However, the contract had been substantially performed. Therefore the Hamills were responsible for the full price less a deduction for the lower cost of the plywood.

Failure to perform in accordance with the contractual terms is a **breach of contract**; this gives the other party the right to cancel. Sometimes a party who *defaults* (fails to perform) notifies the other party to a contract before the time of performance has arrived that he or she will not perform. This is called an **anticipatory breach**. The victim may wait until the promised time of performance, or the victim may treat the default as a breach of contract and immediately sue for damages.

breach of contract: failure to perform the terms as agreed

anticipatory breach: notification, before the time of performance, of refusal to perform the contractual terms as agreed

On January 5, Graham Roofers contracted to remove the old shingles and to install a new shake roof on the home of the Sterlings. The job was to be completed "by March 30, at the latest," because of anticipated heavy spring rains. Late in February, Graham notified the Sterlings that because of a rush of orders, his crews were "swamped" and could not get to the job until late April or early May. This was an anticipatory breach. The Sterlings have the choice of waiting for performance or immediately proceeding as though there were a breach of contract.

Breach of contract by one party may give the other party the right to treat his or her obligation as discharged or terminated. When one party terminates a sales contract because of a breach of the other party, the UCC uses the word *cancellation*.

A contract that calls for payment in money requires payment of the exact amount on the specified date. The one to whom the money is owed need not accept anything else. Therefore, in the problem, Wesley was under no obligation to accept the ring. However, if she does accept, Hudson's obligation to pay the $900 would be discharged.

Frequently a check is given in payment of a debt that is payable in money. Acceptance of the check merely suspends the debt while the check is being processed in the banking system for collection. The debt is not discharged until the check is paid by the bank on which it was drawn.

When a contract states that performance must be completed on or before a specified date, and that "time is of the essence," failure to perform by that date is generally regarded as a breach of contract. However, if no loss is caused by a delay, time is not critical. In such cases, the "essence" clause may be ignored by the courts. When no precise date is specified, performance within a reasonable time suffices.

IN WHAT OTHER WAYS CAN CONTRACTS BE DISCHARGED?

PROBLEM: Diaz was the owner of a landscape service. He contracted to maintain the yard of Reingold while the latter sailed around the world in a 45-foot yacht. Reingold planned to write and take photographs for a national magazine and had no fixed itinerary for the journey. When would the contract with Diaz terminate?

In addition to discharge by complete or substantial performance, a contract may be discharged by:

1. agreement,
2. impossibility of performance, or
3. operation of law.

1. By Agreement

When the parties prepare their contract, they may agree that it will terminate:

a. on a specified date or upon the expiration of a specified period of time (for example, a fresh food supply contract on the last day of school);
b. upon the happening of a specified event (in the problem, the contract to maintain the yard would terminate when Reingold returned);
c. upon the failure of a certain event to happen (for example, a loan contract upon failure to get a building permit); or
d. at the election of either party upon giving notice (for example, when one partner decides to retire from business and gives the required notice).

The parties who have made a contract may later mutually agree to change either the terms of the contract or the nature of their relationship. They may do so without any liability for breach.

By *rescission* the contracting parties may agree to terminate the existing contract entirely, returning any consideration received and placing the parties in their original positions. Or they may agree that the present contract is not what they want, and so they may replace it with a new one. This is discharge by **substitution**. The parties may also agree to change the obligation required by the original contract. An agreement to make such a change is known as an **accord**. Performance of the new obligation is called a **satisfaction**. A compromise of a disputed claim or a composition of creditors (see pages 202-203) is an accord. Carrying out the new agreement is the satisfaction. Thus, the previous obligation is discharged by an **accord and satisfaction**. Also, as you may recall, a contract can be terminated, and a new one formed, through novation.

substitution: replacement of one contract with another

accord: agreement to change a contractual obligation

satisfaction: performance of a new contractual obligation

accord and satisfaction: agreement to change a contractual obligation, followed by the agreed-upon substituted performance

> Vanvoor was a skilled handyman who had borrowed $650 from Banta. Vanvoor could not repay the loan on schedule. The parties then agreed that Vanvoor would work off the debt by doing 60 hours of painting, electrical, and plumbing work in Banta's home during the next three months. The agreement to change the required performance was an accord. Vanvoor's completion of the agreed-upon work was the satisfaction. Together, this accord and satisfaction discharged Vanvoor's original obligation to pay $650.

2. By Impossibility of Performance

As a general rule, a contract is not discharged when some unforeseen event makes performance more costly or difficult for one of the parties. For example, increased prices of needed supplies, a strike of needed workers, difficulty in obtaining materials or equipment, or some natural disaster such as a flood or earthquake may delay performance. But, generally, these events do not discharge the contractual obligations; they should be anticipated as possibilities when the contract is made. A party who fails to perform because of these events could be held liable for breach of contract.

> Sundstrum was a wholesaler. He contracted to supply various airplane parts to Arcadia Airport at a price of $17,686. However, Sundstrum later defaulted. He claimed that it was impossible to deliver at the contract price because manufacturers had increased their prices to him by more than $8,600. The court held him to the contract. The fact that the contract was no longer economically profitable did not mean that it was legally and physically impossible to perform.

However, the parties may, and commonly do, include "escape hatch" language in the contract. Such language permits modification, or even termination, of performance without liability for damages in the event of inability to perform on schedule because of specified conditions such as foul weather and labor strikes.

Note also that under unusual circumstances recognized by the UCC, a contract for goods may be discharged by conditions which make performance impracticable. Increased cost alone is not enough. But a possibility not thought of by the parties, such as a surprise war or an unexpected *embargo* (legal stoppage of commerce) may suffice. Even a shutdown of major supply sources could discharge the contract if it prevented the seller from getting supplies or if it caused an extreme increase in cost beyond what could be reasonably anticipated.

Other situations in which a contract is discharged by impossibility include:

Destruction of the subject matter. Sometimes performance depends upon the continued existence of some specific thing. The destruction of that thing terminates the contract if the destruction was not the fault of the party who is sued for nonperformance.

Vitesse was a famous jockey. He contracted to ride the thoroughbred "Black Phantom" in the Kentucky Derby. A week before the race, the horse stumbled during a workout, broke a leg, and had to be destroyed. Vitesse's employment contract was discharged. He was free to ride another horse in the Derby.

The result of destruction of the subject matter is different if the seller has many sources of supply and the parties did not specify one and only one source as acceptable. For example, suppose a wholesale broker of lumber loses one supply source, perhaps because of a fire. However, the broker has access to other sources of lumber. In addition, the broker's contract does not specify any one source. Thus, the broker is required to perform at no higher price to the buyer. This is true even if the resulting cost is much higher to the broker.

Performance declared illegal. If a contract which is legal when made later becomes illegal, it is discharged. Illegality might be caused by a new statute, by a court ruling, or by an administrative decision.

Tippner contracted with Barnell to build a warehouse on land owned by Barnell. Before construction began, the city council passed a zoning ordinance restricting the site to residential dwellings. The contract was discharged because of this ordinance.

Death or disability. If the contract requires personal services, the death or the disability of the party who was to provide such services terminates the agreement. This rule would not apply when other persons are available to perform, as in partnerships or corporations which continue to do business. Likewise, it would not apply where the contract simply called for payment of money, delivery of goods, or transfer of title to land by the decedent. In each such case, the decedent's personal representative is required to perform.

The *Daily Press* employed Bodrig for a two-year term to supervise the installation and operation of a computerized system for the newspaper's newsroom, pressroom, circulation department, and business office. Nine months after beginning work, Bodrig suffered a nervous breakdown and was unable to continue. His contractual obligation was discharged by impossibility.

3. By Operation of Law

A contract may be discharged or the right to enforce it may be barred by operation of law. This happens when the promisor's debts are discharged in bankruptcy. It also happens when the statute of limitations has run (the time allowed by statute for enforcement of the contract has elapsed).

alteration: change in contractual terms without the consent of the other party

Alteration of a written agreement also usually discharges the agreement by operation of law. **Alteration** is a change in the terms of a contract without consent of the other party. To discharge the contract, the alteration must be:

a. material, thus changing the obligation in an important way;
b. made intentionally, and not by accident or mistake;
c. made by a party to the agreement, or by an authorized agent; and
d. made without consent of the other party.

Koplan's Komplete Kleaners contracted to clean all rooms and public spaces of Dahl's office building. A contractual clause in small print allowed a 10 percent discount if the charges were paid in advance in one lump sum instead of in 12 monthly installments. After the contract had been signed by both parties, and before giving Dahl her copy, Koplan secretly crossed out the clause referring to the discount. This material alteration released Dahl from the contract. Dahl could insist on reinstatement of the clause or seek damages through court action. Proof could be difficult, however, if Koplan lied about the incident under oath.

WHAT IS THE EFFECT OF TENDER OF PERFORMANCE?

PROBLEM: Zamorski, a professional artist, agreed to paint Quincy's portrait for $5,000. Five sittings of two hours each were scheduled at times selected by Quincy, but he failed to appear for any one. To accommodate her client, Zamorski then offered to come to Quincy's home or office for rescheduled sittings at the latter's convenience. Quincy rejected this proposal. Is Zamorski's legal obligation discharged? Is Quincy liable for damages?

An offer to perform an obligation is a **tender**. If the obligation requires the doing of an act, a tender which is made in good faith but is rejected will discharge the obligation of the one offering to perform. In the problem, Quincy refused Zamorski's offer to perform as agreed. Thus, Zamorski's obligation was discharged, and Quincy is liable for damages.

tender: offer to perform an obligation

If the obligation requires the payment of money, rejection of an offer to pay the money does not discharge the debt nor does it prevent the creditor from collecting later. It merely relieves the debtor of court costs or future interest that might otherwise become due. To be valid, the tender of money must consist of the exact amount due in legal tender. **Legal tender** is currency or coins—including Federal Reserve Notes—of the United States of America. Checks are not legal tender, but as noted earlier, they are frequently given and accepted, conditional on payment by the bank on which they are drawn.

legal tender: United States currency or coins

PREVENTING LEGAL DIFFICULTIES

To Protect Yourself . . .

1. as the prospective assignee, determine whether the assignor is subject to any defense that may affect your claim. Do this by promptly checking with the obligor (debtor). Remember that you, as the assignee, acquire only such rights as the assignor possessed;
2. do not forget that the assignor does not agree to pay the debt if the debtor fails to do so. If you wish the assignor to remain liable, include a provision to that effect in the written assignment agreement;
3. be sure to notify the obligor of the assignment as soon as practicable;
4. be aware that "time is of the essence" in many contracts. If a contract calls for performance by a certain time, failure to perform may be a breach of contract. When appropriate, include this requirement in your contracts. State that failure to perform at the time agreed may be treated as a breach; and
5. remember that hardship and higher costs do not make performance impossible. Hardship could be caused by bad weather, fires, strikes, inability to obtain materials, or similar difficulties. To be protected against damages for failure to fulfill a contract because of such events, include a clause in the contract to that effect.

Strengthening Your Legal Vocabulary

accord
accord and satisfaction
alteration
anticipatory breach
assignee
assignment
assignor
breach of contract
delegation of duties
discharge of contract
legal tender
novation
obligor
performance
satisfaction
substantial performance
substitution
tender

1. Agreement to change a contractual obligation, and the performance of the new obligation.
2. Transaction by which a party transfers contractual rights to another.
3. Notification, before the scheduled time of performance, of refusal to perform contractual terms as agreed.
4. Termination of contractual obligations.
5. Currency or coins of the United States.
6. Material change in the terms of a contract, made intentionally by one party without consent of the other.
7. Fulfillment or accomplishment of the contract as promised.
8. One who transfers contractual rights.
9. Turning over to another party one's routine duties under a contract.
10. One to whom contractual rights are transferred.

Reviewing Important Points

1. A party may generally assign rights under a contract as long as the performance will not thereby be materially changed. One is not released from contractual duties by making an assignment. Some duties may be delegated. They may not be delegated when they involve personal judgment or skill, as with artists and professional experts. When duties are delegated, the original party remains liable for proper performance.
2. An assignee acquires only such rights as the assignor has under the contract. The assignee takes the rights subject to any existing defenses, such as prior payment.
3. Until notification of assignment is received, the obligor is justified in believing that performance may still be properly made to the original contracting party.
4. Contracts are usually discharged by performance or by substantial performance.
5. A breach of contract generally permits the other party to regard his or her obligation to perform as discharged. The same is true in anticipatory breach of contract. In either case, the victim may seek relief in court.

6. Discharge by agreement of the parties may be accomplished by doing any of the following:
   a. including provisions for termination in the contract,
   b. rescinding the existing contract,
   c. substituting a new contract,
   d. replacing a party through novation, or
   e. making an accord and satisfaction.
7. Difficulty of performance or unforeseen high costs generally do not relieve a promisor of the obligation to perform. However, contractual duties may be discharged because of actual impossibility when:
   a. the subject matter is destroyed,
   b. a change in the law makes performance illegal, or
   c. either party dies or becomes disabled, if the contract required the personal services of the individual.
8. The obligation of one party is discharged when a written contract is materially and intentionally altered by the other party without the consent of the former.
9. An obligation calling for an act is discharged by a tender of performance that corresponds exactly to the agreement. A tender of payment does not discharge an obligation to pay money. It does relieve the debtor of court costs and future interest charges.

Applying Law to Everyday Life

1. Zack bought an automobile insurance policy. The policy contained a clause prohibiting assignment of the policy without written consent of the insurer. Later, when the car was stolen, Zack notified the insurer. After several months, during which the car had not been recovered, Zack assigned to Pragg his claim for reimbursement. The insurance company refused to pay because its written consent to assignment was missing. Must the insurance company pay?

2. Cullen purchased a Holee Donuts franchise. The contract contained a clause which forbade transfer of the business without consent of the franchisor. After six years of successful operation, Cullen wanted to sell the business to his manager. Was he legally permitted to do this?

3. MacMahon contracted with Hidden Valley School District to provide a bus and to serve as the driver for a five-year period. After two years, MacMahon died and his adult son became owner of the bus. He proposed to become the driver and complete the remaining three years of the contract. Must Hidden Valley accept his services?

4. Bradmaker operated a profitable lunch bar in a downtown business district. He sold the business to Olefson for $60,000. Olefson was to pay 25 percent down and the balance in equal monthly installments over a five-year period,

with interest at 10 percent a year on the unpaid balance. Olefson later assigned the contract to Ogden with Bradmaker's knowledge and consent. By then only $30,000 of the debt remained to be paid. Within six months, however, Ogden closed the lunch bar. He also stopped making payments. Bradmaker sued Olefson for the unpaid balance. Is Olefson liable?

5. Ferrazzi, a distinguished Italian sculptor, contracted to create a large bronze abstract design for the lobby of the Martindale Mart. He was to receive $75,000. Shortly thereafter, Ferrazzi was injured in an accident. Unable to fulfill his agreement, he asked his friend Drinano to do the work for him. Drinano was an equally competent sculptor. Must Martindale Mart accept Drinano's services?

6. Ohler Oil Company contracted to sell and to deliver 500 barrels of fuel oil on the first of each month for one year to the Monson Mushroom Factory (an indoor farm). Ohler delivered the oil for the first two months, but none during the third month. Ohler said there was unprecedented demand and it was allocating available supplies to all customers. Monson notified Ohler that it was canceling the contract because of Ohler's breach. Was Monson justified in its action?

7. The Laroffs had looked for a long time to find the right color for the exterior of their recently remodeled home. Finally, they contracted with Redi & Able Painters to do the job. Paint brand, color, and quality were specified in the contract. It was also specified that two coats would be applied by brush, not sprayed or rolled on. One week later, when the Laroffs came home from a vacation, they were dismayed to find their dream house painted in the wrong color. Also, they learned that the paint had been sprayed on and that only one coat had been applied. It was not the brand of paint that the Laroffs had specified. But it was a more expensive brand, and the maker guaranteed that "one coat covers any surface." Had Redi & Able Painters breached, or had they substantially performed the contract?

Solving Case Problems

1. The defendant, Kyle, bought a car from Milliken Chevrolet, Inc., on a conditional sales contract. As is customary under such contracts, Milliken retained the legal title (ownership), but Kyle had possession and use of the car as the owner of the equitable title. Milliken immediately assigned the sales contract to General Motors Acceptance Corporation (GMAC). The sales contract was illegal because it did not comply with the state law for full disclosure of all costs including extras, registration fees, and insurance. After making two payments to GMAC, Kyle learned of the illegality of the contract and refused to continue making payments. GMAC repossessed the car and Kyle sued to recover its value. In defense, GMAC claimed that it did not know that the sales contract was illegal when the sales contract was

purchased from Milliken. Accordingly, GMAC denied responsibility for Milliken's actions. Is GMAC liable to Milliken? (*General Motors Acceptance Corporation v. Kyle*, 351 P.2d 768, Cal.)

2. Partin sold a mechanical water softener to the defendants, Earl Walker and his wife Billie, for their dairy farm. Although a written installment contract was signed by the Walkers, Partin orally agreed that if milk production did not increase enough to pay for the machine, Partin would remove it without charge. Partin also orally agreed not to assign the contract. In fact, he did assign the contract to the plaintiff, Associates Loan Company. The Walkers made no payments, but Partin and a successor did. Ultimately the softener was removed because milk production did not go up as promised. Associates sued the Walkers to collect the balance due. Who should win? (*Associates Loan Co. v. Walker*, 416 P.2d 529, N.M.)

3. In August, Tanner contracted to pay $300 to the Swanola Club to have his minor daughter participate as one of eight maids in the following year's carnival ball. Tanner paid $50 down, but one month later, he notified Swanola that his daughter would not participate because it might interfere with her college studies. He failed to pay the balance of $250 due before December 15. The contract gave Swanola "the option either to cancel the agreement and retain the cash portion paid as damages, or, in the alternative, to enforce payment of the entire consideration." Tanner claimed that Swanola was not entitled to the full contract price because it had never tendered performance by delivering the ball gown and other items as agreed. (Tanner's daughter had been measured for her gown by the Swanola dressmaker. Also, the daughter had found time to participate as a maid in a ball sponsored by another organization that same carnival season.) Only seven maids appeared in the Swanola ball. Six months after the ball, Swanola sued for the $250 balance. The trial court allowed Swanola to retain only the $50 deposit. Swanola appealed. Decide. (*Swanola Club v. Tanner*, 209 So. 2d 173, La.)

4. The defendant, Sunset Packing Company, contracted to buy Schafer's strawberry crop. It also contracted to furnish 150-200 laborers to harvest the crop beginning June 1. A recruiting fee of $15 per laborer was to be paid by Schafer, who gave Sunset a check for $2,000 as advance payment. Sunset recruited the laborers in Texas, but they went to Idaho to work in the sugar beet harvest. Two days before June 1, Sunset notified Schafer that it would be impossible to supply the laborers as agreed. Sunset said, however, that it would make available 100 laborers from its own labor force if Schafer would pay Sunset an extra $20 per ton of harvested strawberries. Schafer then recruited his own labor force, but at a greater cost. Later he sued Sunset for $17,880 in lost profits. Sunset claimed that it was discharged from its contractual obligation because of impossibility of performance. Do you agree with Sunset? (*Schafer v. Sunset Packing Company of Oregon*, 474 P.2d 529, Or.)

5. The Washington Trader was a giant oil tanker owned by the plaintiff, American Trading and Production Corporation. In March, 1967, the defendant, Shell International Marine, Ltd., contracted for the ship to carry a load of oil from Texas to India. The total fee agreed upon was $417,327.36. No reference was made in the contract for the route to be taken; this was to be a decision of the shipping company. The route around Africa's Cape of Good Hope was an acceptable route; however, the price was based on passage through the Suez Canal (the invoice contained a Suez Canal toll charge). The Washington Trader headed for the Mediterranean Sea and the Suez. When the ship reached Gibraltar, it was warned of possible violence in the Middle East. Nevertheless, it continued. Upon reaching the Suez Canal, the ship found the Canal closed by the Arab-Israeli War. The ship turned back and took the long route around Africa, at an added cost of $131,978.44. It arrived in Bombay some 30 days later than originally expected. American Trading then billed Shell for the full amount; when Shell refused to pay, it sued. American claimed that the war made it impossible to perform as originally agreed. Shell, it said, should pay the extra cost because otherwise Shell would be unjustly enriched. Decide. (*American Trading and Production Corp. v. Shell International Marine Ltd.*, 453 F.2d 939, 2d Cir.)

15

Remedies for Breach of Contract

1. An asphalt surface is applied on the gravel road in front of your home by a construction crew working under a contract with the county. The asphalt is not properly applied, and the surface develops large cracks and bubbles. Claiming rights as a taxpayer and co-owner of all public county facilities, your father sues the paving contractor for damages. Should he win?

2. A college basketball coach has a winning record. The coach also has two years remaining on a three-year employment contract. He is induced by the owners of a professional basketball team to break the contract in order to coach their team. Does the college have any legal recourse?

3. You are hired to work as an aid at a youth camp in Alaska for three months beginning on June 10. Because of higher camp fees and airfares this season, enrollments drop sharply. After the first of six scheduled two-week camp sessions, the camp no longer needs as many aids. Therefore you are fired. Do you have any legal remedy?

WHO HAS RIGHTS UNDER A CONTRACT?

PROBLEM: Shortly after Royter was born, his elderly uncle bought an endowment life insurance policy naming Royter as the beneficiary. The policy was to mature when Royter reached the age of 18 or when the uncle died, whichever came earlier. The proceeds were intended for Royter's college education. Although the insurance company and the uncle were the parties to the endowment contract, does Royter have any legal rights under it which he could enforce in court?

In general, a person who benefits from something such as an insurance policy or other contract is called a *beneficiary*. Every person benefits directly from countless contracts executed by other people over the years. The machinery of agriculture and industry, the warehouses and stores of commerce, and the planes, trains, and ships of transport are the result of a maze of interrelated contracts. All persons who use these facilities or enjoy their products and services are incidental beneficiaries. An **incidental beneficiary** is one who benefits from a contract (for example, from any of the underlying contracts that made the above facilities possible), yet is not a party to the contract and may not enforce it.

incidental beneficiary: one who benefits from a contract but is not a party to it and cannot enforce it

As a general rule, only parties who have entered into a contract have enforceable rights under it. This is true even though other persons may gain some advantage by having the contract performed. There are two important exceptions to this rule:

1. most enforceable rights that arise under a contract can be transferred to a third person by assignment and can then be enforced by that person as discussed in the preceding chapter; and
2. when a contract is made with the primary intention of benefiting a third person, that person is entitled to enforce the agreement.

Contracts made specifically for the benefit of a third party can usually be enforced by that person. The **third party beneficiary**, then, is the one for whose benefit such a contract is made. Life insurance contracts are the most common form of third party beneficiary agreements. Parents, for example, in contracts with insurance companies, often name their children as beneficiaries. In the problem, Royter was a third party beneficiary. Therefore he could compel the insurance company to pay him when the policy *matured* and the face value became due.

third party beneficiary: one who is not a party to a contract but benefits from it and can enforce it

WHAT REMEDIES DOES THE INJURED PARTY HAVE?

PROBLEM: Dunken Pools contracted to install an outdoor swimming pool in Taber's yard by June 15. "Time was of the essence" to permit full use during the warm summer months. By June 15, Dunken had not even begun to excavate. He said he would not be able to begin for at least one more month, claiming problems with work crews, with weather, and with equipment. On July 15, Dunken said the pressure of bigger orders made it impossible to begin work for at least another month, but then he would work with two shifts on the job "under lights if necessary." Taber then contracted to have Crystal Clear Pools, Inc., do the job immediately. However, Crystal charged an extra $5,200. Does Taber have any enforceable claim against Dunken?

When one party to a contract refuses to perform or fails to perform properly, the other party suffers a legal injury. The injured party is entitled to be "made whole" and to get "the benefit of the bargain" as made. Accordingly, such a party may seek any one of several remedies for the breach. A **remedy** is the means to enforce a right or to compensate for an injury. Remedies vary with the type of contract and differ in effect or result. In the problem, Dunken failed to perform his obligation under the contract. Taber had a choice of remedies as discussed below.

remedy: means used to enforce a right or compensate for an injury

Sometimes one party may not wish to enforce a contract or a provision in it. When one intentionally and voluntarily gives up a contractual right, the right is said to be *waived*. Reasons for waivers are many in number: the damages may be very limited; the victim may be glad to be free of any obligation; the legal cost of suing may be prohibitive; the outcome of a lawsuit may be too uncertain; the defendant may be judgment-proof; or the suit may be bad for public relations.

When Lister bought her new automobile, she received a customary limited warranty from the manufacturer. It provided protection against defects in materials or workmanship of most components of the car for one year or 12,000 miles, whichever came first. One door did not fit properly and a whistling of wind could be heard when Lister drove faster than 50 miles per hour. Also, in heavy rains, water leaked into the trunk. Because Lister drove only in town, at low speeds, in good weather, she never bothered to complain about the defects. By her failure to act within one year, she waived her right to claim a breach of warranty.

Remedies for breach of contract include the following:

1. rescission of the contract, either voluntarily or by court order,
2. cancellation of the contract (in cases of sales of goods),
3. recovery of monetary damages, and
4. specific performance or an injunction.

1. The Injured Party Has the Right of Rescission

PROBLEM: A certain type of doll was in such demand that the manufacturer could not fill all orders. Dealers therefore put their customers on waiting lists. In October, one retailer required a $15 deposit with every order and promised to deliver "no later than December 1." In fact, the supply remained inadequate until the new year. Hundreds of depositors did not get dolls for Christmas. Were they entitled to refunds or must they accept late delivery?

If one party breaches the contract by failure to perform, the other party may usually consider any obligation as discharged. Thus, in the problem, customers who received no dolls before Christmas had a right to be restored to their original position—as if there had been no contract—by getting full refunds.

rescission: return of parties to position before contract was made, with no damages

This remedy is the right of **rescission**. Each party returns any consideration received and gives credit for what cannot be returned. The entire contract must be rescinded, not just a part of it. It may be done by voluntary agreement of the parties, or it may be done by court order at the request of the injured party. Neither party gets damages.

2. The Injured Party May Have the Right of Cancellation

cancellation: ending contract for sale of goods because of breach, while retaining other remedies

Cancellation is a variation of rescission. It exists under the UCC, but only for breach of contract for the sale of goods. The injured party—either buyer or seller—may cancel the contract, return consideration received, and still retain other remedies.

Bowen's Gift Bazaar ordered one thousand solid brass unicorns from the East-is-East Import Co. The items were advertised in Bowen's Holiday Gift Catalog and were expected to generate a net profit of at least $7,500. When the first of ten crates arrived, a receiving clerk accidentally dropped one of the unicorns on its head. The horn broke off, revealing a pot metal base with only a plated brass surface. Bowen returned the crate and canceled the order. Bowen could also sue for damages for breach of contract and possibly for the tort of fraud.

3. The Injured Party Has the Right to Damages

PROBLEM: Wanous contracted with Holling to install some pinball machines in Holling's snack bar. When Wanous attempted to deliver the machines, Holling said he had changed his mind and canceled the contract. What rights did Wanous have?

When a breach of contract occurs, the injured party is entitled to be put in the same position he or she would have been in if the contract had been performed. The parties frequently negotiate a settlement directly or with the help of their lawyers. If they do not reach a settlement, the injured party may sue to recover damages—money awarded by the court for loss or injury caused by incomplete performance or failure to perform. In the problem, Wanous could sue Holling for any injury suffered, including the loss of anticipated reasonable profits as a result of Holling's breach.

Note, however, that the victim of the breach of contract is required to **mitigate** damages. This means that damages must be reduced by any means reasonable under the circumstances. For a victimized buyer it might require buying substitute goods elsewhere or getting someone else to perform the service. For an employee unfairly discharged, it could require promptly seeking and accepting similar employment elsewhere.

mitigate: to reduce damages if reasonably possible

DeForce was hired on a three-year written contract to be the French representative of an American advertising agency. DeForce's salary was $3,000 a month plus expenses. After two years, DeForce's employer told him that changes in company plans required DeForce's dismissal. Instead of seeking new employment, DeForce went to a resort on the coast of the Mediterranean for twelve months of rest and relaxation. His failure to mitigate the damages by seeking other comparable employment will substantially reduce any damages he can recover from the advertising agency.

4. The Injured Party May Compel Specific Performance or Get an Injunction

PROBLEM: Kelly contracted to buy 160 acres of land from the McCalls. She planned to develop an amusement park on the land. When the McCalls learned of her plan, they refused to deliver the deed. Did Kelly have any recourse?

Sometimes money damages are not an adequate remedy for breach of contract. Therefore a court may give the injured party a form of special relief termed specific performance. *Specific performance* is the actual completion of the agreement as promised. The court simply orders the defaulting party to perform as agreed.

Generally money damages suffice as a remedy for breach of contract in cases involving the sale of personal property. The victim may use the money to buy similar property from someone else. If the property is unique, however, so that it cannot be obtained elsewhere, specific performance may be awarded. An example would be a rare work of art. This remedy is also generally available when the contract is for the sale of real property because every parcel of land is unique, if only as to location. Accordingly, in the problem, Kelly could sue the McCalls and require them to specifically perform by delivering the deed.

Specific performance is ordinarily denied by the court when:

a. money damages would be adequate,
b. the court is not able to supervise performance,
c. the contract is immoral, fraudulent, or illegal,
d. specific performance will work undue hardship on the other party to the contract, or
e. the contract involves personal service or employment.

In employment contracts, the court of equity will not compel a person to work against his or her will. Such an action would resemble slavery. However, the court may prohibit the defaulting party—such as a football coach or a rock concert star—from working for anyone else during the contractual period of employment. Note that the person who breached the contract would still be liable for any monetary damages suffered by the employer. Thus, the defaulter may decide to perform as agreed rather than be without work, yet liable for damages.

In some cases, when money damages or specific performance would not be appropriate, the court may order rescission or grant an injunction to prohibit specified acts.

HOW ARE DAMAGES MEASURED?

PROBLEM: In a valid contract, Hall agreed to sell his used ski outfit (skis, boots, jacket, and pants) to Cornall for $600. Then Hall changed his mind. He said, "Sue me if you must, but I'm not selling." Cornall, seeking to mitigate damages, immediately searched for comparable equipment. He found a better outfit at a college campus "Ski Swap," and it cost only $450. Can he still collect damages from Hall?

In awarding damages for breach of contract, the court tries to place the injured party in approximately the position that party would have been in had the breach not occurred. The amount awarded as **compensatory damages** is usually determined by the extent of the injury. One party is not permitted to increase the damages by continuing to perform the contract after notice of the other's breach or intention to cancel. As noted earlier, the injured party is also required to mitigate damages if reasonably possible.

compensatory damages: amount awarded to make good the plaintiff's loss

Failure to perform a duty under a contract is a legal wrong. Therefore courts will award **nominal damages** even when there is no actual injury. This could happen when, after a breach, the plaintiff finds a satisfactory product at a lower price. Such would be the case with Cornall in the problem. Nominal damages are granted in recognition of the rights that have been violated. Such damages may consist of a few cents or a dollar. The plaintiff is usually pleased to have proved a point, to have embarrassed the defendant and imposed legal costs, or to have established a precedent for the future.

nominal damages: token amount awarded when there is no actual injury

At the time of entering into a contract, the parties may agree upon an amount of money that, in case of default, is to be paid by the person who breaches. This sum is known as **liquidated damages**. This arrangement is common when actual damages would be difficult to prove. It is enforceable if the amount is reasonable. If damages are not reasonable, the court will deem them to be a penalty and will not enforce the agreement but will award reasonable damages if proved. Penalties are imposed for crimes and intentional torts but not ordinarily for breaches of contract. To do so would be to discourage free and active trade.

liquidated damages: amount agreed upon in advance of possible breach

The Bethlehem Steel Company contracted with the City of Chicago to supply and erect the steelwork for a certain section of a superhighway. The price agreed upon was $1,734,200. The contract also provided that the steel company would pay as liquidated damages $1,000 for each day the work was extended and uncompleted beyond a specified date. The work was completed 52 days after the date agreed upon. The court held that it was difficult to determine the actual amount of damages. It also held that the amount of damages provided for in the contract was reasonable, and therefore was not a penalty. The company was liable for $52,000.

Under certain circumstances, such as when a tort is involved in a breach of contract, the courts will award exemplary or punitive damages. Such damages are awarded in addition to the actual damages. The purpose of *exemplary* or *punitive damages* is to punish and to make an example of the defendant. This could happen, for example, when a defendant seller defrauds a plaintiff buyer.

HOW MAY THE INJURED PARTY LOSE THE REMEDY?

PROBLEM: Raley sold a used videocassette recorder to his friend and neighbor, Parr, for $395 on credit. Over a six-year period, Parr always had some excuse for not paying when Raley tried to collect. Exasperated, Raley finally filed suit in small claims court. Will the court consider the claim even though it is old?

Under certain circumstances, a remedy for breach of contract will be denied or barred. For example, a debtor who is too poor to pay a debt may avoid the obligation by having it discharged in bankruptcy. Also, a creditor who is tardy in pressing a claim or seeking a remedy may lose otherwise available legal rights. Such would be the case with Raley in the problem. It would be unfair to permit a person to wait an unreasonable length of time before bringing suit. Circumstances change, witnesses move, memories fade, and records may be lost or destroyed. Then, too, there is a greater tendency toward fraud and perjury in proving stale claims, and many courts are already overcrowded with current cases. The courts do not want to be bothered with old disputes which often can no longer be decided fairly.

1. The Remedy May Be Barred by a Statute of Limitations

> **PROBLEM:** Morin purchased equipment for her beauty salon after she borrowed $10,000 from Sanders to pay for it. In a written loan contract, Morin agreed to repay the debt plus interest in monthly installments of $200. The contract also provided that the unpaid balance of the debt would be due immediately if she defaulted on any payment. After making payments for 18 months, Morin failed to pay. The beauty salon was profitable. However, Morin spent every weekend in the neighboring state, gambling—and usually losing. The applicable statutory period of limitations was four years. Sanders made repeated attempts to collect but never filed suit until four years after the default. Could he collect?

A creditor may lose a legal right of action against a debtor by waiting too long before filing suit. Statutes in all states deny creditors a right of action for damages for breach of contract after the lapse of a specified time. These statutes prevent harassment of debtors by lawsuits based on stale claims. As you may recall, such a law is called a *statute of limitations*. If the injured party does not begin an action in court within the prescribed time, the debt is an **outlawed debt** and the creditor may not sue. The period of time varies among the different states. Within the same state, it may vary according to the nature of the contract. In most states, a statute bars action after a period of three, four, five, or six years from the time the debt was due and payable. About half the states allow more time to sue on written contracts than on oral ones.

outlawed debt: one that cannot be legally enforced because of the statute of limitations

The UCC provides that an action for breach of a contract of sale of goods must be *commenced* (begun) within four years after the cause of action arises. The statute begins to run from the moment there is a right to sue for a breach or a default. However, while the defendant is out of the state, "the clock stops," and statutory time does not cumulate. Such was the case in the problem. Thus, Sanders could still sue and collect.

In the case of minors and others who lack capacity to contract, allowance is made for their period of incapacity. Thus, a minor is given a reasonable time after reaching majority to start the action.

Statutes of limitations ordinarily do not discharge debts. Instead, they merely bar the remedies of the injured parties. The bar may be waived and the right of action may be revived if the debtor makes a new promise. Since the new promise is a waiver, it need not be supported by consideration. However, in some states, it must be in writing. The new promise may be express or implied, as in the case of a partial payment or a payment of interest. The period specified in the statute, during which an action must be commenced, begins to run anew from the date of the new promise.

Friedman borrowed $500 from McAnulty for one year at 7 percent interest. Each year for ten years, Friedman sent the interest but no payment on the principal. Finally, McAnulty decided she must take steps to collect the debt. So she filed suit. Friedman pleaded that the statute of limitations outlawed the debt. However, this was not a good defense. His annual payments of interest acknowledged the existence of the debt and kept it alive.

2. The Remedy May Be Barred by Discharge of the Debtor in Bankruptcy

PROBLEM: Greene had overextended himself financially by buying too many items on installment plans. Then he lost his job. His wife required major surgery and was hospitalized for almost two months. Soon after, Greene was found guilty of negligence in an auto accident and was held liable for $155,000 more than his insurance policy coverage. Greene can see no way of paying his creditors, yet bill collectors are at his door almost daily. Is there anything he can legally do to get rid of his debts?

Years ago, a person who could not or did not pay debts as they came due could be jailed. Such punishment is costly for society, impractical, and unreasonable. A debtor cannot earn money to pay a debt while in prison. Moreover, the debtor's dependents may be forced to rely on public relief for support. Under the United States Constitution, Congress has established uniform laws on bankruptcies which permit the discharge of debts. Under these laws, debtors can get a fresh start, and creditors share fairly in whatever assets are available. **Bankruptcy** is the legal proceedings whereby a debtor's assets are distributed among creditors and debts are discharged.

bankruptcy: legal proceedings whereby a debtor's assets are distributed among creditors and debts are discharged

In the problem, Greene should file a proper voluntary petition with the bankruptcy court. If the petition is approved, he possibly would be permanently excused from paying all of his debts. Note that if Greene had willfully and maliciously caused the auto accident, the judgment debt of $155,000 would not be discharged (excused). Bankruptcy proceedings are discussed more fully in Chapter 19.

PREVENTING LEGAL DIFFICULTIES

When Seeking a Remedy for Breach of Contract . . .

1. negotiate, and possibly use mediation or arbitration, before resorting to litigation. A lawsuit should be the final resort because it is costly;
2. as a creditor seeking payment of an overdue debt, try to get at least a partial payment. In most states, such payment extends the time for filing suit before the claim is barred by the statute of limitations;
3. do not delay too long. If the debtor is uncooperative or defiant, sue. To rest on legal rights is to risk losing them;
4. if you wish to rescind or cancel your obligation, you must show that the other party breached the agreement in a material way. If you have paid anything, you may be able to recover what has been paid. If you have performed any service, you are entitled to be compensated;
5. always keep accurate records and be prepared to show that you actually suffered a monetary loss if you seek more than nominal damages. You must also show that you made a reasonable effort to mitigate the damages; and
6. if you seek specific performance, you must show that money damages will not adequately compensate you for your loss. You must also show that you are able, willing, and ready to perform your obligation.

Strengthening Your Legal Vocabulary

bankruptcy
cancellation
compensatory damages
incidental beneficiary
liquidated damages
mitigate
nominal damages
outlawed debt
remedy
rescission
third party beneficiary

1. One who benefits from a contract but is not a party to it and cannot enforce it.
2. Damages that are agreed upon in advance of possible breach of contract.
3. Legal proceedings discharging debts and distributing assets.
4. Means used to enforce a right or compensate for an injury.
5. Ending a contract by placing parties in the same position as if there had been no contract; neither party gets damages.
6. To reduce damages if reasonably possible.
7. One who is not a party to a contract but benefits from it and can enforce it.
8. Ending a contract for the sale of goods because of a breach, and returning consideration and retaining other remedies.

9. Token amount awarded when rights have been violated, but there is no actual injury.
10. Amount of money awarded to compensate for a plaintiff's loss.

Reviewing Important Points

1. As a general rule, one who is not a party to a contract has no rights or duties under the contract. However, a third party beneficiary may enforce a contract made for such party's benefit. An assignee may also acquire rights or assume duties under another party's contract.
2. In case of a breach of contract, the injured party has various remedies. An injured party may: (*a*) rescind or cancel the contract, (*b*) recover the amount of loss through damages, and (*c*) in certain cases, require specific performance.
3. After default, the injured party usually may recover the amount already spent in carrying out the obligations incurred as part of the contract. But the injured party should not increase the damages. Instead, the damages should be mitigated—that is, reduced if reasonably possible.
4. Generally a party to a contract has the option of breaching it. The courts will not punish such action by awarding punitive or exemplary damages unless a tort is involved. Rather, the court will award compensatory damages. Sometimes the court will award either liquidated or nominal damages.
5. When the legal remedy of damages is not adequate, the court may grant the equitable remedy of specific performance, or it may prohibit specified acts.
6. At the time of entering into a contract, the parties may agree to pay a specified, reasonable amount of damages if actual damages would be difficult to prove in case of default. Such damages are known as liquidated damages. The amount must not be so excessive that it would constitute a penalty.
7. A remedy for breach of contract may be barred (*a*) by the lapse of the time period prescribed by a statute of limitations or (*b*) by the debtor's discharge in bankruptcy.

Applying Law to Everyday Life

1. When Gallo sold his bookshop to Blake, there were balances due to 12 different publishing companies for books sold on account to Gallo. In their contract for sale of the shop, Blake agreed to pay these accounts payable, and Gallo reduced his selling price by an equivalent sum. Now Blake refuses to pay the publishers, claiming Gallo overcharged him for the store. Do the publishers have a cause of action against Blake?

2. Fulton sold traffic signal equipment to the City of Philadelphia. The City installed the equipment, put it to use, and found that it did not work satisfac-

torily. The City claimed the equipment did not meet specifications and so notified Fulton. The City refused to pay the purchase price. Nevertheless, the City continued to use the equipment. The City did not claim damages. Was the notice of failure to meet specifications a good defense against a suit for purchase price?

3. Hoglund reneged on his promise to sell his 1981 Camaro coupe to Elsen. Elsen immediately went to nearby Los Angeles and found a 1982 model with lower mileage, in better condition, and priced $500 below Hoglund's model. Nevertheless, Elsen was incensed by Hoglund's conduct and was determined to sue him "for all he's got." What damages, if any, is Elsen entitled to?

4. Van Denton agreed in writing to sell directly to Wallister 5,000 shares of stock in a major corporation listed on the New York Stock Exchange. By not going through stockbrokers they would save the usual sales and purchase commissions. The market price of the stock was $7 per share. For reasons he refused to disclose, Van Denton told Wallister, "Our deal is off. Sue me if you must." Wallister could have purchased the shares through a stockbroker, paid the commission, and sued Van Denton for reimbursement of the commission. Instead, he hesitated for three weeks, wondering whether he really wanted to buy the stock. By the time he bought, the price had more than doubled to $15 a share. Now he sues Van Denton for the extra cost of $8 a share plus the commission he had to pay as a percentage of the total price. Is he entitled to judgment?

5. Madison Unified High School District had plans to build a new high school. Madison awarded the contract for construction to Empire Builders, Inc., which bid $1,600,000. The contract contained a liquidated damage clause. The clause provided for payment of $1,000 a day for every day that completion was delayed beyond the expected 18-month construction period. Could the liquidated damage clause be enforced?

6. Goodman contracted to build a house for Stein according to Stein's plans. After the house was completed, there were several defects which Goodman refused to fix. Stein then contracted with Madden to do the necessary corrective work for $8,000. Stein then sued Goodman for $8,000 in compensatory damages plus $10,000 in exemplary damages. He sued Goodman for the exemplary damages "to punish him and set an example to warn others." How much is Stein entitled to?

7. Henderson was found guilty of manslaughter for causing the death of another driver in an auto accident. Henderson had been drinking and had been "showing off" his car to the passengers. At the trial, all of the passengers testified that they had tried to get him to stop, but he would not do so. In a separate civil action, judgment was rendered against Henderson for a total of $450,000 for willful and malicious battery. Although he had no liability insurance, Henderson just laughed. He said that when he got out of jail, he would "go through bankruptcy and shake the debt off." Can he do so?

Solving Case Problems

1. The plaintiffs filed a class action suit against the State of Colorado, certain officials, and the contractors on a tunnel construction project. The purpose of the suit was to seek recovery of funds alleged to have been expended unlawfully in the construction. The plaintiffs claimed that as citizens and taxpayers, they were beneficiaries of the contract for the tunnel construction. Therefore, they claimed, they were entitled to sue on the contract that was made on their behalf even though the contract was made with the State of Colorado and did not mention any individuals by name as beneficiaries. May these plaintiffs properly sue? (*Gallagher v. Continental Insurance Company*, 502 F.2d 827, 10th Cir.)

2. Seismic & Digital Concepts, Inc., was a manufacturer of computer hardware. Digital Resources Corp. produced computer software. Digital Resources sold software to Seismic and sued when Seismic refused to pay for the software. Seismic countersued for damages because of late delivery of the goods—they were delivered 10 to 25 days after the date specified in the contract. There was no indication in the contract that "time was of the essence." Moreover, Seismic had accepted and used the software, and for about five months had even asked Digital Resources to do additional work. Is Digital entitled to judgment? (*Seismic & Digital Concepts, Inc. v. Digital Resources Corporation*, 590 S.W.2d 718, Tex.)

3. Union Oil Company was the owner of a truck stop. Union sued the general contractor and subcontractors who had constructed the large service station to recover the cost of repairing the cracked parking area pavement. Union claimed the defendant had not followed specifications for the base material used for fill. When the contractor refused to make the needed repairs, Union had the work done by others at a cost of $58,659 and now sought to recover this sum. The defendant's superintendent admitted under oath that he had not followed the specifications, but he said that Union had approved the substitute material. Union denied this, and the notes of Union's representative supported Union's testimony. The defendant's witnesses could not remember times or dates or present any records on the matter. Should Union win? (*Union Oil Company of California v. Kennon Construction*, 502 F.2d 792, 6th Cir.)

4. Under a written contract, plaintiff Shirley MacLaine Parker agreed to play the female singing-dancing lead in defendant 20th Century-Fox Film Corporation's planned production of a musical entitled "Bloomer Girl," to be filmed in Los Angeles. Fox Films was to pay MacLaine a minimum of $53,571.42 a week for 14 weeks, starting May 23. Before then, Fox decided not to produce the picture. In a letter dated April 4, Fox offered to employ MacLaine in a dramatic, western-type movie to be produced in Australia instead. She was given one week in which to accept. She did not, and the offer lapsed. She then sued for the agreed $750,000 guaranteed compensation. Fox defended by saying MacLaine had unreasonably refused to miti-

gate damages by rejecting the substitute role. Decide. (*Parker v. 20th Century-Fox Film Corporation*, 474 P.2d 689, Cal.)

5. Knutton operated a music company. Cofield was the owner of a restaurant. Knutton and Cofield contracted for the installation of a jukebox in the restaurant, agreeing to share the receipts obtained. The contract provided that if Cofield discontinued use of the jukebox before the end of the agreed period, he would pay Knutton a sum of money for the unexpired time. The sum would be based on the average of the amount paid to Knutton per day while the machine had been used. Before the contracted time expired, Cofield disconnected the jukebox and installed one from another supplier. Knutton sued for damages for breach of contract. Cofield claimed the damages sought were a penalty for the breach and not liquidated damages, as claimed by Knutton. Was Cofield correct? (*Knutton v. Cofield*, 160 S.E.2d 29, N.C.)

SPECIAL SECTION: Choosing an Attorney

All too often, individuals find themselves immediately in need of legal services, and they are forced to choose an attorney without the benefit of adequate time to evaluate the alternatives. This may result in an unsatisfactory selection. The prudent person deliberately establishes an ongoing working relationship with a qualified attorney early in adult life and maintains the relationship through the years by practicing preventive law. Preventive law involves consulting your lawyer often in order to anticipate, identify, and confront legal issues before they become legal problems.

Your attorney should be someone with whom you can talk comfortably and in whom you have confidence. Although the working relationship is typically person to person, resources of firms with multiple members can be important. Especially in smaller urban and rural areas, the size of the firm often affects the size of its library and computer research capability. It also determines the pool of specialized experience available to your lawyer. Inquiries among relatives, friends, perhaps your banker, accountant, and insurance agent can provide information about the reputation of the lawyers you are considering. Newspaper reports of legal actions are sometimes helpful. The work load of a lawyer is significant because an attorney who is successful but is too busy to give your situation the attention it needs will not be a good choice for you. You may want to visit the offices of more than one attorney (and determine applicable fees for services) before you decide.

Even if you have selected a personal attorney, your situation may at times require an attorney who is a specialist in a particular area. Criminal law, patent and copyright law, constitutional law, environmental law, antitrust law, family law, and administrative law are all specialized subject areas.

Attorneys often identify their field(s) of specialization in the Yellow Pages of telephone directories. Also, the multivolume Martindale-Hubbell directory of attorneys, published annually, and available in large public libraries, lists most practicing attorneys and law firms in the United States. It indicates specializations, broadly states the reputations among peers, and lists business clients of large firms. Local bar associations often can provide lists of attorneys in specialized areas of practice.

Unit Four
BUYING AND SELLING GOODS

UNIT OBJECTIVES

UPON COMPLETION OF THIS UNIT, you should be able to

1. distinguish the sale of goods from a contract to sell, barter, conveyance of real property, lease, assignment, bailment, gift, and negotiation of commercial paper.
2. explain why sales of goods for a price of $500 or more must generally be evidenced by a writing.
3. list exceptions to the preceding rule.
4. discuss how a true owner may *always* transfer ownership (title) of goods owned, while a thief may *never* do so, and how other categories of persons may *sometimes* do so.
5. describe how a person who does not have possession of goods may nevertheless suffer the loss if the goods are lost or destroyed.
6. define and explain the differences among existing, identified, and future goods.
7. define and explain the difference between a sale on approval and a sale or return.
8. distinguish between implied and express warranties.
9. discuss the importance of careful, informed buying whether or not warranties are given by the seller.
10. understand how an express warranty may actually provide less protection than the implied warranty of merchantability, but that the latter may be limited or excluded by the seller.
11. explain the difference between a full warranty and a limited warranty.
12. recognize a situation where one may seek relief on the theory of strict liability if injured by a defective product, whether or not a warranty is in effect.

16
The Sales Contract

1. You are unable to go to a rock concert for which you already have a ticket. Therefore a friend who wants to go to the concert persuades you to trade your ticket for some record albums. Is this barter really a sale and therefore governed by the UCC?
2. A young couple selects matching wedding bands from a catalog in a jewelry store. The couple agrees to pay in full upon delivery. Has a sale been made?
3. A bride-to-be wants her wedding gown to be custom-made from a unique new fabric. A bridal shop quotes a price of $1,750. When she orally agrees, the shop special-orders the fabric and cuts it to fit. Then the wedding is canceled. The young lady seeks to avoid the contract because it was not in writing. Can she do so?

WHAT IS A SALE?

PROBLEM: At the Big Department Store, the Allertons signed a contract to buy a microwave oven. The store expected to receive the microwave from the wholesaler within 30 days. While shopping, the Allertons left their car in the store's automobile service department to have the engine's idling speed adjusted and to have squeaks in the door eliminated. The charge for labor was $45; there was no charge for the lubricant. The service attendant recommended replacement of the car's tires and the Allertons agreed. The cost of the tires was $200, plus $25 for balancing and installation. The Allertons also bought a new battery for $59, and it was installed free of charge. Were all of these agreements sales?

sale: contract in which ownership of goods passes immediately from the seller to the buyer for a price

A **sale** is a contract in which *ownership* of (also known as *title* to) goods transfers immediately from the seller to the buyer for a **price**. The UCC deals with sales or contracts to sell **goods**, that is, tangible, movable personal property, such as a jet plane, clothing, growing crops, or the unborn young of animals. By definition in the UCC, goods do not include the following:

price: consideration for a sale or a contract to sell

1. money (except rare currency or rare coins),
2. intangible property (such as rights under a contract, which are transferred by assignment rather than by sale),
3. patents and copyrights, and
4. real estate (although the transfer of title to real property is commonly called a sale, it is technically a conveyance).

goods: items of tangible, movable personal property

The price for the goods may take the form of money, services, or other goods. However, when the parties to a sale exchange only goods for goods, without involving money or services, the sale is known as a **barter**.

barter: exchange of goods for goods

Under the UCC, a sales contract may be made in any manner sufficient to show agreement, and the contract suffices if the parties by their actions recognize the existence of a contract. This is true even though a court might not be able to determine precisely when the contract was made, and even though one or more terms generally are left open.

payment: buyer's delivery and seller's acceptance of the price

receipt of goods: buyer's taking of physical possession or control of goods

Payment occurs when the buyer delivers the agreed price and the seller accepts it. **Receipt of goods** means that the buyer takes physical possession or control of them. Receipt usually involves actual delivery. However, delivery may be constructive, as when one gets the keys to a car or receives a warehouse receipt for stored goods.

Acceptance of goods means that the buyer has agreed, by words or conduct, that the goods received are satisfactory. Acceptance is shown when the goods are used, resold, or otherwise treated as if they were owned by the buyer. Acceptance may also be indicated when a buyer fails to reject the goods within a reasonable time, if the buyer has had adequate opportunity to inspect them.

acceptance of goods: buyer's approval of goods

In general, the law of contracts has been simplified and made less strict in its application to sales of goods. For example, the price for goods usually is fixed in the contract. However, the parties may indicate that the price is to be set in a certain way at a later date. This method is especially used in long-term contracts when considerable instability of prices is expected. Ordinarily, when nothing is said about the price, a contract results if all other essentials are present, and provided the parties do not express a contrary intent. In such a case, the buyer is required to pay the price that is reasonable at the time of delivery.

In many situations, the contract is primarily for personal services. Such contracts are not sales because any goods supplied are merely incidental. In the problem, the work on the car engine and the doors was strictly a contract for services; goods (lubricants) supplied were incidental, and no specific charge was made for them. The transfer to the Allertons of title to the tires was a sale of goods, even though a small charge was made for related labor. The battery was acquired in a sale of goods, with no charge for labor. The Allertons' agreement to buy a microwave oven at a later date was not a sale. Instead, it was a **contract to sell**—a contract in which ownership of goods is to transfer in a sale in the future. Both present sales of goods and contracts to sell goods are governed by the law of sales found in the UCC. In both types of transactions, the seller is known as a **vendor**. The buyer is known as the **vendee** (also called the *purchaser*). The transaction involving a vendor and a vendee is called a "sale" by the seller and is called a "purchase" by the buyer.

contract to sell: contract in which ownership of goods in a sale is to pass in the future

vendor: seller

vendee: buyer

WHAT IS THE EFFECT OF OWNERSHIP?

PROBLEM: Leister won $2,000,000 in a state lottery. When he received the first of 20 promised annual payments of $100,000, he went on a spending spree. He bought a new car which he carelessly wrecked, clothes which he never even wore, and a mink coat for a casual friend he met in a bar. He staged a wild New Year's Eve party for 50 new friends, during which the revelers smashed their crystal champagne glasses in a fireplace. Through court action, relatives now seek to stop Leister from using his money and goods so wastefully. Will they succeed?

It is important to know the difference between a sale and a contract to sell because both benefits and burdens generally go with ownership. Therefore it is necessary to know when ownership transfers from one party to another. When one person *sells* (transfers to another party the ownership of goods), he or she says, in effect, "I hereby transfer to you the legal right to use, control, and dispose of these goods."

Ownership carries valuable rights. Any rise in value (as in prices of securities, output of land, or increase in animal weight or number) belongs to the owner. Moreover, goods generally may be enjoyed and used as the owner pleases. They may be squandered or even destroyed, as in the problem. Leister's relatives will fail unless they can prove he has become mentally incompetent, which is unlikely.

Ownership also involves duties and burdens. The owner may be taxed in proportion to what is owned. The freedom to use one's property may be limited by government regulations for the common good, as by speeding and zoning laws. Property should be protected and maintained. If it is cared for improperly or used in a manner which interferes with the rights of others, the owner may be liable for resulting torts (see Chapter 5). In some cases, this responsibility may extend to the use of the goods by another person. For example, in some states, the owner of an automobile is responsible for injuries arising out of the operation of the car by another person if that person has the owner's permission to be operating the car.

An owner of goods must also bear any loss that occurs when those goods deteriorate because of the action of natural forces—sun, wind, rain, snow, and oxidation. When goods are destroyed, stolen, lost, or damaged without the legal fault of any person, the owner must take the loss unless the goods were covered by proper insurance. For example, if a storm damages or destroys camping equipment that you own, you suffer the loss unless the equipment was properly insured.

In spite of all this, ownership does not always determine who shall take losses for goods. As will be discussed in Chapter 17, the UCC sometimes places the risk of loss on someone other than the owner.

HOW DO SALES COMPARE WITH SIMILAR TRANSFERS OF OWNERSHIP AND POSSESSION?

PROBLEM: Both Brian and Cowan became electronic data processing specialists during their service in the U.S. Army. When they retired from the Army, they decided to open their own retail electronic specialty store. Using savings, some borrowed funds, and (a) money donated by their parents, they (b) purchased a parcel of land which had a suitable building. They (c) rented the empty lot next to the building to use as parking space, under a contract for a five-year period. They (d) bought a supply of personal computers and related equipment and (e) agreed to purchase an equal quantity of a new PC model scheduled for production within six months. They (f) traded their two sports cars for a company truck, and (g) raised additional money by transferring, to a buyer, a note receivable (commercial paper) for $27,000 which Brian had received in partial payment when he sold his house trailer. To get more cash for working capital, (h) Brian and Cowan transferred to a bank all rights to collect on a group of accounts receivable which they had obtained from sales made on credit. They (i) obtained all their store display cases by renting them from the manufacturer. In every instance noted, Brian and Cowan obtained possession of property needed for their business. What types of transactions did they utilize?

In the problem, Brian and Cowan became merchants after retirement from the Army. Most of the transactions they henceforth engage in will be sales. This will be true when they acquire inventory and other equipment from suppliers, and when they sell their stock in trade to customers. However, as noted in the problem, they could acquire property in a variety of other transactions. The transactions lettered in the problem are identified as follows, in Table 16-1: (a) - 9 (gift); (b) - 4 (conveyance); (c) - 5 (lease); (d) - 1 (sale); (e) - 2 (contract to sell); (f) - 3 (barter); (g) - 6 (negotiation); (h) - 7 (assignment); and (i) - 8 (bailment).

In most cases, the UCC treats all buyers and sellers alike. In some cases, it treats merchants differently from casual sellers. A **merchant** is a seller who deals regularly in a particular kind of goods or otherwise claims to have special knowledge or skill in a certain type of sales transaction. A **casual seller** is one who sells only occasionally or otherwise does not meet the definition of merchant. For example, you would be a casual seller if you sold your private automobile. A used-car dealer selling the same car would be a merchant. In general, the UCC holds merchants to a higher standard of conduct than it does casual sellers. Merchants may be required to have

merchant: one who regularly sells a particular kind of goods

casual seller: one who sells occasionally

Transaction	Type of Property Involved	Involvement of a Contract	Transfer of Ownership	Transfer of Possession	Evidence of Transaction
1 **Sale**	Goods (Tangible Personal Property)	Yes	Yes	Usually yes	Contract; Bill of Sale
2 **Contract to Sell**	Goods	Yes	No	Usually no	Contract
3 **Barter**	Goods	Yes	Yes	Usually yes	Contract
4 **Conveyance**	Real Property	Usually*	Yes	Usually yes	Contract; Deed
5 **Lease**	Real Property (Usually)	Usually*	No	Yes	Lease
6 **Negotiation**	Negotiable Instruments	Usually*	Yes	Yes	Commercial Paper
7 **Assignment**	Contract Rights	Usually*	Yes	Yes, when contract is performed	Contract
8 **Bailment**	Personal Property	Usually*	No	Yes	Contract (in commercial bailment)
9 **Gift**	Personal or Real Property	No	Yes	Usually yes	Usually none; Deed for Real Property

*May be gratuitous.

Table 16-1. Comparison of Sales with Similar Transactions

licenses to sell. They are also usually subjected to special taxation and closer regulation by the government.

As already noted, sales contracts may be made through a traditional exchange of offer and acceptance. But the UCC recognizes alternative methods. It adds another way of accepting an offer to buy. Instead of phoning or mailing an acceptance, the seller may simply ship the goods and thereafter notify the buyer of this action.

The Tastie Treat Shop mailed an order for 500 one-pound boxes of bonbons to the Chocolate Castle Company. Chocolate Castle could have accepted the order by mail, telephone, or wire. Instead, it immediately shipped the candy, thus creating a contract. The usual price was simply added to the next invoice mailed to Tastie Treat Shop.

Under the UCC, an offeror may expressly state that the offer to buy or to sell goods must be accepted exactly as made or not at all. Otherwise the offeree may accept and still change some terms of the contract or add new ones. Recall that in most contract negotiations such changes would end the original offer and would be considered a counteroffer. Under the law of sales of goods, the new term is treated as a proposal for addition to the contract.

This provision of the UCC helps to avoid what courts have called the "battle of the forms." This battle occurs when a merchant buyer makes an offer with a preprinted *purchase order form.* It contains detailed terms, often including many which clearly favor the buyer. In response, a merchant seller accepts by using a *sales order form* with differing terms, which favor the seller.

When both parties are merchants, a new term inserted by the offeree automatically becomes part of the contract if the offeror fails to object within a reasonable time. However, the new term must not materially alter the offer, and the original offer must not expressly bar such changes. If the new term is a *material* (important) alteration, it is included in the contract only if the offeror expressly agrees to be bound by it.

A pottery manufacturer offered to sell flowerpots in three sizes to a department store. The store accepted the offer, but it specified that the pots had to be packaged in sets of three rather than individually as described in the offer. Instead of objecting, the pottery maker shipped the goods as requested. A contract resulted with no other change in terms.

MUST DELIVERY AND PAYMENT BE MADE AT THE SAME TIME?

PROBLEM: Ross bought Hanukkah gifts for his children during the Sunrise Center's Lay-Away Sale in October. Ross was to take delivery early in December and agreed to pay with no charge for credit before January 31 of the next year. Did he own the gifts in October?

In the basic sales transaction, payment, *delivery* (transfer of possession), and transfer of title take place simultaneously at the seller's place of business. Even if payment or delivery, or both, take place later, title still passes when the buyer selects (identifies to the contract) and agrees to buy the goods in the seller's store. At the appropriate time fixed in the sales contract, the buyer normally has a duty to pay, and the seller has a duty to transfer possession. Generally neither is obligated to perform until the other does. Thus, unless it is otherwise agreed or is the custom of the trade, the seller may retain the goods until the buyer makes payment in full. Similarly, the buyer may refuse to pay the price until the seller delivers all the goods. The buyer is entitled to a receipt when payment is made.

bill of sale: receipt serving as written evidence of the transfer of ownership of goods

A **bill of sale** is a receipt that serves as written evidence of the transfer of ownership of (title to) goods. Neither a bill of sale nor a sales contract need identify the parties or explain the terms of the transaction. Such a document is sometimes required by statute, as in the case of automobile sales. If a bill of sale is signed by the seller, buyer, or both, it can satisfy the requirements of the statute of frauds for a signed writing.

A bill of sale makes resale of the property easier because it provides the owner with written evidence of ownership. When goods are lost, stolen, or destroyed, as in a fire, the document can be used to help prove value for insurance purposes. If the owner borrows money and uses the goods as security, the bill of sale ensures the creditor that the debtor owns the goods pledged. Of course, other persons may have acquired claims against the goods since the bill of sale was issued. Also, dishonest persons may forge such documents to help dispose of stolen property.

To encourage business, most sellers extend credit to qualified buyers, including other business firms. Some retailers do most of their business selling to customers who use credit cards or charge accounts, or who pay in installments (see Unit 5). Thus, the buyer may get both title and possession before payment. In the problem, assuming the goods were set aside for Ross at the time of the sale, he received title in October, possession in December, and paid for the goods in January.

HOW DOES THE STATUTE OF FRAUDS APPLY TO SALES?

PROBLEM: Chilton orally agreed to buy an imported camera from the Open Shutter Shop for $748.98. No camera was in stock, but a shipment was expected any day. Therefore the salesclerk prepared a memo of the sale, signed it, and gave Chilton a copy. A week later the clerk phoned and said, "Your camera is ready." Chilton replied that he did not want it because he had learned that the identical model could be purchased for much less by mail from a New York City discount store. Is Chilton liable to Open Shutter for breach of contract?

Sales or contracts to sell, like other contracts, are generally valid and enforceable in court whether they are oral, written, or implied from the conduct of the parties. However, as you may recall, under the statute of frauds sales of goods for $500 or more must be evidenced by a writing to be enforceable in court.

In good business practice, both parties sign if a written sales contract is used. Each party gets a copy. This provides both parties with a useful legal record. It shows mutual good faith. Normally both parties expect to perform, but either party might break the contract. If that should happen, the injured party can seek the aid of a court. The writing would help to prove the existence of their agreement.

In the problem, the price of the goods was $500 or more. Therefore the sale was governed by the statute of frauds. Open Shutter is bound because its clerk signed the contract. Chilton is not bound because he did not sign, but he could enforce the agreement against Open Shutter if he so desired.

Not all the terms of a sales contract have to be in writing to satisfy the statute of frauds. Essentially, all that is required is a writing, signed by the party being sued, which satisfies the court that a contract to sell, or a sale, has been made. The number or quantity of goods involved in the transaction must be contained in the writing, and the contract is not enforceable beyond the stated amount. However, the time and manner of performance, credit and warranty terms, and even the price need not be included for the writing to satisfy the statute. If necessary, these items can be supplied later by oral testimony in court.

Between merchants, the signature of the party who is suing may suffice to prove an otherwise unenforceable sales contract. If a merchant sends a written confirmation of an oral contract to another merchant within a reasonable time after the agreement is made, the confirmation binds both parties. However, if the second merchant sends a written objection to the confirmation within ten days, the confirmation is not binding.

WHEN IS A SIGNED WRITING NOT REQUIRED UNDER THE STATUTE?

PROBLEM: La Fargo telephoned an order to Hoban's Brick and Tile Works for some kitchen tile priced at $663. The proper tile was delivered. However, when La Fargo checked the shipment later that day, he decided it was not quite what he wanted. He immediately notified Hoban of his refusal to accept the goods, but Hoban insisted the oral contract was binding. La Fargo refused to pay, and Hoban sued for the price. Who won?

Under certain circumstances, oral contracts for the sale of goods worth more than $500 may be held valid and enforceable. These exceptions to the requirements of the statute of frauds include the following:

1. When the Goods Have Been Received and Accepted by the Buyer

Receipt of the goods alone does not make an oral contract binding under the statute of frauds. Both receipt and acceptance are necessary. A buyer may receive goods without accepting them, as in the problem when La Fargo promptly exercised his right to reject. Normally if goods are properly delivered and conform to the contract, the buyer is bound. However, the statute of frauds enabled La Fargo to avoid his obligation. Hoban could have prevented this costly problem by requiring the buyer's signature on a suitable writing before shipment.

Note that if the buyer has received and accepted only some of the goods, the oral contract is enforceable only for those goods received and accepted.

Ramirez visited Petrosiki's Paint Pot and orally ordered 40 gallons of shingle stain. The stain was priced at $13 a gallon. It was to be charged to his account and delivered the following Monday. Nothing was signed. Ramirez took one 5-gallon can home with him. However, his wife was displeased with the color, and he disliked the way it went on. Therefore he refused to accept the balance of the order. Ramirez was within his rights in doing so. Ramirez was bound by the contract only for the five gallons which he had received and accepted.

2. When the Buyer Has Paid for the Goods in Full and the Seller Has Accepted Payment

When payment in full has been accepted by the seller, the contract is enforceable in full. When *partial* payment has been accepted by the seller, the oral contract is enforceable only for the goods paid for if the goods can be divided and the price can be apportioned fairly. If the goods are indivisible and there can be no dispute as to quantity, the contract is enforceable in full.

> At an auction, Zutto bought a handmade, oak rolltop desk from Winslow for $650. Zutto paid $350 on the bill and left to get a truck and the balance due. When Zutto returned, Winslow told him the desk had been sold to another person for $850. Winslow explained that the contract with Zutto was oral and therefore not enforceable. Winslow was wrong; Zutto's partial payment for the indivisible goods (the oak desk) made the oral contract enforceable. If the goods had been divisible (for example, 50 reams of paper) the contract would be enforceable only for the quantity paid for.

3. When the Goods Are to Be Specially Manufactured for the Buyer and Are Not Suitable for Sale to Others in the Ordinary Course of the Seller's Business

A seller can enforce an oral contract for nonresellable goods in either of the following two situations:

a. if the seller has made a substantial beginning in manufacturing the goods, or
b. if the seller has made contracts to obtain the goods from third parties.

4. When the Party Against Whom Enforcement Is Sought Admits during the Course of Legal Proceedings that the Oral Contract Was Made

A party against whom enforcement of an oral contract is sought may admit in legal pleadings or testimony that a contract was made. In this case, a signed writing is not necessary for the enforcement of the part of the contract which was admitted.

> Richardson was sued by the seller, Olmstead, for breach of an oral contract to buy 300 sides of prime Kansas beef. Because the order exceeded $500, the contract should have been evidenced by some signed writing

to be enforceable. In his testimony during the trial, Richardson admitted that there had been an oral agreement, but he said that it was for only 100 sides. Richardson is bound to perform or pay damages for breach of contract for the reduced quantity because of his admission of the existence of the oral contract.

PREVENTING LEGAL DIFFICULTIES

In Sales, Be Informed and Aware that . . .

1. during your lifetime, you will probably enter into more sales contracts (usually as buyer, but often as seller) than any other type of contract. It helps to know the law of sales;
2. your best protection against shoddy merchandise is knowledge of goods and their value, followed by careful comparison shopping;
3. your best protection against sales fraud is the integrity of the seller (as reflected in the seller's established reputation) coupled with your caution;
4. when you make a major purchase, make sure your insurance is adequate. Your insurance should provide for coverage against possible loss of the purchased property. If appropriate (as in automobile purchases), it should also provide protection against possible liability for injury to others;
5. it is a good idea to put a sales agreement in writing even if it is for goods worth less than $500. Although this is not required by the statute of frauds, doing so can avoid misunderstandings and prevent costly litigation. If the goods are worth $500 or more, insist on compliance with the statute of frauds;
6. the other party should sign the contract or memorandum and give you a copy. The other party may properly require that you sign too;
7. you are bound by an oral contract for goods over $500 to the extent that you have received them and accepted delivery. You may be bound in full or in part if you have made some payment. You usually are bound when you order custom-made goods; and
8. for expensive "big ticket" items, you should get a bill of sale marked "paid" when you pay the full price.

Strengthening Your Legal Vocabulary

acceptance of goods
barter
bill of sale
casual seller
contract to sell
goods
merchant
payment
price
receipt of goods

sale **vendor**
vendee

1. Contract in which ownership of goods passes immediately from the seller to the buyer for a price.
2. Consideration in money, goods, or services, which is given in return for the transfer of title to goods.
3. Buyer or purchaser.
4. Contract to transfer ownership of goods at a later date.
5. Seller who deals regularly in a particular kind of goods or otherwise claims to have special knowledge or skill in a certain type of transaction.
6. Exchange of goods for goods.
7. Tangible personal property that is movable.
8. Receipt serving as written evidence of the transfer of ownership of goods.
9. Buyer's taking of physical possession or control of goods.
10. Buyer's indication that the goods received are satisfactory.

Reviewing Important Points

1. Both sales and contracts to sell are governed by a combination of basic contract law and special UCC provisions on sales. Transfers of ownership of other types of property, such as intangible personal property and real estate, are governed by different laws.
2. Both benefits and burdens go with ownership of goods.
3. Merchants generally are held to a higher standard of conduct by the UCC than are casual sellers.
4. Neither payment nor delivery is essential for transfer of title.
5. Unless it is otherwise provided by statute, sales or contracts to sell may be oral, written, or implied from the conduct of the parties.
6. To be enforceable, a sale or contract to sell goods for a price of $500 or more must be evidenced by a writing. The writing must specify at least a quantity of the goods involved and must be signed by the party who is sued or by that party's agent. The writing is not essential when:
   a. the buyer has received and accepted the goods,
   b. the buyer has paid for the goods in full and the seller has accepted payment,
   c. the goods are custom-made for the buyer, are not readily resellable in the ordinary course of business, and the seller has begun purchasing parts or necessary manufacturing, or
   d. the party seeking to avoid the contract admits during the legal proceedings that the oral agreement was made.
7. Price may consist of anything, such as money, services, or goods, as agreed upon by the parties as consideration.
8. Payment occurs when the buyer delivers the price and the seller accepts it.
9. Receipt of goods occurs when the buyer takes physical possession or control of the goods when they are tendered by the seller.

10. Acceptance of the goods occurs when the buyer indicates that the goods received are satisfactory.
11. A bill of sale provides evidence of the transfer of ownership of goods.

Applying Law to Everyday Life

1. The Caribbean Mill sold a quantity of standard electrolytic copper bars to Pollard. The contract was complete in all respects except that it failed to state the price. Was the contract a valid one, thus enforceable in court?

2. At Mrs. Johnson's request, her doctor prescribed and injected her with a drug. The drug had been tested and had been approved for sale by the federal Food and Drug Administration. It had been manufactured by Maker A, sold to Wholesaler B, then sold to Retail Pharmacy C which sold it to the doctor. The doctor charged Mrs. Johnson $15 for the drug and $50 for his services. Twenty years later, Mrs. Johnson's daughter developed a cancer traceable to the drug which her mother had taken. Was the doctor a seller and therefore liable for breach of warranty?

3. As Brackston was examining a large Swedish glass vase in the Nook and Cranny Shoppe, the vase slipped from her hands. It smashed into countless pieces when it hit the floor. After the proprietor had swept up the mess, she pointed to a sign on the wall which said, "Handle with Care! If You Break It, You Buy It." She then rang up a sales charge of $300 plus $18 sales tax. Was Brackston the vendee in a sales contract?

4. Every two weeks, Ericson held a garage sale to resell items she had purchased at other such sales. When the city and state governments tried to tax her sales, Ericson claimed that she was merely a casual seller. Therefore, she claimed, she did not have to pay a sales tax. Was Ericson correct?

5. When Soule bought a sweater for his wife, the clerk deliberately lied to him. She said that the garment was a pure silk and mohair, handknitted import from Italy. In fact, it was a machine-made, domestic, polyester-and-wool mix. Did the clerk violate the statute of frauds by her conduct?

6. Grant had long admired Kahn's collection of records featuring the big bands of the 1930s. One day Kahn orally agreed to sell the collection to Grant for $275. When Grant appeared with the money, however, Kahn said she had changed her mind and refused to deliver. Moreover, she insisted she was acting within her legal rights. Kahn said she had learned that her collection was actually worth at least $1,000. Therefore, she said, a signed writing was required to make the contract enforceable. Has Kahn stated the law correctly?

7. Harrison orally agreed to buy two electric guitars and a matched set of drums from Rudolph. The price was $1,250, payable with $800 in cash and a bass saxophone. Harrison paid the price in full. However, Rudolph

refused to deliver the guitars and drums, and he sent the saxophone back and mailed a certified check for $800 to Harrison. He explained that he had decided to start another rock group. Rudolph claimed that their oral agreement was not enforceable. Is he right?

Solving Case Problems

1. Gillispie, a minor, was injured when two bottles of a soft drink exploded. The accident occurred as Gillispie was carrying the bottles to the checkout counter in the defendant's self-service store. Had a sale taken place even though Gillispie had not yet paid for the goods? If so, the store could be liable for the injury. Decide. (*Gillispie v. Great Atlantic and Pacific Tea Company,* 187 S.E.2d 441, N.C.)

2. Shriber, an officer of Nelly Don, Inc., orally agreed with a representative of the defendant DHJ Industries, Inc., to buy 75,000 yards of colorfast fabric from DHJ. A few days later Shriber confirmed this agreement by telephone, and then sent a Nelly Don purchase order form. The form included these words, "This purchase order shall become a binding contract when acknowledged by Seller, or upon whole or partial shipment by Seller." In response, Shriber received a DHJ sales order form. At the bottom, just above the lines for signatures, this statement appeared, "THIS CONTRACT IS SUBJECT TO ALL THE TERMS AND CONDITIONS PRINTED ON THE REVERSE SIDE." On the reverse side was a clause requiring settlement of any controversy by arbitration. Shriber signed. Later, a dispute arose as to whether the fabric delivered was colorfast and machine washable. The plaintiff buyers claimed fraud and sued. The defendant sellers said the dispute had to be settled by arbitration and not in court. Was the arbitration clause binding? (*N & D Fashions, Inc. and Nelly Don, Inc. v. DHJ Industries, Inc.,* 548 F.2d 722)

3. Cargill Incorporated, the plaintiff, is a large grain company. Warren, an agent of Cargill, managed its grain elevator in Hingham, Montana. On August 24, Warren orally contracted to buy from Wilson, the defendant farmer, 28,000 bushels of wheat at $1.48 per bushel and 6,000 bushels of higher protein wheat at $1.63 per bushel. Warren prepared two standard grain purchase written contracts. He signed them for Cargill, as its agent, and he also signed Wilson's name. A few days later, he delivered copies to Wilson who made no objection. On August 30, Wilson received a $10,000 loan from Cargill. The check was attached to a detachable part of the standard grain contract, and it incorporated the two contracts by specific references to their numbers. Wilson indorsed and cashed the check. The loan was interest-free because it was actually an advance payment for the wheat. During September and October, Wilson delivered 11,000 bushels of ordinary wheat at the agreed price of $1.48, and 6,000 bushels at the then-current, higher market price. Then Wilson refused to deliver any more

wheat. Cargill sued for damages. Wilson claimed he was not bound because of the statute of frauds. Who should win? (*Cargill Incorporated v. Kenneth L. Wilson*, 532 P.2d 988, Mont.)

4. Smigel orally offered to sell to Lockwood a used Rolls Royce for $11,400. Lockwood orally accepted the offer, paid $100 down, and agreed to pay the balance on delivery. However, Smigel failed to deliver the car and notified Lockwood that he had sold it to someone else. Lockwood sued to enforce the oral contract. Decide. (*Lockwood v. Smigel*, 18 Cal.App.3d 800, 96 Cal.Rptr.289)

5. Jordan Paper Products, Inc., sued to recover $22,089.48 owed to it under an oral contract by Burger Man, Inc., an Indiana fast-food chain. The contract was for various paper products that Jordan had prepared at Burger Man's order, to specially identify the fast-food chain to its customers. Burger Man maintained that the oral contract was unenforceable because of the statute of frauds. Decide. (*Burger Man, Inc. v. Jordan Paper Products, Inc.*, 352 N.E.2d 821, Indiana)

17

Transfer of Ownership and Risk of Loss

1. In good faith, you purchase a set of cross-country skis from an acquaintance who then disappears with the money. Later, you find out that the skis were stolen property. You learn this when the rightful owner demands that the skis be returned. Must you return them?
2. Paying the price in advance, you order a professional-type hair dryer from a mail-order house. If the shipment is lost en route, who bears the loss?
3. You agreed to a 10-day free home trial of a new motion picture camera. During the trial period, a thief broke into your home. The camera, a television set, and some sterling silver flatware were stolen and never recovered. Must you pay for the motion picture camera?

WHO MAY TRANSFER THE OWNERSHIP OF GOODS?

PROBLEM: Brad stole a tape recorder from Fuller's car. He then sold it to Standon who knew it was stolen. Did either Brad or Standon receive good title to the tape recorder? Would it make any difference if Standon did not know or suspect that the recorder was stolen?

Generally only the true owner of goods may legally transfer ownership of those goods. Also, as a general rule, the buyer of goods receives only the property rights that the seller has in the goods and nothing more. Therefore the person who buys stolen goods from a thief receives possession, but not title, because the thief did not have good title to give. This is true whether the buyer is innocent or, as in the problem, knows that the goods have been stolen. In reality, stolen goods usually are not recovered. If recovered, they are often not identifiable as the property of the victim and therefore are not returned. (The police simply sell them at auctions.)

As with most general rules, there are exceptions to these rules about transfer of ownership. Such exceptions include the following:

1. Persons Authorized to Do So May Transfer Another's Title

Persons may validly sell what they do not own if the owner has authorized them to do so. Salesclerks in retail stores are so authorized. Auctioneers and sheriffs are also authorized when they sell goods under court order.

2. Fraudulent Buyers May Transfer Better Title than They Have

If an owner of goods is induced by fraud to sell the goods, the buyer obtains a voidable title (see Chapter 12). Upon discovering the fraud, the victimized seller may cancel the contract and recover the goods unless an innocent third party has already given value and acquired rights in them. Such a third party is known as a **good-faith purchaser**. Thus, a fraudulent buyer with voidable title may transfer valid title to a good-faith purchaser. To act in good faith, the purchaser must not have reason to suspect the person who has the voidable title. The defrauded seller must seek damages from the original buyer, if the person can be located and is not judgment-proof (without enough assets to be able to pay a judgment).

good-faith purchaser: innocent third party who gives value and acquires rights in goods

Downy lied about his income and assets when he bought a dinette from Furniture World on credit. After making the first of twelve payments, Downy defaulted. Furniture World then checked Downy's credit record and discovered the fraud. But Downy had already sold the dinette to Tilly, who honestly thought that Downy was the owner. As a good-faith buyer, Tilly received good title to the dinette. Furniture World must suffer the loss unless it can locate Downy and recover from him.

3. Holders of Negotiable Documents of Title May Transfer Better Title than They Have

In business, certain documents are often used as a substitute for possession of goods. Examples are warehouse receipts issued by public warehouses, and bills of lading and airbills, issued by common carriers. These documents may be non-negotiable or negotiable. If the documents are negotiable, the goods are to be delivered to the bearer (the person with possession) of the document or to the order of a named party. Such persons, also known as holders, are deemed to have title to the goods. They may transfer ownership of the goods by transferring the documents alone. A holder who is named in the negotiable document must sign as well as deliver the document to transfer it to a third party.

4. Merchants Who Keep Possession of Goods They Have Sold May Transfer Better Title than They Have

Occasionally a buyer will allow the merchant seller to temporarily retain possession of the goods after the sale. If, during this period, the merchant resells and delivers these goods to a good-faith buyer, the latter receives good title. But the merchant must replace the resold goods or be liable in damages for the tort of conversion.

When their new home was almost finished, the Howlands bought a set of new living room furniture from Eaton's Fine Furniture Shop. Eaton was to retain possession of the furniture under a layaway plan until the house was completed. Eaton assumed that she would have no trouble replacing the furniture before this completion date. Therefore she sold the Howlands' furniture to Hopkins, a good-faith buyer who took immediate delivery. Hopkins thus obtained a valid title. If Eaton is unable to replace the set when the Howlands demand delivery, she will be liable to them for damages.

WHAT IS REQUIRED FOR TRANSFER OF OWNERSHIP?

PROBLEM: O'Dell was preparing for a gala charity ball. He could not decide which of three tuxedos to buy from Signet Styles. At O'Dell's request, the manager set all three aside until the next day so O'Dell's friend could come in to help decide. That night a fire destroyed the store and its contents. Must O'Dell pay for the tuxedos which were set aside?

existing goods: goods that are physically in existence and are owned by the seller

identified goods: goods that are specifically selected as the subject matter of a particular contract

For transfer of ownership of goods in a sale, the goods must be both existing and identified. **Existing goods** are those that (1) are physically in existence even though they may not be in a fully assembled and immediately deliverable condition and (2) are owned by the seller. **Identified goods** are those that have been specifically designated as the subject matter of a particular sales contract. The identification of such goods may be done by the buyer, by the seller, by both, or by a mutually agreed upon third party. When identified, the goods are typically marked, separated, or in some other way made distinct from similar goods that the seller might have on hand.

In the problem, there was no intent to buy all three tuxedos, and no selection had been made of the one to be bought. Therefore, even though the goods were existing, they had not been identified. Thus, there never was a contract to buy any one tuxedo. Consequently, ownership and risk of loss for all three items remained in the seller.

future goods: goods that are either not existing or not identified

Unless goods are both existing and identified, they are **future goods**. Any contract for the sale of future goods is a contract to sell. Neither ownership nor risk of loss passes at the time of the agreement.

fungible goods: goods of a homogeneous nature

An important exception to the process of identification is made for **fungible goods**. These are goods of a *homogeneous* (essentially identical) nature in which, by nature or trade usage, each unit is regarded as equal to every other unit. Examples would be a quantity of corn or oil of a given variety and grade or thousands of cases of identical canned fruit in a warehouse. In many states, ownership and risk of loss in fungible goods pass at the time of the agreement and without identification. The buyer becomes the owner of an undivided portion or share of the mass.

WHEN DOES OWNERSHIP TRANSFER?

PROBLEM: Wu, of the People's Republic of China, ordered $2,500,000 worth of electronic equipment from Inter-Continental Traders, a Seattle exporter. The sales agreement, signed by both parties, stated that title and risk of loss would pass "when all necessary government permits are obtained." The Chinese government granted an import permit and necessary clearance to allow the exchange of Chinese currency into dollars to pay for the order. However, the U.S. State Department refused to grant an export permit because of the classified nature of some of the equipment. Did a sale take place?

Once goods are existing and identified, disputes may arise over who has title to the goods at particular times. Sometimes creditors of the seller, or creditors of the buyer, may claim possession in order to collect moneys due. Other disputes may concern who bears the risk of loss if the goods are damaged or destroyed before the transaction is completed. A risk-bearer may want or need the protection of casualty insurance. Generally the person who has title to the goods will bear the loss, but this is not always the case.

In deciding when title transfers from the seller to the buyer, courts first examine the sales agreement to see if the parties have clearly specified when they intended that title was to pass. If they have expressed such intent, courts will generally uphold their agreement. In the problem, no sale took place. The agreement said that title and risk of loss would pass "when all necessary permits" were obtained. Therefore Inter-Continental Traders would retain its goods because this condition had not been met.

If the parties do not clearly specify when title is to pass, courts decide if a recognized trade custom or usage exists to settle the question. If there is no agreement on the matter and no available trade custom or usage, courts refer to the UCC for a solution.

Common situations involving transfer of title are discussed below. Generally accepted rules are given. Note that neither the method nor the time of payment governs the outcome.

1. If the Seller Is to Deliver the Goods to Their Destination

If the contract requires the seller to deliver the goods to their destination, title passes when the goods are tendered at that specified destination. **Tender of delivery** means that the seller (1) places (or authorizes a carrier to place) the proper goods at the buyer's disposal and (2) notifies the buyer so that delivery can be received. The manner, time, and place for tender are determined by the agreement and the UCC. When the seller is required to do additional work, title does not pass until such work is completed.

tender of delivery: placing of goods at the buyer's disposal with notification that delivery may be taken

Ozark Electric ordered a new type of electric generator for its power plant. Because of the generator's complexity, the seller was required to deliver it to Ozark's plant site and then install and test run it. Title to the generator passed to Ozark Electric when the delivery, installation, and test run were properly completed.

2. If the Seller Is to Ship, but Not Deliver, the Goods to Their Destination

If the contract requires or authorizes the seller to ship the goods but does not obligate the seller to deliver them at the destination, title passes to the buyer at the time and place of shipment, when possession is transferred to the carrier.

The San Pedro Unified School District ordered from the Papyrus Products Company of Quebec, Canada, 5,000 reams of paper suitable for high-speed photocopying. The buyers specified shipment via the Dolphin Lines Steamship Company with transit through the Panama Canal. Title passed when the seller delivered the paper to the carrier.

3. If the Seller Is to Deliver a Document of Title

When it is customary, or when the parties have agreed that the seller is to deliver a document of title (such as a negotiable warehouse receipt), title passes when and where the document is delivered.

Degory bought five thousand tons of rice from the Diamond Delta Rice Growers' Cooperative. The rice was stored in a public grain elevator. Title passed when an authorized agent of Diamond Delta delivered the negotiable warehouse receipt for the goods to Degory. Degory planned to withdraw the goods at a later date.

4. If the Buyer is to Take Possession of the Goods Where They Were Purchased

If the seller is to tender the goods at the place of sale, title passes at the time and place of contracting.

The Petaluma Pet Shoppe bought 300 delicate tropical fish from a wholesale breeder. Because of special handling problems, the buyer insisted on taking delivery at the seller's place of business. Title passed at the time and place of contracting.

WHEN DOES RISK OF LOSS TRANSFER?

PROBLEM: Alda had stored 200,000 pounds of potatoes in Berle's warehouse. On December 17, Alda sold 25,000 pounds to Clark. On December 20, Alda notified Berle, who issued a negotiable warehouse receipt to Clark for 25,000 pounds. On February 15, Clark paid the storage charges and ordered shipment of the potatoes to New Orleans. On February 16, Berle shipped the goods. When did the risk of loss transfer to the buyer, Clark?

The transfer of the risk of loss from seller to buyer does not always occur when title transfers. But it is important to know just when the transfer of risk of loss takes place. Important possibilities are discussed below.

1. If the Seller Ships the Goods by Carrier

If the seller is required to deliver the goods to a particular destination but is allowed to use a carrier, such as a railroad, to make the delivery, the risk of loss passes to the buyer at the destination, upon tender of delivery. This is true even if goods which are shipped by carrier are still in possession of the carrier.

Oregon Indian Industries Corporation sold a carload of cedar shingles to Orange County Developers, Inc., a construction company. Oregon Industries was to deliver the goods but could use a carrier to do so. When the railroad (the authorized carrier) delivered the car on a siding at the buyer's warehouse, unloading was delayed. The reason for the delay was that Orange County Developers hoped to save handling costs by transferring the shingles directly to delivery trucks for a subdivision project underway. A full week passed before the railroad car was opened. If the contents had been damaged or destroyed during those days, the buyer would have taken the loss. Risk of loss had passed upon the initial tender of delivery by the carrier. Moreover, the carrier could have charged a fee for the delay in unloading the car.

Suppose the seller is not required to deliver the goods to the buyer at a particular destination. If the seller then uses a carrier to transport the goods, the risk of loss passes to the buyer when the goods are delivered to the carrier.

Kook's Xmas Tree Korner ordered 50 cases of fragile ornaments from a wholesaler. The contract did not require delivery at Kook's store or at any other designated destination. The wholesaler routinely shipped the ornaments to Kook by using a licensed common carrier trucking company. The shipment was destroyed when the truck ran off the highway in a snowstorm. Unless Kook can prove that the accident was caused by the truck driver's negligence, Kook must bear the loss. Insurance would have prevented this result.

FOB: shipment term which means "free on board"

Commercial buyers often use the shipment term **FOB**, which means "free on board." For example, assume that the seller is in Atlanta and the buyer is in New York City. In such case, "FOB Atlanta" means the seller agrees to deliver the goods no further than the carrier's truck or freight station in Atlanta. Title and risk of loss transfer to the buyer at that point. If the terms are "FOB, buyer's warehouse, New York City," the seller must deliver the goods to the buyer's warehouse in New York City. The title and the risk of loss remain with the seller until delivery takes place. In the absence of contrary arrangements, the buyer pays the transportation charges in the first example. In the second example, the seller pays the charges.

In shipments from foreign countries, it is not uncommon for the seller to quote a *CIF (cost, insurance, freight)* price. This means that the seller contracts for adequate insurance and for proper shipment to the named destination and then adds these items to the price or cost of the goods. The risk of loss passes to the buyer when the seller delivers the goods to the carrier.

2. If the Goods Are Held by a Bailee

bailee: one who holds temporary possession of goods of another, in trust

Sometimes goods are held for a seller by a **bailee**, one who has temporary possession of goods that belong to another, holding them in trust for a specified purpose. A public warehouse is an example of a bailee. The goods may be sold by the owner, yet the contract may call for delivery to the buyer without the goods being moved. The risk of loss transfers to the buyer under such circumstances in any of the following situations:

a. when the buyer receives a negotiable document of title covering the goods (such as a negotiable warehouse receipt);

b. when the bailee acknowledges the buyer's right to possession of the goods; or
c. after the buyer receives a non-negotiable document of title (such as a non-negotiable warehouse receipt) or other written direction to a bailee to deliver the goods. (The buyer must have had a reasonable time to present the document to the bailee, who must have honored it.)

In the problem, the risk of loss passed to Clark on December 20, when Berle issued the negotiable warehouse receipt.

3. If Either Party Breaches After the Goods Are Identified

The seller sometimes breaches by providing goods so faulty that the buyer has the right to and does reject them. In such a case, the risk of loss remains with the seller until the defects are corrected.

Warren shipped a truckload of women's three-speed bicycles to Billington's Bikes, Inc. Billington had actually ordered the ten-speed men's model, FOB, seller's factory. The truck was hijacked en route, and the shipment was stolen. The loss fell on the seller. Had the proper goods been shipped, the risk of loss would have been on the buyer.

Sometimes the buyer breaches the contract as to properly conforming goods that have been identified to the contract. To the extent that the seller lacks insurance coverage, the loss falls on the buyer. This protection for the seller lasts, however, only for a commercially reasonable time after the seller learns of the breach.

4. If the Goods Are Neither to Be Shipped by Carrier Nor to Be Held by a Bailee

In any case not covered previously, the risk of loss falls on the buyer upon receipt of the goods if the seller is a merchant. If the seller is not a merchant, the risk of loss transfers to the buyer as soon as the seller makes a tender of delivery.

Abraham bought a camper trailer at a garage sale. The seller said that the trailer could be taken home by Abraham at any time. Abraham went home to get a pickup with a trailer hitch. Upon returning, Abraham was told that during his absence, an unidentified person had backed into the trailer and had done extensive damage to it. If the person cannot be found, Abraham will have to bear the loss. That is because the seller was not a merchant and the seller had made an effective tender prior to Abraham's leaving to get the pickup.

WHEN DO INSURABLE PROPERTY INTERESTS TRANSFER?

PROBLEM: Frosty-Frolic Company was a fresh-food packer and processor. In a sales contract with Goodman, Frosty-Frolic agreed to pack a quantity of head lettuce grown near Salinas, California, and to place the "Soaring Eagle" brand label on the cartons. The lettuce was routinely dehydrated, cooled, packaged, placed in the special cartons, and stacked on pallets in Frosty-Frolic sheds for daily shipment as ordered by Goodman. At what point did Goodman obtain the right to insure the goods against possible loss?

The buyer obtains a special property interest in goods at the time of their identification to the contract. This special interest gives the buyer the right to buy insurance on the goods. The physical act of identifying goods usually takes the form of setting aside, marking, tagging, labeling, boxing, branding, shipping, or in some other way indicating that the specific goods are to be delivered or sent to the buyer in fulfillment of the contract. Thus, in the problem, Goodman obtained an insurable interest when the lettuce was identified as his, probably when it was placed in "Soaring Eagle" cartons. If the goods already exist and have been identified to the contract, the property interest of the buyer arises when the contract is made.

In addition to the insurable interest, the buyer has the following rights:

1. to inspect the identified goods at a reasonable hour,
2. to compel delivery if the seller wrongfully withholds delivery, and
3. to collect damages from third persons who take or injure the goods.

WHEN DO THE TRANSFER OF OWNERSHIP AND RISK OF LOSS OCCUR IN SPECIFIC TRANSACTIONS?

PROBLEM: Cutting Edge, Inc., a manufacturer, sold 250 gasoline-powered chain saws to Valu-Line, a large retailer. The full price was due in six months, and Cutting Edge agreed to accept the return of any saws not sold by then. Two months later, after only 25 saws had been sold, Valu-Line filed a bankruptcy petition. Cutting Edge demands return of the unsold saws. Valu-Line's other creditors claim that title to the saws had passed to the retailer. Therefore, under the bankruptcy law, all creditors should share in the claim to the saws. Who is right?

The following transactions merit special attention because of the frequency with which they occur or because of the uniqueness of the rules that apply to them.

1. Cash-and-Carry Sales

When the buyer in a sales contract is a consumer who pays cash and takes immediate delivery, title passes to the buyer at the time of the transaction. This is the most common type of transaction when the goods are groceries or low-priced sundries. Risk of loss passes upon the buyer's receipt of the goods from a merchant and on tender of goods by a casual seller.

The seller may insist on payment in legal tender. Checks are commonly used but are not legal tender. Acceptance of a check by the seller is not considered payment until the check is paid at the bank. But use of a check by the consumer in a cash-and-carry sale does not affect the timing of the transfer of title or risk of loss.

2. Sales on Credit

The fact that a sale is made on credit does not affect the passing of title or risk of loss. A **credit sale** is simply a sale which, by agreement of the parties, calls for payment for the goods at a later date. Ownership and risk of loss may pass even though the time of payment or delivery is delayed.

credit sale: sale in which, by agreement, payment for goods is made at a later date

3. COD Sales

Goods are often shipped **COD**, which means "collect on delivery." The carrier collects the price and transportation charges upon delivery and transmits this amount to the seller. If the buyer does not pay, the goods are not delivered. Thus, in effect, the seller retains control over the possession of the goods until the price is paid. In a COD arrangement, the buyer loses the right otherwise available to inspect the goods before payment. Nevertheless, ownership and risk of loss transfer just as though there were no such provision.

COD: shipment term which means "collect on delivery"

For years Global Reach, Inc., had sold postage stamps to collectors by direct mail. Losses from bad checks and uncollectible accounts continued to grow and were reducing the company's profits. Therefore, the owners adopted a new policy: all sales would be COD. This eliminated bad debt losses.

4. Sale or Return

sale or return: completed sale in which a merchant buyer has the right to return goods

When goods are delivered to a merchant buyer in a **sale or return**, the ownership and risk of loss pass to the buyer upon delivery. This is true whether the sale is made for cash or on credit. However, the buyer has a right to return the goods to the seller. Such a transaction is a true sale, but if the buyer returns the goods within the fixed or a reasonable amount of time, ownership and risk of loss pass back to the seller. The returned goods must be in substantially their original condition. Normally goods held on sale or return are subject to the claims of the buyer's creditors, who can seize the goods under court order. Thus, in the problem, all of Valu-Line's creditors share in the claim to the saws. Cutting Edge was but one of many claimants.

On November 27, Distributors, Inc., sold 100 pairs of ladies' hose, each in Christmas packaging, to Andy's Supermarket. Under the terms of the contract, Distributors, Inc., would buy back all the hose that the supermarket had not sold by January 1. This agreement would be classified as a sale or return.

5. Sale on Approval

sale on approval: sale in which there is no transfer of ownership and risk until the buyer approves of the goods

Sometimes goods are delivered to the buyer in a **sale on approval,** "on trial," or "on satisfaction." In such a case prospective ownership and risk of loss do not pass until the prospective buyer approves of the goods. This may be done by words, by payment, by any conduct indicating approval, or by retention of the goods beyond a specified or reasonable time. While in possession of the goods, of course, the prospective buyer is liable for any damage to them caused by his or her negligence. Normally the prospective buyer may reject for any reason.

Gardner filled in and mailed a magazine coupon for a series of best-selling books. The advertisement and descriptive folder both said the subscriber would have "ten days free trial." When the first book was delivered Gardner carelessly placed it on the metal cover over a steam radiator in her old Victorian house. She forgot about the book until she returned two weeks later from a winter skiing vacation. By then the heat from the radiator had permanently warped the binding of the book. The loss was Gardner's. Risk of loss had passed to her at the end of ten days. Even if the damage had taken place during the trial period, she would still be responsible because the damage resulted from her negligence.

6. Sale of an Undivided Interest

A person who sells a fractional interest in a single good or in a number of goods that are to remain together makes a **sale of an undivided interest.** Ownership and risk of loss pass to each buyer at the time of the sale of each undivided interest.

sale of an undivided interest: sale of a fractional interest in a single good or in a number of goods that are to remain together

Clarke bought a one-half interest in a traveling carnival. On the day after the purchase, the truck and trailer carrying the big tent to the next city were totally destroyed in a crash and fire. Clarke claimed that he should not have to bear any part of the loss because the owners had not yet determined which part of the carnival belonged to whom. However, the contract showed an intent to continue the carnival's operation under joint ownership. There was no intent to divide the various properties into separately owned parts. Therefore Clarke was wrong. From the time of the purchase, he was part owner of all the carnival properties. As such, he had to suffer one-half of the loss.

7. Auctions

An **auction** is a public sale to the highest bidder. When an auctioneer decides that no one will bid any higher for the goods on sale, the bidding is closed by letting the "hammer fall" or by another appropriate signal. In doing so, the auctioneer accepts the bid on behalf of the owner of the goods, and ownership passes to the buyer at that time. Risk of loss passes whenever the auctioneer acknowledges the buyer's right to possess the goods.

auction: public sale to the highest bidder

Auction sales are "with reserve" unless specifically announced in advance to be "without reserve." "With reserve" means that if nothing to the contrary is stated in the conditions of the sale, an auctioneer may withdraw the goods anytime before announcing completion of the sale. If "without reserve," the goods must be sold to the person who makes the highest bid even if it is ridiculously low.

WHAT PROCEDURE MUST BE FOLLOWED IN A BULK TRANSFER OF GOODS?

PROBLEM: Tinker rented a small retail store building in a resort town in Massachusetts. She planned to stock it with toys and souvenirs and was pleased when Turner, a local merchant, offered to sell her his entire inventory of such goods at his wholesale cost. Turner gave Tinker a list of creditors of his business. What should Tinker do with this list?

bulk transfer: transfer of all or a major part of the goods of a business

A **bulk transfer** is the transfer of all or a major part of the goods of a business in one unit at one time. Such goods would include materials, supplies, merchandise, and equipment if sold with the inventory.

The law protects creditors of the occasional dishonest merchant who would otherwise sell out secretly, keep the proceeds, and disappear. The UCC requires notice to the seller's creditors before the bulk transfer is made. The seller is required to list all creditors. The buyer is required to notify those creditors of the forthcoming transfer of ownership and to pay their claims or to make other arrangements with them. In the problem, Tinker would be required to take this action. If the buyer does not do this, creditors of the seller may make claims against the inventory and equipment after the buyer takes possession.

An innocent third party who in good faith buys some or all of the goods from a bulk transferee gets good title. But if such third party pays no value or knows that the buyer failed to comply with requirements of the bulk transfer law, the creditors can retake the goods.

PREVENTING LEGAL DIFFICULTIES

When Dealing with Personal Property. . .

1. remember that ownership of goods will not necessarily prevent transfer of title to them contrary to your wishes when:
   a. you have authorized others to sell the goods for you (They may violate your instructions.),
   b. you have been defrauded in a sales transaction and have given a voidable title to the wrongdoer. (Before you cancel the contract and try to get your goods back, the wrongdoer can transfer good title to a good-faith buyer.),

c. someone has wrongfully obtained possession of a negotiable warehouse receipt, a negotiable bill of lading, or a negotiable airbill for your goods (The wrongdoer can give good title by negotiating the paper.), or
d. you have allowed the person who sold to you to keep possession of your goods (The person who sold them to you might sell them again.).

Be alert to such possibilities;

2. it is generally wise to act promptly in identifying goods to the sales contract and in completing performance. Delay may lead to complications;
3. ideally, important written sales contracts specify precisely when title to and risk of loss of goods is to transfer;
4. as a buyer or a seller, carry adequate insurance when appropriate to cover any insurable interest you may have in goods subject to the sales contract;
5. assure yourself of the integrity and financial responsibility of buyers before selling to them goods on credit, on sale or return, or on approval.
6. when the buyer's credit is questionable, sell for cash or on a COD basis; and
7. if you buy an entire business inventory or a major part of one, be sure to comply with the UCC rules governing bulk transfers.

Strengthening Your Legal Vocabulary

auction
bailee
bulk transfer
COD
credit sale
existing goods
FOB
fungible goods
future goods
good-faith purchaser
identified goods
sale of an undivided interest
sale on approval
sale or return
tender of delivery

1. Goods of a homogeneous nature in which each unit, by nature or trade usage, is treated as equal to every other unit in the mass.
2. Shipment term which forces the buyer to pay before being allowed to take delivery of the goods.
3. Transfer of all or a major part of the goods of a business.
4. Completed sale in which the buyer has a right to return goods within a reasonable or fixed amount of time.
5. Sale to the highest bidder.
6. Goods that are selected and designated for a particular contract.
7. Goods that are not identified or are not in existence.
8. Sale in which payment for the goods takes place, by agreement, at a future time.
9. Placing of the proper goods at the buyer's disposal with notification that delivery can be taken.
10. Sale of a fractional interest in a single good or in a number of goods that are to remain together.

Reviewing Important Points

1. Generally the owner of goods is the only one who can legally transfer title to them. Exceptions are made for a party who:
   a. is authorized by the owner to sell the goods,
   b. has obtained title to the goods by fraud,
   c. is the holder of a negotiable document of title, or
   d. is a seller who has retained possession of sold goods.
2. Before ownership in goods can pass, goods must be both existing and identified.
3. In determining when title and risk of loss pass in a sales transaction, the terms of the sales contract are given top priority. If those terms do not provide an answer, then trade usage may provide the determining customary rule. If not, UCC rules are used to make the determination.
4. A special, insurable property interest is transferred to the buyer at the time of identification of the goods to the contract.
5. In cash-and-carry sales, title passes at the time of the transaction. If a check is used, the payment is conditional until the check is paid.
6. COD terms by a seller do not affect the time of transfer of ownership or of risk of loss. But the terms do reserve control of the goods to the seller until payment is received.
7. At an auction, title passes when the auctioneer signifies acceptance of the bidder's offer. Unless otherwise announced, the auctioneer may refuse all bids and withdraw the goods.
8. Notice of a bulk transfer of the inventory and equipment of a business must be given to creditors of the seller before the sale takes place.
9. An innocent third party who in good faith buys some or all of goods from a bulk transferee gets good title.

Applying Law to Everyday Life

1. After Raviza refurbished her home, she held a yard sale of furniture and equipment she no longer needed. Included was a large cross-cut saw which she sold to Sutro, not knowing that her husband had borrowed the tool from a neighbor. Did Sutro become the owner?

2. Smith's Bookstore handled rare books. Needing money desperately, Smith's sold an old edition of the Bible to Aubley, a collector. Smith's received a deposit of half the purchase price of $20,000. The remainder was to be paid upon delivery of the book. Smith's then sold the same book to another collector, James, on the same terms. Finally, Smith's sold and delivered the book to Salmon for the full $40,000. All three buyers acted in good faith and without notice of the other transactions. Who gets title to the book?

3. Some years ago, OPEC (the Organization of Petroleum Exporting Countries) boosted oil prices. Since then, fuel conservation has become increasingly

important. Accordingly, the Enterprise Tower Corporation contracted for installation of a computerized system of temperature control for their 30-story office building. The seller, Minnesota Systematics, was required to deliver, install, and successfully test run all equipment involved in the new system. When did Enterprise Tower become the owner of the goods?

4. Donatti, of San Francisco, ordered 400 pounds of fresh blueberries from Margeson, a produce broker in New Zealand. The terms called for shipment by airfreight, FOB Donatti's cold-storage plant, in Los Angeles. The blueberries were properly packed and shipped by airline common carrier, but they were mishandled upon arrival at the Los Angeles International Airport. Delivery was delayed, and when the fruit was finally delivered it was not edible. Who must suffer the loss?

5. Burby was a dealer in fuel and related supplies. Burby sold a quantity of oak firewood to Buckminster. Nothing was said about delivery to a carrier or transfer to a bailee. After the goods were set aside and were ready for delivery, they were stolen by burglars. Who suffers the loss?

6. To finance a trip for the high school band, the director bought "safe and sane fireworks" priced at $4,000 wholesale. He paid cash in a sale-or-return contract. Band members took turns as salesclerks in the 4th of July booth provided by the distributor. Several items did not sell at all. The wholesale price of those fireworks sold by midnight on July 4th was only $1,286.50. What should the director do?

7. After ten years as a retail stationery and gift dealer, Ashford decided to sell out and move to Europe. Shortly before the lease on his store expired, he sold his entire inventory, all cabinets and shelving, accounting equipment, and accounts receivable to Bogler for $48,950. Bogler planned to open a store in a new location under her own name. Ashford owed $13,950 to 14 trade creditors. He assured Bogler that he would pay them off out of the sales price so that "she would not be pestered and could start out with a clean slate." The creditors were not notified of the bulk transfer. What can they do when they learn that Ashford has disappeared somewhere in Europe with the sales proceeds?

Solving Case Problems

1. In 1945, during World War II, Lieber was in the U.S. Army and was one of the first soldiers to occupy Munich, Germany. Lieber entered Adolf Hitler's apartment with some companions and removed some of "der Führer's" clothing, decorations, and jewelry. In 1968, Lieber was living in Louisiana when his chauffeur stole the collection and sold it to a dealer. The dealer then sold the collection to Mohawk, in New York. Mohawk bought the collection in good faith. Through collectors' circles, Lieber learned that Mohawk had his collection. He demanded its return. Decide. (*Lieber v. Mohawk Arms. Inc.*, 314 N.Y.S.2d 510, N.Y.)

2. Lane was in the business of selling boats in North Carolina. In February, he sold a new boat, a 120-HP motor, and a trailer to a man who represented himself to be "John Willis." Willis gave Lane a check for $6,285 and left with the goods. The check proved to be worthless. Less than six months later, Honeycutt bought the three items in South Carolina from a man whom he had known for several years as "John R. Garrett." In fact, this was Willis, using an alias. Later, while searching for Willis under the alias of "John Patterson," the F.B.I. contacted Honeycutt. Honeycutt said that (a) he had paid a full price of only $2,500; (b) Garrett had nothing to show he was the owner; (c) he did not know from whom Garrett got the boat; (d) Garrett said he was selling the boat for someone else; (e) Garrett signed what he called a "title" (the document was nothing more than a "Certificate of Number" issued by the state Wildlife Resources Commission, not the "certificate of title" required by statutes); (f) Garrett forged the signature of the purported owner, one John F. Patterson, on the so-called "title." Plaintiff Lane now claims that defendant Honeycutt was not a good-faith purchaser and therefore should return the boat to him, with damages for a wrongful detention. Decide. (*Lane v. Honeycutt*, 188 S.E.2d 604, N.C.)

3. Consolidated Chemical Industries purchased three heat exchangers at a cost of $12,500 from Falls Industries, in Cleveland. The contract specified that after identification, the machines were to be crated securely. They were then to be delivered, without breakage, at the destination, the Consolidated plant in East Baton Rouge. Because the machines were not crated securely, the exchangers were badly damaged in transit. Consolidated refused to accept them, and Falls sued. Falls claimed that risk of loss had passed when the goods were delivered to the carrier. Do you agree? (*Falls Industries, Inc. v. Consolidated Chemical Industries, Inc.*, 258 F.2d 277)

4. The plaintiff, a Los Angeles manufacturer of men's clothing, sold a variety of clothing to the defendant, a retailer in Westport, Connecticut. The plaintiff prepared four invoices covering the clothing and stamped them "FOB Los Angeles," and added the words "GOODS SHIPPED AT PURCHASER'S RISK." The plaintiff delivered the goods to the Denver-Chicago Trucking Company. When the truck arrived in Connecticut with the goods, the defendant's wife was in charge of the store. She ordered the driver to unload the cartons and place them inside the store. The driver refused and left with the goods. The defendant complained to the plaintiff, who filed a claim against the trucking company. No reimbursement was obtained by the plaintiff, and the defendant never received the goods. Now the plaintiff seller sues the defendant buyer for the purchase price. Decide. (*Ninth Street East, Ltd. v. Harrison*, 259 A.2d 772, Conn.)

5. In June, plaintiff Multiplastics, Inc., contracted with defendant Arch Industries, Inc., to make and to sell 40,000 pounds of plastic pellets which were to be delivered at the rate of 1,000 pounds a day after Arch gave "release instructions." Multiplastics produced the pellets within two weeks. Arch

refused to give the release orders, citing labor difficulties and its vacation schedule. On August 18, Multiplastics wrote, "We have warehoused these products for more than forty days . . . however we cannot warehouse . . . indefinitely, and request that you send us shipping instructions." Multiplastics followed this with numerous telephone calls seeking payment and delivery instructions. In response, on August 20, Arch agreed to issue the release orders but never did. On September 22, the Multiplastics factory, including the 40,000 pounds of this order, was destroyed by fire. The pellets were not covered by Multiplastics' fire insurance policy. Therefore Multiplastics sued Arch for breach of contract and also claimed that the risk of loss had passed to the buyer. Decide. (*Multiplastics, Inc. v. Arch Industries, Inc.*, 348 A.2d 618, Conn.)

18

Warranties and Product Liability

1. Shortly after buying a new jacket, you become displeased with its color, fit, style, and price. As you think back, you also decide that the merchant was rude, delivery was slow, and credit terms were harsh. Can you, as a consequence, return the goods and claim a breach of warranty?

2. You enter a hardware store and tell the salesperson, "I need some stuff that will remove varnish from an old oak desk I'm refinishing." The salesperson urges you to buy a product called Strippo-Speedo. "It works like a charm," he says. When you apply the product, it gums up the varnish but does not remove it, and it scars the wood. Is the seller liable?

3. Your parents buy a new sofa for the family room. Less than six weeks after the purchase, they discover that the upholstery is starting to wear thin. In some places, the stitching is starting to unravel. Do your parents have any legal recourse?

WHAT ARE EXPRESS AND IMPLIED WARRANTIES?

PROBLEM: Bligh, a sales agent employed by Total Environments, persuaded the Fletchers to install a central air-conditioning system. Bligh assured them that "this unit will keep all rooms at 68° even on the hottest summer days and the coldest winter mornings." The unit failed to perform as promised. Do the Fletchers have any rights against Total Environments?

To induce prospects to buy, sellers often claim impressive qualities for their products. An example was Bligh's statement in the problem. When such a statement becomes a part of the bargain, the seller has promised that the product, in truth, has the indicated qualities. The price paid is consideration for the product and any warranty. In sales, a **warranty** is a statement about the product's qualities or performance which the seller assures the buyer to be true.

warranty: a statement of product qualities which the seller assures is true

Warranties may be either express or implied. Because they involve sales of goods, they are governed by the UCC. An assurance of quality or promise of performance explicitly made by the seller is an **express warranty**. An example would be: "Use our brand of oil and you won't need to change your engine oil for 10,000 miles." In the problem, Bligh made an express warranty. As an employer and a principal of Bligh, Total Environments is liable because the warranty was breached. Note that a breach of warranty is a breach of contract. There is no intent to deceive, so it is not the tort of fraud for which punitive damages might be claimed and collected.

express warranty: warranty explicitly made by the seller

An express warranty may be oral or written. (See the example in Figure 18-1.) It may even be implied by conduct. If the contract is written, the warranty must be included in the writing, or it probably will be excluded from the agreement by the parol evidence rule. However, if the warranty is made after the sale, it may be oral even though the sales contract was written. A warranty or any other term may be added to a sales contract later by mutual agreement, and no new consideration is required.

Under the Magnuson-Moss Warranty Federal Trade Commission Improvement Act, the Federal Trade Commission (FTC) has established certain minimum standards which must be met by sellers who give written warranties on products that cost $15 or more, that are sold to consumers, and that normally are used for personal, family, or household purposes. Sellers are not required to give these

Motorparts PART NO. **CX-83** ADJ. PERIOD **60 MO.**

BATTERY LIMITED WARRANTY

This Motorparts Battery is warranted by Steeley Motor Co. to the original retail purchaser for the time shown above when it is used in a private passenger car or light truck. If the battery fails to hold a charge due to a defect in material or workmanship it should be returned to a Motorparts retailer or wholesaler. THIS CARD AND YOUR DATED PURCHASE INVOICE ARE REQUIRED FOR WARRANTY REPLACEMENT.

PLANT CODE GRN 0846

Name *Al F. Kelley* Date Purchased *8-6-87*
(Date Installed for Service Fleet)

Address *1020 Elm* City *Akron* State *OH*

SERIAL NUMBER A 464476

If a failure occurs, the owner will pay a percentage of the replacement cost based on the Motorparts user exchange price (fleet price for fleet users) at the time of the adjustment. Shown below are the adjustment tables for privately owned passenger cars and light trucks and fleet, farm, marine and other commercial vehicles.

Adjustment Table

Mo.'s After Purch.	0-3	4-5	6-10	11-15	16-20	21-25	26-30	31-35	36-40	41-45	46-50	51-55	56-60

Owner's Percentage Replacement Cost

Car/Lt. Truck	0%	8%	17%	25%	33%	42%	50%	59%	67%	75%	84%	92%	97%
Fleet/Commercial*	0%	16%	35%	50%	67%	84%	100%	*Farm, Marine & Other Commercial					

IMPORTANT: Further Warranty information is on the reverse side of this card.

NOTE: Detach and KEEP with your purchase invoice.

The Motorparts Limited Battery Warranty does not cover:

1. Failure as a result of use in applications other than those recommended in Motorparts catalogs
2. Damage to case, cover or terminals caused by abuse, negligence, freezing or improper installation
3. Cost of recharging or use of a rental battery
4. Labor to remove and replace battery in the vehicle
5. To the extent allowed by law, loss of time, inconvenience, loss of use of the vehicle or other consequential damages

THERE IS NO OTHER EXPRESS WARRANTY ON MOTORPARTS BATTERIES. ANY IMPLIED WARRANTY OF MERCHANTABILITY OR FITNESS IS LIMITED TO THE DURATION OF THE WRITTEN WARRANTY. SOME STATES DO NOT ALLOW THE EXCLUSION OR LIMITATION OF CONSEQUENTIAL OR INCIDENTAL DAMAGES OR HOW LONG AN IMPLIED WARRANTY LASTS, SO THE ABOVE LIMITATIONS AND EXCLUSIONS MAY NOT APPLY TO YOU.

THIS WARRANTY GIVES YOU SPECIFIC RIGHTS, AND YOU MAY HAVE OTHER RIGHTS WHICH VARY FROM STATE TO STATE.

Inquiries concerning this warranty should be directed to:

Warranty Administration, Steeley Parts and Service Division
7800 River Road Pittsburgh, Pennsylvania 15227

Figure 18-1. Express Limited Warranty

warranties, but if they do they must make available to consumers prior to the sale a single document, in simple and readily understandable language, with the following information:

1. to whom the warranty is extended (for example, if it is limited to the original buyer),
2. a description of the product and any excluded parts,

3. what the *warrantor* (one who makes a warranty) will and will not do in the event of a breach of warranty,
4. when the warranty begins (if different from purchase date) and when it ends,
5. the step-by-step procedure to follow to obtain performance of warranty obligations,
6. the availability of any informal methods of settling disputes,
7. any limitation on how long implied warranties last,.
8. any exclusion or limitation on incidental or consequential damages, and
9. the words "This warranty gives you specific legal rights, and you may also have other rights which vary from state to state."

When an express warranty obligates the seller to repair or to replace a defective product without cost to the buyer and within a reasonable time, it is a **full warranty**. If a warranty does not provide as much protection as a full warranty, it is a **limited warranty**, and the seller must describe it as such.

full warranty: warranty that obligates a seller to repair or to replace a product without cost and within a reasonable time

limited warranty: warranty that provides less protection than a full warranty

Sellers may decide whether or not to give express warranties. However, the law imposes certain warranties to ensure minimum standards of quality and performance even if no explicit promises or representations are made by the seller. A warranty obligation imposed by law is an **implied warranty**.

implied warranty: warranty imposed by law

ARE SELLERS' CLAIMS ALWAYS WARRANTIES?

PROBLEM: Kanssar was trying to persuade Ana to buy a new car. "Just stand back and admire it," he said. "There's nothing finer on the road. It's sleek as a leopard. Fast as a jaguar. Tough as a tiger. Test drive it and you'll think you're floating on a cloud—at 80 m.p.h. And look at our terms. You can't find a better deal in town!" Not one of these claims was strictly true. But Ana, who knew little about cars, was persuaded and made the purchase. Does she have any resulting legal rights against Kanssar?

Sellers often exaggerate the merits of the goods they are trying to sell. The making of such statements as "superb quality," "you can't buy a better book," or "most beautiful" is known as **puffing**—exaggerated sales talk. Such words are not warranties or statements of fact. They are merely personal opinions. Buyers generally are not able to rely on such opinions. In the problem, Kanssar's description

puffing: exaggerated sales talk

of the car and the deal was an example of puffing. Thus, Ana has no resulting legal rights.

Sometimes, however, the buyer has good reason to believe that the seller is an expert. If a buyer asks for the seller's opinion as an expert, the seller's word as to the quality of the article becomes part of the basis of the bargain and may be taken as a warranty. This is particularly true with merchants. For example, a statement by a jeweler that a diamond is flawless may thus constitute a warranty.

WHAT IS MEANT BY "CAVEAT EMPTOR," "CAVEAT VENDITOR," AND "GOOD FAITH"?

PROBLEM: The Stephensons bought a personal computer from Outer Space Outfitters. Within two weeks, while taking a course on how to use computers, the Stephensons learned that although their PC was a standard brand sold nationally, it was not highly regarded by experts in the field. It was comparatively slow, had limited capacity, and could not be used with many of the best software programs. Moreover, it was overpriced. In fact, some stores were already selling the same model at 30 percent below the list price paid by the Stephensons. Security analysts predicted that the manufacturer would soon file a bankruptcy petition. Can the Stephensons legally demand and get their money back from Outer Space Outfitters?

According to common law, a person who inspects goods or who fails to use the opportunity to inspect them, yet purchases, cannot later complain of defects that would be detectable by ordinary inspection. As you know from Chapter 7, *caveat emptor* is Latin for "let the buyer beware." This warning applies to all buyers. The buyer may get the "worst of the bargain" because of a failure to define needs, to study values, and to compare available brands (and unbranded items) and prices before buying. Persons who fail to observe many limitations in the quality and worth of goods bought must live with their mistakes. Of course, many sellers voluntarily agree to accept a return and make a refund or exchange, or give credit toward a future purchase. In the problem, the Stephensons cannot recover their purchase price. They could have avoided their situation by becoming more knowledgeable before they bought. The law does not protect buyers against poor taste in color, style, or fit, nor does it direct all buyers to the very best car or cake or computer available at any price level.

To a considerable extent, the effect of caveat emptor has been reduced in modern times by **caveat venditor**, which is Latin for "let the seller beware." Under this doctrine, important warranties are implied by law to benefit buyers if the seller is a merchant. Numerous statutes have been enacted to protect consumers. Also, courts have helped buyers with an expanded concept of strict product liability.

caveat venditor: let the seller beware

The UCC declares the general rule that every contract under the Code includes the obligation of the parties to act in good faith in the contract's performance and enforcement. **Good faith** is defined as honesty in business conduct and transactions. Moreover, for merchants, good faith requires observance of reasonable commercial standards of fair dealing.

good faith: honesty in business conduct and transactions

WHAT WARRANTIES ARE IMPLIED BY LAW IN ALL STATES?

PROBLEM: While building a new family room, the Shihs asked Beta's Electrical Shop what size of circuit breaker they would need to carry the current load. After reviewing a list of the appliances that would be in the room, Beta recommended a 15-ampere breaker. Following installation, however, the breaker consistently cut the power off whenever two or more of the listed appliances were operating at the same time. The breaker was mechanically perfect, but it was not adequate for the current load. Do the Shihs have any legal rights against Beta?

The following warranties are made by both the casual seller and the merchant to their purchasers unless there is a specific agreement between the seller and the purchaser to exclude one or more of the warranties:

1. Warranty of Title

In the very act of selling, the seller implicitly warrants that he or she has title to the goods and the right to transfer them. This warranty is implied by law. It may be excluded from the bargain in circumstances where it is obvious that the seller does not have title. An example would be when a sheriff, by court order, sells a debtor's goods to satisfy a judgment. This warranty may also be expressly excluded from the bargain by agreement of the parties.

> Donnell found a gold ring on a busy downtown street. The ring had no identifying marks. Unable to determine its owner, Donnell sold the ring to Leesen. They agreed that since Donnell had found the ring there would be no warranty of title. If the true owner appeared and could prove ownership, the ring would have to be returned, and Leesen agreed to take the loss.

2. Warranty against Encumbrances

encumbrances: claims of third parties

Also implicit in the act of selling is the seller's warranty that the goods shall be delivered free of all **encumbrances** (claims of third parties) of which the buyer is not aware at the time of contracting. This warranty, which is implied by law, does not ensure that the goods are free of encumbrances at the time of sale. Instead, it ensures that the goods shall be free at the time of delivery. This distinction is important. It enables a seller who has encumbrances against the goods to avoid a breach of the warranty by paying off the encumbrances before delivering the goods.

> Kossel sold a portable copying machine to Nansen and promised delivery in two weeks. Kossel did not mention that he owed $850 to the bank, with the machine as security. Kossel can avoid breaching the implied warranty against encumbrances by paying off the loan before delivering the machine.

3. Warranty of Fitness for a Particular Purpose

A buyer who needs goods for a specific purpose often tells the seller about that purpose. Then the buyer relies on the seller's skill and judgment for a selection of appropriate goods. In such circumstances, the seller impliedly warrants that the goods delivered to the buyer are reasonably fit for the indicated purpose. If they prove to be unfit, the buyer has a right of action for breach of warranty. Therefore, in the problem, the Shihs have a right of action for breach of an implied warranty of fitness for a particular purpose.

This warranty does not arise in any of the following situations:

a. when the buyer personally selects the goods,
b. when the buyer orders the goods according to the buyer's own specifications, and

c. when because of independent testing or for other reasons, the buyer does not rely upon the skill and judgment of the seller to evaluate the quality of the goods.

The warranty may exist even though the buyer has asked for goods by patent or brand name. This would apply if the seller knew the purpose for which the goods were required and if the buyer relied upon the seller in the actual selection. For example, the buyer might ask for a chain saw to fell a stand of trees with trunks two feet in diameter. The seller selects the proper model. On the other hand, a buyer who insists on getting goods of a particular brand and specifies the model, size, or number obviously is not relying on the seller's knowledge. Consequently, in such case, there is no warranty of fitness for a particular purpose.

WHAT EXPRESS WARRANTIES CAN BE MADE BY SELLERS?

PROBLEM: The Metropolitan Unified School District bought a large quantity of blackboard chalk from the Cliffs-of-Dover Corporation. The purchase was based on the sales agent's statement that the chalk was nonirritating, nontoxic, and would not scratch. In fact, however, the chalk often made a loud scratching sound when used. It also produced a fine dust which caused many users to sneeze and develop skin rashes. Can Metropolitan recover from Cliffs-of-Dover for the false statements?

1. Warranty of Conformity to Seller's Statement or Promise

In addition to warranties implied by law, every seller is bound to any express statement of fact or promise that is made part of the basis of the bargain. It is desirable to have such statements in writing. Thus, in the problem, Metropolitan can recover for the false statements made about the chalk.

2. Warranty of Conformity to Description, Sample, or Model

When a description of the goods or a sample or model is made part of the contractual agreement, there is an express warranty that all the goods shall conform to the description, sample, or model—whichever is used. This is true even if the words "warrant" or "guarantee" are not used in the contract. It is also true even if the seller did not have any specific intention of making a warranty.

The Space Rockets, a professional football club, contracted for new uniforms from Arkwright Mills. At the time of the order, sample uniforms in particular colors and fabrics were referred to and included as part of the agreement. Arkwright is legally obligated to provide goods which match the samples.

WHAT ADDITIONAL WARRANTIES ARE IMPLIED BY LAW FOR MERCHANTS?

PROBLEM: Marquez built and sold to Frobisher, a candy manufacturer, a special machine for wrapping individual pieces of candy in foil. The machine was built according to directions and specifications provided by Frobisher. Unknown to either party, Rodmann, a European candy manufacturer, held a Swiss patent on such a machine. She had also registered it with the United States Patent Office to protect the American monopoly rights. Rodmann sued Marquez for an injunction against further production and for damages. Rodmann won the suit. Must Frobisher reimburse Marquez for the loss?

Merchants are typically held to higher standards in their dealings with consumers than are casual sellers. This is certainly true in the area of warranties. In addition to the warranties previously discussed, which are made by all sellers, the following warranties are, by law, also made by merchants:

1. Warranty against Infringement

A merchant warrants that the goods in which he or she normally deals shall be delivered to a buyer free of any third party's claims for patent, copyright, or trademark *infringement* (unauthorized use). This warranty, implied by law, may be excluded by agreement between the parties.

If the buyer furnishes specifications to the seller which lead to a claim of infringement against the seller, the buyer is under an obligation to compensate the seller for any loss suffered. Accordingly, in the problem, Frobisher must compensate Marquez. Frobisher is also liable to Rodmann.

2. Warranty of Merchantability

merchantable: reasonably fit for normal use

An implied warranty that the goods are **merchantable** goes with a sale by a merchant who customarily deals in goods of that kind.

The buyer may be either a consumer buying the goods for use or a merchant buying the goods for resale.

Basically this warranty requires that the goods be reasonably fit for the ordinary purposes for which they normally are used. Thus, a radio must bring in broadcasts, soap must clean, and an umbrella must provide protection from rain. All goods sold must pass in the trade under the sales contract description; buyers must not balk at accepting them. If the goods are fungible, like grain, they must be at least of fair, average quality. Within variations permitted by the contract, goods must run of even kind, quality, and quantity. If required by the contract, they must be adequately contained, packaged, and labeled. Finally, they must conform to any promises or affirmations of fact made on the label or container.

Huang was a gift shop owner. Huang bought a shipment of ceramic flower vases from Kwo, a Singapore exporter. After Huang had sold many of the vases, customers started coming back with the complaint that the vases leaked water. Kwo has breached the warranty of merchantability. She must take back all unsold and returned vases, refunding payment in full. Huang has likewise breached the warranty of merchantability to customers. Therefore he must make refunds or other adjustments acceptable to the customers.

This very important implied warranty of merchantability greatly increases the merchant's duties of care and performance beyond those of the casual seller. It extends, for example, to food sold, which must be wholesome and fit for human consumption. It includes foods and drinks which are sold and served to be consumed elsewhere or on the premises, as in restaurants and in fast-food shops. Note however that buyers of perishable foods must treat them properly to keep them edible. For example, common knowledge tells us not to eat inadequately cooked pork nor to eat mayonnaise that has been exposed to heat. Drugs for human use must also be safe and wholesome.

Merchantability requires that any warranty protection that is customary in the trade be extended to the buyer. For example, the seller of a pedigreed animal, such as a dog or horse, is expected to provide documentation of the lineage of the animal because such proof is customary in the trade.

The warranty of merchantability may be expressly excluded by agreement of the parties. Also, when a buyer has examined the goods, sample, or model before contracting, there is no implied warranty of merchantability as to those defects which a reasonable examination would have revealed. This would also apply if the buyer refused to examine the goods, sample, or model before contracting.

Heathe bought a bolt of cloth that was marked down in price because of a flaw in the weave. The flaw was obvious under casual inspection. Heathe cannot later return the goods, claiming a breach of warranty of merchantability.

WHEN AND HOW MAY WARRANTIES BE EXCLUDED?

PROBLEM: At a sale in a discount store, Doty bought twenty pounds of shelled walnuts. They were packed in one-pound sealed plastic bags and were sold at a bargain price "as is." When Doty's wife opened one package, she discovered that the walnuts were edible but were stale and unpalatable. Doty claims a breach of warranty of merchantability. Is he entitled to a refund?

A seller may offer to sell goods without any warranties. This may occur if the goods are known to have defects or if they are a new design or model. To sell goods without a warranty, the seller must:

1. refrain from making any express warranties, and
2. use appropriate language that will exclude implied warranties.

disclaimer: notice of exclusion

For example, to exclude or modify the broad warranty of merchantability or any part of it, the seller must mention "merchantability" in a disclaimer. A **disclaimer** is a notice of exclusion. To exclude or modify any implied warranty of fitness, the exclusion must be in writing and must be conspicuous (easily seen or noticed). A statement such as this would suffice for both merchantability and fitness: "There are no warranties of merchantability or fitness which extend beyond the description on the label."

Unless circumstances indicate otherwise, all implied warranties are excluded by expressions such as "with all faults," "as is," or other similar words. Thus, in the problem, Doty is not entitled to a refund because the walnuts were bought "as is."

When express warranties of quality are given, they exclude all inconsistent implied warranties except the one for fitness for a particular purpose. No warranty arises, however, as to fitness for use when a casual seller disposes of used goods. An example would be when someone holds a garage sale to dispose of assorted second-hand possessions. On the other hand, if the seller is a merchant, such a warranty would be implied according to the conditions discussed earlier. Note, however, that no disclaimers allow the manufacturer or merchant seller of the goods to avoid liability for injuries caused by defects in those goods.

An auto manufacturer gave a new-car warranty which limited recovery to replacement of defective parts and necessary labor "for one year or 12,000 miles, whichever occurs first." The manufacturer stated that the warranty was "in lieu of all other warranties, obligations, and liabilities, including the warranty of merchantability." Mackenzie bought one of the cars and operated and maintained it in accordance with the *Owner's Manual*. Nevertheless, when Mackenzie was driving at a normal highway speed 14 months later, the steering wheel suddenly failed to work properly. As a result, the car left the road and overturned. Despite the disclaimer of liability, the manufacturer may be liable in tort on the theory of strict liability.

WHAT IS PRODUCT LIABILITY?

PROBLEM: Tacky removed a safety guard from his electrically-powered radial saw. This was contrary to a warning prominently printed on the guard. Because of a defect in the manufacture of the saw, a saw blade broke. Since the safety guard was not in place, the blade hit and seriously injured Tacky. Can Tacky recover for the injury caused by the defective product?

The rules for determining who is legally liable for injuries caused by a defective product have been expanded in recent years to protect injured plaintiffs. For example, at common law, warranty liability depended upon the contract between the buyer and seller, who were said to be in **privity of contract**. Only the immediate buyer was permitted to sue and this could be done only against the immediate seller. Thus, an injured consumer could sue the retailer, but not the wholesaler nor the manufacturer, who might be primarily responsible for the defect and better able to pay.

privity of contract: relationship of persons who are parties to the same contract

Now, however, the UCC broadens the common-law rule so that all injured persons who are in the buyer's family or household, including guests, may sue. Moreover, courts in most states now permit the injured party, even a nonuser, to sue retailers, intermediate sellers, and manufacturers.

Today, a manufacturer or producer who makes inaccurate or misleading statements in advertising or labels is liable for resulting injuries to consumers. If the goods are defective and therefore dangerous, the maker is similarly liable for resulting harm. In either case, not only the manufacturer or producer but also intermediate sellers and the immediate supplier may be liable. **Product liability** may be based on a breach of warranty. It may also be based on the torts of fraud or negligence, or, increasingly, on the tort of strict liability.

product liability: responsibility for injury caused by a defective product, based on warranty, fraud, negligence, or strict liability

While there are many alternative legal theories, it may still be difficult for the injured consumer to recover. A person injured by a defective product might find that there is no warranty, that the warranty is not applicable, or that the warranty has expired. The injured person, even if defrauded, might also discover that the seller's misbehavior is difficult to prove. Fraud requires proof of intent, an elusive element. Finally, negligence, even if present, is difficult to prove because the defective product may have been made many months or years before in some distant factory by workers who cannot be identified or located.

Today, a person injured by a defective product is most likely to recover damages by relying on strict liability. The trend in many states is to hold the manufacturer, wholesaler, and retailer strictly liable if someone is injured because of a defective product condition which caused it to be unreasonably dangerous to the user or consumer. The liability is imposed without reliance on warranties and regardless of the presence or absence of fraudulent intent or negligence. At the time of the writing of this edition, efforts are being made in Congress and in some state legislatures to limit the scope of strict liability and to require the proof of fault. Some proposals would place ceilings on the amount of punitive damages that could be awarded.

There is no liability if the injury was suffered while the product was being used for a purpose for which it was not intended (for example, using gasoline to clean clothes or using a screwdriver as a chisel) or which could not reasonably be foreseen (such as trying to climb a mountain using ropes made for tying packages). Likewise, liability may be barred if the product has been altered by the user (for example, lengthening a ladder by nailing extensions to its legs). Liability may also be barred if the injured person is personally found guilty of improper conduct which causes the accident. (Examples of this would include driving on a defective tire after discovering the defect, failing to service or maintain an engine, or taking an overdose of medication.) Of course, there is generally no liability if one is hurt when improperly using a product that may be dangerous when misused (for example, sharp knives and cutting tools, firearms, and various chemicals).

In the problem, Tacky's removal of the fully adequate safety guard bars his recovery. Legally, the injury was the result of Tacky's foolish action, not the defect in the saw blade.

PREVENTING LEGAL DIFFICULTIES

When Purchasing Goods. . .

1. be aware that not every assurance of quality or performance made by a seller is a warranty. Often such statements are deemed by the law to be "puffing" and cannot be the basis for breach of warranty action;
2. know the implied warranties and watch for sellers' statements of limitation and exclusion of such warranties;
3. when appropriate, tell the seller how you intend to use the goods. If the seller has superior knowledge and advice upon which you reasonably rely, you will be protected by an implied warranty of fitness of the goods for your particular purpose;
4. generally request that express warranties be placed in writing. This helps to avoid later disputes as to their meaning or existence. If the seller unreasonably refuses to warrant the goods, go elsewhere, or realize that any disappointing product quality and performance will be your burden; and
5. use special care in buying goods "as is." Inspect the goods to be sure that you are willing to take them without the benefit of warranties.

Strengthening Your Legal Vocabulary

caveat venditor
disclaimer
encumbrances
express warranty
full warranty
good faith
implied warranty
limited warranty
merchantable
privity of contract
product liability
puffing
warranty

1. Promise that a statement of product qualities is true.
2. Exaggerated sales talk.
3. Warranty that is explicitly made.
4. Warranty imposed by law.
5. Reasonably fit for normal use.
6. Relationship of persons who are parties to the same contract.
7. Creditors' claims.
8. Liability of manufacturer or producer, wholesaler, or retailer when a defective product causes injury to a consumer or to the consumer's property.
9. Let the seller beware.
10. Notice of exclusion of a warranty.

Reviewing Important Points

1. Warranties may be express or implied. Express warranties are oral or written promises by the seller of product quality or performance. Implied warranties are imposed by law.
2. The following warranties are made by both casual sellers and merchants:
   a. that the seller has title to the goods and the right to transfer them (implied),
   b. that the goods shall be delivered free of all encumbrances unknown to the buyer (implied),
   c. that the goods are fit for the purpose of the buyer when the seller knows of the buyer's intended use and the buyer relies on the skill and judgment of the seller for selection (implied),
   d. that the goods will conform to the seller's statements or promises (express), and
   e. that goods sold by description, sample, or model will conform to such description, sample, or model (express).
3. The following warranties are made only by merchants:
   a. that the goods are free of any patent, copyright, or trademark infringement claims by third parties (implied), and
   b. that the goods are merchantable—that is, of fair, average, saleable quality and fit for the ordinary purpose for which they normally are used (implied).
4. The buyer from a casual seller should examine the goods for defects before making the purchase. That is because the buyer has no legal right (in the absence of fraud by the casual seller) to complain of defects that might have been detected by ordinary inspection. It is prudent, of course, to also inspect goods sold by merchants. However, merchant sellers normally are bound by implied warranties of merchantability.
5. Generally any person injured by a defective product may bring suit against any manufacturer or merchant in the chain of distribution of that product. Depending on the circumstances, the suit may be based on warranty, fraud, negligence, or strict liability.

Applying Law to Everyday Life

1. When the Grand Motor Car Company introduced their new model, sales lagged. After three months, only 7,500 cars had been sold. To stimulate sales, Grand added four years to its standard one-year warranty. It also extended the warranty on the cars already sold. Is Grand legally bound to the early buyers for the extra four years even though no new consideration was paid?

2. It had been an exhausting year of hard work for Dryden. The Paradiso Resort advertisement in a national magazine promised "The perfect holiday. Escape from it all on the beaches of Kauai—your paradise on earth! Surf and relax in the sun. Dine and dance like royalty. Return refreshed, revitalized, renewed!" Dryden used all his savings for a month-long stay. After the vacation, he was still physically exhausted and mentally frustrated with his work. Is the Paradiso Resort liable for breach of an express warranty?

3. While in Florida, Van Loon decided to go fishing for tarpon. Visiting Stanton's Sports Shop, Van Loon explained the specific need to the salesclerk. Van Loon then bought the rod, reel, and line that the salesclerk recommended. During the first trip out, Van Loon had repeated strikes, but the line was too light for the weight of the fish. As a result, the line broke every time even though it was being handled properly. What legal rights, if any, does Van Loon have against Stanton?

4. The Motleys entered Penn's Nursery and asked for a 50-pound sack of ZAP, a brand-name weed killer, to use to eliminate narrow-leaved devil grass from their lawn. ZAP was advertised as "effective, when properly used, against crabgrass and other broad-leaved weeds and grasses." The Motleys applied the chemical according to directions, but the devil grass survived. Therefore they sued the manufacturer, claiming a breach of warranty. They also sued Penn for failure to give them proper advice as to what kind of weed killer they should buy. (a) Will the Motleys win their suit against the manufacturer? (b) Will they win their suit against Penn?

5. Using a newspaper want ad, Canby sold his slightly used stereo equipment to Pegler. A week later, Pegler tried to return the merchandise to Canby. Pegler claimed that there was a breach of the warranty of merchantability because the record changer did not work properly. Is Canby liable?

6. Gallo, an experienced glider pilot, rented a glider at a commercial glider port. While in flight during ideal weather, she lost control because of a defect in the cables for the tail assembly. As a result, the glider crashed while landing, and Gallo was permanently disabled. The glider, which was several years old, had been properly maintained. There was no warranty in effect on the plane. Does Gallo have any legal recourse?

7. When Winslow decided to install a brick walk in front of his home, he bought three sacks of standard Pyramid brand mortar mix from the U-Can-

Do store. Instructions on the bags warned against direct contact with skin. Although Winslow had sensitive skin, he repeatedly touched the wet mix with his bare hands because he was not skilled in using a trowel. This burned his hands and he developed an allergic rash. Is either U-Can-Do or Pyramid liable to him under any theory of product liability?

Solving Case Problems

1. Every week for a year and a half, Newmark was given a shampoo and set by employees of Gimbel's. Then a new product ("Candle Wave," made by the Helene Curtis company) was applied to Newmark's hair. As a result, Newmark suffered contact dermatitis of the scalp, with substantial loss of hair. Newmark sued Gimbel's for breach of the implied warranty of fitness for a particular purpose. Gimbel's argued that it was providing a service and not selling goods in this transaction. Therefore it could not be held liable for breach of warranty with reference to the product of Helene Curtis. It could only be held liable, it claimed, if its own employees were proved negligent. Could a jury find Gimbel's liable if the wave solution was defective and caused the injury? (*Newmark v. Gimbel's Incorporated*, 258 A.2d 679, N.J.)

2. While trying on a pair of slacks in a Mode O'Day Frock Shop, Flippo was bitten by a poisonous brown recluse spider concealed in the slacks. Flippo was hospitalized for 30 days because of the bite. Was Mode O'Day liable for a breach of the implied warranty of merchantability? (*Flippo v. Mode O'Day Frock Shops of Hollywood*, 248 Ark. 1, 449 S.W.2d 692)

3. Mahaney purchased a used car from Perry Auto Exchange. Mahaney was told that the car was in "perfect, A-1, and first-class condition." A written statement given to Mahaney at the time of the sale described the car as being in "good operating condition." Mahaney had no opportunity to investigate the truth of these statements. Later, it was determined that the car had a bearing knock and a growl in the differential and had no brakes at the time of the sale. Mahaney sued for rescission. Were Perry's statements merely puffing or were they warranties upon which the rescission could be based? (*Mahaney v. Perry Auto Exchange*, 85 N.E.2d 558, Ohio)

4. Edwin Green, Sr., died of lung cancer. His widow, Mary Green, sued the defendant American Tobacco Co. for damages. She claimed a breach of the implied warranty of merchantability, saying that "Lucky Strike" cigarettes were not fit and wholesome for consumption by the public and had caused her husband's cancer. Expert witnesses for the plaintiff testified that cigarette smoking caused lung cancer in a sizeable part of the smoking population (one out of ten heavy smokers). Experts for the defendant testified that the cause of cancer is not really known and that they did not believe there is a causal connection between smoking tobacco and lung cancer. On direct and cross-examination the plaintiff's experts also conceded a lack of knowl-

edge as to the cause of cancer. Should Mrs. Green be awarded damages? (*Green v. American Tobacco Co.*, 409 F.2d 1166)

5. On January 1, plaintiff Werner bought the "White Eagle," a wooden sloop, from defendant Montana, and the parties signed a bill of sale. During the previous October they had signed an intent to purchase and sell. During their negotiations, the seller had assured the buyer orally that the hull would "make up" from swelling when placed in the water and would be watertight. At the end of June, Werner put the boat in the water. He allowed more that six weeks—a sufficient time—for the planking to swell to form a watertight hull. But the hull still leaked. The boat could not be sailed. Werner then checked the hull and for the first time discovered extensive dry rot which required substantial repairs. In a letter in September, he demanded that Montana take the boat back and refund the purchase price of $13,250. The defendant refused, and so Werner sued for rescission. Montana argued that the oral assurances he had given of watertightness could not be admitted at the trial because of the parol evidence rule. Who should win? (*Werner v. Montana*, 378 A.2d 1130 N.H.)

SPECIAL SECTION:
How to Deal with an Attorney

Although attorneys take some cases at the request of the court or as the attorney's conscience dictates without expecting a fee in return, attorneys usually expect to be paid for their services. It is important to determine in advance how your lawyer is to be paid. Most attorneys either charge an hourly rate or are paid on a contingency-fee basis. A typical contingency-fee schedule calls for payment to the attorney of 25 percent of the recovery if the case is resolved without trial. If a trial is required, the attorney might get 33 percent of the recovery, and if the judgment is appealed, the percentage might go up to 40 percent. If the case is lost, the attorney gets nothing. With the hourly rate, the attorney is paid regardless of whether the case is won or lost. Attorneys often take tort suits, antitrust, and contract actions on a contingency-fee basis, but only if they believe there is a good chance of recovery. To avoid misunderstandings, it is a good idea to have a written agreement about compensation before the attorney begins working on your case.

Some urban areas have legal clinics. These clinics set a flat fee for various types of legal services. For example, a name change might cost $125. Uncontested divorces, simple wills, and other legal services frequently can be obtained through such a clinic. Of course, the more complex the service required, the more expensive it will be and the less likely it can be provided by a clinic.

When dealing with your attorney, you must provide every bit of information that can be used to pursue your interests. When first meeting with your attorney about a given problem, bring a detailed, chronological, written summary of relevant events, together with any supporting correspondence or other documents. Too often, clients withhold useful information that they consider irrelevant or embarrassing only to find later that without it their attorney was misdirected, and possible success in court was jeopardized.

Always listen to your attorney's advice and weigh it carefully. Never forget, however, that it is your reputation, your resources, or your freedom that is at stake—not the attorney's. Therefore ask detailed questions about what is happening. Utilize your attorney's legal experience to the utmost, but also realize that your experience is superior regarding the facts about your case. You must integrate what the attorney says is legally possible into your plan to achieve your ends.

If you feel that your case is being handled carelessly or incompetently, tell your attorney so. Frequently the problem is one of communication, such as the attorney's failure to inform you about the progress of the case. If the problem persists, consult another attorney; you are free to change your counsel. If your dispute is over the fee charged, or other matters, you may contact the local bar association and possibly settle through arbitration. If all else fails, you can sue the attorney for damages, claiming malpractice.

Unit Five
USING CREDIT

UNIT OBJECTIVES

UPON COMPLETION OF THIS UNIT, you should be able to

1. identify the parties in a debtor/creditor relationship.
2. understand the relative legal positions of the parties in a debtor/creditor relationship.
3. discuss the laws which protect creditors.
4. discuss the laws which protect debtors.
5. recall the special laws that apply to the use of credit cards.
6. distinguish between a secured and an unsecured transaction.
7. explain how a security interest is created.
8. discuss how security interests in both tangible and intangible property are protected.
9. describe how a security interest is properly terminated.

19

Debtors, Creditors, and Bankruptcy

1. You are considering borrowing a sum of money to make a major purchase. Is there a limit on how much interest a lender can charge you? If, instead, you decide to buy the item "on time," is there a limit on how much finance charge a credit seller can add to the price of the goods?
2. An acquaintance brags to you that she is going to finance her college education with government student loans and then use bankruptcy to avoid paying them. Is this possible?
3. All five of your credit cards are stolen from your motel room while you are skiing. Fortunately you discover the loss immediately upon your return to your room and notify the credit card companies within a few hours. However, in the next few days, the thief uses the cards to charge $1,875 in a series of small purchases. Each credit card company then bills you for $50 of the purchases made with its card. Why did they do this, and must you pay them?

WHO ARE DEBTORS AND CREDITORS?

PROBLEM: Dante, a college student majoring in physics, won a $1,500 prize in a science project competition. She deposited the money in her checking account at the First National Bank. As far as her checking account is concerned, is Dante a debtor or creditor of the bank?

debtor: one who owes a debt

debt: that which is owed

creditor: one to whom a debt is owed

A **debtor** is a person or a business that owes money, goods, or services to another. Whatever is owed is generally called the **debt**. The **creditor** is the one to whom the debt is owed.

A legally enforceable debt normally arises out of a contract where something of value has been exchanged for a promise to provide money, goods, or services. In the problem, Dante has transferred her money to the bank in exchange for the bank's promise to keep it safe and to return it or pay it to someone else immediately upon Dante's demand. Therefore the bank is the debtor and Dante the creditor in the relationship.

During the Middle Ages, charging any interest on loans was illegal; today it is legal and borrowing is deemed beneficial to growth and productivity in our society. As a consequence, the debtor/creditor relationship is encouraged and protected by our laws. This protection extends not only to creditors, by making them more secure in the lending of resources, but to debtors, by making the system fairer and by providing bankruptcy as a last resort.

WHAT LAWS PROTECT THE CREDITOR?

PROBLEM: Bandai borrowed $2,500 from Ndem. Bandai promised to repay the money in 12 months with interest at 9 percent per year. Bandai gave Ndem shares of American Telephone Company common stock, which had a market value of $3,000, to hold as security for the payment. The stock was to be returned to Bandai when the debt was paid. What was Ndem's legal status?

When an individual or a business becomes a creditor, its primary concern is whether or not it will be repaid. If the debt is not repaid or if it is expensive to collect, the creditor must bear the loss initially. If the creditor is to continue making loans, it must charge its other borrowers more to make up for the bad debts. Therefore it is in society's interest to see that a creditor who has made a fair and proper loan can collect on it with minimal difficulty.

As a consequence, the law provides a number of ways in which a creditor can be protected.

1. Laws Allowing Secured Debts

The most important of the laws protecting creditors allow the creditor to acquire a legal interest in (that is, a right in or claim to) some specific property of the debtor. This interest is enforceable if the debtor defaults (fails to pay according to the terms of the agreement) and is called a **security interest**. The debt is referred to as a **secured debt**. A creditor who holds a security interest, as did Ndem in the problem, is a secured creditor.

security interest: the creditor's right to enforce the debt against specific property of the debtor

secured debt: debt in which a promise to pay is reinforced by a direct claim against some property

When a creditor has a security interest in specific property, there is a **lien** against that property. A lien gives the creditor the right, if necessary, to sell the property and to use the proceeds from the sale to pay the debt.

Usually, the debtor keeps possession of the liened property as long as the debt is not in default. Mortgages on homes are very common examples of this type of secured debt. However, if there is a default, the creditor is allowed to peacefully repossess the secured property if it is movable, such as a car or TV.

lien: a security interest giving the creditor the right to force the sale of the property to recover the debt amount

Some secured debt arrangements permit the *creditor* to have possession of the property until the debt is paid. One such lien is the **pledge**, which arises when personal property is given to a creditor as security for the payment of a debt, or for the performance of an obligation. The property may be either goods or documents representing property rights (for example, corporate stock). The **pledgor** voluntarily gives up possession of the property. The **pledgee** receives possession.

pledge: situation in which personal property is given to a creditor as security

In the pledge, the pledgee must treat the property with reasonable care. The property may be repledged to a third party on terms which do not impair the debtor's right to get the property back. In the event of default by the pledgor, the pledgee may sell the property after proper notice to the pledgor. The UCC gives the pledgee the right to make either a public or a private sale. However, the pledgee must act in good faith and in a manner which is commercially reasonable. If the amount received, after the deduction of expenses and interest, is more than the amount of the debt, the excess must be paid to the pledgor. If the amount is less, the difference still must be paid by the pledgor. Upon performance of the obligation, the pledgor has a right to the return of the property.

pledgor: debtor who voluntarily gives up possession of personal property to a pledgee

pledgee: creditor who receives possession of personal property from a pledgor

pawn: pledge of tangible personal property

pawnbroker: person licensed to loan money on the security of tangible personal property

A **pawn** is a pledge of tangible personal property, usually of small size and high value. This type of pledge includes items such as jewelry, cameras, or musical instruments. It excludes such items as stocks or bonds or other documents of value. A **pawnbroker** is a person in the business of lending money at interest who requires such tangible personal property as security. The nature of the pawn business makes it easy for thieves to dispose of stolen property. Therefore the business is regulated by special statutes. These laws usually provide that the pawnbroker must obtain a license, post a bond, and keep accurate records open to police inspection. If stolen goods are found in the pawnshop, they may be seized without compensation to the pawnbroker. Also, maximum limits are imposed on the rate of interest that may be charged.

The borrower who pawns goods is given a receipt known as a *pawn ticket*. The pawnbroker is required to redeliver the goods when the debt is paid with interest due and the pawn ticket is surrendered.

Goods that are pawned must be held for a certain length of time after the loan is due before they can be sold. In some states, this length of time is one year. In most states, the rights of the parties to the proceeds of sale are usually the same as in ordinary pledges. In other states, ownership passes to the pawnbroker at the end of a specified time.

mechanic's lien: lien against the real property of the debtor for the unpaid value of labor and materials

artisan's lien: lien against the personal property of the debtor being held by the creditor for value of the repair or service provided

Although most liens are created with the consent of the debtor/owner, statutes in many states create liens in favor of the creditor without such consent. These involuntary liens include the mechanic's lien and the artisan's lien. The **mechanic's lien** allows a person who has not been paid for labor or materials furnished to build a home, building, or other real property improvement to file a lien on the realty. If the lien is not paid, the realty can be sold and the lienholder collects the amount owed out of the proceeds even before a mortgageholder on the same property gets any money.

The **artisan's lien** (generally the same as the garage or hotelkeeper's lien) allows persons who have not been paid for services, such as the repairing of a car or the providing of a hotel room, to collect what they are owed by selling the debtor's personal property, such as the car or luggage, possessed by the creditor.

2. Laws Involving Third Parties

In addition to liens, a number of other means of protection are available to creditors. For example, a creditor who wishes assurance beyond the debtor's word that a debt will be paid may get a third party to assume liability. **Suretyship** is a contractual relation in which a third party becomes primarily liable for the debt or obligation if payment or performance becomes overdue. Three parties are involved. The **principal debtor** is the party who originally owes the debt or obligation. The creditor is the one to whom the obligation is owed. The **surety** is the third party who promises to be liable in case of the default of the principal debtor. The surety may be bound by an oral contract since a suretyship is a primary obligation, but such agreements are usually put in writing. If the surety is required to pay the creditor, he or she has a right to collect from the principal debtor.

suretyship: relationship in which a third party becomes primarily liable for a debt upon default of the principal debtor

principal debtor: one who originally owes a debt in a three-party arrangement

Suretyship contracts are discharged in much the same way as other contracts. If the debtor pays, the surety is discharged. The surety is also discharged if the creditor releases the debtor or alters the obligation, as by extending the time of performance, without the surety's consent.

surety: third party who promises to pay a debt in case of default by the principal debtor

Alston was the surety on a debt owed by Baxter to Clark. When Baxter was unable to pay on the due date, Clark agreed to allow an extra month to raise the money. Because the creditor did this without notifying and getting Alston's consent, Alston was released from the obligation as surety.

If there are cosureties, any cosurety who pays the full debt may get a judgment against the other cosureties for their proportionate share of the debt. This is called the *right of contribution.*

Like suretyship, the **guaranty** relationship protects the creditor. In it, the third party, the **guarantor**, agrees to pay if the principal debtor fails to do so. But unlike a surety, the guarantor is only secondarily liable. This means that the creditor must first sue the defaulting debtor and get a judgment that proves to be uncollectible. In a suretyship, such a suit is not necessary. The contract creating the guaranty relationship must be in writing and signed by the guarantor to be enforceable under the statute of frauds. This is because a guaranty contract is a contract to pay a debt of another person.

guaranty: relationship in which a third party becomes secondarily liable for a debt upon default of the principal debtor

guarantor: third party who promises to pay a debt if the creditor cannot collect by suit from the principal debtor

3. Laws Concerning Unsecured Debts

At times, when the debt is small or the credit standing of the borrower is very good, the creditor may be willing to take an

unsecured debt: debt based only on a promise to pay

unsecured debt. This is a debt based only on the oral or written promise of the debtor.

Upon default, an unsecured creditor is in a much weaker position than a secured creditor because, in order to collect, the unsecured creditor must sue the debtor for breach of contract. Then, upon obtaining judgment, the creditor must take legally prescribed steps to collect. This is costly and time consuming. Moreover, some debtors may prove to be dishonest and may move away without leaving a forwarding address. Or they may have no assets that the creditor can take. In other instances, debtors may even avoid some of their obligations by going into bankruptcy. It is certainly better for the creditor to have a security interest in some asset of the debtor. For example, in the problem at the beginning of this section, the common stock could be converted into cash by the secured creditor (Ndem) in case of default by the debtor (Bandai).

4. Laws Allowing Garnishment of Wages

garnishment: court-granted right to intercept a debtor's wages for the purpose of paying a debt

One other method for creditor protection is the **garnishment** of wages. Once a creditor's claim is shown to be legally valid and fair in a court hearing, the creditor may receive a portion of the debtor's wages directly from the debtor's employer. The amount that can be garnished by all creditors, however, is generally limited by the Consumer Credit Protection Act to 25 percent of the debtor's take-home pay.

WHAT LAWS PROTECT THE DEBTOR?

PROBLEM: The Santaros decided to rent an unfurnished apartment. Reliable Finance Company was among the sources they used for funds to buy the furniture they needed. Reliable gave them a copy of the loan contract showing only the amount to be paid per installment and the number of payments. Could they demand further information?

Generally laws protecting debtors are of five types: (1) laws setting maximum interest rates, (2) laws requiring clear and complete disclosure of loan terms, (3) laws correcting specific abuses of the credit system, (4) laws requiring the creditor to record a public notice that the debt has been paid, and (5) laws allowing a debtor to cancel most debts and start over.

1. Laws Setting Maximum Interest Rates

Laws that set maximum interest rates, called usury laws, were discussed in Chapter 10. Usually such laws apply only to transactions involving the lending of money, not the buying of goods on credit, where much higher limits on finance charges apply, if they exist at all. Also, the usury laws do not protect corporations because they are considered to be adequately protected by the abilities of their professional managers.

2. Laws Requiring Clear and Complete Disclosure of Loan Terms

A **consumer loan** arises when a person borrows money primarily for personal, family, household, or agricultural purposes. It is often called a personal loan to distinguish it from a business or commercial loan.

consumer loan: money borrowed for personal, family, household, or agricultural purposes

By requiring complete and clear disclosure of loan terms, the federal Truth in Lending Act is the primary example of a law which protects consumer debtors. In particular, the Truth in Lending Act, part of the Consumer Credit Protection Act, requires a creditor to furnish a debtor with certain information. The creditor must make a full disclosure of interest and finance charges whenever the consumer loan is repayable in four or more installments or carries a finance charge. The **finance charge** is the total added cost when one pays in installments for goods or services. The creditor must also declare the true equivalent annual interest rate. Thus, 1½ percent a month must be stated as 18 percent a year. Under the law, a credit sales contract must also state such details as the cash price of the item, the down payment or trade-in allowance, if any, itemized list of finance charges, and total amount to be financed. In the problem, Reliable Finance is obligated to tell the Santaros the total cost of their loan expressed in dollars and cents, and to show the actual annual percentage rate.

finance charge: added cost for the payment in installments for goods or services

The Truth in Lending Act does not apply to first mortgage loans on homes. It also does not limit the interest or finance charges which can be made on any loans. It merely requires full disclosure of the terms.

Any creditor who willfully and knowingly violates the Truth in Lending Act may be fined, imprisoned, or both. The violator must also pay the debtor twice the finance charge (but no less than $100 nor more than $1,000) plus court costs and attorney fees.

An increasing number of consumers lease automobiles and other equipment instead of buying the items. A big advantage of leasing for some persons is that it requires no down payment. However, in the end, the total price paid is usually higher than a purchase would be. The federal Consumer Leasing Act extends the protection of the Consumer Credit Protection Act to consumer lessees. Before the contract is signed, the lessor must comply with full disclosure requirements.

3. Laws Correcting Specific Abuses of the Credit System

Specific laws have been enacted to correct problems such as the relative inability of women to get credit, unfair debt-collection practices, and inaccurate credit reports.

The federal Equal Credit Opportunity Act. The federal Equal Credit Opportunity Act makes it unlawful for any creditor to discriminate against an applicant because of sex or marital status. In the past, women had difficulty in obtaining credit. This was true even for employed women. It was especially true for married women. The act was created to make such discrimination illegal. Major provisions of the act are:

(1) A creditor may not refuse, on the basis of sex or marital status, to grant a separate account to a credit-worthy applicant.
(2) A creditor may not ask the applicant's marital status if the applicant applies for an unsecured separate account.
(3) A creditor may not prohibit a married female applicant from opening or maintaining an account in her maiden name.
(4) A creditor shall not request information about birth control practices or childbearing intentions or capability.
(5) Married persons who have joint accounts have the right to have credit information reported in both their names in order to provide a credit history for both. In the past, upon divorce or upon death of the husband, the wife would often be denied credit because the joint account had been listed in the husband's name only.

The federal Fair Debt Collection Practices Act. The federal Fair Debt Collection Practices Act makes abusive and deceptive debt-collection practices illegal. The act applies to professional bill collectors or agencies who regularly try to collect consumer debts for clients. Prohibited are such practices as:

(1) Harassment (such as a series of letters with menacing language, or repeated night and day telephone calls).
(2) Abusive and profane language.
(3) Threats of violence.
(4) Contact with third parties (such as relatives, neighbors, friends, and employers).
(5) Communication with the debtor at work.

The act is aimed at certain aggressively irresponsible agencies. It does not apply to personal "in-house" debt collection efforts of the creditor, employers or lawyers of the creditor, or certain other persons. However, an abused debtor may sometimes bring a civil action against any debt collector for damages due to defamation, assault, invasion of privacy, and intentional infliction of mental suffering.

The federal Fair Credit Billing Act. The federal Fair Credit Billing Act provides somewhat similar protection to credit card holders. It also includes a provision that allows merchants to offer discounts to customers who pay cash instead of using credit cards. The act further provides that:

(1) Creditors must mail bills at least 14 days in advance of the due date, must acknowledge billing inquiries within 30 days, and must settle any complaints within 90 days.
(2) Creditors are prohibited from sending repeated, insistent letters demanding payment until disputes over the billing are settled.
(3) Credit card holders have the right to withhold payment for items that prove defective without being held liable for the entire amount owed. This applies only in case of purchases of more than $50 made in the buyer's state or within 100 miles of the buyer's home.

The federal Fair Credit Reporting Act. The federal Fair Credit Reporting Act regulates those companies that review personal financial records for business firms so that those firms can decide whether to extend credit to applicants. These companies, such as the Retailers Credit Association (an organization of retail merchants who sell on credit) review the applicant's personal financial records in order to determine for the business firm the applicant's credit

credit rating: evaluation of one's ability to pay debts

rating. A **credit rating** is an evaluation of one's ability to pay debts. If credit is denied because of information in a credit report, the company denying credit must tell the applicant. The applicant may then demand that the reporting agency disclose the general nature of the contents of its file (except medical information) and the names of parties who were given this information. Names of those who provided the information need not be disclosed, however. If there is any error, the credit reporting agency must correct the record. Upon request, it must notify the inquirers who were misinformed. The agency must make the disclosures and reports without charge if the applicant acted within 30 days of getting notice of a denial of credit. Similar rules apply when an individual is denied an insurance policy or employment contract because of an unfavorable credit report.

4. Laws Requiring Notice of Debt Payment to be Recorded

As a practical matter, debtors should always request receipts, especially when paying in cash. In some states, a debtor is not required to pay a debt unless such a receipt is given. A canceled check returned by the bank serves as a receipt if it bears a notation showing the purpose for which payment was made. Even without such a notation it is useful evidence of payment. When a secured debt is paid in full, the law generally permits the debtor to require the creditor to record that fact in the public records.

5. Laws Allowing Debtors to Cancel Most Debts and Start Over

Bankruptcy laws have been enacted to help debtors who have become overburdened with debts. These laws allow an individual or business to be released from most debts. This release is called a **discharge**. Discharges through bankruptcy are available to a particular debtor only once every six years. A record that debts were discharged in bankruptcy generally stays on the debtor's record for ten years. This reduces the debtor's ability to get credit during that period. Nevertheless, bankruptcy remains as an alternative to a debtor. Bankruptcy offers protection from an overwhelming debt burden. It also aids creditors by ensuring a fair and orderly distribution of the debtor's assets among the creditors.

discharge: release from debt obligations through bankruptcy

Under the federal Bankruptcy Code, there are several forms of relief for debtors. Liquidation, or "straight bankruptcy," involves the collection and liquidation (conversion to cash) of the property of the debtor and the distribution of the proceeds to creditors. Liquidation results in the discharge of most of the debtor's financial obligations. Relief may also be obtained through the *reorganization* of debtor corporations, partnerships, or individuals in business. Under a reorganization, the debtor keeps assets, stays in business, and reaches a settlement with the majority of creditors. A third form of relief, available only to debtors with regular income, is to gain approval for a plan to reduce debt payments by extending the repayment period.

Liquidation may be voluntary or involuntary. With a few exceptions, any person, business, or other association may request **voluntary bankruptcy**. Any person or business, except farmers and charitable institutions, owing $5,000 or more and unable to pay debts when they come due may be forced into **involuntary bankruptcy**.

voluntary bankruptcy: status of one who has requested and been granted bankruptcy

involuntary bankruptcy: status of one forced into bankruptcy by creditors

In either voluntary or involuntary bankruptcy proceedings, the debtor must file a list of all creditors and amounts owed, a list of all property owned, and a list of current income and expenses. A trustee is then selected. The trustee's duties are to find and to protect the assets of the debtor, liquidate them, and pay the claims against the debtor's estate with the proceeds. Such claims would include court costs, back wages owed to the debtor's employees, taxes, and claims of the general creditors. Secured creditors would seek payment of the secured debts directly against the collateral. Secured debts would be enforced ahead of any of these other claims. In addition, there are certain types of claims that are not dischargeable by bankruptcy. These include:

a. certain taxes,
b. alimony and child support,
c. student loans,
d. judgments against the debtor for willful and malicious injury to another,
e. judgments against the debtor resulting from driving while intoxicated, and
f. any claims not listed by the debtor.

In addition, certain assets of the debtor are exempt from use to satisfy creditor's claims. Under the federal law these exemptions include:

a. up to $7,500 in equity in a debtor's home,
b. up to $1,200 of a debtor's interest in one motor vehicle,
c. up to $750 of a debtor's interest in the tools of the debtor's trade, and
d. alimony and support payments, Social Security payments, and certain welfare and pension benefits.

States may pass legislation disallowing the use of these federal exemptions and some have done so. In such states, only the state exemptions are available.

WHAT SPECIAL LAWS APPLY TO CREDIT CARDS AND THEIR USE?

PROBLEM: Tomlinson applied for and received a gasoline credit card. After using it several times, Tomlinson sold the automobile, bought a bicycle, and laid the card aside. Several weeks later, she received a bill for $79 from the oil company for purchases made by someone else. Tomlinson realized that the card had been lost or stolen and so notified the company. Must she pay the $79?

credit card: small plastic form which identifies the holder as entitled to obtain goods or services on credit

Instead of carrying large sums of cash or checks that may not be honored by a retailer, many of today's consumers buy goods and services by using credit cards. A **credit card** identifies the holder as entitled to obtain goods or services on credit. Usually a credit card is made of plastic, is embossed with the holder's name and identification number, and has a place for the holder's signature. (See Figure 19-1.) Credit cards are used to make billions of dollars of credit purchases annually. Credit cards may be good for certain types of expenses. (For example, the AMERICAN EXPRESS®, Carte Blanche®, and Diners Club International® cards are commonly used for travel and entertainment.) Some cards are limited in use to a certain retail store or chain (cards for a local department store or a national oil company). Some are all-purpose cards which cover any type of purchase from any cooperating seller authorized to honor them. (Banks are generally the issuers of this type, which includes such cards as MasterCard™ and VISA®.)

A credit card is usually issued in response to a consumer's written application. When the consumer signs the card, he or she is bound in a contractual relation with the issuer. Generally the cardholder is liable for all purchases made with the card by the holder or by others with the holder's permission.

Under federal law, the cardholder is also liable for unauthorized use of the credit card by any other person, such as a thief or a dishonest finder. This liability is limited, however, to $50 and is imposed only if:

1. the cardholder had asked for and received the credit card or had signed or used it,

Figure 19-1. Credit Card

2. the card issuer had given adequate notice of the possible liability for unauthorized use,
3. the card issuer had provided the cardholder with a description of how to notify the card issuer in the event of loss or theft of the card,
4. the card issuer had provided positive means for identification on the card, such as space for the holder's signature or photograph, and
5. the unauthorized use took place before the cardholder had notified the issuer that the card had been lost or stolen.

Thus, the loss or theft of a credit card should be reported immediately to the issuer. In the problem, Tomlinson would probably be liable for $50 of the charges. The thief would, of course, be criminally liable for forgery and larceny.

Most credit card agreements require the cardholder to pay the amount charged on the card within 30 days of being billed for it. If the cardholder fails to do so, he or she is contractually obligated to pay interest on the unpaid balance. Some states set limits on the interest rates that can be charged to credit card holders, although these limits may be relatively high.

Although credit cards may offer convenience and protection for the consumer, they can add greatly to the cost of the goods that the consumer purchases. This is true even when the balances due are paid before the interest charges apply. The seller must pay the credit card company for its service. Generally this charge is between 3 and 6 percent of the sale. Such amounts paid to the credit card company are usually passed on to both cash and credit customers through higher prices for the goods.

In addition, credit cards have a great potential for abuse through overuse by owners and misuse by thieves or finders of lost cards. Some consumers fail to plan and save for their purchases. Instead, they impulsively use their credit cards to purchase goods and services. Often the payments for these purchases, when added to other living expenses, total more than the debtor's income. As a consequence, debt counseling services have opened around the country. These services assist debtors in budgeting their incomes in such a way as to pay off creditors and to avoid being forced into bankruptcy.

PREVENTING LEGAL DIFFICULTIES

Using Credit Wisely . . .

1. in applying for credit, always be completely accurate and honest. Any temporary advantage gained by misleading a creditor will generally lead to trouble. Credit information about customers is exchanged freely by stores and other creditors. Lies about one's credit history are, thus, easily exposed;
2. if you put up property as security for a debt, be sure it is returned or properly released when the debt is paid. Otherwise you may later have difficulty selling the property or using it as security again;
3. protect your rights by learning them and, where appropriate, exercising them. The Fair Credit Reporting and Billing Acts, Equal Credit Opportunity Act, Fair Debt Collection Practices Act, and other similar statutes are of no use without consumer demand for their enforcement;
4. be cautious about entering into a credit agreement as a surety or a guarantor; and
5. a person who repairs your TV, watch, car, or other personal property can exercise an artisan's lien on the property. The person can keep the repaired item until paid or sell the item if you do not pay. Be sure you deal with reputable individuals. Get a detailed estimate of the bill before the repair is begun and authorize work only if you can afford the price.

Strengthening Your Legal Vocabulary

artisan's lien
consumer loan
credit card
credit rating
creditor
debt
debtor
discharge
finance charge
garnishment
guarantor
guaranty
involuntary bankruptcy
lien
mechanic's lien
pawn
pawnbroker
pledge
pledgee
pledgor
principal debtor
secured debt
security interest
surety
suretyship
unsecured debt
voluntary bankruptcy

1. Small plastic form which identifies holder as entitled to receive goods or services on credit.
2. Debt supported only by the debtor's promise to pay.
3. The creditor's right to enforce the debt against specific property of the debtor.
4. One to whom a debt is owed.
5. Third party who agrees to be secondarily liable for the debt of another if such other defaults.
6. Situation in which personal property is deposited with a creditor as security for the payment of a debt.
7. Claim that is filed against real property for the unpaid value of labor and materials.
8. Third party who agrees to be primarily liable for the debt of another if such person fails to pay the debt when due.
9. One who lends money at interest and has possession of personal property as security for the money.
10. Court-granted right of the creditor to intercept wages of the debtor to pay overdue debt.

Reviewing Important Points

1. When one owes money to another, a relationship of debtor and creditor exists.
2. A debt may be secured or unsecured. If it is secured, the debtor gives the creditor a lien against specified property until the obligation is performed. If it is unsecured, the creditor does not have a lien against specified property.
3. A lien gives the creditor the right to sell specified property of the debtor to pay the debt. Any excess money received goes to the debtor. If there is a deficiency or shortage, the creditor normally may sue for the balance due.

4. Goods or documents representing property rights may be delivered to the creditor as security for a loan. This creates a pledge and gives the creditor the right to sell the goods or the documents in case of default. Upon performance of the obligation, the pledgor has a right to the return of the property.
5. Creditors may proceed against the general assets of the debtor in the following two cases:
   (a) when secured debts are in default and are not paid in full by proceeds from sale of the property pledged, and
   (b) when unsecured debts are not paid.
6. In answering for the debt of another upon default, the surety assumes a primary liability. The guarantor is liable secondarily after the creditor has exhausted all remedies against the debtor, including judgment and execution.
7. Debtors are protected by usury laws, laws requiring disclosure of loan terms, laws providing equal credit opportunities, laws requiring fair billing, laws controlling the collection of debts, laws regulating fair reporting of credit standing, and laws allowing debt discharge through bankruptcy.
8. A signed credit card binds the cardholder and the issuer in a contractual relationship. In case of loss or theft of a card, the cardholder generally is liable for unauthorized purchases up to a limit of $50 unless the issuer had been notified previously.

Applying Law to Everyday Life

1. When Dodrill started her own copying and duplicating business, she entered into a number of contractual arrangements. First, she bought $900 worth of paper from Springfield Business Supply, promising to pay the money within the next 30 days. Then, using her bank credit card, she purchased a computer and word processing software. Next, Dodrill leased a large copying machine from its manufacturer. In addition, she bought several desktop copying units from the same manufacturer on a 24-month installment purchase plan. The plan permitted the seller to repossess the machines if Dodrill defaulted on payments. Finally, Dodrill borrowed $2,000 from the Ozark Region National Bank to meet current expenses, giving a United States Treasury Bond as security for repayment. (a) Which of the transactions entered into by Dodrill involved a debtor/creditor relationship? (b) Which relationships were secured? Which were unsecured?

2. Glenn needs money on short notice. He has a very expensive watch and a very poor credit rating. Where might he be able to raise the funds he needs?

3. Buckley owed $1,750 for furniture purchased from Taylor's store. When Buckley failed to pay, Taylor asked Buckley to get a surety to stand good for the debt. Young readily agreed to act as surety. However, when Buckley defaulted and Taylor demanded payment from Young, Young refused. Could Taylor compel Young to pay for Buckley's debt?

4. Langley had owed $7,340 to St. John's Hospital for more than one year. Finally, the hospital went to court and obtained an order directing Langley's employer to pay a sum of money out of each of Langley's paychecks towards the bill. What creditor protection device has St. John's utilized? What is the maximum amount of Langley's check which is available to the hospital?

5. During the warranty period, the Arnaudos returned their home computer for repair to the seller, Computerville, Inc. Later, after the warranty period had expired, the Arnaudos stopped making their regular monthly $100 payments for the computer because the same problem continued. Computerville then gave its claim for the $1,900 balance to Bulldog Services, a collection agency. Bulldog had a clerk telephone the Arnaudos at least once a day and once a night. Every Sunday, a uniformed Bulldog agent would park the company truck in front of the Arnaudos' house. The truck had these words in large type on both side panels: "Bulldog Services. We chase deadbeats." The agent would then try to talk about the claim with any person entering or leaving the house. Was Bulldog Services acting legally?

6. Mathew, a recent college graduate, applied for credit at a large department store. Unfortunately the store denied her application, citing an unfavorable credit report from the Superior Protective Investigations Credit Bureau. Mathew felt that the unfavorable credit rating stemmed from a dispute she had recently had with a major retail chain which had billed her inaccurately. What may Mathew do to correct this situation?

7. McCormack owed the Coopersmith Variety Store $67.50 for goods purchased. She paid the bill with a personal check after noting the purpose on the face of the check. The check was indorsed and cashed by Coopersmith and returned to McCormack properly canceled. Coopersmith then billed her again for the same obligation. What should McCormack do?

Solving Case Problems

1. Medias and other pawnbrokers objected to an Indianapolis city ordinance which regulated their business. The ordinance required an applicant for a pawnbroker's license to establish good character by the certificate of three landowners. The ordinance also provided that the licensee keep specified records and supply information to the chief of police. Finally, the ordinance specified that the licensee hold all pledged articles for 96 hours, and it required that the licensee take the thumbprints of all persons from whom he or she bought or received goods. Are these regulations arbitrary and unreasonable? (*Medias et al. v. City of Indianapolis*, 216 Ind. 155, 23 N.E.2d 590)

2. Wiggins, a general contractor, contracted with Von Ber Mar, Inc., to build a residence on land owned by the corporation. Von Ber Mar then obtained a

construction loan and permanent financing from the Searcy Federal Savings and Loan Association to construct the residence. Wiggins completed the job but was not paid in full. Therefore he claimed a mechanic's lien for an amount in excess of $20,000. He had furnished the last items on August 21, and he filed suit to enforce his lien on October 1. Under Arkansas law, an account must be filed within 120 days to *perfect* (protect) the lien. The first pleading in which Wiggins gave an account and asserted a claim of priority over the mortgage owned by Searcy was filed on April 1 of the following year. Does Wiggins's lien have priority over the Searcy mortgage? (*Wiggins v. Searcy Federal Savings and Loan Association*, 486 S.W.2d 900, Ark.)

3. Todd was one of seven cosureties. When the principal debtor defaulted, Todd paid the debt and sued the other cosureties. Is Todd entitled to a judgment for one-seventh of the debt against each of the cosureties or to a judgment for six-sevenths of the debt against each? (*Todd v. Windsor et al.*, 118 Ga.App. 805, 165 S.E.2d 438)

4. In his divorce decree, Elliot was ordered to pay $102 of his weekly wages of $467.47 from his job at a General Motors plant for child support. Months later, U. S. Life Credit Corporation (USLC) recovered a judgment against Elliot in municipal court. With court approval, USLC then garnished 25 percent of Elliot's $467.47 per week to pay off the judgment amount. The U. S. Secretary of Labor, whose job it is to see that the provisions of the federal Consumer Credit Protection Act relating to garnishment are properly enforced, then filed a lawsuit against the municipal court and USLC contending that the payments to USLC and for child support, taken together, violated the 25 percent of disposable income restriction on garnishments imposed by the Act. Decide. (*Donovan, Secretary of Labor, v. Hamilton County Municipal Court*, 580 F. Supp. 554)

5. When Hardison filed for bankruptcy, one of his main creditors was General Finance Corporation (GFC) to whom he owed $2,800. After the GFC debt and others were discharged as a result of the bankruptcy procedure, he received a letter from GFC informing him that his credit was still good with them. By telephone, Hardison then arranged for a $1,200 loan from GFC. However, when he appeared to pick up the money, GFC informed him that they were going to make the loan only if he agreed to pay back not only the $1,200 but an additional $1,200 from the first loan. Hardison then signed a consumer credit contract agreeing to those terms. Later, Hardison filed a lawsuit claiming that GFC should have included the amount from the previously discharged debt in the "total finance charge" in the Truth in Lending statement shown him at the time of the transaction, rather than as a part of the "total amount financed." Hardison wanted damages available under the Truth in Lending Act. Should he receive them? (*Hardison v. General Finance Corporation*, 738 F.2d 893)

20

Secured Transactions

1. A friend considers buying a used car advertised in the newspaper. How can she be sure that some third party does not have a creditor's claim against the car?
2. You buy a new compact disc read-only memory unit for your personal computer under a contract that permits the seller to repossess it if you miss a payment. The seller has officially recorded these facts. If you sell your personal computer and the memory unit to a friend before you have paid for the unit in full, does your friend get clear title?
3. You need to take out a loan. You offer as security a very expensive component stereo system that you purchased on credit over a year ago and have since paid for in full. Unfortunately the bank informs you it cannot lend money on the system because the public records show that the previous creditor still has a claim. What can you do?

WHAT IS A SECURED TRANSACTION?

PROBLEM: Andrus loaned a friend, O'Shea, $300 cash for a down payment on a new type of videodisc player that would also play compact audiodiscs. O'Shea financed the remaining $900 of the purchase price through the seller, giving the seller a security interest in the goods. Later, O'Shea stopped making payments while she still owed Andrus the $300 and the retailer $500. The retailer repossessed the player and resold it for $480. Would Andrus get a share of the $480 to help pay back the $300 O'Shea borrowed from him?

All purchases are made either by cash or by credit. No debt is involved in a cash transaction. In a credit purchase, however, payment is delayed and a debt, owed by the buyer to the seller, is created.

In a credit transaction, the buyer may agree to allow the creditor to have a superior position over other creditors of the buyer. This normally is done by giving the seller (creditor) a security interest in the goods sold. When a security interest is granted, the transaction is referred to as a **secured transaction**. As mentioned in the previous chapter, a security interest may allow the creditor, upon the debtor's default, to sell the goods and use the proceeds of the sale to pay the debt. If there is any money left over, it goes to the debtor's other creditors or to the debtor. This is true even if the debtor goes through the legal steps of bankruptcy. Therefore, the secured creditors, because of the priority of their claims brought about by the security interest, are much more likely to be paid.

secured transaction: business deal in which a creditor gets a security interest in personal property

In contrast, a creditor with an unpaid, *unsecured* claim must bring suit, get a court judgment, and then execute (put into force) that judgment against the debtor's property. Other creditors of the debtor may have equal rights in that property. If the debtor's financial obligations are discharged in bankruptcy, the unsecured creditor may receive nothing or only a few cents for each dollar of the unpaid debt rightly claimed.

In the problem, the retailer could keep the full $480 because of its security interest in the player. It could also sue O'Shea for the remaining $20 of the $500 owed, for which it would have the right of an unsecured creditor such as Andrus.

HOW ARE SECURITY INTERESTS CREATED?

PROBLEM: Trup needed to pay medical bills. She borrowed from her brother and gave him an IOU for the amount. Was the IOU a pledge, making the loan a secured transaction?

Before the Uniform Commercial Code was enacted, many types of legal transactions gave creditors special rights in the property of debtors. Each type had distinct rules for its creation, maintenance, and execution. These rules varied from state to state. Their number and technicality created a situation which enabled unscrupulous individuals to take advantage of the unsuspecting or uninformed.

The UCC, however, did away with many of the problems by making secured transactions the only legal means of giving a creditor a security interest in another's property. The creditor in such a transaction is the **secured party**, and the personal property subject to the security interest is the **collateral**. Note that these UCC provisions apply only to personal property. Contracts involving real property as security, such as mortgages and deeds of trust, are still governed by other widely varying state laws.

secured party: creditor in a secured transaction

collateral: personal property subject to a security interest

As previously mentioned, a security interest under the UCC can be created only with the agreement of the debtor. This agreement can be expressed either orally or in writing, depending upon which one of two basic types of secured transactions is being used.

1. When the Creditor Retains Possession of the Collateral

In the first type, the creditor retains possession of the collateral. This transaction, which may be based upon an oral or written agreement, is called a pledge (see Chapter 19). The debtor may be buying the property, or the property may already be owned by the debtor but is now being put up as security for a loan of money. No pledge was created by Trup in the problem because an IOU is merely a written acknowledgment of a debt. It is not security given to ensure payment. Therefore the agreement was not a secured transaction.

Upon default of the debtor in a pledge, the creditor has a right to sell the property. The creditor applies the proceeds of the sale to the debt. Any surplus is returned to the debtor. Any deficit remains an obligation of the debtor and may be collected as an unsecured claim through a lawsuit.

2. When the Debtor Retains Possession of the Collateral

security agreement: written contract which creates a security interest

In the second type of secured transaction, the debtor retains possession of the collateral. In such cases, the secured party enters into a written contract with the debtor. This contract creates or provides for the security interest. Such a contract is called a **security agreement**. In addition to being in writing, the security agreement must be signed by the debtor and contain sufficient information to identify the collateral reasonably.

It is this second type of secured transaction which enables a consumer to buy an automobile, major kitchen appliances, or other costly items on credit. The debtor gets immediate possession and use of the goods. But the seller or finance company has the right to take them back if a payment is missed or if the contract is breached in any manner.

In a similar way, a merchant can buy goods on credit and sell them routinely to customers. The merchant gets money to pay the debt. The creditor-seller is protected by retaining a security interest in the unsold goods.

This type of secured transaction is not limited to buying on credit. It is also used in borrowing money. Suppose one wants to borrow funds from a bank. By giving the bank a security interest in a car, the debtor's promise to repay is strengthened by the car's value. If the bank approves the loan, which it is very likely to do with this added security, the borrower obtains the desired money and still has the use of the car.

Of course, when the debtor retains possession of the collateral, the secured party may have problems repossessing the goods in case of default. Repossession must be accomplished without committing a breach of the peace, that is, without violence, actions likely to produce violence, or a breaking of the law. The secured party may find that the collateral has been improperly cared for or even disposed of, or subjected to the claims of other creditors. However, the UCC gives the secured party maximum protection against most such occurrences provided the security interest has not only been properly created but has also been "perfected."

HOW DOES A CREDITOR PERFECT A SECURITY INTEREST?

PROBLEM: The Old Salt Fishing Supply sold a newly developed fish-locating sonar on an installment plan to Abernathy, who used it on his commercial fishing boat. The seller retained a security interest in the sonar and filed a financing statement. Before the sonar was paid for, Abernathy sold it to Thornton. Thornton was a purchaser in good faith who knew nothing about Old Salt's security interest and who purchased the sonar for her own fishing boat. Can Old Salt enforce against Thornton its security interest in the radio?

It is possible for a debtor to agree to give many different creditors, each unaware of the others, a security interest in the same goods. The UCC therefore specifies that the first creditor to perfect a security interest has priority over all the others. Such priority generally allows that creditor to take as much of the proceeds from the sale of the collateral as necessary to completely satisfy the amount owed to that creditor by the debtor. A **perfected security interest** results when the creditor gives proper notice of the existence of the security interest to all other potential creditors. Such notice may be given in a number of ways. For example, a creditor in possession of the collateral, as in a pledge, needs to take no additional steps for protection. Possession alone is notice to any possible subsequent buyer or creditor of the debtor that a security interest may exist. The creditor who has possession has a perfected security interest. Note that if a creditor is able to repossess collateral upon default, the act of retaking possession also perfects the security interest even though the interest had not been perfected previously.

perfected security interest: protected interest resulting from the creditor's possession of collateral or the creditor's filing of a financing statement

When the debtor has the goods, it may be necessary for the creditor to file a financing statement to perfect the creditor's interest.

A **financing statement** is a brief, written notice of the existence of a security agreement. (See example in Figure 20-1.) It must include the following:

financing statement: brief, written notice of the existence of a security agreement

1. the names and addresses of both the debtor and the creditor,
2. the signature of the debtor (although the creditor may also sign and commonly does), and
3. a statement describing the items of collateral.

If crops or property attached to buildings or land are involved, the land where such property is located must also be described. If the security agreement extends to products to be derived from the original collateral, such as the calves of cows, or proceeds from the resale of such collateral, these facts must be stated. The security agreement itself may be filed instead of the financing statement if it meets these same requirements.

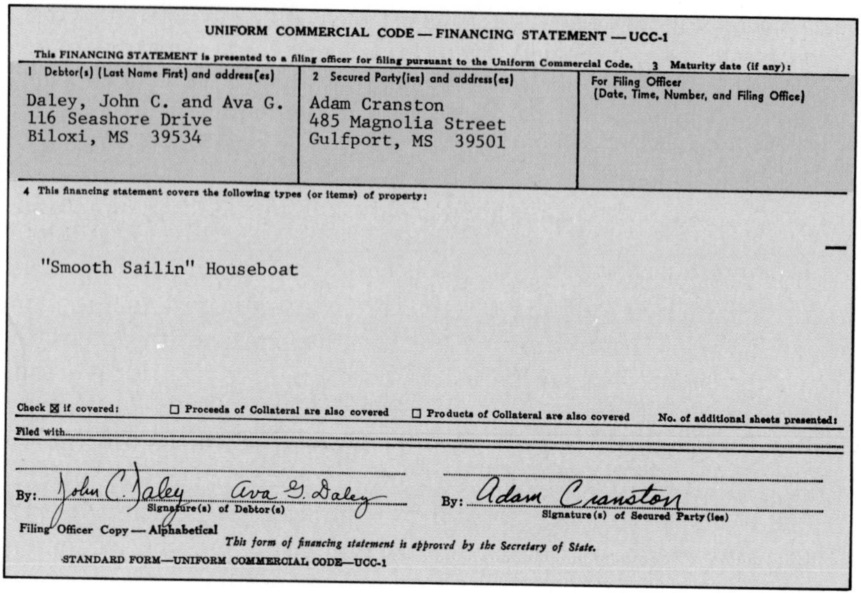

UNIFORM COMMERCIAL CODE — FINANCING STATEMENT — UCC-1

This FINANCING STATEMENT is presented to a filing officer for filing pursuant to the Uniform Commercial Code. 3 Maturity date (if any):

1 Debtor(s) (Last Name First) and address(es)	2 Secured Party(ies) and address(es)	For Filing Officer (Date, Time, Number, and Filing Office)
Daley, John C. and Ava G. 116 Seashore Drive Biloxi, MS 39534	Adam Cranston 485 Magnolia Street Gulfport, MS 39501	

4 This financing statement covers the following types (or items) of property:

"Smooth Sailin" Houseboat

Check ☒ if covered: ☐ Proceeds of Collateral are also covered ☐ Products of Collateral are also covered No. of additional sheets presented:

Filed with.

By: John C. Daley Ava G. Daley
Signature(s) of Debtor(s)

By: Adam Cranston
Signature(s) of Secured Party(ies)

Filing Officer Copy — Alphabetical

This form of financing statement is approved by the Secretary of State.

STANDARD FORM—UNIFORM COMMERCIAL CODE—UCC-1

Figure 20-1. Financing Statement

constructive notice: knowledge, presumed by law, of facts on file

consumer goods: goods used primarily for personal, family, or household purposes

farm products: crops, livestock, unmanufactured farm products, and farm supplies

inventory: business goods that are intended for sale or lease

On the financing statement, any description that reasonably identifies the property is sufficient even though it might be necessary to ask questions to determine just what property was intended. It is not essential to have a detailed description or to include serial numbers. However, confusion and disputes often may be avoided by giving greater detail than is required.

Filing gives constructive notice to the world that a security interest in specific property exists. **Constructive notice** means that the law presumes one has knowledge of the facts on file even if one actually does not. Anyone sufficiently concerned may get actual notice by checking the public records. The place of filing is specified by the UCC and depends upon the nature of the collateral.

1. Tangible Property

When tangible property is used as collateral, the procedure for perfecting the creditor's security interest depends on whether the goods are (a) **consumer goods**—used primarily for personal, family, or household purposes, (b) **farm products**—crops, livestock, unmanufactured products of the farm and farm supplies, (c) **inventory**—business goods that are intended for sale or lease, or (d)

equipment—goods used by a business in performing its function, such as a computer used by a secretary for word processing.

equipment: goods used by a business in performing its function

Goods can be in only one of these four classes at a given time. Their classification may change, however, if their use changes. For example, a television set is classified as inventory if it is held by a dealer for resale. If the television set is used as a closed circuit system in the store for security, it is equipment. If the set is purchased and taken home by you, it is classified as consumer goods.

Consumer goods. Filing is not required to protect the seller's security interest in consumer goods against other creditors of the buyer. This rule relieves retail merchants, who sell many thousands of articles on installment plans, of what would be a heavy burden in paperwork and in payment of filing fees. In case of default, the creditor may, nevertheless, repossess the goods from the original buyer.

Filing would be required for consumer goods if the consumer already owned the goods and was simply borrowing against them as security. Filing is also necessary, even in initial purchases, if the seller wants protection against a third person who might innocently buy the good for personal, family, or household use from a dishonest debtor. Such a buyer of consumer goods, who gives value and does not know of the security interest, acquires clear title if there is no filing. On the other hand, if there is a filing, the third person is bound by the security interest even if that person is unaware of its existence.

Ale bought a household refrigerator for $750 from Sandon in a secured transaction. Sandon did not file a financing statement. When $500 was still due, Ale sold the refrigerator to a neighbor, Vard, who paid $600, assuming that Ale had clear title. Sandon may not repossess the refrigerator from Vard if Ale fails to make any payment. Instead, Sandon must sue Ale. Vard obtained clear title because Sandon had not filed a financing statement.

In the problem at the beginning of the section, Thornton did not get good title because Old Salt had filed a financing statement. Thus, Old Salt can enforce its security interest by repossessing the sonar. It may do so without compensating Thornton, who must pursue Abernathy for money lost in the deal. In contrast, if Old Salt had not filed the financing statement, Thornton would have acquired clear title. In that case, Old Salt would have to sue Abernathy for damages.

For motor vehicles, most states provide that instead of filing as above described, a security interest is perfected by noting its existence on the certificate of title to the vehicle. An exception to the filing requirement is also made when fixtures are sold on credit. Fixtures are items of personal property attached to real property in a manner that makes the law treat them like real property. A filing to protect a security interest in fixtures must include in the financing statement a description of the real property involved.

Farm Products. A security interest in farm products is perfected by filing or by taking possession of the products upon default. This applies both to farm products bought on credit and those put up as security for loans. Most states require the filing of the financing statement for farm products to be made at the county courthouse.

Inventory. A security interest in inventory is perfected by filing or by taking possession of the inventory upon default. This is true whether the inventory is bought on credit or is put up as security for a loan. However, since inventory generally is purchased by business firms for the very purpose of reselling, a person buying from such a debtor in the ordinary course of business will get clear title even when aware of the security interest. For example, if you buy a stove at the appliance store, you get title to it free of the security interest held by the unpaid manufacturer who originally sold it to the store on credit.

Equipment. A security interest in equipment is perfected by filing or by taking possession of the equipment upon default. This applies whether the equipment is bought on credit or is put up as security for a loan. If the equipment is a motor vehicle, a notation on the certificate of title may substitute for filing in perfecting the interest. As with inventory, perfection of a security interest in equipment requires filing with the state government, usually with the Secretary of State.

intangible property: real value in rights to money, goods, or contractual performance; generally evidenced by documents

2. Intangible Property

The second major classification of collateral, **intangible property**, represents real value in rights to money, goods, or contractual performance. Intangible property generally is evidenced by documents or writings. It includes the accounts receivable of a business, the rights to performance under a contract, bills of lading or airbills, warehouse receipts, commercial paper, and bonds or stocks.

As with tangible property, the procedure used in perfecting a security interest in intangible property varies with the classification of that property. A security interest in accounts receivable or contractual rights which cannot be possessed in a physical sense must be perfected by filing unless the transaction does not cover a significant part of the debtor's accounts or contractual rights. For documents, such as bills of lading, airbills, and warehouse receipts, the creditor may either file a financing statement or take possession of the goods upon default. To perfect a security interest in paper (such as promissory notes, stock certificates, or bonds), possession by the creditor, upon default of the debtor, is essential.

HOW ARE SECURED TRANSACTIONS TERMINATED?

PROBLEM: The Nosmans bought a new flat-screen wall TV for their recreation room for $2,000. They paid $400 down and agreed to pay the balance in $200 monthly installments. The seller, Silitech, Inc., retained a security interest in the TV. After making six payments, the Nosmans defaulted. Silitech repossessed the TV. What must Silitech do to be able to legally keep the set in settlement of the unpaid $400 balance?

Most secured transactions are terminated by the debtor's paying the debt in full and the creditor's then releasing the security interest in the collateral. If the creditor has filed a financing statement, this release is made when the creditor files an acknowledgment of the full payment, called a **termination statement**, with the governmental body that has the financing statement. Filing the termination statement is a way to inform the potential buyers and creditors that the property is no longer collateral. In the case of a security interest in consumer goods, the termination statement must be filed within 30 days of the payoff or within 10 days of a written request by the debtor, or the creditor must pay $100 plus damages to the debtor.

termination statement: publicly filed acknowledgment that a secured debt has been paid off

When the debtor fails to pay as promised, the secured creditor who does not have possession of the collateral may take possession of it. This may be done without legal proceedings, provided it does not involve a breach of the peace. Then the creditor may sell, lease, or otherwise dispose of the collateral. (Note that this right of sale also applies to the secured creditor who has retained possession of the property.) The proceeds of disposition are applied to the reasonable expenses of retaking, holding, preparing for resale, and reselling. They are applied also to payment of reasonable attorney's fees and other legal expenses incurred. What remains of the proceeds then goes to pay off the secured debt. In some cases, other creditors may have subordinate or secondary security interests in the collateral, and these are now paid off if proper claims have been made. Finally, if any surplus remains, it goes to the debtor. If there is any deficiency, the debtor is obligated to pay it unless otherwise agreed.

Even when in default as to payment or other performance of the security agreement, the debtor does not forfeit all rights. For example, the debtor may pay the balance due and the expenses of the creditor, and redeem the collateral any time before the creditor has disposed of it or contracted for its disposal.

As an alternative to resale, the secured creditor may retain the collateral in full settlement of the debt. Written notice of the creditor's intention to keep the collateral must be given to the debtor. If the debtor (or any other person entitled to receive notice) objects in writing within 21 days, the creditor must dispose of the collateral in a commercially reasonable manner by a public or private sale.

Additional protection is given to consumers who have paid 60 percent or more of the debt. In these situations, the creditor may not keep the collateral in satisfaction of the debt unless the consumer agrees in writing. In the absence of such a written agreement, the creditor must sell the collateral within 90 days after the repossession. This law seeks to protect consumers in situations where the value of the goods exceeds the amount of the debt. In the problem, the Nosmans paid $400 down and $1,200 in monthly installments. The total ($1,600) was far more than the 60 percent ($1,200). Therefore Silitech must obtain the Nosmans' written consent before Silitech can keep the TV. Without that consent, the TV must be resold in a commercially reasonable manner.

When the creditor sells the collateral, reasonable notice must be given to the debtor unless the goods (1) are perishable, (2) threaten to decline speedily in value, or (3) are of a type usually sold on a recognized market where prices are determined openly and fairly. The secured creditor may be the highest bidder and get title. If the proceeds fail to equal the balance due, including all costs of repossession and resale, the debtor is liable for the deficiency unless otherwise agreed. In the unlikely event that a surplus exists, it belongs to the debtor.

PREVENTING LEGAL DIFFICULTIES

Suggestions for Buyer or Borrower in a Secured Transaction. . .

1. be sure you understand the entire security agreement before you sign it. If you have any doubts, have your lawyer, banker, accountant, or other counsel examine the form and explain it to you;
2. never sign any security agreement that has blank spaces to be filled in later. Draw lines in any blank spaces not used;
3. know what any charges are for, especially service charges. Ask for a detailed listing if it is not offered;
4. find out if there are any penalties for late payment of installments or if there are any discounts for making payments before they are due;
5. include express warranties or other promises of the seller in the written contract to avoid later difficulty of proof under the parol evidence rule;
6. always get a copy of the agreement signed by the other party; and
7. check to be sure that a termination statement has been properly filed after payment in full.

Strengthening Your Legal Vocabulary

collateral
constructive notice
consumer goods
equipment
farm products
financing statement
intangible property
inventory
perfected security interest
secured party
secured transaction
security agreement
termination statement

1. Business deal in which a creditor is given a security interest in personal property as protection in the event of default by the debtor.
2. Goods to be used primarily for personal, family, or household purposes.
3. Knowledge, presumed by law, of facts on file.
4. Officially filed acknowledgment of the end of a creditor's security interest.
5. Any personal property in which the creditor has a security interest as protection against default by the debtor.
6. Creditor (lender or credit seller) in a security agreement.
7. Brief, written notice of the existence of a security agreement.

Reviewing Important Points

1. Secured transactions are of two types: (a) those in which the creditor has possession of the collateral (called pledges) and (b) those in which the debtor has possession.

2. Property used as collateral is classified as either tangible property (called goods) or intangible property. Goods are further classified as (a) consumer goods, (b) farm products, (c) inventory, or (d) equipment. In perfecting a security interest, proper classification of the property must be known. Intangible property includes such things as accounts receivable, bills of lading, airbills, warehouse receipts, notes, bonds, and other contractual rights.
3. A security interest may be perfected by the creditor having or taking possession of the collateral or by the filing of a financing statement. An exception may apply in the case of a motor vehicle; some states provide that such a security interest is perfected by a notation on the certificate of title.
4. The financing statement is used to give notice that a security interest in specific property exists. The statement identifies the parties and the collateral. Usually the financing statement and the security agreement are separate writings. However, the security agreement may be filed in place of the financing statement if it meets the proper requirements.
5. After default in a secured transaction, the debtor has the following rights:
   (a) To pay all that is owed and to redeem the collateral held or repossessed by the creditor at any time before the creditor arranges to dispose, or actually does dispose, of it.
   (b) Under certain specified circumstances, to demand that the collateral be sold and the proceeds applied to the payment of the debt.
6. Upon the debtor's default, the secured creditor has the following rights:
   (a) To sell or otherwise dispose of the property. If the creditor does not have the property, he or she may repossess it.
   (b) Under certain specified circumstances, to retain the property in settlement of the debt.
7. When the debtor has fully paid the obligation in accordance with the security agreement, the secured party has the responsibility for clearing the official records by filing a termination statement.

Applying Law to Everyday Life

1. The Lawsons bought a set of color-coordinated bedspreads and draperies at the Mercantile Mart Department Store. They paid for the $987 purchase by using a nationally recognized credit card. When the monthly statement arrived, they defaulted. Could Mercantile Mart repossess the goods?

2. Taft borrowed $50 from a friend, agreeing to repay $5 each week. Although the agreement was informal and oral, Taft gave the friend her high school class ring to hold until the debt was paid in full. Did the friend have a perfected security interest in the ring?

3. The Bartons needed money to have their child's teeth straightened. They used their microwave oven, electric range, and refrigerator as security for a loan from the Home and Health Finance Company. Did Home and Health

have a perfected security interest in these consumer goods as soon as it gave the money to the Bartons?

4. Cuisine International sold kitchen equipment on credit to the Shoreline, a large resort. In the security agreement and in the financing statement, the collateral was identified as "food service equipment delivered to the Shoreline resort." When the Shoreline was unable to pay its creditors, including Cuisine, some creditors claimed that the collateral description was too vague to create a valid security interest. Were they correct?

5. Conant was the owner and operator of the Tipperary Tavern. She purchased two color television sets on installment. One set was for home use and the other set was for the tavern. How would each set be classified?

6. Ortega sold Ford a small household robot and retained a security interest. When Ford defaulted after paying 25 percent of the purchase price, Ortega decided that she would keep the robot and give it to some friends for a gift. What must she do to be able to retain the robot in full settlement of the debt?

7. D'Artole, an accountant, bought for her personal use a new portable computer with a hard disk for $7,500. She paid $1,000 down and then paid $150 per month for several months under a security agreement she had signed with the seller, the Computer Clinic. Finally, she paid off the remaining balance with her Christmas bonus. The next May she needed a $5,000 loan to take advantage of a business opportunity. She offered the computer as collateral, but the lender refused, saying there was still a security interest in favor of the Computer Clinic on file. D'Artole did not get the loan as a result. What are her rights in this situation?

Solving Case Problems

1. Shelton purchased an automobile on credit from Erwin. Both Shelton and Erwin clearly intended to create a security interest in the car in favor of Erwin. As a consequence, they signed a bill of sale that set out the terms of payment of the balance due and that also required that Shelton should insure the auto until paid for in full. Shelton later obtained a title certificate from the state that clearly showed Erwin as the holder of a first lien on the car. Did these actions and documents give Erwin a security interest in the car? (*Shelton v. Erwin*, 472 F.2d 1118)

2. Speigle fell behind in his car payments to Chrysler Credit Corporation. He had made 14 monthly payments on a 36-month contract, and Chrysler had accepted several late payments. Then he was out of work and money, and he was almost a month in default on a current payment. Speigle visited the Chrysler office to negotiate a solution to his problem. While in the office, one employee of Chrysler parked a car behind Speigle's car, blocking it so it could not be moved. Another employee told him it was repossessed. Speigle

sued, claiming that Chrysler's conduct was inequitable and in breach of the peace. Do you agree? (*Speigle v. Chrysler Credit Corporation*, 56 Ala. App. 469, 323 So. 2d 360)

3. The Uniform Commercial Code excludes "money" from its definition of goods. As a consequence, a perfected security interest cannot be obtained in money merely by the creditor's taking possession of it. Midas Coin Co. transferred possession of some rare United States coins to the St. Johns Community Bank as security for a loan. Did the Bank have a perfected security interest? (*In re Midas Coin Co.*, 264 F.Supp. 193)

4. The Franklin State Bank repossessed the Parkers' automobile because of the Parkers' delinquency in payments. At the time, Mr. Parker and his son were giving the engine of the car a tune-up in their garage. The vehicle was not mechanically operational because the spark plugs, points, condenser, and air filter had been removed. Franklin did not try to determine why the car was not mechanically operational. Instead, after a three-day notice to the Parkers, the bank sold the car at a private sale to an auto parts dealer for $50. The bank then sued the Parkers to recover the substantial balance of the purchase price remaining and unpaid. Decide. (*Franklin State Bank v. Parker*, 136 N.J. Super. 476, 346 A.2d 632)

Unit Six
WORKING FOR OTHERS

UNIT OBJECTIVES

UPON COMPLETION OF THIS UNIT, you should be able to

1. identify and describe the types of employment contracts.
2. describe the duties of employers and employees.
3. recognize when an employer is liable for an employee's acts.
4. explain how and when employment contracts can be terminated.
5. describe the way government regulates employment.
6. discuss workers' rights which are protected by the law.
7. identify and describe unfair labor practices.
8. discuss the ways the negligence of an employer can be established and the defenses an employer may use.
9. describe the coverage and benefits of workers' compensation.
10. describe the functions of OSHA.
11. describe the ways agency authority is created and identify the type of agency.
12. identify the duties owed by the agent to the principal and by the principal to the agent.
13. recognize when an agent or principal is liable to a third party.

21
Contracts of Employment

1. Your brother applied for a job as a hairdresser. The employer told him only women were hired for such jobs. Does he have any recourse?
2. A friend gets a job as a ride operator with a traveling carnival. At a county fair, he carelessly fails to secure the safety bar over the seat in a roller coaster. Two riders are thrown out and seriously injured. Who is liable for the injuries—the carnival, your friend, or both?
3. You have been employed as an accounting clerk at a local auto parts store for the past three years. In formal performance evaluations, your supervisor has consistently ranked you "superior." Now the company is installing a computerized accounting system and plans to fire you and hire someone who has computer experience. Can your employer legally fire you when you have done nothing wrong?

WHAT IS EMPLOYMENT?

PROBLEM: Phil and his teenage son and daughter trimmed the branches from a large, dead tree in front of their house. They also dug around the base and chopped up most of the roots. Then they tried to pull the main trunk down with a long, heavy rope. Seeing them struggle, a neighbor, Steve, came out and helped. Are the children employees of Phil? Is the neighbor an employee of Phil?

employer: party who engages another to work for pay

employee: party who agrees to work for another for pay

employment: a contract to pay for supervised work

Employment is a legal relationship based upon a contract. The parties to this contract are called the employer and the employee. The party who pays is the **employer**; the party who does the work is called the **employee**. In general, **employment** exists when an employer contracts to pay an employee to do work under the employer's direction and control. This contractual process is sometimes called *hiring*. If there is no contract to pay for work, or if there is no direction and control by an employer, the relation between the parties is not one of employment. Thus, in the problem, neither the children nor the neighbor, Steve, were employees. There was no contract for pay. The children were helping in a cooperative family chore; Steve was a friendly volunteer.

Sometimes people use the words *employment* and *hiring* to refer to relationships which are not actually relationships of employment. This occurs most frequently when someone contracts to have a job done, but has neither the intent nor the ability to supervise or control the worker. For example, suppose some homeowners promise to pay $3,500 to a roofing company to install a new roof on their home. There is a contract here. Also, it is a contract to pay for work. However, because the homeowners will not direct and control the work, this is not a contract of employment. Rather, it is what the law calls the retaining of an independent contractor. In general, an **independent contractor** agrees to produce a finished job, whereas an employee agrees to do tasks as directed and controlled by the employer.

independent contractor: one retained to accomplish a specific result without supervision

Power to control the details of the work is the major test for distinguishing between employees and independent contractors. Secondary tests sometimes help to prove the status, which affects questions of liability, workers' compensation, and income taxation. Employees are typically paid for their time, and they typically work at the place of their employer, work the hours specified by the employer, and use the employer's tools. Independent contractors are paid by the job; they usually work at their own place of business, set their own hours, and provide their own tools. Many activities can be performed by either an employee or an independent contractor. For example, employees often perform secretarial services. This usually involves someone who is paid by the hour or week, who works at the employer's place of business using office equipment provided by the employer, and who performs the tasks in the order requested by the employer. In contrast, secretarial work can also be performed by an independent contractor; this might involve a contract to pay for the end product, such as a 25-page typewritten report. Independent contractors generally use their own office equipment, set their own hours, and use their own judgment about how and when to perform each task.

Julio engaged Sara as a gardener to maintain his lawn, shrubbery, and trees. Sara set her own time for work and decided what to do and how to do it, although Julio occasionally made suggestions. Sara was an independent contractor because she was responsible for the finished job. She was not under the direction and control of Julio.

WHAT ARE THE TERMS OF THE EMPLOYMENT CONTRACT?

PROBLEM: Sid applied for a part-time job as a cook in a fast-food restaurant. Sid and the manager, Leslie, discussed hours and agreed that Sid would work from 3:00 p.m. to 5:30 p.m. on Mondays, Wednesdays, and Fridays and would be paid $2.95 per hour. In addition, Leslie told Sid how she wanted the food cooked. What are all the terms of this employment contract?

In most contracts, the terms are drawn almost completely from the agreement between the parties as expressed in their communications. Employment contracts are different because the terms are usually drawn from a variety of sources. In general, the terms of each employment contract are based on combinations of the following sources:

a. the express and implied agreement between the employer and employee;
b. state and federal statutes, administrative rules and regulations, and cases;

c. the labor union-management contract, if there is one, affecting the job; and
d. state and federal constitutions.

1. The Express and Implied Agreements Between the Employer and Employee are Terms of the Employment Contract

Only a small percentage of employment contracts are completely express. An express employment contract generally exists only when there is a written document signed by both the employer and the individual employee. A detailed, written employment contract is uncommon, but is used, for example, in professional sports and for top-level management positions.

Most contracts of employment are partly express and partly implied. Often express terms are oral rather than written. In the problem, Sid's hours have been expressly agreed upon. Thus, this is an express term. However, Sid and Leslie have not said anything about the length of time Sid will be employed. Will he work for one month or for twelve months? When hiring hourly workers, custom, or trade practice, determines this. Sid, like most other employees, is employed in a job which is "terminable at will." This means that he can be fired at any time because there has been no agreement about the length of employment. This term of the employment contract is implied from custom—from the way most people understand employment agreements. Often the employer and employee expressly agree on a length of time required for *notice* of termination. Sometimes reasonable notice is an implied term.

Frequently there are other terms which are implied from the way individual employers supervise their employees. For example, in a particular restaurant there may be an implied term which requires waiters and waitresses to pool their tips and to share them with the people who clear tables. Factory workers may be required to provide their own safety shoes and gloves. A ten or fifteen minute break may be permitted in mid-morning and mid-afternoon. Such implied terms come from the rules of a particular employer rather than from customs of the industry or trade group.

2. State and Federal Case and Statutory Laws Provide Many Terms of the Employment Contract

State and federal laws provide very important terms for each employment contract. In general, these laws deal with such issues as minimum wage, overtime pay, employment discrimination, child labor, unemployment insurance, workers' compensation, labor union negotiations, and job safety. Each of these laws becomes, in effect, a part of each employment contract to which it applies. In the problem, Sid is entitled to receive, and Leslie is required to pay, the minimum wage specified by federal law—$3.35 per hour. Even though Sid and Leslie have expressly agreed upon a lower amount, federal law would dictate this part of Sid's employment contract.

3. Labor Union-Management Agreements Specify Most of the Terms for Some Employment Contracts

A **labor union** is an association of workers organized for the purpose of securing favorable working conditions. A labor-managment contract arises when labor union officials representing employees negotiate an employment contract with managers representing the employer. Such a contract is usually written in great detail, and it becomes the principal source of the terms and conditions of employment. Of course, the terms must comply with employment laws.

labor union: organization of employees formed to negotiate with employers

4. Constitutions Determine an Important Term for Some Employment Contracts

State and federal constitutions influence employment contracts mainly when the employer is a *governmental* organization. The main employment term created by constitutions is that the governmental employer must grant to each employee *due process*. This means that a governmental employer must be able to show that it has acted reasonably in its treatment of every employee. It cannot treat a governmental employee arbitrarily.

The terms of the employment contract come from different sources for different jobs. Almost all employees have employment contracts which contain some express and some implied terms. Every employee can look to state and federal laws to determine certain rights and duties. Those who are union workers can read their union contracts to learn many of the terms of their employment. Those, such as public school teachers, who work for a government have a constitutional right to due process as a term of their employment contracts.

WHAT CONTRACTUAL DUTIES ARE IMPOSED BY LAW ON THE EMPLOYEE?

PROBLEM: Vito employed Winston as a welder. Vito required all welders to wear protective helmets and goggles while working. Winston, who had long hair which made it difficult to wear the helmet, refused to do so. Was Vito within her rights in discharging Winston?

An employee has a duty to produce adequate work for the wages paid. But the employee has other duties too, including the following:

1. Obedience

An employee has a duty to obey reasonable orders and to comply with reasonable rules of the employer. An employee agrees, usually by implication, to carry out the lawful and reasonable orders and rules of the employer, including the reporting of accidents and the using of prescribed safety devices. Thus, in the problem, the company would be within its rights in discharging Winston because the rule that Winston disobeyed was a reasonable one. However, an employee cannot be required to do anything that is illegal, immoral, or contrary to public policy.

2. Reasonable Skill

PROBLEM: Lark was hired by the March Construction Company to operate a heavy-duty road-grading machine. Actually Lark had misrepresented past work experience. Lark was qualified to handle heavy-duty earth-moving tractors but not graders. Would March be justified in firing Lark?

One who enters into a contract to work implies to the employer that he or she possesses to a reasonable degree the skill, experience, or knowledge that will be necessary to perform the duties. (This would not be true for someone hired as a trainee, however.) The employer need not retain the employee nor pay damages for discharging the employee if the employee does not perform reasonably well. Thus, in the problem, March would be justified in discharging Lark.

3. Loyalty and Honesty

PROBLEM: Ashworth was the assistant to the president of Piños Point Properties. Ashworth had confidential information that her company was going to make an offer to purchase a certain plot of land for $250,000 but would be willing to pay as much as $350,000. Ashworth told this to the owners of the land, who agreed to give her half of any amount over $250,000 that they received. After the purchase was made for $350,000, Piños Point learned of Ashworth's action. Piños dismissed Ashworth and sued her for damages. Was the company within its rights?

An employee owes the duties of loyalty and honesty to the employer. In entering into a contract of employment, an employee implies that he or she will not engage in any activities contrary to the interest of the employer. By committing or aiding in the commission of a fraud upon the employer, or by revealing confidential information about the business, an employee (like Ashworth in the problem) may be justifiably discharged. Such a worker may also be liable for damages. Although an employer cannot require an employee to use or to recommend company products, the employer may expect that the employee will do nothing that will harm the employer's business.

4. Reasonable Performance

PROBLEM: Despite several warnings, Katz, a salesperson of Barker's Bootery, continued to take more time for lunch than was allowed. Katz said she always made up her time by coming in early or working late, and this was true. Nevertheless, Barker was annoyed. One day several prospective customers left during the noon hour because there was no one to serve them. When Katz returned from lunch, 30 minutes late, Barker said, "Enough is enough. You're through!" Was Barker acting within his rights?

"An honest day's work for an honest day's pay" is a principle recognized by the law. Hence, an employer is justified in discharging an employee who materially breaches the agreement by failing to perform assigned duties at the prescribed time and in the prescribed manner. Barker would be justified in discharging Katz because Katz was not available to perform her duties at the proper time. Occasional minor failure to perform as expected ordinarily is not sufficient grounds for dismissing a governmental employee. On the other hand, any employee justifiably may be discharged if unable to perform with reasonable efficiency because of illness or injury.

5. The Duties Agreed Upon by the Employee and the Employer

PROBLEM: Perkins was employed by Babbson's Bakery, which was unionized. The union had negotiated with the bakery an employment contract that specified that all full-time employees would work eight hours a day, five days a week. Perkins wished to work ten hours a day, four days a week, and Babbson's was agreeable. Could Perkins follow the special schedule?

The employee owes to the employer a duty to comply with the terms of the employment contract. These terms can come from communications between the employer and the employee, from the way such employment relationships are customarily handled, and sometimes from a formal labor-management agreement. In the problem, Perkins could not follow the special schedule because it conflicts with the labor-management contract.

WHAT ARE THE BASIC DUTIES OF THE EMPLOYER?

PROBLEM: Dale hired Frey to run her office for one year for $1,800 a month. The agreement provided that Frey was to be paid on the fifteenth and the last business day of each month. One month, Dale had financial problems and temporarily withheld $100 from Frey's paycheck. Dale promised to make it up the next payday, which she did. Three months later, Dale withheld $200, and so Frey quit. Was Frey legally justified in quitting?

Employers owe a variety of duties to employees. Some of these duties, if breached, give the employee alone the right to sue for breach of contract. In other cases, both the employee and a governmental agency have the legal power to act against the employer for breach of the duty. The following are the principal duties which the employer owes to the employee.

1. Compensation

The right to compensation is at the heart of the employment relationship. **Compensation** consists of wages or salary paid for labor or services. In reality, compensation also includes **fringe benefits** such as free life and health insurance, paid holidays and vacations, and in-plant dining and recreational facilities. In addition, many employers supplement social security with private pension plans. Such plans are set up voluntarily by the employers to pay a fixed sum to their workers after retirement. The plans are regulated by the federal government, for the protection of the workers, under the Employees Retirement Income Security Act (ERISA).

compensation: wage or salary paid in return for supervised work

fringe benefits: special compensation paid in excess of wage or salary

The amount of compensation for a particular job may be expressed or implied. It may be fixed and definite, as a weekly or monthly salary. Or it may be conditional (1) upon production ("piecework"), (2) upon the amount of sales, or (3) upon a time basis, as per hour or day. Compensation may be a combination of these and other terms.

Failure by the employer to pay the agreed or implied compensation gives the worker the right to abandon the job without any liability for breach of contract. Accordingly, in the problem, Frey was justified in quitting.

The right to compensation depends upon the employee's proper performance of the contract obligations. In the absence of an agreement to the contrary, if an employee is ready, able, and willing to perform for a specific period of time the service required by a contract, the employer must pay the agreed-upon wages. Tips belong to the worker unless otherwise agreed.

> Van Camp hired Baker as a factory timekeeper for an agreed period of six months. The day Baker went to work, however, other employees went on strike. Therefore Baker had nothing to do. Baker came in every day and remained at the assigned post but did no work. Baker finally quit, but Van Camp was obligated to pay for all of Baker's hours on the job.

Statutes in most states require certain industries to pay wages monthly, semimonthly, or even weekly. In most states, when one's employment is terminated, the wages due must be paid at that time or within a specified period. In some states, if an employer does not pay wages that are rightfully earned, the employee may apply to the state labor commissioner or other state official for help in collecting the wages. In the problem, Frey could do this.

By law and by agreement, deductions may be made from the employee's wages before the employee is paid. Social security payments and income taxes must be withheld where applicable and then paid directly to the entitled state or federal government. By agreement, deductions may be made for other purposes, such as union dues, insurance, and United States savings bonds.

2. Safe Working Conditions

> **PROBLEM:** Pittman operated a forklift for Corder Moving and Storage Co. The brakes on the forklift were not holding properly, and the lift was slipping. On three separate occasions, Pittman reported these defects to her supervisor. However, no repairs were made. After a near-accident caused by these unsafe conditions, Pittman walked off the job. Did she have a right to do so?

An employee is entitled by law to reasonably safe working conditions (including tools, equipment, machinery, and the building itself). That is, the working conditions must not be harmful to the employee's health, safety, morals, or reputation. If the employer does not provide safe working conditions, the employee may quit without breaching the contract. In the problem, Pittman had this right. She also had the right to report the unsafe conditions to the Occupational Safety and Health Administration (OSHA) in the U.S. Department of Labor. (The rights of an employee to proper working conditions and the rights of an employee in case of injury on the job are explained in detail in Chapter 23.)

3. Reasonable Treatment

> **PROBLEM:** Gerhardt had been hired as a vacation replacement for clerical employees of the Dairyland Creamery. When Gerhardt made a number of mistakes, his supervisor reprimanded him and called him "a stupid fool." Was Gerhardt within his rights in quitting his job?

An employer is required to treat the workers in a reasonable manner. If the employer commits an assault or battery upon an employee (Chapter 5), the employee may quit the job without liability for any damages resulting from breach of the employment contract. The injured employee could even sue for damages. In the problem, however, there was no assault or battery. There was only an insult and reprimand, which did not constitute unreasonable treatment. Normally, under such circumstances, an employee, like Gerhardt in the problem, would have no right to quit and could be held liable for breach of contract if he did quit.

4. Agreed-Upon Duties

PROBLEM: Howard was hired as a server in the coffee shop of the Pine Lodge Resort. When she reported for work, she was told she would also have to help prepare food and operate the dishwasher. She refused and returned home. Could she be held liable for breach of her agreement?

When the employer insists upon the performance of services not contemplated in the agreement, the employee may rightfully withdraw from the employment. The employee may not, however, abandon the employment merely because of the severity or unpleasantness of the task if the task is within the scope of the job for which the employee was hired. Thus, in the problem, Howard could rightfully withdraw from the employment. That is because helping to prepare food and operating a dishwasher were not within the usual scope of the job of server.

WHAT FEDERAL LAWS REGULATE EMPLOYMENT?

PROBLEM: As a condition of employment, Duke Moving Co. required a high school education or a satisfactory score on a general intelligence test. Neither requirement was specifically related to the jobs to be performed. Both requirements were designed simply to improve the overall quality of the work force. Griggs, a member of a minority group, claimed that the test discriminated against him. Griggs said that, as a minority member, he had not had the educational opportunity afforded others. Moreover, he said, the test related to skills and qualifications which were not necessary for the work which he had applied to do. Was Griggs correct?

There are some duties owed by the employer to the employee which, if breached, not only allow the employee to recover for breach of contract but also give a governmental agency the legal right to investigate, to sue in civil court, or to fine the employer. Breaches of these duties are particularly serious offenses since these duties are owed to both the employee and to society at large.

Several of the laws creating these duties have been enacted by Congress. One of the most important is the National Labor Relations Act, which regulates relations between unions and management. This law is discussed in detail in Chapter 22. Another major federal law of this type is the Occupational Safety and Health Act. which attempts to make the work place safe; this law is discussed in Chapter 23. Federal laws regulating wages and hours of work are discussed in Chapter 22.

Other federal laws are designed to ensure that each worker is evaluated only on the basis of her or his individual performance. These are sometimes called fair employment practices laws. They include the Civil Rights Act of 1964, the Equal Pay Act, and the Age Discrimination in Employment Act.

1. The Civil Rights Act of 1964

With some exceptions, this act applies to all employers with 15 or more workers. The act forbids employers, employment agencies, and unions from discriminating in hiring, paying, training, promoting, or discharging employees on the basis of race, color, religion, national origin, or sex. Under this act, unintentional discrimination is just as illegal as intentional discrimination. Any questions asked of a female applicant, for example, which are not asked of a male applicant seeking the same job are discriminatory. Questions asked in an interview must be job related. Testing or screening of applicants is not forbidden. However, the tests and educational requirements cannot defeat the goal of affording equal opportunity to every person qualified to do the job. Therefore tests and educational requirements must be related to specific job requirements. An employer may discriminate in selecting one worker over another if the standard set is necessary for proper performance of the job. For example, a prospective pilot of a jet airplane may be required to understand radar and navigation equipment. That person may also be required to react quickly to emergencies and to be free of potentially fatal heart diseases. Such requirements are legal because they relate specifically to job performance.

In the problem, Griggs was correct in claiming that the test discriminated against him. Although the evidence showed that whites, as a group, scored higher on the test than did minority members, such higher scores did not show that the whites were better fitted to do the actual work. In addition, the minority members scored lower on the tests because of a lack of equal educational opportunities.

In addition to hiring, the law applies to wage payments, promotions, working conditions, and every other aspect of the employment relationship. Benefits once given only to women are now generally also given to men.

The act sets up the **Equal Employment Opportunity Commission (EEOC)**. The EEOC has the authority to investigate and conciliate complaints of job discrimination and to prosecute suspected offenders.

Equal Employment Opportunity Commission (EEOC): federal agency which enforces the Civil Rights Act

Federal courts may require any employer who violates the Civil Rights Act of 1964 to adopt an **affirmative action plan**. Under such a plan, the employer agrees to seek out, hire, and promote minority members and women who have been discriminated against in the past. Most employers who contract with the federal government must also submit affirmative action plans. These positive steps are aimed at offsetting past discrimination by bringing the percentages of minorities and women in the work force up to their corresponding percentages in the local community. Because the federal government is the biggest buyer of goods and services in the country, most large employers are directly affected by affirmative action.

affirmative action plan: positive program to hire more minorities and women

2. Equal Pay Act of 1963

This act prohibits wage discrimination on account of sex. Women who do the same work as that done by men must be paid at the same rate. This means that when the same skill, effort, and responsibility are required and when the job is performed under similar working conditions, women must be paid the same as men.

> Jarrett was employed in a glass factory. Her job was to inspect and pack glass jars in cartons. Men were also employed in the same capacity, but they were occasionally required to lift the packed cartons. The women were paid 10 percent less than were the men. The court held that Jarrett and the other women were entitled to equal pay for equal work and that "equal work" did not mean identical duties.

3. Age Discrimination in Employment Act of 1967

This act forbids discrimination against workers between the ages of 40 and 70 in any employment practice (such as hiring, discharging, retiring, promoting, and compensating). As with the Civil Rights Act, this act applies to employers, unions, and employment agencies. Exceptions are made when age is a necessary consideration for job performance. Such occupations would include bus drivers, fire fighters, and police officers.

Laws such as the Civil Rights Act of 1964, the Equal Pay Act, and the Age Discrimination in Employment Act have been enacted because of past injustices in the hiring, paying, training, transferring, and discharging of workers. Most states and many cities have enacted similar laws. In addition, the Supreme Court has interpreted the Fourteenth Amendment to apply to employment. The Supreme Court has also extended to employment the civil rights laws passed in 1866 and 1870. These efforts have modified the old common-law concept which provided that an employer has complete freedom in hiring and, subject to liability for breach of contract, freedom in discharging workers. Essentially, current laws, regulations, and court decisions require that job applicants be judged on their merits as individuals, not as members of any group or class.

IS THE EMPLOYER LIABLE FOR THE TORTS OF EMPLOYEES?

PROBLEM: Walker was an electrician for Centurion Electrical Service. One day Walker was sent to repair mixing machines at Molecular Chemical Company. Walker did the work in a negligent manner, causing several thousand dollars worth of damage to the machines. Was Centurion liable for the loss?

If an employee, acting within the scope and in the course of the employment, commits a tort (injures another person or that person's property), the employer is liable for the damages. It is immaterial that the employer did not authorize the act. Thus, in the problem, Centurion was liable for the damage Walker caused. Even if an employee intentionally causes damage, in some states the employer may be held liable if the employee has acted with the intention of furthering the employer's interests.

The fact that the employer is liable for the torts of an employee does not relieve the employee from personal responsibility for such acts. Furthermore, if an employee commits a tort but is *not* acting within the scope or in the course of the employer's business, the employee alone is liable for any injuries that result.

Generally if a person is an independent contractor rather than an employee, the person who retained the contractor is not liable for the contractor's torts. However, if the job is *inherently dangerous*, such as blasting, the party retaining the independent contractor may be liable to those injured by the inherently dangerous activity.

HOW IS THE EMPLOYMENT CONTRACT TERMINATED?

PROBLEM: After suffering a stroke, Koa-Ching hired Vennet as a nurse and companion. Four months later, Koa-Ching died. Was Vennet's contract terminated?

Contracts of employment are terminated in the same ways as are other contracts (see Chapter 15). The usual method is by performance. However, in the problem, the contract was terminated by impossibility of performance as a result of the death of Koa-Ching. Disability of either party which prevents proper performance would also justify discharge.

As you also recall, breach of contract is cause for termination of a contract. For example, suppose an employer fails to fulfill obligations to the employee, thereby breaching the contract. In such a case, the employee would be justified in quitting or abandoning the job without liability for breach. Similarly, if the employee fails to live up to the obligations of the job, the employer may treat the contract as broken and can discharge the employee without liability. In both cases, the breach must be material.

As with other contracts, courts look to the terms of the employment contract to determine the liability of the parties for an *unjustified* termination. The express and implied terms, and those implied in law, play a large role in determining liability for unjustified termination.

1. Employment Contracts Terminable at Will

Many employment contracts with private employers, especially where a union is not involved, are terminable at the will of either the employer or the employee. This occurs because the employer and employee generally do not specify a length of time for the employment relationship. The law then assumes that, provided the termination does not violate any laws, such as the Civil Rights Act of 1964, either party may terminate employment at any time without liability. For example, if an auto repair shop hired a mechanic for $8.00 per hour and a competitor later offered the mechanic $9.00 per hour, there would generally be no liability for quitting the $8.00-per-hour job. However, there may be liability if reasonable notice is required and is not given.

2. Employment Contracts for a Specific Length of Time

If the employment contract is for a certain length of time, it is breached if one party terminates it early. For example, if a basketball star signed a three-year contract for $600,000 a year to play for a professional club, this would be a contract for a specific length of time. If the player breached the contract by deliberately refusing to come to scheduled games (a breach of the employee's duty of obedience), the employer would probably be justified in terminating the contract. In addition, since the player caused the termination, the player may be liable for damages. Thus, if the club had to pay $1,000,000 to obtain the services of an equally talented replacement, the player might be liable to the club for the difference of $400,000.

3. Employment Contracts Negotiated by Unions

Contracts of employment negotiated by unions usually state a specific period of employment, such as one, two, or three years. In addition, the contract identifies specific procedures to be followed in discharging employees covered by the contract. Generally employers are permitted to lay off employees for economic reasons such as declining sales. On the other hand, if there is a discharge for noneconomic reasons, such as poor performance, the collective bargaining agreement usually requires the employer to show "good cause" for the discharge. This usually involves presenting evidence which indicates the poor performance.

4. Employment Contracts with Governments

In general, public employees (that is, those who work for a government) are entitled to due process before being discharged. This means that they are entitled to *notice* of the reasons for the discharge along with a *hearing* where they are given the opportunity to present their own evidence and to challenge the claims of the governmental employer. For this reason, it is often very difficult to discharge public employees.

The terms of the employment contract vary significantly from one job to another. Therefore it is necessary to carefully consider each employment contract to determine *all* the terms of employment.

5. Right to Unemployment Compensation

Workers who have been terminated even though they have complied with all the terms of their employment contract are said to have been discharged "without cause." This means the cause of the discharge was not the employee's conduct. If an employee is discharged "without cause," he or she is entitled to unemployment compensation benefits. This is money paid by the government to workers who have lost their jobs through no fault of their own.

If an employee has been discharged because he or she violated a duty created by the employment contract, then the discharge is said to be "for cause." If a worker is discharged "for cause," the worker generally is not entitled to unemployment compensation.

Unemployment compensation payments are made by the states in cooperation with the federal government under the Social Security Act of 1935. There is usually a time lag of one week, and then a percentage of the regular wage is paid to the unemployed person every week for 26 weeks. The payment may be continued for additional weeks to persons who remain jobless in an area where unemployment is extensive.

Unemployment compensation generally is not available to those who quit voluntarily, strike, or refuse to accept similar substitute work. Unemployment compensation covers employees only—not independent contractors.

PREVENTING LEGAL DIFFICULTIES

When You Become an Employee. . .

1. realize that you and your employer are parties to a contract in which you both have rights and duties;
2. before you go to work, learn as much as you can about the job. Find out about hours, pay, duties, dress, fringe benefits, and any other related matters;
3. avoid unnecessary tardiness and absenteeism. Both can lead to *demotion* (reduction to a lower grade or rank), delayed promotion, or even discharge;

4. remember that in addition to reasonable skill and performance, you owe your employer loyalty, honesty, and obedience; and
5. remember that you are personally responsible for your own negligent acts. This is true even though the injured party may also be able to recover from your employer or from the employer's insurance company.

Strengthening Your Legal Vocabulary

affirmative action plan
compensation
employee
employer
employment
Equal Employment Opportunity Commission (EEOC)
fringe benefits
independent contractor
labor union

1. Contractual relationship in which one party engages another to work for pay under the supervision of the party paying.
2. Party who engages another to work for pay.
3. Organization of employees formed to negotiate with the employer.
4. Wage or salary paid for labor or services.
5. One who contracts to do something for another but is free of the latter's direction and control.
6. Party who agrees to work for another for pay.
7. Special compensation paid in excess of wage or salary.
8. Positive program to hire and to promote minority members and women.

Reviewing Important Points

1. Employment is a form of contract.
2. An employee is distinguished from an independent contractor by the fact that an employer has the power to direct and to control the employee's work. An independent contractor is not subject to the direction and control of the person with whom the contract is made, but is responsible for the finished job, as promised.
3. Contracts of employment may be express (oral or written) or implied (shown by conduct). Those made between an employer and an individual employee are usually oral, and the terms are partly express and partly implied. Those made between an employer and a unionized group of employees through their representatives are generally in writing with detailed express terms.
4. Among the basic duties of the employer are (*a*) compensation, (*b*) safe working conditions, (*c*) reasonable treatment, and (*d*) agreed-upon duties.
5. Among the duties of the employee are the duties to (*a*) obey reasonable rules and orders, (*b*) perform the prescribed duties reasonably well, (*c*) be loyal and honest, and (*d*) perform the prescribed duties at the proper time and in the proper manner.

6. An employer is liable for injuries to the person or property of third parties if the injuries are caused by employees acting within the scope and in the course of their employment. The employee is also responsible for such acts.
7. Contracts of employment are terminated in the same ways as are other contracts. Material breach of contract by the employee is cause for discharge. The employee is justified in quitting if the employer does not fulfill an important part of the agreement.

Applying Law to Everyday Life

1. The High Country Lumber Company hired Mason to haul trees from a forest site to a mill 25 miles away. Mason used his own truck, began and ended work when he pleased, paid for his own gasoline, and worked by himself. He was paid $8.50 per log. Was Mason an employee of High Country Lumber Company?
2. Myron was the owner of Crossroads Service Station. Myron directed Jerry, an employee, to put re-refined oil into the unlabeled oil jars displayed for sale. Jerry knew that the law required that re-refined oil be so labeled for sale to the public. Therefore Jerry refused to fill the jars. Was Jerry's disobedience grounds for discharge? If discharged, could Jerry collect unemployment compensation?
3. Amit was the night clerk at the Indian Inn. He had several duties besides working at the main desk. Therefore he was not allowed to sleep while on the job even if business was slow. On several occasions, the manager of the inn found Amit sleeping and warned him not to do so. If Amit continued to fall asleep on the job, would the manager be justified in discharging him? If discharged, could Amit collect unemployment compensation?
4. A fast-food restaurant conducted a survey of its customers to determine their preference for food servers. The survey indicated that the customers clearly preferred girls over boys as servers. Therefore the restaurant advertised for and hired female servers only and this caused their business to increase substantially. Biff applied for a job but was denied an interview because of his sex. Is Biff entitled to an interview for this job? What governmental agency might help Biff resolve this problem?
5. Suppose you were in charge of hiring 15 workers to assemble very small electrical components to make a toy. If you believed that females of Asian ancestry were most likely to do this type of work well, would you limit your interviews to this group of persons only? Would your decision be different if you were *certain* there would be no legal risk?
6. Boyce's mother, Martha, went to college after her husband died. She studied accounting and graduated when she was 52 years old. When she applied for positions with large accounting firms, she was never seriously considered

because of her age. The firms seemed to hire people in their 20s and 30s only. Has Martha been the victim of illegal employment discrimination?

7. Swenson had been employed by a neighborhood service station as a mechanic for 12 years. His boss had always praised his job performance. After a competing station was built nearby, Swenson was given a 30-day notice of termination. He protested, claiming he had always been a very good employee. Was Swenson discharged "for cause"? Can Swenson collect unemployment insurance?

Solving Case Problems

1. Gale, an umpire, was a member of the Greater Washington Softball Umpires Association. During a game in which Gale was officiating, a player objected to his decision on a play. The player then struck Gale with a baseball bat, causing injuries to Gale's neck, hip, and leg. Gale claimed that he was an employee of the association and so sought workers' compensation for his injuries. The association asserted that its members were independent contractors. It based this assertion on the fact that the umpires had full charge and control of the games, and that the association did not direct the worker in the performance or manner in which the work was done. The evidence presented showed (*a*) that the umpires were paid by the association from fees collected from the teams; (*b*) that the umpires, while assigned to the games by the association, were not obligated to accept the assignments; (*c*) that the association conducted clinics, administered written examinations, and required members to wear designated uniforms while officiating; and (*d*) that the umpires had to meet with the approval of committees of the association who observed a member officiating during a probationary period. Under these circumstances, do you believe Gale was an employee of the association or an independent contractor? (*Gale v. Greater Washington Softball Umpires Association*, 311 A.2d 817)

2. United Airlines had certain minimum requirements for the position of flight officer. The applicant had to have 500 hours of flight time, be 21 to 29 years of age, have a commercial pilot's license and instrument rating, and have a college degree. When Spurlock, a black, applied for the position, no one knew his race. At the time, he had only 204 hours of flight time and only two years of college, mostly in music education. His written application was rejected. Therefore Spurlock sued United, claiming racial discrimination in violation of Title VII of the Civil Rights Act. He pointed out that of approximately 5,900 flight officers in United's employ at the time, only nine were blacks. Was United guilty of illegal discrimination? (*Spurlock v. United Airlines, Inc.*, 475 F. 2d 216)

3. Walgreen Company planned to open a restaurant in Duluth, Minnesota. A district manager for Walgreen, A. J. Gatzke, was sent to Duluth to supervise

preparations for the opening. Gatzke obtained a room—paid for by Walgreen—in a motel owned by Edgewater Motels, Inc. One day, after working many hours, Gatzke quit work at 12:30 a.m. and, with another Walgreen employee, went to a bar near the motel. There Gatzke drank four brandy Manhattans (three were doubles) in about an hour. At the bar, Gatzke discussed the planned operations of the new restaurant.

Gatzke went back to his motel room where, apparently, he smoked several cigarettes after completing an expense account report. The butt of one cigarette was apparently thrown into a wastebasket in the room. The room caught on fire and spread to the entire motel. Gatzke escaped uninjured but the damage to the motel was over $330,000. Edgewater Motels sued both Gatzke and his employer, Walgreen Co. Who is liable? (*Edgewater Motels, Inc. v. Gatzke*, 277 N.W.2d 11, Minn.)

4. Lucky Stores, Inc., hired Q.R.I. Corporation as an independent contractor to remove from a building owned by Lucky a large sign spelling "ARDENS." The work of removal was inherently dangerous because each letter was about 6 feet high and 2½ feet wide and weighed between 50 and 60 pounds. Q.R.I. workers safely removed the letter "A" and loaded it on their truck. They also safely removed the letter "R" and leaned it against the truck. Then for a moment, one worker negligently released his hold on the letter. A gust of wind blew the letter into contact with the 79-year-old plaintiff, Smith, injuring her seriously. Is Lucky liable to Smith for damages? (*Smith v. Lucky Stores, Inc.*, 61 Cal. App. 3d 826, 132 Cal. Rptr. 628)

SPECIAL SECTION:
Rules of Professional Conduct for Attorneys

The Model Rules of Professional Conduct adopted by the House of Delegates of the American Bar Association define a lawyer's responsibilities to the profession, to clients, and to the public. These responsibilities fall into different categories. For example, many rules cover the lawyer-client relationship. Others cover the lawyer's role as counselor and advocate, transactions with persons other than clients, the lawyer's role in law firms and associations, public service by lawyers, the communication of information about the legal services that lawyers provide, and the maintenance of the integrity of the profession.

The rules governing the lawyer-client relationship call for the lawyer to provide competent representation and to act with reasonable diligence and promptness in representing clients. The lawyer must keep the client reasonably informed about the status of the matter at hand and provide understandable explanations to permit the client to make informed decisions regarding the representation. Fees charged must be reasonable, and, when the lawyer has not regularly represented the client, the basis or rate of the fee must be communicated to the client before or within a reasonable time after commencing the relationship. A lawyer cannot reveal information relating to the representation unless the client consents or the lawyer has to do so to prevent the client from committing a criminal act likely to result in imminent death or substantial bodily harm. Potential conflict of interest situations are also closely regulated by the rules.

Under the rules governing the lawyer as an advocate, the lawyer is called on to make reasonable efforts to expedite litigation—as long as the client's interests are not jeopardized—and to refrain from bringing frivolous matters before the court. The lawyer must act with candor in relations with the court and must not unlawfully obstruct access to or falsify evidence. Publicity initiated by the lawyer that might materially prejudice a trial is prohibited in many instances.

The rules call on the lawyer to render public-interest legal aid by providing professional services at no charge or for reduced fees to persons of limited means, to public service groups, and to charitable organizations.

Every lawyer who knows that another lawyer has committed a serious violation of the Rules of Professional Conduct is required to inform the appropriate professional authority. Also, any lawyer with knowledge of similar misconduct by a judge must inform the appropriate authority.

The Rules of Professional Conduct are the foundation of an internal control system designed to maintain the integrity of the legal profession.

22

Unions and Laws Affecting Employment Conditions

1. Friends of your family own a large bakery. They claim their workers are not allowed to join a union because all of the workers are paid union-scale wages or better. Are your friends correct in their assumption?
2. You are employed as a fruit picker at a large orchard. You and your coworkers are greatly dissatisfied with your wages and working conditions. If most of you organize into a union and ask your employer to discuss the disputed issues, must she do so?
3. An adult man, an adult woman, and a teenager of 17 are employed by the same firm to do the same type of work. The man is paid $10 a week more than the woman, and the woman gets $5 a week more than the teenager. Is this legal?

HOW IS EMPLOYMENT REGULATED?

PROBLEM: Jerry was employed as a typist in an electronic component factory which shipped its products throughout the United States and to many countries of the world. Was his employment subject to state employment law, federal employment law, or both?

The U.S. Constitution gives the federal government certain powers and reserves other powers to the states and to the people themselves. However, in certain areas such as labor-management relations and employment conditions, both federal legislation and state legislation exist. These two types of legislation usually do not conflict because most industrial states have followed the federal example and have enacted similar labor laws. State laws are limited, of course, to intrastate commerce (trade within one state). Also, a federal agency—the National Labor Relations Board (NLRB)—has adopted guidelines stating which employers are not subject to federal jurisdiction even though engaged in interstate commerce. Thus, if a retail store sells less than $500,000 worth of goods annually, it is regarded as an intrastate firm and is governed by the state, even if it actually does business in more than one state. In general, however, if a conflict between state and federal jurisdiction arises, federal law prevails.

At either the federal level or the state level, and sometimes at both, laws exist which deal with such labor matters as:

1. the right of employees to form, join, and assist labor unions and to bargain collectively with employers over wages, hours, and conditions of employment,
2. the basic rights of union members,
3. minimum wages and maximum hours of work,
4. protection of young persons against harmful work,
5. the right to get a job and be promoted without regard to race, color, religion, sex, national origin, or advanced age (see Chapter 21),
6. training of apprentices in some crafts,
7. proper working conditions and compensation for injury suffered on the job (see Chapter 23), and
8. security payments in case of unemployment caused by discharge or disability or by retirement (see Chapter 21).

In the problem, Jerry's employment was subject to both state and federal laws governing the previous items.

HOW ARE UNIONS ESTABLISHED?

PROBLEM: Phil was an employee of Long Distance Trucking, Inc. Although his department had been unionized by a majority vote of the bargaining unit, Phil was not a member of the union. In addition, Phil did not like the contract the union had made. Therefore he tried to make an individual contract with the company. Could he do so?

Employees may organize into unions and bargain collectively with their employers through representatives of their own choosing for wages, hours, and working conditions. Or they may voluntarily decide not to organize into unions and instead to bargain individually. An employer is not required to bargain over such things as prices, product designs, plant location, or quality of products. These are strictly management matters even though they do affect the company's ability to pay wages.

If some workers in a company desire to establish union representation, they go through a series of steps. One step involves determining which employees should be associated. Within a company, any group of employees represented by a union is called the **bargaining unit**. It is common for different types of workers, such as clerical and maintenance workers, to be in different bargaining units. Sometimes one union represents several bargaining units in negotiating with a single employer. Some companies have many bargaining units, each represented by a different union. Each unit is entitled to select its own union to bargain with the employer. A large corporation may find itself bargaining with dozens of different unions. Whether they are union members or not, all workers in each bargaining unit are bound by the collective agreement reached between the union and the employer. Thus, in the problem, Phil could not make an individual employment contract with his employer.

bargaining unit: group of workers joined together to select a bargaining representative and to negotiate with an employer

To establish a union, the organizing employees must obtain signatures asking the NLRB to conduct a representation election. At least 30 percent of the employees in the company or in the bargaining unit must sign. If the 30 percent requirement is met, the NLRB will conduct hearings to determine the bargaining unit and to decide who is eligible to vote in the representation election. Managerial employees are not permitted to vote or to be represented by a union. This is because their duties differ from those of the nonmanagerial employees whom they direct. Moreover, the company owners should be able to rely on the undivided loyalty of their managers in negotiations with unions. For the selection of a bargaining representative (a union), a secret vote of the workers in the bargaining unit is required. The NLRB supervises the voting. The union selected by majority vote becomes the exclusive spokesperson for all the employees in the bargaining unit in making employment contracts and in dealing with the employer. A majority of the employees in the bargaining unit can reject representation by any union. In such a case, workers continue to negotiate individually with the employers. If employees who are represented by a union decide they would prefer to have a different union represent them or if they decide they no longer want to be represented by any union, they can ask the NLRB to conduct another election. At this election employees can reject representation by their current union.

> For six weeks, union organizers conducted an intensive campaign to get workers in a particular bargaining unit of the MGM Cabinet Works to join the union. Picketers carried placards which read "MGM IS UNFAIR TO ORGANIZED LABOR." They did this even though the company paid the union-scale wage or higher in all categories of work. An election was finally held under the guidance of the NLRB to determine whether the union should have the exclusive right to represent the workers in making the contract of employment with the company. By a close margin, the workers in the bargaining unit rejected the union. Under NLRB rules, the union may not picket or call for another election for at least one year thereafter.

union shop: establishment in which all workers must join the union within a prescribed period

agency shop: establishment in which nonunion members must pay union dues

open shop: establishment in which nonunion members do not pay union dues

closed shop: establishment in which only union members may be hired

Even after an election which recognizes a union, workers are not required to join a union unless the employer has agreed to have a union shop. In the **union shop**, nonunion employees may be hired, but they must join the union within a stated maximum period, usually 30 days. The agency shop is a variation of the union shop. In the **agency shop**, employees are not required to join the union, but if they do not, they must nevertheless pay union dues as a condition of employment. The union, in effect, acts as their agent in dealing with the employer. Thus, employment contracts are binding on all workers. In the **open shop**, employees are not required to belong to a union. There may, nevertheless, be a recognized union that bargains collectively with the employer and agrees to an employment contract binding all workers. However, the nonmembers do not have to pay union dues. The **closed shop** was one in which the employer agreed that workers had to belong to the recognized union before they could be hired and that the workers had to remain members of the union while employed. The closed shop was outlawed by the Labor Management Relations Act because it created "too great a barrier to free employment," according to a Congressional report.

Right-to-work laws have been enacted by 20 states. Such laws prohibit compulsory union membership and ban the union shop as well as the closed shop and agency shop. In states with right-to-work laws, unions may function, but only with open shops.

right-to-work-laws: state laws which ban both the union shop and the closed shop

WHAT LAWS GOVERN LABOR-MANAGEMENT RELATIONS?

PROBLEM: Mulroy worked in a factory where leather goods were manufactured. During lunch hour and after work, Mulroy was active as an organizer for a labor union which sought to be recognized as the sole bargaining agent for the employees. Mulroy's employer said he paid better than union-scale wages and did not want to deal with any union. He fired Mulroy because of the organizing efforts. Was he legally permitted to do so?

Employment is a contractual relationship. Usually there is a contract between the employer and each employee. However, unions negotiate employment contracts on behalf of large groups of people. Federal labor laws are designed to ensure that employers treat unions and union members fairly, and that unions treat employers and union members fairly.

1. The National Labor Relations Act and the Labor Management Relations Act

The National Labor Relations Act (1935) as amended by the Labor Management Relations Act (1947) covers union-related activities in businesses engaged in interstate commerce. However, this Act excludes railways and airlines, which are governed by separate legislation. It also excludes farm laborers, domestics employed in homes, and supervisors and others who are considered part of the management team. In California, a state law gives farm laborers the right to organize and to bargain collectively with employers. Eventually other states and the national government may enact similar legislation. The National Labor Relations Act requires that employers treat unions fairly by allowing them to organize and by engaging in good faith negotiations (collective bargaining) with unions. The National Labor Relations Act, together with the Labor Management Relations Act, defines certain actions of employers and of unions as **unfair labor practices** and prohibits such actions. In an effort to compel both employers and unions to respect the rights of employees related to union activity, the following practices are forbidden.

unfair labor practices: union or employer acts which violate the rights of employees with respect to union activity

Unfair Labor Practices of Employers. The National Labor Relations Act, as amended by the Labor Management Relations Act, makes it illegal for employers to:

(1) interfere with employees in their rights to form, join, and assist unions,
(2) dominate or interfere with the formation or administration of any labor organization, or give financial or other support to it,
(3) discriminate in any term or condition of employment to encourage or discourage union membership. In the problem, Mulroy's employer was guilty of an unfair labor practice. He could be required to rehire Mulroy and pay Mulroy wages lost while barred from the job,
(4) discharge or otherwise discriminate against an employee for filing charges of labor law violations, and
(5) refuse to bargain collectively in good faith with the union which is the representative of the employees.

blacklist: to place the names of employees on a list of undesirables to be sent to other employers

In addition, employers may not threaten to **blacklist** employees (place their names on a list of undesirables sent to other employers with the purpose of making it difficult for the employees to find work). Employers may not threaten to stop operations, replace workers with machines, or move the factory, just to avoid unionization.

> Kent and Rimski were trying to get their coworkers to join a clerical union. The manager of their department threatened to fire them. He also threatened to blacklist them by sending their names as "known troublemakers" to a trade association for distribution to other employers. Because of these acts of the department manager, the employer was guilty of two unfair labor practices.

Unfair Labor Practices of Unions. The National Labor Relations Act, as amended by the Labor Management Relations Act, makes it illegal for unions to:

(1) attempt to force employees to join a union or to restrain employees from organizing into unions or to interfere with their right to bargain collectively. Of course, if a majority of the workers select a union, all are bound by its contracts with the employer,
(2) attempt to cause an employer to discriminate against an employee because of union-related activities,
(3) refuse to bargain collectively in good faith with the employer,
(4) require payment of an excessive or discriminatory fee for initiation into the union,
(5) attempt to force an employer to pay for services not performed or not to be performed (called **featherbedding**). If the work is actually performed, however, there is no featherbedding even though the work may be unnecessary,
(6) **picket** (patrol with signs) an employer to try to force the employer to bargain with that union or to try to force employees to select that union as their representative within 12 months after losing a valid representation election, and
(7) engage in certain kinds of strikes and boycotts. A **strike** is a work stoppage by a group to force an employer to give in to union demands. (Its counterpart is a **lockout**, which occurs when an employer temporarily closes down operations to resist union demands or to induce the union to agree to the employer's proposals.) Most strikes are not illegal if conducted without violence.

featherbedding: forcing an employer to pay for work not done or not to be done

picket: walk with signs at employer's business to publicize dispute or influence opinion

strike: concerted work stoppage by employees to bring pressure on the employer

lockout: shutdown of operations by an employer to bring pressure on employees

If a strike is *economic* (one over wages, hours, or conditions of employment), an employer may permanently give any striking employee's job to someone else. On the other hand, if the strike is an *unfair labor practice strike* (caused by a violation of the National Labor Relations Act by the employer), the employer may not permanently give the striking worker's job to someone else. When an unfair labor practice strike is over, the employer must reinstate the striking worker even if this requires transferring or discharging the replacement.

Strikes of public (governmental) employees are generally prohibited even though such workers may unionize and bargain collectively. Despite this ban, in recent years many public workers (including police officers, teachers, and fire fighters) have gone out on strike, or they have stayed away from work, claiming illness. In such cases, the workers and their leaders are willing to accept penalties for defying court orders to return to work.

boycott: refusal to deal with the goods or services of an employer

primary boycott: boycott directed mainly against the struck employer

secondary boycott: boycott directed mainly against third parties who deal with the struck employer

A **boycott** is basically a refusal to have anything to do with the products or services of an employer. A **primary boycott**, which is legal, involves the employees' refusals to buy their employer's products or services. Typically, a primary boycott is accompanied by a strike and by picketing at the employer's place of business. Usually the striking employees attempt to cause neutral third parties, such as suppliers and customers of the struck employer, to refuse to deal with the employer. Sometimes, however, striking employees try to get customers of the neutral third party to stop buying from the third party. Such action against a third party is known as a **secondary boycott**. The strikers refuse to buy from the neutral third party, refuse to work for or handle any products of such third party, or try to persuade others not to deal with the third party. Although generally illegal, secondary boycotts are legal when the National Labor Relations Act, or similar state statutes, do not apply. Such would be the case with farm labor in most states.

> A union was on strike against a New York manufacturer of women's dresses. Members of the union set up picket lines at retail stores which were neutral, independent buyers of dresses from the New York manufacturer. The pickets tried to persuade customers of the stores to refuse to buy from the stores because they dealt with the New York manufacturer. This action was an illegal secondary boycott by the union. The picketing would have been legal if it only urged customers of the stores to stop buying dresses made by the New York manufacturer.

The federal govenment and most of the states have organized services that are designed to help prevent strikes and to settle labor-management disputes by voluntary methods. When collective bargaining breaks down or becomes deadlocked, a government representative may try to bring the parties together to settle their differences. In **mediation** (also known as *conciliation*), a mediator (conciliator) talks with both sides and attempts to achieve a compromise. However, such a person has no power to compel agreement.

mediation: attempt by a neutral third party to achieve a compromise between two parties in a dispute

The National Labor Relations Board. In addition to defining unfair labor practices, the National Labor Relations Act sets up a federal agency to regulate labor relations problems. That agency, the National Labor Relations Board (NLRB), administers the rights and duties given to both workers and employers by the act. Representatives of the union and representatives of the employer (as well as individual workers) are entitled to file charges and to take part in hearings before the board. A party who is dissatisfied with an order of the board may seek review in the federal courts.

2. The Landrum-Griffin Act

The Landrum-Griffin Act (1959) is designed primarily to ensure that unions treat their members fairly. It regulates certain relations between the individual union member and the union. For example, the Act regulates voting rights and procedures, disclosure of financial information, and relations between unions. Many states have similar acts to govern employment of an intrastate nature. Both the federal and state acts set up procedures to enforce the rights given workers and employers and to settle disputes between them. Subject to reasonable union regulations, the federal Landrum-Griffin Act provides for union members the rights shown in Figure 22-1.

WHAT OTHER LAWS AFFECT EMPLOYMENT CONDITIONS?

> **PROBLEM:** Janet was employed by Tasty Candy, Inc., as an operator of a candy-bar-packaging machine. She worked 44 hours a week and was paid \$5 an hour. How much did she earn each week?

States and the federal government have many other laws which affect employment conditions. Laws affecting wages and hours, child labor, veterans' preferences, and time to vote are discussed in the following sections.

1. The Fair Labor Standards Act

The federal government has enacted the Fair Labor Standards Act (known as the Wage and Hour Act) to provide minimum wages and maximum hours for all employees considered to be under federal jurisdiction. Minimum wages as of 1986 are \$3.35 an hour. Maximum hours which can be worked at regular rates of pay are 40 per week (with no daily maximum). This means that as of 1986 the

ELECTIONS:	Equality in nominating candidates for union offices; in voting by secret ballot in union elections; and in attending, participating, and voting by secret ballot on other union business at membership meetings.
MEETINGS:	Freedom in meeting and assembling with other members and in expressing any views about candidates or other business.
DUES:	Secret balloting on increases in dues, initiation fees, and assessment levies, after reasonable notice of the intention to vote upon such questions.
LAWSUITS:	Freedom in suing and testifying in court or before any administrative agency or legislative body or in communicating with any legislator.
DISCIPLINE:	Protection against union disciplinary action, unless the member is served with written charges, given time to prepare a defense, and afforded a fair hearing. (Members may be disciplined for nonpayment of dues without such elaborate due process.)
MANAGEMENT:	Freedom to enjoy rights as a member free from violence; to have access to union policy and financial information; to recover misappropriated union funds for the union; to inspect union contracts; and to be informed of provisions of this act.

Figure 22-1. Union Member Rights

minimum pay for a full week is $134. If more hours than the maximum allowed at regular rates are worked in one week, 1½ times the regular rate must be paid for all overtime. However, some union contracts require double the regular rate for work on Sundays and holidays. In the problem, Janet's weekly wage was $230 ($200 for regular time, and $30 for the time over 40 hours figured at the rate of $7.50 an hour). Over the years, as the cost of living has gone up, Congress has raised the minimum wage. When the law was first passed as a Depression remedy in 1938, the minimum wage was 25¢ an hour.

The minimum wage and overtime requirements of the law do not apply to the following:

a. executives, administrators, and professional workers (including teachers and certain salespeople),
b. employees of certain small enterprises (such as retail or service establishments with annual sales under $225,000 and newspapers with circulations under 4,000),
c. employees in such industries as small-farm agriculture and fishing, and
d. casual babysitters and personal companions for aged or infirm persons.

In addition, the hourly provisions apply only partially to workers in seasonal industries. Special rules apply to learners, apprentices, student workers, handicapped workers, and messengers.

Full-time students may be employed at retail stores, service businesses, colleges, and farms at lower than minimum wage on a part-time basis during school and on a full-time basis during vacations. However, it must be demonstrated that the lower wage is necessary and that the jobs would not be offered at a higher rate. Similar exemptions from minimum wages may be authorized by the secretary of labor for students employed by their own elementary and secondary schools. Many people have urged Congress to permit a lower than minimum wage (a "teen wage"). This would be for 16- to 19-year-olds who are full-time or part-time employees, but who no longer attend school. This has not been done thus far because of a fear that it would take regular jobs at higher wages from adults.

2. Child-Labor Laws

PROBLEM: Cushing was age 17 and a recent high school graduate looking for a summer job. Cushing found an opening for working the swing shift (4 p.m. to 12 a.m.) on a saw machine in a lumber mill. Could Cushing qualify for the job?

The federal government and every state regulate child labor because many children are employed for pay. The federal law is part of the Fair Labor Standards Act. Although these federal and state laws vary, they are all based on the three following principles:

a. that in a free society a person's early years are better used for education,
b. that certain work is harmful or dangerous for the young, and
c. that child labor at low wages takes jobs from adults.

These state and federal laws regulate the conditions and types of employment permitted for persons under age 18.

While specific child-labor laws vary, their provisions commonly do the following:

a. set the maximum number of working hours in a day,
b. prohibit night work,
c. prescribe the grade in school that must be completed,
d. set the required age for certain hazardous occupations, and
e. establish whether a child who is working is required to continue school on a part-time basis.

For example, some states require that all minors who work must do so in the period between 5 a.m. and 10 p.m. Moreover, the job must not be classified as hazardous. In the problem, if these particular laws were in effect where Cushing lived, Cushing could not qualify for the job. Some of the federal rules concerning child labor are outlined in Figures 22-2 and 22-3.

Employment of children under age 18 is specifically prohibited in the following hazardous occupations:

1. Mining.
2. Manufacturing explosives, brick, or tile.
3. Operating power-driven hoists.
4. Logging and saw milling.
5. Driving motor vehicles or acting as an outside helper on such vehicles (except for incidental, occasional, and school bus driving).
6. Any work involving exposure to radioactive materials.
7. Operating power-driven woodworking, metal-forming, punching, shearing, baking, or paper-product-producing machines.
8. Slaughtering or meat packing.
9. Operating circular saws, band saws, or guillotine shears.
10. Wrecking or demolishing buildings or ships.
11. Roofing.
12. Excavating.

Figure 22-2. Work Forbidden for Those Under 18

Employment of children between ages 14 and 16 is specifically prohibited in the following nonagricultural occupations:

1. Manufacturing, mining, or processing.
2. Delivering messages to the public.
3. Operating any power-driven machinery other than office machinery.
4. Operating motor vehicles or serving as helpers on such vehicles.
5. Working in transportation, warehousing, and storage (except office and sales work) or communications and public utilities (except office and sales work).
6. Constructing, demolishing, and repairing (except office and sales work away from the site).

Figure 22-3. Work Forbidden for Those Between 14 and 16

Jay, age 17, knows of an available job as a flower maker in a novelty shop. In her state, she may not be employed until she has (1) received a work certificate from the superintendent of schools, (2) enrolled in a continuation school to attend four hours a week until she has reached age 18 or has graduated from high school, and (3) presented a physician's statement certifying that she is in good physical condition. If employed, she will not be allowed to work at night. She will also not be allowed to work more than 8 hours in any one day or more than 48 hours in any one week.

Young persons aged 14 to 16 may work in retail stores, food-service shops, and gasoline stations (except those with pits or racks). The specific jobs they may do in such establishments include office and clerical duties, garden maintenance (without power mowers), in-store selling and cashiering, modeling, advertisement drawing, window trimming, comparison shopping, survey taking, price marking, packing and shelving, and bag carrying for customers.

Children younger than age 14 may be employed in certain nonhazardous occupations. These include:

a. farm work during nonschool hours in the locality where the child resides if the child is under age 12 and is employed by a parent or guardian. Such farm work done for other employers is permitted (a) if the child is age 12 or 13 and has the written consent of a parent or guardian or (b) if the parent or guardian is working on the same farm. Such farm work is permitted without permission of parent or guardian if the child is 14 or older;

b. nonfarm work provided by a parent or guardian in many nonhazardous occupations;
c. dramatic work in motion pictures, radio, TV, or theater;
d. newspaper delivery to consumers;
e. evergreen wreath making in the home; and
f. hand-harvest labor, paid on a piece-rate basis, for up to eight weeks a year if the employer has obtained permission from the government and the child is between ages 10 and 12.

When state child-labor laws have higher standards than those of the federal act, the state laws apply to children in all industries within that state. For employment during school hours, the states are about equally divided in specifying either the age of 14 or the age of 16 as the minimum. All of the states place a limit on the number of hours which a young person may work. The hours of school are often combined with the hours on the job while school is in session. For example, a common maximum is 48 hours of work (school and outside work combined) in one week. Some states place no special limit on the work hours of those young people between the age of 16 and 17 years. However, most states maintain controls over those hours, and most require a work permit if the individual is under the age of 17 or 18 years.

3. The Military Selective Service Extension Act

PROBLEM: Follard enlisted in the United States Army for a three-year period. After her honorable discharge from the service, she wished to return to her former job. However, her employer said the job was now held by another person and refused to rehire her. What, if any, were Follard's rights?

The Military Selective Service Extension Act of 1950 requires that certain military persons must be reemployed after honorable discharge from the service unless their employment at the time of induction was temporary. Such persons would be those who have (1) been drafted, (2) enlisted, or (3) been recalled to active duty.

Upon honorable discharge, such veterans must still be able to do their former work to be reemployed. If a service-connected disability makes this impossible, they are entitled to jobs with duties they can perform. The veteran must not have been away for more than five years and must apply for reemployment within 90 days after discharge. Hence, Follard in the problem must be reemployed if she applies within the time limit.

4. Laws Allowing Time to Vote

More than half the states provide that workers must be given sufficient time off with pay, at a time convenient to the employer, to vote in regular primary and general elections.

PREVENTING LEGAL DIFFICULTIES

If You Are an Employee, Remember . . .

1. neither employers nor unions may legally discriminate against you on the basis of race, color, religion, sex, national origin, or advanced age. If you feel you have been discriminated against unfairly, consult an attorney, your union officer, your state or federal labor or employment office, or your state or federal legislative representative;
2. you and your coworkers generally have the legal right to organize into unions and bargain collectively with your employer;
3. an employer may not legally discharge you for engaging in a lawful strike. An employer who does so is guilty of an unfair labor practice; and
4. if you belong to a union, you have a right to vote for your officers in secret elections and to see accurate and timely information on union finances and activities.

If You Are an Employer, Remember . . .

1. it is generally illegal to discriminate against employees or prospective employees because of race, color, religion, sex, national origin, or advanced age. You may, however, select, train, or promote on grounds such as appropriate educational preparation, skill, or experience when such factors are truly job related and necessary for the particular work to be done;
2. unions are legal. If they represent your workers, you should cooperate with them in good faith for the common good of all parties involved;
3. you may not discharge or otherwise discriminate against your workers because they join a union or because they refuse to join a union (unless there is a legal union shop); and

4. you must bargain collectively in good faith with representatives of any union chosen by a majority of the workers in each bargaining unit. You are not obligated to make any concessions, such as boosting wages, reducing hours, or changing conditions of employment. If you refuse to compromise and make some concessions, there may be a strike, and it may continue indefinitely. If it is an economic strike (for higher wages, for example), you are free to hire permanent replacements for the strikers and to resume production. However, this is not always a feasible alternative. If it is an unfair labor practice strike, you may not hire permanent replacements for the strikers.

Strengthening Your Legal Vocabulary

agency shop
bargaining unit
blacklist
boycott
closed shop
featherbedding
lockout
mediation
open shop
picket
primary boycott
right-to-work laws
secondary boycott
strike
unfair labor practices
union shop

1. Acts which violate the rights of employees with respect to union activity.
2. State laws which ban both the union shop and the closed shop.
3. Establishment in which all employees must belong to the union, either when they are hired or within a specified time after they are hired.
4. Boycott directed mainly against the struck employer.
5. Concerted stoppage of work to force an employer to yield to union demands.
6. Patrolling by union members with signs, alongside the premises of the employer, during a labor dispute.
7. Requiring an employer to pay for services not performed or not to be performed.
8. Attempt by a neutral third party to achieve a compromise between disputing parties.
9. Employer's shutdown of operations to bring pressure on employees.
10. Establishment in which nonunion members do not pay union dues.

Reviewing Important Points

1. The federal government regulates the employment of persons in enterprises engaged in interstate commerce. The state governments have similar power over intrastate commerce.

2. Certain basic rights of workers are protected by law. These include the rights to:
   a. organize and join labor unions,
   b. bargain collectively with employers,
   c. strike, and
   d. secure jobs without regard to race, color, religion, sex, national origin, or advanced age.
3. Certain acts of employers and of labor unions are termed *unfair labor practices* and are prohibited by law.
4. With certain exceptions, workers considered to be covered by the federal minimum wage law must be paid a minimum of $3.35 an hour (as of 1986) for 40 hours of work in any one week. Further, they must generally be paid time and one-half for all hours worked over 40.
5. All states and the federal government restrict the employment of children and have laws designed to protect such workers.

Applying Law to Everyday Life

1. When a national union sent organizers to try to persuade Baker's workers to join the union, Baker called three of her most trusted employees to her office. She urged them to organize a new union limited to company employees. She offered to provide the union with office space and free time for officers. Baker then gave the three workers money to buy printed notices and refreshments for an organization meeting. Was Baker's action legal?

2. In the first year of its operation, a local union, attempting to increase membership, threatened to slash the tires of nonunion members. Union members trailed nonunion members to their homes and picketed there. The union fined a member for accusing the union of an unfair labor practice. Were these actions legal?

3. A strike at the Titan Stone Works was in its fifth week when Pax, a federal mediator, was called in. After long discussions with both sides, she persuaded the union representatives to accept certain terms. The terms were a major concession on the part of the union but seemed to her to be fair to all parties involved, including the buying public. Titan rejected the terms even though it was financially able to meet every demand. Can Pax compel Titan to sign the proposed contract?

4. Employees of the City of Locale became dissatisfied with their working conditions. As a result, 35 percent petitioned the NLRB for a representation election. They established a local, unaffiliated union which won the election. When they were unsuccessful in their negotiations with the city council, they went on strike. Is any conduct by these employees illegal?

5. The Electrical Workers Union of Westport represented most of the assembly line workers in the General TV Plant. In a dispute over wages, the union

went on strike and began picketing the plant. They also picketed nearby stores which carried the General brand of TV sets, asking that shoppers not purchase the General TVs. Is any of this conduct illegal?

6. Phyllis started work with Consolidated Auto Supply as a parts clerk. She never worked more than 40 hours per week without getting time and one-half for overtime. Phyllis was promoted to assistant supervisor, then supervisor, and finally to plant superintendent—an executive position. Her base salary increased to $55,000. Can she claim time and one-half now when she works her customary 10 to 20 hours overtime per week?

7. Sara, 13 years old, was offered a summer job at the Sunrise-Sunset Country Club. The job had three duties: serving as a golf caddy, operating the riding power mower, and unpacking and shelving goods in the golf pro's shop. Could she legally perform all three of these duties?

Solving Case Problems

1. During a union organizing campaign at Portage Plastics Company, some members began wearing union buttons on the job. Then the president of Portage prohibited the wearing of either union or nonunion badges at work. The president made the order because a button had fallen into a grinder and caused loss of material and because of the rising feelings among the employees. Other jewelry and hair attachments were still permitted even though such ornaments had also fallen into equipment and caused losses on prior occasions. Immediately thereafter, a strike started in protest of the order. (a) Was the company rule on union badges an unfair labor practice? (b) Would it make any difference if the union agreed, after the order, that its members would not wear badges? (*Portage Plastics Company v. International Union, Allied Industrial Workers of America, AFL-CIO,* 163 N.L.R.B. No. 102)

2. Kuebler was a member in good standing of the lithographers union when it struck the Art Gravure Company. Several months after the strike began, Kuebler met in a nonsecret meeting with 12 or 13 other strikers at the home of one. Their purpose was to discuss "the widening gap" between the labor and management bargaining committees and to "try to straighten this thing out to where we could get back to work." Then a three-person committee from the group communicated its views to the Union Negotiating Committee. Kuebler returned to the picket line. When the strike finally ended, the trial board of the local union charged and found Kuebler guilty of attending "a meeting . . . held for the purpose of undermining the Union Negotiating Committee." Kuebler was suspended from the union for three months and was fined $2,000. He filed a notice of appeal to the membership and requested several items: copies of charges against him, with supporting facts; names of the persons on the executive board who had accused and

also tried him; a copy of the decision in writing showing how each member had voted; and a copy of the transcript of the evidence and proceedings at his trial by the union trial board. This information was refused, and so Kuebler sued for relief in the United States District Court. (a) Had the union violated Kuebler's rights? (b) Had Kuebler been denied a fair hearing? (*Kuebler v. Cleveland Lithographers and Photoengravers Union Local,* 473 F.2d 359)

3. The Greenpark Nursing Home hired a firm to handle the maintenance of its facilities. The company hired was First National Maintenance. This firm in turn hired employees to work for it on the premises of the nursing home. These employees of First National Maintenance formed a union. Shortly thereafter, First National Maintenance decided, for purely financial reasons, to cancel its maintenance contract with Greenpark Nursing Home. In anticipation of a complete layoff, the union sought to negotiate with management over the decision to terminate this contract. Management refused to negotiate on this issue. Was this refusal to negotiate legal? (*First National Maintenance v. NLRB,* 452 U.S. 666)

4. Mary Weatherman was the personal secretary to the president of Hendricks County Rural Electric Membership Corporation. One of her friends, who also worked for the same firm, was involved in an industrial accident which resulted in the loss of one of his arms. Shortly after the accident he was dismissed. Mary, concerned about the plight of her friend, signed a petition seeking his reinstatement. Because of this conduct Mary was also discharged. Mary filed a charge with the NLRB, alleging an unfair labor practice. The company defended by claiming that because Mary was a confidential secretary, she was not covered by the National Labor Relations Act's definition of "employee." Who is right, Mary or the company? (*NLRB v. Hendricks County,* 102 S. Ct. 216)

5. Truck drivers employed at Arkansas-Best Freight Systems, Inc., were paid in two ways—one for their time and the other for the number of miles driven. For example, they were paid for the time they spent doing paperwork at the beginning and end of each trip. In addition, they were paid for the distance traveled on a trip at a "driving rate." Arkansas-Best required that the drivers conduct a careful safety inspection of their trucks before beginning each trip. However, the drivers were required to conduct this inspection after they had punched out on the time clock. As a result, the drivers were not being paid for the time they spent on the safety inspections. They complained to their union. The union entered into arbitration with the employer under the terms of the collective bargaining agreement, but the claim for wages for the time spent on the safety inspection was denied. One of the drivers, Barrentine, did not like the decision and sued Arkansas-Best, claiming violation of the Fair Labor Standards Act. Arkansas-Best defended on the grounds that the union contract takes precedence over the FLSA. Who is correct? (*Barrentine v. Arkansas Best Freight Systems, Inc.,* 450 U.S. 728)

23
Employee Injuries

1. Smith started a phone-answering business in his home. He hired one person—Jones—to work for him. Smith agreed to pay Jones a flat fee for one week's work because the job was temporary. They agreed that Jones would receive no fringe benefits of any kind and that there would be no workers' compensation coverage. During his second day on the job, the very old chair Jones was sitting in collapsed, and his spinal cord was severely injured. Is Smith liable for Jones' injury?

2. Jameston, a school custodian, is injured when some student lockers fall on him while he is cleaning the hallway. All of the school's employees are covered by the school's workers' compensation insurance policy. What are Jameston's legal rights?

3. A friend of yours worked in a plastic-processing plant. She complained to her supervisor that fumes in the plant were causing eyeburn, headaches, and nausea. She asked that exhaust fans be installed, but this was not done. Therefore she reported the problem to the Occupational Safety and Health Administration (OSHA). Shortly after her employer learned that she had reported the problem to OSHA, her employer told her that her services were no longer needed. Can your friend use the law to get her job back?

HOW DOES OUR LEGAL SYSTEM DEAL WITH EMPLOYEE INJURIES?

PROBLEM: Cowley was a steelworker employed on a high-rise apartment project. His employer, Nu-Dimensions, Inc., provided all workers with protective helmets as required by law. One day, because of the intense heat, Cowley removed his helmet and worked bareheaded while the supervisor was off duty. A small section of steel plate fell and hit Cowley's head, causing a skull fracture. Is Cowley entitled to receive money for medical expenses and lost wages? Is Nu-Dimensions likely to be fined?

Our legal system has developed three ways of dealing with injuries to employees. The earliest approach, developed under the common law, involves the injured employee suing the employer for negligence. If the employee can prove in court that the employer's negligence caused the injury, the employer must pay damages. This system attempts to make the party at fault bear the financial loss associated with the injury. By making employers liable for injuries caused by their negligence, this system encourages employers to do many things to help ensure the safety of employees. Until the early 1900s, this system was the only recourse of workers injured on the job.

However, the common-law system is highly unsatisfactory. The injured worker (or spouse of a worker killed on the job) is at an obvious disadvantage in suing the employer. Moreover, the employer can, and usually does, avoid all liability by proving (a) that the worker was guilty of negligence which contributed to the cause of the accident and injury, (b) that negligence of a coworker was the cause, or (c) that the employee had voluntarily assumed the risk of being injured or killed while doing work known to be dangerous.

Because injured employees had great difficulty in winning negligence suits, state legislatures enacted **workers' compensation statutes** in the early 1900s. These laws require most employers to obtain insurance to pay benefits to injured employees. If an employee is covered by workers' compensation insurance and is injured in the course of employment, the benefits will be paid. This is so even when the employer is not the cause of the injury. This statutory system acts as a substitute for negligence suits. Today, if an injured employee is covered by workers' compensation—and almost all are—then no suit is allowed against the employer. This system attempts to provide injured workers with the money to make them

workers' compensation statutes: laws creating an insurance program for injury to employees

well without regard for fault. Because the amount an employer must pay for workers' compensation insurance is related to the firm's safety record, employers have an incentive to maintain a safe workplace.

Occupational Safety and Health Administration: federal agency which tries to prevent employee injuries

The third approach relies on workplace safety standards enacted and enforced by federal and state administrative agencies. The **Occupational Safety and Health Administration (OSHA)** inspects workplaces, and when it finds violations of its regulations, it can impose fines and even shut down plants. OSHA does not allocate loss based on fault, or provide money for medical expenses without regard to fault; rather, it seeks to prevent injuries to employees by eliminating some of their causes.

In the problem, Cowley probably could not recover from his employer in a suit for negligence because Cowley's failure to wear his helmet was a cause of his injury. Cowley was more at fault than the employer. If, as is most likely, the employer had workers' compensation coverage for Cowley, then Cowley would not be allowed to sue his employer. Workers' compensation would probably pay some of Cowley's lost wages and all of his medical expenses. The injury might lead to an OSHA investigation. If OSHA finds that any of its safety regulations have been violated, it would require that the unsafe condition be eliminated and would perhaps fine the employer.

WHEN CAN THE INJURED EMPLOYEE WIN A SUIT AGAINST THE EMPLOYER FOR NEGLIGENCE?

PROBLEM: During a two-year period in the late 1800s, a long steel suspension bridge was built over the entrance to a coastal bay. The work was very hazardous. Twelve workers were killed and many more were injured before the job was done. Some workers were killed when they lost their balance and fell while climbing up to their workplaces. One was killed because of the horseplay of coworkers. Others were killed when the safety lines supplied by the employer broke when subjected to normal pressure. Is the employer liable in negligence for any of these deaths?

Under certain circumstances, an employee who is injured on the job or the family of an employee who is killed on the job can sue the employer and win a negligence judgment for damages.

1. When, by Violating a Duty Owed Employees, the Employer Caused the Injury

The law imposes on employers the general duty to provide reasonably safe working conditions for employees. This duty may be violated in a variety of ways. For example, an employer might fail to provide a safe workplace, safe tools, or safe machinery. Similarly, the employer would violate a duty owed employees if there were an insufficient number of coworkers to do a job safely or if there were inadequate safety instructions. Also, violation of an OSHA regulation may violate the duty to provide reasonably safe working conditions.

When the employer violates the duty to provide safe working conditions and this causes injury to workers, the employer has probably committed the tort of negligence. Thus, in the problem, the employer was probably negligent in providing defective safety lines.

2. When There Are *No Defenses* to the Employer's Negligence

Even if an employer's negligence causes injury to an employee, the employee may not be able to collect under the common law. This is true when the employer proves any one of the following defenses:

a. the employee *assumed the risk* involved,
b. the employee was *contributorily negligent*, and
c. the *negligence of a coworker* caused the injury.

A person who is aware of a danger before it causes injury but voluntarily remains in the dangerous situation assumes the risk. In the example, the employer probably was negligent in failing to provide safety nets. Still, the employer could probably avoid liability for the deaths of the workers who fell by proving that the employees knew that it was dangerous to climb to the top of the bridge without safety nets, yet they carried out this activity. In doing so, the employees assumed the risk of any harm that might occur to them during their climb.

Contributory negligence means that the employee carelessly did something which contributed to the injury or death. This employer's defense might also be available against those employees who fell while climbing to their work sites; it could be argued that they were unlikely to fall unless they were somehow careless.

Negligence of a coworker also defeats recovery from an employer. Thus, in the problem, the horseplay leading to the death of a worker would prevent the employee's family from winning a suit for negligence against the employer.

3. When the Employee is Not Covered by Workers' Compensation Insurance

If a worker is covered by workers' compensation, then a suit for negligence against the employer usually is not permitted. On the other hand, if state law requires that an employee be covered, but the employer has not purchased such insurance, the injured, uncovered employee may claim negligence and sue the employer. Moreover, in such cases, the employer generally may not use the employers' customary common law defenses listed in the previous section. Thus, the employee has the possibility of recovering large sums of money while the employer is almost defenseless. This possibility scares some employers into purchasing workers' compensation coverage even if it is not required.

In most instances, an injured employee not covered by workers' compensation must be willing to sue in order to obtain a fair out-of-court settlement from an employer. This generally means that an attorney must be hired. The fee in these cases is usually a percentage of the money won. It may range from 20 percent to 40 percent depending upon how complicated the case is and whether or not the case is settled before trial.

In the problem, all the employees could have maintained negligence suits since the injuries occurred before workers' compensation statutes were enacted. In all cases, the employer has probably violated the basic duty of providing reasonably safe working conditions. However, those who lost their balance while climbing the bridge probably assumed the risk and/or were contributorily negligent. Therefore they could not recover from the employer. The victims of horseplay would probably be in the same position because of the negligence of their coworkers. The first employee injured when the safety line broke could probably recover from the employer. However, employees injured after the first safety line accident might be subject to the assumption-of-the-risk defense.

HOW DO WORKERS' COMPENSATION LAWS HELP EMPLOYEES?

PROBLEM: Turpin was a production-line worker in a steel desk factory. His job was to use a hydraulic shear to cut large pieces of sheet metal into smaller sizes for drawers. One morning while Turpin was setting up his shear, his friend and coworker, Gillis, watched. Gillis believed that the main power supply for the machine was off. As a joke, he pressed the "ON" buttons while Turpin's arm was under the shear's blade. Turpin's arm was cut off. Can Turpin recover from his *employer* for the loss of his arm?

Negligence suits under the common law were risky for both employers and employees. Most injured employees collected nothing because of the employer's defenses. However, when employees did win, they sometimes were awarded amounts which would bankrupt the employer.

Today's workers' compensation laws reflect a public policy objective of moving away from allocating costs based on *fault* and toward *insuring* that injured employees will recover medical expenses and some of their lost wages. The cost of this insurance is passed along to consumers in the form of slightly higher prices for goods and services.

Thus, in the problem, Turpin would recover workers' compensation benefits even though the injury was caused by a coworker and the employer was not at fault. Note that before workers' compensation, no money would have been paid since Turpin's only right at that time would have been to sue for negligence. He probably would have lost this suit against his employer because of the defense of negligence of a coworker. Although the coworker, Gillis, was legally responsible, he was probably judgment-proof (had no money to pay a judgment).

1. Recovery under Workers' Compensation Insurance

PROBLEM: Boal assembled fire hydrants for the Richmond Foundry. The job required Boal to lift finished fire hydrants weighing up to 140 pounds. One day, while lifting fire hydrants, Boal suffered a hernia. Can he collect workers' compensation benefits?

Employees are generally protected by workers' compensation insurance if they are injured (1) by accident or disease, including job-stress related illness, (2) in the course of their employment, and (3) from the risks of that employment. Generally these requirements are satisfied if a worker is injured while on the job and the injury is caused by the work. Thus, in the problem, Boal could collect benefits. On the other hand, a worker who suffered a hernia while picking a piece of paper off the floor might not collect benefits. That is because the injury may not have been caused by the job; it probably was caused by weak abdominal muscles. Similarly, if one intentionally injures oneself, perhaps to obtain benefits, there has not been an accident and benefits usually are denied. Workers who are injured in fights they started or because they were intoxicated often are denied benefits on the grounds that there has been no accident. Also, one who suffers a heart attack while at work may or may not collect benefits depending upon whether the "risks of the employment" caused the attack. An air traffic controller might recover benefits while a delivery person probably would not.

If a worker covered by workers' compensation is injured because of the job, the worker becomes entitled to benefits. Sometimes there is a small, lump-sum payment to cover such things as pain and suffering, injuries such as loss of a hand, or loss of life. In nearly every case, the payment is less than if the injured party had won a negligence suit. Medical expenses usually are covered up to some maximum amount. Most states will also pay a percentage of lost wages; 80 percent is a common amount. In addition, most states also pay for job retraining if an accident makes it impossible for a worker to continue in the former job. This retraining is called **vocational rehabilitation.** Often the amount of the benefit is increased if the employer is grossly negligent or reduced if the employee is grossly negligent. A 10 percent increase or reduction is typical.

vocational rehabilitation: job retraining

Workers' compensation benefits are paid from one of three sources. Employers may purchase a workers' compensation insurance policy from an insurance company, participate in a state-administered workers' compensation fund, or be self-insured. Insurance companies and state funds charge amounts which reflect the riskiness of the business and each employer's particular safety history. Of course, the amount paid out by those who are self-insured depends upon their safety practices. The cost of workers' compensation coverage gives employers an incentive to make the workplace safe.

2. The Coverage of Workers' Compensation Laws

Not all workers are required to be covered by a plan of workers' compensation. Frequently companies with three or fewer employees are not required to provide workers' compensation insurance.

Similarly, in most states **casual workers** need not be covered. Casual workers are those who do not work for a particular employer regularly. If a company hired a troop of Scouts on a one-time basis to wash all the company cars, the Scouts would be casual workers. In addition, domestics—such as housekeepers—and agricultural workers often are not required to be covered. Generally employers can obtain coverage for employees even though the state statute does not require that they be covered.

casual workers: those who do not work for an employer regularly

Two groups of employees usually cannot be covered—sole proprietors and partners (and their families). This limitation is intended to prevent fraudulent claims for benefits.

Rather than being covered by state workers' compensation laws, employees of railroads, airlines, trucking firms, and other common carriers engaged in interstate commerce are governed by a special federal act. Longshore and harbor workers also operate under a different federal law and are not subject to state workers' compensation laws.

3. Winning a Workers' Compensation Award

The decision about whether a person is entitled to benefits is made at a hearing conducted by a state administrative agency. This agency is often called the Workers' Compensation Board or the Industrial Accident Commission. Hearing procedures are much less complicated than those of a trial. Accordingly, for small claims the injured worker does not need a lawyer. However, when the claim or injury is significant, one should be represented by a lawyer, preferably a specialist in the field. Lawyers specializing in workers' compensation cases frequently charge a fixed fee for representing injured employees. In some states, these fees are regulated by statute and are a part of the benefits awarded.

4. Effect of Workers' Compensation Statutes on Suits for Negligence

Injured workers who are not required by state law to be covered by workers' compensation may sue their employers for negligence. Sometimes employers fail to pay the required insurance premium for some or all employees. This may happen when the employer is in financial trouble or, for example, when the employer mistakenly classifies someone as a casual employee. If injured, these illegally uncovered employees can recover if they prove that the employer's negligence caused the injury. The employer may not use the employer's defenses of assumption of the risk, contributory negligence, or negligence of a coworker. In a few states, such employees are entitled by statute to recover all of their expenses plus an additional 50 percent of the expenses as a penalty to the employer.

In a few states, the injured employee can elect to file under workers' compensation or to sue the employer for negligence. Employers generally can use the employer's defenses in these cases.

HOW DOES OSHA PROTECT EMPLOYEES?

PROBLEM: Browning Processing Company is engaged in preparing fruits and vegetables for the market. An OSHA inspector ordered the company to install clutches on the prune-pitting machines and to provide electrical grounding of all electric typewriters and word processors. Must Browning comply?

In 1970, the United States Congress enacted a law called the Occupational Safety and Health Administration Act. This law created the Occupational Safety and Health Administration and empowered it to enact rules and regulations designed to achieve safety in the workplace. Both the law and the federal administrative agency are commonly referred to as "OSHA." The basic policy behind this legislation was to directly prevent injuries by requiring that workplaces be safe.

1. The General Duty Clause

In general, OSHA enforces two types of laws. The first type is called the general duty law or clause. It requires that employers provide a place of employment which is free from hazards which are likely to cause death or serious physical harm. If this general duty requirement is violated, OSHA can fine the company and/or shut down the plant.

2. Specific Regulations

The second type of OSHA law includes specific workplace safety regulations. Many of these regulations were hastily established shortly after this federal administrative agency was formed. In many cases, OSHA simply adopted private industry and trade association safety standards. As a result, many regulations were poorly worded and inappropriately applied. In recent years, many rules have been improved.

These rules cover most aspects of work. They spell out safety training requirements, safety clothing and equipment to be worn by workers, and the construction, maintenance, and shielding of equipment. Minimum standards are established for lighting, ventilation, and sanitation. For example, OSHA specifies that spray paint booths must be vented to the exterior of the building and that they must be constructed of metal rather than wood. Another example is the requirement that hair protection (such as hair nets) be worn when working in the area of moving equipment such as drills.

Minor violations of OSHA regulations usually are resolved by bringing the workplace into compliance, although employers can be fined up to $1,000. OSHA is more concerned with eliminating risks to workers than with collecting fines. In fact, it has a low-interest loan program to help small businesses finance the costs of bringing their workplaces into compliance with OSHA's regulations.

In the problem, Browning Processing would be required to comply with OSHA's demands because the lack of clutches and electrical grounding violate specific OSHA regulations. If the company did not comply, it could be fined.

3. Workplace Inspection

OSHA uses workplace inspections to ensure compliance with its general duty law and specific regulations. While an employer may deny OSHA inspectors access to the workplace, inspectors can easily obtain a search warrant giving them authority to inspect. Employers are required to file periodic safety reports which describe work-related injuries and deaths. These reports often prompt inspections. Also, employees may anonymously report safety violations simply by calling OSHA. When this occurs, OSHA will send inspectors to this workplace. Employers may not discriminate against workers who have informed OSHA of safety violations.

4. Dealing with OSHA Violations

In most cases involving violations, employers deal with OSHA officials without legal representation. The problems usually involve technical engineering and safety issues rather than legal issues. Inspectors and company supervisors are better equipped to deal with these problems than are lawyers.

Sometimes OSHA violations become very serious because the cost of compliance is prohibitive. Some companies can be pushed into bankruptcy by the cost of OSHA compliance requirements. In these situations, expert legal help is needed immediately. Unless one acts quickly, some rights to appeal the citation may be lost.

PREVENTING LEGAL DIFFICULTIES

As an Employee. . .

1. follow all safety precautions, use all safety devices prescribed for your job, and follow the employer's safety regulations;
2. determine whether you are covered by workers' compensation insurance;
3. try to think about those elements of your work which might cause injury to you or to a coworker. If there are serious risks, discuss them in a friendly way with your boss. If your boss is not helpful, consider discussing the situation with the people at OSHA; and
4. if you are covered by workers' compensation, investigate the benefits to which you are entitled.

As an Employer. . .

1. inspect your workplace to identify and to eliminate risks to the safety and health of your workers;
2. verify that all your workers are covered by workers' compensation. If some are not covered, ask an attorney to review their status;
3. if you hire casual workers who are not covered by workers' compensation, ask a lawyer for advice on how to limit your liability for injuries to them;
4. consider asking OSHA inspectors to conduct an informal inspection of your workplace; and
5. identify lawyers in your area who specialize in workers' compensation law.

Strengthening Your Legal Vocabulary

casual workers
Occupational Safety and Health Administration (OSHA)
vocational rehabilitation
workers' compensation laws

1. Retraining of an injured worker.
2. Laws that provide compensation for workers (or their dependents) when the workers are injured (or killed) in the course of employment.

3. Federal agency which administers the Occupational Safety and Health Act.
4. Persons who do not work regularly for a certain employer.

Reviewing Important Points

1. Negligence suits are based on determining who is at fault. These suits cannot be brought if the injured worker is covered by workers' compensation. In a small minority of states, covered workers can elect between workers' compensation benefits and suing the negligent employer.
2. In a suit for negligence, the worker must establish that the employer was *negligent* and this *caused* the injury. Negligence can be established by showing that the workplace, tools, equipment, safety instructions, or number of coworkers is unsafe.
3. Even when the employer is negligent, the worker cannot win if the employer can establish any of the employers' defenses. If the state required that the injured employee be covered by workers' compensation, but the employer failed to do so, the employer may not use the employers' defenses in a negligence suit by an injured employee.
4. Workers' compensation pays benefits to those injured on the job in the course of their employment. The benefits usually include all medical payments, some lost wages, and sometimes vocational rehabilitation.
5. The employer pays the workers' compensation premiums. The amount is based in part on the safety record of the employer.
6. OSHA enforces both a general duty clause and specific workplace regulations.
7. OSHA inspectors can obtain search warrants to inspect the workplace. Most violations do not involve a fine if the violation is eliminated. Serious violations can lead to heavy fines and plant closings.

Applying Law to Everyday Life

1. Owens was hired by Moonglow Drive-In Theater to carry in a parade a banner advertising the theater. While carrying the banner, Owens was injured by an automobile. Was Moonglow liable?

2. Baldauf worked for West Oregon Lumber Co. as a wood sorter. In violation of Oregon law, the company did not carry workers' compensation insurance. While sorting wood on a table, Baldauf knocked off a piece which fell and hit his foot. The employee sued the employer for negligence. The lumber company asserted contributory negligence as an employer's defense. Will Baldauf win?

3. Lambert hired Mayer to apply anhydrous ammonia, a fertilizer, to the soil on her farm. Lambert was not required to provide workers' compensation insur-

ance, so Mayer was not covered. Lambert said to Mayer, "Be careful when you handle this stuff; it might burn you." However, Mayer had never used this type of equipment before, and Lambert did not explain to Mayer how to handle the tank or hose or what to do if Mayer were sprayed on the body. The hose got out of control and sprayed Mayer in the face, blinding him in one eye. He sued Lambert for negligence, claiming that he was not properly instructed in how to handle the equipment. Who wins?

4. Atlas Warehouse was equipped with an old-fashioned freight elevator that had a manually operated gate on each floor. Any employee using the elevator could operate it personally. When the elevator reached a floor, the employee had to raise the gate and then lower it after getting off. Lacey, a supervisor delivering a message to Ritter, stepped off the elevator after raising the gate. But Lacey did not lower the gate because she intended to get back on immediately. While she was talking with Ritter the elevator was moved to another floor. After completing her conversation, Lacey returned to the elevator. However, she failed to note that it had been moved, and so she stepped into the shaft and fell to her death. (a) What would be the liability of the employer in a suit for negligence? (b) What would be the employer's liability under workers' compensation statutes?

5. Fricke and Bracton were employed as truck drivers by different companies. Both Fricke and Bracton were covered by workers' compensation. Late one afternoon, Fricke was rushing to make a delivery before quitting time. In haste, Fricke rammed into Bracton's truck, which was legally parked. Bracton suffered fatal injuries. Bracton's widow later received a lump-sum workers' compensation benefit of $55,000. Is this all she can collect?

6. Randle worked at the Hide Tanning Co. which employed only two people. The company was not required by the state to carry workers' compensation insurance and it did not do so. A large wooden vat of acid with an open top was mounted on a wooden stand six feet off the ground. Because the stand was old and rickety, the people working near it were afraid that it would collapse and spill the acid on them. An OSHA inspector cited the company for violation of the general duty clause and threatened to close down the production operation. After negotiations, the company was given 30 days to correct the problem. Two days after the citation, the vat broke—spilling acid on Randle. Randle sued the employer and introduced the citation as evidence of the negligence of the company. The company objected, claiming that OSHA inspections have nothing to do with suits for employer's negligence. Is the company correct?

7. Circo-Pacific manufactured circuit boards—the base upon which electrical components are mounted by soldering. Peery worked as a "dip solderer," inserting the bare boards into a small tub of molten solder to coat the copper circuits. The building in which this work was done leaked and, when it rained, water dripped into the tub and splashed molten solder onto Peery's

arm, causing numerous slight burns—some as large as the size of a pencil eraser. Peery complained to his boss about the problem several times but the complaint was dismissed with the statement, "Don't be such a sissy." Peery finally complained to OSHA. An inspector arrived at the plant and cited the company. The fine was $500. A month later, Peery was transferred to another job which paid much less than that of dip solderer. He complained to OSHA that he was being discriminated against because of his complaint. Is he correct? What is the result?

Solving Case Problems

1. Abell lost his life when he was struck by a tractor while working. Abell and his brother had been hired as laborers to help prepare the grounds for the county fair. They were to be paid by the hour and were to furnish their own tools. No understanding was reached concerning the length of their employment, but it was understood that it would be "for one or two weeks." The work to be done consisted of "odd jobs," such as cleaning up and making minor repairs. In light of these facts, were Abell's survivors entitled to worker's compensation benefits? (*Wood v. Abell,* 300 A.2d 665)

2. Norbert Crow was the 14-year-old son of the vice president and general manager of Harry Crow and Son, Inc. Norbert was killed by a tractor while working for the corporation during the summer vacation. He had no work permit and was paid irregularly by his father, who was not reimbursed by the corporation. Norbert's job usually required answering the telephone, weighing materials, and at times, loading materials on trucks. When the parents were awarded death and burial benefits by the Industrial Accident Commission, the corporation appealed the award. The issue was whether Norbert was an employee at the time of the accident despite the fact that the workers' compensation law provided that members of a family are not so considered and the fact that Norbert had no work permit. What should the appellate court have decided? (*Harry Crow and Son, Inc. v. Industrial Accident Commission,* 18 Wis. 2d 436, 118 N.W.2d 841)

3. Thornton was employed as production foreman with the defendant corporation. On several occasions, Thornton had reprimanded an employee, Sozio, for failure to wear safety glasses and had reported this to the employer. On one occasion, Sozio threatened Thornton, saying, "I'll take care of your eyes later." Nine days after Sozio's employment had been terminated, Thornton saw him in a bar. At that time Sozio said, "Remember me, remember me?" and attacked Thornton, causing Thornton to lose the sight of one eye. Thornton claims that he is entitled to workers' compensation benefits because his injuries arose out of and had their origin in his employment and because the injuries were in the course of the employment. His employer claims that the injuries did not occur on the job even though they did arise out of the employment. Sozio, no longer an employee, had deliberately

inflicted the injuries. Therefore, the employer argues, Thornton is not entitled to workers' compensation benefits. Is Thornton entitled to benefits? (*Thornton v. Chamberlain Manufacturing Corporation*, 62 N.J. 235, 300 A.2d 146)

4. Bailey managed a gasoline station. He was required to use his station wagon to make emergency calls for the station. Tools were carried in the car, and the service station paid for the gas and oil it used. Bailey owned another car which was used as a "family car." One morning while driving to work, Bailey was struck and killed by a train. His wife filed a claim for workers' compensation benefits. The Industrial Commission denied the claim, stating that travel to and from work is not covered by workers' compensation insurance. Was Bailey's death caused by his work? Is his widow entitled to the death benefit? (*Bailey v. Utah State Industrial Commission,* 16 P.2d 208, Utah)

5. Eckis, age 22, was a full-time employee of Sea World, an amusement park. Eckis served as secretary for Burgess, the director of animal training. Eckis, who was an excellent swimmer, had worked as a model. When Burgess asked her to ride "Shamu, the Killer Whale" in a bikini for some publicity pictures, she eagerly agreed. Burgess knew Shamu was conditioned to being ridden only by persons wearing wet suits and had attacked riders in ordinary bathing suits. Eckis was warned in general terms of the danger, and she fell off during one practice session while wearing a wet suit. When a trainer told Eckis he would not watch her ride Shamu "because it was really dangerous," Burgess reassured Eckis and she rode Shamu three different times. Each time she wore a bikini instead of a wet suit. During the second ride, Shamu's tail was fluttering, indicating that the whale was upset. During the third ride, Eckis fell off and Shamu then bit her on her legs and hips and held her in the tank until she was rescued. As an employee, Eckis qualified for modest workers' compensation payments but had no other insurance benefits. Therefore she sued for more money in a civil action. She claimed that the employer was negligent, had defrauded her, and was liable for the acts of an animal with dangerous tendencies. The jury awarded Eckis damages of \$75,000. Sea World appealed. Was workers' compensation Eckis's only remedy? (*Eckis v. Sea World Corporation,* 64 Cal. App. 3d 1, Cal. Rptr. 183)

24
Agency

1. The Wilderness Shop has a big sale scheduled for next weekend, but you will be out of town. Can you authorize another person to buy a pair of binoculars in your name? Are you both liable for the purchase price?
2. Jefferson hired Sally as his real estate broker to help sell his home. While trying to sell the home, Sally lied to the buyer about the need for repairs on the roof. The buyer now sues Jefferson and Sally. Who is liable to whom?
3. You know a friend is looking for a weight-lifting bench and a set of barbells. When you find a good buy, you give the seller a down payment in the name of your friend. Is your friend liable for the down payment and for the balance? Are you liable for the balance?

WHAT IS AN AGENCY?

PROBLEM: Jeff worked at the Civic Center Service Station. His duties included selling gasoline, oil, and accessories for which he either collected cash or made out credit tickets. Jeff also changed oil and filters, provided lubrication services, and cleaned the premises. Was Jeff an agent or an ordinary employee?

You have learned that one who does work under the direction and control of another person (for example, typing letters, packing groceries, or repairing radios) is an ordinary employee. But there is another kind of employee—one who makes contracts with third parties for his or her employer.

agent: one who makes contracts for and on behalf of another

principal: one who authorizes an agent to make contracts

agency: relationship in which one person represents another in making contracts

scope of authority: within the range of authorized acts

A person who makes contracts for and on behalf of another is an **agent.** The person who authorizes such action is a **principal**. When a person is authorized to act for another in contracting with third persons, the relationship of **agency** exists. In the problem, Jeff was an employee when he changed oil and filters, lubricated cars, and cleaned the premises. He was both an employee and an agent when he sold gas, oil, and accessories because he was making contracts for and on behalf of the service station's owner. The transfer of authority to contract is the core characteristic of agency relationships.

If the agent acts within the **scope of authority**—that is, within the range of acts authorized by the principal—and, as the principal's representative, thereby negotiates a contract with the third party, the principal is bound by the contract. If the agent has acted outside the scope of authority, the principal is not bound.

Smiley bought a minibike from The Hot Wheels Shop. The salesperson who sold Smiley the bike gave her a signed card offering a free engine adjustment anytime within three months of purchase. If the salesperson changed jobs or was out of the shop when such an adjustment was requested, Smiley could look directly to Young, the owner of the shop, for performance. The signature of the salesperson was binding on the owner as principal, just as if the owner had personally signed the card.

Generally, agents are not personally liable for the contracts which they negotiate on behalf of their principals. However, when the agent acts outside the scope of authority and the third party suffers an injury because the contract cannot be enforced against the principal, the third party can recover from the agent. In the problem, Jeff's scope of authority is probably limited to selling the products usually offered for sale by gas stations. His scope of authority clearly does not include authority to sell the real estate owned by the firm. If Jeff did sign a contract to sell the real estate and the third party was injured because it could not enforce the contract, the third party could recover from Jeff.

While agency law generally follows the principles of contract law, there is one area where it differs dramatically. In contract law, the parties to a transaction should be able to identify all the terms and conditions of the contract merely by reflecting on the conduct and communications among the parties. In contrast, parties to an agency contract have additional obligations called **fiduciary duties**. In essence, fiduciary duties (which include loyalty, obedience, and care) require that the agent behave with scrupulous good faith and serve the best interests of the principal.

fiduciary duties: duties which require one to serve the best interests of another

WHO CAN BE A PRINCIPAL OR AN AGENT?

PROBLEM: Carvey, a minor, wished to sell her surfboard. She agreed to pay Fischer 10 percent of the sales price of $100 if Fischer would sell the board. Fischer agreed, but after Fischer had found a buyer, Carvey decided not to sell. She claimed that, as a minor, she had no power to appoint an agent. Was Carvey correct?

Anyone who has the capacity to contract can be a principal and act through an agent. That is because the authorized acts of the agent are legally the acts of the principal. For the same reason, one who is not competent to contract cannot escape that incompetency by appointing an agent.

A minor lacks capacity to contract (see Chapters 6 and 12). Hence, if a minor—such as Carvey in the problem—appoints an agent, the appointment is generally regarded as voidable by the minor. In most states, Carvey would have the power to appoint an agent. However, she would also have the power to avoid any contract the agent might make on her behalf.

Anyone, regardless of capacity or incapacity to make contracts, may, in theory at least, be an agent. This is true because the agent represents the principal and is not one of the parties to the contracts that are made. Thus, minors (who lack legal capacity to act for themselves) can act for and bind adults in contracts. The adult principals cannot later avoid the resulting contracts because of the minority of their agents.

To protect the public against unqualified workers, all states require that agents in certain occupations be licensed (see Chapter 7). For example, this usually involves successful passing of professional examinations by persons who want to serve as auctioneers, insurance agents, lawyers, and real estate brokers.

HOW IS AGENCY AUTHORITY CREATED?

> **PROBLEM:** In planning a Christmas party, Floris asked her friend Logan to buy the cake. Logan agreed. Floris told her to charge the cake to Floris's account at the bakery. Floris also gave Logan the keys to her car. What agency authority does Logan have?

Agency authority is created when a principal authorizes an agent to represent the principal in the contracting process. When the principal agrees to pay the agent, the agency relationship arises from a contract between the agent and the principal. In other instances, there is no contract. One person, such as Logan in the problem, may simply agree to help another in contracting with third parties. In cases where the agent receives no consideration, the agency is called a **gratuitous agency**.

gratuitous agency: agency relationship in which the agent receives no consideration

Agency authority may be created in a variety of ways. These include: (1) an express grant of authority, (2) an implied grant of authority, (3) appearance, and (4) ratification.

express authority: authority delegated to an agent by words

1. Express Grant of Authority

power of attorney: writing that appoints an agent

Express authority is communicated by the principal to the agent. It may be oral or written. In the problem, Floris gave Logan express authority to purchase the cake. If written, the grant may be in an informal letter or in a carefully drafted document. Any writing which appoints someone as an agent is called a **power of attorney**.

implied authority: authority to do anything reasonably necessary to carry out expressly authorized duties

2. Implied Grant of Authority

An agent is automatically given **implied authority** to do anything which is reasonably necessary or customary to carry out the duties expressly authorized. Thus, an agent's implied authority flows out of the express authority. In the problem, there may be implied authority for Logan to buy some gas for the car and charge it to Floris if that is necessary to complete the purchase of the cake.

Implied authority may be expanded in an emergency. In the problem, if Floris's car caught on fire while Logan was driving it on the errand, Logan would have implied authority to promise money to someone to assist in extinguishing the fire. Floris would be liable to pay for this help.

3. Appearance

PROBLEM: Redman drove into Milton's Motors with the intention of trading her car for another one. The only person present was Davis, who was seated at the sales desk. Davis had been left in charge by Milton. Milton had instructed Davis to answer the telephone and to ask any in-person callers to wait until Milton returned from the bank. Davis, upon learning of Redman's purpose, suggested that Redman inspect the new models on display while Davis test-drove the old car for appraisal purposes. Davis drove Redman's car off the lot and never returned. Would Milton be liable for the value of Redman's car?

Agency authority may sometimes result from the appearance created by the principal. This does not create a conventional agency because there has been no agreement between the principal and the agent. Nevertheless, if an action on your part leads others to reasonably believe that a particular person is your agent, you will be held liable to them for the actions because you have granted **apparent authority**. Because the principal is always the source of authority in an agency, such authority must always come, or appear to come, from the principal's words or acts. It can never arise from the words or conduct of the agent alone. Thus, in the problem, Milton's conduct—allowing Davis to take charge of the office—reasonably led Redman to believe that Davis was Milton's agent with authority to make appraisals and sales. A person who intentionally or unintentionally misleads another into thinking that a particular individual has agency authority will generally be barred from denying the apparent agency. Apparent authority creates an **agency by estoppel** in which a principal cannot, because of the principal's conduct toward third parties, deny the existence of an agency. Milton's conduct stops him from claiming that he did not appoint Davis as his agent. Thus, Milton would be liable for the value of Redman's car.

apparent authority: power the agent appears to have

agency by estoppel: relationship in which a principal is stopped from denying the existence of an agency, due to the principal's conduct toward third parties

The Wiltons were displeased with a power lawn mower they had purchased from Lacey's Department Store. It was very difficult to start the engine even after repeated adjustments. Barkdoll, who was in charge of Lacey's Customer Relations Department, had express authority to handle exchanges and to give credit slips for returned goods. In this case, he allowed the Wiltons to return the mower, and he gave them a full cash refund. Barkdoll assumed that Lacey's would return the mower to the manufacturer. Later, Watson, the store manager, told the Wiltons they should have complained directly to the manufacturer. She then asked them to return the refund. They need not do so because Barkdoll had apparent authority to bind the store.

4. Ratification

If a person acts without express, implied, or apparent authority (that is, acts outside the scope of his or her authority), the principal is not bound. However, the principal who later assents to the transaction will be bound. This approval of an unauthorized act is called **ratification**. A principal impliedly assents to an agency transaction by knowingly accepting its benefits.

ratification: approval of a previously unauthorized act

For a valid ratification, the following conditions must be met:

a. the third person must have believed that by dealing with the principal's agent, he or she was making a contract with the principal,
b. the principal must have full knowledge of all material facts,
c. the principal must show an intent to ratify,
d. the principal must ratify the entire act, not just those parts that may benefit him or her, and
e. the principal must ratify before the third person withdraws, as the third person could do upon learning that the agent lacked authority.

Norman was a collector of music boxes. One day her friend Wadell discovered a particularly attractive Swiss music box that he thought Norman would want. Therefore Wadell bought the music box for $750, making a down payment of $100 in Norman's name but without her knowledge. When Wadell described the transaction, Norman took the music box and paid Wadell the $100. She is liable for the remaining $650 because she has ratified Wadell's unauthorized conduct.

WHAT ARE AN AGENT'S FIDUCIARY DUTIES?

PROBLEM: Martaen gave Wallace an antique Chinese bronze mirror to sell for her at the highest possible price. Wallace, an antique collector himself, bought the mirror for his wife. However, he did not reveal that fact when he paid Martaen. If Martaen discovered what Wallace had done, could she avoid the contract?

In many respects, the agent's duties to the principal are the same as those of an ordinary employee. However, the agent has the power to bind the principal in business dealings with others. Therefore great trustworthiness and loyalty and the utmost honesty and good faith are required of the agent. The law encourages this with four fiduciary duties which agents owe principals. These duties are: (1) loyalty, (2) obedience, (3) care and skill, and (4) accounting.

1. Loyalty

One of an agent's most important duties is that of loyalty. This means that an agent must inform the principal of anything that affects the principal's interest. Thus, the agent may not secretly benefit from transactions completed in connection with the agency. Indeed, agents should avoid placing themselves in situations where there is a possible conflict of interest and where there is the opportunity to place their own well-being above that of their principals. Any profits agents earn in performing their duties belong to their principals unless otherwise agreed. Agents may not buy from nor sell to themselves (or relatives or friends) without prior approval of their principals. If an agent does so, as in the problem, the principal may avoid the contract even if the principal suffers no monetary loss.

An agent may not secretly represent other persons in a transaction being performed for the principal unless all parties are informed and give their consent.

Phillips was a newspaper broker. She located prospective buyers and prospective sellers of weekly and daily newspapers. She would skillfully match the demands for one with the supply of another. If a sale were concluded, she would collect a commission from both. However, before any negotiations began, she would inform both parties of her dual role and expectation. Thus, she could legally serve both parties.

2. Obedience

PROBLEM: McGill authorized Fernandez to sell his van for cash only. Fernandez sold the van but accepted the buyer's personal check made out to Fernandez. The check was dishonored when it was presented for payment. Must McGill suffer the loss?

The agent must obey the lawful instructions of the principal, and is liable for damages that result from failure to follow proper instructions. Thus, in the problem, Fernandez, not McGill, must suffer the loss unless, of course, he can recover from the defaulting buyer. It should be obvious that an agent should not follow instructions to do an illegal or immoral act. For example, a sales agent should not lie about a product even if the principal has ordered such fraudulent conduct.

3. Care and Skill

PROBLEM: The Merritts owned the Pony Express Inn. Because the Inn was located far from any community, security was a problem. Therefore the Merritts limited the cash on hand by dropping all excess receipts into a floor safe controlled by an automatic timer. DeMille, the weekend manager, thought this was too bothersome, so she simply left the receipts in the cash drawer and dropped the excess in at the end of her shift. One Sunday, robbers held up DeMille. They escaped with the $3,000 that was in the cash drawer at the time. Is DeMille liable for the loss to the Merritts?

In performing a transaction for one's principal, an agent is required to exercise the degree of care and skill that a reasonably prudent person would use in a similar situation. Failure to do so renders the agent liable to the principal for any loss or injury sustained. Thus, DeMille could be held for the loss of the $3,000. This is because a prudent person would not have left so much money in the cash drawer when a safe was available.

4. Accounting

PROBLEM: Rich, who often donated animals to the city zoo, sent his agent, Gruff, to Africa to buy an elephant. Rich gave Gruff $9,500 for travel and other expenses. Upon his return, must Gruff report his actual expenses to Rich?

An agent, like Gruff in the problem, must account to the principal for all money and property of the principal that comes into the agent's possession. The agent must promptly notify the principal of the receipt of money from third parties and must make an accounting within a reasonable time.

The agent is required to keep any personal funds and property separate from those of the principal. If the agent's property is mixed with that of the principal in such a manner that they cannot be separated, all the property can be claimed by the principal. Money of the principal held by the agent should be deposited in a bank, in the name of the principal. If the money is deposited in the agent's name and the bank fails, the agent is liable for any loss.

WHAT DUTIES DOES A PRINCIPAL OWE AN AGENT?

PROBLEM: James signed an agreement with Jesse, appointing Jesse to find a buyer who would pay $35,000 for James's antique Lincoln. If Jesse found a buyer who was ready, willing, and able to buy the car, Jesse was to receive a commission of 10 percent of the price. Jesse found Anderson, who was ready, willing, and able to buy the car for the price, but James refused to enter into a sales contract. Was Jesse entitled to the commission?

A principal has many of the same obligations to an agent that an employer has to an ordinary employee. Failure of the principal to fulfill these obligations gives the agent the right to quit and to collect for any damages.

The principal's main obligation is the duty to pay the agent. Thus, a principal promises to pay for agency services, then the principal, like Rich in the problem, is legally obligated to pay. In addition, if an agent properly incurs expenses—as when a private investigator hired by a lawyer to investigate a client's accident incurs travel expenses—the principal must reimburse the agent.

WHEN IS A PRINCIPAL LIABLE TO THIRD PERSONS?

PROBLEM: Carol authorized Stanich, her agent, to sell a quantity of out-of-style ladies' shoes at a very large discount. However, Stanich was authorized to sell them for cash only. Stanich sold the shoes to the Bargain Mart for 10 percent cash and the balance on three month's credit. When Stanich told Carol it was "the best deal I could get for that junk," Carol accepted the cash. Two days later, however, Carol changed her mind. Must she complete the contract and deliver the shoes?

As long as an agent acts within the scope of the authority given by the principal, the principal is liable to the third party for performance of any contract made in the principal's name. The principal is also liable when, as in the problem, the unauthorized acts of the agent are ratified. By accepting the cash down payment, Carol ratified the contract made by her agent. Thus, Carol must deliver the shoes or be liable in damages.

If torts or fraudulent acts are committed by an agent who is acting within the scope of the authority granted, or if such actions are ratified, the principal is liable to third parties for the actions. For example, if an agent who has authority to sell defrauds a customer in order to make a sale, the principal is liable for any damages that result. The agent is also liable for harm caused by any torts or fraudulent acts that he or she personally committed.

Bridges was the credit manager of White Appliances. Bridges wrongfully took possession of Halvorson's truck while attempting to collect a past-due account from Halvorson. White Appliances was liable to Halvorson for damages because Bridges, its agent, had committed the tort of conversion while acting within the scope of his authority. Bridges was also liable for the wrongdoing.

Usually, the principal is not liable for an agent's crime unless the crime itself has been authorized or ratified. As an exception to this rule, the principal is generally liable for the illegal sale, by the agent, of intoxicating liquor or adulterated foods. Thus, the principal, a bar owner, would be liable if the agent, a bartender, illegally served liquor to a minor.

A principal is deemed to have received any legal notice or other information given by a third party to an agent who is acting within the scope of his or her authority. Thus, when a third party gives notice or knowledge to an agent, it is the same as giving it to the principal.

Gaspar was the agent in charge of the New Jersey branch office of the Kay-O Corporation. As such, Gaspar was authorized to receive legal notices for Kay-O. When Landlubber Company sued Kay-O, it served Gaspar with the necessary summons and complaint. Gaspar failed to transmit these documents to headquarters of Kay-O, and so no answer was filed within the time allowed by law. As a result, Kay-O lost the action by default because notice to Gaspar was deemed to be notice to Kay-O.

WHEN IS AN AGENT LIABLE TO THIRD PERSONS?

PROBLEM: Sara was authorized to sell rugs and carpeting for the Magic Carpet Company, Inc., but she was not authorized to make purchases. While on a sales trip to New York, Sara had a rare opportunity to buy a quantity of small oriental rugs at low "distress sale" prices. She did not have enough time to contact her home office. Therefore she simply signed the contract as a purchasing agent for Magic Carpet. Is Sara liable for the purchase price?

If an agent acts without authority from the principal, the agent becomes personally liable to the third party. That is because the agent impliedly warrants the authority that she or he purports to have. This type of situation usually arises when an agent exceeds the authority given by the principal. For example, in the problem, Sara was personally liable because she exceeded her authority. However, if Magic Carpet Company, Inc., later ratified the purchase, Sara would no longer be personally liable. In some cases, a person will act as agent for an alleged principal when absolutely no authority has been given for any action. Again, only the "agent" is liable to the third party unless the "principal" ratifies the contract (or unless the principal has given apparent authority, as in an agency by estoppel).

Alice knew that a friend, Jill, wanted to sell a matched set of luggage. When Raza revealed that she was about to leave on a trip to South

America, Alice sold her Jill's luggage set for $300, promising prompt delivery. Jill refused to ratify the sales contract and so Raza had to buy a comparable set elsewhere for $375. Alice is liable to Raza for $75 in damages.

The agent warrants the principal's capacity to the third party. If it turns out that the principal does not exist, or that the principal is able to avoid the contract for lack of capacity, the agent will be liable.

undisclosed principal: principal whose identity may not be disclosed by the agent

Sometimes an authorized agent is not allowed to disclose the principal's identity. The principal in such a case is known as an **undisclosed principal.** With a simple contract, the third party may generally elect to hold either the principal (if and when that person's identity is later disclosed) or the agent liable. But the third party may not hold both liable. This would not be true, however, for formal contracts—that is, for contracts under seal and for commercial paper, such as notes and checks—that are made in the agent's name alone. In those cases, the agent alone is liable.

Normally to bind the principal and to avoid personal liability (except in the case of an undisclosed principal), an agent will sign the name of the principal to a contract and add words to indicate that the signature is by an agent.

Costa contracted for a supply of paper bags and cartons for her employer, Tasti-Town Tamales. She properly signed the contract as follows: "Tasti-Town Tamales, by Maria Costa, Purchasing Agent."

HOW IS AN AGENCY TERMINATED?

PROBLEM: Daisey entered into a one-year written contract with the Sweet Magnolia Wholesale Nursery as a sales agent in North Carolina, South Carolina, and Georgia. After six months, total company sales dropped far below expectations as a result of a general economic recession. Because Daisey was the last to be hired, she was the first to be fired even though her manager admitted that her performance had been satisfactory. Did the nursery have a legal right to terminate the agency?

Generally, both the agent and the principal have the power, but not the right, to terminate the agency at any time. The principal terminates by revoking the agent's authority. Thus, in the problem, the nursery could revoke Daisey's authority. It had the power to do so but not the right. Therefore it would be liable in damages for breach of the one-year employment contract, since Daisey's performance had been satisfactory.

In a similar way, the agent has the power to quit at any time. However, he or she may lack the right to do so unless the principal has breached the contract. If an agent wrongfully terminates the agency before the contract expires, the principal is entitled to damages.

An exception arises when the agent has a financial interest in the agency other than the customary compensation. This is called an **agency coupled with an interest**. In such a case, the principal has neither the right nor the power to terminate the agency.

agency coupled with an interest: agency in which the agent has a financial interest beyond compensation

Swanson borrowed $85,000 from Olson to construct a small office building which Swanson leased to various tenants. As security for the loan, Swanson appointed Olson as her agent to collect the rent and to apply 50 percent of the rent to reducing the loan. The relationship of Swanson and Olson was an agency coupled with an interest. The agency could not be terminated by Swanson until the debt was repaid.

An agency is also ordinarily terminated upon the death, insanity, or bankruptcy of either the principal or the agent. In most states, however, this is not true when the agency is coupled with an interest. Thus, in the case of Swanson and Olson, the death of either party would not terminate the agency. A successor could act for the deceased party.

There is no difference between the way a gratuitous agency may be terminated and the way an agency created by contract may be terminated. There is, however, a difference in the remedies that are available for wrongful termination. Usually, a gratuitous agent cannot recover any damages if the authority is revoked. Likewise, a principal normally cannot recover any damages from a gratuitous agent who abandons the agency.

When the authority of an agent is terminated by the principal's voluntary act, the principal should promptly notify third persons who have previously dealt with the agent. If the principal does not give such individualized notice, the agent is likely to have apparent authority to make binding contracts between the principal and such third persons so long as the third persons do not know of the termination. Others who may have heard of the agency are also entitled to notice, but this can be given by publishing the fact of the termination in a newspaper of general circulation in the area.

PREVENTING LEGAL DIFFICULTIES

If You Are a Third Person Dealing with an Agent, Remember That . . .

1. you should learn the extent of the agent's authority from the principal;
2. if you pay an agent money, be sure that the agent has authority to accept it. You should also obtain a receipt with the name of the principal on it. The receipt should state the date, amount, and purpose of the payment and should be signed by the agent; and
3. if you are uncertain about the authority or honesty of the agent, make payment by a check payable to the principal.

If You Are an Agent, Remember That . . .

1. when you sign anything for your principal, make it unmistakably clear that you are signing as an agent. Always write the name of your principal first, then add "by" and your signature followed by the word "agent";
2. you must be loyal to your principal and exercise reasonable care and skill in obeying all proper instructions; and
3. if you handle your principal's money or other assets, you should keep them separated from your own.

If You Are a Principal, Remember That . . .

1. your agent, in effect, stands in your shoes. Your agent's acts become your acts. Therefore use care in selecting an agent; and
2. if you discharge your agent, protect yourself by notifying those with whom the agent has been dealing in your name. To inform all others who may have heard of the agency, publish a notice in a journal of general circulation in the area.

Strengthening Your Legal Vocabulary

agency
agency coupled with an interest
agency by estoppel
agent
apparent authority
express authority
fiduciary duties
gratuitous agency
implied authority
power of attorney
principal
undisclosed principal
ratification
scope of authority

1. One who makes contracts for and on behalf of another.
2. Duties which require a person to serve another's best interests.
3. Authority of an agent to do anything necessary or customary to carry out expressly authorized duties.
4. Authority creating an agency by estoppel.
5. Agency in which the agent has a financial interest beyond compensation.
6. Authority directly granted by a principal to an agent orally or in writing.
7. An agency that is not based on a contract.
8. Principal's assent to unauthorized acts of an agent.
9. A writing which grants agency authority.
10. One who authorizes an agent to make contracts.

Reviewing Important Points

1. The relationship of principal and agent is created when one person authorizes another to act on his or her behalf in contracting, or assisting in contracting, with third persons.
2. Principals are bound by the contracts negotiated by their agents when the agents have acted within the scope of their agency authority.
3. Agency authority may be created by express grant, implied grant, or may result from appearance. Unauthorized action may also be created through ratification.
4. Agents owe fiduciary duties to their principals. These duties include the duties of loyalty, obedience, reasonable care and skill, and accounting.
5. The agent is liable to the third party if the agent acts outside the scope of authority and thereby injures the third party.
6. Both the principal and the agent have the power, but not the right, to terminate most agency relationships. An agency coupled with an interest may not be terminated by only one party.

Applying Law to Everyday Life

1. Newman authorized Sanchez to sell his car at the highest price possible but for not less than $2,800. Sanchez received an offer of $3,000 from Hack. Nevertheless, Sanchez sold the car to a buddy, Glenn, for $2,800. When Newman learned of this, he attempted to collect $200 from Sanchez. Would he succeed?

2. Jane asked Kroger to represent her in selling her real property, which consisted of a farm and certain pastures. She executed a formal power of attorney authorizing Kroger to negotiate a sale and to execute all necessary documents in order to transfer title to her real property. Then Jane left for a three-week vacation. When she returned, she learned that Kroger had sold the farm and pastures at an attractive price. But he had also sold two tractors

and a truck. Is Jane bound by Kroger's conduct in selling the farm? In selling the tractors and the truck?

3. Baroni asked her boyfriend, Sid, to help her sell her car. She promised to pay Sid 10 percent of the sale price. Sid agreed. Later, when trying to sell the car, Sid stated that a rebuilt engine had just been installed. This was not true. Kate bought the car. When she discovered the deception, she sued Baroni. Is Baroni responsible?

4. Vasquez owned a large clothing store, and he hired Juan, a business broker, to help him sell it. The contract between Vasquez and Juan only authorized Juan to "find a ready, willing, and able buyer." Juan found a buyer, Jerry, who offered an attractive price. Juan executed the documents of sale on behalf of Vasquez. When Vasquez discovered this, he said the price was too low and that he would not be bound by the contract of sale. Meanwhile, Jerry had moved his family across the country, spending about $5,000 to do so. Is Vasquez bound by the contract of sale? Can Jerry recover his expenses from Vasquez? From Juan?

5. Peach Farms authorized Cook to purchase 500 peach trees from Darcy Nursery unless Cook could save money by purchasing the trees elsewhere. Violating his instruction, Cook purchased the trees from Russell at $10 a tree more. Peach Farms complained of the price but nevertheless planted the trees. Can Russell collect the purchase price from Peach Farms?

6. Vance borrowed $10,000 from Jose. As security Vance gave Jose bonds worth $15,000 with a power of attorney authorizing Jose to sell the bonds and to apply the proceeds to repayment of the loan if Vance did not repay it when it became due. Could Vance revoke Jose's authority to sell the bonds?

7. When Kraus discharged Stamford and terminated their agency relationship, Stamford became angry. To "get even," Stamford made three contracts that included terms that were unfavorable to Kraus, yet were reasonable in the competitive market. The first contract was with an old customer, A. The second contract was with a new customer, B, who had heard of the agency but had never been contacted by Stamford. The third contract was with a total stranger, C, who had never heard of the agency. Is Kraus liable on any of these three contracts?

Solving Case Problems

1. Nissan Motor Corporation appointed McKnight as its Denver area agent and dealer for the sale of its automobiles. McKnight purchased automobiles and parts from Nissan. He then sold them as he desired and at prices he set without any control from Nissan. The question arose as to whether an agency existed. What is your judgment? *(United Fire and Casualty Company v. Nissan Motor Corporation,* 164 Colo. 42, 433 P.2d 769)

2. The manager of a retail butcher shop owned by Serges borrowed $3,500 from David for use in the butcher shop. Serges claimed that the manager had no authority to borrow money. Nevertheless, Serges made payments of $200. Serges also told David upon several occasions that the full sum would eventually be paid. Was Serges liable? *(David* v. *Serges,* 373 Mich. 442, 129 N.W.2d 882)

3. Desfossess was a mobile home park developer. He hired Notis, a licensed real estate broker, at a weekly salary. Notis's job was to assist Desfossess with a special assignment of acquiring land for mobile home parks. Desfossess requested Notis to negotiate on his behalf for the purchase of a tract suitable for a mobile home park. Notis suggested a certain parcel and received authority to purchase it in his own name, with Desfossess as the undisclosed principal. Notis reported to Desfossess that the land would cost $32,400, although Notis knew it could be and was purchased for $15,474.62. It also appeared that Notis, before becoming the agent of the plaintiff, had obtained an option for $1,000 to purchase the land but did not reveal this to Desfossess. Desfossess sought the return of the difference in what he had paid Notis and the cost of the land. Notis claimed that if Desfossess, as his former principal, had any right at all, it would be only to rescind the contract and to return the land to Notis. Who was correct? *(Desfossess* v. *Notis,* 333 A.2d 89)

4. Smith and Edwards operated a sporting goods shop in Brigham City, Utah. Sponsors of the Golden Spike Little League made arrangements with the store to purchase at a substantial discount baseball uniforms and equipment. The sponsors picked up $3,900 worth of merchandise without making any payments. After a demand for full payment, Smith and Edwards sued the sponsors. The sponsors defended by asserting that they were agents of Golden Spike Little League, acting within the scope of their authority, and thus were not personally liable. The trial judge found that Golden Spike Little League was a loosely formed voluntary association and thus not a legal entity upon which liability could be imposed. Are the sponsors liable? If the sponsors avoided liability, do you think this would be ethical? (*Smith and Edwards* v. *Golden Spike Little League,* 577 P.2d 132, Utah)

5. William Kirchberg was a food broker. He represented O'Day in 55 transactions for the purchase of lettuce from Arakelian Farms. In each transaction Arakelian Farms sent bills to O'Day and he paid them. Then Kirchberg terminated the agency relationship with O'Day. Arakelian Farms was not notified of the termination. Thereafter, Kirchberg placed 20 more orders, purportedly on behalf of O'Day. Arakelian Farms delivered the lettuce and billed O'Day but was not paid. Arakelian Farms sued O'Day. At the trial O'Day's defense was that Kirchberg was not his agent. What is the result? *(O'Day* v. *Arakelian Farms,* 540 P.2d 197)

SPECIAL SECTION:
Discipline of Attorneys for Misconduct

If an attorney embezzles funds entrusted to his or her care, neglects a case, is involved in a conflict of interest, charges excessive fees, uses improper advertising, or in other ways injures clients and violates the Rules of Professional Conduct, there are different ways in which the misconduct may be punished.

Sometimes the injured party may sue for damages, claiming malpractice. The success of some of these suits has been noted by the media, as well as by the insurance companies that issue coverage against such claims.

In addition to being named defendant in a civil suit, the attorney may be disciplined by the state authority that licenses lawyers. Typically, the highest court of a state is responsible for maintaining the professional standards of the attorneys who are members of that state's bar. To carry out its responsibility, the court publishes Rules of Professional Conduct. Administrative committees investigate complaints against attorneys, charge the practitioners with violations of the Rules, hear the cases, and make recommendations on disciplinary action to the court. Although complaints generally come from nonlawyers, in most states other lawyers, judges, and the committee members themselves may also initiate complaints. The investigative committees are usually made up of members of the legal profession, as well as nonlawyers representing the public.

In most disciplinary actions, the attorney who pleads innocent to the charges has the right to a trial by the high court sitting *en banc* (all together). The rights of due process—for example, rights to a hearing and to counsel—are afforded the attorney charged.

If the lawyer is found guilty, a number of sanctions can be imposed as punishment. These sanctions range from a simple letter of censure which admonishes the attorney against repeating the violation, to suspension of the attorney's license to practice, and sometimes even disbarment (permanent revocation of the license).

Unit Seven
PROTECTING AGAINST LOSS

UNIT OBJECTIVES

UPON COMPLETION OF THIS UNIT, you should be able to

1. explain insurable interest and the importance of this concept.
2. identify the various types of insurance.
3. understand how the law of contracts applies to insurance.
4. recall the risks covered by and the procedure for collecting under fire insurance.
5. discuss the way coinsurance provides protection at reduced cost.
6. describe the various applications of liability insurance.
7. identify the types of coverages available in an automobile insurance policy.
8. explain how no-fault insurance works.
9. understand the advantages and disadvantages of the various types of life insurance policies.
10. discuss the rights of the beneficiary and the duties of the insurer under a life insurance policy.
11. explain the concept of social insurance.
12. recall the various coverages of the social insurance program.
13. describe the eligibility requirements for coverage under the social insurance program.

25

Nature and Kinds of Insurance

1. You buy a car from a person who has just renewed the insurance on it. Will the insurance automatically be transferred to you along with the title to the car?
2. Your parents become concerned about the advancing age of their parents. Consequently, they apply for life insurance on the lives of each of your grandparents to be used to pay for funeral and other death expenses. Will the application be accepted?
3. While still in school, you start a small but successful business. You hire an employee and apply for fidelity insurance on her. You know she has served a prison term for larceny, but, because you are sure she has been rehabilitated, you do not report this information to the insurer. Would this affect the insurance?

WHAT IS INSURANCE?

PROBLEM: Ramirez is about to open a robot sales, exchange, and repair store. She does not know how large a market there is for such an enterprise. Therefore she asks an insurance agent to write a policy that would pay back any amount she might lose from business operations. Will the agent be able to sell her a policy that insures her against the risk of loss in doing business?

insurance: contract to pay for a specified loss if the loss occurs

indemnify: to make good a loss

policy: written contract of insurance

face value: stated maximum amount to be paid in the event of the insured loss

insurer: party who agrees to indemnify

insured: party who is protected by insurance

beneficiary: recipient of the policy proceeds

premium: consideration for an insurance contract

risk: possible loss covered by an insurance contract

Insurance is a contractual arrangement in which one party (usually an insurance company) agrees to pay up to a preset amount of money to a named recipient if a specified loss occurs. The loss may be the death of a person, property damage from fire, or damage resulting from exposure to many other risks. The party who pays to compensate for such a loss is said to **indemnify** or to make good the loss.

Insurance makes an important contribution to society. By collecting relatively small premiums from a large number of persons, an insurance company builds a fund from which payments can be made to indemnify the comparatively few who suffer losses.

A written contract of insurance is called a **policy**. The **face value** of a policy is the stated maximum amount to be paid in the event of the loss covered by the policy. A person who suffers a loss covered by insurance recovers no more than the actual value of the loss, even if this amount is less than the face value of the policy.

The party who agrees to indemnify is called the **insurer**. The party who is covered or protected is the **insured**. The recipient of the amount to be paid is the **beneficiary**. In some cases, notably in life insurance contracts, the insured will not be the beneficiary.

The consideration for a contract of insurance is the **premium**. The possible loss arising from injury to or death of a person or from damage to property from a specified peril is called the **risk**.

The risk of most financial losses can be covered by insurance. The risk of certain losses, however, cannot. The problem illustrates one of the most important risks for which a policy of insurance cannot be written. The risk of doing business is too unpredictable and too subject to the control of the would-be insured. If she were insured, Ramirez could simply neglect the business and yet collect on the insurance when the store failed. The best protection against the risk of doing business is found in hard work, good products, and excellent service.

WHAT IS AN INSURABLE INTEREST?

PROBLEM: When DePaulo bought Smith's car, she offered to pay Smith an extra $100 for the two months of protection still remaining on Smith's automobile insurance policy. Smith refused, saying he did not have the power to transfer its protection to her. Was he correct?

Insurance is said to be a personal contract; it is a contract between the insurer and the insured. Therefore the insured cannot transfer or assign the benefits of the policy to a third person in the same way that the insured goods could be sold. Accordingly, in the problem, Smith was correct. The insurer must approve any transfer of the rights under an insurance policy. Merely selling goods which have been insured does not automatically transfer the benefits of the insurance policy to the new owner of the goods. However, anyone who has capacity to enter into a contract may become an insured if such a person also possesses a financial interest known as an **insurable interest** in that which is being insured. Exactly what is required for an effective insurable interest differs for property and life insurance.

insurable interest: direct financial interest in the life of the insured or in the insured property

1. Insurable Interest in Property

PROBLEM: Tudor sold Clark a mobile home for $12,500 cash. Rather than canceling the insurance he held on the home, Tudor decided to let it run for the three months that were left on the policy. One month after Clark bought the mobile home, it was totally destroyed by fire. Tudor immediately filed a claim for the loss of the mobile home with his insurance company. Would he be able to collect?

Any person who would suffer a direct and measurable monetary loss if specified property was damaged has an insurable interest in that property. A person with an insurable interest need not hold all of the property rights in the insured property. Therefore many individuals may have an insurable interest in the same property. For example, in a long-term commercial lease, both a landlord and a tenant of a building may carry fire insurance on the building.

The Patrami Paving Company was renting Ruben's asphalt paving machine for use on a large highway job. The First National Bank had a security interest in the paving machine. Patrami Paving, Ruben, and the First National Bank all had insurable interests in the machine.

In order for the insurer to be legally obligated to pay the face amount of a property insurance policy, the insurable interest must exist at the time of the loss. In the problem, this was not the case. When Tudor sold the mobile home to Clark, his insurable interest was terminated. Therefore he could not collect on the policy.

It is possible to obtain coverage on property in which the insured does not have, but anticipates having, an insurable interest. For instance, it is quite common for a shipper to obtain marine insurance coverage on cargo not yet purchased.

2. Insurable Interest in Life

PROBLEM: Buck and Shannon formed a partnership to market a new type of computer memory device that Buck had developed. Shannon, who was in poor health, had all the business contacts that would make the venture a success. Buck worried that she would lose her $100,000 investment if Shannon should die. Therefore Buck insured Shannon's life for $100,000. A year later Shannon quit the partnership. Buck decided to keep the insurance in force, however, and when Shannon died eight months later, Buck sought to collect the $100,000 from the insurance company. Will she be successful?

Everyone with lawful capacity (that is, anyone who is qualified and competent) has an insurable interest in his or her own life. Also, a person may have an insurable interest in the life of another if the latter's death would directly deprive the former of some economic benefit. For instance, business partners may insure one another, and creditors may take out life insurance policies on their debtors. However, if the amount of the insurance far exceeds the amount of the debt, the courts will declare the policy void.

Generally a husband and wife have insurable interests in each other. However, courts frequently hold against (1) brothers and sisters having insurable interests in each other and (2) adult children having insurable interests in their aging parents.

Unlike in property insurance, in life insurance the insured is not required to have an insurable interest at the time of loss—that is, at the death of the person whose life is insured. But the insured must have had an insurable interest when the insurance was taken out. Therefore, in the problem, Buck should collect the $100,000. Unless he or she contracted for the life insurance, the beneficiary of the policy need not have an insurable interest at any time.

WHAT ARE THE COMMON TYPES OF INSURANCE?

PROBLEM: The citywide organization of PTAs contracted with a well-known precision flying and parachuting team to appear at a weekend fund-raiser. What kind of insurance would protect the PTAs against liability for negligence or other torts causing injury to individuals attending the fund-raiser?

Insurance can be divided into seven major categories (see Figure 25-1). These categories are (1) life insurance, (2) fire insurance, (3) casualty insurance, (4) social insurance, (5) marine insurance, (6) inland marine insurance, and (7) fidelity and surety bonding insurance.

1. Life Insurance

This type of insurance pays a predetermined amount of money to a beneficiary upon the death of a specified person. (Life insurance will be discussed in Chapter 28.)

2. Fire Insurance

A typical fire insurance policy indemnifies for loss or damage resulting from fire and usually smoke as well. In addition, the policy may cover loss due to perils such as windstorm, earthquake, rain, and hail. (Fire insurance will be discussed in Chapter 26.)

3. Casualty Insurance

Casualty insurance provides coverage in a variety of specific situations in which the intentional, negligent, or accidental acts of others or mere chance may result in loss. Some of the most important types of casualty insurance include:

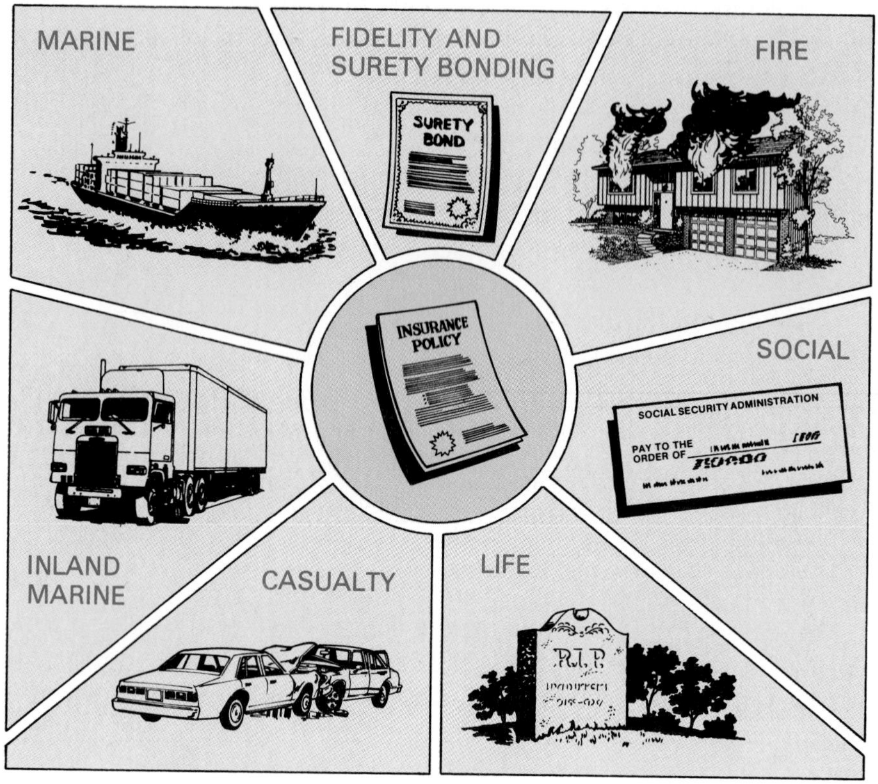

Figure 25-1. Major Categories of Insurance

Burglary, robbery, theft, and larceny insurance. Such insurance protects against losses resulting from identifiable criminal behavior. It also protects against the mysterious disappearance of property—that is, when the cause of the property's vanishing cannot be ascertained.

Automobile insurance. This type of insurance indemnifies for losses arising from the ownership and operation of motor vehicles. (Automobile insurance will be discussed in Chapter 27.)

Liability insurance. Such insurance provides protection against claims of third persons who suffer injury or loss as a result of negligence or other torts committed by the insured. Product liability insurance is a form of liability insurance. In the problem, if the organization of PTAs was insured under a suitable liability policy, it would be protected against claims arising from the weekend fund-raiser.

Workers' compensation insurance. This type of insurance is a casualty coverage that protects employees from injury or death on the job. (Workers' compensation insurance is discussed in Chapter 23.)

Disability or accident and health insurance. Such insurance generally provides for the making of payments according to a fixed schedule when the insured is injured, disabled, or ill.

4. Social Insurance

Under the provisions of the Social Security Act and related laws, millions of Americans insure themselves against unemployment, disability, poverty, and medical expense problems typically incurred in their later years. A detailed coverage of the programs set up by society to handle these problems is presented in Chapter 29.

5. Marine Insurance

Marine insurance indemnifies for loss of or damage to vessels, cargo, and other property exposed to the perils of the sea. It is perhaps the oldest type of insurance, dating back to ancient times.

6. Inland Marine Insurance

Inland marine insurance covers personal property against loss or damage caused by various perils while such property is being transported (other than on the oceans) or wherever such property is located. (This insurance is discussed in Chapter 26.)

7. Fidelity and Surety Bonding Insurance

This insurance provides coverage against financial loss caused by dishonesty. Such dishonest acts would include embezzlement or failure of one person to perform a legal obligation to another, such as constructing a building as promised. Contracts of fidelity insurance are often in the form of surety bonds. (See Chapter 19.)

HOW DOES THE LAW OF CONTRACTS APPLY TO INSURANCE?

PROBLEM: Frye bought a new sports car at Elegance Cars' downtown sales lot. Before driving off in the $48,000 vehicle, he called his insurance agent to get fire, theft, liability, and collision protection. The agent told him to "enjoy driving, you're covered." The car was stolen from Frye a few minutes later when he stopped to eat on the way home. Will the insurance agent's company cover the loss although it has not received a premium or issued a written policy on the car?

Generally the law of contracts applies to the field of insurance with relatively minor changes. Mutual assent, consideration, capacity, proper form, and legality are all significant in resolving insurance-related legal issues. If the insurance contract is ambiguous, its meaning is construed against the insurer, as the party who drafted the contract. However, specific changes from contractual law, required mainly by detailed governmental regulation of the insurance industry, need to be noted:

1. Offer and Acceptance

In an insurance contract, the insured is generally the offeror. The insurance company or insurer is the offeree. The offeror makes an application (the offer) to the insurance company by communicating risk-related facts which have been requested by the company. On the basis of these facts, and frequently upon further investigation, the insurer determines whether it will accept or reject the application.

Most insurance companies are corporations and operate through agents. Therefore the law of agency (see Chapter 24) is involved in insurance. However, most agents do not have the authority to alter or to vary the actual written terms of the insurance contract which appear in the company's printed forms. Insurance agents are typically well trained and frequently must pass qualifying examinations to be licensed. In addition, in casualty insurance, it is customary for the agent to have the power to make a preliminary, oral agreement to insure an applicant. When this is done, a written notation (called a **binder**) is issued as evidence of the oral contract, and the insurance is placed in force immediately. However, the company reserves the right to cancel the policy after reviewing the facts, unless a loss has occurred. In the problem, Frye was covered even though the policy itself had not been issued. Thus, he would be able to collect in accordance with its terms.

binder: agent's written notation of an oral agreement to insure

In life insurance, the agent also has the power to issue immediate coverage. This coverage, however, is usually conditional upon the agent having the first premium in hand and upon the insured passing the insurance company's physical exam if required.

2. Form

Most states require by statute that a contract of insurance be written. In fact, much of the wording used within the contract to describe the relationship between the parties is prescribed by state law. State law also prescribes the size of type used to print the contracts. Even when a standard policy is used, each state has certain variations in its requirements. The nature and location of the property and the kind of protection provided change the level of risk and therefore affect the insurance contract.

3. Consideration

Payment of the premium for an insurance contract is usually made in advance of the time for which protection is provided. Installment payments, however, are commonly permitted so that large premiums can be spread over the length of the policy period.

4. Capacity of Minors

Minors, because of their statutory lack of capacity, can avoid most contracts, including insurance contracts. However, most states have statutes which prevent minors from avoiding contracts for health, life, or disability insurance.

WHO MAY BE AN INSURER?

PROBLEM: Coleman carried no insurance on his life or property because he objected to the large profits made by the major insurance companies. One day his friend, Van, told him that there were insurance companies where the insureds were the owners. Is Van correct?

Because of its importance to society as well as to the insureds, the business of insurance is ordinarily limited to corporations organized for that purpose. In most states, any group or company that deals in insurance is under the supervision of a state insurance commissioner. New applicants must obtain a charter from the state and must meet certain other requirements before they can start an insurance business. One such requirement is that the applicants must have sufficient financial reserves to pay for losses. The only meaningful way to classify sellers of insurance is by their type of business organization, such as:

1. Stock Insurance Companies

stock insurance company: profit-making insurance company owned by shareholders

A **stock insurance company** has capital stock owned by shareholders who contribute the original capital and share the future profits or losses. A stock company is ordinarily governed by rules applicable to other corporations.

2. Mutual Insurance Companies

mutual insurance company: insurance company owned by the insureds

participating policies: life insurance policies on which dividends are paid

A **mutual insurance company** has no capital stock, and the members are both the owners and the insureds, as Van correctly noted in the problem. At periodic intervals, the members contribute, usually through premiums, to a fund that is used in paying losses and expenses. Because the policyholders are the owners of mutual companies, they are entitled to refunds if losses are low. These refunds are known as dividends. Such dividends are not taxable income but are instead a refund of excess premiums charged. Life insurance policies on which dividends are paid are **participating policies**. All mutual company policies are participating. Many stock life insurance companies also issue participating policies.

3. Other Types of Insurers

Certain lodges and fraternal societies, such as the Knights of Columbus and the Grange, provide various lines of insurance for their members. State and federal government insurance for a variety of perils is also available. For example, workers' compensation insurance, disability insurance, and certain other forms of casualty insurance are provided by some states. In addition, the federal government issues or sponsors:

a. life insurance to members of the armed forces and to veterans,
b. crop insurance to farmers,
c. mortgage insurance to those who lend money for the construction or repair of buildings,
d. flood insurance,

e. deposit insurance to depositors' banks, savings and loan associations, and credit unions, and
f. retirement, survivors', disability, and health insurance.

Finally, as an insurer of last resort, there is Lloyd's of London, England. Lloyd's is famous for assuming a wide diversity of risks ranging from injury to pianists' fingers to the sinking of massive oil tankers. Lloyd's rarely, if ever, handles an ordinary life insurance policy. With that exception, for the customer willing to pay the premium, Lloyd's will issue an insurance policy to cover practically any risk.

WHAT IS THE IMPORTANCE OF REPRESENTATIONS AND WARRANTIES?

PROBLEM: In the application for fire insurance on his building, Elza stated that the building had an automatic sprinkler system even though it did not. As a consequence, the insurance policy was issued at a reduced rate. When fire damaged the building shortly thereafter, the insurance company discovered the truth and refused to pay for the loss. Was it legally correct in refusing to pay?

A person who applies for insurance usually is given an application form containing questions about the nature of the risk. If the applicant wants insurance on property, the form will ask for information as to the age, use, description and condition of the property. It will also ask for facts about the property's location, value, or cost. An application for life insurance will ask for such facts as the age, occupation, and habits of the applicant, any prior illnesses or accidents, and the health of the applicant's parents.

If the statements made by the applicant are used by the insurer in determining whether to accept the application but are not made part of the final writing (the policy), they are called **representations.** A false representation can render the contract voidable by the insurer only if it is material or is so important that it significantly increases the risk. Accordingly, in the problem, because the presence or lack of an automatic sprinkler system would certainly be a material fact when securing fire insurance, the insurance company was legally justified in avoiding the contract and refusing to pay.

representations: statements of an applicant which are not part of the final insurance contract

If statements of past or existing fact or promises as to future behavior made by the applicant are included as part of the final

warranties: statements of an applicant that are part of the final insurance contract

contract of insurance, they are called **warranties**. False warranties make the contract voidable by the insurer whether the matter is material or not. This means that they must be literally true or the policy can be avoided even though the insured honestly believed the statements to be true and acted in good faith.

WHAT IS THE EFFECT OF CONCEALMENT OF MATERIAL FACTS?

PROBLEM: Andu applied for and was issued a life insurance policy for $175,000 naming her husband as beneficiary. On the application she was required to check boxes beside the names of diseases she had previously had. She intentionally did not check the box beside cancer although she had previously been treated for skin cancer. The insurance company discovered this fact three years later, immediately after Andu had died of cancer. As a consequence, the company refused to pay. Can it legally be forced to pay the $175,000?

concealment: failure to reveal material facts

The parties to a contract of insurance are required to act with the utmost good faith, especially in regard to material facts. In insurance, the materiality of a fact usually can be determined by asking the following question: "If this fact had been known, would the insurer have issued the policy on the same terms?" Failure to disclose such facts is known as **concealment**.

incontestable clause: clause which disallows insurer's avoidance of a contract due to misrepresentation or concealment by the applicant

Generally, in property and casualty insurance contracts, however, one need not volunteer information to the other contracting party. Further, a special rule governs life insurance contracts. Insurers may require medical examinations and answers to long questionnaires. The applicant generally may assume that if nothing is asked about some ailment, nothing need be volunteered. However, if a material fact has been concealed with intent to defraud the insurer, the contract may be rescinded and any claim denied. There is one major exception to this rule. That exception occurs in most states due to a statutory requirement of an **incontestable clause** in each life insurance policy. Usually this clause provides that after two years from the date of issuance, any insurer's claims of misrepresentation or concealment by the insured cannot be used to avoid the contract. Therefore, in the problem, because the policy was three years old, it is most likely that the insurance company would have to pay the $175,000.

PREVENTING LEGAL DIFFICULTIES

To Purchase and Use Insurance Wisely . . .

1. make your insurance agent as aware as possible of your personal financial situation, property holdings, and insurance needs as you see them. Consider your agent's advice as to additional types of insurance coverages that may be desirable, even though one may prudently assume some risks and should not over-insure;
2. compare costs from various companies for the insurance you require and check on the financial stability of these insurance companies;
3. periodically check the extent and level of your life and property insurance coverage to see if changes need to be made;
4. be truthful in answering all questions on insurance applications. A material false representation may render the contract voidable. A false warranty, material or immaterial, may also render the contract voidable;
5. disclose all facts that may be material to the risk. Concealment may also render the contract voidable;
6. read the "fine print" to understand any stated exclusions and conditions. You may also find some coverages and benefits you do not know you have; and
7. keep an itemized list of insured property with each item's purchase price and date of purchase. In the event of a general loss of your goods, such a list would allow you to recover more fully on your property insurance policy.

Strengthening Your Legal Vocabulary

beneficiary
binder
concealment
face value
incontestable clause
indemnity
insurable interest
insurance
insured
insurer
mutual insurance company
participating policies
policy
premium
representations
risk
stock insurance company
warranties

1. Recipient of the amount paid on an insurance claim.
2. Written contract of insurance.
3. Consideration in an insurance contract.
4. Possible loss covered by an insurance contract.
5. Stated maximum amount to be paid in the event of the insured loss.
6. Contract in which one party promises to pay the other a sum of money from a common fund if the latter experiences a specified loss.

7. To make good the actual loss suffered.
8. Written evidence of a preliminary, oral contract of insurance.
9. Party who agrees to indemnify.
10. An insurance contract clause which prevents an insurer from challenging the validity of a policy because of misrepresentations or concealment on the part of the insured, as long as the policy has been in existence for the required length of time.

Reviewing Important Points

1. Although insurance is an excellent way to protect against possible loss, certain risks, such as that of doing business, cannot be covered.
2. A person has an insurable interest in property when a direct financial loss would be suffered by that person if the property were damaged or destroyed. The insurable interest must exist at the time of the loss.
3. A person always has an insurable interest in her or his own life. One also has an insurable interest in the life of another if it can be reasonably expected that the death of such person would cause financial loss to the party contracting for the insurance. Such an insurable interest in life need exist only at the time the insurance is obtained.
4. Generally an insurer can avoid a life insurance policy if, within the first two years it is in force, the insurer discovers that facts material to the risk have been concealed by the insured.
5. In applying for insurance, statements of fact called representations can render the contract voidable only if they are both false and material.
6. Statements included as part of the policy or final contract are called warranties. A false warranty makes the contract voidable even if the matter is not material.

Applying Law to Everyday Life

1. Nan contracted for fire insurance coverage for the full value of her $125,000 home at an annual cost of $783. The policy was issued by Harvest States Insurance Company. Identify: (a) the insurer, (b) the insured, (c) the subject matter, (d) the risk, (e) the face value, and (f) the premium.

2. Browning farmed hundreds of acres. She bought a harvesting machine for $173,000. The seller, Equipment Unlimited, retained a security interest. The next summer, Mundo, a neighboring farmer, leased the harvester. Of these parties, which one(s) had an insurable interest in the harvester?

3. An abandoned factory surrounded by high, dry weeds stood on a frequently traveled road near Rydman's home. Rydman realized that the factory building would be destroyed if just one cigarette butt were thrown from a passing vehicle. Therefore she decided to insure the building against loss by fire. After she obtained the insurance, there was a fire. Could Rydman collect on the policy?

4. Claudia James took out a $100,000 life insurance policy on her husband and named herself as beneficiary. Three months later they were divorced, and a month after that the husband died in a car accident. Claudia sought to collect on the policy, but the insurance company refused to pay, stating that she lacked an insurable interest both at the time the policy was taken out and at the time of death. Is the company legally obligated to pay?

5. Rouse was about to be married and thought he should have some life insurance. He called Collins, an agent, and told him he would like to have $20,000 coverage. Collins said, "O.K., you're covered. Come in and sign the papers when you get back from your honeymoon." While on the honeymoon, Rouse was killed. Could his widow collect?

6. Sentacks, a minor, took out a personal life insurance policy at age 14. One month before reaching majority, Sentacks sued to avoid the policy and collect the premiums previously paid. Will Sentacks be successful?

7. Benesh applied for life insurance. The insurance company had him undergo a medical examination. Although he had been under treatment for diabetes for seven years, Benesh did not volunteer the fact because he thought it was unimportant and because the examiner did not ask about it. Will the insurance company be able to rescind the contract and deny any claim because of the lack of such information?

Solving Case Problems

1. Antrell made an offer to purchase a building on the Leech Lake Indian Reservation in Minnesota for $300. He paid $100 cash at the time he made the offer, and he received keys to the building from the tribal council. Without examining the property, the defendant insurance company issued a policy with a face value of $16,000. Several months after the policy was issued, fire totally destroyed the building. At the time of the loss, Antrell had not paid the balance of the purchase price nor had the title been transferred. The company claims that the plaintiff had no insurable interest in the building. If this is true, the company is not liable on the policy. What is your judgment? (*Antrell v. Pearl Assurance Company, 252 Minn. 118, 89 N.W.2d 726*)

2. Lakin sued the Postal Life and Casualty Insurance Company for their failure to pay him, as beneficiary, under a life insurance policy on his business partner, Hankinson. Evidence presented at the trial showed that Hankinson had contributed neither capital nor skills to the alleged partnership, that he could not issue partnership checks, and that he could not hire nor fire employees. In addition, it was disclosed that Lakin paid the policy premiums and had made no settlement of "partnership" interests after Hankinson's death. Should the insurance company be ordered by the court to pay the $25,000 face amount to Lakin? (*Lakin v. Postal Life and Casualty Insurance Company*, 316 S.W.2d 542, Mo.)

3. The plaintiff and her then husband were issued an automobile policy with liability coverage in which both were named as insureds. Two automobiles, registered in the names of both parties, were covered by the policy. The husband and wife separated, and the separation agreement gave one car to each party. A few months later, the husband requested the defendant insurance company to change his address. When the policy renewal notice was received, he asked that the coverage on his former wife's car and her name as an insured be deleted from the policy. The plaintiff received no notice of renewal nor of the deletion of her car and herself from the policy. After renewal of the policy, as changed, the plaintiff had an accident, and the insurer was immediately notified. She then learned of the deletion of her automobile and her name from coverage. Shorty thereafter, an injury suit arising out of the accident was initiated against the plaintiff. Therefore she instituted this action to determine her rights under the policy issued to her former husband by the defendant. Does she have any? (*Broquedis v. Employers Mutual Liability Insurance Company of Wisconsin*, 360 N.Y.S.2d 735)

4. Milburn carried automobile damage and theft insurance on his Cadillac sedan as required by the creditor on his car loan. When the car payments became burdensome, Milburn turned the car over to an auto salesperson to sell. The salesperson failed and ultimately disappeared with the car. The insurer, Manchester Insurance Company, refused to pay, and World Investment Company, Milburn's creditor on the loan, sued this insurer. The insurer claimed that the policy only insured against a theft, which involves a taking *against the owner's will*. Since Milburn voluntarily delivered the car to the salesperson, no theft had occurred. World Investment Co. claimed instead that the word "theft" should be given its common meaning of "steal" and that, as a consequence, the insurance company should pay. Decide. (*World Investment Co. v. Manchester Insurance and Indemnity Co.*, 380 S.W.2d 487, Mo.)

5. Davison was injured while riding as a passenger in a car driven by Wilson. Both were employees of the Wisconsin State Employment Service and were on an official trip for the service when the accident occurred. When Davison sued Wilson to recover for his injuries, Wilson's insurer, the Dairyland Insurance Co., denied liability. The insurance company stated that the policy on Wilson excluded coverage of injuries to more than one employee of the service occurring in any single accident. Davison contended that the exclusion of coverage on himself was invalid because it did not comply with a Wisconsin state statute requiring exclusions to appear in a color or type of print different from the rest of the policy. The insurance company pointed out that although the exclusion did not appear in a different color or type of print, it was located in a section of the policy clearly labeled "exclusions." Should the exclusion be held invalid, thus allowing Davison to collect? (*Davison v. Wilson*, 71 Wis. 2d 630, 239 N.W.2d 38)

26

Property and Casualty Insurance

1. When an electrical fire suddenly starts in your home, you begin moving valuable personal property out of the house. Unfortunately, while moving your new color TV, you drop it and it is damaged beyond repair. Will your fire insurance cover the loss of the TV set?

2. A friend is injured when the Slithering Serpent ride at the local amusement park jumps its track. What kind of insurance would protect the owner of the park if your friend sues?

3. Tract left her riding lawnmower unattended while it was running. It slowly started moving down the incline on which she left it. Gathering speed, it ran through Benton's stained-glass house door and into Benton's living room where it sheared his three-inch shag carpet to within one inch of the floor. Benton's insurance company paid him for the damage and now claims the right to sue Tract for her negligence. Can it do so?

WHAT ARE PROPERTY INSURANCE AND CASUALTY INSURANCE?

PROBLEM: The Neilallens' house was severely damaged during a tornado. What kind of insurance would have protected them against financial loss from such an occurrence?

property insurance: insurance that indemnifies for loss to the personal and real property of the insured

casualty insurance: insurance that indemnifies the insured for loss due to accident, chance, or negligence

The general type of insurance intended to indemnify for harm to the insured's personal or real property brought about by perils such as fire, theft, and windstorm is termed **property insurance**. In the problem, property insurance would have protected the Neilallens from loss. The type of insurance that indemnifies for losses resulting from accident, chance, or negligence is referred to as **casualty insurance**. There is some overlap between these two. Certain types of casualty insurance (for example, automotive policies) are written to indemnify for casualty and property losses. Examples of casualty insurance include workers' compensation, disability insurance and health insurance. Liability insurance, which protects the insured against other parties' claims of negligence or other tortious conduct, is also a type of casualty insurance.

The purpose of all property and casualty insurance is indemnification for loss. As you recall, this means that a person who experiences a loss recovers no more than the actual value of the loss. This limitation on the amount that can be recovered applies even if the insured has policies with more than one company.

exclusions: exceptions to insurance coverage

Although property and casualty insurance can be obtained to indemnify for almost any peril that might cause a loss, certain circumstances relieve the insurance company from paying. These exceptions to coverage, known as **exclusions**, are expressly stated in the policy. Many states make certain that any exclusions are easily noticeable within a policy by requiring such exclusions to be set in a different style and larger size of type, in a different color of print, or both. Examples of common exclusions include losses due to war, invasion, insurrection (rebellion), nuclear disaster, and depreciation.

WHAT IS A COMPREHENSIVE INSURANCE POLICY?

PROBLEM: The Augusts are a busy couple. Their careers make heavy demands on their time. As a consequence, they do not want to take the time to investigate what types of property and casualty coverages they should have, nor do they want to be bothered with keeping many separate policies current. What should they do to acquire proper insurance coverage?

comprehensive policy: policy that provides a variety of property and casualty coverages

A **comprehensive policy** (which may also be called an all-risk, package, or homeowner's policy) is a policy that may be written to contain all the real property, personal property, and liability coverages needed by the average family. Losses from fire, theft, legal liability, windstorm, hail, vandalism, glass breakage, and other causes may all be insured against under such a policy. In the problem, the Augusts should purchase a comprehensive policy.

As with all insurance policies, there may be certain exclusions. Exclusions with this type of policy could include losses caused by termites, earthquakes, floods, and insurrections. Also excluded could be losses which normally are covered by other insurance. Such losses could be those arising from the ownership and operation of motor vehicles, boats, and aircraft, as well as those arising from business activities. "All-risk" policies cover losses from all perils except those that are specifically excluded in the policy.

In some cases, it may be better to insure against individual risks in separate policies rather than to insure against many risks in a more expensive comprehensive policy. Therefore it is important to know as much as possible about the individual types of property and casualty insurance.

WHAT RISKS DOES FIRE INSURANCE COVER AND HOW DO YOU PROVE THAT A LOSS SHOULD BE INDEMNIFIED UNDER SUCH A POLICY?

PROBLEM: Tapton placed $10,000 in bearer bonds on a footstool in her living room. A visiting friend, not recognizing what they were, used them to start a fire in the fireplace. The ashes were discarded. Could Tapton collect for the loss under her fire insurance policy?

The risk which is covered by fire insurance alone is the direct loss to property resulting from fire, lightning strike, or removal from premises endangered by fire. Any fire insurance contract written to

standard fire policy: fire policy composed of basic provisions required by state law

forms: modifications of the standard fire policy that make it apply to the specific type of property being insured

endorsements: modifications of the standard fire policy and forms to make them apply to special needs

extended coverage endorsement: endorsement that adds protection against several other perils

cover these risks is composed of a basic or **standard fire policy** and one or more **forms** that modify the standard policy to make it apply to the specific type of property being insured. The standard fire policy itself is composed of basic policy provisions required by the law of the state in which the policy is written. All the states have such provisions. Some forms include a Dwellings and Contents Form for homes and a Mercantile Building and Stock Form for businesses. For those who have no need for policies to cover the building itself, such as renters and tenants, there are special forms covering only the contents and other personal property.

The standard policy and forms may also be modified by **endorsements** (also known as *riders*). These endorsements are attached to the policy and forms to provide for special and individual needs. For example, difficulty often arises in determining whether a loss was the direct result of fire, lightning, windstorm, explosion, or some other peril. Suppose that a truck crashes into a building and explodes causing a fire. In such a case, it would be hard to tell how much of the loss was caused by the impact of the truck, how much by the explosion, and how much by the resulting fire. To avoid this difficulty, a fire insurance policy may be issued with an **extended coverage endorsement.** This endorsement adds coverage for damage by windstorm, hail, explosion, riot, smoke, aircraft, and vehicles. Therefore it would not be necessary to determine the exact cause of the damage, since all possible causes would be covered. Because of the frequency of the losses covered by an extended coverage endorsement, such an endorsement usually is added routinely to the Dwellings and Contents Form.

In order to prove that a particular loss should be indemnified by fire insurance you need to:

1. Show that There Was an Actual Fire (Glow or Burning)

The mere scorching or blistering of property by heat is insufficient for establishing loss by fire. There must be an actual fire--that is, either a glow or a burning.

hostile fire: fire started by accident, negligence, or arson; or friendly fire that becomes uncontrollable

friendly fire: fire in its intended place

2. Show that the Loss Was Caused by a Hostile Fire

A **hostile fire** is either of the following:

a. fire started by accident, negligence, or a deliberate act; or
b. **friendly fire** (fire in its intended place) that escapes from its intended place or for other reasons becomes uncontrollable.

For example, any damage caused by smoke escaping from a fireplace or overheated stovepipe is not considered to be from a hostile fire unless the fire actually escapes from the fireplace or stove. In the problem, Tapton could not recover because the fire was not hostile. It is, however, immaterial whether a hostile fire results from an act of ordinary negligence of the insured or from the act of an arsonist. Of course, a hostile fire deliberately set by the insured or someone controlled by the insured voids the insurance policy, thereby releasing the insurer from any obligation.

3. Show that the Hostile Fire Was the Proximate Cause of the Damage

If it can be shown that it was reasonably foreseeable that certain damage or loss might naturally occur as a result of a hostile fire, the fire will be acknowledged as the proximate cause of the damage. (As you recall from Chapter 5, *proximate cause* is that which is the natural and foreseeable cause of loss or injury.) Without the showing of proximate cause, a recovery for loss is impossible. Generally fire is considered the proximate cause not only of damage by burning but also of losses due to scorching, smoke, water used in extinguishing a fire, broken windows or holes chopped in the roof by fire fighters, and the hasty removal to a safe place of goods endangered by fire.

Zantini's grocery store caught fire. Although total destruction was prevented by the efficiency of the fire department, the damage was substantial. Considerable water damage, window and case glass breakage, and smoke contamination of grocery products occurred. Because the fire was the proximate cause of the losses, Zantini's fire insurance would indemnify her.

WHAT IS COINSURANCE?

PROBLEM: Blackrock's fire insurance policy had an 80 percent coinsurance clause. At the time of a fire that totally destroyed the structure, the building was valued at $100,000, and Blackrock had $80,000 of face value coverage. How much of the $100,000 loss would the insurance policy cover?

Over the years, as the capability of fire departments to respond to and contain fires improved, the number of total losses of buildings and contents decreased significantly. Consequently, insureds felt that they needed only to keep the face value of their insurance at a level sufficient to cover part of their property. This, of course, greatly reduced premiums. However, in the event of a total loss, there was the possibility of ruin. Therefore, in response to this situation, insurance companies sensitive to the needs of their clients began offering *coinsurance.*

coinsurance: policy clause resulting in the insurer and the insured sharing the risk of fire loss

Coinsurance is a clause in an insurance policy that requires the insured to maintain coverage equal to a certain percentage of the total current value of the insured property. The coverage amount, therefore, must be increased as the property value increases. In the event of loss, the insurance company will indemnify up to the face amount of the policy unless the insured has failed to keep that face amount at the proper level. For example, suppose that the insured's property has a current value of $50,000 and that the policy has an 80 percent coinsurance clause. Therefore the insured will have to have a $40,000 (80 percent of $50,000) face value on the policy. If the insured has this, the insurance company will pay any loss in full up to a limit of $40,000. The insured will have to bear any amount of loss in excess of the $40,000.

If the insured does not increase the face value of the policy as the property value increases, the insurance company will pay for a smaller portion of the loss. For example, assume that the above insured's property value increases from $50,000 to $100,000, yet the insured keeps the face value at $40,000. If a $50,000 loss occurs, the insurance company will not pay the face value of the policy or $40,000. The insurance company will pay an amount equal to the loss ($50,000) times the fraction of insurance actually carried ($40,000) divided by the amount that should have been carried ($100,000 × 80 percent = $80,000). As a consequence, the company will pay for one-half of the loss. The insured would have to bear the other $25,000.

Remember that the insurance company will never pay more than the face amount of the policy. In the problem at the beginning of this section, even though Blackrock was carrying the full amount required by the coinsurance provisions ($80,000) he would still have to bear $20,000 of the loss ($100,000 − $80,000).

The system of coinsurance is somewhat complex, but it can result in up to a 70 percent savings in premium amounts for policies covering fire-resistant buildings in areas with good fire departments.

WHAT DOES INLAND MARINE INSURANCE COVER?

PROBLEM: While the Bradys were on vacation and traveling by car from New Orleans to Galveston, a suitcase containing more than $700 in personal items was stolen from them. Would their inland marine insurance policy with a personal property floater cover the loss?

Modeled after insurance covering goods being transported on the high seas, **inland marine insurance** was developed by fire insurance companies to indemnify for loss to most personal property while it is being transported across land. However, the carrier, such as the automobile, airplane, or railroad car, is not covered by this insurance. In response to the changing needs of insureds over time, the basic inland marine policy was altered to produce a second type called a **personal property floater.** This was issued to cover any and all of an insured's personal property against practically any peril regardless of the location of the property. The term **floater** means that the protection floats with, or follows, the property. Rather than have the policy written to cover all the insured's personal property, it is also possible to contract for coverage of scheduled (specifically identified) property such as jewelry, furs, stamp collections, musical instruments, livestock, athletic equipment, wedding presents, and photographic equipment. One can also arrange to insure a single piece of personal property, such as an organ or a neon sign. Mail order dealers frequently take out a blanket policy to cover all losses, including breakage and mysterious disappearances of goods shipped. Laundries and dry cleaners may take out policies covering possible losses to customers' property in their possession. Such a policy is known as bailee insurance.

inland marine insurance: insurance that indemnifies for loss to certain personal property in transit

personal property floater: policy providing all-risk coverage of the insured's personal property wherever located

floater: insurance protection that follows the property

Like other all-risk policies, personal property floaters do not cover all risks of loss. There are certain exclusions and limitations. For example, generally excluded losses are those caused by repairing, wear and tear, dampness and extremes in temperature, war, confiscation, and dishonesty of a bailee. In the problem, the Brady's personal property floater would cover the loss of their stolen suitcase and all its contents.

WHAT IS LIABILITY INSURANCE?

PROBLEM: Mercel invited some friends over to her apartment to watch a televised baseball game. While there, one of her friends slipped on a throw rug and broke an ankle. Would Mercel's liability insurance protect Mercel from a lawsuit and possible judgment stemming from the incident?

liability insurance: a type of casualty insurance protecting against claims arising from the insured's negligence

Liability insurance is a type of casualty insurance that protects the insured against claims arising from torts that cause personal injury or property damage to other persons for which the insured may be legally liable. Since many liability insurance claims arise from the operation of motor vehicles, a special type of policy has been developed in response. It will be discussed in Chapter 27. In addition to automobile insurance, however, most individuals, especially business firms, apartment dwellers, and owners of buildings, should carry liability insurance. For most, the cost is small in relation to the protection afforded. In the problem, Mercel's insurer would pay for her defense in court as well as for any settlement or court judgment up to the dollar limit of the policy. If Mercel had included optional medical payments coverage in her policy, the insurer also would pay for any medical expenses, without regard to the fault of the insured.

Persons engaged in providing personal services, such as beauty shop operators, usually carry liability insurance. Persons rendering professional services, such as hospital operators and physicians, usually are covered for malpractice by liability insurance. Television and radio broadcasting companies also carry liability insurance to protect against liability for defamation.

HOW DOES AN INSURED COLLECT AFTER A LOSS?

PROBLEM: Late one summer afternoon, a severe hail and windstorm hit Allen's town. While it was raging, a door to Allen's gift shop was blown open and back against a wall. The expensive etched glass in the door was shattered. What must Allen do to be indemnified under his insurance policy?

Generally, in order to secure indemnification, a demand for payment of a loss covered by an insurance policy is filed with the insurance company. (This procedure applies to all areas of insurance and particularly to property and casualty insurance.) This demand is called a **claim**. Payment of a claim is conditional upon the insurer receiving proper notice of loss and proof of loss from the insured.

claim: demand for payment of an insured loss

Notice of loss must be made in the way required by the contract or by statute. It is usually given to the agent who wrote the policy. Most insurance contracts require immediate notice of loss, often written, if it is practicable. If not, loss must be reported within a reasonable time. If legal action is commenced against the insured, immediate notice to the insurer is required. Prompt notice enables the insurer to investigate and to take other suitable action while the evidence is fresh and witnesses are available. The insured is required by the insurance contract to cooperate with the insurer not only in such an investigation but by helping settle claims and by testifying in court, if necessary. However, the insured should not independently settle claims that should legitimately be handled by the insurance company. If the insured does so by making payments or transferring property without proper authorization from the insurer, the insurance company may rightfully refuse to reimburse the insured.

notice of loss: statement informing the insurer of the loss

Proof of loss must be in writing and must be submitted within 60 to 90 days of the time of loss. Proof of loss is a sworn statement including information as to:

proof of loss: written evidence of an insured loss

1. origin and time of loss,
2. value of and damage to any property,
3. injuries suffered,
4. names of any witnesses, and
5. other insurance carried.

Accordingly, in the problem, Allen must both give notice of loss and furnish the insurer with proof of loss. The proof of loss is usually made out on a form supplied by the insurer. Note that it is extremely helpful to the insured who must file proof of loss to have accurate records of the property for which a claim is being filed. Ideally, these records would contain invoices and photographs of the property.

Once an effective claim is made, the insurer has the option to pay for the loss or to repair, rebuild, or replace the property destroyed or damaged with property of like kind or quality. Depending on the insurance contract, any payment will be equal either to the actual cash value of the property or to the replacement cost of the property. The **actual cash value** is the purchase price less an allowance for age and use. The **replacement cost** is the amount that it would currently take to replace the damaged or destroyed item. Coverage on terms of replacement cost instead of actual cash value can at times be obtained by the payment of an additional premium. In the problem, the insurer would probably have the door glass replaced

actual cash value: property's purchase price less allowance for age and use

replacement cost: current cost of replacing the damaged or destroyed item

or pay for the replacement arranged by Allen rather than pay any money directly to Allen. This method discourages deliberate, fraudulent destruction of property by the insured simply to collect its value.

subrogation: assigned right, by operation of law, to recover damages

Policies generally provide that upon settlement of a loss, the insured gives up and the insurer obtains, by law, the right to recover damages from liable third parties. This is known as **subrogation**.

Uttle cut down a hedgeapple tree in her yard. As a consequence of her negligence, the tree fell across her property line and onto Simpson's garage. Simpson's insurer paid his claim for damage to the garage and its contents and, by so doing, acquired the right to proceed against Uttle for the amount it paid to Simpson.

Subrogation prevents the insured from collecting more than the actual cash loss. For instance, in the example, if Simpson's insurer did not have the right of subrogation, Simpson would collect under the policy and then would possibly recover again in a legal action against Uttle.

Property and casualty insurance policies generally may be assigned only with the consent of the insurer because insurance is a personal contract. However, after a loss has occurred, the insured may assign the right to the money proceeds of the policy without such consent.

HOW IS AN INSURANCE POLICY TERMINATED?

PROBLEM: Pompli's house was totally destroyed by fire. The insurance company paid the full face value of the policy, $125,000, in settlement. Did this terminate the fire insurance policy?

Property or casualty insurance policies generally may be terminated either by cancellation or by expiration of the specified time period. In addition, it is possible that payment of a claim for a total loss will terminate the policy as such payment completes performance of the insurance contract. Even payment of a partial claim may reduce the face value of the policy by the amount of the claim. However, this is not true of all insurance. The standard fire policy for dwellings and for business and personal property provides that the full amount of insurance remains in effect despite the payment of any loss. Thus, Pompli's policy was not terminated. Also, in many casualty policies, the policy also remains in effect despite the payment of any claims.

1. Termination by Cancellation

A policy may be canceled at any time by mutual consent. Statutes and policies usually provide that either party may cancel a policy upon giving notice in accordance with the terms of the contract. The standard fire insurance policy prescribes 5 days' notice by the insurer to cancel the coverage. Other types of insurance may require 10 or 15 days' notice by the insurer.

The courts typically require strict compliance with the appropriate contractual or statutory cancellation procedure. This requirement is especially directed at insurance companies that elect to cancel. That is because the notice provided to the insured by the canceling company may be the only one that the insured will receive. Upon receiving such notice, the insured must immediately find other insurance coverage or else run a significant risk. Of course, the insured may cancel by giving notice to the insurer at any time.

When a policy is canceled, the insured has a right to the return of the unused portion of the premium if it is not voluntarily tendered by the insurer. The amount varies. When the insurance company cancels a policy, the premium is prorated. **Prorate** means to divide proportionately. For example, if a company cancels a one-year policy at the end of four months, it must return to the insured the premiums paid for the eight remaining months. That is, it must return eight-twelfths of the total premiums paid. If the insured cancels the policy, a part of the premium is returned, but the share is less than if the insurance company had canceled the policy. The amount refundable by the insurer is shown in a short rate table in the policy.

prorate: to divide proportionately

2. Termination by Expiration of the Policy

If not previously terminated, most property or casualty insurance policies will go out of force upon the expiration of the time period for which premiums have been paid. The usual time period is one year. If a fire or other peril commences during the policy period and causes damage either before or after the time of expiration, the policyholder is insured. Likewise, if damage is sustained during the life of the policy, the policy covers any consequences of the damage realized after the policy expires.

PREVENTING LEGAL DIFFICULTIES

In Purchasing Insurance. . .

1. consider first those possible losses that would cause serious financial hardship. Be sure to protect yourself against those hardships through the service of an agent and insurance company in which you have confidence and the assurance of good service in case of loss;
2. obtain comparative price quotations. Premiums charged by insurance companies are not uniform for the same coverage;
3. read your insurance policies carefully. Be sure any exclusions do not negate the protection you expect from the policy;
4. read and comply with the notice of loss and proof of loss provisions of your policies. Keep accurate records and photographs of your insured property;
5. know the expiration dates of your policies as well as the methods by which your policies can be canceled. Move quickly to acquire other coverage if a policy lapses or is terminated; and
6. acquire appropriate liability coverage in addition to that provided in your automobile insurance policy.

Strengthening Your Legal Vocabulary

actual cash value
casualty insurance
claim
coinsurance
comprehensive policy
endorsements
exclusions
extended coverage endorsement
floater
forms
friendly fire
hostile fire
inland marine insurance
liability insurance
notice of loss
personal property floater
proof of loss
property insurance
prorate
replacement cost
standard fire policy
subrogation

1. Policy clause in which the insured shares the risk of loss with the insurer in return for lower premiums.
2. Coverage against claims for damage caused by one's torts.
3. Addition to the standard fire policy giving protection against several other perils.
4. Fire that is accidental or that escapes from its intended place.
5. Policy covering movable personal property wherever located.
6. Demand for payment of an insured loss.
7. A right, by operation of law, of the insurer to recover for loss from liable third parties.

8. Protection against losses caused by chance, accident, or negligence.
9. Insured property's purchase price less an allowance for age and use.
10. Modifications of a standard policy that are attached to it to provide for individual insurance needs.

Reviewing Important Points

1. The purpose of all property and casualty insurance is indemnification. This means that one who suffers a loss may recover only (1) the actual value of the property at the time of the loss or (2) the amount of the damage if the loss is not total.
2. A fire insurance policy is payable only when hostile fire or lightning is the proximate cause of the loss. The fire policy will protect against other perils if it has appropriate endorsements, such as the extended coverage endorsement.
3. The personal property floater of inland marine insurance may be written to cover any and all of an insured's personal property against practically any peril regardless of the location of the property.
4. Liability insurance is a form of casualty insurance which protects an insured against damage claims arising from unintentional torts for which the insured is legally liable.
5. When loss occurs, the insured must normally give notice of loss to the insurer as soon as practicable. Proof of loss must also be submitted by the insured within a specified time from the date of loss.
6. Property and casualty insurance policies are terminated by expiration of the time for which they are written. Both insurer and insured have the right to cancel before the expiration of the policy period.
7. A property or casualty insurance policy can be assigned only with the consent of the insurer. The right to recover from an insurer a loss which has already been sustained may be assigned by the insured without consent of the insurer.
8. Coinsurance requires the insured to keep the face value of the policy equal to a certain percentage (usually 80 percent) of the current value of the insured property. Coinsurance usually requires significantly lower premiums from the insured.
9. Payments for damaged or destroyed property may be either the actual cash value or the replacement cost, depending on the the insurance contract.

Applying Law to Everyday Life

1. Baird was insured against fire by Scandinavian Fire Insurance Company. One day while ironing, he left to answer the telephone and negligently forgot to turn off the iron. The iron fell from the ironing board, and the carpet caught fire. The fire then spread to the drapes. As flames engulfed the room,

smoke damaged the remainder of the house. Will the loss be covered by the policy?

2. To protect her inventory, Bistol, owner of an appliance store, carried a coinsurance fire policy. The policy required that Bistol carry insurance in the amount of 80 percent of the current inventory value. Late one night, fire totally destroyed the inventory, which was valued at $100,000 when the loss occurred. The face value of Bistol's policy was $80,000. For how much of the $100,000 loss will the insurance company pay?

3. Dr. Bray performed a tympanoplasty (eardrum replacement) on Azle. The operation appeared to be successful, but one year later the ear canal was found to be completely closed due to the growth of scar tissue from areas where Dr. Bray had drilled improperly. What type of insurance would protect Dr. Bray from a malpractice suit by Azle?

4. Abner was seriously injured when an employee of Jay's Fixit Shop stumbled and pushed her into a glass display case. Jay forgot about the matter and did not notify his insurer until Abner filed suit six months later. Would this delay release the insurer from liability coverage?

5. Following a fire on his property, Tony was paid the face value of his homeowner's policy, $22,000, by the insurer. During the rebuilding of the property, a windstorm did $4,000 more damage. Could Tony collect for the second loss, or had his policy been terminated by payment of the fire loss?

6. The day before her medical and hospitalization insurance was to expire, Natel was injured in a skiing accident. Her hospitalization lasted over a month. Did her insurance benefits end after one day, or did they cover her entire stay in the hospital?

7. When he sold his comic book collection, Turk canceled the insurance contract covering the books. He had paid a year's premium of $120 just three months earlier. Will the insurance company return $90 of the premium?

Solving Case Problems

1. Suit was brought by the insured for failure of the insurer to comply with a "Mexico coverage" endorsement on an automobile policy. Such endorsements are required for coverage when an insured uses his or her car for trips into Mexico. This endorsement limited coverage to within 100 miles of the border. It also referred to collision coverage only, but it carried a "warning" recommending insurance coverage by a Mexican company. While in Nogales, Sonora, Mexico, the insured struck a pedestrian who subsequently died as a result of the injuries. The insured paid medical bills of the victim and reported this and the accident immediately to the insurer, who agreed to reimburse the insured. Under Mexican law, when an automobile acci-

dent causes personal injuries, a settlement has to be reached within 72 hours or the case is transferred to a criminal court. For this reason, when the insurer had not completed its investigation within that time, the plaintiff negotiated the settlements personally. Later when the victim died, the insured also paid the funeral expenses without consent of the insurer. He now seeks reimbursement following refusal of the insurer to pay him. He also asks damages for the refusal of the insurer to defend him in Mexico on criminal charges resulting from the accident. Should the insurer be liable? (*Pacific Insurance Company of New York* v. *Del Monte*, 530 P.2d 380, Ariz.)

2. Sager was injured in an automobile accident. He hired an attorney to handle his case. The suit was dismissed over three years later for failure to prosecute, due to what the trial court found to be the attorney's negligence. The suit was not reentered, as it could have been, before the five-year statute of limitations had run. Sager sued the attorney and received a judgment for $15,000 plus court costs. Nothing was paid on the judgment, so Sager then sought to recover against the insurance company that insured the attorney with professional liability insurance. It refused to pay, claiming in part that if the attorney had notified it after the suit was dismissed, it would have seen that the suit was reentered before the five-year statute of limitations had run. Instead, the attorney notified the insurer only after the five years had passed. Is this an adequate defense for the insurance company? (*Sager* v. *St. Paul Fire and Marine Insurance Company*, 461 S.W.2d 704, Mo.)

3. The Schaeffers' insurance company refused to pay when portions of their roof separated on the third day of a period of high winds, even though coverage against "windstorm" was clearly in the policy. The roof separation allowed rain to fall into the interior of the insured structure and portions of the roof, wood, brick, and plaster followed. The winds were clocked at the nearby Weather Bureau Office at 40, 31, and 14 mph respectively on each of the three days. The insurance company claims that the winds did not constitute a "windstorm" and that, since the collapse occurred when the strength of the wind was only 14 mph, a structural defect caused the damage. Decide. (*Schaeffer* v. *Northern Assurance Company*, 177 S.W.2d 868, Mo.)

4. Taff and Hardwick were in an automobile accident that resulted in a $5,000 judgment for Taff against Hardwick. This is an action by Taff to collect the amount of the judgment. The defendant insurance company denied liability claiming failure of the insured, Hardwick, to cooperate in defending the action, as required in the policy. The policy reads as follows: "Insured shall cooperate with the company and upon the company's request shall attend hearings and trials, and shall assist in effecting settlements, securing and giving evidence, obtaining the attendance of witnesses, and in the conduct of suits." The insurer presented evidence that it had unsuccessfully sought to locate Hardwick by letter, telephone calls, and investigators so that he could cooperate in his defense. Is the insurer released from its obligation to pay the judgment? (*Taff v. Hardwick and Empire Fire and Marine Insurance Company of Omaha*, 419 S.W.2d 482, Mo.)

5. On June 1, 1969, New York Underwriters Insurance Company issued a fire and windstorm policy covering the ice cream stand of Beach Treat, Inc. The policy was to expire June 1, 1972. The policy called only for "a five days written notice of cancellation." The policy did not require that Beach Treat inform New York of changes of address. On January 20, 1971, New York tried to cancel the policy. The written notice sent by New York was returned undelivered as Beach Treat had changed addresses. No other action was taken until after April 6, 1971, when the roof of the ice cream stand was damaged by a windstorm. Beach Treat filed a claim with New York on April 9, 1971, and was greeted with notice of the cancellation and the offer of a premium refund effective January 20, 1971. Was the insurance company legally obligated to pay for the damage? (*Beach Treat, Inc. v. New York Underwriters Ins. Co.*, 301 A.2d 298, Del.)

27

Automobile Insurance

1. You buy a new sports car and immediately purchase automobile insurance. You allow a friend to take the car for a test drive. He carelessly loses control on a curve and demolishes the car. Your friend is unhurt but lacks insurance and money or other financial resources needed to pay for the loss. Will your automobile insurance cover the loss?
2. While on vacation you legally park your car alongside a road in order to walk along a nature trail. When you return, you find that your car has been sideswiped by a hit-and-run driver. The other driver is not apprehended and repairs to your car will cost more than $1,200. Must you bear the loss?
3. When you are returning to an out-of-state school after the holidays, your new car catches fire due to faulty wiring. Your clothes, skiing equipment, and tape deck are all destroyed with the car. Will the comprehensive coverage of your automobile insurance cover all the losses?

WHAT KINDS OF PROTECTION ARE AVAILABLE IN AN AUTOMOBILE INSURANCE POLICY?

PROBLEM: Lisso is at fault in an automobile accident in which two of his passengers are injured. Will Lisso's full-coverage automobile insurance policy pay for their medical treatment?

Automobile insurance offers protection to the insured from loss or liability in the following four major instances:

1. when the insured is liable for injury to or death of other people, or for damage to the property of others, resulting from the ownership, maintenance, or use of the specified motor vehicle;
2. when the insured must pay for the medical treatment of occupants of the insured's car who are injured in an accident. Therefore, in the problem, Lisso's policy would pay for his passengers' medical treatment;
3. when the insured's own vehicle is damaged, destroyed, or stolen; and
4. when the insured is involved in an accident with a driver who is liable but is uninsured and potentially insolvent or who is a hit-and-run criminal.

WHAT IS THE EXTENT OF THE LIABILITY PROTECTION AVAILABLE UNDER AN AUTOMOBILE INSURANCE POLICY?

PROBLEM: Jerry was driving his friend Bill's car, at Bill's request, when he negligently smashed into the rear of Green's station wagon. Jerry's parents had an automobile policy that covered Jerry while he was driving someone else's car. In addition, Bill's policy covered anyone driving Bill's car with permission. Which insurer will have to pay for the property and personal damage liability claims made by Green?

Liability coverage under an automobile insurance policy provides for the defense of the insured—and protects against the payment of damages by the insured—for negligent ownership, maintenance, or use of a motor vehicle. The coverage is generally found in a Family Automobile Policy or a Personal Automobile Policy. It extends to all drivers who are members of the named insured's household and to any person not in the household who drives the insured's car with proper permission. (In the latter case, the policy makes the driver an additional insured.) The coverage of these parties is through a policy provision known as an **omnibus clause**. Some companies require that policies on cars whose owners are students or members of the armed forces must have a special endorsement. This endorsement declares that the coverage is void if the car is driven by anyone other than the insured or a member of the insured's family.

omnibus clause: clause which covers all drivers who are members of the insured's household and any person who is not a member but is permitted to drive the insured's car

Liability insurance also commonly provides coverage for the insured and members of the insured's family when such persons are operating nonowned vehicles with the owner's permission. This coverage applies to all borrowed or substitute automobiles. Examples would include those automobiles used when the car described in the policy has broken down or is being repaired or serviced. Also, if one purchases another automobile to replace the insured car, generally all the coverages under the policy apply to the replacement car for a limited time as specified in the policy.

When one becomes liable for damage or injury while driving a nonowned vehicle, the car owner's policy provides the primary coverage. The driver's policy then provides coverage up to its face amount for any excess liability. In the problem, Bill's insurer would pay any liability claims up to the policy limit and the remainder would have to be paid by the family policy of Jerry's parents.

Because insurers are contractually liable for legitimate claims against their insured, the insurers have the right to either settle such claims out of court or to defend their insured in court. Since the insurer has potential liability under the policy, only the insurer can make a settlement with claimants against the insured. If the insurer requires the presence of the insured as a witness at any legal hearings, most automobile insurance policies provide for payment of lost wages to the insured.

Liability claims against the insured which the insurer may have to pay include bodily injury or death of third parties (that is, persons other than the insured or insurer) and damage to the property of third parties.

1. Bodily Injury and Death Coverage

PROBLEM: While driving in a state with a guest law, Stearns was involved in an accident when she negligently forgot to signal her turn. Her passenger was an acquaintance, Harshaw, whom she was giving a short ride home. The other driver was not negligent. Can Harshaw recover for his injuries against either driver?

bodily injury insurance: insurance which protects against liability for bodily injury to or death of others

The first of two major types of coverages provided by automobile liability insurance is for bodily injury. **Bodily injury insurance** protects the insured against liability for bodily injury to or death of other persons. This type of coverage is usually issued with top limits for each injured person and for each *occurrence* (accident). For example, coverage of $25,000 for each person and $50,000 for each occurrence may be obtained. In the insurance industry's "shorthand," this is called 25/50. By paying comparatively small additional premiums, an insured may have substantially higher limits, such as 50/100 or 100/300. Damages in excess of the policy limits would have to be paid for by the insured.

guest laws: claims which disallow suits based on ordinary negligence, brought by guests against drivers

Some states have statutes known as guest laws, although the number of states that still have guest laws in effect is decreasing. **Guest laws** provide that a guest in a car does not have a legal right to sue the driver for damages for injury caused by the driver's ordinary negligence. That is, a guest can sue for injuries only if the driver was grossly negligent (for example, drove while intoxicated) or willfully caused the accident. A *guest* is defined as a nonpaying rider or a person who regularly participates in a car pool. In the problem, Harshaw was a guest. Because Stearns was negligent (not grossly negligent) and because the other driver was not negligent, Harshaw cannot recover against either driver. Guest statutes do not, of course, prevent guests from suing negligent drivers of other cars who cause injury to them.

collusion: agreement to misrepresent facts to gain an advantage

Guest laws relieve drivers from the fear of lawsuits from casual passengers. Guest laws also help to prevent collusion. **Collusion** is an agreement between parties to misrepresent facts in order to gain an advantage. Prior to guest laws, such an act typically involved the passenger (guest) and the driver of the other car in the accident. Together, they would falsely testify to the negligence of the driver of the car in which the passenger was riding. They would then collect damages based on the alleged negligence. Because a guest law prohibits a passenger from bringing suit for mere negligence, the motive for collusion disappears.

2. Property Damage Coverage

PROBLEM: Samuels parked his van on a steep hill but failed to set the brakes properly. The van rolled down the street, jumped the curb, and crashed into the Mashburns' car, which was parked in their driveway. The van also took off a corner of their home, damaging some furniture. The Mashburns claimed $2,400 damage to the car, $9,000 to the residence, and $1,400 to the furniture. They also claimed the cost of renting a substitute car while their own was being repaired. Was Samuels's insurer required to pay for all the damage and for the rental of the substitute car?

The second major area of coverage provided by automotive liability insurance is for property damage. **Property damage insurance** protects the insured against liability for damage to a third person's property. This coverage includes not only the property itself but also any other related losses proximately caused by the loss of the property. Hence, the Mashburns were correct in claiming not only the cost of damages to their house, car, and furniture but also the amount of rental paid for the substitute car.

property damage insurance: insurance which protects against liability for damage to the property of third persons

Property damage liability coverage may be written for $10,000. However, this amount may not cover the loss. Higher coverage is available for a small additional premium. A policy with bodily injury coverage of $25,000 and $50,000 and property damage coverage of $25,000 would be indicated as 25/50/25.

WHAT IS THE EXTENT OF THE MEDICAL PAYMENTS COVERAGE AVAILABLE UNDER AN AUTOMOBILE INSURANCE POLICY?

PROBLEM: Bean was hit by a car while she was jogging. The driver of the car was not at fault. Bean's medical bills were large. Could she use the medical payments coverage of her automobile insurance policy to help pay them?

Medical payments coverage pays for the reasonable medical claims of occupants of the insured's vehicle who are injured in an automobile accident. An *occupant* is defined as one who is in a vehicle, is upon a vehicle, is entering a vehicle, or is leaving a vehicle. The coverage also applies to the insured and the insured's family members while such persons are driving or riding in another's auto. This kind of coverage is mainly for car occupants. However, it also covers the named insured and the family members if such persons

medical payments coverage: coverage for the reasonable accident-related medical claims of the occupants of the insured's vehicle

are struck by an automobile while walking, riding bikes, roller skating, or sledding. Therefore, in the problem, Bean's automobile insurance policy would help pay for her medical expenses.

With medical payments coverage, payment will be made even if the driver is not liable and the state has a guest law. Necessary medical, surgical, dental, and X-ray services, and even funeral expenses, will be paid for up to the per-person limit in the policy. The limit is usually $1,000 to $5,000 per person, but there is no limit per accident. The expenses must be incurred within one year from the date of the accident, however.

As with liability coverage under an automobile insurance policy, medical payments coverage generally requires that when a loss is suffered while the insured is driving another's vehicle, the car owner's policy provide the primary coverage. Nevertheless, medical payments coverage provides an important portion of the overall insurance coverage many motorists desire.

WHAT PROTECTION IS PROVIDED BY HAVING COLLISION OR COMPREHENSIVE INSURANCE COVERAGE FOR YOUR AUTOMOBILE?

PROBLEM: Reel had failed to have the brakes of her car serviced when they began to show signs of wear. One day, when she was driving down the steep driveway from her home to the street, the brakes failed. Before she could use the emergency brake, the car slammed into the side of a truck driven by Holmes. There were no injuries but Reel's car sustained $1,700 in damages, and it cost $875 to repair the truck. How will the damage claims be handled?

collision insurance: insurance which protects against damage to the insured's vehicle caused by collision or by upset

comprehensive insurance: insurance which protects against damage to the insured's vehicle from causes other than collision or upset

Two kinds of insurance indemnify insureds for damage to their own vehicles. The first, **collision insurance**, protects against direct and accidental damage to the insured's vehicle caused either by collision with another object or by upset. The second, **comprehensive insurance**, also known as *other than collision insurance*, covers all damage to the insured's vehicle from causes other than collision or upset. These causes include fire, theft, water, vandalism, and breakage of glass for any reason.

Under collision insurance, only the actual cash value of the loss is payable. If the insured carries full coverage, the insurer pays the entire amount up to the limit of the policy. Generally the coverage will be subject to a *deductible* (stated initial amount not paid by the insurer). The amount of the deductible varies from $50 to $500. It usually is either $100 or $200. The deductible is applied to each loss that occurs during the policy period. Thus, for each such loss, the insured pays for the loss up to the amount of the deductible, and the insurer pays any excess.

In the problem, because the accident was Reel's fault, the full $875 in damages to Holmes's truck would be covered by Reel's automobile liability (property damage) insurance. The $1,700 in damages to Reel's car would be paid by Reel's insurer under her collision coverage. If Reel had a deductible for her collision insurance, as most insureds do, she would receive $1,700 less the amount of that deductible. For example, if the deductible were $500, she would receive $1,200 and would have to pay the remaining $500 portion of the loss herself. If neither party were determined to be at fault, both would have to look to the collision coverage of their own policies for indemnification.

Deductibles are utilized to lower the premiums the insured must pay for the coverage. Deductibles are especially effective in bringing lower premiums for collision insurance because most "fender bender" collision claims are relatively small compared to the relatively high costs of investigating, inspecting, and settling such claims.

In the event of loss from collision or upset, the insured must give notice to the insurer "as soon as practicable." Failure to do so releases the insurer from its obligation. The insured also has an obligation to protect the automobile from further loss. Once proper notice of loss and proof of loss have been received, the insurance company has the option of either paying for the loss or repairing or replacing the lost or damaged property.

Like collision insurance, comprehensive insurance will pay only the actual cash value of the loss. Also, a deductible is usually written into the policy so that the insured will have lower premiums. Comprehensive insurance is basically an all-risk coverage excluding collision and upset. Definitions of the various perils covered by comprehensive insurance are the same as those for other property insurance. For example, theft includes loss not only of the car but also of any part of the car, such as hubcaps. However, loss of clothing and other personal property left in the car generally is not covered unless the loss is by fire. Similarly, most policies require extra premiums to cover citizen band radios and tape decks. Any damage done to a car, such as broken locks, is covered.

Yakane's car, which contained some gifts and a camera, was stolen. When the car was recovered, the gifts and camera were missing. Also, the car tools and tires had been removed, and the locks had been smashed. Under his comprehensive coverage, Yakane could recover for the loss of the car tools, tires, and locks. However, comprehensive insurance would not cover the loss of either the gifts or the camera.

The typical comprehensive policy provides that the insured must notify the police in the event of theft of an automobile. Also, as with all insurance losses, the insured must notify the insurer of any loss as soon as practicable. In case of theft, the typical policy also provides that the insurer will reimburse the insured for expenses (up to a specified amount each day for 30 days) for the use of a substitute automobile or for taxicab fares.

WHY CARRY UNINSURED MOTORISTS COVERAGE?

PROBLEM: Brace worked in an exclusive restaurant to earn money for college. While he was driving home from work late one evening, another vehicle, driven by a drunken driver, ran a red light and struck his car. Brace was severely injured and incurred thousands of dollars of medical costs. In addition, he could not work for the remainder of the summer. Unfortunately Brace could recover no damages from the other driver, who had no liability insurance and few personal assets. Must Brace absorb the loss personally?

Sometimes accidents occur which are caused by the negligence of drivers who are either uninsured and potentially insolvent or who leave the scene of the accident and cannot be located. In either situation, the innocent party's own collision and medical payments insurance may help absorb that party's loss. However, all the medical expenses may not be covered. Also, payments for lost wages or support and for pain and suffering would not be collectible. Consequently, many car owners carry **uninsured motorists coverage.**

uninsured motorists coverage: coverage for losses caused by the negligence of uninsured drivers and hit-and-run drivers

Such coverage allows the insured motorist to collect damages from his or her own insurance company when the loss is caused either by a negligent driver who is uninsured and financially unable to pay or by a hit-and-run driver. In the problem, Brace could collect his medical expenses, as well as compensation for lost wages and for pain and suffering, from his own insurer if he had uninsured motorists coverage. In most states, the coverage is limited to compensation for bodily injury, death, lost wages or support, and pain and suffering. Generally payment for property damage is excluded.

Some insurance companies are now offering **underinsured motorists coverage,** which compensates the insured when a negligent driver does not have sufficient insurance to cover the losses incurred by his or her negligence. Underinsured coverage excludes payment for property damage as does uninsured motorists coverage.

underinsured motorists coverage: coverage for losses not compensated for by the insurance of minimally insured drivers

The liability of the insurer in uninsured motorist cases depends upon establishing that the uninsured motorist, or the hit-and-run driver, was negligent and would be liable if sued. In addition, in an accident with a hit-and-run driver, the collision must have been immediately reported to the police. Also, a reasonable attempt to locate the hit-and-run driver must have been made. Such requirements help to prevent fraud such as a driver involved in a one-car accident reporting it as a hit-and-run accident. Finally, for uninsured motorists coverage to apply, actual contact with another car is required. Thus, injuries to the insured caused by the insured swerving off the road to avoid a collision with another car would not be covered.

In a governmental attempt to solve the problems caused by hit-and-run drivers and uninsured motorists, a few states have **unsatisfied judgment funds**. Such a fund is financed by taxes on insurance companies and by automobile license fees. Under this plan, a party suffering damage must first obtain a judgment. If the judgment is not collectible, a claim may be made to the fund to satisfy the judgment.

unsatisfied judgment funds: pools of money used to pay uncollectible judgments

In addition, most states have **financial responsibility laws**. These laws require that in an accident resulting in injury, death, or property damage greater than a specified amount, the driver or owner must show proof of the ability to pay a liability judgment. In some states, the showing may be accomplished by producing an insurance policy in a specified amount. In other states, either a security deposit large enough to pay any judgment that might be rendered or a signed release from the other driver is required. Failure to comply typically results in the suspension of the driver's license, suspension of the vehicle registration, or suspension of both. Unfortunately these statutes do little to protect the victim of the first accident of a financially irresponsible person. In addition, there are only a very few states which require that liability insurance be obtained before a driver's license is issued.

financial responsibility laws: laws that require owners and drivers to furnish evidence of the ability to pay damages to third parties

Some car owners find it difficult to obtain liability insurance to satisfy the requirements of the financial responsibility law of their state. Such difficulty may be due to the person's age, driving record, traffic violations, or other reasons. To enable such persons to comply with this law, an **assigned risk plan** has been devised. (It is also known as an *automobile insurance plan*). Under such a plan, a person who has been refused insurance can apply to be assigned to an insurance company that will issue to that person the minimum liability insurance required by the state. The premium, however, is usually much higher than that charged other drivers for similar coverage. Often this type of insurer voluntarily will insure such a person at regular rates if there has been a clear record for a year or two.

assigned risk plan: plan under which a person who has been refused automobile insurance can obtain the minimum required amount of coverage

HOW DOES NO-FAULT INSURANCE WORK?

PROBLEM: Benjamin made an illegal U-turn in front of Lombardi's car. A crash occurred. Benjamin and Lombardi each had full insurance coverage. Benjamin's car sustained $1,350 in damages; Lombardi's, $1,700. In addition, Lombardi had $2,200 of damages from medical expenses and lost wages. How would the claims for damages be settled in a state with a no-fault insurance law?

No-fault insurance is insurance that requires that parties to an automobile accident be indemnified by their own insurance company regardless of who is at fault. Thus, an injured person does not have to go to court and prove that the other party caused the accident. In this respect, no-fault insurance is similar to workers' compensation (see Chapter 23) and medical coverage insurance.

no-fault insurance: insurance that requires parties to an automobile accident to be indemnified by their own insurance company regardless of fault

No-fault insurance takes the place of any damages that might be awarded in a court action. However, no-fault statutes often provide that an injured person with medical claims larger than a designated amount, or with permanent injuries, may sue for all damages caused by the party at fault, including claims for pain and suffering.

In most states that provide for no-fault insurance, such insurance is mandatory and usually applies only to bodily injury and death (not to property damage). The statutes of most of these states provide that claims may cover medical costs, including hospitalization up to a specified amount, such as $5,000. Also provided for are (1) payment for loss of income or of wages for a maximum period of time, (2) a death benefit, and (3) limited payments to survivors in case of a death. In some states, general damages (including payment for permanent disability and disfigurement) may be recovered. In return for these payments, injured parties give up their right to sue the other party for damages. Or the injured parties are severely restricted in their right to sue for general damages.

Accordingly, in the problem, under most no-fault laws, Benjamin's insurer would have to pay the $1,350 less deductibles from the collision coverage of Benjamin's policy. Lombardi's claim of $1,700 in vehicle damage would similarly be collected from Lombardi's insurer. Lombardi's additional claim for $2,200 in medical expenses and lost wages would also be collected from Lombardi's insurer, up to the allowable maximum, under the no-fault provisions of the policy.

PREVENTING LEGAL DIFFICULTIES

For Automobile Insurance, Remember that . . .

1. one of the most frequently incurred and potentially disastrous liabilities is that resulting from a lawsuit based on bodily injury and property damage in an automobile accident. Consequently, to protect yourself, carry adequate automobile liability coverage.
2. too many drivers fail to carry insurance. Because often such drivers are also potentially insolvent, they are judgment-proof. Therefore, if it is available, carry uninsured motorists coverage. Or if your state requires no-fault insurance, obtain that type of coverage.
3. if you are sued as a result of an accident and you have complied with the policy requirements, your insurer is required to defend you. Therefore, if you are involved in an accident, report it to your insurer immediately no matter how trivial it may appear. Failure to notify the insurer may release the insurer from liability on your policy. Such failure may also excuse the insurer from defending the suit against you.
4. you should deal with a reputable insurance agent. In selecting the proper coverage, and especially in case of an accident, your agent can be of great help.
5. you should read your policy carefully; it is your contract. If you wait until an accident occurs, it may be too late. If there is something about your policy that you don't understand, ask your agent to explain it.
6. if you buy a car in a secured transaction, you will probably be required to protect the seller's interest with collision and comprehensive coverages.
7. your medical payments coverage covers you not only while you are driving another car but if you are struck by a vehicle while you are afoot.

Strengthening Your Legal Vocabulary

assigned risk plan
bodily injury insurance
collision insurance
collusion
comprehensive insurance
financial responsibility laws
guest laws
medical payments coverage
no-fault insurance
omnibus clause
property damage insurance
underinsured motorists coverage
uninsured motorists coverage
unsatisfied judgment funds

1. Insurance which protects the insured against liability for damage to the property of third persons resulting from his or her operation of a motor vehicle.
2. Clause which covers all drivers who are members of the insured's household and any person who is not a member but who has permission to drive the insured's car.
3. Arrangement that enables a person whose application for automobile insurance has been rejected to obtain the minimum amount of coverage.
4. Coverage that pays the reasonable medical claims of occupants of the insured's vehicle who are injured in an automobile accident.
5. Insurance coverage that allows insured motorists to collect damages for bodily injury and death from their own insurers if the accidents are caused by the negligence of uninsured motorists with limited resources or hit-and-run drivers.
6. Insurance covering loss or damage to the insured's car from all causes other than collision or upset.
7. Type of automobile insurance program in which recovery of most losses is sought from an insured's own insurance company regardless of who was legally responsible for the accident.
8. Statutes denying nonpaying riders the right to sue the car's driver for injuries sustained in a car accident caused by the driver's ordinary negligence.
9. Insurance covering direct and accidental loss to the insured's car caused either by collision with another object or by upset.
10. Insurance which protects the insured against liability for bodily injury to or death of third parties resulting from his or her operation of a motor vehicle.

Reviewing Important Points

1. The basic purposes of automobile insurance are:
   a. to pay claims for personal injury or property damage resulting from an auto accident which was caused by the insured's negligence,
   b. to pay accident-related medical expenses for occupants of the insured's vehicle,
   c. to indemnify the insured for damage to the insured's vehicle, and
   d. to indemnify the insured when he or she is involved in an accident with a

driver who is liable but is uninsured and has inadequate financial resources, or who is a hit-and-run driver.

2. Under an omnibus clause, insurance coverage may be extended to others who drive the insured's car as well as to members of the insured's family who drive the cars of others with permission.
3. With uninsured motorists coverage, the insured can collect from his or her insurer damages for bodily injury or death caused by negligent drivers who are uninsured and financially limited, or who are hit-and-run drivers.
4. Most states require motorists to furnish evidence of their ability to pay damages when they are involved in an accident. For those persons unable to obtain insurance, assigned risk plans are available.
5. No-fault insurance, which indemnifies the insured for various losses sustained in an auto accident regardless of who had legal responsibility for the accident, is now required by a number of states.
6. The amount that the insurer pays on a claim under collision or comprehensive insurance is reduced if one chooses to carry deductibles to hold down premium costs.

Applying Law to Everyday Life

1. Tyson negligently backed into Wyatt's car. Tyson was very apologetic and, after a few minutes of negotiating, paid Wyatt for the damage. Tyson then asked his automobile insurance company to reimburse him under its liability coverage for the amount he had paid Wyatt. Must the insurance company do so?

2. Park carried 25/50/10 liability insurance. Park borrowed the pickup of his brother-in-law, Dyer, to get a load of firewood. Dyer had the minimum liability coverage required in his state, 10/25/5. Park struck a pedestrian, Stafford, who sued and received judgment for $20,000. How would Stafford collect on this judgment?

3. McMurray was injured when she lost control of her panel truck on a curve and ran off the road. McMurray was insured for bodily injury and property damage. She sought to collect from her insurance company for hospital and medical expenses, loss of wages, and damage to her truck. Will she be able to collect?

4. Temerant's son, Don, sustained a broken arm in an accident while riding in Smith's car. There was a guest law in the state, and Smith was not grossly negligent. Smith had the minimum liability insurance coverage required by law. What other insurance coverage might be available to cover the expenses of treating the broken arm?

5. Beuttrie took a shortcut over a graveled road while driving home one evening. A piece of gravel hit his windshield and broke it. The windshield cost

$400 to replace. Beuttrie's collision deductible was $500 and his other than collision deductible was $400. How much of the damage amount would his insurer pay?

6. Flanagan's car was hit broadside by Scott's sports car. Flanagan had the car repaired for $480. However, she was indemnified by her insurer for only $380, since she had a $100 deductible. When Scott's insurer declined to pay, Flanagan filed suit in small claims court and received judgment for $480. Could Flanagan keep the entire $480?

7. While in high school, Blount had received a number of traffic tickets and had been at fault in several auto accidents. Therefore Blount's driver's license was revoked. A few months after graduation, Blount again became eligible for a license. To obtain a license, Blount needed liability insurance. However, no company voluntarily would insure Blount even though Blount needed to be able to drive to work. What can Blount do to obtain the needed insurance?

Solving Case Problems

1. Gary Stallings was on active duty with the National Guard when a three-quarter-ton truck he was driving overturned and caused a fellow Guard member and passenger, Robert Ward, bodily injury. Stallings was the named insured in Michigan Mutual Liability Company's "Auto-Guard" Family Insurance Policy. When Ward sued Stallings for the injuries, Michigan Mutual refused to defend Stallings and denied responsibility to pay any judgment that might result. In addition to other coverages, the policy obligated the company to defend and pay judgments up to the policy limit if the insured was driving a "nonowned automobile." The company maintained that the three-quarter-ton army truck with canvas top and doors was not an automobile. Decide. (*Michigan Mutual Liability Co. v. Stallings*, 523 S.W.2d 539, Mo.)

2. Jackson purchased a 1968 Chevrolet Caprice automobile and insured it with Teachers Insurance Company. Four months after her purchase, the car was reclaimed from her by members of the Los Angeles Police Department. The car previously had been stolen from the National Research Chemical Company and was returned to its rightful owner. Jackson then filed a claim under the Teachers policy for loss due to theft. Although the Teachers policy included theft coverage, the company refused to pay. Therefore Jackson brought suit. Should she recover? (*Jackson v. Teachers Insurance Company*, 30 Cal. App. 3d 341, 106 Cal. Rptr. 208)

3. The Sacketts' automobile engine was extensively damaged when a service station attendant did not properly replace the radiator cap. The coolant escaped, and so the engine overheated and was damaged. The Sacketts'

insurer, Farmers Insurance Exchange, refused to cover the $336 loss under the comprehensive clause in the automobile policy. The comprehensive portion of the policy covered "loss . . . by any accidental means except collision" but excluded "loss . . . due to mechanical failure." The Sacketts brought suit against the insurer. The insurer justified its refusal to pay by claiming that the damage was due to mechanical failure. Decide. (*Sackett v. Farmers Insurance Exchange,* 47 Cal. Rptr. 350)

4. Gallup had a family insurance policy on his motor vehicles. Under medical coverage, the policy obligated the insurer to pay all reasonable expenses for necessary medical care for injuries "caused by accident . . . through being struck by an automobile." Gallup's son, Keith, was riding his motorbike from school on his way to lunch when he ran into the rear of an automobile that was stopped, signaling to turn left. Keith was injured in the accident. Did Keith's injuries result from being struck by an automobile? (*Gallup v. St. Paul Insurance Company,* 515 S.W.2d 249)

5. Nancy Brake, the plaintiff, was left a widow with five minor children when her husband was killed in an automobile accident caused solely by the negligence of Donald Miller. Because Miller maintained only the minimum amount of insurance required under the state's motor vehicle operator's financial responsibility law, she was able to recover only $4,000 of the $50,000 in damages she alleged. The Brakes had their own automobile insurance policies with a total of $40,000 uninsured motorists protection. Nancy Brake brought suit against her and her deceased husband's insurer for the $40,000. She claimed that the definition of "uninsured," contained in the state statute which required uninsured motorists coverage to be made available by insurers, was ambiguous and that it should be construed to mean "underinsured" as well. Otherwise she could not collect from her insurer and actually would have been better off if Miller had no insurance whatsoever rather than the small amount he actually carried. Should Nancy Brake be allowed to collect under the uninsured motorists provisions of her policies? (*Brake v. MFA Mutual Insurance Company,* 525 S.W.2d 109, Mo.)

28

Life Insurance

1. When she entered graduate school two and a half years ago, one of your acquaintances bought a $100,000 life insurance policy and named her parents as beneficiaries. Last week, severely depressed over personal problems, she committed suicide. Must the insurance company pay $100,000 to the parents?
2. In good health but concerned about the financial consequences for her family if she were to be killed in an accident, your friend's mother buys a $50,000 triple indemnity personal life insurance policy. How much would the insurance company pay to her beneficiaries in the event of her accidental death?
3. A student contracted for life insurance, naming his mother as beneficiary. Later, he married and wished to make his wife the beneficiary. Could he do so?

WHAT IS LIFE INSURANCE?

> **PROBLEM:** Borrego had faithfully paid premiums on his life insurance policy for more than 28 years when he developed a life-endangering kidney disease. When he was about to pay the next premium, he received from the insurance company a notice that his policy had been canceled. Is the insurance company legally permitted to cancel?

Life insurance is a contractual arrangement under which an insurer promises to pay an agreed upon amount of money to a named party upon the death of a particular person. Given the uncertainties of today's world and its fast-paced mode of living, such insurance is crucial to families, businesses, and responsible individuals throughout our society. As a consequence, it is very important to know how such insurance varies from the other types of insurance that have been discussed. For example, with life insurance:

life insurance: insurance in which an insurer promises to pay a specified amount upon the death of a person

1. The Event Insured Against—Death—Is Bound to Happen

The risk is not whether it will happen, as with property and casualty insurance, but that it will happen at some unknown and possibly premature time in the future, when the individual still has one or more dependents.

2. There Is No Possibility of Partial Loss

In life insurance, the amount payable is the *face value* (face amount) of the policy less any outstanding loans which may have been made against the policy.

3. The Purpose Is Not Primarily to Indemnify for Loss

Although it is possible to estimate the potential lifetime earnings of an individual, such a figure would not be an accurate value of the life. Because it is impossible to calculate such a value, face amounts for policies can vary widely—even for persons of the same age—and yet be legally enforceable.

4. A Savings Function May Be Incorporated into the Policy

Many policies include a clause under which part of the premium is invested by the insurance company for the benefit of the policyholder. The investment accumulates earnings over the life of the policy.

5. The Probability of Loss Increases Each Year

The likelihood of death increases with age. Therefore the older one is when entering a life insurance contract, the higher the premium is.

6. Insurable Interest Requirements Change

Whereas an insurable interest in property must exist at the time of the loss (see Chapter 25), an insurable interest in a life is required only at the time of contracting.

7. The Right to Cancel Is Restricted

The insurer agrees that if there was an insurable interest and the premiums are paid when they are due, the contract will remain in force. This is a very important feature of life insurance. The insurance company cannot cancel the contract at any time it wishes. Only the policy owner has this right. Therefore, in the problem, the insurance company could not cancel.

8. The Right to Assign the Policy Is Expanded

Consent of the insurer is required before a property insurance contract can be assigned. However, a life insurance policy can be assigned without the insurer's consent.

9. A Minor's Contractual Rights Are Expanded

In most states, minors' contracts for life and disability insurance are valid if the contracts are either on the minors or on their dependents.

WHAT KINDS OF LIFE INSURANCE POLICIES ARE AVAILABLE?

PROBLEM: Simpkins wants a life insurance policy which provides adequate coverage on her life and also builds up a cash value that earns interest comparable to current money-market investments. What type of insurance would be best for her?

Within the past few years, a variety of new life insurance plans have been developed by the insurance industry to meet the demands of competition from other investment opportunities offering a savings function. Underlying all of the life insurance plans, however, are the two basic types of coverage that have been offered for decades. The first of these types involves the payment of the minimum premium necessary to buy only life insurance on the insured for stated periods of time, generally one, five, or ten years. At the end of that period or upon payment of the face value at the death of the insured, the contract ends with no further obligation on either party. This type is generally called **term insurance**.

term life insurance: insurance which covers the life of the insured for a specified period only

The second type of coverage requires the policyholder to pay a premium significantly larger than the minimum premium necessary for term insurance coverage. The surplus amount of the premium is then placed in one of the various savings, investment, or endowment plans run by the insurance company. For many years, this second type or *combination* coverage was favored because the necessity of maintaining the life insurance protection by paying the premium forced participation in the savings or investment plan. Without such a discipline, many families would not have put money aside as a reserve. During the inflation of the recent past, however, the rates paid on other forms of savings, for example certificates of deposit or money-market mutual funds, increased much more rapidly than the rates paid on the savings element in ordinary life insurance policies. As a consequence, the established types of combination policies declined in popularity. Several new combination plans have been introduced with higher interest rates and greater flexibility. These have been popular, and Simpkins, in the problem, would be wise to consider such new combination policies.

The most common term and combination policies available today are:

level term life insurance: term insurance which pays the same amount regardless of when the death occurs in the term

1. Term Life Insurance Policies

decreasing term life insurance: term insurance in which the amount to be paid upon death declines during the term

There are two basic types of term insurance. The first, **level term life insurance**, requires the payment of the same premium amount throughout the term in return for a face value that will not change during that term. The second and less expensive type is **decreasing term life insurance**. It requires the payment of the same premium amount throughout the term in return for a face value that will steadily decrease during that term. Decreasing term can be used to insure that a credit instrument such as a mortgage (which steadily declines in amount) would be paid off if the primary wage earner should die.

Term insurance often is sold on an individual basis with the policies having high face values, for example to young parents who need maximum protection at the lowest price. It is also often sold to cover a relatively large number of similarly situated people, each for a moderate face value. For example, an employer may want to provide pure life insurance for employees at a minimum cost per person.

group life insurance: insurance that covers all members of a group

Insurance sold to cover many similarly situated people is called **group life insurance**. It is typically term insurance and is most frequently utilized by employers to cover their workers.Typical coverage ranges from $10,000 to $50,000 per worker, with the specific amount depending on the worker's salary or classification. The employer is generally considered to be the agent of the employee in making payments. If the employer fails to pay the group premiums, the insurance will lapse and the insurer will not be liable to the employee or the beneficiary. Employment by the firm is usually the only requirement for participation. Since working groups are usually made up of healthy, active people, no medical examination is required, and death claims are low. An employee who leaves the group has no further interest in the group policy but is commonly permitted to convert it to an ordinary policy within 30 days without taking a medical examination.

Certain specialized forms of insurance such as credit life, travel, and industrial are actually term policies.

credit life insurance: group insurance that pays the debt upon the death of the debtor

Credit life insurance pays a lender the amount of an outstanding debt upon the death of the debtor. It is made available by a lending institution to individual debtors of that lender. Credit life insurance often is used to cover purchases of cars and other large consumer items made on installment plans. The insured in such a policy is usually the primary income earner in a household. Should the insured die, the insurance would pay off the debt and prevent the family from being burdened by it. It is unlawful for a lender to turn down a would-be debtor's application for a loan because the applicant refuses the lender's offer of credit life insurance.

travel insurance: insurance that pays if the insured dies while using a particular mode of travel

Travel insurance is a special type of life insurance which is sold to air and other types of travelers. It is often sold from coin-operated vending machines. Travel insurance is similar to term insurance.

That is because travel insurance is in effect for only a certain period of time—the time that the insured is using a particular commercial mode of travel.

Industrial life insurance is generally designed for those who are financially unable to buy ordinary life insurance. The face amount of an industrial policy is low—typically less than $1,000. Premiums are low, but handling costs are high. Two factors make industrial insurance costly for the insurance company and relatively expensive, per dollar of protection, for the insured:

industrial life insurance: insurance with a low face amount and frequent payment of premiums

a. industrial policy premiums usually are paid weekly or monthly, and
b. the premiums are often collected from door-to-door.

Industrial policies may or may not have provisions similar to those of ordinary policies. A medical examination generally is not required.

2. Combination Policies

For many years, two basic combination policies—endowment and whole life—dominated the market. Upon the death of the insured, an **endowment policy** requires the insurer to pay the beneficiary the policy's face amount during the period of coverage (usually for 20 years or until the insured reaches retirement age). However, if the insured lives to the end of the coverage period, the owner of the policy (usually the insured) is paid the face value. The premiums are comparatively high, but the necessity of having a large lump sum of money available at a set point in time (for example, to buy a retirement home upon reaching age 65) has attracted many to this type of insurance.

endowment life insurance: insurance which pays the face value upon death or at the end of a specified time

Whole life insurance, another standard type of policy, provides that in return for level premiums paid at regular intervals, the face amount of the policy will be paid upon the death of the insured, or at age 100 when most whole life policies mature. *Level premiums* remain the same as long as the policy is in force. Whole life policies are also known as *ordinary, straight life, permanent,* or *continuous premium policies.* Premium payments are made for as long as the insured lives, or until age 100, rather than for a specified term, such as 20 years.

whole life insurance: insurance which pays the face amount upon death or at age 100 in return for premium payments made during the insured's life

Obviously, few people live to the age of 100 to collect the face value. However, the amount of the premium of a whole life policy is set significantly higher than what would be required for term insurance of the same face value. The surplus goes into a savings program that pays a low return that is nontaxable until received. Gradually over the years, the whole life policy acquires a cash value from this savings function. This cash value provides a savings reserve for the insured that can be borrowed against at a relatively low interest rate. Should the insured die, the face value of the policy less any outstanding loans against it is paid to the beneficiary.

As interest rates paid on other investment forms increased dramatically in the last decade, the use of whole life or endowment policies decreased due to their low rate of return. Instead, many insureds bought term insurance as cheaply as possible and invested the difference. The insurance industry responded with a variety of new types of insurance, the most successful of which has been universal life. A **universal life** policy provides death coverage from term insurance plus a minimum guaranteed return on the cash value roughly the same as in a whole life policy (4 to 4.5 percent). In addition to the guaranteed return, the insurance pays "excess" interest, the rate of which depends upon the success of the insurance company's investment of the funds. Over short periods, such as one year, the policy may pay rates close to those of the money-market funds. Another type of policy, **variable life,** allows the insured to invest in several types of funds, such as common stocks, bonds, and money-market instruments. The premium amount is fixed, but the death benefit varies depending upon the success of the investments.

universal life insurance: insurance that combines term life insurance coverage with a forced premium savings plan with interest close to money-market rates

variable life insurance: fixed-premium life insurance in which the death benefit varies depending upon the success of the investment of the premiums

The possibility of a relatively high return combined with the forced savings, tax-free cash buildup, and flexibility (being able to have the cash value utilized to make the premium payments during periods of unemployment, for example) has caused a renewal of interest in combination term and savings policies.

WHAT ARE THE RIGHTS OF THE BENEFICIARY OF A LIFE INSURANCE POLICY?

PROBLEM: Pumbro was worried that his wife, who was the beneficiary of his life insurance policy, might die in an accident when she was traveling with him and that he might die within a few days without regaining consciousness. Consequently, he feared that the insurer would have no one to pay. What should he do to solve the problem?

A **life insurance beneficiary** is the recipient of the proceeds of the policy that are paid upon the death of the insured. Possible beneficiaries include:

life insurance beneficiary: party who receives the policy proceeds

1. the estate of the insured,
2. partnerships, corporations, or individuals who have taken out life insurance on the insured because they would suffer the loss of the insured's services if the insured were to die, or
3. third persons who are named in the policy but are not otherwise parties to the insurance contract (for example, a spouse or the children of the insured).

It is also possible to have two or more beneficiaries. They may share equally, or they may be primary and contingent beneficiaries. A **primary beneficiary** is the one designated by the policy to receive the proceeds if that person is still alive at the death of the insured. A **contingent beneficiary** is one designated to receive the proceeds if the primary beneficiary dies before the insured. In the problem, Pumbro could solve his problem by naming a contingent beneficiary, such as a relative, a friend, or a charity. If there were no contingent beneficiary, the insurance proceeds would go to his estate to be distributed under his will or as provided by law if he left no will.

primary beneficiary: beneficiary designated to receive the policy proceeds if still alive at the time of death of the insured

contingent beneficiary: beneficiary designated to receive the policy proceeds if the primary beneficiary dies before the insured

Policies generally give the insured the right to change the beneficiary by giving the insurance company written notice. As a precaution, state law typically provides that any beneficiary who has feloniously killed the insured is not entitled to the policy proceeds.

The **proceeds** of a life insurance policy equal the face of the policy less any amount borrowed against it. When payable to a living beneficiary, the proceeds of insurance are not subject to any claims of creditors of the insured.

proceeds: money paid to the beneficiary of the policy

WHAT OTHER PROVISIONS ARE COMMONLY FOUND IN A LIFE INSURANCE POLICY?

PROBLEM: Jameson was the beneficiary of her uncle's term life insurance policy. When her uncle, a Navy pilot on active duty, was killed in a terrorist bomb explosion overseas, the insurance company refused to pay the policy's face value of $100,000. Can it legally be forced to do so?

The insurer of life agrees to pay to a named beneficiary or to the insured's estate the amount stated in the policy, in accordance with the policy provisions. However, life insurance policies sometimes contain provisions that exempt the insurer from liability when death is due to certain causes, such as the crash of a private airplane. Policies may also provide for exemption from liability in case of the policyholder's death during military service abroad or at home. Therefore, in the problem, if such an exemption were in Jameson's uncle's policy, the insurance company could not legally be forced to pay the $100,000. In cases where death occurs under an exemption, the insurer is liable for return of the premiums paid or cash value (less any indebtedness), instead of the proceeds.

Most states have adopted uniform policy provisions which are a part of all ordinary life insurance policies. The following provisions are commonly included in life insurance policies for the protection of the insured:

1. Incontestable Clause

As you learned in Chapter 25, an incontestable clause prohibits the insurer from refusing to perform due to any fraud or misrepresentation committed by the insured at the time the policy was issued. The prohibition takes effect after a certain length of time, usually two years, following the date of issuance. After that time, the company may not cancel the policy or refuse to pay the proceeds even if the company had relied on the false representation. However, the incontestable clause does not bar an insurance company from claiming that the insured's death (for example, if it occurred while the insured was in military service overseas) was not covered by the policy.

2. Days of Grace

days of grace: period during which the policy remains in force after the premium is due

Life insurance contracts provide for a period of time during which the policy remains in force even though a premium which is due is not paid. The period of time is usually one month after the premium due date. This period is called the **days of grace.** (It is commonly known as the *grace period*.) If a policy is to remain in force after the days of grace, however, the overdue premium must be paid before that period ends. The laws of some states require the insurance company to send notices of premiums due. However, most companies automatically send such notices as a matter of courtesy and good business practice.

Mehr was very ill. As a consequence, she failed to pay the premium on her $50,000 term life insurance policy by the due date of March 3d. Mehr died on March 30th without making the payment. However, since her death occurred within the grace period, the insurance company would have to pay the $50,000 (less the amount of the premium) to the beneficiary.

3. Lapses and Reinstatement

When the insured fails to pay a premium before the grace period expires, the policy is said to **lapse**. This is one method of terminating the contract. Policies usually give the policyholder the right to **reinstate** (to place the policy back in force) within three to five years after lapse. However, the policyholder must still be in good health and must pay, with interest, all premiums due during the lapse.

lapse: to no longer be in effect because a premium was not paid

reinstate: to place a policy back in force

4. Misrepresentation of Age

PROBLEM: Garoutte, age 34, gave his age as 29 when he applied for his life insurance policy. If Garoutte died, would the company pay his beneficiaries anything?

Misrepresentation of age, while material to the life insurance risk, does not void the policy. The insurer does, however, make an adjustment so that the amount of proceeds payable is only that which the premiums paid would have purchased at the insured's correct age. Thus, in the problem, in making a settlement to Garoutte's beneficiary, the company would figure the amount of insurance which the premiums Garoutte had paid would have purchased for a person 34 years of age. It would then pay the beneficiary that amount.

5. Suicide

Life insurance policies require only the return of premiums as proceeds if the insured commits suicide within one or, in some cases, two years of issuance. After that time, however, the face amount of the policy is paid.

6. Nonforfeiture Options

PROBLEM: For 18 years, Juliard paid premiums on a whole life insurance policy with a built-in savings plan. Unfortunately, Juliard's financial situation had become so bad that Juliard could no longer make the premium payments. Will Juliard lose the money paid into the savings plan as a consequence?

nonforfeiture options: ways of using the cash value if the policy lapses

As was mentioned earlier, many ordinary life insurance policies have built-in savings plans. These plans cause the premiums for those policies to be substantially higher than for term insurance with the same face value. Eventually, significant cash values may accumulate under such savings plans. As a consequence, all the states have passed statutes to guarantee that in the event of lapse of the policy the money accumulated will be used for the benefit of the insured. Thus, these statutes require policies to include alternatives for beneficial use of accumulated funds. These alternatives are called **nonforfeiture options**. At the time of application, the insured selects one of the options. Then if a lapse occurs, the insurance company treats the policy's cash value according to the terms of the option selected. The options usually available include the following:

a. taking the cash surrender value,
b. borrowing up to the loan value,
c. taking an automatic premium loan,
d. buying a reduced amount of paid-up life insurance, or
e. extending the present policy's face value for as long as possible by converting it to term insurance.

cash surrender value: amount of savings and accumulated interest of the policy

loan value: same as the cash surrender value; may be borrowed against the policy

Thus, an insured has the right to demand the **cash surrender value** of the policy if the policy is allowed to lapse. This is the amount of savings and accumulated interest (usually at a relatively modest annual rate) in the policy. This sum is also the **loan value** of the policy because the insured may, instead of taking the cash, borrow that amount or any part of it from the insurer by making the necessary arrangement. In the problem, Juliard could surrender the policy and take the cash surrender value or, if he preferred, he could borrow the policy's loan value at the rate of interest stated in the policy.

Often a cash surrender or loan value is not available until the policy has been in force for a certain length of time, usually two or three years. That is because much of the first year's premium is paid to the insurance agent as commission, and other initial costs must be paid by the company. Group policies usually do not have a cash surrender value because they are term insurance without a savings element.

An **automatic premium loan** keeps a lapsed policy in force on its original plan. The policy becomes the security for a loan to pay current premiums. These may later be repaid by the insured, or they may be deducted from the proceeds in case of death or matured endowment. If the policyholder desires to resume payment of premiums, such payment may be done without the necessity of submitting proof of insurability by a medical examination.

automatic premium loan: option that keeps a policy in force in case of lapse

After her father's death, Anne Talbot discovered that the premiums on his $30,000 whole life policy had not been paid for the past two years. Fortunately when he bought the policy some ten years before, he had selected the automatic premium loan option. Consequently, the policy was still in effect despite the lapse, and Anne, the beneficiary, collected the proceeds of the policy less the amount loaned to pay the premiums.

The **reduced paid-up life insurance** option, upon lapse of the policy, uses the cash value to purchase as much ordinary life insurance as possible. The amount of the policy so purchased is significantly lower than the original. However, no further premium payments are required to keep the new policy in force.

reduced paid-up life insurance: option that uses the cash value of the original policy to buy ordinary life insurance without further premiums

Strocke, age 40, was unable to keep up the premiums on her $20,000 limited-payment life insurance policy, which she had had for 15 years. Strocke decided to let the policy lapse and to take a paid-up policy for the amount listed in the table in her policy. This amounted to $831 per thousand of insurance. There would be no further premium payments, and the company would pay the beneficiary $16,620 upon her death.

Under the **extended term insurance** option, the cash value of the policy is used to purchase as much term insurance of the same value as possible. If the insured makes no selection of a nonforfeiture option, most insurers automatically use this one. In this way, the insured is covered for a specific period of time with the same amount of insurance as in the original policy. No further premiums are required.

extended term insurance: option that uses the cash value of the original policy to buy term insurance without further premiums

In the example, if Strocke wished, she could request that she be covered, as listed in the table in her policy, with $20,000 term insurance for a period of 37 years with no further premium payments. At that time, the policy would expire.

WHAT ADDITIONAL COVERAGES CAN BE PLACED IN A LIFE INSURANCE POLICY?

PROBLEM: Crowonwing had a $50,000 life insurance policy on himself with double indemnity coverage. When Crowonwing died of pneumonia at age 34, Crowonwing's brother, the beneficiary, claimed the insurance company owed him $100,000 because Crowonwing had died of a disease from which most afflicted persons survive. Is the brother's claim valid?

Two additional coverages often are written into life insurance policies. Each coverage requires the payment of an additional premium amount. These two types are known as double indemnity coverage and disability coverage.

double indemnity coverage: coverage which provides that the insurer pay double if the insured's death is accidental

Under **double indemnity coverage,** the insurer is required to pay double (triple or quadruple coverage may also be purchased, if desired) the face amount of the policy if the death of the insured is accidental. Policies commonly require that the death result "from bodily injury effected solely by external, violent, and accidental means, independently and exclusively of all other causes and within 90 days after such injury." Some policies also require a visible wound on the exterior of the body, except in cases of death by drowning or asphyxiation. Because the probability of accidental death is very small, the added premium charge is low. In the problem, the brother's claim is not valid. Crowonwing's early death by disease, rather than by accident, does not obligate the insurance company to pay more than the $50,000 face value of the policy.

Double indemnity coverage generally excludes such causes as suicide, illness or disease, physical or mental infirmity, service in military or naval forces during time of war, and certain airplane accidents. It is also usually inapplicable after age 65 or 70.

disability coverage: coverage for permanent incapacity to work due to injury or disease

Disability coverage provides for protection against the financial effects of total permanent disability. *Disability* is usually defined as "incapacity, resulting from bodily injury or disease, to engage in the customary occupation of the insured." A total disability that has been continuous for a period specified in the policy, usually not less than four or six months, is presumed to be permanent. Proof of continued disability must be furnished to the company from time to time.

rider: attachment to a policy that alters the terms

There are actually two types of disability riders. (A **rider** is an attachment to an insured's policy that changes the terms in some respect.) One disability rider (a **waiver of premium**) provides that no premiums are required while the insured is totally disabled. The other disability rider pays a cash benefit that is called *disability income*.

waiver of premium: rider which provides that no premiums are required while the insured is totally disabled

HOW ARE LIFE INSURANCE CONTRACTS SETTLED?

> **PROBLEM:** Holly made Laurel the beneficiary of Holly's life insurance policy. Afraid that Laurel might spend the money foolishly, Holly wanted the insurance company to pay out the proceeds to Laurel in equal monthly installments. Is that possible?

Upon the death of the insured, notice of death and proof of death are required by the insurer. Proof of death is generally an official death certificate or a physician's written statement certifying the date and the cause of death. Proof of age may also be required.

Most ordinary life insurance policies allow the party contracting for the insurance to select from a number of options as to how the proceeds of the policy are to be paid. These **settlement options** may apply to death proceeds paid to beneficiaries or to liquidation of the cash value of the contract paid to the insured. Most policies provide that the beneficiary may not change the settlement option. Usually the method chosen calls for the payment of the face amount in a single lump sum. However, other options frequently used include:

settlement options: ways that the proceeds of a life insurance policy may be paid

1. The Interest Option

The company retains the proceeds as a principal sum and pays interest thereon to the beneficiary until the principal is demanded by the beneficiary.

2. The Time Option

The company pays out the proceeds in equal monthly installments over a number of years. In the problem, Holly would simply have to specify this method of payment.

3. The Amount Option

The company pays equal monthly installments of the amount specified by the party contracting for the insurance or the beneficiary, such as $150, as long as the proceeds and the interest thereon last.

4. The Lifetime Income Option

annuity: option that pays the beneficiary a specified sum at regular intervals until death

The proceeds are used to buy an **annuity**. Such an option pays the beneficiary a specified sum at regular intervals until the beneficiary dies.

A policy of life insurance, like any other claim for money, ordinarily may be assigned. However, in the case of life insurance, written notice to the insurer is usually required. A life insurance policy may be assigned by the beneficiary after the death of the person whose life was insured. It may also be assigned by the insured before her or his death if there is no restriction imposed by the agreement or by statute. The assignee need not have an insurable interest in the life of the insured.

PREVENTING LEGAL DIFFICULTIES

When Considering Life Insurance . . .

1. study your own needs, and select the type or combination of types that will fit them best. All life insurance policies are not alike;
2. study the insurance contract and choose the most desirable nonforfeiture options and settlement options;
3. check your policies every few years or whenever there is any significant change in family, occupation, or financial situation. Be sure that the beneficiaries and the options are still what you wish and that the old coverages and arrangements are still satisfactory;
4. consider buying decreasing term life insurance to age 65 and investing the premium savings over whole life, if you can discipline yourself to do so. If not, evaluate the term-plus-savings options in the new universal life policies; and
5. use credit life insurance and other optional coverages to protect against the loss of income due to the death or disability of a family wage earner.

Strengthening Your Legal Vocabulary

annuity
automatic premium loan
cash surrender value
contingent beneficiary
credit life insurance
days of grace
decreasing term life insurance
disability coverage
double indemnity coverage
endowment life insurance
extended term insurance
group life insurance
industrial life insurance
lapse
level term life insurance
life insurance
life insurance beneficiary
loan value
nonforfeiture options
primary beneficiary
proceeds
reduced paid-up life insurance
reinstate
rider
settlement options
term life insurance
travel insurance
universal life insurance
variable life insurance
waiver of premium
whole life insurance

1. Sum of money payable if the policy lapses or is canceled.
2. Insurance contract in which an insurer, in consideration of a specified premium, promises to pay a certain sum upon the death of a person.
3. A type of combination life insurance policy that includes term insurance and a savings program that guarantees a minimum return close to that of a whole life policy but may, on a period-by-period basis, pay a much higher return on savings.
4. Attachment to a policy changing it in some respect.
5. Time period during which a policy remains in effect even though a premium which is due is not paid.
6. Insurance that pays only if death occurs within a specified period.
7. Party to whom the proceeds of a life insurance policy are payable.
8. Coverage under which the insurer pays twice the face amount if the death of the insured is accidental.
9. The amount due to be paid to the beneficiary under a life insurance contract, equaling the face value less any loans against the policy.
10. Person designated to receive the amount due under a life insurance contract if the primary beneficiary dies before the insured.

Reviewing Important Points

1. Life insurance policies may be pure term insurance or they may be a combination of term and a savings component.
2. It is possible and prudent to specify a primary beneficiary and one or more contingent beneficiaries to a life insurance policy.

3. The beneficiary of a policy may be the insured's estate, a person who takes out insurance on the life of another, or a named third person who is not otherwise a party to the contract.
4. Most policies contain an incontestable clause and provide for days of grace, reinstatement in case of lapse, assignment, and various methods of settlement.
5. In the event that a policy lapses, the holder may usually receive the cash surrender value or borrow the loan value. Or the holder may elect that a premium loan, reduced paid-up insurance, or extended term insurance automatically be put into effect.
6. Also, in event of lapse, the policyholder may reinstate the policy by paying the unpaid premiums plus interest and furnishing evidence of insurability.
7. For an additional premium, a policy may provide for double indemnity, for a waiver of premiums in case of disability, and for disability income.

Applying Law to Everyday Life

1. Mr. and Mrs. Beal disagreed on the relative merits of term versus combination life insurance policies. Mr. Beal maintained that it was better to buy the same amount of term insurance (at a lower rate) and to invest the difference between that rate and the higher whole life rate. Mrs. Beal pointed out that they probably would spend the premium savings rather than invest them and that the insurance company would have better investment opportunities. What is your opinion?

2. Woolsey was employed as a keypunch operator by Starfast Company and was insured under the company's group life insurance policy. When she left the company, Woolsey insisted that she could keep the policy in force by continuing to pay the premiums. Can she do so?

3. Tolentino's life insurance premium was due on January 15. (a) If she did not pay it by that date, would the policy lapse? (b) If so, on what date?

4. When Moon died, he owed Studer $7,500. Studer claimed the proceeds of Moon's policy, which was payable to Moon's wife. Will Studer prevail?

5. While intoxicated, Mr. Baxter drove over and killed his wife. He was convicted of the felony of vehicular manslaughter. Can he still collect the proceeds as beneficiary of her $100,000 double indemnity policy?

6. When Henecker took out his life insurance policy, he misrepresented his age as 27. In reality, he was 34. Will the insurance company be required to pay on the policy when Henecker dies?

7. Shuster had a $100,000 triple indemnity policy. Three years after contracting for it, she committed suicide. Will the insurance company have to pay $300,000?

Solving Case Problems

1. The plaintiff, Duke, was insured by the defendant company against disability that was total and permanent resulting from accidental bodily injury. The policy provided disability income benefits if "such disability requires the insured to be under the regular care and attendance of a legally qualified physician." After two years of medical treatment, the plaintiff's condition became static and did not require regular care and attendance by a physician. The plaintiff's physician testified that on occasion he talked with his patient over the telephone, but he did not prescribe any medication or treatment and he did not keep a record of the calls. The Court of Appeals stated that a contract clause requiring regular medical treatment is inapplicable when such treatment would not improve the insured's condition. In light of the wording of the policy, should the Supreme Court reverse the decision of the lower court and award judgment to the insurer? (*Duke v. Mutual Life Insurance Company of New York,* 210 S.E.2d 187)

2. While married to his first wife, Lavender took out a $5,000 life insurance policy on his own life. He named his wife beneficiary and his three minor children as contingent beneficiaries. Marital difficulties later resulted in divorce. The court decreed that Lavender was to keep the policy "in full force and effect" with his former wife as beneficiary and the three children as contingent beneficiaries in the event the plaintiff (wife) remarried or died. Both parties remarried, and Lavender changed the beneficiary of the policy to his new wife. Lavender and his second wife were later divorced, but the divorce decree made no mention of the life insurance policy. When Lavender died, the proceeds were claimed by the children, now adults, and the second wife. The first wife made no claim to the proceeds of the policy. The insurer, being aware of both the first divorce decree and the change of beneficiary, paid the proceeds into the court with a request that the court determine the rights of the parties. Decide. (*Travelers Insurance Company v. Lewis,* 531 P.2d 484)

3. Mr. Dupont took out life insurance on himself. The policy was prepared by the Carolina Life Insurance Co. on October 30. However, the company marked the date of issue on the policy as October 28. The policy provided for a one-month grace period. Mr. Dupont paid the first premium. However, he had not paid the second one when he died in a fire at the Dupont's home on December 30. The insurance company refused to pay. It claimed that the policy had lapsed after the expiration of the grace period on December 28. Mrs. Dupont, on the other hand, claimed that either (a) the policy was in force because the insurance took effect on November 24 when the policy was delivered and the first premium paid or (b) the grace period was still running on December 30 because the policy was actually issued on October 30. Decide and state the reason for the decision. (*Carolina Life Insurance v. Dupont,* 141 So. 2d 624)

4. After purchasing all of the capital stock of the Laclede Packing Co., the new stockholders—Mickelberry's Food Products Co. and others—sought to collect the cash surrender value of $36,945.51 on two life insurance policies. The two policies were on the lives of the former president and the former secretary-treasurer of the Packing Co., Haeussermann and Ackermann. Haeussermann and Ackermann were the principal stockholders and officers in the Packing Co. from its inception until the new stockholders took over. When the policies were taken out, several years before the takeover by the new stockholders, the stockholders were obligated to pay the premiums and were also named as the beneficiaries. The defendants, Haeussermann and Ackermann, claim that the new stockholders have no insurable interest in the lives of the former officers and that, as a consequence, the new stockholders are not entitled to the proceeds. Decide. (*Mickelberry's Food Products Co. v. Haeussermann*, 247 S.W.2d 731, Mo)

5. One month after his release from the Missouri State Penitentiary, Frank Bird insured his own life in a double indemnity policy issued by John Hancock Mutual Life Insurance Company. A little over two months later, the insured was killed while attempting to hold up a cocktail lounge. The insurance company refused to pay the proceeds to the beneficiaries, Harry and Edna Bird, even though the policy contained no provision exluding liability if the insured died as a result of a violation of the law. John Hancock stated that to pay even innocent beneficiaries under such circumstances would be against public policy and might foster criminal behavior. Decide. (*Bird v. John Hancock Mutual Life Insurance Company*, 320 S.W.2d 955, Mo.)

29

Social Insurance

1. Your friend says that paying social security tax is a waste. "You're just paying for someone else's retirement, and you won't receive any benefits for 30 or 40 years, if you live that long." Is this true?
2. Your uncle is just turning 65 and is looking forward to receiving social security benefits. However, he has not applied for them. Will he lose them if he fails to make a timely application?
3. A friend of your family is receiving social security retirement benefits and working at a part-time job. Will the wages from the job reduce the benefits?

WHAT IS SOCIAL INSURANCE?

> **PROBLEM:** Gerdan was employed by a supplier of transmissions for the large automakers. Because of a decline in car buying, the automakers cut back on production. In turn, Gerdan's employer had to lay off many of its employees, including Gerdan. Does Gerdan have any protection from an immediate, total loss of income?

social insurance: indemnification from financial consequences of unemployment, retirement, and other social concerns

RSDHI: Retirement, Survivors', Disability, and Health Insurance

Social insurance indemnifies persons at least partially from the harsh financial consequences of unemployment, disability, death, or forced retirement. Since the late 1930s, programs under the federal government's Social Security Act have been instrumental in providing such protection. Coverages provided under this Act (frequently labeled **RSDHI**—**R**etirement, **S**urvivors', **D**isability, and **H**ealth **I**nsurance) include:

1. Unemployment compensation	Temporary income for persons laid off from paying jobs
2. Retirement insurance	Supplementary retirement income for workers, age 62 and over, and their dependents
3. Survivors' insurance	Income for widows, widowers, and their dependents
4. Disability insurance	Income for disabled workers and their dependents
5. Health insurance	Hospitalization and medical care (popularly known as Medicare) for persons over 65 and certain others under 65 who are disabled

The Social Security Administration coordinates and administers most of the programs that provide the above benefits. As a consequence, before beginning a first job, every person should report to or write to the nearest office of the Social Security Administration. This office will assign a permanent number and will provide a card—called a Social Security Number Card—which bears one's name, a line for signature, and a nine-digit number. When a person's name is changed by marriage, adoption, or court order, he or she must apply for a new card which is issued showing the new name, but the number always remains the same. Because of the possibility of errors, it is important for individuals to check periodically with the Social Security Administration to make sure they are receiving the proper credit for wages earned.

The financing for these social insurance programs, except for unemployment and medical insurance, comes primarily from payroll taxes on both workers and employers. The workers' taxes are withheld from their pay by the employers. These **payroll deductions** are then matched in amount by employer contributions, and the total is paid into the appropriate government trust fund. The amounts of the taxes and the benefits usually are set as recommended by the Standing Committee on Social Security in Congress. However, the taxes and benefits from unemployment insurance are determined by the various states which administer them in coordination with the federal government. The taxes which support the unemployment insurance programs are paid by the employers only.

payroll deductions: money withheld from paycheck for taxes and other purposes

Each of these social insurance programs is discussed in detail in the following sections.

WHO IS ENTITLED TO UNEMPLOYMENT COMPENSATION?

PROBLEM: Plumb had been employed for five years as an expeditor at a shipyard. When government contracts were cut back, he was discharged. Was he eligible for unemployment compensation?

Unemployment compensation is designed to lessen the financial hardship of losing one's job. Although the program generally is controlled by the federal government, under the Social Security Act, the states are allowed considerable freedom in determining taxes and benefits and in administering the program. For a worker to receive unemployment benefits, it is typically required that:

unemployment compensation: governmental payment to lessen consequences of job loss

1. the worker must have been working on a job covered by the state law;
2. the worker must have been employed by a firm that employed one or more workers on at least one day in each of 20 weeks during the calendar year. In the alternative, the firm

must have paid wages of at least $1,500 during a calendar quarter; and

3. the worker must have received a minimum amount of pay from, or have worked a minimum amount of time on, covered jobs during the year or two before losing the job.

Today, most workers are covered by the program, but this was not always true. For example, only in recent years has coverage been extended to include agricultural workers, most workers for nonprofit organizations, and government workers. Still not covered by the act are the self-employed, those who work for their spouse or parent, and a variety of others. Plumb, the worker in the problem, meets the requirements of the program and is eligible for unemployment compensation.

HOW IS UNEMPLOYMENT COMPENSATION OBTAINED?

PROBLEM: Immediately upon being laid off from a secretarial job with a magazine agency, Kirchner applied to the proper state office for unemployment compensation. Could Kirchner get compensation immediately?

Unemployment benefits are usually figured as a certain percentage of the worker's average wages while employed. Thus, the higher the wages, the higher the unemployment benefits up to a specified maximum. There is usually a minimum weekly payment as well. Benefits vary widely in amount from state to state and may be subject to increases as the cost of living rises. If a worker receiving compensation finds part-time work, most of the worker's pay is deducted from the benefit amount.

To obtain unemployment benefits, generally a worker must:

1. be totally unemployed for a specified period of time;
2. register for a job at a public employment office;
3. be ready, willing, and able to work if a suitable job is offered, and in most states, actually be looking for work. To be considered suitable, a job offered must be one in which the worker is trained or experienced even if it pays less than the former work. It must be within a reasonable distance from home; and
4. file a claim for the benefits.

After a worker has filed a claim for benefits, a substantial number of states require a one-week waiting period before the benefits actually begin. A growing number, however, pay benefits immediately. In the near future this policy of paying immediately may be required of all states. Thus, in the problem, Kirchner would have to wait one week before drawing benefits unless he lives in one of the eight states which require no waiting period. Benefits are payable while the unemployment continues, but only up to a certain maximum time—usually 26 weeks. With assistance from the federal government, the time may be extended if unemployment reaches a specified high level and persists.

The employee who is absent from work because of illness cannot collect unemployment benefits in most states. However, such a person might qualify for disability insurance.

WHEN IS UNEMPLOYMENT COMPENSATION DENIED?

PROBLEM: After repeated warnings, Speilman and a fellow employee, Brown, were fired for racing their forklifts around the company loading dock in violation of safety regulations. Were they entitled to unemployment compensation?

Under certain circumstances, an otherwise qualified unemployed person may have benefits reduced or denied. Typical state rules provide that benefits are partly or completely denied if a worker:

1. quits work voluntarily without good cause;
2. refuses to apply for, or to accept, suitable work;
3. loses the job through an economic strike or a labor dispute in which the worker is involved;
4. intentionally misrepresents the facts about his or her job qualifications;
5. is discharged for misconduct connected with the work, such as refusal to obey proper orders or company regulations;
6. is discharged for criminal conduct;
7. is attending school full-time; or
8. receives other payments, such as a company pension or social security retirement benefits.

In the problem, Speilman and Brown were fired for work-related misconduct. As a consequence, they would be barred from receiving any of the unemployment compensation to which they might otherwise have been entitled.

WHO CAN BE COVERED BY RETIREMENT, SURVIVORS', DISABILITY, AND HEALTH INSURANCE?

> **PROBLEM:** As a result of an automobile accident, Skyler suffered from total, permanent kidney failure. Treatments on the dialysis machine at a local hospital were life preserving, yet were too expensive to continue for long. Is there a social security program that will help keep Skyler alive?

retirement insurance: governmental program providing supplementary income to eligible retirees

survivors' insurance: governmental program to indemnify worker's dependents when worker dies

disability insurance: governmental program to indemnify workers and their dependents should the worker become disabled

Medicare: governmental program to help pay hospital and other bills for eligible persons

The remaining four major programs under the Social Security Act currently provide various benefits to more than 36 million Americans. Unlike unemployment compensation, the benefits from these programs are uniform throughout the United States, and all are administered by the federal government. More than half of the people receiving these benefits are retired. The **retirement insurance** program provides monthly payments for workers and their dependents when the wage earners retire at the age of 62 or older. **Survivors' insurance** provides monthly insurance benefits for dependents when the wage earner dies. **Disability insurance** provides monthly insurance benefits for workers and their dependents if the worker is unable to do any substantial work for pay because of sickness or injury. The ailment must have lasted, or be expected to last, at least one year, or end in death. Health insurance, or **Medicare**, provides hospital insurance and optional medical insurance to most persons 65 or older. Regardless of age, persons who are insured under social security and who have received disability payments for 24 consecutive months or who have permanent kidney failure are also eligible for Medicare. In the problem, for example, Skyler would be eligible for Medicare assistance payments if he is over the age of 65. Skyler would also be eligible if under the age of 65 if he is insured by social security or if he is the spouse or dependent child of someone insured under the system.

Although workers in almost every kind of employment and self-employment can be covered by these social security insurance programs, certain categories are subject to special, detailed provisions under the Act. These categories include persons under 21 working for a parent, those working for a spouse, parents working in the home of a child, individuals working in the private home of an employer, students employed at a school or college, farm workers, and those working in a job where they receive tips. Persons in these categories should contact their social security office for information about their status under the social security program.

HOW DOES A PERSON BECOME ELIGIBLE FOR BENEFITS?

> **PROBLEM:** Copeland worked steadily for six years for Carlo's Custom Lamp Shop; for the last five years he has worked for Busy-Buzz Electric Supplies. Would Copeland be covered under the Social Security Act?

A person becomes eligible to receive the various social security benefits by obtaining credit for a specified number of **quarters of coverage**. Prior to 1978, a quarter of coverage generally was awarded for each calendar quarter (a three-month period starting January 1, April 1, July 1, or October 1) in which the worker was paid $50 or more in nonfarm wages. Prior to 1978, separate coverage requirements were applied to farm workers, domestic workers, and the self-employed. Since 1978, all employees and self-employed people have earned quarter credits in the same way—that is, by earning more than a set amount ($440 in 1986, the amount increases automatically each year as average wages go up). A quarter of credit, up to a maximum of four per year, is awarded each time the set amount is earned.

quarters of coverage: a measurement used to determine eligibility for various social security benefits

The number of quarters of coverage obtained by a worker determines only eligibility for benefits, not the amount of the benefits or when they will be paid. According to the number of quarters earned, a worker is determined to be either uninsured, currently insured, or fully insured. Whether one is currently or fully insured governs the type of benefits which are paid. A worker who has six quarters of coverage within the past three years is **currently insured**. This makes the worker's spouse and children eligible for certain survivor's benefits payable upon the death of the worker and makes the worker eligible for disability payments under the program. To be **fully insured**, that is, eligible to receive benefits under all the major

currently insured: status making the worker eligible for disability and the worker's spouse eligible for survivors' benefits should worker die

fully insured: status making a person eligible to receive benefits under all major social security programs

programs, a worker must receive the proper number of quarters of coverage required by each program. Once a worker is fully insured, the worker remains so for life. However, a worker can be fully insured and yet not be currently insured because the worker has not earned six quarters of coverage within the past three years. The current quarterly requirements to be fully insured are shown in Figure 29-1.

To be eligible for retirement benefits:

If a worker reaches age 62 in:	Quarters of coverage needed:
1987	36
1991 or later	40

To be eligible for disability and death benefits:

If a worker was born after 1929 and became disabled or died at age:	Quarters of coverage needed:
28 or younger	6
30	8
32	10*
62 or older	40

To be eligible for Medicare:

A person need only be 65 or older or be insured under the disability program if under 65.

*Note: The number of quarters of coverage needed for eligibility for disability and death benefits increases at the rate of 2 for each additional 2 years of age until age 62 or older, when a maximum of 40 quarters of coverage are required.

Figure 29-1. Current Quarterly Requirements to be Fully Insured

In the problem, Copeland would be fully insured under the Act because he had more than 40 quarters of coverage. He would be currently insured because he has worked at least six quarters within the immediate past three years.

WHERE DOES THE MONEY COME FROM TO PAY THE BENEFITS?

PROBLEM: While talking about social security during a discussion after school, Carmen insisted that "the benefits are paid out of federal income taxes, and that's why those taxes are so high." Is she correct?

As in previous years, today's Social Security Act benefits are financed primarily by the Social Security Tax. The amounts subject to this tax (up to $42,000 of each employee's earnings in 1986) are to rise yearly as worker's earnings rise in the economy as a whole. Both the employer and employee will pay amounts over 7 percent (from 7.15 percent in 1986 to 7.65 percent in 1990) of the employee's earnings for a total of more than 14 percent for the period 1986-1990. The employee's half of the total tax is deducted from wages each payday. The employer adds the other half of the tax and forwards the total to the appropriate United States Depository. A worker who is self-employed pays the self-employment tax along with the individual income tax return. The self-employed rate will be between 12 percent and 13 percent for the near future. In the problem, Carmen was wrong. Social security and income taxes are separate and distinct taxes, even when paid at the same time.

Most benefits are paid from funds received from social security taxes. However, certain costs of the program have been paid from general funds which include income tax receipts. In addition, the federal government uses general funds to provide grants to the states and to local governments for welfare programs, medical care, and social services to certain needy persons not covered or inadequately covered by the basic social security program. Thus, many persons who receive social security benefits also qualify for federal food stamps or for other welfare benefits. Those who are helped include persons who are needy and over 65, blind, permanently and totally disabled, dependent children of an unemployed parent, and those in need of medical care or general assistance. The benefits vary among the states, but all states do participate.

HOW DOES AN ELIGIBLE PERSON QUALIFY TO RECEIVE RETIREMENT INSURANCE BENEFITS AND ARE THE BENEFITS REDUCED IF THE PERSON WORKS?

PROBLEM: Kubler, age 69, a retired worker receiving monthly benefit checks, works part-time as a salesperson for T-Biskit-Cookie and earns $600 a month in commissions for a total of $7,200 per year. Kubler also receives $2,000 in dividends from a stock investment. What effect will this income have on Kubler's retirement benefits?

An eligible person may elect to begin receiving retirement insurance checks as early as age 62 or may wait until age 65. However, the amount of the monthly income differs considerably between the two options, in favor of the person who retires at the age of 65. Also, it is important to remember that, whatever option is chosen, the checks from the social security retirement insurance program are meant to provide supplemental income only. Too often, individuals rely solely on the checks for their retirement income. This is not the purpose of the program. During the working years, each individual is responsible for accumulating savings to provide enough income which, when added to the social security retirement amount, will allow an adequate standard of living during the retirement years.

All too often, persons retire only to find that they have to return to some form of employment to make ends meet. This working income, earned after retirement, may or may not reduce the worker's retirement insurance payments, depending on the worker's age and the amount of the income from the job. Generally a retired worker older than 70 will not have his or her benefits reduced regardless of the amount of income earned. However, individuals between retirement age and age 70 may have their social security retirement checks reduced if they work and receive earnings that exceed a certain amount. Through the first part of 1985, retirees between 65 and 70 years of age could earn up to $7,320 (retirees under 65 could earn up to $5,400) without having their benefits reduced. When earned income exceeds the exempt amount, the benefit check is reduced $1 for each $2 over the exempt amount. Note, though, that earnings from savings, investments, or insurance are not counted as income for this purpose. Therefore, in the problem, using 1985 limits and because the $2,000 in dividends is not countable, Kubler is not over the exempt amount. As a consequence, Kubler will not lose benefits while adding $9,200 to the social security income.

WHEN ARE SURVIVORS' BENEFITS PAID?

> **PROBLEM:** Garcia was fully insured by the survivors' insurance coverage of social security. Garcia died at age 47. Garcia's 73-year-old mother was thereby left without support. Will she be eligible for any survivors' benefits?

Figure 29-2 shows the persons to whom survivors' benefits can be paid and the conditions under which they will be paid. Note especially the importance of being fully insured versus currently insured.

Monthly payments are made to the worker's:	If the worker was:
*Widow or widower 60 or over or disabled widow or widower 50 or over	fully insured.
*Widow or widower (regardless of age) if caring for your child who is under 18 (or disabled) and is entitled to benefits	either fully or currently insured.
Dependent children (or, under certain conditions, grandchildren)	either fully or currently insured.
Dependent parent 62 or over ...	fully insured.

A lump-sum death payment is made if the worker was either fully or currently insured.

*Note: All types of widow(er)'s benefits may be paid to a surviving divorced wife (husband) under certain conditions.

Figure 29-2. Recipients of Survivors' Benefits

In the problem, because Garcia was fully insured, Garcia's mother will receive benefits under the survivors' insurance. This would not be the case if Garcia were only currently insured.

WHEN ARE ELIGIBLE PERSONS QUALIFIED TO RECEIVE DISABILITY BENEFITS?

PROBLEM: Sterling, 33 years old, had been working steadily for a construction company for ten years and was fully insured. Then Sterling lost a leg and an arm as a result of an accident while on the job. Does Sterling qualify for disability benefits?

To be eligible for disability benefits, a worker must (a) be under age 65, (b) be fully insured, (c) have worked at least five years (20 quarters) in a covered occupation during the ten-year period ending when he or she becomes disabled, (d) have a severe and long-lasting disability, and (e) have filed an application for benefits. If disabled before reaching the age of 24, the worker needs credit for only one and a half years of work in the three years before becoming disabled. From the ages 24-31, the worker needs credit for one-half the time between age 21 and the time when unable to work. A worker disabled by blindness needs enough credit to be fully insured but does not need to meet the requirement for recent work.

Benefits for the disabled worker's family are also available and are the same as though the worker were 65 and retired. Disabled widows and widowers age 50 or older receive benefits if their disability begins not later than seven years after the death of the insured husband or wife or the end of a widow's or widower's right to benefits as a mother or father caring for her or his children.

A severe, long-lasting disability is one that prevents the worker from being able to "engage in any substantial gainful activity." Before any payments can be made, it must be established that the condition is physical or mental, is expected to continue indefinitely or result in death, and has lasted—or is expected to last—for at least 12 months. The worker must not refuse reasonable medical treatment. The following ordinarily are considered severe enough to meet the test of disability: loss of both arms, both legs, or a leg and an arm; heart and lung diseases that cause pain or fatigue on slight exertion; progressive cancer; brain damage that results in loss of judgment or memory; loss of vision; inability to speak; and deafness. In the problem, Sterling qualified for disability benefits because of being severely disabled, being under 65 years of age, having worked in a covered occupation for more than five of the past ten years, and being fully insured.

Disability of a dependent does not qualify such person for benefits. However, if a retired, disabled, or deceased worker has a son or daughter who was disabled before reaching 22 years of age, who has remained disabled ever since, and who is unmarried at the time of the application, such child is eligible for benefit payments. A disabled child does not need work credit to be eligible.

WHEN DOES AN ELIGIBLE PERSON QUALIFY TO RECEIVE MEDICARE BENEFITS?

PROBLEM: Hoffener's 65th birthday is approaching. His wife advises him to sign up for the voluntary medical insurance available under Medicare. He maintains Medicare's hospital insurance is enough protection from the financial consequences of illness. Is he correct?

In the last two decades, the costs of medical care have risen so dramatically that a major illness involving extended hospitalization and treatment threatens not only the physical well-being but the financial livelihood of the patient and the patient's family. As a consequence, **health insurance**, which indemnifies against the cost of medical care necessary to regain physical well-being after an illness, has become very important. Medicare provides such coverage primarily for those over 65, and private insurance companies provide similar coverage for those not protected by the Social Security Act.

health insurance: indemnification against most of the costs of medical care for those eligible

Medicare consists of two basic programs. The first, **hospital insurance**, helps pay for hospital expenses and the costs of follow-up treatment. To actually receive payments under this program, an eligible person (as mentioned earlier, nearly all persons over 65, those with severe kidney problems, or those covered for extensive periods by the disability program if under 65 are eligible) must enter a hospital for necessary treatment. After a hospital stay, this program will also help pay for care in a skilled nursing facility or in the home by a home health agency for a period of time. Current benefit figures are available from any Social Security office.

hospital insurance: indemnification against the costs of hospital and follow-up treatment

Not all costs of hospital and extended care are covered by Medicare. Many individuals take out supplemental insurance from a private company to pay what Medicare's hospital insurance does not.

Medical insurance, the second basic Medicare program, helps pay for items not covered by the hospital insurance. These include services of physicians and surgeons. Also included are services such as ambulance charges, X rays, radium treatments, laboratory tests, surgical dressings, casts, and home visits by nurses or therapists as

medical insurance: indemnification against the costs of doctor's fees and related services ordered by a doctor. The patient pays relatively small yearly deductibles, and then medical insurance generally pays either a large percentage or all of the costs of the covered services. All of these items can be very expensive. Consequently, in the problem, it is advisable for Hoffener to follow his wife's suggestion and to sign up for the medical insurance coverage.

Unlike hospital insurance coverage which is financed primarily from the social security tax, the contracting for medical insurance coverage and the payment of the premiums are voluntary. Each person currently enrolled in the medical insurance plan pays a monthly premium. An equal amount is paid by the federal government out of general revenues.

A person must apply for Medicare, just as one must apply for all other social security benefits. However, Medicare differs from other Social Security Act benefits in that application must be submitted within three months before or after the month in which one's 65th birthday occurs. Failure to sign up within the prescribed period will result in a six- to nine-month delay in protection, and the premium for medical coverage will then cost more.

Not all medical costs are covered by Medicare. For example, ordinary dental care, routine physical examinations, eye or ear examinations for prescribing, fitting, or changing eyeglasses or hearing aids, strictly cosmetic surgery, and drugs which are not furnished as part of hospitalization are excluded. Therefore most persons should consider buying supplemental private health insurance coverage.

Medicaid: state-administered program for those without the income or resources to meet medical expenses

In addition to the Medicare program, the **Medicaid** program will assist those in financial need in covering medical costs. Medicaid is federally sponsored but is administered by the states, generally through their divisions of family services.

PREVENTING LEGAL DIFFICULTIES

Remember This About Social Insurance . . .

1. if you have not already secured a Social Security Account Number Card, do so now. You must have one before beginning your first covered job;
2. be informed and aware of the benefits to which you or members of your family might be entitled as a result of dependency, unemployment, disability, or old age;
3. unemployment benefits may be reduced or denied under certain circum-

stances. Be sure that you do not jeopardize your rights to unemployment benefits by actions on your part;

4. should you become eligible for any benefits under social security, file an application promptly. There is a waiting period and benefits are not paid retroactively;
5. there are periodic changes in the Social Security law. Keep up-to-date so that you are aware of the costs to you and of the benefits to which you are entitled;
6. try to maintain, at a minimum, a status of having received credit for one quarter of coverage out of the last two possible until you become fully insured under the social security program; and
7. check your social security earnings record for accuracy about every three years. Your social security office will provide you with a free postcard form for this purpose.

Strengthening Your Legal Vocabulary

currently insured
disability insurance
fully insured
health insurance
hospital insurance
Medicaid
medical insurance
Medicare
payroll deduction
quarter of coverage
retirement insurance
RSDHI
social insurance
survivors' insurance
unemployment compensation

1. Monthly insurance benefits for dependents when a worker dies.
2. Money withheld from worker's pay by employer for taxes or for other purposes.
3. Retirement, Survivors', Disability, and Health Insurance.
4. Status required in order to be eligible to receive benefits under all major social security programs.
5. Benefits which are payable to persons over 65 and which cover most of the costs of hospitalization, post-hospital care, and certain home health services.
6. Payments designed to lessen the financial hardship of temporary, involuntary unemployment.
7. Federal health insurance program which includes both hospital and medical benefits.
8. Monthly insurance benefits for workers and their dependents when the worker retires.
9. A worker with at least six quarters of coverage within the three years before death.
10. Monthly insurance benefits for workers and their dependents when a worker sustains a severe, long-lasting disability.

Reviewing Important Points

1. Every employee and self-employed person in covered work obtains a Social Security Card with an account number. This same number is used all the worker's life to ensure that contributions are properly credited to the individual's account.
2. Unemployment compensation provides weekly benefits for a limited time for workers on covered jobs who have been employed a minimum time and have been discharged.
3. To obtain unemployment benefits, a worker must make proper application, register for a job at a public employment office, be unemployed for a specified time, and be able and available to work a suitable job.
4. Since unemployment insurance is administered by the state, benefits vary widely.
5. Retirement insurance provides monthly benefits for a worker and dependents when the worker retires at age 62 or later.
6. Survivors' insurance provides benefits for dependents when the worker dies.
7. Federal disability insurance provides monthly benefits for a worker and dependents if a severe, long-lasting disability is suffered.
8. Most individuals over 65 and those disabled under 65 are eligible to receive social security payments under Medicare's hospital insurance. Such payments greatly aid in meeting the cost of necessary hospitalization and nursing care.
9. An important supplement to the hospital insurance under Medicare is the medical insurance available to eligible parties upon the payment of a monthly premium. The medical insurance helps meet costs for which assistance is not available under the hospital insurance, for example, doctor bills and X rays.
10. Employers and employees share retirement, survivors', disability, and health insurance tax burdens equally. In most states, employers alone pay for unemployment insurance.

Applying Law to Everyday Life

1. Podesta was laid off when the fruit and vegetable canning plant where she worked cut back on production. After a week, she began receiving unemployment benefit checks. Shortly after, a new semester began at the local state college. Podesta enrolled as a full-time student but continued to accept the benefit checks because she said she was ready, willing, and able to go back to work full-time. If called, she would either rearrange her classes or quit school. Was she entitled to unemployment benefits?

2. Chadwick began working full-time when he graduated from high school at age 18. He joined a union and got a job driving a heavy caterpillar-type

tractor in road construction. By putting in many hours of overtime, he earned about $15,000 a year for four years. He married and soon after a child arrived. Then tragedy struck. Chadwick's tractor overturned on a mountainside, throwing him and permanently paralyzing his lower body. Will social security help Chadwick and his family?

3. Montebello had often said, "If you retire, you're on the shelf. Might just as well be in a box six feet under." And so he continued to work full-time until he died at the age of 81, never missing a day because of illness or accident. By then his wife had died, and his children were married and self-sufficient. Montebello had paid social security taxes for more than 40 years. Will his estate or his heirs receive any benefits?

4. Collin was self-employed as a sharpener of knives and scissors. She drove from town to town in a large van which served as her mobile home and shop. Business gradually declined, and after 17 years, she quit because she could not make a living with her service. Is Collin entitled to unemployment compensation?

5. When the cost of living rose, Bollinger's employer refused to boost the wages of his workers because costs were up and sales down. After weeks of fruitless negotiations, Bollinger and his fellow union members demanded a pay boost and went out on strike. This cut Bollinger's income to nothing and he applied for unemployment compensation. Does he qualify?

6. Porter was convicted of stealing a typewriter from his employer and was promptly sentenced to 30 days in the county jail. After waiting one week, Porter insisted that he was eligible for unemployment compensation to feed his family. Was he correct?

7. McMurty, who was 70 and covered by Medicare, slipped and fell down a flight of 15 steps. She broke her hip and her jaw and required dental surgery as well as plastic surgery to restore her face. Would the necessary medical attention be provided under Medicare?

Solving Case Problems

1. Lenore and William Moss brought suit against the Secretary of the Department of Health, Education, and Welfare for refusing to grant Mr. Moss derivative spouse's benefits under the Social Security Act. To receive the benefits, Mr. Moss had to show that he received at least one-half of his support from his wife. He had been unable to do so. However, the one-half of support test was applied only to the husbands of insureds and not to wives who were in a similar position of claiming the derivative benefits. For this reason, the Mosses claimed the qualifying test for receiving benefits represented a denial, on the basis of sex, of equal protection under the due process clause of the 5th Amendment to the United States Constitution. The

Secretary argued that the distinction was necessary for administrative convenience. Decide. (*Moss v. Secretary of H.E.W.*, 408 F. Supp. 403)

2. Dawkins had been employed as a sheet metal worker by the Sun Shipbuilding and Dry Dock Co. When World War II ended and shipyard work declined, he expected to be laid off. Therefore he quit to go into business for himself as a roofing contractor. Within four months he had to shut down because he could not get materials. Now he asks for unemployment compensation, claiming he left his job at the shipyard for good cause. Is he entitled to unemployment benefits? (*Sun Shipbuilding and Dry Dock Co. v. Unemployment Compensation Board of Review*, 358 Pa. 224, 56 A.2d 254)

3. For years Mary Sizer had lived on and helped manage a small farm owned by her mother and brother. When the mother became an invalid, Mary entered into a contract with her brother under which she would receive from him $15 per week for caring for their mother and doing chores at the farm. Five years later her mother died, and her brother inherited the farm. Mary now claims that the contract evidenced an employer-employee relationship between her and her brother that entitled her to claim social security hospital benefits. She further states that an outsider hired to perform the duties she did would fall under the protection of the Act. The Social Security Administration denies that benefits should be paid, claiming that the relationship was merely a close family cooperative arrangement based on mutual love and affection. Decide. (*Sizer v. Weinberger, Secretary of H.E.W.*, 401 F. Supp. 109)

4. Club Hubba Hubba hired some Japanese women and brought them to Hawaii where they were to work as nightclub entertainers for six months. The club impounded their passports on arrival, gave them room and board and other benefits, and advertised them as the "Hubba Hubba Girls." The women were not permitted to work for anyone else without the consent of the Club. If the Club consented to their working elsewhere, the Club was compensated for their services and it, in turn, paid the women. The Club claimed the women were independent contractors, like most traveling entertainers, and therefore it was not necessary to pay social security taxes for them. Was the Club correct? (*Hubba Hubba v. U.S. & Evans*, 239 F. Supp. 324)

5. Joe Fitzgerald, a laborer, injured his back. Physical therapy did not help, and his doctor recommended injecting oil into his spinal canal for X rays (myelogram), a painful but safe procedure. If the results were positive, the doctor would recommend surgery, which would require six months for recovery. Joe refused this treatment and claimed disability benefits. Is he entitled to such benefits? (*Fitzgerald v. Finch*, No. 1862, E.D. Ky.)

Unit Eight
USING COMMERCIAL PAPER

UNIT OBJECTIVES

UPON COMPLETION OF THIS UNIT, you should be able to

1. discuss the importance of commercial paper.
2. identify the types of commercial paper.
3. explain the concept of negotiability and why it is so important.
4. recall the elements necessary to make an instrument negotiable.
5. understand the implications of each type of indorsement.
6. distinguish between the various types of holders.
7. recall the limited and universal defenses.
8. explain how commercial paper is discharged.

30

Nature and Kinds of Instruments

1. You want to buy $1,200 worth of sporting goods from a discount seller in a distant state. Unfortunately you have no credit cards, the seller will not take a personal check, and it would be risky to send cash through the mail. What special type of check could you use for the purchase?
2. When you ask a business associate for $200 she owes you, she writes a message to her bank on a blank sheet of paper. The message directs the bank to pay $200 from her checking account to you or to your order whenever you demand it. She signs the paper, dates it, and gives it to you. Is the paper a check?
3. You loan $1,000 to someone who is to repay you a year or more in the future. If you do not wish to rely on the person's oral promise to repay you, what other two options are available to you?

WHAT IS COMMERCIAL PAPER?

PROBLEM: Benito boasts to his friend Sanguine that he has loaned money to the Intercontinental Bank, because it holds his checking account with $327 on deposit. "It's a demand loan and they've got to pay me whenever I say so!" Sanguine disputes Benito's claim that the bank is his debtor. Who is right?

commercial paper: unconditional written orders or promises to pay money

Commercial paper consists of unconditional written orders or promises to pay money. The most common form of commercial paper, the personal check, is familiar to us all. Like other forms of commercial paper, it was developed hundreds of years ago to serve as a relatively safe substitute for money. Rather than carry their gold and silver with them, merchants would leave such precious metals with bankers. Then, when merchants wanted to pay a seller for goods they were buying, they merely wrote an order addressed to their bank. The order directed the bank to deliver a specified amount to the person or the place of the seller's choice. The bank could tell if it was receiving an authentic order by comparing the merchant's signature (and perhaps a seal) on the order with the signature the bank had on file. The bank would comply with such written orders because, once the merchant had made a deposit, the bank was legally indebted to the depositor for that amount. Consequently, if the merchant demanded return of the deposit, the bank had to give it back. The same is still true today. Banks still are debtors of their depositors, as Benito correctly noted in the problem. Also, checks are still known as demand instruments because they allow depositors to get their money out of banks or have it paid in accordance with the depositor's order. The laws governing the use of commercial paper are found mainly in Article 3 of the Uniform Commercial Code.

WHAT ARE THE DIFFERENT TYPES OF COMMERCIAL PAPER?

PROBLEM: Nightwing purchased a personal computer to help her with her new business. After comparing software, she selected an integrated accounting and inventory program for the machine. The program cost more than $400, and she had to borrow the money temporarily from her friend Fyffe. In exchange, Nightwing gave Fyffe an IOU for that amount. The IOU was signed and dated. Was it commercial paper?

Today commercial paper can be grouped into two broad categories. The first is composed of unconditional *orders* to pay money. In this category are the draft and the check. A check is a special kind of draft. The second category is composed of unconditional *promises* to pay money. In this category are the promissory note and the certificate of deposit.

Unconditional, as used in the definition of commercial paper, means that the legal effectiveness of the order or promise is not dependent upon any other event. Accordingly, an instrument that reads "Pay to the order of Sam after he delivers a new ten-speed bike to me" would not be commercial paper because its enforceability is conditional upon delivery of the bike. Also, unlike unconditional orders or promises to pay a sum of money, an IOU, such as the one given to Fyffe in the problem, is merely an acknowledgement of a debt. It is not a formal promise or order to pay the money at a certain time or on demand to the bearer or someone's order. Therefore an IOU is not commercial paper.

Now examine each of the four main types of commercial paper:

1. Drafts

A **draft** is an unconditional written order by which one party directs a second party to pay to the order of a third party or to the bearer a certain sum of money on demand or at a definite time (see Figure 30-1). A draft is also known as a *bill of exchange.*

The usual purpose of a draft is to collect money owed. A draft initially involves three parties—the drawer, the drawee, and the payee. The **drawer** is the one who executes or draws the draft and orders that payment be made. The **drawee** is the one directed to pay the draft. The **payee** is the party to whom commercial paper is made payable.

draft: unconditional written order by one party to a second party to pay a third party a certain sum on demand or at a definite time

drawer: one who executes a draft

drawee: one directed to pay a draft

payee: one to whom commercial paper is payable

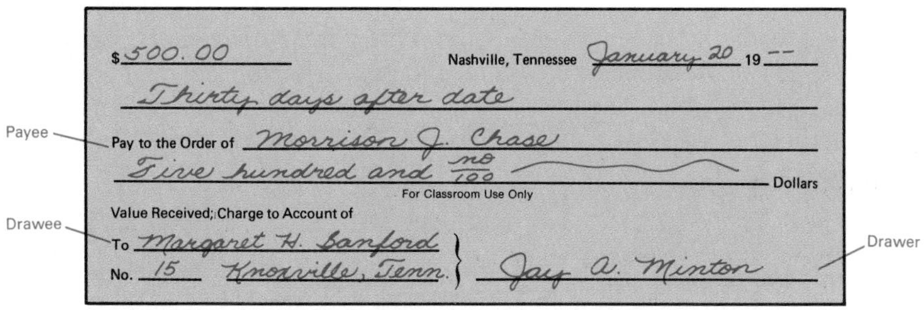
$500.00 Nashville, Tennessee January 20 19--
Thirty days after date
Pay to the Order of Morrison J. Chase
Five hundred and no/100 Dollars
For Classroom Use Only
Value Received; Charge to Account of
To Margaret H. Sanford
No. 15 Knoxville, Tenn.
Jay A. Minton

Figure 30-1. Time Draft

In Figure 30-1, Sanford presumably owes Minton $500 as a result of a previous transaction. Therefore Sanford is likely to honor the draft by paying Chase and in that way be relieved of her debt to Minton.

sight draft: draft payable on sight

time draft: draft payable at a specified time or after a specified period

acceptance: drawee's promise to pay the draft when due

Drafts are sometimes described in terms of the time of payment. If the draft is payable at sight or on demand—that is, when it is presented to the drawee by the one holding the draft—it is a **sight draft.** The drawee is expected to pay when the draft is presented.

If a draft is payable at a specified time, or if it is payable at the end of a specified period after sight or after the date of the draft, it is a **time draft,** as is illustrated in Figure 30-1. When a time draft is payable a number of days or months after sight, it must be presented to the drawee for acceptance in order to start the running of the specified time. **Acceptance** is the drawee's promise to pay the draft when due. When the draft states it is payable a number of days or months "after date," the time starts running immediately from the date of the draft.

Clinton sold Devue an amplifier for an electric guitar. Devue paid Clinton $100, which left a $700 balance. Clinton then bought a state-of-the-art, low-distortion speaker system from Downtown Audio. As partial payment to Downtown, he drew a draft on the $700 owed him by Devue. To be sure Devue had adequate time to get the money together, Clinton made the draft payable to the order of Downtown Audio 30 days after sight. Upon receiving the draft, Downtown immediately presented it to Devue who indicated her willingness to pay in 30 days by writing the date and her signature on the front of the paper along with the word *accepted.*

2. Checks

PROBLEM: Hubble gave a check for $385 to Honest John's Auto Repair for the repair of her car's transmission. When the job proved to be defective, she telephoned her bank and ordered it to stop payment on the check. Three weeks later, however, the bank allowed Honest John's to cash the check and paid the $385 out of Hubble's account. Can Hubble legally force the bank to recredit the $385 to her account?

check: a type of draft in which a depositor orders his or her bank to pay deposited funds to a third party or to bearer

A **check** is a special type of draft by which a bank depositor orders the bank to pay money, usually to a third party (see Figure 30-2). Checks are usually written on special forms provided by the

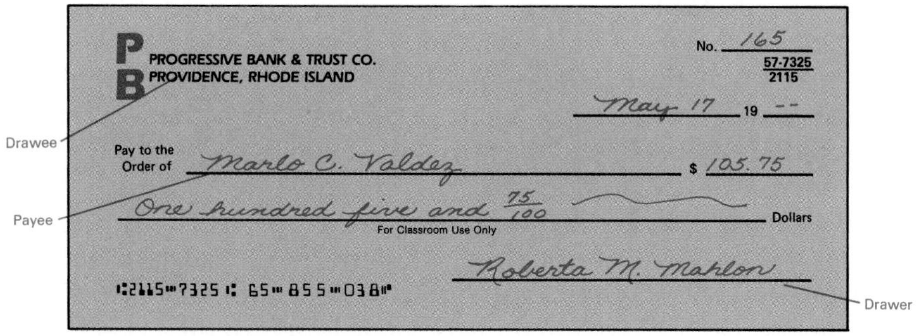

Figure 30-2. Check

bank for a fee. The forms provided by the bank usually are magnetically encoded to make check processing easier for the banking system. However, checks may be written on blank sheets of paper, forms provided by the depositor, or other materials and still be legally effective. The drawee, though, must always be a bank for the instrument to qualify as a check.

The bank, according to the contracts with its depositors, agrees to **honor** (pay when due) each check as long as sufficient funds remain in the depositor's account. As a debtor of the depositor, the bank owes the duty to honor checks in return for the right to use the depositor's funds until the depositor demands their return. Of course, the bank must retain a sizable percentage of all funds deposited so that it can pay properly drawn checks when they are presented. The remainder of the deposited funds is loaned at interest to pay for the bank's operations and to earn a profit for the bank's owners.

honor: to pay an instrument when due

A person who deliberately issues a check with the knowledge that the funds in the account will be insufficient to pay the check when it is presented at the drawee bank, is guilty of a crime. The bank will **dishonor** (refuse to pay when due) the instrument and the payee or current owner of the check will not get any money for it from that source. In addition, if a check is issued to pay a debt, the payoff is not effective until the check is presented to the drawee bank and honored.

dishonor: to refuse to pay an instrument when due

When a check has been lost or stolen, the drawer should direct the bank not to pay it. Such an instruction is called a **stop payment order.** Banks usually charge a small fee to stop payment on a check. If, by mistake, the drawee bank disregards the stop payment order and pays the check, the bank must recredit the account. The bank—not the depositor—must bear any loss. Oral stop payment orders

stop payment order: an order directing a bank not to pay on a check

are good only for two weeks unless they are confirmed in writing. Written stop payment orders are good for six months and lapse at the end of that time unless renewed. Therefore, in the problem, Hubble could not force the bank to recredit her account because more than two weeks had elapsed and she had not sent a written stop payment order to the bank.

Reasonable care must be taken when writing or accepting checks. When you write a check, be sure not to leave room for someone to insert figures and words to change the amount of the instrument. Do not give anything of value in return for a check that appears to have been altered in any manner. In addition, do not accept a check that may have been issued in connection with illegal activities, for example, gambling. Such instruments are usually considered void by the courts. Finally, never sign a blank check.

3. Promissory Notes

promissory note: unconditional written promise by one party to pay a certain sum of money to the order of another party on demand or at a definite time

maker: one who executes a promissory note or a certificate of deposit

> **PROBLEM:** Burger was the owner and the president of a small manufacturing company. She also owned the land and the buildings the company used. When she needed to raise cash to finance a major expansion, her financial advisors told her that the best way to do so was by using the building and the land as a source of funds. How could Burger do this?

A **promissory note** is an unconditional written promise by one person to pay to the order of another person or to the bearer a certain sum of money on demand or at a definite time (see Figure 30-3). Promissory notes initially involve only two parties—the maker and the payee. The **maker** is the one who executes or makes a prom-

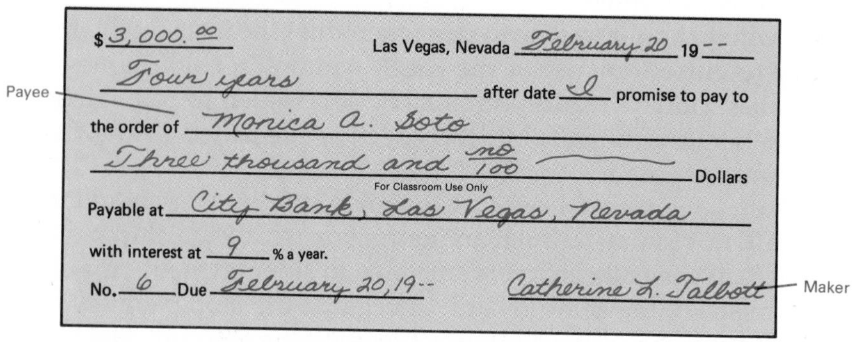
$3,000.00 Las Vegas, Nevada February 20 19--
Four years after date I promise to pay to
the order of Monica A. Soto
Three thousand and no/100 Dollars
For Classroom Use Only
Payable at City Bank, Las Vegas, Nevada
with interest at 9 % a year.
No. 6 Due February 20, 19-- Catherine L. Talbott

Figure 30-3. Promissory Note

issory note (or a certificate of deposit) and promises to pay. (Certificates of deposit will be discussed later in this chapter.) If two or more parties join in executing the note, they are **comakers** and are equally liable for payment.

comakers: two or more makers of a promissory note

Personal property may be pledged to secure performance—that is, to ensure payment—of a note. When this fact, together with a description of the property, is stated on the face of the note, the paper is a **collateral note.** The property pledged in collateral notes is usually in the form of documents of title, such as bonds, a warehouse receipt, or a life insurance policy. A collateral note typically provides for the sale of the security by the payee if the note is not paid when due.

collateral note: note secured by personal property

If real property is the security for the payment, the note is a **mortgage note.** In the problem, Burger could borrow funds by signing a mortgage note and giving a mortgage on the land and the building as security for repayment. Thus, Burger would not have to sell the building to raise the capital. If the payment is not made when due, however, the payee can force a sale of the real property and use the proceeds for payment.

mortgage note: note secured by real property

When a note authorizes the owner to have a court judgment entered against the maker upon failure to pay, without notice to the maker and without lawsuit, the instrument is a **judgment note.** In such a case, the one holding the note can get judgment and can obtain execution speedily against the assets of the maker. Judgment notes are outlawed in some states because they deprive the debtor of a "day in court," where the debtor might present an acceptable reason for not paying.

judgment note: note that authorizes judgment without notice to the maker and without a lawsuit

4. Certificates of Deposit

PROBLEM: Paruzzi wanted to buy a new car in a year or so. He had just received a large income tax refund which he intended to use as a down payment. However, he was afraid that he might spend the money before he was ready to contract for the car. Therefore Paruzzi was looking for an investment that would pay a good interest rate, allow him access to the money in a year, and discourage him from spending it in the interim. Should Paruzzi consider buying a certificate of deposit with the refund?

certificate of deposit: unconditional written promise of a bank to repay with interest a deposit of money at a certain future date

A **certificate of deposit** is a written acknowledgment by a bank of receipt of money, with an unconditional promise to repay it (see

Figure 30-4). The stated amount is payable with interest at a definite future time, normally ranging from several months to several years. A certificate of deposit is often called a CD.

By federal law, banks are prohibited from paying out CD's or other long-term deposits before maturity unless the depositor is penalized. Usually the penalty is a sharp reduction in the amount of interest payable on the funds. This inhibits depositors from withdrawing funds prematurely and leaves the banks free to lend the funds to others on a long-term basis. As a consequence, interest rates on CD's are usually significantly higher than on savings or checking accounts, where the depositor is far more likely to withdraw funds. Therefore, in the problem, Paruzzi should consider buying a certificate of deposit that would mature in a year. It would offer a relatively high interest rate, the security of having a federally insured savings association's or bank's backing, and, considering the interest penalty for early withdrawal, an incentive to save funds until they really are needed.

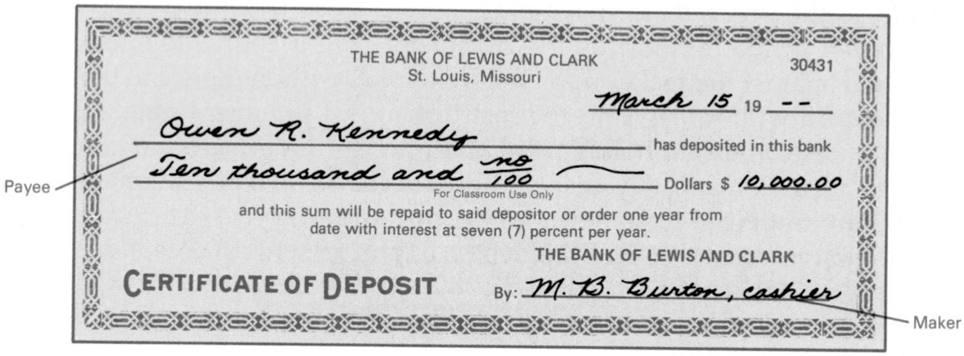

THE BANK OF LEWIS AND CLARK
St. Louis, Missouri
30431

March 15 19 --

Owen R. Kennedy has deposited in this bank

Ten thousand and no/100 Dollars $ 10,000.00

For Classroom Use Only

and this sum will be repaid to said depositor or order one year from date with interest at seven (7) percent per year.

THE BANK OF LEWIS AND CLARK

CERTIFICATE OF DEPOSIT By: M. B. Burton, cashier

Figure 30-4. Certificate of Deposit

WHAT ARE SOME OF THE SPECIALIZED FORMS OF COMMERCIAL PAPER IN USE?

PROBLEM: Dr. Ho in Santa Ana, California, needed a shipment of expensive drugs to treat a rare disease in one of his patients. The supplier of the drug, a New York company, would not ship COD, extend credit, or accept personal checks from customers outside the state. What other means of payment could Dr. Ho use to satisfy the New York company?

Although the four types of commercial paper described in the previous section are the most frequently used, certain variations of the forms are available for specialized needs. These include:

1. Certified Checks

A person to whom a personal check is offered as payment may fear the bank will not honor the check because of insufficient funds in the drawer's account. However, accepting a check is much safer if the bank already has agreed to pay the check, because only the unlikely event of the bank's failure will prevent the payee or current owner of the check from receiving the money due. A personal check that has been accepted by a bank in advance of payment is known as a **certified check.** At the time of certification, the bank draws sufficient funds from the depositor's account and sets them aside in a special account to pay the check when it is presented. In addition, the bank marks the front of the check with "accepted" or "certified," the date, and the bank's signature. In the problem, Dr. Ho could use a certified check if the New York firm would accept it.

certified check: personal check accepted by the bank in advance of payment

2. Cashier's Checks

A check that a bank draws on itself and which is issued by an authorized bank officer is a **cashier's check** (see Figure 30-5). Such checks are used by banks to pay their own obligations. They also may be purchased from a bank by persons who wish to send *remittances* (payments) but who either have no personal checking account or do not wish to use their personal checks. A cashier's check would also be a satisfactory way for Dr. Ho to pay for the drugs.

cashier's check: check drawn by a bank on itself

Figure 30-5. Cashier's Check

3. Bank Drafts

bank draft: draft drawn by one bank as a depositor in a second bank

A draft drawn by a bank on funds that it has on deposit with another bank is a **bank draft**. Thus, such a document is a draft drawn by one bank on a second bank. Banks use these drafts in their own transactions. Sometimes a person or a business firm wishes to make an initial purchase for a sizable sum. The seller refuses to accept checks of customers whose credit is not established. Therefore such customers may use bank drafts purchased from a bank. This would be another possibility open to Dr. Ho.

4. Money Orders

money order: draft used to transfer money using the credit of the issuer of the money order

Money orders are often used by persons who do not have checking accounts. A **money order** is a draft issued by a post office, bank, express company, or telegraph company for use in making payment or transferring funds upon the credit of the issuer. Money orders serve the same purpose as checks. For example, a money order is purchased from one post office, which orders payment by another post office in the hometown of the payee designated by the purchaser. A money order could be used by Dr. Ho.

5. Traveler's Checks

traveler's check: check drawn by a reliable financial institution on itself, and then sold to a traveler who signs at the time of issue and of use

Hotels and retailers around the world understandably prefer to take checks from persons they know and can trust only. At the same time, travelers are reluctant to carry cash on journeys. To meet the needs of both the traveler and the merchant, traveler's checks have been devised. A **traveler's check** is a check drawn by a reliable financial institution (such as Bank of America or American Express Company) on itself or its agent. Traveler's checks may be purchased from banks and other institutions. At the time they are purchased, each check is signed by the buyer. Either in the U.S.A. or in a foreign land, when cashing one of the checks the traveler writes in the name of the payee and again signs her or his name as originally written on the check. This is done in the presence of the payee who can compare the signatures. The payee, who knows and trusts the drawee bank or issuing company, is usually willing to take the traveler's check. Thereafter, the payee may deposit and collect the traveler's check in the same manner as other checks. Although traveler's checks are still used, the greatly expanded use of credit cards throughout the world has reduced the need for them.

PREVENTING LEGAL DIFFICULTIES

Commercial Paper Can Be as Good as Money if You . . .

1. prepare commercial paper accurately and handle it with care, appreciating its value. Be sure not to leave blank space where a wrongdoer might insert figures and words that change the amount of the instrument;
2. make certain that the other party's credit is good before you accept a check or lend money in exchange for a note. Be ensured that the check or note will be honored when due. If practicable, ask for security, such as collateral or a mortgage, for repayment of notes;
3. consider using a certified check, cashier's check, bank draft, money order, traveler's check, or credit card if a creditor is hesitant about accepting your personal check;
4. use your right to stop payment of checks to prevent your bank from honoring a lost or stolen check. Or use the process if a payee breaches the underlying contract which led you to write the check; and
5. remember that an oral stop payment order is good for only 14 days unless confirmed in writing. A written stop payment order is good for six months and can be renewed.

Strengthening Your Legal Vocabulary

acceptance
bank draft
cashier's check
certificate of deposit
certified check
check
collateral note
comakers
commercial paper
dishonor
draft
drawee
drawer
honor
judgment note
maker
money order
mortgage note
payee
promissory note
sight draft
stop payment order
time draft
traveler's check

1. Check drawn by a financial institution on itself and then sold to a person who signs it at the time of issue and again at the time of use.
2. Party directed by the drawer to pay a draft.
3. One who executes a promissory note or a certificate of deposit.
4. Unconditional written promise by one party to pay a certain sum of money to the order of another person or to the bearer on demand or at a definite future time.
5. One who executes a draft.

6. Special form of draft by which a depositor orders his or her bank to pay money to a third party.
7. Party to whom a promissory note or other commercial paper is payable.
8. An unconditional written order or promise to pay money.
9. Drawee's promise to pay a draft when due.
10. To pay an instrument when due.

Reviewing Important Points

1. Commercial paper was developed hundreds of years ago to serve as a safer, more convenient substitute for precious metals and currency.
2. There are four important types of commercial paper: (a) drafts, (b) checks (a special type of draft), (c) promissory notes, and (d) certificates of deposit.
3. In general, drafts are unconditional orders to another party to pay a certain sum of money on demand or at a definite future time. Checks, a special type of draft, are unconditional orders to a bank to pay a certain sum of money on demand. Initially three parties are involved in drafts and checks: the drawer, who gives the order to pay; the drawee, who gets the order; and the payee, to whom payment is to be made.
4. A check differs from other types of drafts in that:
   a. the drawee of a check is always a bank,
   b. a check is drawn against funds the drawer has on deposit in the bank, and
   c. a check is always payable on demand.
5. Promissory notes and certificates of deposit are unconditional promises to pay a certain sum of money on demand or at a definite future time. Initially two parties are involved; the maker, who promises to pay; and the payee, to whom payment is promised.
6. Various forms of checks and drafts have been devised for special purposes. These forms include (a) certified checks, (b) cashier's checks, (c) bank drafts, (d) money orders, and (e) traveler's checks.

Applying Law to Everyday Life

1. Joseph McReynolds gave the following signed instrument to Helen Harrison after borrowing $5,000 from her: "This will acknowledge my legal duty to pay Helen Harrison $5,000." It was dated and signed by McReynolds. Is the instrument commercial paper?

2. Grier executed the following commercial paper. Identify the paper as to type and identify the parties.

Portland, Maine
June 1, 19--

On September 1, 19--, I promise to pay to the order of J. Cameron Curtis one thousand dollars ($1,000).

Anna C. Grier
Anna C. Grier

For Classroom Use Only

3. Nelson executed the following commercial paper. (a) Identify the paper as to type and parties. (b) Under what circumstances would Campbell be legally obligated to pay the amount as ordered?

Chattanooga, Tennessee
January 15, 19--

Thirty days after date, pay to the order of Corita J. Clifford the sum of fifteen hundred dollars ($1,500) with interest at the rate of seven (7) percent per year.

To: J. C. B. Campbell
15 Mountain View Road
Asheville, North Carolina

Arthur G. Nelson
Arthur G. Nelson

For Classroom Use Only

4. Catron executed the following paper. (a) Identify the paper as to type and parties. (b) What could happen if Catron had started the words "Three hundred" farther to the right, near the middle of the check?

Mother Lode Mining & Refining Bank
Fairbanks, Alaska

No. 8116
89-73/1252

November 15, 19--

Pay to the Order of John G. Barbour $300.00

Three hundred and no/100 Dollars

For Classroom Use Only

Louise L. Catron

⑆1252⑈0073⑆ 4156⑈2222⑈

5. Sutherland wanted to order some novelty costume jewelry which she saw advertised in a national magazine. The ad expressly said, "Send no cash or personal checks. No COD orders accepted." How should Sutherland pay?

6. Rivera ordered by mail a programmable electronic doorbell for her townhouse. She paid with a personal check. When the doorbell arrived, it would not work. Rivera immediately called the bank and told them to stop payment on her check. She then shipped the doorbell back to the seller. The next day she confirmed the stop payment order in writing. Seven months later the seller sent her check through the interbank collection process, and Rivera's bank paid it. Rivera was furious and demanded that the bank recredit her account for the amount which was paid in spite of the stop payment order. Must the bank recredit her account?

7. Thruster owns the Discovery Electronic Works, a small company that manufactures portable computers. The company is doing well but needs to expand and update its product line. Thruster plans to use credit to do both. What specific types of commercial paper will be used if: (a) The Works borrows $15,000 of the $20,000 needed to pay for a shipment of integrated circuit chips and uses the chips as security for payment? (b) The Works borrows $65,000 of the $100,000 needed to buy a building in which a new assembly line is to be housed and uses the real property as security for payment?

Solving Case Problems

1. While in Shreveport, Louisiana, Claypool wanted to play poker for money stakes at the Crystal Bar. He persuaded Parker to *stand good* (pay) for any losses he might have. Before the night was over, Claypool's losses swelled to $3,500. Then Parker added another $2,500 to help Claypool "get even." This too, was lost. Thereafter, Claypool gave Parker a promissory note for $10,473.14 to cover the $6,000 lost. The balance was to repay money that had been previously advanced by Parker to Claypool to buy oil and gas leases. When the note came due, Claypool refused to pay. Is Parker's claim barred because the note was given in part for an illegal gambling debt? (*Parker v. Claypool*, 223 Miss. 213, 78 So. 2d 124)

2. Blayton was president of a trucking company. The company was delinquent in rental payments for equipment leased from Mason. On November 4, when Mason threatened to sue, Blayton gave Mason his personal check for $3,000 to cover the amount due. However, Blayton asked Mason to withhold action on the check until November 6, when the company would be able to pay. On November 6, the company failed to pay, and Mason deposited Blayton's check. It was dishonored because Blayton had stopped payment, claiming there was no contract in writing, as required by the statute of frauds, to bind him. (a) Was the check a sufficient contract? (b) Was Blayton justified in stopping payment? (*Mason v. Blayton*, 119 Ga. App. 203, 166 S.E.2d 601)

3. Gunn contracted to sell Tak, a broker from Hong Kong, 60,000 metric tons of UREA, a fertilizer, at $400 a ton. In connection with this $24,000,000 sale, Gunn entered another contract agreeing to pay Tak a commission for all Tak's sales of the fertilizer. After 10,000 tons of UREA had been sold, paid for, and delivered, Gunn bought and delivered to Tak a cashier's check from the Empire Bank of Springfield for $150,000 payable to the order of Tak. Shortly thereafter, Gunn learned that the balance of the order for the remaining 50,000 tons of UREA had been canceled by Tak. Therefore Gunn ordered the bank to stop payment on the check because of the cancellation of the contract and the alleged fraud of Tak. The court issued an injunction ordering the bank not to pay the check. Shortly after the court order, the cashier's check was transferred by Tak to Lai, who claims the right to collect the face amount. Should the bank honor the stop payment order, or must it pay Lai the face amount of the check? (*Lai v. Powell, Judge*, 536 S.W.2d 14, Mo.)

4. In a Missouri Circuit Court, Kleen was convicted of issuing an insufficient funds check. He appealed, pointing out that he had merely signed a blank check form in Missouri and then given the form to his truck driver. The truck driver carried the signed blank check form to Memphis, Tennessee, where someone at the Herring Sales Company filled in the company name as the payee and also filled in the amount. Herring then kept the check in return for a truckload of meal that was transported by Kleen's truck and driver back to Kleen's business in Nevada, Missouri. Kleen therefore contended that, even though the check was drawn on the Citizen's Bank of Nevada, the alleged criminal act occurred in Tennessee, where the signed blank form was completed. Kleen argued that, as a consequence, Missouri had no jurisdiction and that the conviction should be overturned. Decide. (*State v. Kleen*, 491 S.W.2d 244, Mo.)

5. Henry Thomas purchased a new car on October 22 and gave Frazier Buick Company a check for the full amount. The company then signed over the certificate of title to Thomas. However, Thomas died the next day, and Frazier Buick immediately repossessed the car without cashing the check. The administratrix of Thomas' estate then sued the company on behalf of the estate for $500 actual damages as she "had (the car) sold" for $500 above the price Thomas had paid for it at Frazier Buick. She also asked for $2,500 in punitive damages for the company's abrupt and insensitive action in repossessing the car. Will the estate recover? (*Hickerson v. Con Frazier Buick Co.*, 264 S.W.2d 29, Mo.)

31
Negotiability

1. An acquaintance asks you to cosign a promissory note so that the seller of a car will accept the note as a partial payment. "Be a pal," the acquaintance says. "It won't cost you a cent. And I'll let you borrow the car when you need it." You sign the note. Could you later be required to pay the full amount of the note?
2. On April Fool's Day, a friend gives you a check for $25, deliberately postdated a full year ahead. Will you be able to collect in a year and thus enjoy the last laugh?
3. Using a pencil, a friend writes a check to your order for $100 on the back of a restaurant napkin. Is the check legally valid?

WHAT IS NEGOTIABILITY AND WHY IS IT SO IMPORTANT?

PROBLEM: Hunsak wanted to open a farm supply store. While talking with her accountant, Hunsak indicated that she wanted to do business on a cash-only basis because taking checks or promissory notes was too risky. Is she correct?

If commercial paper is to be accepted instead of cash, the person or business receiving it must have confidence that the instrument will be paid. Today such assurance is provided to some extent by the UCC each time a negotiable instrument which has been issued by a financially responsible person is properly transferred. The UCC empowers an innocent new owner to overcome many of the otherwise legitimate and effective defenses which the obligor might raise against paying. **Negotiability** refers to the quality of a properly transferred instrument to be transferred so as to convey such powers to qualified transferees. **Negotiation**, in turn, means the proper transfer of negotiable instruments. An instrument must be negotiable to be classified as commercial paper. However, even when commercial paper is negotiable, if it is not properly transferred (negotiated) it is considered to have been assigned only. As a consequence, the assignee receives only the rights of the transferor. These rights may fall far short of the rights that accrue to the innocent transferee of properly negotiated commercial paper.

negotiability: quality of a properly transferred instrument which protects qualified transferees against certain defenses

negotiation: the proper transfer of a negotiable instrument

This chapter discusses what is required for a written instrument to be considered negotiable and then explains how to negotiate such an instrument properly. In the problem, Hunsak is incorrect. The law would provide significant protection if she were to accept properly transferred negotiable instruments from financially responsible customers. Such protection would reduce the risk of not being able to collect. Not taking commercial paper would probably mean losing customers because they would be denied the safety and convenience of using checks and notes.

WHAT IS REQUIRED TO MAKE A WRITTEN INSTRUMENT NEGOTIABLE?

PROBLEM: Deborah Harvel had a rubber stamp made that read "Downtown Furniture Store, by Deborah Harvel, Treasurer." To save time, she used the stamp to sign the company's payroll checks. Were the checks legally signed without her handwritten signature?

Whether or not an instrument is negotiable generally is determined by what appears on its face at the time it is issued. To be considered negotiable and therefore eligible for classification as commercial paper under Article 3 of the UCC, an instrument:

1. must be in writing and must be signed by the maker or drawer,
2. must be an unconditional promise or order,
3. must be payable in a sum certain in money,
4. must be payable on demand or at a definite time, and
5. must be payable to the bearer or to someone's order.

It is not required that the instrument state that value has been given for the paper or that a date appear on the instrument. Of course, identifying the value given is often a good idea and will not defeat negotiability. If a date is not on the paper, the paper is regarded as having the date of the day on which it is made and delivered to the payee. Sometimes, however, the date is essential to the meaning of the paper (for example, as with a draft payable "30 days after date"). In such a case, any owner in possession of the paper who knows the true date may write it in if authorized to do so, thus making the paper negotiable. The paper may be **antedated** (dated earlier than the date of issuance). Or it may be **postdated** (dated later than the date of issuance). However, in either case, the date must not be used to defraud.

antedated: dated earlier than the date of issuance

postdated: dated later than the date of issuance

Each of the requirements of negotiability is discussed in detail in this chapter.

1. A Writing Signed by the Maker or Drawer

To be negotiable, a paper must be in writing; thus, it is subject to the parol evidence rule (see Chapter 13). The paper must also be signed by the maker or drawer with the intent that it create a legal obligation.

The writing may be done entirely in ink or on a typewriter. It may consist of a printed form with the terms written or typed in. Pencil may be used, but the impression is not durable and may invite alteration. Legally, any medium may be used for the writing surface and inscription as long as the end result is recognizable as a writing. If there is a conflict between provisions written by hand and those typed or printed, the handwriting prevails. The theory is that the handwriting is more recent than the typing or printing. Thus, it is more likely to reflect the true intention of the party. Similarly, typewritten terms prevail over commercially printed ones. Typed terms are more recent, personalized, and customized than are printed terms. In addition, an amount expressed in words prevails over an amount expressed in figures. For example, *seven dollars and fifty cents* would be seen as correct when compared with a conflicting figure of *$75.00* in the same instrument.

The form of the signature generally does not affect its legality as long as the person intended it to be his or her signature. For example, an effective signature may be made with a rubber stamp, as in the problem.

A trade or assumed name is effective if it is intended as one's signature. Examples would be Outer-Space Suits Co. or Kris Kringle. One person may legitimately sign another person's name if authorized to do so as an agent (see Chapter 24). Any individual who cannot write because of illiteracy or a physical handicap may sign with a mark, such as an X. It is commonly required that another person insert the name of the signer next to the mark and also sign as witness.

The location of the signature is also generally immaterial as long as it appears somewhere on the face of the instrument. Thus, the signature may appear in the body of the instrument's text as long as the signer's status as maker or drawer is clear.

2. An Unconditional Promise or Order

To be negotiable, a promissory note or a certificate of deposit must contain an unconditional promise to pay money. Similarly, a check or a draft must contain an unconditional order. Simply acknowledging a debt as in "I owe you $100" is not enough, because the statement is not a formal promise or order to pay the money at a certain time or on demand to the bearer or to someone's order. The word *unconditional* means that the promise or order to pay money must be absolute, that is, free of any limits or restrictions. "I promise to pay Herbert Wilcox $1,000 if his horse wins the sixth race" would be conditional upon an event that might not occur; therefore, the instrument that bore the statement would not be negotiable.

Likewise, to promise payment out of a certain fund or account *only* or to make payment *subject to* another agreement would make the obligation conditional on there being enough money in the account or on the agreement being properly performed. Such conditions would restrict the free flow of commercial paper since a cautious potential recipient or buyer of the paper would not know whether the condition had been satisfied, and would not want to take the time and effort to find out.

Courteous or considerate language, on the other hand, such as *please pay to the order of* or listing the obligor's bank account number (without the word *only* following) for the convenience of others does not affect negotiability. However, contrary to other rules, government checks that are restricted to payment from one account (such as *Pay out of Social Security Account 87509 only*) are still negotiable. Finally, instruments that merely acknowledge the source of the obligation, as in *Pay to the order of Janet Warho as per contract*, are also negotiable.

3. Payable in a Sum Certain in Money

money: any official currency or coin acceptable as a medium of exchange

To be negotiable, a paper must call for the payment of a sum certain in money. **Money**, for this purpose, is any official currency or coin acceptable as a medium of exchange either in the United States or in any foreign country at the time the commercial paper is made. Thus, a paper which is collectible in the United States but which has the amount expressed in an acceptable foreign currency is negotiable. Normally the foreign currency is simply changed into American dollars on the day the paper is payable. However, if the paper requires that the foreign currency be used as the medium of payment, the commercial paper is payable in that currency.

Payment must be solely in money and not in money plus another good or service. On the other hand, paper may give the holder a choice of money or something else, for example, "I promise to pay to the order of Leslie Wexler $10,000 or 35 ounces of gold at the holder's option," would be negotiable since the holder could choose money as payment. If the choice to pay in money or a good or service was the obligor's, the instrument would not be negotiable.

An instrument is still negotiable if it requires that the amount be paid:

acceleration clause: clause which makes the entire balance due if an installment is missed

a. with interest or discount,
b. by installment, perhaps with an **acceleration clause** (clause which makes the entire balance due and payable if any installment is missed),
c. with bank charges for exchanging one national currency into another, or

d. with costs of collection and reasonable attorney fees in case the paper is not paid at maturity.

In fact, most of these provisions usually tend to make the paper more attractive to prospective owners.

4. Payable on Demand or at a Definite Time

Negotiability also requires that an instrument be payable at a definite time or be **payable on demand**, that is, expressly made payable *at sight, on presentation, on demand,* or without a time of payment being specified.

payable on demand: due when proper request for payment is made

Alternatively, **payable at a definite time** requires the instrument to be payable on or before an identified calendar date. It is also acceptable for an instrument to be payable within a set period after an identified calendar date or a fixed period, such as 90 days, after sight. An instrument is not negotiable if it is payable at or after a date that is sure to occur but that cannot be determined beforehand. For example, a note payable *30 days after the death of Larue Dobbs* would not be negotiable. A promise reading in such a way might be honored by the person making it or it might be legally enforceable as part of a contract, but that has nothing to do with whether the instrument is commercial paper and can therefore be negotiated.

payable at a definite time: payable on or before an identified calendar date

5. Payable to the Bearer or to Someone's Order

The final requirement is that the paper contain the words of negotiability by being made payable to the bearer or to the order of a specified person or firm.

When commercial paper is made payable to the bearer, it is legally collectible by the party in possession of it (who is termed the **bearer**). The instrument is called **bearer paper**. To qualify as such, the face of the commercial paper can read *pay to the order of bearer, pay to bearer, pay to (a named party) or bearer, pay to cash,* or any other way that does not identify a specific payee. Bearer paper is also created when the last indorsement is only a signature and does not specify a particular person to whom the paper is transferred.

bearer: the party in possession of bearer paper

bearer paper: paper issued or indorsed so as to be collectible by the party in possession of it

In contrast, when commercial paper is made payable to the order of a specified payee, it is called **order paper**. Such phrasing shows the intent of the maker or drawer to have the paper payable to the named payee or to anyone to whom the paper is subsequently negotiated by order of the payee. Order paper may read *pay to the order of Louis Desmond* or whatever specific party the maker or drawer

order paper: paper that is issued or indorsed to the order of a specified person

intends. It may also read *pay to Louis Desmond or order*. However, if it reads *pay to Louis Desmond*, it is not negotiable. (Note that it is also possible to change bearer paper to order paper with a special indorsement. Special indorsements are discussed on pages 561-562.)

Order paper may be made payable to the order of more than one party—either jointly, such as *pay to the order of J. J. Adamson and Greenwood School* or, in the alternative, *pay to the order of Ashleigh Adamson or Greenwood School*. In the former example, both parties have to sign the instrument to negotiate it further, and, in the latter example, either party (Ashleigh Adamson or Greenwood School) acting alone can sign and cash it.

HOW IS COMMERCIAL PAPER TRANSFERRED?

PROBLEM: When Charleton visited his dentist's office, the receptionist told him he still owed $175 for previous treatment. By coincidence, Charleton had with him a check made out to his order in that amount, and so he gave it to the receptionist. The receptionist returned it and asked him to sign the back. Was his signature necessary?

As mentioned previously, commercial paper is usually transferred by negotiation. This process allows the transferee greater rights than if the paper is merely assigned because, in the case of assignment, the transferee receives only the rights of the transferor. However, when commercial paper is negotiated, the transferee may receive more rights than those held by the transferor. In particular, negotiation to an innocent party may cut off many defenses that the party obligated to pay might have otherwise used, such as breach of contract or failure of consideration. (These defenses are explained in the next chapter.) If commercial paper is improperly transferred, it is legally considered as having merely been assigned. Hence, it is important to know the proper way to transfer an instrument. The proper way is dependent on whether the instrument is order or bearer paper.

indorsement: a signature on the reverse side of commercial paper

indorse: to sign on the reverse of the paper

indorser: the indorsing party

If an instrument is order paper (payable to the order of a named person), the named person must sign the paper on its reverse side, as requested in the problem, and then deliver it for the transfer to be complete and proper. Such a signature is termed an **indorsement**. An owner of commercial paper who signs on its reverse is said to **indorse** the paper and is an **indorser**. The party to whom the paper is indorsed is the **indorsee**. A party who has physical possession of commercial paper that is payable to his or her order or who is in possession of bearer paper is termed a **holder**. Thus, a bearer is a holder, and so is a person in possession of paper payable to his or her order.

indorsee: the party to whom the paper is indorsed

holder: a party in possession of bearer paper or paper payable to the possessor's order

If the paper is bearer paper, it may be negotiated by delivery alone. The bearer may simply hand the paper to the transferee, for example. Many transferees, however, will require the bearer to indorse the paper. This generally allows the new owner to pursue the transferor for the paper's value if there are problems collecting it from the maker or drawee.

WHAT ARE THE KINDS AND RESPECTIVE LEGAL EFFECTS OF INDORSEMENTS?

PROBLEM: Arlene Clark paid George Rogers for rent due by indorsing her pension check with her name only and delivering it to him. However, during Rogers's bus ride home, a pickpocket stole his wallet, which contained the check. The thief promptly bought goods with the check at the In-N-Out Market, which accepted it in good faith. In-N-Out can collect on the check. How could Rogers have avoided this loss?

All indorsements are either blank or special. However, by the use of appropriate phrases, each of these two basic types may also become qualified and/or restricted in their effect.

1. Blank Indorsements

A **blank indorsement** does not specify a particular person to whom the paper is transferred. Thus, it transforms order paper into bearer paper, which even a finder or a thief can cash. A blank indorsement consists of just the indorser's signature (see Figure 31-1). Because it is easy and fast to write, the blank indorsement is commonly used. It is satisfactory and safe for the indorser (1) if value is immediately received or (2) if the paper is deposited in a bank at the time of indorsement.

blank indorsement: indorsement that consists of the indorser's signature only

2. Special Indorsements

special indorsement: an indorsement that makes the paper payable to the order of a designated party

A **special indorsement** is one that makes the paper payable to the order of a designated person. In an indorsement, unlike on the

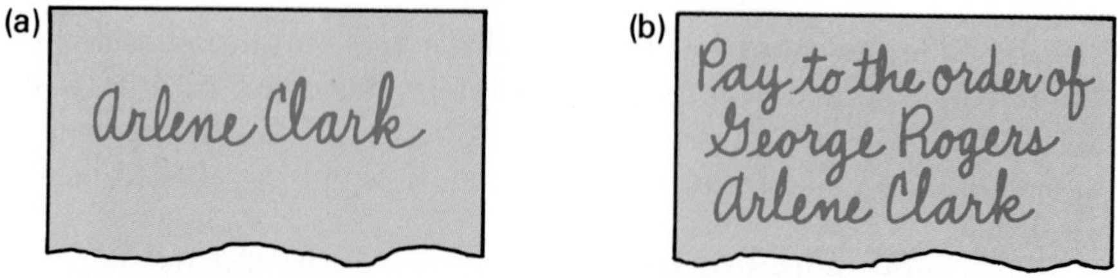

Figure 31-1. (a) Blank Indorsement and (b) Blank Indorsement Converted to Special Indorsement

face of the instrument, the more concise wording "Pay to George Rogers" is as effective as "Pay to the order of George Rogers." The paper will be order paper as a result of either wording.

The transferee who receives paper with a blank indorsement may be protected by writing above the signature of the blank indorser a statement that the paper is payable to the indorsee or the indorsee's order. This notation converts the blank indorsement into a special indorsement. It thus restores the order character of the paper. In the problem, Rogers could have written the words "Pay to the order of George Rogers" or "Pay to George Rogers" just above Clark's signature. (See the converted blank indorsement in Figure 31-1.) Then only Rogers could have collected on the check. If the check had been stolen, the thief would have had to forge George's name to collect. A forged signature used as an indorsement on commercial paper does not pass title, so In-N-Out could not have collected on it.

In some cases, a forgery of a payee's name will be effective. Suppose a dishonest employee fraudulently gets an employer to sign a check payable to a nonexistent party or to a real party who is not entitled to any payment. The employee has no intent to deliver the check to the **fictitious payee**. Or suppose an *imposter* (one who fraudulently claims to be someone else) tricks the maker or drawer into issuing an instrument made payable to the person being impersonated. In either case, the dishonest person (or anyone else) may then forge the fictitious payee's signature as indorser. The forger could then get value for the paper from some innocent person because the signature of the drawer or maker is genuine.

fictitious payee: real or nonexistent party not entitled to money but dishonestly named as a payee

3. Qualified Indorsements

Unless blank or special indorsements are qualified by adding "without recourse" or equivalent words such as "not liable for payment" over the signature, the indorser will be an **unqualified**

indorser and will remain liable to later transferees to pay the instrument if the maker or the drawee does not pay. A **qualified indorsement** eliminates this secondary liability based on a signature.

unqualified indorser: an indorser with signature-based liability to later transferees

Even though secondary liability is avoided, certain warranties implied by law as given by all transferors may still require the indorser to pay if the instrument cannot be collected. These warranties include that the indorser has good title or authority to transfer the paper for another; that all signatures are genuine; that there has been no material alteration of the instrument; that the indorser has no knowledge of a bankruptcy proceeding against the maker, drawer, or drawee; and that there are no defenses of any type good against the indorser. In the case of a qualified indorser, this last warranty is altered to state that the indorser has no knowledge of such defenses. Regardless, the warranties are quite broad and protect later transferees as well. Even the transferor of bearer paper who does not indorse it (and therefore does not acquire secondary liability on his or her signature as an indorser) still is accountable for these warranties, but only to the immediate transferee.

qualified indorsement: an indorsement that eliminates an indorser's signature-based liability to later transferees

To be totally without potential liability on commercial paper, a qualified indorser might add "without warranties" and thus also eliminate warranty liability. However, it would generally be extremely difficult to find a transferee who would give significant value to a potential transferor under such circumstances. An exception would be a holder who is merely an agent of the transferee.

4. Restrictive Indorsements

A **restrictive indorsement** specifies the purpose of the indorsement. That is, it prescribes the use to be made of the money proceeds from the paper. (An example would be "Pay to Jay Scott to be held in trust for the Valley Charity Hospital.") A restrictive indorsement might also impose conditions on payment. Such conditions would destroy the negotiability of the paper if included on its face. But they do not prohibit further negotiation when made by an indorser. However, a future holder must apply the funds received for the paper in accordance with the indorsement.

restrictive indorsement: indorsement that indicates the use of the proceeds or imposes a condition on payment

Restrictive indorsements include indorsements for deposit or collection ("for deposit only"), indorsements for the benefit of the indorser or another party ("pay to Marilyn Mobley, Guardian, for the benefit of Jesse Kohler, Ward"), or conditional indorsements ("pay to Oscar Leopold if he delivers his 1982 Lincoln sedan to me, James Garrett, at 702 N. Mountain View").

WHAT IS AN ACCOMMODATION PARTY?

PROBLEM: Alimadi was new in the city. When he made a down payment on some furniture, he asked his employer, Byron, to indorse the check for him as a courtesy. Otherwise, the seller, Rumsfeld, would refuse to accept it. What, if any, was Byron's liability on the check?

accommodation party: one who lends name and credit by signing another's commercial paper

guarantor of payment: accommodation party who is primarily liable

Sometimes a person who desires to borrow money or to cash a check is not well known in the community or has not established credit. To make commercial paper acceptable, such a person may arrange—as in the problem—for someone who is known and has a good credit rating to join in signing the paper. Such a signer is an **accommodation party**, whether the signature is given as a favor or for some consideration. The accommodation party may sign as a maker, a drawer, an acceptor, or an indorser (as did Byron). An accommodation party who writes "payment guaranteed" or the equivalent becomes a **guarantor of payment**. As such, the person is primarily liable even though the holder does not try to collect from anyone else when the paper comes due.

An accommodation party is liable to all subsequent holders of the paper who give value for it but, of course, not to the party accommodated. In the problem, Byron would be liable to Rumsfeld if the check were dishonored when presented to the drawee bank for payment. Byron would also be liable to any subsequent holder, but she would not be liable to Alimadi.

PREVENTING LEGAL DIFFICULTIES

Using Commercial Paper . . .

1. when you issue a paper payable on demand, realize that the paper is immediately collectible even though the holder might not press for prompt payment. Thus, be prepared to pay;
2. when you are the payee of commercial paper, include a clause for payment of reasonable attorney fees by the maker in case of default;
3. if you are the payee or holder of commercial paper, do not "rest on your rights" when the paper comes due. The statute of limitations begins to run immediately from the due date of the commercial paper;
4. a paper which is lacking an element required for negotiability is not a

commercial paper. However, the paper may still be a valuable contract or creditor's claim;

5. when commercial paper payable to your order is delivered to you and you plan to indorse it in blank, do not indorse it until you are ready to deposit it or to immediately transfer it and receive value in exchange;
6. generally do not issue bearer paper unless you expect to get value for it immediately. Bearer paper is so similar to cash that it can be easily misused by unauthorized persons; and
7. do not lend your name to commercial paper as an accommodation party unless you are prepared to pay the full amount of the instrument. Although you are not liable to the party you accommodate, you are liable to pay the holder if the accommodated party does not pay. Then you are burdened with the task of trying to collect from the party you accommodated, who was supposed to pay in the first place. If you become a *guarantor* of payment, you become primarily liable.

Strengthening Your Legal Vocabulary

acceleration clause
accommodation party
antedated
bearer
bearer paper
blank indorsement
fictitious payee
guarantor of payment
holder
indorse
indorsee
indorsement
indorser
money
negotiability
negotiation
order paper
payable at a definite time
payable on demand
postdated
qualified indorsement
restrictive indorsement
special indorsement
unqualified indorser

1. To be paid at the time the paper is presented.
2. Dated later than the date of issuance.
3. Clause making the entire balance due upon default.
4. Indorsement that eliminates the indorser's secondary liability to pay.
5. Indorsement consisting only of the signature of the indorser.
6. Person who signs as maker, drawer, acceptor, or indorser to lend name and credit to another person.
7. Indorsement that indicates the use of the proceeds or imposes a condition on payment.
8. Indorsement that makes a paper payable to a particular party or to his or her order.
9. Real or nonexistent payee who is not entitled to the money but whose name is used dishonestly in properly signed commercial paper.
10. Accommodation party who is primarily liable.

Reviewing Important Points

1. To be negotiable, a paper:
   a. must be in writing and must be signed by the maker or drawer,
   b. must contain an unconditional promise (if it is a note or a certificate of deposit) or an unconditional order (if it is a draft or a check),
   c. must call for payment of a sum certain in money,
   d. must be payable on demand or at a definite time, and
   e. must be payable to the bearer or to the order of a specified person.
2. In conflicts between provisions written by various methods, the handwritten version prevails over the typewritten version, and the typewritten version prevails over the printed version. Also, amounts expressed in words prevail over amounts expressed in figures.
3. The order or promise of commercial paper to pay money must be unconditional. However, certain terms, including the following, may be added without destroying negotiability:
   a. charging a particular account as a matter of convenience or record keeping,
   b. charging a particular account or fund if a government is the drawer or maker,
   c. collecting interest or deducting a discount,
   d. paying in installments,
   e. accelerating payment of the total principal in case of default,
   f. requiring payment of bank charges for changing one currency into another,
   g. requiring payment of collection costs and reasonable attorney fees in case in default,
   h. identifying the consideration received or to be given for the paper,
   i. providing that cashing or indorsing by the payee acknowledges full satisfaction of the debt, or
   j. identifying collateral or real property pledged as security for payment and providing for its sale in case of default.
4. Commercial paper payable to order may be negotiated only by indorsement and delivery. Commercial paper payable to the bearer may be negotiated by delivery alone.
5. There are two basic forms of indorsement: blank and special. By the use of appropriate phrases either kind may become qualified and/or restrictive.
6. Even qualified indorsers have some potential liability on an instrument unless they place "without warranties" above their signatures, along with "without recourse."
7. An accommodation party is liable to all subsequent holders of the paper who give value for it, but an accommodation party is not liable to the party accommodated. The extent of liability is governed by the capacity in which the accommodation party signed, such as guarantor of payment, indorser, or maker.

8. Although a forgery normally would not result in title passing to a transferee, cases involving fictitious payees or imposters may result in the loss falling upon the maker or the drawer.

Applying Law to Everyday Life

1. Korry handwrote the following: "I, John Korry, promise to pay to the order of Allison J. Nagy $2,500." Korry then delivered it to Nagy. In a dispute that arose later, it was argued that the instrument was not negotiable because it lacked Korry's signature, was not dated, and was without a time of payment. Do you agree?
2. Winslow was the maker of a promissory note payable to Homer. The note was complete and correct in all respects but contained the following additional terms:
   a. "This note is prepared as a result of a service contract between the parties, dated 6/15/--.
   b. This note is secured by a mortgage on the maker's residence at 445 Copperdome Court, Butte, Montana, U.S.A.
   c. This note is payable in Canadian dollars, with exchange, and shall be charged to the maker's foreign operations fund if the balance therein is adequate on due date.
   d. This note shall be extended six (6) months if services, as agreed, are not completed by payee as of due date.
   e. This note is payable at the Calgary Crown Imperial Bank, Calgary, Alberta, Canada."

   Do any of the added terms destroy the negotiability of the note?
3. Smith paid Coleman $500 for possession of a bearer note made out in the amount of $750. The note is payable upon the death of Coleman's uncle. Is the note negotiable?
4. Anton drew a check for $750 payable to the bearer. Anton gave the check to Brewster. Brewster negotiated the check by delivery to Charlois. Charlois negotiated it by delivery to Deltoid. Deltoid tried to collect but found that Anton's bank account lacked the necessary funds for payment. May Deltoid collect from either or both of the prior holders?
5. DeBrul received a promissory note for $500 payable to the bearer. She indorsed it "to Cindy Frankel or order." Later, Frankel simply delivered the note to the Tiperrary Antique Shop in exchange for merchandise. Was Frankel's action a proper negotiation?
6. Heart indorsed a draft "without recourse" and delivered it to Shefner. On the day the draft came due, the drawee refused to pay Shefner because the drawee had proof that the signature of the drawer (a certain L.J. Marks) was a forgery. Shefner sued Heart for payment. Must Heart pay?

7. Krosby was starting a new business and needed cash. He persuaded the Federated Finance Bank to lend him $10,000 against his new equipment. However, the bank insisted that his prominent friend, Hopper, or someone of equal financial means, indorse the note which Krosby signed. Therefore Hopper indorsed the note. What is Hopper's liability?

Solving Case Problems

1. Associates Discount Corporation sought court enforcement of a note they held. The note stated that Fitzwater owed a large sum of money for a tractor that had been delivered to him. Fitzwater, the signer and obligor on the note, sought to introduce evidence to show that the tractor was never delivered. Can he do so? (*Associates Discount Corporation of Iowa v. Fitzwater*, 518 S.W.2d 474, Mo.)

2. Brookshire was convicted of issuing a check with intent to defraud. On January 1, 1957, Brookshire had written a check dated December 31, 1957 to pay his taxes for 1956. On January 7 or 8, 1957, Brookshire's bank dishonored the check due to insufficient funds. The State of Missouri brought charges resulting in the above conviction on May 8, 1957. Was an intent to defraud evidenced by the use of the postdated check? (*State v. Brookshire*, 329 S.W.2d 252, Mo.)

3. In May, 1963, Ferri executed a note promising to pay $3,000 to Sylvia's order "within ten years after date." Two years later, Sylvia demanded payment. When refused, Sylvia sued Ferri. Is the note due at a definite time, and if so, when? (*Ferri v. Sylvia*, 100 R.I. 270, 214 A.2d 470)

4. Obie received a check drawn to her order by the Atlanta Federal Savings & Loan Association, Inc., for $2,000. Obie transferred the check to Jett for valuable consideration but neglected to indorse it. Later, the drawee bank refused to pay the check because it was not indorsed. Therefore Jett sued Atlanta and Obie. Are they liable? (*Jett v. Atlanta Federal Savings and Loan Association, Inc.*, 104 Ga. App. 688, 123 S.E.2d 27)

5. Shine and Buck, as comakers, executed a promissory note to Stelfox. Buck was actually an accommodation party. Later, Stelfox assigned the note to Reed. When the note was not paid, Reed sued Buck alone because the whereabouts of Shine were not known. Buck argued that he was only an accommodation party and as such could not be sued alone. Thus, he claimed, Shine should be joined as a defendant in the action. Decide. (*Reed v. Buck*, 370 S.W.2d 867, Mo.)

32

Rights and Defenses of Holders

1. A girl at your school, age 17, contracts to pay $2,500 for a 12-month course in modeling. She pays $100 down and gives a note for the balance payable in 24 monthly installments. Advertisements for the course promised "exciting, high-paying jobs." Within weeks, however, it becomes clear that the only jobs offered are to model clothes for various local schools' home economics exhibitions. The teenager decides to avoid the contract but is told that the note has been transferred to a bank that is a holder in due course. Must she pay as promised?

2. You contract for aluminum siding to be put on the exterior of a building you have purchased for your business. As a partial payment, you sign a promissory note for $10,000 payable to the order of the siding company. The siding company goes out of business without doing the job. Soon after, a local bank demands payment of the note which has come due. Having purchased the note in good faith from the siding company for $9,500, the bank is a holder in due course. Are you legally required to pay the note?

3. Someone breaks out a window of your locked car and steals a book of your blank checks from the glove compartment. By forging your signature, the thief makes purchases at various stores, all of which qualify as holders in due course. Are you legally required to pay when the checks are presented to your bank?

WHO CAN BE A HOLDER IN DUE COURSE AND WHY IS IT SO IMPORTANT?

PROBLEM: Trevail paid Saxton $500 for a promissory note that had a face value of $10,000. The note was signed by Erman and was made payable to the bearer. Saxton refused to indorse it, explaining that he had to leave town and therefore his indorsement would be of no use. Trevail knew Saxton had recently been indicted for his role in an alleged blackmail scheme. When Trevail tried to collect on the note, Erman refused to pay. He claimed he had signed the note only because Saxton had threatened to tell the IRS certain incriminating facts about unreported income. Will Trevail be considered a holder in due course by the court and therefore collect despite Erman's defense?

One who has possession of bearer paper or of order paper made out or indorsed to such person is a holder. All holders have the power to assign, negotiate, enforce payment, or discharge the paper (with or without payment in return). However, certain types of holders have additional rights.

holder in due course (HDC): a holder who takes in good faith, for value, and without notice of defect or dishonor

holder through a holder in due course: a holder who acquires an instrument previously held by an HDC

Compared to an ordinary holder, a **holder in due course** (HDC) or a **holder through a holder in due course** is able to overcome more of the defenses that the obligor might raise against having to pay on the paper. To be an HDC, a holder has to take the paper in good faith, give value for it, and not know of any defect in the paper or that it is overdue. A holder through a holder in due course is any holder who takes commercial paper after an HDC. A holder through a holder in due course normally has the same rights as an HDC.

Taking paper in good faith requires that the holder act honestly, not only in the immediate transaction, but with regard to all circumstances surrounding the paper. In addition, although the courts generally do not test the adequacy of the value given for the paper, sometimes what is given has very small value compared to the face amount of the instrument. In such cases, fraud or some other unconscionable act that would prevent the holder from being considered an HDC may be implied. In the problem, Trevail's knowledge of Saxton's alleged criminal activities, the suspicious circumstances of the purchase, and the small value given by Trevail ($500 for a $10,000 note) will probably disqualify her from being an HDC.

In addition to giving value in good faith, an HDC must not know the paper is overdue. For example, a time instrument is overdue the day after the maturity date; if payments are to be made in installments, the paper is overdue if even a single installment is late. If an instrument is due on demand, it is overdue a reasonable time after it is issued. The UCC presumes a check is overdue 30 days after issue. Every holder is charged with knowledge of what is on the instrument, so failing to check the date is no excuse. However, if the date has been altered, as from May 5 to May 15, and the alteration is not recognizable by a reasonable person, an innocent holder is accountable only in accordance with the date as altered—in this case May 15.

Finally, to qualify as an HDC, a holder must not know of any defenses against enforcement of the paper, any claims of ownership from third parties, or any previous dishonor of the paper. Any such knowledge attributable to the holder when taking the paper would prevent that holder from qualifying as an HDC.

Defenses that are good against everyone except an HDC or a holder through an HDC are **limited defenses**. Defenses that are good against all obligees are **universal defenses.**

limited defenses: defenses good against all but an HDC or a holder through an HDC

universal defenses: defenses good against all obligees

WHAT ARE THE LIMITED DEFENSES?

PROBLEM: Chisholm sold Boutell a large truck and trailer for use in Boutell's trucking business. In payment, Boutell gave Chisholm $5,000 down and a promissory note for $20,000. Chisholm had assured Boutell that the odometer reading of 25,275 miles was true. Later, Boutell learned that the true odometer reading was 125,275 miles. Boutell decided to avoid the contract because of the fraud. Chisholm had already negotiated the note to the Continental Bank, an HDC. Must Boutell pay Continental the $20,000 as promised?

While the emphasis in this and the next section is on defenses, most commercial paper is enforceable according to its terms and is promptly paid. Defenses to collection seldom arise. When they do, however, the holder's risk of not being able to collect is greatly diminished if he or she is an HDC and thereby able to overcome the limited defenses.

Limited defenses, which are also called personal defenses, are varied. Against ordinary holders they are just as effective in barring collection as universal defenses. The following are limited defenses:

1. Breach of Contract or Failure of Consideration

Often commercial paper is issued as part of a contractual agreement. Ordinary holders are subject to defenses that stem from the terms of the contract not being fulfilled or the lack or failure of the consideration that was to go to the person who issued the instrument. However, an HDC is not subject to such defenses. For example, Jones buys some furniture from The Furniture Outlet and gives his personal check for $375 in payment. The store never delivers the furniture and shortly after goes bankrupt. Meanwhile, the check passes into the hands of an HDC who can enforce it despite the defense of lack of consideration.

2. Fraud in the Inducement

If a person used fraud to induce another to make out commercial paper (as Chisholm did to Boutell in the problem), the defrauded party has a limited defense useable against holders who seek to collect. However, in the problem, Continental Bank is an HDC, and therefore Boutell must pay the note. Boutell can then seek to recover from Chisholm. Fraud in the inducement, where the issuer is aware that an obligation based on commercial paper is being created, should not be confused with fraud in the execution, where the issuer is unaware that an obligation based on commercial paper is being created or is unaware of the nature or essential terms of the commercial paper. Fraud in the execution is a universal defense covered later in this chapter.

3. Incapacity to Contract (Excluding Minority)

Temporary loss of capacity due to insanity or intoxication produces contractual obligations that are voidable and also produces a personal or limited defense against commercial paper issued during such periods.

4. Ordinary Duress

Duress as a defense can be either limited or universal depending on whether or not the duress is so severe as to deprive the signer of control. If a person issues commercial paper because of fear of losing property or because of the fear of being exposed in a scandal, the person has only a limited defense to the paper's enforcement. On the other hand, if an immediate threat of force or violence to the issuer's person (or spouse, child, or parent) compels the issuer to sign against his will, the defense is universal.

5. Prior Payment or Cancellation

If the obligation on commercial paper is discharged prematurely by payment without the paper being turned over to the obligor, the instrument could continue circulating. If it has not been marked paid, it could end up in the hands of an HDC. Such a party could then enforce it against the obligor a second time because prior payment or cancellation produces only a limited defense.

6. Conditional Delivery or Nondelivery

A check or a note may be delivered under a separate agreement that it is to be enforced only upon the happening of a certain event. If it is nevertheless negotiated when the condition has not been fulfilled, the resulting defense is good only against ordinary holders. For example, promoters give a $10,000 earnest money check (partial payment to indicate the intention and ability to carry out a contract) to the agent of a famous rock group. The agent is to cash the check only if the group appears for the performance. If the group does not appear yet the agent indorses the check to an HDC for some new sound equipment for the group, the promoters will have to pay it and try to collect their loss from the agent or the group. Similarly, if an instrument is made out to pay someone for a good or service that is not provided, the drawer or maker has only a limited defense of nondelivery. This defense is good solely against ordinary holders. For example, if the owner of a home leaves a $200 bearer instrument on the dining room table as intended payment for the carpet cleaners and, before the service is performed, someone finds and cashes the instrument, the homeowner who wrote the instrument would have to pay a holder in due course.

7. Unauthorized Completion

A maker or drawer who signs a negotiable instrument but leaves the amount blank runs a great risk. Typically, in such an instance, someone else is authorized to complete the paper when, for example, a final price is negotiated. If the amount actually entered is not within authorized limits and the instrument is transferred to an HDC, the amount as completed would have to be paid to the HDC because unauthorized completion is only a limited defense.

8. Theft

A thief or an ordinary holder cannot enforce payment of a stolen instrument. An HDC can require payment, however. By definition, an HDC cannot acquire an instrument through theft. The theft would have had to occur in a prior transaction and be unknown to the HDC.

WHAT ARE THE UNIVERSAL DEFENSES?

PROBLEM: Duker was drunk when she saw the automobile of her dreams. She convinced the owner, Concha, to sell the car to her and agreed to pay $30,000—triple the current market price—for it. Duker wrote Concha a $6,000 check and a $24,000 promissory note. When she sobered up the next day, Duker called her bank to stop payment on the check, but Concha had already cashed it. Shortly thereafter Duker was notified by the First National Bank that it had purchased the note and that Duker should begin making payments to the bank in accordance with its terms. Duker replied that she was not legally required to pay the note even to a holder in due course because she was drunk when she issued it. Is she correct?

Universal defenses (also known as real defenses) are valid against all obligees of an instrument, even holders in due course. These defenses include:

1. Minority and Other Incapacity to Contract

Minority is a universal defense. Therefore it is good even against an HDC. It does not matter whether the minor's contracts are void or voidable. A minor who signs commercial paper as maker, drawer, or acceptor may refuse to pay as promised.

Insanity, intoxication, or other contractual incapacity is a universal defense only if its effect is to make a contract void. For example, all contracts of a person judicially declared insane are void. Therefore an insane person who signs commercial paper as maker, drawer, or acceptor would not be responsible for payment. If the contractual capacity renders the contract only voidable, the defense is limited. A person must be declared an alcoholic by the court and have a guardian appointed by the court in order for the person's contracts to be void because of intoxication. Therefore, in the problem, Duker's temporary intoxication produces only a limited defense at best. She would have to pay the note when collection is sought by an HDC.

2. Illegality

If the law declares void a commercial paper made in connection with certain conduct, the defense of illegality may be used against any holder. For example, in states where gambling is illegal, commercial paper given in payment for a gambling debt is void.

3. Forgery or Lack of Authority

When one person signs the name of another with intent to defraud, the resulting forgery is a crime, and it is a universal defense good against all holders. If the intent to defraud is lacking, but the person is signing without authorization, the signer does not commit forgery. However, the effect on third parties is the same. An example would be if a well-meaning agent indorsed the principal's name on a note without authority to do so. No holder could collect from the principal. However, the agent could be liable. Note that the principal would be liable as maker if he or she later *ratified* (approved) the signing. The principal would also be liable if he or she were barred for some good reason from denying liability on the note (for example, if the note had been given in payment for goods ordered by the principal).

> While working as a file clerk for Johnson, Zolo found a check for $50 made payable to the order of Johnson. Zolo indorsed the check in blank by forging Johnson's name. She then transferred the check to Springston, an HDC. Forgery is a universal defense, and Johnson need not pay Springston. However, Zolo would be liable to Springston.

4. Material Alteration

Sometimes a dishonest holder fraudulently and materially alters commercial paper. An example of such an alteration would be a change in the maturity date, the amount due, the rate of interest, or the place of payment. Prior parties who have not agreed to such changes are generally discharged from liability on the paper as altered. They are, however, liable according to its original terms if the paper is in the hands of an HDC. Therefore, if the amount payable on a check is boosted from $15 to $150, the HDC could collect $15, not $150. Thus, material alteration is a partial universal defense.

5. Fraud as to the Nature of the Paper or Its Essential Terms

Sometimes trickery is used in such a way that even a careful person who signs does not know and has no reasonable opportunity to learn the nature or essential terms of the document. Such person has a defense of fraud against all holders. For example, suppose a celebrity signs an autograph on a blank sheet of paper, and a dishonest person then prints or writes a promissory note around the signature. Or suppose the signer of a paper might not be able to read because he or she is illiterate in English or may have broken glasses, and the person planning to defraud gives a false explanation of the essential terms or substitutes one paper for another before the signing. No one (not even an HDC) who subsequently comes into possession of a paper in any of these cases has the right to collect.

6. Duress Depriving Control

Duress is a universal defense only if it deprives control. For example, suppose a person points a gun at another person and threatens to shoot if that person does not sign a commercial paper. Suppose a person uses physical force to compel a person to sign. In either case, the defense of duress raised by the signer would be a universal defense.

7. Claims and Defenses Stemming from a Consumer Transaction

Although not defined as a universal defense by the UCC, by Federal Trade Commission (FTC) rule any defense or claim that the debtor in a consumer credit transaction could assert against the seller of the good or service involved can be asserted against any type of holder. Common examples would be fraud in the inducement, breach of contract, and failure of consideration. However, notice must be given (in bold print on the instrument) that the commercial paper originated in a consumer transaction (a transaction in which a party buys goods or services for personal or household use) and that the debtor's defenses are good against holders. The consumer in such transactions may refuse to pay for goods or services when the contract is not properly performed, just as if the consumer were still dealing with the original seller. This rule was made because too often in the past, sellers on credit would defraud buyers or go out of business and thus default on warranties. Nevertheless, the buyers would still have to pay the financiers who bought the related commercial paper. Often, such holders knew or should have suspected the unfair trade practice of the sellers.

It is very important that the note itself indicate that it arose in a consumer transaction. If it does not do so, the consumer is not protected by the FTC rule and may not use any limited defenses against an HDC. However, a few states have special rules to protect consumers in such cases.

HOW IS COMMERCIAL PAPER DISCHARGED?

PROBLEM: MacLean owed $3,700 on a note held by Duvall. On the due date, MacLean offered Duvall a prize quarter horse worth more than $3,700 as payment instead of cash. Must Duvall accept the quarter horse as payment, or can he demand cash?

The obligation to pay commercial paper may be discharged in a number of ways:

1. By Payment

A note or a certificate of deposit is usually paid by the maker. A check is usually paid by the bank on which it is drawn. Other types of drafts are usually paid by the drawees. The terms of commercial paper must call for payment in money, and payment must be made in money unless the holder is willing to accept something else. For instance, the holder may voluntarily take another commercial paper in payment. Or the holder may take other kinds of property. In the problem, MacLean's offer of the quarter horse did not legally meet the terms of his obligation to Duvall. Duvall has the right to demand payment in money or to consider MacLean in default. If, however, Duvall agreed to accept the substitution, the note would be discharged.

When you pay a holder for commercial paper, you should obtain possession of the paper at the time of payment. Otherwise, a dishonest holder who retains the paper might later falsely claim that it has not been paid and demand a second payment. Or the dishonest holder might negotiate it wrongfully to an innocent third party who then might also be entitled to payment. Even if the paper is paid only in part, this fact should be shown by appropriate notation on the paper itself.

2. By Cancellation

cancellation: any act that shows an intent to end the obligation of payment of commercial paper

Commercial paper is also discharged by a cancellation. **Cancellation** in this case consists of any act by the holder that indicates an intent to end the obligation of payment. An example of such an act would be the deliberate destruction or mutilation of a paper by the holder.

3. By Alteration

A fraudulent and material alteration of commercial paper by the holder will discharge the obligation of all prior parties. For example, suppose that a holder changed the rate of interest payable on a note from 7 percent to 9 percent. In such a case, neither the maker nor any persons who may have previously indorsed it would be obligated to pay the note. However, the original parties to the paper would still be bound to make payment in accordance with the original terms if the paper later came into the hands of an HDC.

WHAT ARE THE LEGAL IMPLICATIONS OF ELECTRONIC TECHNOLOGY IN COMMERCIAL PAPER AND BANKING LAW?

PROBLEM: Kinton was unaware that he had lost the plastic card obtained from his bank for use in its automated teller machines. The day after the card was lost, it was used for an unauthorized withdrawal of $400 from Kinton's account. Must Kinton bear this loss?

electronic fund transfer (EFT): an account-altering order given electronically to a financial institution

Electronic fund transfer (EFT) is an order or authorization given to a financial institution by phone, magnetic tape, or computer to cause the institution to debit or credit an account. It is a fairly recent development which may someday make the use of commercial paper somewhat obsolete. EFTs are basically conducted without traditional instruments such as checks or drafts. Automated teller machines throughout a community, point-of-sale terminals in stores, and a clearinghouse network that automatically credits government checks directly to accounts are examples of an emerging electronic banking system. As a consequence, Congress enacted the

Electronic Fund Transfer Act as a part of the Consumer Credit Protection Act. The EFT Act was then clarified and placed in the form of working rules by Regulation E of the Federal Reserve System.

The EFT Act emphasizes that the use of such transfers is to be purely voluntary. When an EFT is used, the consumer must receive a written receipt at the time and later must receive a statement of all transfers over a particular period. A consumer who detects an error resulting in overbilling must, within 60 days of the date the statement was sent, report the error to the institution responsible for the EFT. The institution then has 45 days to investigate, during which time the consumer has the funds returned for use. This rule applies unless the institution makes a reasonable determination within ten days of the report.

In the case of unauthorized transfers, Congress rejected the idea present in commercial paper law requiring full liability on the part of a depositor who negligently allows such a transfer (by losing a check, for example). Instead, Congress chose to cause the risk of unauthorized transfers to be shared between the consumer and the financial institution, even if the depositor is negligent. As a consequence, the consumer is responsible for the lesser of $50 or the value obtained in an unauthorized transfer prior to notification of the financial institution that an unauthorized transfer has occurred or may occur. The institution must absorb the rest of the loss. The consumer must, however, report loss or theft of a card within two business days after the consumer learns of the loss or theft or the consumer may be responsible for up to $500. In the problem, Kinton would lose $50 and his bank would lose $350 if he reported the loss of the card within two business days of learning of its loss.

Although the EFT Act has helped, there are many other legal questions developing as the trends toward nationwide banking and electronic financial networks continue. As it has in the past, applicable law will change to reflect and to facilitate responsible business practice.

PREVENTING LEGAL DIFFICULTIES

For Your Protection . . .

1. it is better to be a holder in due course than it is to be an ordinary holder. Therefore, generally:
   a. acquire commercial paper only in good faith.

b. pay value for commercial paper. (You are not an HDC if the paper was intended as a gift. However, you could be a holder through a holder in due course if you received the paper from an HDC.)
c. do not accept commercial paper when you know that it has been dishonored, that there are claims to it, or that some defense exists against payment.
d. do not accept overdue commercial paper.
e. do not accept altered commercial paper.

There will, of course, be times when you may decide to take paper as an ordinary holder because you are only reasonably sure that there are no defenses against payment and that the credit of the party or parties legally obliged to pay is good;

2. be careful about accepting (as a transferee) commercial paper from anyone you don't know. Require identification, but remember that ID cards can be stolen or forged. Generally it is helpful to require indorsement in your presence. This permits comparison of signatures. Thus, you should "know your indorser" and be reasonably certain that such person can and will pay when the paper comes due if the debtor with primary liability (maker or acceptor) does not pay. Sometimes you can help to protect yourself by insisting that an accommodation party known to you also sign the paper as maker, drawer, acceptor, or indorser. It may also be wise to place a dollar limit on the commercial paper which you are willing to accept;

3. if you receive paper as a payee from the maker or drawer, you can minimize the possibility of a defense being used against you when you try to collect if you:

a. properly perform your part of the underlying contractual bargain.
b. commit no fraud in inducing the other party to contract or to sign the paper.
c. avoid dealing with persons who may lack capacity to contract, such as minors, unless a legally responsible person also signs the paper as an accommodation party.
d. never use duress or undue influence in connection with the paper or the underlying contract.
e. refuse to accept delivery of paper subject to conditions, or if conditions are present, comply with them.
f. refuse to accept incomplete commercial paper, or if there are blanks, fill them in only in strict compliance with the intent of the issuer and the authority given you.
g. never steal commercial paper or tolerate any dishonesty or illegality in connection with it.
h. never materially alter commercial paper.
i. stay alert to the possibility that the person who deals with you may be a poor credit risk, or worse, a forger.
j. surrender the commercial paper when you are paid;

4. if you pay your obligation on commercial paper in full, have the paper so marked and signed by the holder; then obtain possession of it immediately. Have partial payments noted on the paper as well; and
5. when using EFT, retain your receipts and use them to verify your statements.

Strengthening Your Legal Vocabulary

cancellation
electronic fund transfer
holder in due course
holder through a holder in due course
limited defenses
universal defenses

1. One who takes a paper at any time after a holder in due course and has the same rights.
2. Holder who takes a paper for value, in good faith, and without knowledge that it is overdue or that there are any defenses, claims, or dishonor as to the paper.
3. Defenses that are valid against any holder, including a holder in due course.
4. Defenses that may be valid against any holder except a holder in due course.
5. One method by which commercial paper can be discharged.

Reviewing Important Points

1. To be a holder in due course, one must take a commercial paper for value, in good faith, and without knowledge that it is overdue or that there are any defenses, claims, or dishonor as to the paper.
2. Limited defenses include:
   a. breach of contract or failure of consideration,
   b. fraud in the inducement,
   c. incapacity to contract (excluding minority),
   d. ordinary duress,
   e. prior payment or cancellation,
   f. conditional delivery or nondelivery,
   g. unauthorized completion, and
   h. theft
3. Universal defenses include:
   a. minority and absolute incapacity to contract,
   b. illegality,
   c. forgery or lack of authority,
   d. material alteration,

e. fraud as to the nature of the paper or as to its essential terms,
f. duress depriving control, and
g. claims and defenses stemming from a consumer transaction

4. Commercial paper may be discharged by payment, cancellation, or alteration.
5. The consumer's liability on an unauthorized EFT is limited to $50 if, within two business days after the consumer learns of loss or theft of a card, the consumer reports the loss or theft to the financial institution.

Applying Law to Everyday Life

1. Menninger sold Klebb, a carpenter, a 200-piece professional metric tool set in exchange for Klebb's note for $495 payable in six months. After receiving and examining the tool set, Klebb objected. Klebb said that some of the pieces were not made of stainless steel as Menninger had promised. Klebb therefore demanded a reduction in price. Menninger rejected this claim and indorsed the note to Hench, who knew nothing about the dispute. (a) Can Hench collect? (b) Would your answer differ if Hench had been present when Klebb argued with Menninger about the quality of the set?

2. When a rock star arrived at the local airport, a young woman persuaded him to sign an autograph on a blank sheet of paper. The woman was a skilled typesetter. She went home and printed all the essential language of a promissory note around the signature. After filling in the amount of $15,000 and inserting her name as payee, she sold the note to an HDC. Is the star legally obligated to pay the $15,000?

3. Lammot owed Good $400 for a shotgun purchased the year before. Good had received only $100 in partial payment, so he was becoming extremely exasperated. When he met Lammot in a restaurant one day, Good loudly demanded either cash or a signature on an interest-bearing note "here and now or I'll haul you into court and sue you for all you've got!" Lammot signed, and Good promptly sold the note to Livingston, an HDC. Now Lammot refuses to pay the note, claiming that it was signed under duress. Is this a valid defense?

4. Tilly gave Worth a check for $275 in payment for a used freezer. Worth had told her that the freezer was in good working order. However, when the freezer was installed in Tilly's garage, it did not work. Upon removing the back panel, Tilly discovered that the motor had been removed. (a) Does Tilly have a defense against Worth on the check? (b) Is Tilly's defense good against any HDC to whom Worth might negotiate the check?

5. The following paper was indorsed in blank by Willkie and delivered to Lever on November 10, 19—, in exchange for valuable consideration. Did Lever become a holder in due course?

> Fargo, North Dakota
> July 1, 19--
>
> On December 30, 19--, I promise to pay Walter K. Willkie three hundred dollars ($300) with interest at nine (9) percent per year.
>
> Mary Ann March
> Mary Ann March
>
> For Classroom Use Only

6. Plack was an unqualified indorser on a note for $10,000. Busoy, the holder of the note, mistakenly believed that Plack was in financial ruin. Feeling she could not collect on the note, Busoy struck out Plack's indorsement. Is Plack still potentially liable on the instrument?

7. Tudore detected a $350 overcharge against her account resulting from an electronic funds transfer. She reported the error to Hi-Tech Bank. The Bank had not completed its investigation 10 days later. Can Tudore spend the $350?

Solving Case Problems

1. Biggs owned and operated a drive-in restaurant. Cunningham sold Biggs an Ordermatic communication system for use by patrons, for $3,405. Biggs paid $1,005 in cash and, for the balance of $2,400 due, he executed and delivered a note and security agreement. Shorty thereafter, Cunningham sold the mortgage and negotiated the note to Howard for 75 percent of its face value. Cunningham signed the note "with recourse." Then Biggs defaulted. He claimed that the Ordermatic did not operate properly and that the vendor had failed to service it as promised. Biggs also said that the date and the name of the payee were typed in after he had signed the note. Was Howard a holder in due course? (*Howard v. Biggs,* 378 P.2d 306, Ca.)

2. The Pierces purchased siding for their home from the Globe Remodeling Co., Inc. They gave a promissory note for $3,044.40 in payment. In exchange, they were to receive sufficient siding for the job, properly installed, together with $1,200 in cash. Globe indorsed the note to the Gramatan Co., Inc. Gramatan then sold it without indorsement to its affiliate, the plaintiff, Gramatan National Bank, for $2,250. The bank had previously placed Globe on its "precautionary list" because it knew that in other sales, Globe had not performed as promised. The bank also knew that similar Globe notes were being litigated and that federal law enforcement officials had been investigating Globe activities. In this case, only $400 had been paid to the Pierces. In addition, only about half the siding had been

delivered, and none had been installed. The Pierces refused to pay the note, and the bank sued. (a) Is the bank a holder in due course? (b) Is the bank entitled to any payment on the note? (*Gramatan National Bank & Trust Co. v. Pierce*, 121 Vt. 406, 159 A.2d 781)

3. Dorsey was negligent in failing to determine that the paper he was signing was in fact a promissory note. The note passed into the hands of the New Jersey Mortgage and Investment Co., a holder in due course. May Dorsey use fraud as to the nature of essential terms as a defense against New Jersey? (*New Jersey Mortgage and Investment Co. v. Dorsey*, 33 N.J. 448, 165 A.2d 297)

4. Cameron State Bank mistakenly believed that credit life insurance had paid an $8,000 note they held. Consequently, they marked it paid and returned it to the heirs of the maker. Having discovered the mistake, the Bank now asks the court to void the release and enforce the note against the estate. Has the note been discharged? (*Cameron State Bank v. Sloan*, 559 S.W.2d 564, Mo.)

5. Ognibene withdrew $20.00 at an automated teller machine (ATM) through the use of his Citibank card and the entry of his confidential personal identification number. As he did so, he was evidently observed by an individual who was using a phone between Ognibene's ATM and an adjacent ATM. The individual was seemingly reporting to the bank that the adjacent ATM was not working. The person, speaking into the phone said, "I'll see if his card works in my machine." He then borrowed Ognibene's card and inserted it into the other ATM several times, finally stating, "Yes, it seems to be working." Then he returned Ognibene's card. Later, Ognibene discovered $400 had been withdrawn from his account by the person. Ognibene then sued the bank to have the $400 recredited to his account, claiming the transaction was unauthorized under the EFT Act. The bank refused, stating that by giving the other person the card, Ognibene had "authorized" the transaction and was fully liable even though Ognibene obviously had not benefitted from the transaction. Decide. (*Ognibene v. Citibank N. A.*, 446 N.Y.S.2d 845)

Unit Nine
UNDERSTANDING PROPERTY AND BAILMENTS

UNIT OBJECTIVES

UPON COMPLETION OF THIS UNIT, you should be able to

1. distinguish between real and personal property.
2. discuss the ways to acquire and dispose of personal property.
3. describe the different forms of co-ownership.
4. describe limitations on ownership of personal property.
5. understand how, in bailments, one in possession of tangible personal property may transfer it to another person without selling it.
6. identify examples of the most common types of mutual-benefit bailments.
7. explain why hotelkeepers and common carriers have insurer-like liability, but how statutes and contract terms may limit this liability.
8. define negotiable and nonnegotiable bills of lading, airbills, and warehouse receipts.
9. explain the difference between fixtures and trade fixtures.
10. describe how real property is bought, and discuss how one can acquire real property without buying it.
11. describe the uses and types of deeds.
12. describe the types of tenancies.
13. discuss the rights and duties of landlords and tenants.
14. explain the ways leases can be terminated.
15. describe the requirements for a formal will.
16. discuss the ways a will can be revoked.
17. tell how an estate is distributed when there is, and is not, a will.

33

Personal Property

1. Fran bought a prize-winning cow from Carl for $1,500. Three weeks later both Carl and Fran were surprised when the cow gave birth to a calf worth about $400. Both Fran and Carl claim ownership of the calf. Who prevails?
2. While on a skiing trip in Vermont, you (a) find a pair of skis in a parking lot, (b) pick up some firewood along the road, and (c) shoot two rabbits for a meal. Do you acquire ownership rights in these things?
3. You and five friends combine your savings to buy a 32-foot sailboat. What form of ownership should your group use?

WHAT IS PROPERTY?

PROBLEM: Winkler rented her cabin in Ocean City to Hanson for the summer season. Did Hanson acquire property under the lease?

When someone speaks of property, you probably think of many *tangible things* (things that you can see or touch). Tangible things include this book, desks, clothing, buildings and the land on which they rest, airplanes, cars, and boats. Reflection about property will probably bring to mind *intangible things* (things that you cannot see or touch). For example, both the goodwill of a brand name and the secret formula by which a product is made are intangible. Important intangible property is often described by legal documents. Examples include the patent for an invention, the copyright of this book, the franchise to open a particular business in your town, and the right to collect money under an automobile insurance policy.

property: things and the corresponding group of legal rights and interests

According to the law, **property** is not just a thing, tangible or intangible, that is subject to ownership. It is also a group of *rights and interests* that are recognized by society and, therefore, are protected by law.

For example, suppose that you own some land with a house that you correctly call "property." Ownership, a right itself, gives you a number of other legal rights. These include rights to (1) possess, use, and enjoy; (2) dispose of (by gift or sale), consume, or even destroy; and (3) give away by will after death. You also have the right to lease your property to a tenant. Therefore your tenant acquires property—that is, a right to use your land and building. In the problem, Hanson acquired a property interest in the cabin. A person may own all or some of the total group or "bundle" of rights to property.

real property: land and things permanently attached to the land

personal property: tangible, movable property and intangible property

Property can be classified as real or personal. Different rules govern the creation, use, and transfer of real and personal property. **Real property** is land, including not only the surface of the earth, but also the water and minerals on and below the surface. Real property extends downward to the center of the earth. It also includes, with certain limits, the airspace above the land. Real property also includes anything permanently attached to the land, such as buildings. (Real property is discussed more fully in Chapter 35.) **Personal property** includes property which is tangible and movable, such as a car, airplane, musical instrument, sofa, book, or tennis racket. Personal property also includes intangible property. *Intellec-*

tual property is often purely intangible; that is, it has no physical component one can touch. Intellectual property discussed in this chapter includes patents, trade secrets, and trademarks. The creation, use, and transfer of interests in intellectual property are generally governed by federal statutes.

HOW CAN PROPERTY BE ACQUIRED?

PROBLEM: While comparing their wristwatches, some friends explained how each had acquired possession. Appleton had bought his with earnings from a paper route. Baird had received hers as a graduation gift. Cameron had inherited hers from an aunt who had died. Dawson, a skilled watchmaker, had made his own. Engler had found hers on the street. She had tried but could not find the owner. Did each friend have equal ownership rights in his or her own wristwatch?

Real or personal property is most commonly acquired by contract, gift, or inheritance. In addition, personal property may be legitimately acquired by accession, intellectual labor, finding, or occupancy. (Other methods of acquiring real property are discussed in Chapter 35.) In the problem, each friend had equal ownership rights in his or her own wristwatch.

1. By Contract

Any kind of property may be acquired and transferred, or bought and sold, by contract. Most people acquire most of their property by earning money—a form of personal property. This income may be used, in turn, to purchase more personal property.

Clark wanted to earn money to buy a piano. Therefore she agreed to mow the lawns of 15 neighbors once a week during the summer. She should acquire more than $2,000 as a result of contracts with her customers.

2. By Gift

To be valid, a gift must combine an intent to *transfer* ownership with a *delivery* of the property or of something representing it, such as the keys to a car or a deed to real property. As you learned in Chapter 11, a mere promise to make a gift creates no rights.

Schuster dangled a certificate for 100 shares of stock in front of his niece, a senior in high school. "Melinda," he said, "you've been doing so well in all your classes that I'm giving you this stock." Melinda had no ownership rights in the stock because, as yet, there was no delivery. If Schuster had given her the indorsed stock certificate, however, there would have been delivery and ownership would have shifted.

Sometimes a gift is conditional, as when a man gives his fiancee an engagement ring. If the two mutually agree not to get married after all, or if the woman breaks the engagement, the man may generally reclaim the gift. In most states, if the man breaks the engagement the woman is entitled to keep the ring.

Another type of conditional gift is made when a donor expects to die soon. The gift may be conditional upon the death actually occurring. Donors who survive may change their minds and may take back their gifts. Such a gift, made in contemplation of death, should not be confused with one made by a will. With a will, the transfer of possession and title does not take place until after death.

Three friends were flying across the Rocky Mountains in a small airplane. An unexpected storm caused the wings to ice up, and the plane crashed in an isolated area. Only the pilot, Gary, was hurt. However, his injuries appeared to be critical. "I'll never make it," he said. "Here, Jim, take my diamond ring. Lisa, you take my watch." Gary insisted, and so Jim and Lisa accepted the gifts before he lapsed into unconsciousness. Within hours, however, a helicopter rescued the group, and Gary survived. He is entitled to the return of his ring and watch.

For gifts of low value, such as candy, shirts, or perfume, no condition is intended by the parties or implied by law. The title passes upon delivery of such gifts, and the giver may not demand their return.

3. By Accession

accession: right to a natural or man-made increase in property

Personal property may be acquired by accession. **Accession** is the right of an owner of property to an increase in that property. The increase may be natural or man-made. Thus, farm crops and the offspring of animals belong to the owner of the land and the animals. When new parts are put into an article, they generally become part of the article. For example, if a modem is connected to your personal computer, it becomes part of the computer.

If, by mistake, someone improves another's property, courts seek to do justice by letting the improver keep the property after paying fair value for the original item. For example, an innocent trespasser increased the value of lumber 28 times by changing the lumber into barrel hoops. That person then acquired title to the new goods after paying a fair price for the original lumber. As another example, a person who innocently buys stolen property from a thief gets possession but not title because the thief had none to give. If the true owner learns who has the goods, the possessor may be compelled to pay for them or to return them to the true owner. If the innocent buyer has to return the property, he or she may usually remove anything that has been added. However, a thief or willful wrongdoer who improves another's property generally gets to keep nothing.

4. By Intellectual Labor

One may acquire personal property rights by original production. Authors or inventors have exclusive property rights in their own productions prior to the time of publication or the marketing of their inventions. The author or inventor wishing to keep exclusive rights thereafter may do so for a limited time by properly requesting and obtaining a grant from the federal government.

A grant to an author, an artist, or a composer of the exclusive, monopolistic right to possess, produce, and publish or otherwise dispose of an intellectual production is a **copyright**. Copyrights are granted for the life of the author plus 50 years.

copyright: government grant of exclusive right to possess, produce, and publish an intellectual production

> Martin and two friends were musicians who enjoyed improvising. One day Gardner heard them playing and added lyrics. Together, the four musicians put the music down on paper. They protected the property they had thus created by copyrighting it. Later, they sold the copyright to a publisher who paid them *royalties* (compensation that is usually based on sales).

patent: government grant of exclusive right to make, use, and sell a product or process which is novel, non-obvious, and useful

A grant of the exclusive, monopolistic right to make, use, and sell a novel, non-obvious, useful product or process is a **patent**. A patent is good for 17 years and is not renewable. However, an inventor will sometimes add improvements to the original product and will then patent them over the years. This, in effect, extends the duration of the monopoly. Patents are also given for original designs such as a unique chair or house. They are also given for certain new and distinct varieties of plants.

trade secret: unpatented formula or process not known to others and which is valuable in business

Sometimes a business firm will own important trade secrets, which are not patented. A **trade secret** may consist of a valuable formula or process known only to the company owner and to selected employees. If an employee leaves a company and tries to use or to sell the formula or process, the employee and the new employer may be stopped from doing so by means of a court order. If the trade secret is actually used, the true owner may sue to collect damages and to get an injunction against further use or disclosure.

trademark: distinctive word, device, or symbol that identifies a product or service

Business firms may also acquire property rights in trademarks. A **trademark** is a word, mark, symbol, or device which identifies a product of a particular manufacturer or merchant. The mark must be distinctive and serve to identify and distinguish the product from he products of other manufacturers or merchants. For example, the word "Kodak" is a trademark. It is included in the name of the owner, the Eastman Kodak Company, and it identifies products made by that company. However, descriptive words such as "35 mm camera" may be used by any company.

All states and the federal government have trademark registration laws, which simplify proof of ownership. However, registration is not essential. Common-law protection lasts forever if the trademark is used continuously. Sometimes leading American manufacturers develop and give unique trademarks to products which are widely used. The originating company loses its exclusive property right to the trademark if it does either of the following:

a. permits competitors to refer to similar products by the unique trademark, or
b. does not object when the trademark is used generally in the press as a descriptive generic term.

Examples of terms which have become generic are "shredded wheat" and "cellophane." In contrast, the terms "Xerox," "Levi's," and "Scotch Tape" remain the property of the original owners.

5. By Finding

Anyone who loses property has the right to recover it from any finder. One must simply prove true ownership. If the true owner is unknown, either the finder or the owner of the place where the property was found will be able to keep the property. Who has the right to possession depends on whether the found property was *lost* or *mislaid*. Finders keep lost property and owners of the place where the property was found keep mislaid property. Mislaid property is intentionally placed somewhere but then forgotten. If you went into a restaurant and hung your coat on a coatrack while you ate and then you walked out without your coat, it would be mislaid. Anyone finding the coat would be required to turn it over to the restaurant. Since you may come back looking for the coat, this rule of law helps true owners find mislaid property. Property is lost when it is unknowingly or accidentally dropped or left somewhere. If, while you are preoccupied with a football game, your coat falls from the bleachers at a football stadium, and someone finds it on the ground, the finder, not the school, is entitled to possession unless or until you recover the coat. Statutes permit the finder to become the owner if the true owner does not reclaim the property within a stated time.

6. By Occupancy

Occupancy means acquiring title by taking possession of personal property which belongs to no one else. A common example is **abandoned property**—personal property that has been discarded by the owner. In such a case, the finder who takes possession gets absolute title.

occupancy: taking possession of personal property belonging to no one else

abandoned property: personal property discarded by the owner

> A national aluminum company offered to buy used aluminum cans for recycling. One Saturday the members of the Junior Optimist Club picked up a total of three truckloads of such cans from along the sides of a heavily traveled country road. The club members acquired property by occupancy and transferred ownership of the property to the company by sale.

Like abandoned property, wildlife is considered unowned. A properly licensed person who takes possession of a wild animal by killing it on public lands becomes the legal owner. Similarly, one may become the owner of shells by picking them up on a public beach, or one may become the owner of firewood by gathering it along public roads. However, property so acquired on private lands belongs to the owner of the real property unless otherwise agreed.

7. By Inheritance

A person may acquire both real and personal property by inheritance from others after they die.

WHAT ARE THE FORMS OF OWNERSHIP?

PROBLEM: After graduating from high school, Denise became a computer programmer. Her salary was good, and her expenses were low because she lived with her parents. With most of her savings, Denise bought shares in a mutual fund. What form of ownership did she use?

tenancy: ownership interest in property

co-ownership: ownership in the same property by two or more persons

Tenancy is the general name given to the various forms of ownership of real or personal property. One, two, or more persons may hold the title to a single piece of property.

Co-ownership exists when two or more persons have ownership interests in the same property. It differs from situations in which two persons have different legal rights in the same property. For example, landlord and tenant are not co-owners because they have different rights in the realty. The landlord has the right to dispose of the property and to give it away after death; the tenant has the right to possess the property during the term of the lease. If two persons own the same house together, they are co-owners. Similarly, if you and one of your parents own a car together, you are co-owners.

Co-ownership may be in one of several forms—tenancy in common, joint tenancy, tenancy by the entireties, or community property. All forms have two attributes in common. The first is that all co-owners have equal rights of possession. This means that no co-owner can exclude any other co-owner from any portion of the property. This is the most basic attribute of co-ownership.

The second attribute common to all forms of co-ownership is the right to partition. This right allows any co-owner to require division of the property among the co-owners. Sometimes the partition is physical, as when a farm is divided. Usually partition is financial. For example, a co-owned airplane could be sold and the proceeds of sale divided among the co-owners.

1. Tenancy in Severalty

tenancy in severalty: ownership by one person alone

When property is owned by one person alone, it is held in **tenancy in severalty**. In the problem, Denise held her shares in this way.

2. Joint Tenancy

PROBLEM: Neither Jennifer nor her sister ever married. Several years ago, they bought an eight-unit retail store building as an investment. In the event that either dies, they wish the survivor to get the building. What form of ownership should they select?

Co-ownership of property by two or more persons with the right of survivorship is known as **joint tenancy**. The **right of survivorship** means that if one of the joint owners dies, the surviving owner or owners automatically get the deceased owner's interest. For this reason, one would normally not hold property in joint tenancy with strangers, friends, or business associates. One would do so, however, with relatives who are the "natural objects of one's bounty." In effect, each joint tenant uses this form to leave property to the other joint tenant(s) after death, without incurring the costs and delays of probate. In the problem, the sisters could use this form of ownership. A joint tenant's share may not be given to someone else by a will. However, it may be transferred while the joint tenant still lives. This transfer would end the joint tenancy, however, and would make the new owner a tenant in common. While the joint tenancy lasts, the owners have equal rights to possess and to enjoy the property. Their ownership interests must be equal.

joint tenancy: co-ownership with the right of survivorship

right of survivorship: right of one joint tenant to ownership of property when the other joint tenant dies

3. Tenancy in Common

PROBLEM: Smith, Locke, and Pitt were friends and coworkers at a local factory. The three friends could not afford to purchase house trailers individually. Together, however, they were able to buy one which they agreed to share according to their vacation schedules. What form of ownership would be appropriate for the three?

One form of co-ownership is known as **tenancy in common.** The owners are thus called tenants in common. The interest or share of each owner may be unequal. Although all owners have the right of possession, they can agree to give exclusive use to one or the other at certain times. This is true of all forms of multiple ownership. In the problem, tenancy in common would be advisable for the three friends.

tenancy in common: co-ownership with no right of survivorship

In a tenancy in common, there is no right of survivorship. Upon the death of any tenant in common, that person's interest passes to his or her *heirs* (relatives entitled to inherit) or to the beneficiaries designated in the will if there is one. The heirs or beneficiaries then become tenants in common with the other owners. While still alive, each owner can sell his or her share or interest to another person. That person then joins the prior owners as a tenant in common. Together, the owners may agree to sell the entire property and to divide the proceeds according to their shares.

4. Tenancy by the Entireties

tenancy by the entireties: special joint tenancy between spouses

In some states, a joint tenancy between husband and wife is a **tenancy by the entireties.** This differs from the ordinary joint tenancy in that neither spouse acting alone may convey or mortgage his or her interest to a third person. Also, a creditor cannot claim the property unless that person is a creditor of both the husband and wife. Upon death, the surviving spouse gets title by the right of survivorship.

5. Community Property

PROBLEM: All of the property belonging to John and Sally Yaun was community property. Domestic difficulties developed between the two. Although there was no divorce, John made a will in which he left all the community property to his nephews and nieces. Could he legally do this?

community property: property owned equally by spouses

In eight states,[1] all property acquired by husband and wife during their marriage is **community property.** Each spouse owns an undivided one-half interest in such property. Generally, while the spouses are alive, both must consent to disposal of community property. Upon the death of either spouse, statutes in some community property states provide for the right of survivorship. In other states, the spouse who dies is permitted to dispose of his or her half through a will, or that portion goes to the heirs. In either case, it is clear that John in the problem may not legally deprive his widow of at least her half of the community property. In some states, he could will his half of the community property to relatives or strangers.

Property owned by either spouse at the time of marriage or received as a gift or inheritance is *separate* property. Such property

[1]These states are Arizona, California, Idaho, Louisiana, Nevada, New Mexico, Texas, and Washington.

becomes community property only if the owner formally or informally treats it as community property and mixes it with other community assets.

WHAT ARE THE LIMITATIONS ON OWNERSHIP?

PROBLEM: Reed, who lived alone, was very fond of animals. After his retirement, he began to care for stray dogs which he kept in his home and yard. Within a year, he had 27 animals. Neighbors were reluctant to interfere, but the noise became intolerable. Could the neighbors compel Reed to dispose of his animals?

Certain limitations on ownership are necessary in civilized society. The right of an owner to freely use and to dispose of property is therefore subject to restrictions designed to protect the equally important rights of others.

An owner of property is not permitted to use that property in an unreasonable or unlawful manner that injures another. Thus, in the problem, Reed could be compelled to correct a nuisance.

Under its police power, the government may adopt laws for the protection of the public health, safety, morals, and general welfare. This power extends to the use of property. Thus, a city may require that buildings be maintained at a certain level of livability. A city may enact zoning laws which restrict certain neighborhoods to specific uses. It may also enact laws which prohibit the keeping of livestock in certain sections. It may regulate the purity of food and drugs sold to the public. It may even destroy private property, such as shipments of canned fish that are infected with deadly botulism. All such laws limit the owner's absolute ownership and freedom of use.

All property is subject to sale for the payment of its owner's debts unless specifically exempt by statutes. There are legal means by which unpaid creditors may force a sale of debtors' property with the proceeds going to pay judgments for overdue debts.

To help meet the costs of government, a resident may be compelled to pay taxes. These taxes are based on the value of the property owned or upon that person's income. In addition, **assessments** may be made against benefited real property to pay the cost of improvements. Such an improvement might be the initial installation of streetlights or sewers.

assessments: special taxes on real property

If a person fails to pay lawful taxes or assessments, the government may impose a lien on and later sell that person's property. Proceeds are then applied to the payment of the taxes. The balance, if any, goes to the former owner.

Other noteworthy burdens on the owner of property include:

1. risk of loss by fire or theft or injury to others;
2. decline in value from wear and tear or depreciation; and
3. cost of protection and maintenance needed to reduce the ravages of wind, rain, heat, cold, oxidation, and pollution.

PREVENTING LEGAL DIFFICULTIES

Manage and Use Property Wisely . . .

1. understand your various property rights and use them intelligently. You may use and enjoy, let others use, borrow against, sell, or give away what you own;
2. do not misuse your property in any way that injures others;
3. you have a social responsibility to protect the ecology and conserve resources by avoiding waste. Avoiding waste also gives you more for your money;
4. use public property with care. Vandalism, destruction, and theft deprive innocent persons of the benefits of use and also cause higher taxes, which burden all taxpayers;
5. protect your property against seizure through legal process by paying taxes to the government and debts to your creditors when due;
6. be alert to the many ways in which property can be acquired. When prices are high, acquiring property by repairing, making, or growing your own things can be a money-saving hobby. Examples include fixing automobiles, making clothes, and growing vegetables;
7. do not infringe upon the copyright, trademark, or patent of another;
8. if you become a co-owner, be sure to take title in an appropriate form. Use tenancy in common with strangers, associates, and friends. Use joint tenancy with a spouse or other relative whom you want to have the full ownership by right of survivorship when you die;
9. in community property states, be sure to keep separate property separate, with clear independent records, if you do not want it to become community property; and
10. minimize the burdens of ownership through proper use and maintenance of property. Also, be sure to have adequate property and casualty insurance (see Chapter 26).

Strengthening Your Legal Vocabulary

abandoned property
accession
assessments
community property
co-ownership
copyright
joint tenancy
occupancy
patent
personal property
property
real property
right of survivorship
tenancy
tenancy by the entireties
tenancy in common
tenancy in severalty
trademark
trade secret

1. Tangible or intangible thing and the corresponding group of rights or interests that are recognized by society and protected by law.
2. Co-ownership of property without the right of survivorship.
3. Ownership of property by one person alone.
4. Right of an owner of property to an increase in the property.
5. Exclusive, monopolistic right to make, use, and sell an invented product.
6. Means of acquiring title by taking possession of personal property which belongs to no one else.
7. Exclusive, monopolistic right to possess, produce, and publish an intellectual production.
8. Land and things permanently attached to the land.
9. Form of joint tenancy by husband and wife where neither may dispose of his or her interest without the consent of the other.
10. Co-ownership of property by persons who are not husband and wife and who own the property with the right of survivorship.

Reviewing Important Points

1. Technically, property means a group of rights or interests which are recognized by organized society and, therefore, are protected by law. However, the terms may also refer to the things themselves—both real and personal, tangible and intangible—in which one may have legal rights and interests.
2. Property may be classified as real or personal. Legally, each category includes a group of rights which can be owned.
3. Real property is land, including the surface of the earth, surface and subsurface water and minerals, the airspace above, and anything permanently attached to the land. Personal property is any intangible property or tangible property which is movable. Personal property also includes intellectual property—copyrights, patents, trademarks and trade secrets.
4. Both real and personal property may include intangible rights, as, for example, the right to use land or the right to make and to sell a product.
5. Rights in property may be acquired by (a) contract (including employment

and sale contracts), (b) gift, (c) accession, (d) intellectual labor, (e) finding, (f) occupancy, or (g) inheritance.
6. Ownership by one person is tenancy in severalty. Co-ownership may take the form of joint tenancy or tenancy in common. In some states, husband and wife may hold property by tenancy by the entireties. In some other states, their property acquired during marriage is community property.
7. Individual ownership of property may be limited when necessary to prevent infringement on the rights of others.

Applying Law to Everyday Life

1. Your father operates a small lumber business. He owns a tract of land with a stand of trees on it. He cuts down the trees, saws them into construction lumber, and sells the wood to builders. He also is building a house as a business venture. The house is about one-third finished, and half of the framing for the walls is completed. Your father is concerned about his insurance coverage because it covers only personal property. Which parts of his business property are real and which are personal?

2. Howard gave his nephew, Jake, 100 shares of stock in Gold Stake Oil Corp. for his 16th birthday. He handed the shares, worth about $2,000, to Jake right after Jake successfully blew out all 16 candles. Two days later, Gold Stake discovered a very large oil field. The value of the stock increased 10 times to $20,000. As a result, Howard had second thoughts and demanded the return of the shares. Must Jake return the stock?

3. Jeff's school has a computer laboratory. Jeff also has a computer at home and decides to copy the school's word processing program for his personal use. The program is copyrighted by its developer. Is it legal for Jeff to make a copy for himself? Would it be ethical for Jeff to make a copy if he obtains permission from the school's principal?

4. Voilà!, a French firm, manufactured expensive leather goods. It marked all of its products with a crest or seal which was a registered trademark. Imperial sold six counterfeit handbags bearing the Voilà! mark. The purchaser was a private investigator in the employ of Voilà! Voilà! sued Imperial for trademark infringement. Assume that Imperial did not manufacture the handbags but only sold them. Will Voilà! prevail?

5. Foxx, Flynn, and Hammond were amateur auto mechanics. The three also had equal shares in a drag racer as tenants in common. After a disagreement, Foxx wanted to get out of the arrangement. She demanded the engine as her share of the commonly-owned racer. Is she entitled to it?

6. For ten years, Bert and his sister, Trudy, invested their savings in a 12-unit apartment house. They held the title as joint tenants. Then Bert got married. Shortly after the wedding, he was killed in an auto accident. In his will, Burt left all his property to his wife. His sister and his widow are now in a dispute

over who should get his share of the apartment house. Who should get Bert's share?

7. Michael and his wife co-owned, as tenants by the entireties, a chain of record stores. Michael decided he wanted to sell the record stores and go into the plumbing business. Can he sell his one-half interest without his wife's consent?

Solving Case Problems

1. Roberts had an above-ground swimming pool installed on his land. The pool was not permanently attached to the realty. It could be easily disassembled and moved to another location. Shortly after the installation, Roberts received a real estate tax assessment bill with an increased assessed value for his realty because of the pool. Roberts sued for a reduction, claiming that the pool was personal property. Will he prevail? (*Roberts v. Assessment Board of Review of the Town of New Windsor,* 84 Misc. 2d 1017, N.Y.)

2. Joseph's aunt sent him $5,000 as a gift. Later, she sent a letter stating that upon her death the money was to be distributed among Joseph and his brothers and sisters. After the aunt died, Joseph kept the money and was sued. Joseph defended by claiming that a valid gift of the money occurred before the letter was sent, so the letter is of no legal significance. Is Joseph correct? (*In re Gordon's Will,* 27 N.W.2d 900, Iowa)

3. Gem Electronic Distributors installed Make-a-Tape systems in their retail stores. Make-a-Tape is a coin-operated magnetic tape duplicating system. In two minutes it can reproduce on a blank eight-track cartridge the complete musical selections already recorded on another eight-track cartridge that takes 35 to 45 minutes to play. Elektra records sued Gem to restrain it from using Make-a-Tape to produce for customers unauthorized copies of Elektra sound recordings, which are copyrighted. Decide. Would it be ethical for Gem to make the machine available for use by its customers if it knew that 95 percent of its use violated the copyright laws? (*Elektra Records Co. v. Gem Electronic Distributors, Inc.,* 360 F. Supp. 821, E.D.N.Y)

4. Hamilton and Johnson were tenants in common of a parcel of land. Hamilton wanted to end the relationship and brought a suit for partition of the property. A forced sale of the property would be inconvenient for Johnson and would cause him some loss. Must the court, nevertheless, order partition? (*Hamilton v. Johnson,* 137 Wash. 92, 241 P. 672)

5. Alejo Lopez was a married man. Without divorcing, he married a second time. He and his second wife, Helen, purchased property and tried to take title as tenants by the entireties. Later, Alejo divorced his first wife and then remarried Helen. When he died, a question arose as to whether the property was owned in tenancy by the entireties. Is it? (*Lopez v. Lopez,* 243 A.2d 588, Md.)

SPECIAL SECTION:
How and When to be Your Own Attorney

Sometimes the very nature of a legal cause of action dictates that the parties involved should act as their own attorneys. This may be the only cost-effective alternative when the damages which might be recovered are small. In every state, small claims courts are available to decide such cases. The claim for damages generally may not exceed $1,000. You do not need a lawyer to represent you; indeed, some states ban representation by lawyers in small claims courts.

Small claims courts are ideal to hear disputes involving such things as:

—the $273.45 for which your mechanic billed you for fixing your voltage regulator when the problem was really a dead cell in the battery.

—the $328.00 security deposit kept by your former landlord when you moved, even though your apartment was undamaged and in a much cleaner condition than received by you.

—the $134.70 share of the phone bill still owed to you by your ex-roommate.

—the $425.00 check that the bank paid regardless of your stop-payment order on it.

However, before suing, it is always a good idea to try other possible means of getting satisfaction. A lawsuit, even if in a small claims court, requires the expenditure of much time and energy. Courtroom confrontations can be emotionally troubling and physically exhausting, and there is always the possibility of losing. Therefore, before becoming fully committed to a legal battle, contact the other party and clearly state (preferably in writing) your grievance and specify what you expect in the way of satisfaction. Be reasonable. Give a time deadline and perhaps say that you are considering court action but would much prefer an amicable out-of-court settlement. Carefully consider the response to your demand. Be prepared to compromise; that is what will probably happen under court order if you bring the matter before a judge. If you cannot reach a satisfactory solution, pursue the matter in court.

34

Bailments

1. You need transportation for the senior prom, but your car breaks down before the event. What legal relation arises if you borrow a friend's car for the evening, without charge? What legal relation arises if you rent a car from a rental agency?
2. While shopping for lipstick in the cosmetics department of the store, Sara places her handbag on the counter. Minutes later she reaches for it, but it is gone—apparently stolen. Is the store liable for her loss?
3. A local airline serves small cities that are bypassed by all major carriers. Its business is booming, but it lacks the cash and credit to buy two badly needed additional airplanes. How can it use the law of bailments to solve its problem?

WHAT IS A BAILMENT?

PROBLEM: Roberta's parents own a 25-inch TV set and a videocassette recorder. One evening they rent a videotape of a movie Roberta has been wanting to see. What is the legal relation between Roberta's parents and the videotape rental store?

If you lend your ball-point pen to a fellow student, you are involved in the legal relation of bailment. The transaction is neither a sale nor a gift, because your friend is obligated to return the pen to you.

bailment: transfer of possession of personal property without transfer of ownership

bailor: one who transfers possession of the personal property

bailee: one who receives possession of the personal property

custody: care and present control of another's personal property, under the owner's direction

Bailments arise in many transfers of personal property. Whenever one party gives possession of personal property to another under an agreement by which the identical property must be returned or disposed of as agreed, a **bailment** is created. Bailments may be created by express or implied agreements. The purpose of a bailment may be to store the goods, to have them transported, or to have them repaired or serviced. Sometimes the purpose is to use the goods as collateral (security) to ensure repayment of a loan. Often the purpose is simply to let the borrower use the goods for an agreed time. The party who gives up possession of the property is the **bailor**. The party who receives possession is the **bailee**. In the problem, a bailment was created. The rental store was the bailor, and Roberta's parents were the bailees.

It is possible for a person to have present care and control of personal property under the direction of the owner, yet to have no legal interest in the property. This is **custody**, not bailment. For example, a person hired to guard the paintings in an art museum has custody, but is not a bailee. Nor is a clerk using an employer's word-processing equipment in the company offices a bailee. Legally the employer retains possession of the equipment.

WHAT ARE THE CHARACTERISTICS OF A BAILMENT?

PROBLEM: The Slatkins are newlyweds, and their first apartment is in the graduate student housing complex at the state university. They rent an unfurnished apartment from the school and then rent some filing cabinets, a drawing table, and two lamps from Travel Light Furniture Suppliers. Are these contracts bailments?

Every bailment has the following four characteristics:

1. The Subject Is Tangible Personal Property

Real property, such as land or buildings, is not bailed. It is leased under different rules of law. Thus, the apartment rental in the problem was a lease between the school as landlord and the Slatkins as tenants (see Chapter 36). The furniture rental was a bailment because furniture is tangible personal property. Many people refer to rentals of personal property as leases; strictly speaking, these are bailments.

2. Anyone in Possession of the Goods May Bail Them

Usually property is bailed by the owner. However, it may be bailed by anyone in possession, including an agent or employee, a custodian, a finder, or even a thief.

A robber held up the cashier of the snack stand in a theater located in a shopping center. He stuffed the cash into an attaché case and mingled with the crowd of shoppers in the indoor mall. At a nearby restaurant, he checked the case and his topcoat with an attendant. This was a legal bailment for storage.

3. The Goods Must Be Received and Accepted by the Bailee

Transfer of bailed goods is usually actual, as when the bailee receives a rented truck, gets behind the steering wheel, and drives off. Transfer would be constructive if the bailee received keys to the truck which was located elsewhere.

4. The Identical Goods Must Be Returned to the Bailor or to a Designee

The identical goods which have been bailed must be returned to the bailor or to some person designated by the bailor. Of course, the goods may be modified somewhat, as by agreed-upon use, repairs, processing, or aging.

WHAT ARE THE TYPES OF BAILMENTS?

PROBLEM: In preparation for a professional tennis tournament, Page took two of her tennis rackets to the Village Racketeer for restringing. Was this a bailment?

mutual-benefit bailment: bailment which benefits both bailor and bailee

When consideration is given and received by both bailor and bailee, the contracts are called **mutual-benefit bailments** because both parties benefit. Thus, in the problem, Page received the restringing in exchange for the price; the Village Racketeer received the price in exchange for the work.

gratuitous bailment: bailment which benefits only one party

In a **gratuitous bailment** only one of the parties benefits. Thus, it would be a *gratuitous bailment for the sole benefit of the bailor* if your parents accept possession of a neighbor's house plants and agree to care for them without charge while the neighbor is on a vacation. On the other hand, it would be a *gratuitous bailment for the sole benefit of the bailee* if you loaned your pocket calculator to a classmate without charge. Mutual-benefit bailments result from contracts, whereas gratuitous bailments do not because there is no exchange of consideration.

extraordinary bailment: bailment requiring an unusually high standard of care

Certain mutual-benefit bailments are termed **extraordinary bailments** because the bailee is held to an unusually high standard of care for the bailed property. This would be the case when the bailee is a hotel or common carrier. All other bailments are ordinary.

WHAT ARE THE RIGHTS AND DUTIES OF PARTIES TO A BAILMENT?

PROBLEM: During dinner at the Sky-Hi Ski Lodge, Bolo carelessly left his skis near a blazing fireplace in the main lounge. By the time he returned to the lounge, the heat had caused the laminated wood to separate at several points. Bolo took the skis to the Alpenhaus Ski Hut and had them repaired. Now he wants the skis for the coming weekend but has neither cash nor credit to pay for the service. Must Alpenhaus give him the skis and simply bill him? Is Sky-Hi liable to Bolo for the cost of repair?

In any bailment, the bailee has a duty to protect and properly care for the bailor's property. This may require indoor storage of a lawn mower left at a shop for servicing, feeding and exercising a horse boarded at a stable, or loading a rented trailer as prescribed. The bailee should comply with all directions or regulations on how, where, when, by whom, and for how long the property is to be used. Thus, in a bailment for auto repairs, the bailee should do only the work agreed upon. Prior approval should be obtained for any unauthorized work found to be desirable, or even necessary. Although bailees who are victims of contractual violations do not always complain or sue for damages, they have a legal right to do so.

The bailee has a duty to return the property, sometimes modified as agreed. The bailor may be entitled to payment for storage or for services rendered. If so, the bailor may exercise the **bailee's lien** and may retain possession until paid. If payment is unreasonably delayed, the bailee may sell the property to recover the fee and related costs. In the problem, Alpenhaus has the right to retain possession until paid and to sell the skis if not paid within a reasonable time. Sky-Hi is not liable for the cost of repairs because it was not a bailee of the skis.

bailee's lien: right of a bailee to hold goods until payment is received

A bailor who rents to others should inspect for all reasonably discoverable defects before delivery, because in a mutual-benefit bailment there is a duty to provide goods fit for the intended purpose. Thus, a rubber raft rental company should check carefully for damaged spots and slow leaks. Failure to do so could cause injury—or even death—to a bailee later caught in violent river rapids. The bailor in a mutual-benefit bailment who fails to correct, or at least inform, the bailee of any defects which are known or reasonably discoverable is liable for any resulting injuries.

Dermody, owner of a snowmobile business, rented snowmobiles to vacationers at a mountain resort. One particular unit had a defective steering mechanism. The mechanism sometimes locked in a fast turn and could flip the machine over on its side. She failed to mention this defect to Escobar when Escobar rented the snowmobile. Unfortunately the steering mechanism did lock in use, injuring Escobar. Dermody is liable for damages.

A bailee who has been told about or discovers a defect, yet who goes ahead and uses the property and is injured, is barred from collecting damages. The bailee is held to have assumed the risk—to have shown contributory negligence. This could happen, for example, if a bailee drives a rented truck with defective brakes after being told of the dangerous condition.

The bailee cannot be relieved of liability for willful or deliberate injury to the bailor or to the bailor's property. This would be contrary to public policy. When the bailee's liability for negligence is to be limited, this fact must be made clearly known to the bailor, as by prominently posted signs with printing large enough for the average person to read. A mention of the limitation in small print on a claim check is insufficient notice unless the bailor has read it or was specifically told about the limitation. Some states avoid disputes over whether notice was given. By statute or case law they simply prohibit certain paid bailees, such as parking garages, from limiting their liability for negligence.

Disputes sometimes arise when cars left in parking lots are damaged or stolen. Liability is affected by whether or not a bailment exists. The car owner who drives into a lot, parks the car, keeps the key, and can later drive the car away without permission of an attendant continues to have exclusive control of the car. He or she has merely rented space to park. No bailment relationship exists because possession has not been transferred. There is a bailment, however, if an attendant takes possession of the car and gives the owner a claim check which must be surrendered to get the car back.

Questions also arise as to whether the bailment of a car is a bailment of articles enclosed. If the article is normally included, such as a spare tire in the trunk, the bailment covers it without regard to the bailee's knowledge of its presence. Other contained articles are included if the parties reasonably intended or clearly indicated that the articles were part of the goods in a mutual-benefit bailment.

On the other hand, suppose you agree to keep your friend's dog and automobile while the friend is on vacation. These are gratuitous bailments for the sole benefit of the bailor. Unless otherwise agreed, you may not use such goods unless necessary for their preservation. Before transferring possession, the bailor should examine the goods for possible defects. Failure to inform the bailee of known or reasonably discoverable defects makes the bailor liable for any possible resulting injury.

In contrast, friends or relatives often borrow equipment and other personal property from one another without charge. These are also gratuitous bailments, but these are for the sole benefit of the bailee. Thus, one might borrow an extension ladder or some jewelry. The bailee-borrower may use the goods, but only as agreed. The bailor-lender is obligated to inform the bailee only of known defects. Thus, the bailor who knows of a loose rung in a ladder, yet says nothing, may be liable for any resulting injuries suffered by the bailee.

Some courts further refine the definition of the bailee's duty as follows:

1. in a *mutual-benefit bailment*, the bailee must exercise ordinary care and is liable for ordinary negligence. The care could vary with the goods (coal or diamonds), the place (crowded city or isolated farm), the time (day or night), and other circumstances;

2. in a *gratuitous bailment for the sole benefit of the bailee*, the bailee must show great care in preserving property from loss or damage and is liable for even the slightest negligence. This high standard of care is also required of bailees in bailments for storage by hotels or motels and in bailments for transport by common carriers; and
3. in a *gratuitous bailment for the sole benefit of the bailor*, the bailee is required to use only slight care and is liable for gross negligence only.

WHAT ARE THE MOST COMMON TYPES OF MUTUAL-BENEFIT BAILMENTS?

PROBLEM: (a) A Korean automobile manufacturer contracted for shipment of cars from Seoul, Korea to Benicia, California in an ocean-going freighter. (b) When the cars arrived in Benicia they were parked on a lot under contract with the Benicia Port Authority. (c) Within a week, the manufacturer's California representative contracted to have an auto transport company move the cars in truckloads directly to the place of business of People Movers, Inc., a rent-a-car agency located in San Francisco. (d) To comply with California air pollution regulations, People Movers had its employees drive the cars to Hank's Garage, where the smog-control systems were modified under a service contract. (e) As soon as the cars were returned by Hank's to People Movers, they were delivered to rental customers for their personal use. What types of mutual-benefit bailments were involved in the above five events?

The most common types of mutual-benefit bailments are those for (1) transport, (2) storage, (3) hire for use, and (4) services. These and others are discussed below.

1. Bailments for Transport

PROBLEM: Formula-One Chemicals, Inc., requested Pan-World Airlines, a common carrier, to transport 100 glass jars of a certain chemical. The chemical was highly corrosive to metals. Therefore the airline refused to accept the shipment unless the jars were properly insulated against breakage, thus shielding the plane from possible damage from leakage. Must Formula-One comply?

consignor: one who delivers goods to a carrier for shipment

consignee: one to whom goods are shipped

carrier: transporter of passengers or goods

common carrier: transporter of passengers or goods for anyone

demurrage: fees for delay by consignor in loading or by consignee in unloading

carrier's lien: right to hold goods until paid for services

Tremendous quantities and an endless variety of goods are moved every day to supply the needs and wants of society. Raw materials, semifinished goods, and finished goods are transported by train, truck, ship, barge, airplane, bus, and pipeline. The shipper is the bailor and is called the **consignor**. The goods are moved to **consignees** by the bailee who is called a **carrier**.

Common Carriers. Carriers are classified as common, contract, and private. A **common carrier** agrees, for a fee, to transport goods for anyone who applies, provided the goods are lawful and fit for shipment. In the problem, Formula-One must comply with the airline's requirement of insulation, so that the chemical is fit for shipment. Although passengers may be transported by common carriers, only their baggage is governed by bailment law.

Common carriers are generally regulated and licensed. In the past, they were often given exclusive or semi-exclusive rights to serve particular routes. This restrictive favoritism limited competition. However, competition has been stimulated in recent years by the elimination of many regulations.

Traditionally, common carriers have been considered extraordinary bailees with absolute liability for loss or damage to goods. This harsh rule has been modified by statute and common law, and today there are important exceptions. Carriers may now limit their liability by contract, and may charge higher rates for accepting a higher liability.

A common carrier has the right to:

(1) enforce reasonable rules and regulations for the conduct of its business (for example, rules stating how goods must be packed),
(2) demand compensation for its services, as allowed by law,
(3) charge **demurrage** (fees for use of equipment when the consignor fails to load or the consignee fails to unload within a reasonable length of time), and
(4) enforce a **carrier's lien** (right to retain possession of the goods until the charges for transportation and incidental services are paid).

Shooting Star Shippers, an interstate trucking company, transported Morgan's large box of valuable machinist tools to New York. Shooting Star, the carrier, refused to release the box until paid for its services. Morgan said he needed the tools in order to work and earn enough to pay the charges, and he demanded credit. Shooting Star was not required to release the box to Morgan until paid for its services.

Contract Carriers. A **contract carrier** selects its customers and may reject unwanted business. It transports goods under individual contracts, which may limit both service and liability for loss as in any ordinary mutual-benefit bailment.

contract carrier: transporter of goods or passengers under individual contracts

Private Carriers. A **private carrier** transports only its own goods (and/or personnel). Thus, a telephone company may own and operate its own fleet of trucks; no bailment is involved.

private carrier: transporter of goods or members of its own organization only

2. Bailments for Storage

PROBLEM: During the fall harvest, most of the Roman Beauty apples picked at Scott's orchard were immediately placed in the Kool Storage Co. warehouse. When Scott removed some of the apples three months later, many had begun to rot because Kool had carelessly failed to keep the building at the proper temperature. Is Kool liable for the loss?

Warehousers store goods for others for a fee. When they hold themselves ready to serve the public without discrimination, they are subject to state and federal regulation.

warehouser: one who stores goods for profit

The warehouser must return the identical goods received. This rule does not apply, however, where each unit stored is identical to every other unit—as with grain or oil of a certain grade. The warehouser must also maintain the warehouse in suitable condition for the goods stored. For example, an open shed would not be suitable for deluxe furniture but could suffice for drying lumber. In the problem, Kool was liable for the loss because its negligence caused the apples to spoil.

3. Bailments for Hire

PROBLEM: Rosetta rented a house trailer from Beyond the Blue Horizon, Inc., for a week's trip with her children. Because they were having so much fun, she wired the bailor and said she would "take the trailer for another week." This extended use was not authorized. Pressed for time when she got back from the trip, Rosetta asked a recently hired clerk at

> her company to return the trailer. He never did return the trailer or Rosetta's car. Rosetta suspects that the clerk has left the country. What is Rosetta's liability to Beyond the Blue Horizon, Inc.?

A bailment for hire arises when the bailor provides personal property (such as a car, truck, tool, machine, or other equipment) for use by the bailee. The bailee is required to act with reasonable care and would generally be liable for any negligence or other tortious conduct which injures third parties. The bailor, having provided proper equipment, is not liable.

In a bailment for hire, the hirer (the bailee) has the exclusive right to use the property for the purpose and during the time specified in the contract. During the contract period, neither the bailor nor even a creditor of the bailor, has the right to disturb the bailee's possession. The bailee, however, must abide by the contract using the property only for the stated purposes and returning it at the agreed time. In the problem, Rosetta's unauthorized use of the trailer for the second week made her liable for damages. In addition, her failure to return the trailer as agreed made her liable to the bailor for the trailer's full value. Unfortunately her cause of action against the clerk for conversion is probably worthless.

In a bailment for hire, the bailor is entitled to the rent as agreed. This right ends if the property is lost or destroyed through no fault of the bailee. For example, suppose a person rents a light airplane which he properly secures at an airport, yet it is destroyed in a sudden tornado. The bailor has no right to be paid its value or any further compensation for its use. On the other hand, if the bailed property simply requires repairs, the bailment continues. This would be the case if the plane were not destroyed but simply damaged. The bailor normally makes major repairs not caused by the bailee's negligence. An example would be the replacement of a water pump in a rented truck or a tune-up of the engine. The bailee—in the absence of contrary agreement—makes minor repairs, such as replacement of light bulbs, and also pays operating expenses, such as fuel.

Bailments for hire are often used by business firms to obtain costly equipment needed for only a short time. An example would be leasing cranes used for high-rise construction projects. Even a business which needs the machinery for years may lease it because of a shortage of cash or credit required for purchase, or because resources can be used more profitably elsewhere. Thus, railroads often lease freight cars and airlines sometimes lease jet planes.

Sometimes bailment is also preferred in dynamic fields where technology is changing rapidly, as with computers. In such cases, the business manager does not want to equip the firm with soon-to-be-obsolete gear.

4. Bailments for Services

> **PROBLEM:** Systematics Unlimited prepared 1,000 copies of its annual catalog and price list on its own word-processing machines. Then it sent the materials to the Bodoni Bindery for binding into booklets. After the job had been done, a fire broke out in the Bodoni plant. All the booklets were ruined by fire, smoke, and water from the automatic sprinkler system. Must Systematics pay for the job? Under what circumstances would Bodoni be liable for the loss?

When a person delivers goods to be serviced, repaired, or made into a finished article, a bailment results. For example, the bailor may deliver goods to a tailor to have a suit made. Or a bailor may deliver clothes to a laundry to be washed or a watch to a jeweler to be cleaned and oiled. As in the problem, a bailor may send printed materials to a bindery to be made into books. If the goods are damaged or destroyed, but the bailee has exercised reasonable care in their protection, the loss falls on the bailor who owns them. Moreover, the bailor must pay for any work done by the bailee before the destructive accident. In the problem, Systematics must pay for the job. Only if the fire was caused by Bodoni's negligence or intentional wrongful act (for example, arson) would Bodoni be liable.

A bailment for services involves (1) a bailment contract and (2) a contract for services. As a bailee, the business firm has a duty to exercise ordinary care in protecting the goods. As a service company, its duty is to perform as agreed. Thus, the bailee would be liable not only for damage caused by negligence or unauthorized use of the goods but also for failure to do the job as promised.

Return briefly to the five-point problem in the beginning of this section on mutual-benefit bailments. Note that (a) involved a bailment for ocean transport of 50 cars from Korea; (b) a bailment for storage of the cars in Benicia; (c) another bailment for transport, this time by land, to the place of business of People Movers; (d) a bailment for modification services by Hank's, and; (e) individual bailments of hire for use by customers of People Movers.

5. Bailments for Sale

> **PROBLEM:** Werner owned a retail sport shop. Irresistible Lures, Inc., sent Werner a counter card which displayed a new type of fishing lure. Werner thought that neither his customers nor the fish would be interested. But he finally agreed to display the card when the sales agent said, "You pay nothing and return any lures not sold. Just deduct 50 percent of each sale for yourself and send the balance to us." Was Werner a bailee?

consignment: bailment for sale purposes

Sometimes goods are sent on consignment by a manufacturer or wholesaler to a retailer. A **consignment** is a bailment for sale purposes. Until the goods are sold, ownership remains in the manufacturer or wholesaler (the bailor). The retailer who displays and sells the goods, like Werner in the problem, is a bailee. The retailer is also, in effect, an agent authorized to sell goods for the bailor. The retailer's inventory is thus increased without using funds to buy the goods and without risking loss if the goods do not sell. Of course, the retailer gives up some display space, an overhead cost.

Bailment for mutual benefit is also created when a merchant-bailor sends goods on approval to a prospective buyer-bailee. Ownership does not transfer to the bailee unless and until the bailee decides to buy and accepts (as owner) the goods. If the bailee rejects the goods, they must be returned as agreed. This arrangement is common in national merchandising of books, records, and cassettes.

6. Bailments Arising from Other Relations

> **PROBLEM:** In the coat department of Johann's Finery Store, Mandel shopped for a new winter coat. The salesperson helped her remove her coat, and she watched him place it on the sofa next to where she stood. He then brought her several coats which she tried on. "Let me think about it," she finally said. Mandel then reached for her coat, but it had been stolen. Was the store liable as bailee?

Bailments arise in a variety of situations other than those just discussed. The following five are deemed to be most important because they occur so often.

a. If you go into a restaurant and leave any garment with a checker, a mutual-benefit bailment arises. The restaurant must use reasonable care to protect your property and normally would be liable if the garment is damaged or lost. However, there is no bailment if you hang your coat over a chair or on a hook, or even if an attendant hangs it as a courtesy. Legally you retain possession and responsibility for its care. Thus, in the problem, Johann's was not a bailee and was not liable.

b. When you buy an article and leave it with the seller to hold for later pickup or future delivery, a mutual-benefit bailment is created.

c. Were you to borrow money, the lender might ask for collateral as security to ensure repayment. If you pledge personal property, such as jewelry or a camera in a pawnshop, a mutual-benefit bailment arises.

d. When lost, misplaced, or stolen goods come into the possession of someone other than the owner, the person in possession has a bailee's responsibility to the owner. No agreement exists between the parties; there is a **constructive bailment**. If there is no voluntary action on the part of the bailee, the relation is called a **bailment by necessity**.

constructive bailment: bailment created by law when there is no agreement

bailment by necessity: type of involuntary, constructive bailment

> During a severe storm on a lake, a rowboat was torn loose from Compton's pier. The next morning, Sprague found the boat on his beach on the other side of the lake. As a bailee by necessity, Sprague is required to act reasonably in caring for the boat and in seeking the owner. This type of bailment by necessity also arises when mail is delivered to the wrong addressee, who may or may not have a name identical with that of the intended receiver.

A finder of a lost article is not legally required to take possession. If possession is taken, however, the finder becomes a constructive bailee for the sole benefit of the bailor-owner. The finder who says "finders keepers" and makes no effort to locate the owner may be guilty of larceny, although obviously this would be difficult to prove. Unless the goods are of trivial value (for example, a disposable felt-tip pen found on a sidewalk) the finder/possessor should report the find to the appropriate private or public authorities. Typically a valuable find is advertised, and, if the owner does not claim the goods, they are released to the finder to keep. If the owner does appear, the finder is entitled to reasonable expenses incurred in advertising and in caring for the goods. Some states require that a reasonable reward be paid. Sometimes goods are found in a building (such as a hotel) or in a vehicle open to the public (such as a train or plane) under circumstances which indicate that the item may have been intentionally placed but forgotten, or possibly dropped.

Such property is said to be mislaid and should be delivered to the management personnel, who are better equipped to locate the owner.

hotelkeeper: one who furnishes rooms for transients

e. A **hotelkeeper** is a bailee who operates a hotel, motel, resort lodge, or similar business open to the public. As such, the hotelkeeper must accept all transient travelers who arrive in proper condition (not intoxicated, for example) and who pay the fee specified for available accommodations. Formerly, the common law practically made hotelkeepers insurers of the baggage brought in by guests. Today, states generally permit hotels to limit their liability. Nevertheless, hotels usually require that valuables be placed in the hotel safe, and even then a limit of liability may be stated. In contrast, a **boardinghouse keeper** furnishes accommodations to more permanent residents. As such, the boardinghouse keeper has neither the extraordinary liability nor the special rights of the hotelkeeper as described below.

boardinghouse keeper: one who furnishes rooms to permanent residents

Although a hotelkeeper may demand that payment be made in advance, rooms are often rented on credit. If the fee is not paid or properly charged upon departure, the hotelkeeper may retain all goods rightfully in the guest's possession—except clothes actually being worn—until paid. This right is known as the **hotelkeeper's lien.** It may even be asserted against goods owned by third parties, such as sample merchandise belonging to the employer of a traveling salesperson. If the hotelkeeper is not paid within a prescribed time, the goods may be sold at a public sale.

hotelkeeper's lien: right of a hotelkeeper to hold goods until paid for accommodations

WHEN ARE EXTRAORDINARY BAILEES NOT LIABLE FOR LOSSES?

> **PROBLEM:** A large semitrailer was carrying a valuable load of candies from Hershey, Pennsylvania, to Chicago. En route it was suddenly caught by a flash flood which sent it crashing off the highway. The driver survived but the truck was wrecked and the cargo was scattered and destroyed. Was the trucking company, a common carrier, liable for the loss?

Within the limits imposed by statute or contract, hotelkeepers and common carriers as extraordinary bailees are generally absolutely liable for loss or damage to goods in their possession. However, neither the hotelkeeper nor the common carrier is liable if it can prove that the loss was caused by:

1. Act of God

An **act of God** is a violent act of nature that cannot reasonably be foreseen and avoided. Examples are earthquakes, tidal waves, tornadoes, flash floods, lightning, and unusual storms. In the problem, the accident was caused by natural forces beyond the control of the carrier. Therefore the carrier is not liable. Note that appropriate insurance by the consignor, consignee, or carrier could have covered the loss.

act of God: unforseeable, violent act of nature

2. Act of a Public Enemy

A **public enemy** may be a member of the armed forces of a foreign country with which our nation is at war or a foreign *saboteur* (agent) who tries to hinder war efforts. Acts committed by mobs, rioters, strikers, or robbers are not acts of a public enemy.

public enemy: soldier or saboteur from a country at war with the U.S.

3. Act of Public Authority

An act of public authority causes loss when goods are taken from the carrier or hotelkeeper under legal process. Examples would be the seizure of *contraband* (illegal goods) or of contaminated food by law officers.

4. Fault of the Consignor or Guest

The carrier or hotelkeeper is not liable for a loss that results from the bailor's carelessness, as through improper packing or loading. Breakage in transit is a continuing multimillion dollar problem, and it is the source of many disputes between carriers and shippers.

5. Inherent Nature of the Goods

Losses caused by the inherent nature of the goods include decay of fruit or other perishables and evaporation or spoilage of other products. Such losses include spontaneous combustion and injuries inflicted by animals upon one another. To avoid liability the carrier must prove that the loss was due to one of the excepted causes. This is true even though no one knows just what happened and even though the carrier was not negligent. If negligent, the carrier would of course be liable, as when it carelessly fails to maintain the proper temperature in a refrigerated freight car.

A freight train carrying hogs stopped in a desert ravine. Because there was little air circulation, the hogs became overheated. An employee of the owner, who was traveling with the shipment, asked the carrier's crew to move the train. The crew refused, and the hogs died. A court later found the carrier negligent and liable for the loss.

WHAT DOCUMENTS ARE USED BY WAREHOUSERS AND CARRIERS?

PROBLEM: Jacobson, owner of a walnut grove in California, stored 50,000 pounds of shelled walnuts in the Rainbow Valley Warehouse. In return, she received a negotiable warehouse receipt. A month later, she sold the walnuts to Weaver, a broker in Baltimore. How can she conveniently transfer title to the goods to Weaver? Weaver plans to sell the goods to an exporter, who will ship them to England in six months. Can Weaver transfer title without moving the walnuts or getting a new warehouse receipt?

negotiable bill of lading: easily transferable document; contract for land or marine transport, receipt, and evidence of title to goods

negotiable airbill: transferable shipping contract and receipt for goods for air transport

straight bill of lading: assignable shipping contract and receipt for goods for land or marine transport

straight airbill: shipping contract and receipt for goods for air transport

When a carrier accepts goods, it issues a bill of lading to the consignor for land or marine transport, or an airbill for air transport. These documents:

1. state the terms of the contract,
2. acknowledge receipt of the goods, and
3. serve as evidence of title in some cases because the documents may be proof of the ownership or control of the goods.

When negotiable, the documents call for delivery of the goods *to the order* of a person named therein, or to the bearer. A **negotiable bill of lading** or a **negotiable airbill** may be easily transferred to another party by the holder's indorsement and delivery. Or it may be transferred by delivery of the paper alone if it is made out to the bearer. Thus, it is evidence of title and protects the transferee against many defenses.

When the document is a **straight bill of lading** or a **straight airbill,** the goods are consigned to a specified, named person. Thus, the document is not negotiable and the contract rights must be transferred by assignment (see Chapter 14).

When warehousers and carriers act as bailees and accept goods for storage or transport, they issue similar documents to the bailors.

Carriers issue bills of lading; warehousers issue warehouse receipts. In both cases, the documents serve as a receipt, a contract to store or transport, and, if negotiable, as evidence of title to the goods. The documents may be either negotiable or nonnegotiable. A **nonnegotiable warehouse receipt** is transferred by assignment, and the receiver gets only whatever rights in the goods the transferor had authority to give. Thus, before the bailee receives notice of the transfer, the bailee could be required to give the goods to a creditor of the bailor or to a prior buyer of the goods. In contrast, a **negotiable warehouse receipt** may be easily transferred by delivery of the paper alone (if made out "to bearer") or by indorsement and delivery (if made out "to order" of a named person). When such transferee acquires the document (a) in good faith (honestly), (b) without notice of any prior claim to it or defense which would block the transfer, (c) for value, and (d) in the regular course of business or financing, the transferee gets clear title to the goods, free of most defenses or claims that others (such as creditors of the bailor) might have to the goods. Thus, holding the paper is like owning the goods. Of course, if the goods had been stolen before the bailment, the true owner could reclaim them.

nonnegotiable warehouse receipt: assignable storage contract and receipt for goods

negotiable warehouse receipt: easily transferable document; a receipt, a storage contract, and evidence of title to goods

In the problem, Jacobson could transfer title by indorsing the negotiable warehouse receipt to the order of Weaver and by giving Weaver the document. Weaver, in turn, could simply indorse and deliver the paper to the exporter. When ready to pick up the walnuts, the exporter could present the paper to the warehouse.

HOW IS A BAILMENT ENDED?

PROBLEM: Ruden leased a heavy-duty pile driver from Maxima Power Controls for six months with the right to renew upon 30-days notice. Three months later, Ruden was killed in an industrial accident. Was the bailment ended?

A bailment may be ended:

1. By Agreement

The bailment ends when the specified time has elapsed, when a specified purpose has been accomplished, or at any subsequent time when the parties mutually agree to end it.

2. By Act of Either Party

If no time of termination is stated, either party may end the bailment at will. Thus, the bailor might ask for return of the property and if refused, simply retake it peacefully or with legal help, if necessary. Or the bailee may no longer need the property and return it. Of course, if either party violates the agreement, the other may elect to end the bailment.

3. By Destruction of the Subject Matter

If the bailed property is destroyed or damaged so badly that it is not fit for the intended purpose, the bailment ends.

4. By Operation of Law

Death, insanity, or bankruptcy of one of the parties terminates the relation (1) when the bailee's duties cannot be performed by another or (2) if the bailment is one that may be ended at will. Normally, however, if there is a contractual bailment for a fixed period, death or incapacity of a party does not end the relation. The rights and duties of the deceased party are transferred by law to the personal representative (the executor or administrator of the estate). This rule would apply to Ruden's case in the problem.

PREVENTING LEGAL DIFFICULTIES

Practical Pointers for Bailees . . .

1. clearly specify the terms of the contract, preferably in writing, when you accept goods as a bailee for hire, storage, transport, services, security, or sale;
2. before you take possession of or use bailed goods, be sure you are covered by adequate liability and property insurance. You are always liable for your own torts, and you might be required to pay damages if you damage or destroy the bailed property or injure someone with it;
3. if you have performed services on bailed goods, do not return them until you are paid for your services or are satisfied that the bailor's credit is good;
4. when you find and take possession of something of value belonging to another person, you become a constructive bailee. Comply with local

statutes, or otherwise act reasonably, in caring for the property and seeking the true owner; and

5. after you check in at a motel or hotel, read rules (posted in your room) regarding liability for loss of property. Check valuables at the registration desk. Buy adequate insurance on your property before you travel.

Practical Pointers for Bailors . . .

1. because a bailee gets exclusive possession of the bailed goods and may misuse or damage them, try to give your property to responsible persons only;
2. although a bailee may be liable for willful or negligent conduct which damages your goods or injures third parties, it is still wise to carry appropriate property and liability insurance to cover possible losses;
3. spell out the terms of the bailment contract in writing whenever practicable. Always get a receipt for goods transferred to a bailee;
4. if the bailee is to repair or service the goods, be as precise as practicable about prices and work to be done;
5. if you rent a car or other equipment which could be dangerous if in bad condition, inspect it carefully and correct defects before delivering it to the bailee;
6. when you travel by common carrier, you are responsible for clothing and baggage which you retain in your possession. Guard it. Moveover, there are limits on the carrier's liability for baggage you check. For added protection, buy additional coverage from the carrier; and
7. when you ship goods by common carrier, pack, address, and label them properly. Use such terms as "FRAGILE," "PERISHABLE," and "THIS SIDE UP," as appropriate. Again, check the limits of the carrier's liability. For greater protection, buy additional coverage.

In Bailments For Your Sole Benefit . . .

If you alone benefit from a bailment, you must exercise a high degree of care. If you are the bailee, use the goods only as agreed and protect them carefully from possible loss or harm. If you are the bailor, carefully examine the goods for defects that could cause harm and tell the bailee of any found. Failure to perform these duties can make you liable for resulting losses even though you received no consideration.

Strengthening Your Legal Vocabulary

act of God
bailee
bailee's lien
bailment
bailment by necessity
bailor
boardinghouse keeper
carrier

carrier's lien
common carrier
consignee
consignment
consignor
constructive bailment
contract carrier
custody
demurrage
extraordinary bailment
gratuitous bailment
hotelkeeper
hotelkeeper's lien
mutual-benefit bailment
negotiable airbill
negotiable bill of lading
negotiable warehouse receipt
nonnegotiable warehouse receipt
private carrier
public enemy
straight airbill
straight bill of lading
warehouser

1. Bailment which benefits both the bailor and the bailee.
2. Easily transferable document which is a receipt, a contract for land or marine transport, and evidence of title to goods.
3. Violent act of nature which cannot reasonably be foreseen and avoided.
4. Soldier or saboteur from a country at war with the U.S.
5. Right of a bailee to hold goods until paid.
6. One who undertakes, for hire, to transport goods or passengers for anyone who applies.
7. Bailment created by law where there is no agreement.
8. Present care and control of another's personal property, under the owner's direction.
9. Assignable storage contract and receipt for goods.
10. Bailment in which one party receives no benefit.

Reviewing Important Points

1. In a bailment, the bailee has possession of personal property belonging to the bailor. The bailee must return the identical property in the same or altered form, as agreed, to the bailor or to someone designated by the bailor.
2. Every bailment has four characteristics: (a) the subject is tangible personal property; (b) anyone in possession of the goods may bail them; (c) the goods must be received and accepted by the bailee; and (d) the identical goods must be returned to the bailor or designee.
3. Bailments created for the benefit of both parties are mutual-benefit bailments based on contract with an exchange of consideration. Bailments created for the benefit of only one party are gratuitous bailments.
4. The bailee is always required to use reasonable care in protecting and using the bailor's property. More precisely, in a mutual-benefit bailment, the bailee must exercise ordinary care. In a gratuitous bailment for the sole benefit of the bailee, the bailee must exercise great care. In a gratuitous bailment for the sole benefit of the bailor, the bailee need exercise only slight care.

5. In a bailment for hire, the bailor is liable for damages caused by known or reasonably discoverable defects in the property unless the bailee has specifically been informed of such defects.
6. The four most common types of mutual-benefit bailments are those for transport, for storage, for hire, and for services.
7. A bailment for services involves two contractual relations: a bailment between the bailor and the bailee, and a service contract between the serviceperson or repairer and the customer. The bailee has a lien on the goods for service or repair charges.
8. Common carriers enjoy monopolistic advantages. However, they must provide transportation for all who properly apply, and their rates and service are subject to government regulation. Federal controls are currently being phased out to encourage competition.
9. Under common law, hotelkeepers and common carriers, as extraordinary bailees, have insurer-like liability for property. However, statutes and contracts generally limit this liability. Moreover they are not liable for losses caused by (a) act of God; (b) act of public enemy; (c) act of public authority; (d) fault of consignor or guest; or (e) inherent nature of goods.
10. Hotelkeepers and common carriers may demand payment in advance. If a bill is unpaid, a hotelkeeper may retain all goods rightfully in the guest's possession—except clothes being worn—as security for the payment. The common carrier has a similar lien against goods shipped.
11. A negotiable bill of lading or airbill acknowledges receipt of goods, states the terms of the shipping contract, and is evidence of title. It is easily transferable by indorsement and delivery, or by delivery alone. In this respect it is similar to the negotiable warehouse receipt, and both are similar to commercial paper.
12. A warehouser engages in the business of storing goods for profit. The warehouser issues warehouse receipts, must exercise reasonable care only, and has a lien on the goods for storage charges.
13. A constructive bailment is created by law when a finder takes possession of lost goods and when one person comes into the possession of the goods of another by accident, mistake, or theft.
14. A bailment may be terminated (a) by agreement, (b) by act of either party, (c) by destruction of the subject matter, or (d) by operation of law.

Applying Law to Everyday Life

1. Boyd borrowed a lawn edger from her neighbor Eubanks. The edger's circular blade was defective, but Eubanks did not know this. While Boyd was using the edger, the blade snapped. A piece of metal lodged in Boyd's eye, blinding it. Was Eubanks liable for the injury?

2. Widdington inherited an old 90-foot former navy patrol boat. She delivered it to Ol' Jon Silver's Shipyard, which was located near the oceanfront. Widdington contracted with Jon Silver for a conversion of the patrol boat into a

houseboat for $95,000. After the work had been completed but before Widdington came to get her boat, a tidal wave destroyed the shop and all the boats in the immediate vicinity. Is Jon Silver liable for the loss of Widdington's boat? Or must Widdington pay the $95,000?

3. Babbitt rented a paint-spraying outfit from Baronofsky. The equipment was in good working condition, and Babbitt knew how to use it properly. However, when Babbitt was shifting position between two buildings, she carelessly sprayed the neighbor's building and the top of the neighbor's car parked below. The neighbor sued Baronofsky. Is Baronofsky liable?

4. Rolland rented her harvesting machine to Hamsun for the first two weeks of July. After eight days, Rolland needed the machine for her own harvest and insisted on taking it back. Is she enabled by law to do so either by peaceful self-help or by court order?

5. Bortez, a traveling salesman, had a breakfast appointment with Yukich, a retailer/prospective buyer. They were to meet in the restaurant just off the lobby of the Grand Prix Hotel. Bortez left his attaché case, which contained almost $30,000 worth of sample watches, with the clerk in the hotel checkroom. The clerk gave him a receipt which had these words on one side in fine print: "Not liable for loss or damage from any cause beyond a maximum of $100." Bortez, in a hurry, stuffed the stub in his pocket without reading it. The clerk left his post briefly to go to the restroom. When he returned, the case was gone. Is the Grand Prix liable? If so, for how much?

6. Burgoyne customized and sold new vans and serviced old ones. Jake and Jayne Slinker were trusted employees who had been carefully hired and trained and had worked for Burgoyne for ten years. Jake did metalworking and woodworking; Jayne did upholstering. One holiday weekend, the Slinkers and an accomplice stole three vans and disappeared. The first van belonged to Adams, who had brought it in to have the engine tuned. The second van belonged to Yates, a friend who had asked Burgoyne if he could leave the van on the lot with a "FOR SALE" sign. Burgoyne had agreed and did not charge Yates. The third van was a very valuable vehicle, built by Burgoyne, and sold to Mox. Mox had loaned the van to Burgoyne, free, for display in the latter's exhibit at a Civic Auditorium show scheduled for the following week. What is Burgoyne's liability, if any, to Adams? to Yates? to Mox?

7. Kamura Farms loaded a refrigerated trailer owned by Moonlight Express (a common carrier trucking company) with a cargo consisting of properly packed cartons of fresh peaches. The peaches were to be carried from Yuba City, California, to Toronto, Canada. Who must bear responsibility for the loss of the cargo under the following circumstances? (a) Before the truck leaves California, a state inspector halts the shipment and orders destruction of the load. The fruit had been sprayed with chemical insecticides harmful to humans. (b) The truck driver continues at the wheel beyond the limit ordered by Moonlight. He dozes and runs off the highway. The cargo is

destroyed. (c) The peaches were tree-ripened when picked, and many are found to be rotten upon arrival in Toronto. (d) Two escaped convicts hijack the truck, and it is never seen again.

Solving Case Problems

1. Loden shipped a quantity of perishable cucumbers from Yuma, Arizona, to Los Angeles via the Southern Pacific Company railroad. However, the carrier failed to deliver the goods within the ordinary and usual time. Therefore, on January 25, a railroad inspector was sent out to check the track structures. The inspector discovered that heavy rainfall had damaged two bridges near Thermal, California. Repairs were started on January 26, and the tracks were joined on January 28. The making of these repairs further delayed the shipment of Loden's cucumbers. When the cucumbers finally arrived in Los Angeles on January 29, they were spoiled. Loden sued the railroad for $10,000 in damages. Decide. *(Southern Pacific Company v. Loden,* 19 Ariz. App. 460, 508 P.2d 347)

2. Armored Car Service, Inc., had its employees pick up at the Miami Springs Junior High School a locked money bag containing $1,511.25. The money was supposed to be deposited in the proper cafeteria fund account at a certain bank. However, the bag was mistakenly delivered to the First National Bank of Miami. First National provided a receipt for the bag but made no record of the bag's handling or disposition. Presumably, the bag was stolen. Armored Car Service indemnified the high school and now seeks to recover its loss from First National. (a) What kind of bailment was created by the mistake? (b) Is the First National Bank of Miami liable as bailee? *(Armored Car Service, Inc. v. First National Bank of Miami,* 114 So. 2d 431, Fla.)

3. Jackson was a chambermaid in Steinberg's hotel. She was instructed to remove anything that did not belong in the rooms and to take it to the desk clerk if it was of any value. While cleaning a room, Jackson found eight $100 bills concealed under the paper lining of a dresser drawer. She gave them to the desk clerk, but efforts to find the true owner proved unsuccessful. Who is entitled to the money? *(Jackson v. Steinberg,* 186 Ore. 129, 200 P.2d 376, 205 P.2d 562)

4. Plaintiff Wall drove his car into a self-parking lot at O'Hare Airport, Chicago. He entered through an automatic gate and received a ticket bearing the date and time of arrival. He parked, locked the car, and left with the keys. Normally, when ready to depart, he would walk to his car, and, using his keys, would enter the car and drive it to the exit. There, an attendant would take the ticket and compute and collect the parking fee. This time his car had been stolen. He sued the defendant, Airport Parking Company of Chicago, for damages. Is the defendant liable? *(Wall v. Airport Parking Company of Chicago,* 244 N.E.2d 190, 41 Ill. 2d 506)

SPECIAL SECTION: How to Litigate in Small Claims Court

If you cannot achieve a satisfactory out-of-court resolution to a dispute, you may decide to take the case to small claims court. If so, a number of important steps must be taken.

You Must Decide Whom to Sue. Make sure you are correctly naming as defendant(s) the person(s) responsible for your injury.

Many judgments turn out to be uncollectible due to the defendant's lack of resources. Consequently, it is important to bring suit against someone who can pay should you win. However, even individuals who appear to be judgment-proof (without any resources from which to pay a judgment) are not likely to remain so forever. Most jurisdictions allow 10 to 20 years for a judgment to be collected after it is entered.

You Must Decide the Amount for Which to Sue. The damages you claim must be a reasonable approximation of how much you lost due to the defendant's act. The amount cannot exceed the jurisdictional limit of the small claims court.

You Must Properly Serve the Defendant(s) with Process. To give the court jurisdiction, each defendant must receive a summons and a copy of the complaint in person or by certified mail.

You Must Prepare Your Evidence. Although standards of evidence are somewhat relaxed in small claims courts, the documents, exhibits, and testimony you want to present to the court must be logical, concise, relevant, and persuasive.

You Must Appear at the Appropriate Time and Place Ready to Make Your Case. You may be required to appear more than once, especially if the other party has an attorney who asks for a continuance. This request is not uncommon and is often granted once. When you present your case, do so with firmness and control. Even if an attorney is representing your opponent, do not be intimidated. An attorney does not necessarily have an advantage in presenting a case in small claims court.

If You Win, Collect the Judgment. Most defendants will not voluntarily pay the damages awarded. Therefore a successful plaintiff will often have to seek the help of the sheriff to attach (seize) property of the defendant. This property can then be sold and the proceeds used to satisfy the judgment. If the defendant is a wage earner, it may be possible to garnish the wages to satisfy the judgment.

If You Lose. Many jurisdictions allow the defendant, but not the plaintiff, to appeal. If the defendant appeals, seek the counsel of an attorney.

Through all of these steps it is important to remember that the personnel of the clerk of court's office can be a good source of help.

35

Real Property

1. Jerry's mother and father entered into a contract for the purchase of a house. The house contained many desirable improvements such as drapes, a built-in dishwasher, paintings, wall-to-wall carpeting, throw rugs, and a built-in workbench in the garage. The contract signed by Jerry's parents stated only that they had purchased the "real property." Which of the improvements can the sellers take with them and which will stay with the house and become the property of Jerry's family?

2. Your aunt and uncle are about to buy a new house. A friend advises them that it is in their best interest to enter into a mortgage arrangement with the bank, rather than to give a deed of trust. Is the friend correct?

3. By quitclaim deed, a wealthy uncle conveys to you a 160-acre farm. Someone tells you the deed is worthless because your uncle did not warrant good title and you gave no valuable consideration in exchange. Is the deed worthless?

WHAT IS REAL PROPERTY?

> **PROBLEM:** The Bryants owned a condominium and were required to pay property tax on both the real and personal property. The tax rate on the real property was 1 percent of its value. The rate for personal property was 4 percent. The Bryants owned a stereo system which was wired into each room, with speakers concealed in the walls. The receiver, tuner, amplifier, turntable, and other items were permanently attached and wired into a closet which had been remodeled to accommodate the equipment. Should the stereo be taxed at 1 percent or 4 percent of its value?

All property can be classified as either real or personal. Real property includes (1) land, (2) buildings, (3) things permanently attached to land or buildings (called fixtures), and (4) certain rights that a person might have in the real property of others. Personal property, in contrast, is any property that is not real property. In the problem, the Bryants' stereo would be taxed at 1 percent because it was permanently attached to the building and therefore was real property.

Although the definition of real property may seem somewhat simple, the application of that definition is not.

1. Land

> **PROBLEM:** A limb of an apple tree growing on Roeton's land extended over the boundary onto Oster's lot. One day Roeton discovered that Oster had cut the limb off at the point where it crossed the boundary. Had Oster acted illegally?

land: surface of, matter beneath, and airspace above the earth, along with things permanently attached or embedded

Land, in a legal sense, includes not only the surface of the earth, but also the airspace above and whatever is beneath the surface to the very center of our planet. Land also embraces everything permanently attached to the soil—such as perennial grass and trees—and things embedded in the soil—such as minerals, gases, and bodies of water on or below the surface. Annual crops, however, are generally held to be personal property because they are not permanently attached.

An owner of land has a right to the peaceful enjoyment and control of it. Airplanes may fly over the property. But they may not fly so low or so often as to interfere unreasonably with the owner's use and enjoyment of the land. Residents in the flight pattern alongside airports have won damage suits because of noise and vibration caused by the taking off and landing of jet aircraft. Likewise, when limbs or roots of a neighbor's tree overhang or extend into one's adjoining property, one has the legal right to cut them off at the property line. This is seldom done because both owners generally benefit from the vegetation. However, in the problem, Oster did act legally.

2. Buildings

PROBLEM: Vader owns a mobile home. She claims that she can change the home into real property by removing its tires, placing it on a concrete foundation, and installing permanent plumbing. Is she correct?

Buildings are defined by law as structures that are permanently attached to the land. Consequently, a mobile home is generally personal property. However, if a mobile home is set up as described in the problem, it will no longer be movable and therefore will be classified legally as real property—a building.

buildings: structures permanently attached to the land

3. Fixtures

Fixtures are those things which had been personal property but are treated by the law as real property because they are built into or are closely associated with the *realty*. The law uses three tests to determine whether an item so associated with real property is personal or real. These are the tests of annexation, adaptation, and intent.

fixtures: personal property so closely associated with realty that it becomes part of the real estate

Annexation (attachment) is the principal test. If personal property is permanently attached to land or a building and cannot be removed without material damage, then the attachment becomes real property. For example, a built-in dishwasher would be real property under this test, while a free-standing refrigerator would be personal property because it is not permanently attached.

Adaptation refers to things which have been made appropriate or suitable for the purpose for which the real estate is used. Adaptation indicates that the personal property has become part of the realty. For example, cast concrete troughs installed on a dairy farm for feeding and watering the animals would become part of the realty through adaptation.

The third test, *intent*, considers indications of whether the person who affixed the personal property to the real property intended it to become a permanent attachment. For example, a landlord and a tenant might agree to have the tenant install a washing machine in an apartment and retain the right to remove it at the end of the rental period. This washer would be personal property under the test of intent. However, removal would involve only disconnecting hoses. If the real property would be damaged by the removal, the tenant usually must restore the realty to its former condition.

If a homeowner entered into a contract to sell the real property, then the fixtures would go to the buyer. The seller and buyer can agree, however, that certain fixtures are to be removed and kept by the seller of the home.

Tenants are obligated to leave all the real property in the leased premises to the landlord at the end of the lease. This means that if something such as a built-in bookcase is installed by the tenant, it becomes the property of the landlord and may not be removed at the end of the lease. Of course, if the parties agree to treat items as personal property the items would be removable as *personalty* under the test of intent.

trade fixtures: business appliances attached to rented real property used in a business

When they lease space, business tenants frequently install costly equipment and machinery, such as refrigerated display cases. Since most business landlords and business tenants understand that this will occur, under the test of intent, statutes generally treat such items as **trade fixtures** and prescribe that they are personal property. Thus, fixtures installed by a residential tenant generally become the property of the landlord, while trade fixtures installed by a business tenant remain the personal property of the tenant.

4. Rights in the Real Property of Others

PROBLEM: Rudy owned 2,000 acres in Texas. After oil was discovered on Rudy's land, an oil company bought the right to pump the oil from the ground. The company also bought the right to drive on the land with tank trucks in order to transport the oil. What are the legal names of the rights the oil company now holds in Rudy's real property?

easement: right to use land owned and possessed by another party

Rights in the real property of others include easements and profits. An **easement** is the right to a specific use of another's real property even though the other party retains possession of the property. Typically, someone might purchase an easement allowing that person to drive onto another's land. Similarly, a utility company might acquire an easement to hang its power lines over the land of another. A **profit**, on the other hand, is the right to *extract* (remove) something (such as trees, oil, or minerals) from someone else's land. In the problem, the oil company held both an easement and a profit in Rudy's land.

profit: right to extract something from another's land

HOW IS REAL PROPERTY ACQUIRED?

PROBLEM: Eaton, a land developer, wanted to buy a full square block along Michigan Boulevard in downtown Chicago as the site for a new hotel-office-store complex. The property was owned by 12 different individuals and corporations, some of whom refused to sell. Eaton, therefore, asked the city government to use its power of eminent domain to acquire the entire block and then to transfer the block to her. Eaton claimed this was justified because the new facility was badly needed by the public. Also, she said, construction would provide many jobs, and the neighborhood would be improved. Eaton said she would pay fair market value for the property. Could the city comply with Eaton's request?

Ownership of real property is not transferred in the same manner or with the same ease and convenience as is ownership of personal property. The principal ways of acquiring real property today are by deed as evidence of sale or gift, and by wills or inheritance. Other ways are by adverse possession, by dedication or eminent domain, by public grant, and by accretion (gradual accumulation of land by natural causes, such as the deposit of silt by a river).

deed: writing which conveys title and other rights of ownership to real property

grantor: one who conveys real property rights through a deed

1. By Deed as Evidence of a Sale or Gift

If a person buys real property or receives it as a gift, the person should receive a deed as evidence of the transfer. The **deed** is a written document by which an individual conveys title and other rights to real property. The individual who conveys the ownership rights is known as the **grantor**. The individual who receives the rights is known as the **grantee**.

grantee: person to whom real property is conveyed through a deed

The two major types of deeds are the quitclaim deed and the warranty deed. The **quitclaim deed** transfers to the grantee any interest the grantor may have in the real property. If the grantor

quitclaim deed: deed which conveys the grantor's interest without warranties

owned no interest in the property, then the grantee receives nothing. Further, the grantee has no legal claim against the grantor based on the quitclaim deed. The **warranty deed**, however, protects the grantee by providing various legally enforceable warranties about the transaction. Examples of such warranties include:

warranty deed: deed which conveys the grantor's interest with warranties

a. that the grantor is either the owner of the real property or a person who has been given the authority by the owner to transfer the property;
b. that there are no previously unmentioned claims or encumbrances (liens, mortgages, overdue taxes, etc.) against the property; or
c. that the grantee shall have quiet enjoyment of the property (that is, no one with superior title will disturb the grantee's possession).

2. By Will and Inheritance

Even if the title to real property is not received by deed, it may be willed to or inherited by someone in the distribution of properties from the estate of a deceased person.

3. By Adverse Possession

In some situations, a person who publicly occupies another owner's land for a legally specified number of years may be treated by the law as the new owner of the realty. Suppose you bought a 600-acre farm and the legal description of the boundary included ten adjoining acres that really belonged to an absentee owner. If you fenced your farm and included the ten acres, or otherwise occupied the ten acres for the statutory period, you could become the owner of the ten acres. This is because of the doctrine of **adverse possession**. Adverse possession occurs when you "adversely" actually and exclusively possess in an "open and notorious" way the land of another private person "continuously" for a statutory period (5 to 21 years) under claim of right.

adverse possession: means of getting title to another's land by occupation without the owner's permission

a. *Adverse* means that the occupation is without the consent of the owner and is hostile or contrary to the owner's wishes. If an owner said you could occupy the land, either for rent or without charge, you could not become an adverse possessor.
b. *Open and notorious* means that the occupation must be visible to the public, including the owner who may occasionally inspect the land. Erecting fences, planting crops, building

houses or barns, and grazing cattle all constitute open and notorious occupation.

c. *Continuously* means that the occupation is uninterrupted. This element, and the element of "open and notorious," are intended to allow the owner who inspects the land at reasonable intervals an opportunity to become aware of the presence of potential adverse possessors and to evict them.

Many states require that adverse possessors pay the property taxes on the occupied land before they can become owners under the doctrine of adverse possession. To prevent adverse possession, owners of realty, especially raw land, should check it periodically to see if someone is occupying it without their consent.

One can acquire an easement through similar uninterrupted adverse use of another's land without the owner's consent for the statutory period. This may happen, for example, when a landowner does nothing to prevent neighbors from going across the land to reach a main road over an extended period of time. An easement is thus acquired by **prescription**.

prescription: means of getting an easement to another's land by use without the owner's permission

4. By Dedication or Eminent Domain

Dedication typically involves the giving of real property to the government for the government's use as a park or roadway. As with any other gift, the dedication is effective only if the government accepts the property. If the government fails to use the property for the purpose intended by the person making the dedication, the title could be returned to the donor or to the donor's heirs.

dedication: transfer of land to the government by gift

In contrast with dedication (the giving of land to the government), **eminent domain** is the power of the government to take private property for public use in exchange for the fair market price. If the owner is unwilling to sell at a price which the government thinks is fair, the government files what is called a **condemnation proceeding** in court. The owner is entitled to fair compensation and if not satisfied with the price offered, may demand a trial by jury to set a just price.

eminent domain: governmental power to take private property for public use in exchange for the fair market price

Property taken under eminent domain must be for a public use, such as construction of highways, airports, parks, or schools. Privately-owned railroads and utilities may also exercise this power for such essentials as land for tracks and switching yards and for telephone and electric lines. Eminent domain may not be used for other private purposes even though the public may benefit and a fair price is offered. Thus, in the problem, the city could not comply

condemnation proceeding: forced sale through court action under the power of eminent domain

with Eaton's request. However, redevelopment of blighted urban neighborhoods is often done by the government under the power of eminent domain. Some or all of the land is then returned to private ownership by sale after the old buildings are demolished.

HOW DOES A PERSON BUY REAL PROPERTY?

PROBLEM: The Webbs want to buy a house. They have saved $34,000 of the full purchase price of $100,000. They have applied for a loan to make up the difference. What factors will the lending institution consider in deciding whether or not to grant the loan?

Today, real property is most frequently acquired by purchase. The steps that typically make up such a transaction are:

conveyance: transfer of title to real property

1. contracting for the **conveyance** (transfer of title by deed to real property);
2. having a survey of the property made;
3. taking steps to ensure the buyer receives good title to the property;
4. obtaining financing if necessary;
5. closing (completing) the transaction; and
6. recording the deed.

1. Contracting for the Conveyance

The terms of the *contract to convey* (sometimes called a *land contract*) may result from face-to-face negotiations between the buyer and the seller. Or the negotiations may be conducted through, and with the help of, the real estate agents of both parties. Regardless, the contract must be in writing to satisfy the requirements of the statute of frauds (see Chapter 13). Each party to the contract should receive a copy of it signed by the other party or, preferably, signed by both.

2. Surveying the Property

To determine its exact boundaries, the property is often surveyed. The result of the survey can be compared with the legal description of the property, which is usually on file in the office of the county registrar of deeds.

3. Protecting the Title

The buyer of real property wants assurance of getting the title as promised. Therefore, to protect against possible valid claims of others to the same land or parts of it, the buyer may obtain an abstract of title or a policy of title insurance.

An **abstract of title** is a condensed history of a particular parcel of land. It is *abstracted* (taken from) legal records of the "chain of title" over the years. It includes a summary of all conveyances, recorded liens or encumbrances, and other matters that may affect the quality or extent of the title to the land. The buyer may usually rely on the opinion of the attorney who prepares a complete abstract that the title is valid. If the owner has not received the title described in the lawyer's opinion, the lawyer may be liable.

abstract of title: history of transfers of title to a parcel of land

Title insurance, which is now quite common, is an improvement over the abstract of title. It is appropriate to insure titles due to the following reasons:

a. the abstract does not always show every fact that may affect the title;
b. the attorney might give a faulty opinion yet not be liable unless negligence can be proved (which may be difficult to do);
c. the attorney, even if found to be negligent and liable, may be financially unable to pay resulting damages; and
d. the transferor also might be financially unable to make good on warranties or promises made in the deed.

When the title is insured, the pertinent records are examined by attorneys and other employees of the insurance company. In exchange for a premium, the company, if satisfied by the results of the examination, insures that the title is good. This means that the company will pay the buyer for damages suffered if title to the property is not clear.

4. Securing Financing

As in the problem, most individuals do not have the full purchase price of the real property they wish to buy. Banks, savings and loan associations, and similar institutions, however, will normally loan up to 80 or 90 percent of the value of the property to the buyer or buyers. The remaining money must come from the purchaser's savings. In deciding whether or not to make the loan, these institutions will consider many factors, including:

a. the true market value of the property (it may be significantly different from the asking price);
b. the income and outstanding debts of the intended buyer or buyers; and
c. the buyer's expected ability to repay the loan over a 15- to 30-year period. The lending institution in the problem would consider all these factors and more.

If the loan is made and the real property is purchased, the lender will protect itself by requiring that a mortgage or a deed of trust be given in return. Whether the lender requires a mortgage or a deed of trust will depend upon the laws and the business practices of the state in which the transaction takes place. Both arrangements permit the forced sale of the real property to pay off the loan if the debtor fails to make payments. However, the procedure required to force such a sale under the mortgage arrangement differs greatly from that required under a deed of trust.

mortgage: written document allowing the right of foreclosure

mortgagor: debtor who gives a mortgage as security for a loan

mortgagee: lender to whom a mortgage is given as security for a loan

right of foreclosure: right to have property that is subject to a mortgage sold to satisfy the debt

deed of trust: document that is equivalent to a mortgage but that involves a more expedient remedy for default

The **mortgage** is a written document made out by the **mortgagor** (the debtor) in favor of the **mortgagee** (the lender). It allows the mortgagee the **right of foreclosure**. Thus, if the debtor defaults, the mortgagee has the right to ask the court to sell the property to pay off the loan. The foreclosure procedure also allows the debtor to redeem the property by paying the amount due within a certain time after default. In some states, the debtor can redeem the property for up to a year after it has been sold.

In contrast to a mortgage, a **deed of trust** allows a much quicker sale upon default. This is accomplished by a trustee who has the power to cause the sale of the property at a public auction if the debt is not paid as promised. Although the sale must be conducted in a legally prescribed manner, a court generally is not involved. Typically, the sale is swiftly carried out, and the debtor has no right to redeem the property after the sale.

Of course, either the mortgage or the deed of trust will be canceled upon the timely and proper payment of the debt.

5. Closing the Transaction

The *closing* (completing) of the transaction, as required by the contract to convey, most basically involves the exchange of the purchase price in return for a properly executed deed. When there is title insurance, a settlement clerk of the insurance company may work out the details. When there is no title insurance or escrow agent, the grantor and the grantee will adjust the details between themselves.

In some states, the seller may give the deed, the abstract or the title insurance policy, and any other papers to a disinterested third party for delivery to the buyer when the buyer performs as promised. The buyer normally gives the third party the necessary money payment together with a mortgage for the balance due. Papers so delivered to an attorney, bank, title company, or other neutral third party are said to be delivered in **escrow**.

escrow: money or papers delivered to a third party to hold until certain conditions are fulfilled

The third party escrow agent or the settlement clerk normally *prorates* (allocates fairly) the property taxes and fire insurance, if assigned, on the property as of the date of transfer of title. The seller is responsible prior to such date. The buyer is responsible after the date. The escrow agent also prorates rents or other incomes if any are being earned on the property. In accordance with instructions from the parties, a pest control report may be required to assure the buyer that the building is not infested with termites and that any necessary corrective work has been completed. The escrow agent sees to it that all necessary documents are available and are signed if required. If everything appears to be in proper order, the escrow agent delivers the deed to the buyer, the money to the seller, and the mortgage to the bank or other lending institution which financed the sale. When appropriate, money received from the parties is used to pay all fees, including the real estate salesperson's or broker's commission, attorneys' fees, and recording fees.

6. Recording the Deed

Immediately following the sale, the deed should be recorded in the county land records. This is done to protect the grantee against the possibility of the grantor fraudulently reselling the same land to another purchaser. If the deed were not recorded by the grantee, it would not be valid against innocent third parties who may later pay value, in good faith without notice, to the dishonest grantor for the same property.

An unrecorded deed would be good against future claimants who paid no value. For example, it would be good against heirs under the will of a grantor of property who, while still alive, had sold the same property to someone who had failed to record the deed.

Abbott sold 160 acres of undeveloped land to Barney. Before Barney could record the deed, Abbott had a heart attack and died. When Abbott's heirs discovered that the land was in Abbott's name on the public records, they claimed ownership. Nevertheless, the land belongs to Barney.

PREVENTING LEGAL DIFFICULTIES

When Dealing with Real Property . . .

1. if personal property is to be attached to realty, and there is a possibility for future disagreement as to whether it is a fixture, come to a clear understanding before making the contract. Put the entire real property agreement in writing, whether the contract involved is a sale, lease, or mortgage;
2. when purchasing real property, protect your interest by:
   a. having the property properly surveyed if it is an irregularly shaped parcel or has borders which are uncertain,
   b. requiring a deed containing all possible warranties, and
   c. securing title insurance if available;
3. be sure that any deed to land you have purchased is promptly recorded;
4. realize that the services of an escrow agent, where available, are usually worth the modest cost involved;
5. if you inspect your idle real property at reasonable intervals, you can prevent misuse by others. You can also prevent loss of title through adverse possession;
6. if you are asked to convey property and want to be free of possible future obligations, use a quitclaim deed;
7. if you have a choice as a borrower, use a mortgage instead of a deed of trust. A deed of trust gives the holder the power to sell your property upon default, with no right of redemption. If you have a choice as a seller or lender, use a deed of trust; and
8. if the government seeks to take your land by condemnation under its right of eminent domain, consult a lawyer. You have a constitutional right to a trial by jury to determine the fair price that must be paid.

Strengthening Your Legal Vocabulary

abstract of title
adverse possession
buildings
condemnation proceeding
conveyance
dedication

deed
deed of trust
easement
eminent domain
escrow
fixtures
grantee
grantor
land
mortgage
mortgagee
mortgagor
prescription
profit
quitclaim deed
right of foreclosure
trade fixtures
warranty deed

1. Surface of the earth, the airspace above, the matter beneath, and whatever is attached to or embedded in the soil.
2. Personal property attached to the land in such a way that it is regarded as real property.
3. Method of acquiring title by occupying land belonging to another, without the other's consent, for a certain uninterrupted period of time under prescribed conditions.
4. Written instrument executed and delivered by the transferor conveying title to real property.
5. Transfer of title to real property.
6. Condensed history of transfers of title to a parcel of land.
7. Debtor who gives a mortgage as security.
8. Property right allowing one person to extract things, such as minerals and oil, from the land of another.
9. Property right one has in the land of another, such as a right to cross the other's land.
10. Power of the government to take private property for public use upon payment of the fair market price.

Reviewing Important Points

1. Real property includes land, buildings, fixtures, and certain rights in the land of others, such as easements and profits.
2. The steps in buying or selling real property are commonly (a) contracting for the conveyance, (b) surveying, (c) protecting the title, (d) obtaining the financing, (e) closing, and (f) recording the deed.
3. Real property usually is acquired by sale or gift or by will or inheritance. Other less common ways include adverse possession, dedication, and eminent domain.
4. Deeds and other instruments affecting the title to land should be recorded promptly. Otherwise they may not be valid against innocent third parties who later deal with the original dishonest grantor and buy the same land or lend money with the land as security.

5. Two commonly used deeds of conveyance are the quitclaim deed and the warranty deed.
6. If a financing arrangement is necessary to purchase real property, a mortgage is more advantageous to the purchaser than is a deed of trust.

Applying Law to Everyday Life

1. Strolnikov leased an apartment for a period of one year. During this year she hung pictures on the walls, replaced the bathroom sink's chrome faucets with brass ones, installed an under-the-counter trash compactor, and put an Oriental rug in the center of the living room floor. At the end of her lease, what must she leave and what can she take?

2. Brand sold property to Alioto and conveyed it with a quitclaim deed. There was a mortgage on the property that neither Brand nor Alioto knew about at the time of the conveyance. Who will lose money because of this mortgage, Brand or Alioto?

3. Atwater sold a farm to Kent. Atwater conveyed with warranty deed. Later the parties discovered that Atwater was not the owner of about three acres of the land described in the deed. Is Atwater liable to Kent, and if so for what?

4. When Follet purchased her home, she had the property surveyed and the survey matched the legal description contained in her deed. Nearly 20 years later, a neighbor, Swinsen, had his property surveyed and discovered that his deed's description included a parcel extending 10 feet past the common fence into Follet's property. Follet had been paying property taxes on the property for the entire 20 years. Who owns this property?

5. Bentley had been in business at a particular location in Cleveland, Ohio, for many years. When the government Redevelopment Agency sought to buy her land for redevelopment purposes, Bentley refused to sell. Can she be compelled to sell?

6. Ferrera entered into a contract of conveyance which required him to obtain financing within 60 days after signing the contract. In checking with lenders in the area he discovered a wide variety of lending policies. The two best opportunities offered the exact same financial terms. However, one lender wanted a mortgage while the other wanted a deed of trust. Should Ferrera agree to a mortgage or a deed of trust?

7. Wood sold a lot to Roget, who thought her realtor had recorded the deed. In fact, the deed was not recorded. After Wood's death, his executor checked the public records and found that the deed was still in Wood's name in the register. Therefore the executor now claims the property for the estate and the heirs. Can Roget keep the lot?

Solving Case Problems

1. The Pentecostal Tabernacle Church had just built a new church building when dissension broke out and the members divided into two factions. As a consequence, payments on the building loan were not made, and foreclosure resulted. Williams bought the church building at the foreclosure sale. Trustees of the church then brought suit to recover the pews from the building. Williams defended by claiming that the pews were fixtures and were therefore to remain in the building. Evidence disclosed that removal of the pews left holes and broken bolts in the tiled floor. However, the pastor and a trustee of the church testified that when the pews were installed it was intended that they were to be removed later and placed in another wing of the building. Two ex-trustees of the church disputed that intention during their testimony. Decide. (*Sims v. Williams*, 441 S.W.2d 385)

2. Smith bought two lots along the shore of Lake Pepin and built a cottage which he mistakenly extended over the boundary line onto a third lot, Parcel X8. Smith cleaned all three lots, seeded X8 with grass, and used it with the sporadic and seasonal occupancy one would normally use lakeshore property. Burkhardt had a warranty deed to X8 but did not challenge Smith's possession for more than 20 years. Now Smith claims title to X8 by adverse possession. Burkhardt argues that the entire parcel was not actually occupied nor was it usually cultivated. Burkhardt also argues that Smith's possession was not hostile because it was based on a boundary line mistake and because Smith paid no taxes on X8. Does Smith get title to Parcel X8 by adverse possession? (*Burkhardt v. Smith*, 17 Wis. 2d 132, 115 N.W.2d 540)

3. Lober sold a parcel of realty to Brown in 1957. A warranty deed was used. There were no encumbrances listed in the deed. Later, Brown tried to sell a portion of the property to Consolidated Coal Company. At that time, Brown learned that he did not own all of the property described in Lober's deed. Can Brown recover from Lober? (*Brown v. Lober*, 75 Ill. 2d 549)

4. In 1942 a deed properly created a perpetual easement of "right to receive light, air, and unobstructed view" over certain property now owned by Friedman. Friedman erected a TV antenna, and Petersen—as owner of the property benefitted by the easement—sought an injunction to compel removal of the "obstruction." Friedman argues that the parties who created the easement back in 1942 could not have intended to bar such TV installations, since such installations were not even known at the time. Decide. (*Petersen v. Friedman*, 162 Cal. 2d 245, 328 P.2d 264)

5. Cleo Alexander deeded some of her property to Eastwood on December 2, 1958. Later, she deeded the same property to Shedd. Shedd recorded the deed on October 15, 1963. Eastwood did not record his deed until October 16, 1964. Shedd had been unaware of the Eastwood deed. Shedd sued Eastwood to determine ownership of the realty. Who prevails? (*Eastwood v. Shedd*, 442 P.2d 423 Colo.)

36
Landlord and Tenant

1. Several months ago, your brother orally entered into a nine-month lease for an apartment. Now, upon discovering that the apartment can be leased for more money, the landlord has told your brother to vacate. The landlord claims that their oral agreement is unenforceable. Is the landlord correct?
2. You moved into an apartment under a one-year lease. You plan to move out but do not tell the landlord. Two days before the lease expires, while you are packing, the landlord appears and informs you that since you did not give notice of your intent to leave, you owe rent for an additional month. Is the landlord right?
3. Three weeks before you are scheduled to move out of an apartment, the landlord tells you that he wants to begin showing the apartment to other prospective tenants. Must you allow him to do this even though your lease says nothing about showing the apartment?

WHAT IS A LEASE?

PROBLEM: Curtis entered into an oral agreement with Kearne to lease Kearne's cabin for three months during the winter ski season. However, skiing was poor that year because of mild, rainy weather. Therefore Curtis tried to avoid the contract. Curtis claimed that the lease was not enforceable because it was not in writing and because the poor skiing conditions constituted a failure of consideration. Was Curtis correct?

A **lease** is a legal agreement in which one person receives exclusive possession of another's real property for a time in exchange for rent. **Rent** is the consideration given in return for such possession. A lease, therefore, is different from an easement or a profit, where possession of real property remains with the owner (see Chapter 35). The lease creates a relationship between the person conveying possession (called the **landlord** or *lessor*) and the person receiving possession (called the **tenant** or *lessee*). In contrast to rental of real property, rental of personal property (covered in Chapter 34) creates the relationship of bailment between bailor and bailee.

lease: agreement in which possession of real property is exchanged for rent

rent: consideration given for possession of real property through a lease

landlord: person conveying possession of real property through a lease

tenant: person receiving possession of real property through a lease

The agreement that creates the lease relationship may be either express or implied. Thus, although the term *lease* is often used to designate the writing which establishes the relationship, a lease may be oral. Remember, however, that under the statute of frauds, leases which extend for more than one year should be in writing. Otherwise, courts may refuse to enforce them. In the problem, therefore, Curtis was wrong. Because the lease was for only three months, the oral agreement was binding. As the tenant, Curtis was entitled to possession during the three months of the lease. In addition, the landlord had not made any contract to deliver "good weather." The fact that the tenant did not enjoy the occupancy as much as anticipated does not constitute a "failure of consideration."

Even if a writing is not required, it is a good idea to put the important terms of the lease in clear, written form. This will quickly solve or avoid any disputes.

WHAT TYPES OF TENANCIES MAY BE CREATED BY LEASES?

PROBLEM: The two Adams sisters leased an apartment from Pena. They were to pay rent on the first day of each month. No time limit for the lease was specified. What type of tenancy was created?

Depending on the terms, one of the four following basic types of tenancies, or interests in realty, can be created by a lease:

1. Periodic Tenancy

periodic tenancy: a lease for a renewable period with rent due at stated intervals

tenancy from month to month: periodic tenancy with rent paid by the month

When a lease is for a renewable period of time with rent due at stated intervals, it is a **periodic tenancy**. This is probably the most common type of tenancy. A periodic tenancy may be by the week, the month, the year, or any other period of time agreed upon. If the rent is paid by the month, as in the problem, the tenancy is referred to as a **tenancy from month to month**. A periodic tenancy continues for successive time periods until one of the parties ends it by giving proper notice of termination. Leases which create a periodic tenancy usually identify a rental period such as from "week to week," "month to month," or "year to year." Usually notice must be given one period in advance. For example, a lessor could terminate a month-to-month tenancy, or change the terms of the lease, by giving notice one month in advance.

2. Tenancy for Years

tenancy for years: a lease for a definite period of time

When a lease is for a definite period of time, such as six months, one year, or ninety-nine years, it creates a **tenancy for years**. Note that it has this name even when the period of the lease is less than one year. The feature which distinguishes a tenancy for years from a periodic tenancy is the identification of a date for the ending of the lease. Thus, if a lease states that the rental period is from May 1st to August 15th, this is tenancy for years because August 15th is specified as the ending date. At the end of the lease period, a tenancy for years terminates automatically without a requirement of notice.

3. Tenancy at Sufferance

tenancy at sufferance: period during which tenant remains in possession after the lease expires

If a tenant remains in possession after the lease has expired, a **tenancy at sufferance** arises. The landlord may treat such a tenant as a trespasser. However, if the landlord accepts additional rent, a new periodic tenancy is generally created. If the old lease was for a year or longer, the landlord can hold the tenant for another full year's rent. If the old lease was for a month, the landlord generally can hold the tenant for another month's rent.

4. Tenancy at Will

If a party possesses land with the owner's permission but without an agreement as to the term of the lease or the amount of the rent, a **tenancy at will** results. Such a tenancy may be terminated at any time at the will of either party.

tenancy at will: lease for an indefinite period, terminable at will by either party

WHAT ARE THE RIGHTS AND DUTIES OF A TENANT?

PROBLEM: The Bartleys leased a house from Atlas Properties. The lease limited the property to single-family use. To help the family finances, the Bartleys installed bunk beds in the second floor and took in eight college students as boarders. Atlas claims this violates the lease. Is Atlas correct?

The rights and duties of a tenant include:

1. The Right to Possession

The tenant has a right to the possession of the real property starting at the time agreed to in the lease. In addition, unless otherwise provided in the lease, the tenant's possession is to be exclusive of all other persons and is for the duration of the lease.

Landlords generally do not have a right to enter leased premises for inspection unless this right is given in the lease. If a landlord is given the right to enter and inspect the leased premises, most states require that the landlord give reasonable advance notice, such as two days, and require that the landlord inspect at a reasonable time of the day.

Tripe, the landlord of an apartment building, asked to show a tenant's apartment to a prospective renter. Because the lease did not provide for such tours, the tenant could rightfully deny the request. Showing the apartment without the tenant's permission would make Tripe a trespasser.

If the landlord or an agent of the landlord removes the tenant from possession of all the real property covered by the lease, an **eviction** has occurred. Depriving the tenant of the possession of only one part of the real property (for example, one room of an apartment) is termed a **partial eviction**. In either case, the tenant may recover damages from the landlord if the eviction is improper.

In addition, under some circumstances, the tenant may claim **constructive eviction** and refuse to pay rent. This could happen if the landlord failed to perform certain duties as defined in the lease or imposed by statute and the tenant abandoned the premises

eviction: removal of the tenant from possession of all real property by action of the landlord

partial eviction: depriving the tenant of possession of part of the real property

constructive eviction: when property becomes so unfit for habitation through fault of landlord that the tenant is forced to abandon it because of such a breach. Examples would include the landlord's failure to make agreed-upon repairs or failure to heat the premises. If the law requires that the premises be kept in a condition fit for human habitation, an infestation of insects or rodents could amount to constructive eviction if the tenant left the premises because of such condition. The landlord is not responsible for the possible annoying behavior of neighbors.

2. The Duty to Pay Rent

A tenant's most important duty is to pay the agreed-upon rent when it is due. Although rent is usually expressed as a fixed sum of money, it may consist of services or of property. It may also be a share of the crops of a farm or a percentage of the profits of a business. Leases ordinarily require rental payment in advance.

Before leasing property in a tenancy for years or a tenancy from month to month, landlords sometimes require the payment of the first and last month's rent. Thus, if the tenant fails to make prompt advance payment of the next period's rent, the landlord can use the last month's rent for the month during which legal steps are taken to force the tenant to move. In residential rentals, a "cleaning" or "security" deposit is almost always required. The amount of this deposit should be refunded at the end of the lease period if the property is left as clean and undamaged as it was when first occupied, less ordinary wear and tear.

3. The Right to the Use of the Property

The tenant is allowed to use the leased property in the manner specified in the lease. If a particular use is not mentioned in the lease, the tenant may use the property for any purpose for which it is designed or customarily used. A tenant who agrees to lease a house as a single-family residence may not use the building as a boardinghouse. Such would be the case with the Bartleys in the problem.

4. The Duty to Take Care of the Property

A tenant must take reasonable care of the leased property and return it in substantially the same condition it was in when the lease began. The duty of reasonable care ordinarily includes responsibility for making all minor repairs. The tenant is not liable for wear and tear caused by ordinary use. However, the tenant is liable for deterioration or destruction caused by willful misuse or negligence. In some states, by agreement and sometimes by statute, landlords make all repairs. This would include even such minor repairs as replacing faucet washers and electric fuses.

The tenant normally is under no obligation (in fact, has no right) to make major structural changes or repairs or to make improvements without the consent of the landlord. For example, if the roof develops leaks, the necessary repair and replacement are concerns of the landlord. However, in such circumstances, the tenant is legally expected to act reasonably, taking appropriate steps to prevent avoidable damage until the landlord has been notified and can make needed repairs. Also, if the tenant's negligence or misconduct caused damage requiring repairs, it is the tenant's duty to pay for corrective work.

The tenant is obligated to notify the landlord when major repairs become necessary unless the landlord learns the facts by other means, as through routine inspection or notification by local housing authorities. In a few states, the tenant may apply up to a full month's rent towards necessary repairs if the landlord does not make the repairs after reasonable notice.

5. The Right to Assign the Lease or to Sublet

Unless restricted by the terms of the lease, a tenant may assign the lease or may sublet all or part of the premises. An **assignment of a lease** takes place when the tenant transfers his or her entire interest in the lease to a third person. Although the assignee becomes liable to the landlord for the rent and performance of other conditions of the lease, the original tenant also remains liable.

assignment of a lease: tenant's transfer of entire interest to another

A **subletting** occurs when the tenant does either of the following:

subletting: tenant's transferring part of interest to another

a. leases all of the property to a third person for a period of time which is less than the term remaining on the lease, and
b. leases part of the property to a third person for part or all of the term remaining.

When the property is sublet, the original tenant becomes a sublessor in relation to the third person, the sublessee. The original tenant also continues to be directly liable to the owner-landlord for performance of the lease.

Leases often require the landlord's prior approval of assignment or subletting. However, courts have held that the landlord must act in good faith if withholding such consent.

WHAT ARE THE RIGHTS AND DUTIES OF A LANDLORD?

PROBLEM: McElroy leased a store building from Steward for one year. After three months, McElroy moved all her possessions from the building and left town, defaulting on her rent. Steward did not relet the store. Is McElroy liable for the rent for the remaining nine months?

Often, the rights and duties of a tenant find their complements in the rights and duties of a landlord, which are as follows:

1. The Right to the Rent

The landlord's primary right is to the rent agreed upon in the lease. If the tenant fails to pay the rent, the landlord may:

Recover rent if the tenant vacates early. A tenant who vacates the property before the end of the lease may still be liable for the remaining rent. In some states, the tenant is liable for the rent even if the landlord allows the property to remain empty. Other states require that the landlord make a good-faith effort to rerent the property. If it is not rerented, the original tenant is liable for the rent remaining on the lease. If it is rerented, but at a lower rental amount, the original tenant is liable for the difference.

In the problem, McElroy's liability depends on the law of the state where the property is located. In some states, Steward can allow the premises to remain empty and sue McElroy for the unpaid rent. Other states will require that Steward try to re-lease the premises before collecting from McElroy.

Maintain an action to evict the tenant and reenter the property. In the case of breach of the lease by the tenant who remains in possession, the landlord may normally terminate the lease and take legal action to evict the tenant. In some states, the landlord may include the claim for overdue rent in the same action. However, the landlord may not take the law into his or her own hands, bodily evicting the tenant and placing the tenant's belongings on the sidewalk. If the tenant refuses to leave the premises, a court order directing the sheriff or other official to evict the tenant must be obtained.

2. The Duty to Maintain the Premises

The duty to maintain the leased property generally falls on the tenant. However, there are exceptions to this rule. For example, when a number of tenants rent portions of a building, the landlord is responsible for the upkeep of the exterior and the public areas. Such would be the case with apartment houses or office structures. Public areas are those not under the specific control of any one tenant and include common hallways, stairs, elevators, yards, and swimming pools. One who is injured because of the faulty condition of these areas could bring suit for damages against the landlord. In addition, a landlord may be held liable for injuries that result from defective conditions in the property in the tenant's exclusive possession if the conditions are concealed or are not readily apparent.

Finally, when property is leased for human habitation, the landlord is required to provide and keep the quarters in a condition fit for living. In some states and in some cities, the law in the form of a housing code may prescribe in detail the required condition of such rental properties before and during human occupancy. A representative city housing code makes provisions such as these:

a. there shall be no exposed electrical wiring,
b. the roof shall not leak,
c. every ceiling and wall shall be smooth, free of loose plaster and wallpaper, and easily cleanable,
d. outside doors and windows shall have tight-fitting screens,
e. every unit shall have a private bathroom, and
f. gas stoves shall be properly vented and connected.

3. The Right to Fixtures

If a tenant adds fixtures (see Chapter 35) to the property, they belong to the landlord. (Remember, however, that this general rule does not apply to trade fixtures.) Such a situation may provoke disputes. Therefore it is desirable for the parties to agree in advance on which additions are to be considered fixtures and which are to be considered removable personal property.

4. The Duty to Pay Taxes

In the absence of contrary agreement, the landlord pays all real property taxes and assessments to the property leased. However, long-term leases of commercial property commonly provide that the tenant will pay such taxes and assessments, as well as premiums for fire insurance.

HOW CAN A LEASE BE TERMINATED?

PROBLEM: Harpstein leased in a month-to-month tenancy a store in Marx's Shopping Center. Three days before the end of March, Harpstein told Marx that on the first of April she was moving her business to another shopping center. Was Harpstein legally able to terminate the lease on such short notice?

A lease can be terminated in several ways. If it is made for a definite period of time, it terminates at the end of such time. It can also be terminated by agreement before the expiration of the term, as when the tenant surrenders the lease to the landlord and the landlord accepts. Mere abandonment of the premises without assent of the landlord is not surrender, it is a breach of the lease. Any material breach by the tenant generally gives the landlord the right to terminate the lease, and vice versa.

In a periodic tenancy, the party seeking to terminate must notify the other party to the lease. There is usually a requirement that this notice be in writing and be given so many days before it becomes effective or before expiration of the term. Time and method may be specified in the lease, but they generally are subject to statute. Typical notice time for a tenancy from month to month is 30 days. In the problem, Harpstein could not terminate the lease on such short notice unless Marx was willing.

PREVENTING LEGAL DIFFICULTIES

If You Are a Tenant . . .

1. written residential leases are generally prepared by the landlord or the landlord's attorney. Thus, such leases often contain many clauses that protect the landlord's interest. Read with understanding before you sign. If the terms are unacceptable to you, request a change. If you are refused, go elsewhere;
2. you are not permitted to remodel or significantly change the premises without the consent of your landlord;
3. you may be held liable if someone is injured because of the faulty condition of the premises if such condition was caused by your negligence. Normally you, the tenant, have the obligation to make necessary minor repairs and to notify your landlord of the need for major repairs. Protect yourself with careful maintenance and with adequate liability insurance;

4. when you move, do not forget to give your landlord proper notice of your intention if the lease or a statute requires the giving of notice in order to terminate. Such notice is usually the case in periodic tenancies. Failure to give required notice may obligate you to pay additional rent even after you vacate the premises;
5. if you are a tenant in a tenancy for years, be sure to vacate, removing all belongings and trade fixtures, before expiration of the lease or arrange to renew the lease. If you stay beyond the lease period without permission, you could be treated as a trespasser or held liable for as much as another full year's rent; and
6. if a "cleaning" or "security" deposit is required, it is a good idea to conduct an inspection of the premises with the landlord and with witnesses both before occupying and before vacating.

Strengthening Your Legal Vocabulary

assignment of a lease
constructive eviction
eviction
landlord
lease
partial eviction
periodic tenancy
rent
subletting
tenancy at sufferance
tenancy at will
tenancy for years
tenancy from month to month
tenant

1. Tenant's transfer of partial interest in the lease to a third person.
2. Agreement which provides that the tenant shall obtain possession of the real property of the landlord in exchange for rent.
3. Legal action taken to remove a tenant from possession of all real property.
4. Consideration given by a tenant.
5. Depriving the tenant of possession of part of the real property subject to the lease.
6. Periodic tenancy in which the rent is paid by the month.
7. One who, through a lease, transfers to another exclusive possession and control of real property.
8. One who, through a lease, is given possession of real property.
9. Lease which exists for a definite period of time.
10. Tenancy created when the tenant remains in possession after the lease has expired.

Reviewing Important Points

1. The relationship of landlord and tenant always involves real property.
2. A landlord-tenant relationship may be a tenancy for years, a periodic tenancy (for example, a tenancy from month to month or a tenancy from year to

year), a tenancy at will, or a tenancy at sufferance.
3. Generally the tenant is responsible for paying the rent, taking reasonable care of the premises, and using the premises only for the purposes agreed upon.
4. A tenant may assign the lease or sublet the premises unless there is a restriction in the lease which requires prior approval by the landlord.
5. Generally the landlord must deliver possession of the premises, see that the tenant is not deprived of their use, and pay taxes on the property.
6. A lease may be terminated by expiration of the lease period, agreement of the parties, or at the option of either party upon material breach by the other. In a periodic tenancy, either party seeking to terminate must give the other party proper notice.
7. To claim constructive eviction, the tenant must vacate the real property.

Applying Law to Everyday Life

1. Strovic orally leased a restaurant from Quinn for five years. Within a year, Strovic had built a large following, and business was booming. Quinn then demanded more rent. When Strovic refused, Quinn sought to evict him and to lease the now well-established property to someone else who would pay higher rent. Can Quinn do this?

2. Slovin entered into a month-to-month tenancy of an apartment for $450 per month. When he married, his wife moved in with him. The landlord did not discover this until three months later. The landlord told Slovin that he owed an extra $100 per month for the time during which the wife had also occupied the apartment. In addition, he told Slovin that the rent for the next month would be $600. What are Slovin's legal obligations to the landlord?

3. Hirschey moved away to college and rented a room for nine months, to end on the first of June. After her final examinations were over (on the first of June), she moved out of the room without saying anything to the landlord. The landlord now seeks to collect an additional month's rent because Hirschey did not give notice of termination. Can the landlord collect?

4. In the midst of a very cold winter, the heating unit in Manlie's apartment failed to function for a month. Therefore Manlie refused to pay the rent, claiming constructive eviction. Her landlord, however, claimed that the rent was still due because Manlie had not abandoned the premises. Is the landlord correct?

5. Romero rented a farm under a three-year lease. At the end of the lease, Romero and the landlord walked through the farmhouse to inspect for damage. In an empty upstairs room the landlord found a window which was jammed open. It was obvious that rain and snow had come through the open window and damaged curtains and carpeting. Who is liable for this damage, Romero or the landlord?

6. Houser opened a hamburger shop in a building which she leased for five years from Livingston. The long hours impaired Houser's health and after one year she sold the business to Todd, assigning the lease as part of the deal. When Todd later defaulted on rent payments, Livingston tried to collect from Houser. Is Houser liable?

7. Moya rented an apartment in a large complex owned by Johnson. Moya's guest Perkins was injured when he fell on the icy sidewalk leading up to the building where Moya's apartment was located. Perkins sued both Moya and Johnson. Who is liable, Moya or Johnson?

Solving Case Problems

1. Wallenberg leased certain property from Boyar in a tenancy from month to month, beginning October 1. The rent was payable in advance on the first of each month. On November 27, Wallenberg left without notifying the landlord. Is Boyar entitled to rent for the month of December? (*Boyar v. Wallenberg*, 132 Misc. 116, 228 N.Y.S. 358)

2. Lemle rented an expensive home in the Diamond Head area of Honolulu. The home contained six bedrooms and the roof was made in the Tahitian style with corrugated metal covered by woven coconut leaves. After moving in, Lemle and his family discovered the the roof was infested with rodents. For two days after moving in they all slept in the downstairs living room because of their fear of the rodents. After the landlord tried without success to exterminate the rodents, Lemle and his family moved out and demanded return of their deposit and prepaid rent. Is Lemle entitled to the return of the rent? (*Lemle v. Breeden*, 462 P.2d 470, Hawaii)

3. James Kreidel was engaged to be married and planned to attend school. He entered into a lease of an apartment from May 1, 1972 to April 30, 1974. Before the lease period began, James's engagement was broken. James then had no means of support as a student and therefore had no way to pay the rent. On May 19, 1972 he wrote the landlord explaining his situation and stating that he was abandoning the lease. Although the landlord had the opportunity, he did not rerent the apartment until September 1, 1973. Is James liable for the rent from May 1, 1972 to September 1, 1973? (*Sommer v. Kreidel*, 378 A.2d 767, N.J.)

4. Stockton Realty Company rented to Green an apartment in a three-story building which had on the roof a washroom and clothesline for use by tenants. The clothesline ran near the skylight, but there was no guardrail between the clothesline and the skylight. After Reiman, a 14-year-old friend, removed Mrs. Green's clothes from the line, she tripped on some object and fell against the skylight. The glass was too weak to support her weight, and she dropped to the floor below, sustaining injuries. Is the landlord responsible for the condition of the roof, hence possibly liable in damages for the injury? (*Reiman v. Moore*, 108 P.2d 452, Cal.)

SPECIAL SECTION:
Legal Research and Sources of the Law

Ability to do legal research is of prime importance to an attorney (or lawyer). In our common law system, appellate court decisions become precedents for similar cases. Justices of appellate courts usually write opinions which explain their decisions. The West Publishing Company publishes a series of Reporters which contain judicial opinions of the highest state and federal courts. Seven regional reporters (Atlantic, Northeastern, Northwestern, Pacific, Southeastern, Southern, and Southwestern) cover the nation by carrying the opinions of all state appellate courts in the indicated sections of the country. Three other reporters—the Federal Supplement, Federal Reporter, and the Supreme Court Reporter—carry the opinions of the Federal District Courts, Courts of Appeals, and Supreme Court, respectively.

Important legal rules included in the body of each opinion are also printed in summary form as *headnotes* (notes at the beginning of each case) in the particular Reporter. The rules or points of law are grouped into legal categories, such as constitutional law or criminal law, and the groupings are published in encyclopedia-like series of books called Digests. There are Digests for the law of each state and for the United States. An attorney wanting to find out about homicide, for example, could look in the appropriate Digest under Criminal Law and its subcategory, Homicide. There the attorney could read the legal rules that have been stated in cases in the subject area. Citations (or references) are provided in the Digest to the cases where the particular rules appear so that the attorney can look up and read the entire opinion of the cases in the appropriate Reporters.

Other series of books are called *annotations*. Annotations take each state or federal statute or constitutional provision and group with it the pertinent rules from judicial opinions in appellate cases that explain, clarify, or determine the application of the statute or constitutional provision.

In addition to the above-mentioned publications and other more specialized reference works, computers are used to facilitate legal research. Legal information access systems provide on-line service between the attorney's personal computer and massive data bases of legal information. By having the computer search for cases and other legal materials related to key terms that the attorney provides, pertinent information is quickly located and shown on the computer screen. The attorney may then print the needed information, if so desired. Often computer data bases are updated and made available much sooner than the published books containing the same information. Computers enable attorneys to find current information quickly and easily.

37

Wills, Intestacy, and Estate Planning

1. One gloomy, rainy day, you and a friend wonder what would happen to your cars, clothes, books, stereos, and other belongings if either of you should die. You shake hands and agree that whoever survives "gets everything." Will the courts enforce your agreement?
2. Your uncle became angry with your aunt and wrote a will which left her nothing. Does he have the legal power to disinherit his wife?
3. Your friend's grandfather recently died without leaving a will. What will happen to his property?

WHAT IS A WILL?

PROBLEM: Ryan and Susan O'Connor stood on the deck of a cruise ship during their honeymoon. As they discussed plans for the future, Ryan and Susan earnestly assured one another, "What's mine is yours!" Does this effectively take the place of a will?

will: legal expression of how a person's property is to be distributed after the person dies

testator or testatrix: a person who makes a will

intestate: one who dies without a valid will

decedent: one who has died

bequest: a gift, by will, of personal property

devise: a gift, by will, of real property

estate: all the property owned by a decedent at death

beneficiaries: persons who receive real or personal property under a will

heirs: those who receive the property of a person who dies without a valid will

A **will** is a legal expression, usually in writing, by which a person directs how her or his property is to be distributed after death (see Figure 37-1 on page 658). The maker of a will is called a **testator** (if male) or a **testatrix** (if female).

A will takes effect only upon the death of the maker. Therefore it can be changed or canceled at any time during the maker's life. However, this ability to change a will as frequently as the maker wants, coupled with the fact that the contents of a will are proved only after the death of the maker, opens the way to false claims under forged documents. This has, in turn, led to strict rules regarding the preparation and execution of wills.

If a will fails to comply with the legal requirements, courts will not enforce it. The deceased person's property is then distributed as if there were no will. A person who dies without a will, or with an unenforceable will, is called an **intestate**. An intestate's property is distributed according to state statutes rather than according to the expressed wishes of the **decedent**—the deceased person.

Legal requirements for wills are determined by state statute. One normal requirement is that a will be in writing. Therefore, in the problem, the statements of the honeymooners were expressions of their desires or intentions, but they could not take effect as a will.

Personal property that is left by will is a **bequest** (also called a *legacy*). Real property that is left by will is a **devise**. The real and personal property of the decedent is called the **estate**. Those who receive the gifts by will (by testacy) are known as **beneficiaries**. Technically, persons who inherit by virtue of an intestate statute are **heirs** and are always related by blood or by marriage.

WHY MAKE A WILL?

PROBLEM: Winn, a wealthy widow, wanted to make special gifts of money after death to several friends, a favorite nephew, her loyal nurse and companion, her church, and her college alma mater. She also wanted to leave controlling shares of stock in the family business to her older daughter. She wanted to leave a diamond bracelet, which was a family heirloom, to her younger daughter. Winn also was determined to set up a trust to take care of a third child, who was mentally retarded. She also wanted to appoint her sister to take care of this child after Winn died. Should she make a will?

Often individuals with only a limited amount of property do not bother to make a will. Others anticipate that the legal fee for making one will be too large. On the contrary, most property owners can benefit significantly from making a will. In addition, the legal fee charged by an attorney for the making of a will is usually small.

When a proper will is made, the testatrix or testator can take steps that usually make the distribution of property less expensive than if the distribution is governed by state intestacy statutes. For example, the testator can waive any bond otherwise required by law for a personal representative. The will in Figure 37-1 contains such a waiver. In addition, with a clear statement about property distribution, the maker can greatly decrease the possibility of costly litigation. Finally, a well-drafted will can reduce the estate and inheritance taxes.

A proper will can also simplify the administration of the decedent's gifts. For example, if a person with a spouse and two minor children dies without leaving a will, under the typical intestacy statute one-third of the estate will go to the surviving spouse and one-third to each of the children. The court will probably appoint the surviving spouse as guardian of the estates of the children. The surviving spouse will be responsible for taking care of and managing the estates, spending available money as reasonably necessary. The surviving spouse will have to provide a bond ensuring faithful performance of duties and will be required to make periodic reports to the court on the management of the estate until the children reach adulthood. At this point, the children will get control of their shares of the estate regardless of whether they are able to handle them prudently. The time, expense, and annoyance of this procedure could be avoided by a will which leaves everything to the surviving spouse. If this spouse's ability to handle the assets is doubted, the one making the will could set up a **trust** in the will and name a banker or other trustee to manage the estate. The interest earned on the assets, coupled with the right to use the principal if necessary, could be designated as the survivor's income for life. The trust could specify that the children would inherit what is left when the surviving parent dies or when the children reach prescribed ages.

trust: a legal arrangement whereby one party holds title to property for the benefit of another

WILL
OF
CHARLES ALAN COLLIER

I, Charles Alan Collier, of 1875 El Rey Way, San Francisco, California, declare that this is my will. I revoke all wills and codicils that I have previously made.

FIRST: I am married to Janet Lee Collier (nee O'Hara) and we have one child, Charlene Janine, born March 12, 19--.

SECOND: After payment of all my debts, I give my estate as follows:

(A) To my twin brother, Chauncey, I give my personal clothing, my watch, cuff links, hunting guns, and sporting equipment, if he should survive me.

(B) To my beloved wife, Janet, I give all the residue if she should survive me for thirty (30) days.

(C) To our daughter, Charlene Janine, I give all the residue if my wife should not survive me for thirty days and if my daughter should survive me for thirty days.

(D) To the Regents of the University of California (to provide student scholarships and awards without reference to financial need, in order to encourage excellence of effort and achievement), I give all the residue if neither my wife nor my daughter should survive me for thirty days.

THIRD: I nominate my wife as executrix of this will. If for any reason she should fail to qualify or cease to act as such, I nominate my brother, Chauncey, as executor. If for any reason he should fail to qualify or cease to act as such, I nominate the Crocker National Bank, a California corporation, to act as executor. I direct that neither my wife nor my brother be required to post bond as executrix or executor.

IN WITNESS WHEREOF, I have hereunto set my hand this 18 day of January, 19--, in San Francisco, California.

Charles Alan Collier
Charles Alan Collier

The foregoing instrument was subscribed on the date which it bears by the testator, Charles Alan Collier, and at the time of subscribing was declared by him to be his last will. The subscription and declaration were made in our presence, we being present at the same time; and we, at his request and in his presence and in the presence of each other, have affixed our signatures hereto as witnesses:

Susan A. Boyer residing at 432 Third Street
San Francisco, Calif.

Paulette M. Stone residing at 436 Third Street
San Francisco, Calif.

Figure 37-1. A Will

For those who have already made wills, it is important to be aware of the need for keeping the will current. Often a change in the maker's assets, state of residence, possible beneficiaries, or tax laws requires or makes advisable amendment of an existing will or the making of a new one.

If an individual dies without a will and without close relatives, that person's property reverts to the state. This claim of the state on such property is the right of **escheat**. A proper will would prevent this situation and allow the distant heirs to receive what would otherwise pass to the state by escheat.

escheat: passing of an intestate's property to the state because there are no close relatives

In general, then, if there is a proper will, a decedent's property is distributed in the way the decedent desired. If there is no proper will, the distribution is made according to state statutes, and the results may be very different. In the problem, if Winn did not have a will in which she indicated the desired gifts, probably none of her wishes would be fulfilled.

WHAT ARE THE REQUIREMENTS OF A FORMAL WILL?

PROBLEM: Kitt made a will in June. In August of that same year, Kitt was declared insane. Did the will remain valid?

Because a will is subject to specific technical requirements which vary from state to state, it is advisable to have an attorney prepare this document. Unlike some other legal documents, wills are too important and may be too complex for people to prepare without expert help.

There are usually four basic requirements for a valid will:

1. the testator must have *testamentary intent*,
2. the testator must have *testamentary capacity*,
3. the will must be in writing and must be signed, and
4. the will must be witnessed.

1. The Testator Must Have Testamentary Intent

In order to create a valid will, the testatrix or testator must intend to dispose of her or his property upon death. While the writing and the signature usually indicate clear intent, there are some situations where this is not so. For example, some wills are signed by mistake. Occasionally people will mislead a testator into thinking that the document is something other than a will. Also, undue influence may negate testamentary intent. If a person is pressured into signing the document against his or her will, there is no testamentary intent.

> Arturo was 86 years old, confined to a wheelchair, and living with a distant cousin, Alice. He depended upon her for preparing his food, cleaning his clothes, and providing transportation. Alice told Arturo that if he did not sign a will leaving everything to her, she would immediately throw him out of her house. Because of this threat, Arturo did sign. The will is invalid because Arturo acted under undue influence and therefore without testamentary intent.

2. The Testator Must Have Testamentary Capacity

The testator or testatrix must have capacity to make a will and must be able to know at least in a general way the following:

a. the kind and extent of the property;
b. the persons who are "the natural objects of his or her bounty" or generosity, meaning those who could reasonably expect to receive gifts because of family or other relationship; and
c. what is being done in making the will—namely, making arrangements to dispose of the property after death.

If the testator does not have capacity when the will is made, the fact that capacity is later acquired does not invalidate the will. If the testator had capacity when the will was made, as Kitt did in the problem, and later lost it—as by going insane—the will remains valid. In other words, testamentary capacity must exist at the time the will is *made*.

> Dasher was 96 years old and suffering from senility. On some occasions she was lucid and on others she was completely disoriented, unable to recall even her own name. While she was disoriented, her son gave her a document, explained that it was a will, told her that it left everything to him, and asked her to sign. She did. Because she was in a state of disorientation, Dasher did not know what she was doing. The will is not valid because she lacked testamentary capacity. If Dasher had signed the will during a period when she understood what she was doing, she would have had testamentary capacity.

In most states, persons who are under 18 years of age do not have testamentary capacity by law. In a small number of states, individuals younger than 18 can dispose of personal property by will.

3. The Will Must be in Writing and be Signed

Generally a will must be in writing. No particular form or words are necessary so long as the testator's intentions are expressed. The document may be printed, typewritten, or handwritten in pencil or ink. Or it may be any combination of printing, typewriting, and handwriting.

The will must be signed by the testator or by someone directed to sign for and in the presence of the testator. To prevent unauthorized additions to the will, many states require that the signature be placed at the end.

4. Witnesses May Be Required

In most states, witnesses are necessary to attest to the will. Witnessing a will being executed is termed **attestation**. Generally two, and sometimes three, witnesses must attest to a will depending upon the law of the appropriate state.

attestation: act of witnessing the execution of a will

Some states require that the maker of the will inform the attesting witnesses that it is her or his will that is being signed. This is called **publication**. Publication requires only that the witnesses be aware that they are witnessing a will; they need not know what the will provides. In other states, it is enough that the witnesses merely observe the maker signing the document. In addition, in some states, the witnesses must all be present and must sign in the presence of each other and of the testator, and they must all be present when the testator signs (or acknowledges the previously affixed signature to be his or her own).

publication: act of informing attesting witnesses that the document being signed is the testator's will

In most states, a witness who is also a beneficiary under the will is disqualified from receiving the bequest or devise. However, a witness who is an heir receives the gift up to the amount that would have been received if there had been no will.

WHAT ARE THE SPECIAL TYPES OF WILLS?

PROBLEM: Lee was fatally injured in an automobile accident late one evening. As she lay dying, she told three witnesses that she was making a will and that she wanted her valuable collection of paintings to go to her good friend Ross. Unfortunately, Lee died before she could sign anything. Is her oral will valid?

In addition to the ordinary formal will, some states recognize one or more of the following special types of wills:

1. Holographic or Handwritten Will

holographic will: will written entirely in the testator's own handwriting

A **holographic will** is one that is written entirely in the testator's own hand and is signed by the testator. In some states, the will must also be dated in the testator's own hand. In some states, no witnesses are required for a holographic will to be valid.

2. Nuncupative or Oral Will

nuncupative will: oral will made during the testator's last illness

A **nuncupative will** (also called an *oral will*), if recognized in a particular state, is usually valid for disposal of personal property only, and ordinarily the amount is strictly limited. Generally such a will must be made during the testator's last illness, and one or more witnesses are required. The testimony of the witnesses must be reduced to writing within a specified time. Because of these limitations, oral wills are uncommon. In the problem, if the witnesses' testimonies were properly and promptly reduced to writing, this oral will would be valid in most states.

3. Soldier's or Sailor's Will

soldier's or sailor's will: will made by a member of the military, to distribute personal property after death

Some states recognize an oral or written **soldier's or sailor's will**—that is, one in which the testator is a member of the military. Such a will is generally valid for disposing of personal property even though it does not comply with the formalities required for other wills. Such a will remains effective after the maker returns to civilian life, but it can be changed in the same manner as any other will.

HOW CAN A WILL BE REVOKED OR ALTERED?

PROBLEM: Marion had a properly prepared ordinary formal will in a state which required witnesses. Several years later, she used pen and ink to add a new beneficiary. She dated and signed her name next to the addition. No witnesses were present at the signing. Was the addition effective?

Revocation is the ending of the potential of a will to direct the disposition of a testator's property at death. Persons can revoke or alter their wills at any time.

1. By Written Revocation

When someone makes a new will it usually includes a clause which revokes all prior wills. Even without express language, such as, "I hereby revoke all prior wills," a subsequent will containing provisions which conflict with those of a prior will *impliedly* revokes the superseded provisions of the earlier will. Because of this, it is important to date every will.

The testator who wants to modify the will by deletion or substitution of terms, or to change it by addition of new terms, can do so by appropriate deletion or addition of words in a holographic will. It can even be done by an addition of words in an ordinary formal will in those states which do not require witnesses. Such changes should be signed and dated by the testator. But in states which require witnesses, as in the problem, deletions or additions are not effective unless they are made with the same formality required by the original will. Thus, in Maria's will, the addition had no effect, and the old provisions remain in force.

In states which require witnesses, the proper way to change a formal will is by preparing a **codicil**. This is an amendment to the will which adds to, removes, or otherwise alters some of its provisions. A codicil is executed with the same formality as the will itself.

codicil: a modification of a will, executed with the same formality as the will

2. By Operation of Law

It is also possible for a partial or a total revocation to take place solely by action of law. For instance, statutes in some states provide that any will made before marriage is automatically revoked upon marriage. State statutes may also provide that the birth or adoption of a child after the making of a will revokes the will.

In most states, the divorce of the testator does not automatically revoke the testator's will. However, the will may be partially revoked (the provisions for the former spouse may be revoked) by a property settlement resulting from the divorce.

3. By Destroying or Defacing the Will

A testator can revoke a will by doing something to the document which clearly indicates an intent to revoke the will. For example, ripping a will into small pieces would probably revoke it. Similarly, throwing it into a burning fireplace would revoke a will. State statutes specify what physical acts of the testator to the will constitute revocation.

ARE THERE LIMITS ON HOW AN ESTATE IS DISTRIBUTED?

PROBLEM: Forrest was a widower with three adult children. The younger daughter was a successful physician. The son was independently wealthy in a business of his own. The older daughter was still keeping house for her father. She had never pursued a career because she had taken care of her invalid mother for more than 15 years. Could Forrest, the father, elect to leave everything to this older daughter and nothing to his other children?

executor or executrix: personal representative named by the testator to carry out the directions in the will

Although the testator is given wide latitude in disposing of property by will, there are some limitations. The **executor** (if male) or the **executrix** (if female) is a personal representative named by the testator to administer the will. The executrix or executor must pay the lawful debts owed to creditors before distributing any property to the named beneficiaries.

Another limitation is that a surviving spouse can elect to receive either what the testator provided in the will or what the statutes and case law in the state allow. However, a spouse may by consent or by misconduct, such as desertion or nonsupport, give up this right of election.

A few states allow up to only a certain portion of an estate to be given to charity. This limitation may exist only when the decedent is survived by children, grandchildren, or great-grandchildren.

With the exception of the limits just mentioned, generally a testator is not obligated to leave anything to anyone, including close relatives. Contrary to a common, mistaken belief, the testator need not mention a disinherited person, nor bequeath to that person a nominal sum, such as one dollar. However, in some states, a parent who wishes to disinherit any children must either make provision for them while the parent is still alive or explicitly exclude them in the will. Otherwise, they take the shares provided them by state statutes. Thus, in the problem, by using appropriate language, Forrest could leave everything to his older daughter.

HOW IS AN ESTATE DISTRIBUTED IF THERE IS NO WILL?

PROBLEM: Mock, a bachelor living in Maine, had put off making a will for years. Finally, on his deathbed, he made an oral will. Unfortunately such wills were not recognized in Maine. How will Mock's property be distributed?

A person who dies without leaving a will, or whose will is declared invalid (as was Mock's in the problem), is an intestate. In such cases, the court appoints a personal representative known as an **administrator** (if male) or an **administratrix** (if female) to take charge of the intestate's property, to pay all debts including costs of administering the estate, and then to distribute the balance in accordance with the intestacy statutes.

administrator or administratrix: court-appointed representative of an intestate

These intestacy statutes vary from state to state in the shares they award to the various heirs. In addition, some of the states distribute real property and personal property in different proportions among the heirs. Generally, however, a surviving spouse will receive one-third to one-half of all the property. The remainder is divided among the children.

If no children (or grandchildren) survive, the spouse is generally given one-half of the estate and the parents of the deceased share the other half. If the parents are dead, their share goes to the decedent's surviving brothers and sisters if there are any. If any brother or sister has died but has left surviving children, the share of the parent is distributed to the children, who are the nieces or nephews of the deceased.

If the decedent is a single person, his or her parents get the property. In the problem, Mock's parents will get his estate. If neither is alive, the estate will go to his brothers and sisters. If they predeceased him, it will go to their children. If there are no surviving close relatives, and a person dies without leaving a will, the estate will go to the state where the decedent had lived.

HOW IS AN ESTATE MANAGED?

PROBLEM: Benson owed Cane $1,750. Cane did not learn of Benson's death until eight months after it occurred. By that time, the period for presenting claims against the estate had elapsed. Can Cane still legally collect the $1,750 from the estate?

Whether a person dies with or without a valid will, a probate court or surrogate's court will supervise the administration and distribution of the decedent's estate. The estate will be placed in the charge of a qualified executor or administrator depending upon whether or not there is a valid will. Note that if there is no executor appointed in the will or if the executor appointed in the will is not qualified to serve or refuses to serve, the court will appoint an administrator instead.

The primary duties of the executor or administrator are as follows:

1. to assemble and preserve the assets and collect any amount due the estate,
2. to file an inventory of the estate,
3. to pay the just debts of the deceased from the available funds, and
4. to distribute the remaining property in accordance with the will or intestacy statute.

A personal representative will be liable to beneficiaries if she or he fails to reasonably manage the affairs of the estate.

The executor or administrator must publish a public notice to all creditors of the estate, advising them to file their claims. If a claim is not filed within a set time, it will not be paid out of the estate. This is so that an estate can be settled within a reasonable time. Most states allow creditors to file for up to six months from the first notice. In the problem, because Cane did not file within the proper period, the $1,750 claim will go unpaid by the estate.

Unless the testator has waived the bond in the will, the executor must furnish a bond ensuring faithful performance of all duties. The cost of the bond is paid out of the estate. A personal administrator generally is required to give bond, but very commonly, corporate administrators, such as banks and trust companies, need not do so. This is because they are periodically examined and are under the control of a governmental agency to ensure their financial responsibility.

estate tax: tax imposed on the right to transfer property by death

inheritance tax: tax imposed on the right to receive property from a decedent at death

estate planning: arranging one's estate to minimize taxes

HOW IS AN ESTATE TAXED?

The federal government imposes an **estate tax** on large estates before they are distributed to heirs or beneficiaries. Some states impose a similar tax or an **inheritance tax**, which is a tax on the right to receive property from a decedent's estate.

Estate planning is the process of arranging one's affairs so that taxes are minimized and the estate passes smoothly to heirs and beneficiaries. In some instances, families are injured because of a failure to engage in estate planning. For example, if a grandmother owned a profitable business which employed many of her relatives, it might be sold upon her death to raise the cash needed to pay the estate tax. If she had planned her estate, she might have bought enough life insurance so that upon her death there would have been enough cash available to pay the taxes without selling the business.

PREVENTING LEGAL DIFFICULTIES

Since "You Can't Take It with You . . ."

1. the right to decide who shall receive your property after you die is a valuable right. Use it by making a will as soon as you are qualified by law to do so;
2. a will is a technical, legal document. Failure to prepare your will properly may defeat your intentions, lead to lawsuits, add to costs of probate, and increase the tax burden. It can also cause conflicts among those you love. Consult legal counsel before you act;
3. your will is an important document. Keep it in a secure place;
4. for large, complex estates, a corporate executor (bank or trust company) is advisable. For small ordinary estates, a spouse or close relative is often preferable;
5. realize that once a will is made, it should be updated or remade when significant changes occur in your marital status, property, desired beneficiaries, or residency.

Strengthening Your Legal Vocabulary

administrator
administratrix
attestation
beneficiaries
bequest
codicil
decedent
devise
escheat
estate
estate planning
estate tax
executor
executrix
heirs
holographic will
inheritance tax
intestate
nuncupative will
publication
soldier's or sailor's will
testator
testatrix
trust
will

1. A woman appointed by the court to manage the estate of a person who died without a valid will.
2. A handwritten will.
3. A gift of personal property through a will.
4. A man who makes a will.
5. A formal amendment to a will.
6. The property owned by a decedent at death.
7. A woman named in a will to manage an estate of a decedent.
8. An enforceable oral will, valid only for personal property.
9. A gift of real property through a will.
10. One who receives either real or personal property under a will.

Reviewing Important Points

1. The general requirements of a formal will are (a) that the maker have testamentary intent, (b) that the maker have testamentary capacity, and (c) that the will be in writing and be signed by the testator. In most states, the will must also be witnessed and, usually, subscribed by the witnesses.
2. One must execute a will in the manner required by law. This usually requires qualified legal assistance.
3. Since a will does not become effective until after the death of a testator, it can be revoked or changed at any time prior to the testator's death.
4. Creditors' rights to be paid just claims and the rights of a surviving spouse to a share of the estate may not be defeated by a will which attempts to give the property to others.
5. The will may appoint an executor to distribute the property of the deceased according to the terms of the will. When the named executor cannot or will not serve, when the will does not name an executor, or when there is no will, the property is distributed by an administrator or administratrix appointed by the court.

Applying Law to Everyday Life

1. Ray did not get along well with the members of his family. Although he was quite wealthy, he did not want his family to receive any of his property when he died. He told this to the members of his family, his friends, and his coworkers. He died unexpectedly in an automobile accident. He did not have a will. How will his estate be distributed?

2. The Corleys had placed their father in a nursing home because of his need for medical attention. When the nursing home called a member of the family to say that the father was near death, the family decided to have the father execute a will. When the family arrived, they discovered that the father was weak and heavily sedated with drugs. Although conscious, he

was unaware of what was happening around him. One of his daughters placed a pen in his hand and told him to sign the document. He did so. Does this create a valid will?

3. Sid went to his attorney's office and described in detail how he wanted his estate distributed upon his death. The lawyer made extensive notes and prepared a 12-page will. He called Sid and read it to him over the phone. Sid made a few minor changes. After the will was revised, the lawyer arranged an appointment to have the will subscribed and attested to in accordance with the laws of the state. On his way to the appointment, Sid died of a heart attack. Will Sid's estate be distributed according to his wishes or in some other manner?

4. Toa was ill. She did not think she could afford an attorney, so she sat down and wrote on notebook paper what she wanted done with all of her property upon her death. She signed at the end of the document in front of four neighbors who also signed as witnesses. Will Toa's estate be distributed according to her wishes or in some other manner?

5. Hilda executed a will on the first day of January. On the first day of June she executed a second will which contained many provisions in conflict with the first will. She died on the first day of December. Which will governs the distribution of her estate?

6. Eric executed a valid will dividing his property among his wife and three children. The will was not altered for 22 years. Then Eric became furious with his wife. He wrote a second will which left all of his property to their children. After Eric's death, his wife sued to receive a share of his estate. Will she succeed?

7. Simon died without leaving a will. He was survived by his three children. Two were independently wealthy while the third suffered from an incapacitating disease which made it impossible for her to work. How will Simon's estate be distributed among his three children? Do you think this is just?

Solving Case Problems

1. Ralph Mangan was wounded by a gunshot in 1971. He was hospitalized and then moved to a nursing home. There he executed a will dated February 23, 1972. After his release from the nursing home, he was cared for by his brother for a short time. Because of Ralph's advanced age and medical problems, he was again hospitalized. In May of 1972 he returned to the nursing home and in June was adjudicated incompetent. He died in August of 1972. His will was filed for probate and was contested on the grounds that Ralph was disoriented because of his advanced age, heart disease, and the gunshot wound. The will left property to someone described as a nephew when there was no such nephew. Witnesses testified that during

Ralph's first stay in the nursing home he was self-reliant and was able to handle his own business affairs. Ralph's attorney testified that Ralph appeared to be of sound mind at the time he executed the will. Ralph had discussed the details of the will with the attorney and had mentioned a number of nephews, cousins, and other distant relatives. Ralph's physicians testified that Ralph had periods of disorientation and periods of lucidity. Is Ralph's will valid? (*Edward L. Mangan v. Joseph J. Mangan, Jr.*, 554 S.W.2d 418, Mo.)

2. Victor and Agnes, husband and wife, executed a will in 1975 leaving their property to each other and, after the deaths of both, to various relatives. Agnes died and Victor inherited her interest in their property. A niece, Sandra Cook, lived next door to Victor and she began caring for him after Agnes's death. Sandra and her family moved into Victor's house. In 1976 Sandra used Victor's money to buy a new car and a Jeep. She said Victor gave her the money because her car could not get to and from the house during the winter. Later, Victor contacted an attorney about making a new will. Victor visited the attorney's office twice and Sandra was present. On the second visit, Sandra read the will to Victor, then he went into another room without her. There, in front of witnesses, he executed the will, which left all of Victor's estate to Sandra. Sandra said that Victor was upset with his other relatives because they planned to put him into a nursing home. Other relatives testified that there were never any plans to do that. Sandra admitted that she had told Victor that the other relatives did plan to place him in a nursing home. Victor died in 1978, and the 1976 will was filed for probate. The other relatives protested, asserting undue influence. Who prevails? (*Cook v. Loftus*, 414 N.E.2d 581, Ind.)

3. Wallace Kelley executed a will which disinherited all of his heirs at law because "They are capable of caring for themselves." The will was witnessed by three persons, including the person named in the will as the executor. The statute on witnessing wills in that state provided that there must be three witnesses who are not benefitted by the will. A provision in the will stated, "I direct my executor to dispose of my clothing and other personal articles and effects as he in his sole discretion may deem best." The heirs at law challenged the validity of the will on the grounds that it had not been properly witnessed. Who prevails? (*In re Kelley's Estate*, 92 A.2d 724, Me.)

4. Eugene Kraus executed two wills, one in 1964 and the other in 1973. In 1975 Eugene directed the attorney who had prepared the latest will to tear it up because Eugene planned to have a new will prepared. The attorney did as he was instructed. However, Eugene died before he had the opportunity to execute the new will. Both the 1964 will and a copy of the 1973 will were filed for probate. Which of these, if either, is Eugene's will? (*In re Eugene Kraus*, 385 N.Y.S.2d 933)

Unit Ten
UNDERSTANDING BUSINESS ORGANIZATION

UNIT OBJECTIVES

UPON COMPLETION OF THIS UNIT, you should be able to

1. explain what a sole proprietorship is and why it is the most numerous form of business organization.
2. explain what a partnership is and why one should be particularly careful in selecting a general partner.
3. explain what a limited partnership is and why it appeals to busy investors who lack the time and/or ability to participate in management of the business.
4. distinguish among the decisions in a general partnership which one partner may make, which a majority may make, and which all must share in making.
5. appreciate the importance of careful preparation of a clear and complete written partnership agreement.
6. appreciate the importance of profit-seeking corporations in our economy.
7. discuss the advantages and disadvantages of the corporate form of organization.
8. explain how the Subchapter S corporation avoids double taxation yet enjoys corporate advantages.
9. define bonds, common stock, and preferred stock.
10. discuss how the corporate structure is often used effectively for nonprofit organizations.
11. discuss the roles of shareholders, directors, officers, and other employees in the operation of a corporation.
12. understand the importance of the shareholder's right to vote for directors and on important issues, even if done by proxy.

38

Sole Proprietorships and Partnerships

1. At the end of the school year, you buy more than 100 books from other students. During the summer, you clean all the books and rebind some. In September, you sell them at a profit to incoming students. What legal form of business organization are you probably using?
2. Three friends take auto shop in school. The following summer, they combine their savings and buy three old cars of the same make from an automobile dismantling company. They plan to use the best parts to produce two cars. Their expenses, excluding their labor, would total \$1,200. If they sell the two cars for a total of \$3,600, how would the money be divided? What if they decide that not even one running model can be built and they sell the old cars as junk, receiving only \$75?
3. Four partners own a profitable chain of one-hour film processing shops. One partner is seriously injured in a motorcycle accident and is permanently disabled. Is the partnership automatically dissolved because one partner can no longer work?

WHAT IS A SOLE PROPRIETORSHIP?

PROBLEM: Sico wants to open a sporting goods store. She hesitates because she thinks the expenses would be prohibitive. She lists the costs of renting or buying a store, hiring help, buying a computer to keep records, buying a large inventory, obtaining a charter from the state, and paying for licenses and legal fees. Are her fears justified?

There are three principal forms of business organization: (1) the sole proprietorship, (2) the partnership, and (3) the corporation.

sole proprietorship: business owned and controlled by one person

Of the three, the simplest, most flexible, and easiest to start is the **sole proprietorship**, which is owned by one person. The owner has relatively unlimited control over the business and keeps all the profits. However, the sole proprietor (owner) also has unlimited personal responsibility for the losses, debts, and liabilities that the business may incur. In case of breach of contract or tort, nonexempt personal property as well as the business property of the owner may be taken to pay judgments for damages awarded by courts.

Sole proprietorships are by far the most numerous form of business organization. Although corporations are fewer in number, they have a much larger sales dollar volume and employ more workers.

There are no particular legal requirements for organizing or conducting a sole proprietorship. When started, many sole proprietorships are conducted out of the owner's home, garage, or van. No help need be hired, no computer is required for the simple records, and inventory may be limited and may often be purchased on credit. No charter is needed from the state, although a local business license, and perhaps a permit to collect sales taxes for transmittal to the state, may be required. Some types of businesses, such as those selling food or securities, are subject to special government regulations regardless of the legal form of organization. Thus, in the problem, Sico's fears are not justified. She should, of course, make a simple survey of the market and be satisfied that she has the ability, energy, capital, and other requisites for success. Usually it is desirable to have experience as an employee in a similar business.

WHAT IS A PARTNERSHIP?

PROBLEM: Ward and Chang organized and operated the Cinema Theater. They agreed to share profits and losses equally after paying all expenses. The land was leased from Allen for rent which was to be 6 percent of the gross revenue. Chalmer was hired as manager for $1,000 a month plus 3 percent of the net profits. Are all four partners in the business?

According to the Uniform Partnership Act (UPA), which is in force in all states except Georgia and Louisiana, a **partnership** is an association of two or more persons to carry on, as co-owners, a business for profit. A partnership is based upon a voluntary agreement of the persons, who are called **general partners** and who are liable for all debts of their firm. In the problem, Ward and Chang were partners, but the others were not. Neither Allen nor Chalmer owned part of the business. Their sharing of the gross revenue or net profits was merely a method of paying them rent and salary.

partnership: association of two or more persons to carry on, as co-owners, a business for profit

general partners: persons associated as co-owners to carry on a business for profit, and who are liable for all firm debts

The agreement of the partners need not be in writing unless required by the statute of frauds. The statute of frauds requires a writing if a contract cannot be performed within one year from the time it is made. Therefore if the partners agree at the time they form the partnership that the firm is to last longer than one year, the partnership agreement must be in writing to be enforceable. If the partners do not agree on a specific length of time the partnership is to continue, the firm may continue for more than one year based on a verbal agreement. It is always desirable to put the partnership agreement in writing. Doing so encourages thoughtful review of the many problems of a new business and helps to avoid future controversies over rights and duties.

The document containing terms of the agreement is called the **partnership agreement** (or articles of partnership). A qualified lawyer should draft the document.

partnership agreement: document containing the terms and conditions of the partnership

Partnerships can combine and control the capital, labor, skill, and knowledge of two or more persons. Thus, more resources usually are available to a partnership than to a sole proprietorship. Unique abilities are harnessed and utilized through specialization. Partnerships are more flexible and are subject to fewer regulations than corporations.

In a partnership, there is a close relationship and a necessarily heavy reliance of each partner on the others. Moreover, any partner can bind the partnership by contract or incur liability by torts, and all general partners are liable without limit for firm debts. Accordingly, it is usually important that one choose partners who are socially compatible, financially responsible, morally trustworthy, professionally competent, physically fit, and industrious.

Kirk and Kevin had been buddies since kindergarten. After graduation from college, both spent years as sales representatives in Europe. Kirk cultivated a knowledge of French language and business practices, while Kevin became fluent in Spanish and became familiar with Spanish business practices. When Kirk and Kevin returned to the United States, they formed the K & K Company, an export-import trading partnership. It ended within a year because Kirk was constantly in trouble with personal creditors and kept proposing ways to evade export and import laws to boost profits. Kevin, on the other hand, was almost always "last-in and first-out" from their office and resisted any change or expansion.

Under the UPA, a partnership is considered in some respects to be an entity, a single unit that

1. may take title to, and transfer property in its own name;
2. is regarded as a principal, for which each partner may act as agent, making contracts in the firm name; and
3. must use its own assets to pay its creditors before any individual partner's assets may be seized.

For most purposes, a partnership is considered to be an aggregation or group of individual partners. Thus:

1. each partner must pay income taxes on his or her share of the net profit even if it is not distributed. (The firm merely files an information return);
2. the firm, in the absence of a permissive statute, must sue and be sued in the name of all the partners;
3. all debts of the firm not paid out of firm assets are chargeable to every partner;
4. when any partner drops out of the firm for any reason, the partnership is dissolved. (However, prior arrangements can be made to continue operations without interruption).

Persons often join together for social, political, charitable, educational, or general welfare purposes. They do not conduct business for profit, although they may raise money for their activities. Examples are churches, private schools, civic clubs, fraternities and sororities, labor unions, and volunteer fire departments. Such groups may be unincorporated, nonprofit associations. Participating members generally are not liable for debts of the organization. Officers and individual members may voluntarily guarantee its debts. Sometimes such groups organize as nonprofit corporations.

WHAT ARE THE KINDS OF PARTNERSHIPS AND PARTNERS?

PROBLEM: Avery invested $100,000 as a limited partner in a partnership organized to operate an amusement park. On opening day, an accident on a roller coaster severely injured 17 people. The damages awarded to the accident victims totaled nearly $7 million. That amount far exceeded the value of the partnership's assets and insurance coverage. Will Avery be held liable for unpaid liability claims against the partnership?

Partnerships may be classified according to their purpose and according to the extent of the liability of the partners. Classified by purpose, partnerships are either trading or nontrading and are either general or special. A **trading partnership** buys and sells goods and services commercially. A **nontrading partnership** provides professional and noncommercial assistance, such as legal, medical, or accounting advice. A general partnership conducts a general business such as a retail store; a **special partnership** may be formed for a single transaction, such as the purchase and resale of a farm.

Sometimes a construction project (for example, a large dam, bridge, or office building) is too big for a single firm. Two or more firms may then associate, combining their resources in a **joint venture** to complete one complex project only. Because the joint venture is so similar to a partnership, which also may be formed to complete a single job, many courts treat it as such. Another example of a joint venture is a group of individual investors combining their capital and time to acquire a large tract of land to develop for homes. Death of a member does not dissolve the venture; the venture normally continues until the intended project is finished.

Classified by extent of liability of partners, partnerships are either general or limited. In a **general partnership**, all the partners assume full personal liability for debts of the firm, as does a sole proprietor. In a **limited partnership**, at least one partner must be a general partner, with unlimited liability. However, one or more partners may be **limited partners** who are liable only to the extent of their investment in the business.

The Uniform Limited Partnership Act (ULPA) has been adopted (as written or substantially) in all states except Georgia and Louisiana. Unlike a general partnership, a limited partnership can be created only by proper execution, recording, and publication of a

trading partnership: formed to buy and to sell commercially

nontrading partnership: formed for a professional and noncommercial purpose

special partnership: formed to carry out a single transaction

joint venture: association of two or more firms or persons to do a single project

general partnership: partnership in which all partners are fully liable; also, a partnership formed to conduct a general business

limited partnership: partnership in which certain partners have limited liability

limited partner: partner who is not active in management and who has limited liability

certificate stating essential facts about the agreement and identifying the partners. Limited partners contribute capital and share profits and losses with general partners. Because limited partners do not share in the managerial control of the business, their liability for firm debts and losses is limited to the amount of capital they invest. Limited partners who participate in management lose their status and become liable without limit as general partners.

This rule has been relaxed and defined by the Revised Uniform Limited Partnership Act (RULPA), which has been adopted by eleven states as of the writing of this edition.[1]

In the problem, then, presuming that the limited partnership had been properly formed and that Avery had not participated in the management of the business, she would be liable only to the extent of her $100,000 investment.

silent partner: partner who may be known to the public but is not active in management

secret partner: partner who is not known to the public but is active in management

dormant partner: partner who is neither known to the public nor active in management

nominal partner: person who is held out as a partner but is not one

General partners may be further classified as silent, secret, or dormant. A **silent partner** may be known to the public as a partner but takes no active part in management. A **secret partner** is not known to the public as a partner yet participates in management. A **dormant partner** is neither known to the public as a partner nor active in management. All such partners are liable without limit for partnership debts. A **nominal partner** is not a partner. However, such persons hold themselves out as partners, or let others do so. Consequently, if a partnership liability arises, they are liable as partners. A third party, acting in good faith, may rely on the nominal partner and extend credit to the firm. If so, all partners who consented to the misrepresentation are fully liable, on the legal theory of estoppel. If all members consent, the firm is liable. Parents sometimes become nominal partners to assist children who have taken over the family business.

A minor who enters into a partnership agreement generally has special status. In most states, such a partner loses none of the rights and privileges of a minor. Thus, the minor normally can plead minority as a defense if sued by a creditor of the partnership. The minor may also withdraw and thus dissolve the partnership without being liable for breach of contract. Some states do, however, hold a minor liable on contracts made in connection with a business as an individual proprietor or as a partner.

---

[1]As of the writing of this edition, the RULPA has been adopted in Arkansas, California, Colorado, Connecticut, Maryland, Minnesota, Montana, Nebraska, Washington, West Virginia, and Wyoming.

WHAT ARE THE DUTIES OF A PARTNER?

PROBLEM: Fineman was one of five partners in a firm of certified public accountants. Her duties included management of the office. As such, she bought all office equipment. Recently she purchased an advanced word processing system for $25,000, a competitive price. Several days later, she met the seller, Fisher, at a dinner party. Fineman convinced Fisher to give her a 5 percent discount on the price because clients of the CPA firm might be inclined to buy similar equipment when they learned of its use from her. Fineman now claims the $1,250 discount belongs to her alone because she obtained it on her own time after the original contract was signed. Is she right?

By law or agreement each partner must carry out the duties of:

1. Adhering to the Partnership Agreement and Decisions

Each partner must comply with the partnership agreement including later provisions properly added and decisions properly made.

2. Using Reasonable Care

In performing partnership duties, each partner is expected to use reasonable care. However, he or she is not personally liable for honest mistakes, for errors of judgment, or for incompetence, however costly.

3. Acting with Integrity and Good Faith

A partnership is a relationship of utmost trust and confidence. Each partner is legally bound to act with the highest integrity and good faith—always being loyal to the interest of the firm—in dealing with the other partner(s). No partner may personally retain any benefit or profit unless, of course, the other partners consent. In the problem, Fineman was wrong in her claim to the discount. All profits or benefits flowing from firm business belong to the firm.

4. Refraining from Participating in Competitive Business

Unless there is a contrary agreement, a partner may not do any business that competes with the partnership or prevents performance of duties to the firm. A partner may, however, attend to personal affairs for profit, as long as the firm's business is not sacrificed. A partner who withdraws from the firm may compete with it unless validly prohibited by the partnership agreement.

5. Keeping Accurate Records

A partner should keep accurate records of all transactions done for the firm and give the firm all money belonging to it. Moreover, every partner should disclose to the other partner(s) all important information that concerns the firm's business.

WHAT RIGHTS DO THE PARTNERS HAVE AS OWNERS?

PROBLEM: Palm, a partner in the Bobbin' Cork Bait Shops, normally purchased the inventory for the business. Unknown to her, the other three partners voted to no longer deal with Trout Attractions, Inc., one of their main suppliers. Before finding out about their decision, Palm contracted for $1,000 worth of lures from Trout. Is the partnership bound by the contract?

In the absence of contrary agreement, legal rights of partners are shared equally. Partners may, however, agree as to who shall have particular rights and duties. The principal rights are:

1. Right to Participate in Management

Every partner, as a co-owner of the business, has an equal right to participate in its management. Acting alone, a partner may buy, sell, hire, fire, and make other routine decisions in carrying on the ordinary day-to-day activities of the firm. In effect, each partner acts as an agent for the firm and for the other partners (see Unit 6). All are bound unless, of course, the partner lacked the necessary authority, and the person with whom the contract was made knew this. In the problem, the $1,000 contract resulted from a routine decision by Palm, a partner with apparent authority. As a consequence, the partnership is bound.

In addition to routine decisions, each partner may do the things normally done by managers in similar firms. This includes the right to inspect the partnership books at all times, unless otherwise agreed.

When a difference of opinion arises as to ordinary matters connected with the business, a majority vote of the partners decides the issue. Unless otherwise agreed, each partner has one vote regardless of the amount of capital contributed. If there is an even number of partners and they split equally on a question, no action can be taken. A pattern of such deadlocks can eventually lead to dissolution. To forestall such an outcome, it is often helpful to provide in the partnership agreement that deadlocks over specified matters shall be settled by arbitration.

For several years, Gohegan and Briddle had been partners in Dealing In Wheeling, a bicycle retail and repair business. Gohegan wanted to hire two well-qualified mechanics in order to divide the shop work and to give the partners more time for sales promotion. Briddle objected, saying "If you hire; I'll fire . . . We can't afford it now." With the partners deadlocked, no one was hired.

Unanimous agreement of all the partners is required to make any change, however minor, in the written partnership agreement. All partners must also agree to any fundamental change that affects the very nature of the business, for example, changing its principal activity or location. In addition, under the Uniform Partnership Act, unanimous agreement is required for decisions to:

a. assign partnership property to creditors,
b. **confess judgment** (allow a plaintiff to obtain a judgment against the firm without a trial),
c. submit a partnership claim or liability to arbitration, and
d. do any act which would make it impossible to carry on the business.

confess judgment: to allow a plaintiff to obtain a judgment without a trial

The preceding rules which govern the use of managerial authority may be changed by agreement. Often it is agreed that certain partners will have exclusive control over specific activities, such as selling and purchasing or accounting and finance. By specializing according to talents and interests, work is divided and efficiency is increased.

2. Right to Profits

PROBLEM: Laird and Ball were partners in an indoor tennis center. Laird, a wealthy surgeon, contributed all the capital. Ball, a former tennis champion with an international reputation, contributed her name and agreed to work full time at the center. They agreed to split the profits equally. The losses, however, were all to be charged to Laird. Can the partners legally receive different proportions of the losses than the profits?

Partners are entitled to all profits earned. In the absence of contrary agreement, both profits and losses are shared equally regardless of different amounts of capital contributed or time spent. However, the partners may agree to divide the profits and/or the losses in any percentages desired. Often, as in the problem, profits will be shared equally, but a partner with a large amount of outside income may agree, for tax purposes, to take all the losses. Outsiders, however, are not bound by such internal agreements and may hold any or all general partners liable without limit for all partnership debts.

3. Right in Partnership Property

PROBLEM: Adams, Starnes, and Williams were partners in a burglar and fire alarm service. Adams would mount his own camper cabin on the back of one of the company's pickup trucks every weekend and drive it into the country on overnight fishing trips. Starnes would take the company's word processing machine home every weekend to work on her version of the "great American novel." On weekends, Williams used the company's duplicating machine to run off copies of the weekly bulletins for his church. No partner was aware of any other partner's action. Did each have a legal right to borrow the firm's equipment?

tenancy in partnership: co-ownership of firm's property by partners

Partnership property consists of all cash and other property originally contributed by the partners as well as all property later acquired for the firm or with the firm's funds. Such property is held in a special form of co-ownership called **tenancy in partnership.** In such a tenancy, each partner is a co-owner of the entire partnership property and is not the sole owner of any part of it. For example, if a firm of two partners owns two identical trucks, one partner may not claim exclusive ownership of either one of the vehicles. Therefore a partner has no saleable or assignable interest in any particular item of property belonging to the partnership. However, the interest of a partner *in the firm* may be sold or assigned to another party. The buyer or assignee is not a partner but is entitled to the partner's share of the profits, and of the assets upon dissolution.

Each partner has an equal right to use firm property for partnership purposes, but no partner may use firm property for personal purposes unless all other partners consent. Accordingly, in the problem, all three partners were violating their duties to the firm. The breach of one did not excuse the breach of any other.

4. Right to Extra Compensation

PROBLEM: Hudson, De Soto, and Auburn were partners in an advertising agency. Hudson, who spent days playing golf, tennis, or raquetball with prospective clients and friends, brought in most of the firm's accounts. De Soto, a brilliant artist and copywriter, did most of the actual production and often worked ten-hour days as well as weekends. Auburn, who had no creative talent and little energy, spent most of his time delivering and picking up copy and layouts. Are Hudson and De Soto entitled to a larger share of the profits than Auburn?

A partner who invests more capital, brings in more business, or works longer and harder than associates is entitled to no extra pay or share of the profits—unless all the partners so agree. Thus, in the problem, Hudson and De Soto get no more than Auburn, unless all so agree. Common sense and fairness often dictate that a partner who gives more should receive more, but this must be agreed to by all.

WHAT AUTHORITY DOES A PARTNER HAVE?

PROBLEM: Aki, Degas, and Kline were partners in an air-conditioning business. They obtained a $275,000 contract to install units in a candy factory. Long before the job was finished, Kline accepted the final payment of $100,000 and absconded with the money. Must Aki and Degas absorb the loss and complete the job for the $175,000 already paid to them, without being paid an additional $100,000 by the candy factory?

Unless otherwise agreed, each partner has an equal right to participate in management and act as an agent for the firm. Generally the law implies to each member the authority necessary to carry on the business. This includes the right to:

1. Make Binding Contracts for the Firm

Acting within the scope of the particular business, each partner can make binding contracts deemed necessary or desirable, regardless of the possible folly of the deals. Any internal agreement limiting powers of a partner is binding on the partners, but not on third parties who do not know about the limitation. However, a partner who violates such internal agreement is liable to the other partners for any resulting loss. Of course, no partner can bind the firm in contracts which are beyond the scope of the firm's business as publicly disclosed. Partners engaged in an aerial photography business, for example, would not be bound by a contract by one of the partners to use the plane for air ambulance service. Even if a partner has acted beyond authority in making a contract, the other partners may choose to ratify the act. If they do, the partnership is bound as a principal would be in an ordinary agency.

2. Receive Money Owed to the Firm and Settle Claims against the Firm

All partners are bound by payments received, even if the recipient steals the money. Also, each partner may adjust debts of the firm by agreement with creditors. Each may compromise firm claims against debtors, settling for less than is due. Understandably, however, a partner may not discharge a personal debt by agreeing to offset it against a debt owed to the partnership. In the problem, the partnership claim against the factory owners ended when Kline accepted the final payment. Aki and Degas must complete the job. Their claim is against Kline if he can be found.

3. Borrow Money in the Firm Name

In a trading partnership, any partner can borrow for partnership purposes. In such borrowing, the partner can execute promissory notes binding the firm and can pledge or mortgage partnership property as security. Partners in a nontrading partnership generally do not have such power.

4. Sell

A partner can sell in the regular course of business any of the firm's goods and give customary warranties. Acting alone, however, a partner may not sell the entire inventory in a bulk transfer because this could end the business.

5. Buy

Any partner can buy for cash or credit any property within the scope of the business.

6. Draw and Cash Checks and Drafts

A partner can draw checks and drafts for partnership purposes and indorse and cash checks payable to the firm.

7. Hire and Fire Employees and Agents

Each partner has the authority to hire and fire employees and agents to help carry on the business.

8. Receive Notice of Matters Affecting the Partnership

When one partner is served with a summons and complaint against the firm, all are deemed to have received the notice, even if not informed. Likewise, one partner's declarations and admissions in carrying on the business bind all partners even when contrary to the best interests of the firm.

WHAT ARE A PARTNER'S LIABILITIES?

PROBLEM: Pinell and Cotter were in the business of buying and selling used farm equipment. They had privately agreed that Cotter would do all the buying because he was a better judge of value. Nevertheless, one day Pinell had a golden opportunity to buy all the equipment of an elderly farmer who was retiring. Pinell and the farmer agreed on a price and completed the sale. Is the firm bound?

Among themselves, partners may make any agreement they so choose with regard to authority in running the business. Others, however, may not be aware of such internal agreements. If so, the partnership and all partners are liable without limit for all obligations of the firm which arise out of contracts made by any partner within the scope of the firm's business. Thus, in the problem, the firm and both partners are bound. If a loss results, Cotter could seek recovery from Pinell because Pinell violated their agreement.

The partnership and all partners are liable when any partner commits a tort (for example, negligence or fraud) while acting within the ordinary course of the business. The wrongdoer would be obligated to indemnify the partnership for any damages it had to pay to the injured party. Of course, if the other partners had authorized or participated in the tort, all would share the blame and no indemnity would be payable. Liability for certain crimes committed in the course of business, such as selling alcoholic beverages to minors, is also imposed on the partnership and all the partners. Generally, however, if the business of the firm does not as a matter of necessity involve the criminal activity, neither the partnership nor the partners who do not authorize or take part in the crime will be held criminally liable. Thus, a partner who kills a pedestrian while negligently driving a company car on firm business will alone be criminally liable. However, both the wrongdoer and the firm and other partners will be *civilly* liable for damages.

When a judgment is obtained against a partnership, and the partnership assets are exhausted, the individually owned property of the general partners may be seized and sold under process of law for the satisfaction of the debt. Creditors of the individual partners, however, have first claim to such property. Any partner who pays an obligation of the firm with personal assets is entitled to recover a proportionate share from each of the other partners.

A partner cannot escape responsibility for firm debts by withdrawing from the partnership. After withdrawing, one remains liable for all debts incurred while a member. A new partner who joins the firm is liable for both existing and new debts of the business. However, creditors with claims which arose before the new partner joined the firm cannot seize the new partner's nonbusiness property. Such creditors are limited to action against the new partner's share of partnership property.

HOW IS A PARTNERSHIP ENDED?

dissolution: when any partner ceases association in carrying on the business

winding-up period: time during which all business affairs of a partnership are concluded

PROBLEM: Paradiso is a partner in a highly successful firm of certified public accountants. She becomes liable for very heavy damages as the result of an automobile accident while vacationing. She therefore files for bankruptcy and has these and other debts discharged. What effect will this have on the partnership?

When any partner ceases to be associated in the ordinary carrying on of the business, **dissolution** occurs. Dissolution is normally followed by a **winding-up period** which concludes with the actual

termination or ending of the partnership. During the winding-up period, all partnership business in process at the time of dissolution is finished, creditors of the business are satisfied if possible, and each partner's share is accounted for and distributed. When the winding-up process is completed, termination of the legal existence of the partnership actually occurs.

termination: actual legal ending of a partnership

Probably the most common reasons for dissolution are the death or withdrawal of a partner. Often the business is thriving and the remaining partner(s) would prefer to continue without interruption. Therefore partnership agreements, especially in large professional firms, often provide that there shall be no dissolution under such circumstances. This is permitted by statute in a number of states. The survivors continue as partners and simply pay a previously agreed sum to the former partner or that partner's estate for his or her share of the net assets.

Dissolution also often occurs because the agreed term of the partnership's life has ended. Whatever the cause of dissolution, surviving partners may agree to continue as a new partnership without going through the costly formalities of winding up the old one.

Zeno, Smith, and Caspit were partners in Fly by Night, an overnight mail and small parcel airline. When they formed the partnership, the three provided in the partnership agreement for the continuance of the business even in the event of the death of a partner. They did this by agreeing that should one of them die, the others would form a new partnership to continue the business under the same name. In addition, they provided for the proper valuation of the deceased partner's share and a timetable under which the share's value was to be paid to the deceased partner's estate.

Dissolution of a partnership may be caused by any of the following:

1. Action of One or More of the Partners

A partnership may be dissolved by agreement of the parties. For example, if the original agreement is for one year, the partnership concludes at the end of that year. Sometimes a firm is organized for a specific purpose, such as the development of a large tract of farm land into a subdivision for houses. Sale of the last lot and house would end the partnership. Also, as in any contract, the parties may unanimously agree at any time to terminate their relationship.

partnership at will: partnership in which a partner may withdraw at any time without liability

Withdrawal of any partner dissolves the partnership. If the agreement permits such withdrawal, possibly after some reasonable notice, the withdrawing partner would not be liable to those who remain. If withdrawal violates the agreement, however, the withdrawing partner is liable to the others in damages for any injury resulting from the breach. If the organization is a **partnership at will,** a partner normally may withdraw at any time without liability to associates. Under unusual circumstances, the partner could be liable if the sudden withdrawal was unreasonable and did irreparable damage to the firm.

2. Operation of Law

Death of any partner dissolves the partnership. This is a serious disadvantage of the partnership form of organization. Prudent partners anticipate this event and agree upon steps to take when it happens. For example, they may agree that the surviving partner(s) will continue with a new firm and pay for the decedent's share over a period of years. Bankruptcy, a kind of financial death, also automatically dissolves the partnership. This is true whether the bankruptcy is suffered by any of the partners (such as Paradiso in the problem) or by the firm itself. Although uncommon, subsequent illegality also dissolves the partnership. For example a professional partnership of doctors would be dissolved if any member lost the license to practice.

3. Court Decree

Partners, if living, usually arrange for dissolution privately. If necessary, however, one partner may petition a court to order dissolution if another partner has become insane, is otherwise incapacitated, or is guilty of serious misconduct affecting the business. Also a court may act if continuation is impracticable, or if the firm is continuously losing money and there is little or no prospect of success. This could happen, for example, when there are irreconcilable differences between the partners.

PREVENTING LEGAL DIFFICULTIES

Before Going into Business for Yourself . . .

be reasonably sure that your formal education and experience (preferably in a similar established business) have prepared you to do a competent job.

If You Are Starting a Partnership . . .

1. be sure to comply with applicable licensing, registration, and other legal requirements;
2. put the partnership agreement in writing, with the aid of a qualified lawyer. Include appropriate language covering each partner's:
   a. duties and authority,
   b. share of profits and losses, if not intended to be equal,
   c. salary or right to withdraw earnings (drawing account),
   d. vacation and sick-leave rights, and
   e. rights to withdraw;
3. in the agreement, include provisions covering:
   a. periodic valuation of each partner's interest,
   b. methods for raising additional capital,
   c. addition of new partners,
   d. amicable resolution of disputes, as by arbitration, and
   e. possible continuation of the business after dissolution.

Strengthening Your Legal Vocabulary

confess judgment
dissolution
dormant partner
general partners
general partnership
joint venture
limited partner
limited partnership
nominal partner
nontrading partnership
partnership
partnership agreement
partnership at will
secret partner
silent partner
sole proprietorship
special partnership
tenancy in partnership
termination
trading partnership
winding-up period

1. Time during which all business affairs of a partnership are concluded.
2. Persons who associate as co-owners to carry on a business for profit, and who are liable for all firm debts.
3. Partner who is not active in the management and whose liability is limited to the amount of capital invested.
4. Partner who takes no active part in the management of the business but is known to the public as a partner.
5. Legal form of co-ownership of firm property by partners.
6. Actual legal ending of a partnership.
7. When any partner ceases association in carrying on the business.
8. Business which is owned and controlled by one person.
9. Type of partnership in which a partner may withdraw at any time.
10. Association of two or more persons to carry on, as co-owners, a business for profit.

Reviewing Important Points

1. Sole proprietorships are the simplest and most numerous form of business organization. The owner makes all decisions, keeps all the profits, and is liable without limit for all losses.
2. A partnership is an association of two or more persons to carry on, as co-owners, a business for profit. Profits and losses are shared equally unless otherwise agreed. Every general partner is liable without limit to creditors for debts of the business.
3. Unless otherwise agreed, all partners have a right to participate in management with equal authority.
4. Any partner, acting alone, may normally make routine business decisions for the firm. A majority must resolve disputes about ordinary matters. All must unanimously agree on:
   a. changes in the partnership agreement,
   b. fundamental changes in the business of the firm, and
   c. certain matters prescribed by the Uniform Partnership Act.
5. In dealings with one another, partners are bound to act with the highest integrity and good faith. They must keep one another informed about the business, maintain accurate records, and take no secret profits.
6. Partners own firm property as tenants in partnership. Each may use the property for company business but not for personal purposes without consent of the other partners.
7. Limited partnership is a special form in which one or more limited partners contribute capital but not managerial services. The financial liability of a limited partner for debts of the firm cannot exceed the amount of capital such a partner has invested.
8. There must be at least one general partner (with unlimited liability) in a limited partnership.
9. Partnerships may be terminated by:
   a. action of the partners,
   b. operation of law, or
   c. decree of court.

Applying Law to Everyday Life

1. Brinkley, Chapman, and Dodge orally agreed to become partners in a road-paving company. Nothing was said about profits or losses. Brinkley contributed $100,000 in working capital. Chapman contributed used construction equipment with a resale value of $200,000. Dodge, a brilliant civil engineer, contributed no capital. By agreement, Brinkley did no work for the firm, but Chapman and Dodge devoted full-time to the business. (a) A profit of $120,000 was earned during the first year. How should the profit be divided? (b) After ten years, business declines and the firm is dissolved. During the winding-up period, all assets are liquidated. Before the return of invested capital ($300,000) there is only $210,000 in cash. How is the $90,000 loss divided?

2. Gilmore and nine others each invested $10,000 as limited partners in a physical fitness and jazz exercise studio for men and women. Brick, who promoted the business, invested $5,000 as general partner and agreed to manage the studio. An employee improperly explained to a customer how to do bench presses on the exercise machine. As a result, the customer's back was severely injured. What is the extent of possible liability to which each of the partners is exposed?

3. Freeman and Bingham were partners in a wholesale drug company. Their agreement required arbitration of all disputes between the partners. While Freeman was away on a cruise, Stuart, a creditor of the firm, threatened to sue over a disputed supply contract. To save time and money for all concerned, Stuart proposed to avoid litigation by submitting the claim to arbitration. Can Bingham agree to arbitrate without Freeman's approval?

4. Brooke was 17 years old when he entered into a partnership with Beale, age 22. Their agreement to operate a dog training (obedience) school was for three years. After six months, Brooke decided to withdraw. Was he liable for breach of contract?

5. Gary, Mayer, and Solli were general partners in a business that organized fund drives for nonprofit organizations. They received a small percentage of all contributions solicited. When Gary heard of an opportunity to present an outdoor concert by a famous rock group, he proposed that the partners "Do this on our own—we'll make a mint." This went beyond the purposes of the firm as stated in their written agreement. Mayer agreed, but Solli said he would go along only if the others promised to take total responsibility for any liability in case the project failed. They agreed, and the project did fail. As a result, the partnership went bankrupt. Debts exceeded firm assets as well as personal assets of Gary and Mayer. Can creditors seize Solli's personal assets?

6. Jonnas and Schmidt entered into a partnership for five years to conduct a catering business. It proved to be very successful. However, after two years, Schmidt's husband was promoted and transferred by his employer to corporate headquarters in Los Angeles, 2,000 miles away. Schmidt therefore wanted to move. (a) Could she sell out to Topper, a trustworthy, well-qualified assistant, transferring all duties and assigning all her rights, title, and interest in the firm? (b) Could she simply assign her interest to Topper?

7. The written agreement of a professional partnership stated that, during the first year of operations, no partner could draw more than $100 earnings per week, and that no partner could take a vacation. All members would have to rely on personal savings and credit if they needed more funds. The business prospered beyond expectations. After six months, four of the five partners agreed to increase the permitted draw to $200 a week, and three of the five voted to permit up to one week of vacation without pay. Are these modifications legal and binding?

Solving Case Problems

1. Lewis owned a vacant building. He persuaded Dinkelspeel to open and to conduct a business called The Buffet in the property. Together, they purchased furniture, fixtures, and merchandise. They agreed that Dinkelspeel was to run the business and that profits were to be divided equally. The interest of Lewis was not to be disclosed to the public, although he was to raise necessary funds and provide the building space. When the International Association of Credit Men sued both parties for goods sold to The Buffet, Lewis denied liability as a partner. (a) Is he a partner? If so, what kind? (b) If he is a partner, what is his liability? (*International Association of Credit Men v. Lewis, et al.*, 50 Wyo. 380, 62 P.2d 294)

2. On January 1, 1969, Vernon and Engel became partners in a food brokerage business. Later, they disagreed about the way profits were being divided and expenses were being paid. On August 1, 1970, they dissolved the partnership by mutual agreement. Vernon ran the business during the winding-up period. He claimed that Engel had violated their agreement and therefore was not entitled to his share of the profits. Vernon also argued that since he had carried on the business during the winding-up period, Engel was not entitled to any commissions collected during that time. Is Vernon right? (*Engel v. Vernon*, 215 N.W.2d 506)

3. Gast brought suit for back wages against a partnership headed by general partner Petsinger. In order to improve his chances of recovering a court award, Gast maintained that the limited partners in the business were really general partners and were fully liable along with Petsinger. Gast based his claim on the partnership agreement that gave the limited partners the rights and powers to receive distributions of profits and dissolution funds; prevent the transfer of assets of the firm; examine the books and records; attend meetings; hear reports of the general partner; and transfer, sell, or assign their interests to third parties. Should the limited partners in the agreement be considered general partners? (*Gast v. Petsinger*, 228 Pa. Super. 394, 323 A.2d 371)

4. Cooper and Isaacs were partners in a business that sold and distributed janitorial supplies. Their written agreement provided that the partnership "shall continue until terminated by sale of interests, mutual consent, retirement, death or incompetency of a partner." After eight years, Cooper filed an action seeking dissolution because of irreconcilable differences between the partners regarding matters of policy. He also asked for appointment of a receiver to manage the partnership property until the business was wound up. Isaacs claimed such dissolution was in violation of the partnership agreement. Was Cooper's action a wrongful dissolution? (*Cooper v. Isaacs*, 448 F.2d 1202, D.C.)

39

Corporations

1. Several students, all minors, decide to organize a corporation, the Teenagers Trouble-Shooting Company. Can they do so with the ease of forming a partnership?
2. A group of high school teachers are the incorporators, directors, officers, and shareholders of a small corporation that runs boats through the white-water rapids of a nearby river every summer. If a customer is hurt because of the negligence of an employee, who is liable for the damages?
3. As trustees for you, your parents hold 100 shares of stock. Can your parents vote for directors of the corporation in the annual election without going to the meeting which is held in a city far from your home? Could you vote?

WHAT IS A CORPORATION?

PROBLEM: Krug, a prosperous banker, was willing to go into a promising fiberglass boat manufacturing business with Erikson, an engineer. Krug could not devote any time to the business, but she wanted to have some voice on major decisions. Yet she did not want to have unlimited liability if the business should fail. What form of business organization would be appropriate?

corporation: legal entity, created by government grant, existing separate from its owners

A **corporation** is a legal entity (a being) that is created by government grant. Courts speak of the corporation as an *artificial person* with an existence separate from the persons who organize, own, and run it. However, a corporation is created by people and can do nothing without the aid of human agents who act for it.

Most corporations obtain authority to exist as corporations by complying with the incorporation statutes of one of the 50 state governments. Congress, by special legislative act, also creates some corporations (such as the Federal Deposit Insurance Corporation—FDIC) to serve specific national interests.

Although they are far outnumbered by sole proprietorships and partnerships, corporations do most of the business in this country. This is because the corporation has the following attributes which are essential for large-scale enterprises (some of the attributes are attractive to small business ventures, too):

1. Perpetual Life

Unlike the sole proprietorship and the partnership, a corporation is a legal entity separate and distinct from its owners and managers. Therefore it may continue indefinitely if granted a perpetual charter. Many American corporations are more than 100 years old.

2. Limited Liability

Creditors normally cannot collect claims against the corporation from persons who own shares in the corporation. Of course, the corporation itself is liable without limit for its debts; all of its assets may be seized under court order to pay delinquent claims. But the individual stockholders stand to lose only the amount they have invested.[1] It is this limited liability which makes the corporation an appropriate form of business organization for Krug and Erickson in the problem.

3. Transferability of Ownership Interests

A major advantage of the corporate form over the partnership form is the ease of transferring ownership interests. Normally, individual owners can sell their interests in the corporation without disturbing the company's operations or getting the consent of other owners. The stock of most large corporations is traded (bought and sold) on the New York Stock Exchange or the American Stock Exchange. By contacting a stockbroker, any person may buy or sell a reasonable number of shares of any listed stock within minutes when the exchanges are open.

4. Ability to Attract Large Sums of Capital

Because liability is limited to investment, and because owners buy and sell their interests with comparative ease, many persons invest in corporations. Thus, great sums of money are raised. Small and large investments by thousands of persons and institutions are combined to fund the giant corporations.

5. Professional Management

With substantial capital, efficient corporations generally have greater financial strength than do other forms of business organization. This enables corporations to attract superior workers by offering generous salaries and fringe benefits. Moreover, because the corporation is not automatically dissolved by the death of any owner, it usually provides better assurance of continued employment.

In the problem, this advantage would appeal to Erikson, who would probably become a salaried manager. Nevertheless, Krug could participate in major policy decisions as a voting shareholder, and possibly as a director elected by shareholders to oversee the corporation.

---

[1] A stockholder who has not yet paid the full price of the stock may be required to pay the balance due. Also, in a few corporations, such as banks, the stock may be assessable. This means that if the corporation needs money, the directors may call upon each stockholder to contribute, usually up to the price of the share.

WHAT ARE THE DISADVANTAGES OF CORPORATIONS?

PROBLEM: Dorn and several other persons plan to start a business. They reject the partnership form of organization because none of them is willing to become liable without limit for firm debts. They consider the corporate form of organization, but reject it also because they know it could require payment of higher income taxes. Is there an alternative legal form of organization which they could use?

There are some important disadvantages to the corporate form. Net income is taxed by the federal government when earned, and then is taxed again after distribution to the shareholders. Some states also tax the corporation's income, and then the shareholders, on income received. The multiple federal taxation can be avoided by small corporations which elect to be treated as **Subchapter S corporations** under the Internal Revenue Code. To qualify, the corporation can have only one class of stock, and no more than 35 shareholders (husband and wife are considered one), all of whom must be U.S. citizens or resident aliens. For tax purposes only, the business is then treated as a partnership. A Subchapter S corporation would provide a good solution to the problem of Dorn and her associates.

Subchapter S corporation: small corporation taxed as a partnership

It is costlier and more troublesome to organize a corporation than it is to organize a sole proprietorship or partnership (see Figure 39-1). A corporation is subject to extensive regulation of sales of securities to the general public. Juries sometimes tend to favor individuals in legal disputes with corporations. But overall, advantages outweigh disadvantages, especially for big enterprises.

WHAT ARE THE DIFFERENT TYPES OF CORPORATIONS?

PROBLEM: Appleberry, Jackson, and Smythe are urging other members of their urban service club to create a separate organization for a special project. They plan to open a permanent, year-round country farm and camp for underprivileged city children. All farm produce would be used by the campers or given to the poor. All costs would be covered by donations in a fund-raising telethon. Would a corporation be an appropriate form of organization for the group?

Corporations are classified according to their place of incorporation and purpose. If a corporation is chartered in a particular state, it

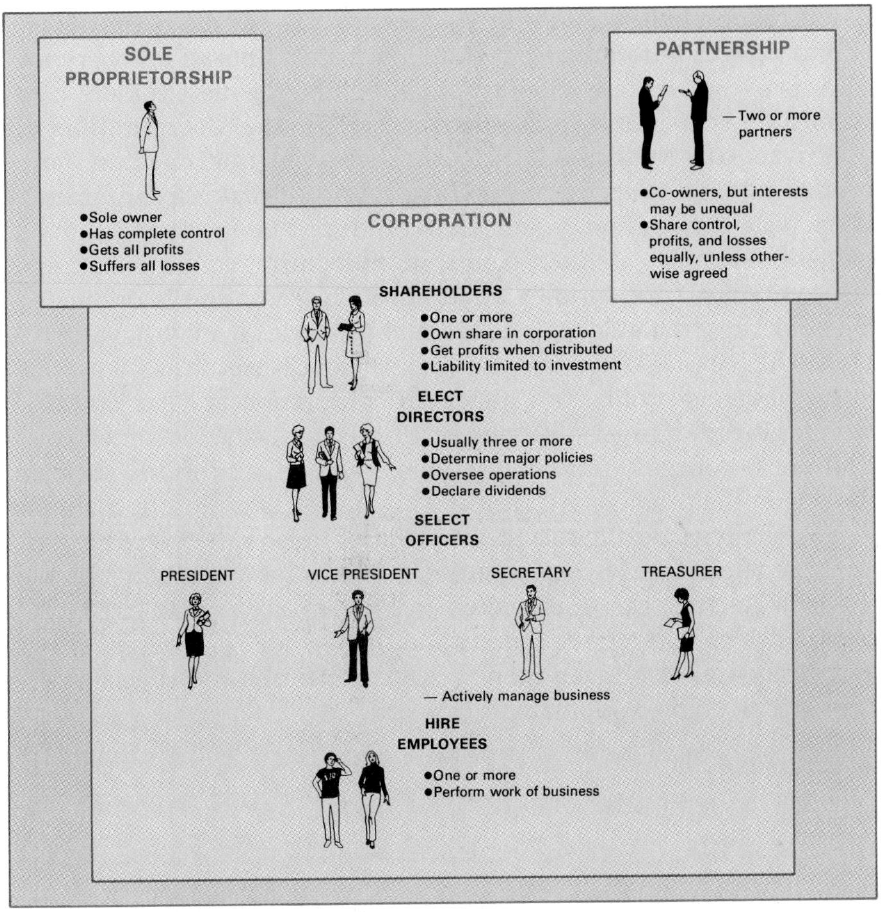

Figure 39-1. Forms of Business Organization

is a **domestic corporation** in that state. Any other corporation doing business in that state is a **foreign corporation** because it was chartered elsewhere.

domestic corporation: chartered in the state in which it is doing business

foreign corporation: chartered in a state other than the one in which it is doing business

> Koba, Ltd., a South Korean corporation, and Tarpon Chasers, Inc., an American corporation incorporated in New Jersey, do business in Florida. Both are foreign corporations in Florida.

public corporation: established for a governmental purpose

private corporation: established by private citizens for a business or charitable purpose

In terms of purpose, a corporation is either public or private. A **public corporation** is established for a governmental purpose. Incorporated cities, state hospitals, and state universities are public corporations. A **private corporation** is established by private citizens for a business or charitable purpose. Sometimes a private corpora-

closely-held corporation: private corporation whose stock is held by one or a few persons

profit-making corporation: private corporation organized to produce a financial profit for its owners

nonprofit corporation: private corporation organized for a social, charitable, or educational purpose; does not return a financial profit to its members

public service corporation: private corporation that provides an essential public service

tion is called public because its stock is broadly owned by the general public. This differentiates it from a private corporation where the stock is owned by only one or a small number of shareholders. The latter type is also known as a **close** or **closely-held corporation**.

Private corporations are further classified as profit-making, nonprofit, and public service corporations. A **profit-making corporation** is a private corporation organized to produce a financial profit for its owners. Examples abound: banks, manufacturing and merchandising companies, and airlines. A **nonprofit corporation** is organized for a social, charitable, or educational purpose. It may have revenues which exceed expenses, but it does not distribute any earnings to members as profits. If a nonprofit corporation engages in business for profit, it must—like any other business—pay income taxes. Churches, colleges, fraternal societies, and organizations such as the one in the problem are typically organized as nonprofit corporations. Finally, a **public service corporation** (also called a *public utility*) is generally a private company that furnishes an essential public service. Electric, gas, and water companies are examples. These companies are closely regulated as to prices they can charge. However, they are often given monopolistic franchises and special powers such as eminent domain.

HOW IS A CORPORATION FORMED?

PROBLEM: Delatronics, Inc., a Delaware corporation, wants to incorporate a subsidiary corporation in another state. The subsidiary will make electronic component parts for Delatronics's products. Could Delatronics serve as an incorporator of another corporation?

promoters: persons who bring together interested persons and take preliminary steps to form a corporation

articles of incorporation: plan submitted to the state as an application for incorporation

Typically, a corporation is formed as a result of the efforts of one or more persons called **promoters**. These individuals bring together interested persons and take the preliminary steps to form a corporation. Regardless of the promoters' efforts, however, the resulting corporation is not liable on any contract made on its behalf. The promoters cannot bind an organization that is still to be created. Usually, though, once it comes into being, the corporation adopts the contracts and is bound by them.

Articles of incorporation are drafted, and when submitted to the proper state official (usually the Secretary of State) they are a plan that serves as an application for incorporation. In most states, when the articles are properly filed, the corporate existence begins. The articles are signed and submitted by one or more persons called **incorporators**. At least one of the incorporators must have legal capacity to enter into a binding contract. Thus, the incorporators cannot all be minors. Either a foreign corporation, such as Delatronics in the problem, or a domestic corporation in a state may be an incorporator. The articles of incorporation are a plan filed by the incorporators and they generally contain:

incorporators: persons who sign and submit the articles of incorporation

1. the name of the corporation;
2. the period of duration, which may be indefinite and everlasting;
3. the purpose, or purposes, for which the corporation is organized. This may be stated broadly, for example: "any purposes legal for a corporation in this state";
4. the number and kinds of shares of capital stock to be authorized for issuance;
5. the location of the proposed corporation's principal office and the name of its agent to whom legal notices may be given;
6. the number of directors or the names and addresses of the persons who are to serve as directors until the first annual meeting of shareholders or until their successors are elected (in some states, the incorporators serve as directors until the shareholders elect their replacements);
7. the name and address of each incorporator; and
8. any other provision consistent with the law.

In some states, the incorporators file a *certificate of incorporation* instead of articles of incorporation, but with the same result. Many years ago, when a corporation was created by a special act of the legislature, a *charter* was issued. Today the word charter refers broadly to the articles (or certificate) of incorporation taken in connection with the governing statutory law. It also may refer to the contract that exists between the state and the corporation.

WHAT ARE SHARES OF STOCK?

PROBLEM: *A* is an incorporator of the newly formed Galaxy Space Research Corporation. *B* is a director. *C* is the president. *D, E,* and *F* are shareholders who own most of the stock. If the corporation buys an electronic microscope, who owns it?

shares of stock: units of ownership in a corporation

shareholder: one who owns corporate stock

stock certificate: written evidence of ownership and rights in a corporation

par value: face value printed on a stock certificate

no-par stock: share with no face value specified

market price: price paid for stock on the market

common stock: basic type of stock, with voting right

dividends: distributions of corporate profits to shareholders

preferred stock: shares with priority claims to dividends and liquidation funds; usually nonvoting

liquidation: sale of corporate assets upon termination

Corporations issue small units of ownership known as **shares of stock**. A person who owns one or more shares of stock is a **shareholder** (also called a *stockholder*).

The corporation uses the money received from the initial sale of stock to buy equipment, supplies, and inventory; to hire labor; and to pay other expenses. As goods and services are produced and sold, more income flows into the business. Often earnings are reinvested. Money is borrowed to provide for further expansion, and sometimes more shares of stock are sold.

A shareholder is issued a **stock certificate**, which is written evidence of ownership and rights in the business. Stock ownership does not transfer title to specific corporate property to the holder. The corporation, as a legal person, remains the owner of all corporate property. Thus, in the problem, Galaxy Corporation owns the electronic microscope.

Stock may have a **par value**, which is the face value printed on the certificate. If it does not have a par value, it is **no-par stock** and is originally sold at a price set by the board of directors of the corporation. When either par or no-par stock changes hands in later transfers, the price may be much higher or lower. This **market price** will be determined by many factors, including economic conditions of the country, the industry, and the company—especially its past profits and future prospects.

Corporations may have one or more types of stock. Those found most frequently are common stock and preferred stock. **Common stock** is the basic type and generally the only kind that allows its owners voting rights in corporate elections. One vote per share may be cast. Common shareholders receive all **dividends** (distributions of corporate profits) unless preferred stock has been issued.

Preferred stock usually lacks voting power but does have priority claim on corporate dividends. For example, by contract with the corporation, the preferred shareholder may be entitled to receive $7 per share each year before any distribution of profits is made to the common shareholders. If profits are high, the common shareholders may get more money than the preferred shareholders. Preferred stock may also have a priority claim on funds generated by a corporate **liquidation** (sale of all assets) if and when the business is terminated.

Preferred stock may be **cumulative**. This means that if the dividend is not paid in a given year, it remains due and payable in the future. Each year the unpaid dividends *cumulate* (add up) and must be paid in full before the common shareholders receive any dividends. In some cases, the preferred stock is also **participating**. For example, in a given year, the fully participating preferred shareholder will receive the contracted amount of dividend per share, and the common shareholder will receive an amount per share equal to that received by a preferred shareholder. Beyond that, any balance of profits distributed is divided equally or in some other specified ratio between the preferred and common shareholders. Most corporations issue little or no preferred stock.

cumulative stock: shares where dividends, if not paid, remain due and payable before common shareholders get anything

participating stock: shares where after regular dividends are received, preferred stockholders share in further distribution of profits with common stockholders

WHO ACTUALLY CONDUCTS THE BUSINESS OF THE CORPORATION?

PROBLEM: Penny was the majority shareholder of the HoarseLion, Inc. Recording Studios. Penny was neither an agent nor an employee of the firm. Supposedly on behalf of HoarseLion, Inc., Penny contracted with Bryant for the installation of a new intercom system in the company headquarters. Did Penny have authority to do this as the majority shareholder?

Although a corporation is a person in the eyes of the law, it must act through human agents elected by the shareholders, appointed by the directors, or hired by the officers. No shareholder, not even one who owns most or all the stock, can act for the corporation or bind it by contract merely because of such ownership. In the problem, Penny had no authority to represent the corporation.

Shareholders indirectly control the affairs of a corporation by electing the directors. They also have the power to vote on major issues such as changing the corporate articles, merging with another company, or selling out in a corporate take over. Antitrust laws do not forbid acquisitions or mergers of dissimilar companies. Large size in itself is not illegal.

The directors, elected by the shareholders, form a corporation's **board of directors**. The directors, who are duty bound to act in good faith and with due care, oversee the corporation and formulate general policies. They must not act fraudulently or illegally. Most states apply the standard of the Model Business Corporation Act. This requires that the director act "in a manner he reasonably believes to be in the best interests of the corporation, and with such care as an ordinary prudent person in a like position would use under similar circumstances."[2]

board of directors: top governing body of a corporation

[2]Model Business Corporation Act, Section 35.

The board of directors may enter into any contract to promote the business for which the corporation was formed. While the board's powers are very broad, they may be limited by statute, by the articles of incorporation, or by its own corporate rules. In any event, the directors are expected to exercise their best personal judgment in arriving at group decisions regarding the corporation. As a consequence, a director may not have another person serve as substitute at a board meeting and vote. This is true even if the substitute acts according to the director's instructions.

The number of directors varies among corporations. Most states allow the shareholders to determine the number. Some states require at least three. Other states require only one director, who can also be the sole officer and sole shareholder. This gives the corporation the attributes of a sole proprietorship plus the advantage of limited liability for its owner. Statutes sometimes require that directors be shareholders. A few states require that directors be adults. Some states require that the president of the company serve as a director, while in many corporations all the directors are officers. This is called an **inside board**, and is not considered ideal because the directors naturally tend to approve their conduct as officers. Better results are sometimes obtained from an **outside board** which has no officers in its membership, and which presumably scrutinizes corporate performance more objectively and critically. Probably the best form is a **mixed board,** with some officers to provide information and detailed understanding, and some outsiders "to ask the embarrassing questions."

inside board: board of directors in which all the directors are officers

outside board: board of directors with no corporate officers

mixed board: board of directors composed of both officers and outsiders

WHAT ARE THE POWERS AND DUTIES OF THE CORPORATE OFFICERS?

PROBLEM: After Kepler was selected as a vice president of a large American electrical products company, it was disclosed that he was a citizen of the German Democratic Republic (East Germany). Several shareholders sought a court order to compel his dismissal. Was Kepler legally qualified to serve in the position?

The directors employ and delegate to the managing officers of the corporation the necessary authority to conduct the firm's day-to-day business. Corporate managing officers generally include a president, a vice president, a secretary, and a treasurer. However, the duties of two or more of these positions may be combined. Other positions may be created as required. Many states and the Model Business Corporation Act permit one person to hold two or more offices, except that the president may not also serve as secretary. This helps to prevent falsification of records. Officers are usually appointed by the board of directors, although they may be elected by the shareholders. Generally there are no restrictions on the selection of officers. Thus, they do not necessarily have to be shareholders or directors, have certain qualifications, or be a certain age. Accordingly, in the problem, Kepler was legally qualified to serve as vice president.

Because the officers of a corporation are its agents, they are generally governed by principles of agency. Limitations may be imposed by the articles of incorporation, by the governing rules of the corporation, and by the board of directors. Like directors, officers are not liable for honest errors of judgment, however costly, but may be held accountable for willful or negligent acts which cause loss to the corporation.

WHAT ARE THE POWERS OF THE CORPORATION?

> **PROBLEM:** Ruiz organized a corporation in which he owned all the stock. His wife and two daughters were directors with him, and they served as vice president, treasurer, and secretary, respectively, under his direction as president. If Ruiz should die, could the business continue indefinitely because it is a corporation?

In general, a corporation can be formed for any lawful purpose. The corporation is then allowed to exercise all powers that are necessary, convenient, and lawful in achieving that purpose.

Powers vary among corporations, but some are inherent in almost every corporation. These powers include:

1. Perpetual Succession

In most jurisdictions, the corporation is the only form of business organization which may be granted the power of perpetual succession. **Perpetual succession** means that regardless of changes in the shareholders (owners), the corporation may continue indefinitely, or for whatever period originally requested by the incorporators. During this time, the death or withdrawal of a director, manager, or

perpetual succession: power by which a corporation continues despite changes in its shareholder membership

shareholder has no legal effect on the corporation's life. Thus, in the problem, Ruiz's business could continue. Of course, even a corporate business may end when a majority of its owners decide to end it or upon the death or retirement of an officer whose services were essential.

2. Corporate Name

A corporation can select any name to identify itself unless that name is identical or deceptively similar to the name of another business already operating in that geographical area. Most states require that the name selected indicate that the business is a corporation, to alert the public of the limited liability of its owners. This can be done by including a descriptive word in the name, such as Corporation, Incorporated, or Limited, or their abbreviations (Corp., Inc., Ltd.).

Note that any form of business organization (not just the corporate form) can use a fictitious name to identify itself. Most states require that these fictitious names be registered.

The power to have a seal which shows the company name is inherent in corporate existence. However, this power is insignificant because of the declining importance of seals.

3. Bylaws

bylaws: rules for the internal management of a corporation

A corporation can make its own reasonable rules and regulations for the internal management of its affairs. Called **bylaws**, these rules specify times for meetings of shareholders and directors, for example, and define duties of officers.

4. Power to Conduct Its Business

In achieving its purpose(s), a corporation may use any legal means to conduct authorized business. Thus, the corporation has the power, in its own name, to:

bonds: long-term secured notes

debentures: unsecured bonds

a. make contracts and incur liabilities;
b. borrow and loan money;
c. make, indorse, and accept commercial paper;
d. issue various types of stock and **bonds** (long-term notes issued in return for money borrowed and usually secured by a mortgage or deposit of collateral). Unsecured bonds are called **debentures**;
e. mortgage, pledge, lease, sell, or assign its property;
f. buy its own stock unless this would make it impossible for

the corporation to pay its debts or to pay off any superior class of stock;

g. acquire and hold stock in other corporations if such action is not in violation of antitrust laws;
h. make reasonable donations or gifts for civic or charitable purposes to promote goodwill in accord with corporate social responsibility;
i. hire agents, independent contractors, and ordinary employees;
j. establish pension, profit sharing, and other incentive plans for employees; and
k. sue and be sued.

5. Other Implied Powers

A corporation may do any legal act which is necessary or convenient for the execution of its express powers. This would extend to such matters as leasing space and equipment, advertising, and buying life insurance for officers and employees.

WHAT ARE THE RIGHTS OF SHAREHOLDERS?

PROBLEM: Berling owns 400 shares of stock in a corporation that has 1,000 voting shares. Niles and Piper, who together own the remaining 600 shares, decide to keep Berling from electing any one of the three directors. Can they do so?

Status as a shareholder does not give one the right to possess any corporate property or to participate directly in management. However, shareholder status does confer the following important rights:

1. The Right to a Stock Certificate

A shareholder has the right to receive a stock certificate as evidence of ownership of shares in the corporation. One certificate may represent one or more shares.

2. The Right to Transfer Shares

A shareholder generally has the right to sell or to give away any shares owned. However, this right is sometimes limited in closely held corporations, where the owners may want to limit ownership to employees or to members of a given family. Accordingly, the corporation's charter may provide that an owner who wants to sell shares must first offer them to the corporation or to other stockholders.

3. The Right to Attend Shareholder Meetings and, in Some Cases, to Vote

A shareholder may attend shareholder meetings and vote shares owned in any class of stock which has the right to vote. Regular meetings are usually held annually at the place and time designated in the articles or bylaws. Notice of the regular meetings usually is not required. Reasonable notice is required for special meetings.

cumulative voting: plan which gives minority shareholders representation on the board of directors

In a corporate election, a shareholder usually is entitled to the number of votes that equals the number of shares of voting stock held. Having a *minority position* means owning less than 50 percent of the voting shares. To safeguard the interests of such shareholders, many states provide for **cumulative voting** in the election of directors. Under this plan, each shareholder has the right to cast as many votes as the number of shares of stock held multiplied by the number of directors to be elected. The shareholder may cast all available votes for one candidate or distribute them among two or more candidates. Thus, in the problem, if three directors are to be elected by cumulative voting, Berling could concentrate his 1,200 votes on one candidate (400 shares × three positions). Niles and Piper have a combined voting power of 1,800 votes (600 × three positions). They can elect two directors by dividing their votes and casting 900 for each. If cumulative voting were not in effect, Niles and Piper could keep Berling from electing anyone to the board because, with only 400 votes for each position, he would be outvoted each time.

proxy: written authorization designating some person to vote in place of the signer in a corporate election

A shareholder who does not wish to attend meetings and to vote personally ordinarily has the right to vote by **proxy** (see Figure 39-2). Most of the millions of persons who individually own comparatively few shares of stock in various corporations cast their votes in this manner. The management, or anyone seeking control of the corporation, mails the necessary proxy forms to all shareholders and solicits their votes. The shareholders may then sign and return the forms. However, if they are satisfied with the corporation's performance, the shareholders usually give their proxies to incumbent directors, giving them authority to cast the votes. Federal law requires that the proxy form give the shareholder an opportunity to specify by ballot approval or rejection of particular proposals. Proxy

THE BACK-PACK CORPORATION

Proxy

The undersigned hereby appoints GEORGE KINNARD and MARY ANN CONNERLY and each of them, proxies, and with power of substitution (i.e. power to name replacements), to attend the Annual Meeting of shareholders of The Back-Pack Corporation, at the company's main office in Green Bay, Wisconsin, on April 15,19--, commencing at 10 a.m. and any adjournment thereof, and there to vote all the shares of the undersigned for election of Directors, and on any other business that may properly come before the meeting.

Dated: March 20, 19-- Roberta J. Hogan (L.S.)
Signature

Proxy # 125413 Roberta J. Hogan
37 Winona Lane
Account # 0590363 Des Moines, Iowa

Figure 39-2. Proxy

voting, especially when there is no right of cumulative voting, usually enables present directors and officers of large corporations to remain in control indefinitely and then to name their successors. The power of proxy should be exercised with a sense of social responsibility, recognizing the rights not only of owners, but also of employees, customers, and others.

4. The Right to Increase the Capital Stock

Shareholders alone have the right to increase the *capital stock* (total shares of stock) of the corporation. This is usually done by majority vote, on the recommendation of the board of directors. In some corporations, when the capital stock is increased, each shareholder may have a right to purchase additional shares to maintain the percentage of interest in the corporation owned before the increase. This is called the **preemptive right**. It enables shareholders to protect their:

preemptive right: shareholder's right to buy a proportionate number of shares in a new issue of capital stock

a. proportionate interest possessed in past and future profits, and
b. proportionate voting power.

Practically, if there is no preemptive power little usually is lost. Most individual shareholders in larger corporations own too few shares to be concerned about their voting power. The sale of new shares to outsiders brings in new capital which should increase the total profits, thus benefitting all shareholders. Sometimes large blocks of unissued shares are needed by the directors to purchase whole companies; the preemptive right could prevent such action.

5. The Right to a Share of the Profits

Each shareholder is entitled to a proportionate share of the profits which are distributed on the class of stock owned. These dividends are usually paid in money, but they may be in the form of stock shares or other property such as products of the company. Even when profits are earned, the board of directors may decide to retain them in the business for future needs of the firm. In effect, the stockholders are thus forced to make an additional investment in the business. Ideally, this should cause the price of stock to go up, and the stockholders can sell out if they so choose. Under unusual circumstances, courts will intervene to compel distribution of dividends at the request of shareholders who claim that there is an unreasonably large surplus of retained and unused or underutilized earnings.

6. The Right to Share in Distributions of the Capital

If a corporation is dissolved, its creditors have first claim upon the assets of the business. After their claims have been satisfied, any remaining assets or proceeds from the sale of assets (liquidation funds) are distributed to the shareholders. Preferred stockholders generally are given priority over the common stockholders in such a distribution.

7. The Right to Inspect Corporate Books of Account

A shareholder has the right to inspect and to make appropriate records of the accounting books of the corporation. However, this inspection may generally be denied if it is not made at a reasonable time and place, in good faith, and with proper motive. This is in contrast to the open inspection permitted to partners. Yet this restriction is understandable when one realizes that many thousands of persons own shares in large corporations. If the books were open to all without restriction, competitors could buy a few shares simply to gain an unfair advantage by such inspection.

UNDER WHAT CIRCUMSTANCES IS CORPORATE EXISTENCE ENDED?

> **PROBLEM:** According to its articles of incorporation, Fun Foods, Inc., was created to operate restaurants and food stands at the state fair for the duration of the event. When the fair ended, how was the corporate existence terminated?

A variety of reasons may cause the dissolution or termination of a corporation. These include:

1. Agreement of the Shareholders

A corporation terminates upon expiration of the agreed period of its existence. Thus, Fun Foods, Inc., in the problem was automatically terminated when the fair ended, as specified in the articles of incorporation. A corporation may end before the agreed upon time if the shareholders (usually those with a majority of the voting power) voluntarily vote to do so.

2. Forfeiture of the Charter

The state may bring judicial proceedings for the forfeiture of the charter of a corporation that has been guilty of certain acts. Examples of such acts would be (1) fraudulent submission of articles of incorporation, (2) flagrant misuse of corporate powers, and (3) repeated violation of the law. Forfeiture is rare because the state does not monitor corporate affairs, and aggrieved persons can seek other private relief in court.

3. Consolidation or Merger

A **consolidation** of corporations can occur with the approval of the boards of directors and a majority of the shareholders in each of the corporations involved. The two corporations cease to exist and a new corporation is formed.

consolidation: when a new corporation is formed from two separate corporations; $A + B = C$

In a **merger** one corporation absorbs the other. The surviving corporation retains its charter and identity; the other disappears. Again, approval must be given by the directors and by the shareholders of the merging corporations.

merger: when one corporation absorbs another corporation; $A + B = A$ (or B)

A combination through either consolidation or merger must not violate antitrust laws by interfering unreasonably with free competition. An illegal monopoly is where one company controls the supply of goods, excludes competitors, and sets prices.

4. Bankruptcy

The bankruptcy of a corporation does not in itself cause dissolution. However, the bankruptcy proceeding typically leaves the corporation without assets with which to do business. In addition, some state statutes provide that when a corporation is insolvent, its creditors may force dissolution.

5. Court Order

In some states, if a corporation's assets are seriously threatened with irreparable harm because an internal dispute cannot be resolved by the board or the shareholders, a court can order dissolution if interested parties petition for dissolution. This is uncommon.

PREVENTING LEGAL DIFFICULTIES

With the Corporate Form of Business Organization . . .

1. directors, even if outsiders, should take their work seriously. They should obey all laws, carefully study the corporate records, and use independent judgment on policy decisions. To "rubber stamp" management proposals is to invite lawsuits by disgruntled shareholders if losses occur;
2. officers of the corporation should be selected with great care because they make most of the decisions. Also, directors tend to rely on the advice of the officers;
3. shareholders should not routinely sign proxies which give officers control. Shareholders should exercise their voting rights in an intelligent manner after studying the annual reports of the corporation and making a comparison of the corporation's progress with that of similar corporations;
4. shareholders with a minority position have a better chance to be represented on the board if the company uses cumulative voting.
5. it is usually risky to buy stock in new or small, closely held corporations because:
   a. they are more likely to fail,
   b. the majority shareholders may favor themselves with high salaries as officers and pay low or no dividends, and
   c. it may be difficult to sell the shares to others; and
6. the buyer of preferred stock who desires greater assurance of receiving dividends should seek cumulative and participating shares.

Strengthening Your Legal Vocabulary

articles of incorporation
board of directors
bonds
bylaws
closely-held corporation
common stock
consolidation
corporation
cumulative stock
cumulative voting
debentures
dividends
domestic corporation
foreign corporation
incorporators
inside board
liquidation
market price
merger
mixed board
nonprofit corporation
no-par stock
outside board
participating stock
par value
perpetual succession
preemptive right
preferred stock
private corporation
profit-making corporation
promoters
proxy
public corporation
public service corporation
shareholder
shares of stock
stock certificate
Subchapter S corporation

1. Stock (usually nonvoting) which has priority with respect to dividends and distribution of assets upon liquidation of the company.
2. Plan submitted to the state as an application for incorporation. When properly filed, corporate existence begins.
3. Governing body of a corporation which determines major policies, declares dividends, and appoints officers.
4. Person who owns one or more shares of stock.
5. Written evidence of ownership in a corporation.
6. Legal entity, created by government grant, existing separate from its owners, directors, officers, or other employees.
7. Distributions of corporate profits to shareholders.
8. Private corporation whose stock is held by one person or by a small group.
9. Written authorization designating some person to vote in place of the signer in a corporate election.
10. When one corporation absorbs and eliminates another corporation.

Reviewing Important Points

1. A corporation can be created only by government grant—available routinely under incorporation statutes in all states—or under unique circumstances, by special legislative acts of the U.S. Congress.
2. In most states, corporate existence begins when properly prepared articles of incorporation are filed in the office of the Secretary of State. (In some states, certificates of incorporation are issued.)

3. Corporations are favored as a form of business organization because of advantages of (a) perpetual life, (b) limited liability, (c) transferability of shares, (d) access to capital, and (e) professional management. A major disadvantage is double taxation (or quadruple taxation in states with corporate and personal income tax laws). Small corporations may eliminate double federal taxation by electing to be taxed like partnerships, under Subchapter S of the Internal Revenue Code.
4. Shareholders have a right to:
   a. receive a properly executed stock certificate (share),
   b. transfer their shares,
   c. attend shareholder meetings, and vote if they hold voting stock,
   d. maintain their ownership percentage by buying an appropriate portion of new stock issues, if there is a preemptive right,
   e. receive a proportionate share of the profits,
   f. share in distributions of capital, and
   g. inspect the corporate books, subject to reasonable restrictions.
5. Certain classes of shares may be nonvoting. If preferred, they have priority in the distribution of dividends, and capital upon termination.
6. The directors can enter into any contract necessary to promote the business for which the corporation was formed. They are liable only for willful or negligent acts which injure the corporation. As fiduciaries, however, they must act with a high degree of good faith and in the best interests of the corporation.
7. Officers of a corporation, governed by the law of agency and employment, must also act with good faith for the best interests of the corporation. They, too, are liable only for willful or negligent acts which injure the corporation, and are not liable for honest mistakes of judgment.
8. The powers of a corporation include those granted by law, and those incidental to corporate existence, as well as those listed in the articles of incorporation.
9. A corporation's existence may be ended by (a) agreement (i.e., vote) of the shareholders, (b) forfeiture of the charter, (c) consolidation or merger, (d) bankruptcy, or (e) court order.

Applying Law to Everyday Life

1. The Lacklands bought 5,000 shares of stock in Space Age Motion Pictures, Inc., a speculative company created to imitate the fabulous success of producers of space dramas such as "Star Wars." Were the Lacklands correct when they said, "At $25 a share, we can't lose more than $125,000; one big hit and we're millionaires!"?

2. Lomax and Widener were among some 5,000 common shareholders of the Commonwealth Commodities Corporation. They owned 15 percent of the stock and were dissatisfied with the performance of the directors and managers because the company had shown a loss on operations for three suc-

cessive years. Therefore they decided to solicit proxies from the other shareholders in order to elect a new "management team." The incumbent managers refused to let the two inspect the books to get the current list of shareholders. The managers called Lomax and Widener "meddlesome troublemakers" and said, "Losses were caused by world overproduction of grains and the strong U.S. dollar which priced us out of the export market." This was true, according to most experts. Can Lomax and Widener get a court order to compel disclosure of the names?

3. Hull organized a corporation to manufacture antibiotics for cattle. She owned most of the capital stock. All went well until a faulty batch of drugs caused the serious illness or death of more than 3,000 cows. After a series of lawsuits, the corporation was forced into bankruptcy with some $200,000 in debts unpaid. Could Hull be held personally liable for these debts?

4. In a discussion with friends, Fascill insisted that a director of a corporation could not also serve as an officer because this would be "a conflict of interest." "Directors select officers," she argued, "and could keep themselves on the payroll as officers this way." Was Fascill right?

5. Plush Play Products, Ltd., produced toy animals and dolls. A new doll called '"Tootsie Twins" proved to be so popular that the factory could not meet the demand. The dolls were commanding premium prices in toy stores. Shortly before Christmas, the board of directors of Plush Play Products voted a dividend which was to include one pair of the "Twins"—valued at the low $10 cost of production—for each stockholder. All shareholders with more than one share would receive the balance of their dividends in cash. Lane, a stockholder, sued the directors to prohibit the doll distribution. He claimed that the corporation could earn more by selling the dolls. Should the injunction be issued?

6. Cox and Cook had an idea for a natural waterslide. They planned to build a small dam and then to release water for the slide as needed. Keeping their plans secret to be certain that the needed stream would be available, they bought a 2,000-acre tract of land for their Wet n' Wild Ride, Inc., a corporation soon to be formed. (a) At this time, are Cox and Cook liable on the contract? (b) Two months later they organized the corporation. Is the corporation now liable on the contract?

7. All directors of the ABC Avionics Corporation were also officers of the corporation. As directors, all were involved in the unanimous decision to follow the advice of De Moreal, the dynamic president of ABC. He had presented engineering and marketing studies in support of a proposal to build a small helicopter that could also be used as a large automobile on public highways. After further study, the directors, as officers, proceeded with the plan to design, produce, and market the novel vehicle. Unfortunately, many unforeseen problems caused abandonment of the project after the corporation had spent, and thus lost, more than $25 million in develop-

ment costs. Acting on behalf of the corporation, several stockholders sued the directors/officers for the full amount. Are they liable?

Solving Case Problems

1. Pillsbury believed that the American involvement in the Vietnam War was wrong. When he learned that Honeywell, Inc., had a large government contract to produce antipersonnel fragmentation bombs, he became determined to stop such production. Pillsbury learned that a trust set up by his grandmother for his benefit owned 242 shares of the stock, but these shares were voted by the trustee. Therefore Pillsbury bought just one share in his own name. As a shareholder, he petitioned the court to order Honeywell to produce its shareholder ledgers and all records dealing with weapons manufacture. He wanted to communicate with other shareholders to change the board of directors and then to have the corporation stop making munitions. Should the court grant his request? (*Pillsbury v. Honeywell, Inc.*, 291 Minn. 322, 191 N.W.2d 406)

2. A group of shareholders of the Manganese Corporation of America sued the corporation and four officers who were also directors. The group of shareholders sought to recover damages for the corporation and all its shareholders. They claimed that the officers and directors had negligently caused the corporation's assets to drop from $400,000 to $30,000 in less than two years. Are the officers and directors liable for the losses? (*Selheimer et al. v. Manganese Corporation of America et al.*, 423 Pa. 563, 224 A.2d 634)

3. General Telephone Company of Florida owned more than 1 percent of the stock of Florida Telephone Corporation. General sought to examine the latter's stock records in order to make a list of the names, addresses, and holdings of all shareholders. Florida refused, claiming that General intended to gain this information in order to buy more shares and thus get control of the corporation. Can General get a court order to compel the disclosure? (*Florida Telephone Corporation v. State ex rel. Peninsular Telephone Co.*, 111 So.2d 677, Fla.)

4. This is a derivative suit, brought on behalf of all the shareholders of the corporation. Schlensky, a minority stockholder in the Chicago National League Ball Club (Inc.)—owner of the Chicago Cubs—sued the corporation and its board of directors, including Philip K. Wrigley. Wrigley also was president and owned about 80 percent of the voting stock. Schlensky alleged negligence and mismanagement for failure to install floodlights to permit night games. He claimed that funds for the installation could be obtained and would be far more than recaptured by increased ticket sales. Allegedly Wrigley thought that baseball was a daytime sport and that night games would have a deteriorating effect on the neighborhood surrounding the ball park and the other directors acquiesced. The trial court dismissed the complaint, and Schlensky appealed. How should the appellate court rule? (*Schlensky v. Wrigley, et al.*, 237 N.E.2d 776, Ill.)

Glossary of Legal Terms

A

abstract of title: history of transfers of title to a parcel of land
acceptance: drawee's promise to pay the draft when due; also, affirmative response to an offer; also, buyer's approval of goods
accord and satisfaction: agreement to change a contractual obligation, followed by the agreed-upon substituted performance
actual cash value: property's purchase price less allowance for age and use
administrative agencies: governmental bodies which administer certain statutes
administrator or administratrix: court-appointed representative of an intestate
adoption: legally taking another's child as one's own
adverse possession: means of getting title to another's land by occupation without the owner's permission
affirmative action: positive efforts to end discrimination
agency: relationship in which one person represents another in making contracts
agency shop: establishment in which nonunion members must pay union dues
annuity: option that pays the beneficiary a specified sum at regular intervals until death
annulment: judicial declaration that a marriage never existed
answer: defendant's statement in reply to the plaintiff's complaint
antedated: dated earlier than the date of issuance
anticipatory breach: notification, before the time of performance, of refusal to perform the contractual terms as agreed
apparent authority: power the agent appears to have
appellate court: court that reviews trial court decisions
arbitrator: one who makes a decision that is binding on parties in a dispute
arraignment: court proceeding where the defendant pleads guilty or not guilty to the formal charge of a crime
articles of incorporation: plan submitted to the state as an application for incorporation
assault: placing another in fear of harmful or offensive touching
assessments: special taxes on real property
assignment: transfer of contractual rights
attestation: act of witnessing the execution of a will

B

bail: deposit of money to guarantee appearance at one's trial
bailment: transfer of possession of personal property without transfer of ownership
bank draft: draft drawn by one bank as a depositor in a second bank
bankruptcy: legal proceedings whereby a debtor's assets are distributed among creditors and debts are discharged
bargaining unit: group of workers joined together to select a bargaining representative and to negotiate with an employer
barter: exchange of goods for goods
battery: harmful or offensive touching of another
bearer paper: paper issued or indorsed so as to be collectible by the party in possession of it
beneficiary: person who receives real or personal property under a will; also, recipient of insurance policy proceeds
bequest: a gift, by will, of personal property
bilateral contract: agreement in which both parties make promises
bill of sale: receipt serving as written evidence of the transfer of ownership of goods
binder: agent's written notation of an oral agreement to insure
blank indorsement: indorsement that consists of the indorser's signature only
board of directors: top governing body of a corporation
bodily injury insurance: insurance which protects against liability for bodily injury to or death of others
bonds: long-term secured notes
boycott: refusal to deal with the goods or services of an employer
breach of contract: failure to perform the terms as agreed
bribery: offering, giving, or receiving money to influence official action
bulk transfer: transfer of all or a major part of the goods of a business
burglary: illegally entering a building with the intent to commit a crime
business: production or sale of goods or services for a profit
bylaws: rules for the internal management of a corporation

C

cancellation: ending a contract for sale of goods because of breach, while retaining other remedies; also, any act that shows an intent to end the obligation of payment of commercial paper
capacity: ability to understand the nature and effects of one's actions
carrier: transporter of passengers or goods
case law: law created by appellate courts
cashier's check: check drawn by a bank on itself
cash surrender value: amount of savings and accumulated interest of an insurance policy
casualty insurance: insurance that indemnifies the insured for loss due to accident, chance, or negligence
caveat emptor: let the buyer beware
caveat venditor: let the seller beware
certificate of deposit: unconditional written promise of a bank to repay with interest a deposit of money at a certain future date
certified check: personal check accepted by the bank in advance of payment
check: a type of draft in which a depositor orders his or her bank to pay deposited funds to a third party or to bearer
citation: order requiring a defendant to appear in court
citizenship: membership in a civil and political community
civil disobedience: peaceful violation of a law thought to be unjust
civil law: law concerned with private wrongs against individuals
civil rights: personal, natural rights guaranteed by our Constitution
class actions: legal suits brought on behalf of large groups
closed shop: establishment in which only union members may be hired

closely-held corporation: private corporation whose stock is held by one or a few persons
COD: collect on delivery
codicil: a modification of a will, executed with the same formality as the will
coinsurance: policy clause resulting in the insurer and the insured sharing the risk of fire loss
collateral: personal property subject to a security interest
collective bargaining: negotiations between representatives of employees and employers
collision insurance: insurance which protects against damage to the insured's vehicle caused by collision or by upset
collusion: agreement to misrepresent facts to gain an advantage
commercial paper: unconditional written orders or promises to pay money
common law: case law, reflecting customs of the people
community property: property owned equally by spouses
comparative negligence: system in which damages are awarded in proportion to the plaintiff's negligence
compensatory damages: amount awarded to make good the plaintiff's loss
complaint: first paper in a civil action, filed by the plaintiff, stating the claim for judgment
composition of creditors: agreement of all creditors to accept a proportion of their claims as full payment
compounding a crime: accepting something of value for a promise not to prosecute a suspected criminal
compromise of a disputed claim: mutual promises to refrain from bringing suit
concealment: failure to reveal material facts
confess judgment: to allow a plaintiff to obtain a judgment without a trial
consent order: voluntary agreement to stop an illegal practice
consideration: what one gives and receives in a contract
consignment: bailment for sale purposes
consolidation: when a new corporation is formed from two separate corporations; $A + B = C$
conspiracy: agreement to commit a crime
constituents: those who elect someone to represent them
constitution: a supreme source of law for a government
constructive bailment: bailment created by law when there is no agreement
constructive eviction: when property becomes so unfit for habitation through fault of landlord that the tenant is forced to abandon it
constructive notice: knowledge, presumed by law, of facts on file
consumer: a buyer of goods primarily intended for personal, family, or household use
contempt of court: willful disrespect to a court or disobedience of its orders
contingent beneficiary: beneficiary designated to receive the policy proceeds if the primary beneficiary dies before the insured
contract: legally binding agreement
contract of adhesion: contract in which the more powerful party dictates all the important terms
contributory negligence: system in which recovery is barred if the injury is partly the result of carelessness by the plaintiff
conversion: wrongfully depriving another of possession of personal property
conveyance: transfer of title to real property
copyright: government grant of exclusive right to possess, produce, and publish an intellectual production
corporation: artificial legal person, separate and distinct from its owners, created under the laws of a state or the nation
counteroffer: reply to an offer, with new terms; ends the original offer
court: tribunal established to administer justice
creditor: one to whom a debt is owed
credit rating: evaluation of one's ability to pay debts
credit sale: sale in which, by agreement, payment for goods is made at a later date
crime: a punishable offense against society
criminal law: law concerned with public wrongs against society
cumulative stock: shares where dividends, if not paid, remain due and payable before common shareholders get anything
cumulative voting: plan which gives minority shareholders representation on the board of directors
custody: care and present control of another's personal property, under the owner's direction

D

damages: monetary compensation for loss or injury
days of grace: period during which an insurance policy remains in force after the premium is due
debentures: unsecured bonds
debt: that which is owed
decedent: one who has died
deed: writing which conveys title and other rights of ownership to real property
deed of trust: document that is equivalent to a mortgage but that involves a more expedient remedy for default
defamation: injury of a person's reputation by false statements, oral or written
default judgment: judgment given (without a trial) to the plaintiff when the defendant fails to answer the complaint
defendant: person against whom a criminal (or civil) action is brought
delegation of duties: turning over to another party one's routine contractual duties
demurrage: fees for delay by consignor in loading or by consignee in unloading
deposition: pretrial questioning of the opposing party and witnesses under oath
devise: a gift, by will, of real property
disaffirmance: refusal to carry out a voidable contract
disclaimer: notice of exclusion
discovery procedures: court-ordered means of getting facts about the dispute from the opposing party and witnesses before the trial
dishonor: to refuse to pay an instrument when due
dissolution: when any partner ceases association in carrying on the business
dividends: distributions of corporate profits to shareholders
domestic corporation: chartered in the state in which it is doing business
dormant partner: partner who is neither known to the public nor active in management
draft: unconditional written order by one party to a second party to pay a third party a certain sum on demand or at a definite time

drawee: one directed to pay a draft
drawer: one who executes a draft
due process: the constitutional requirement that investigations and trials be conducted in fair and orderly ways
duress: overpowering of another's free will through coercion or by illegal imprisonment

E

easement: right to use land owned and possessed by another party
emancipation: release by parents of their parental rights
embargoes: laws banning export and import trade with specified countries
embezzlement: fraudulent taking of money or other property entrusted to one's care
eminent domain: governmental power to take private property for public use in exchange for the fair market price
employment: a contract to pay for supervised work
encumbrances: claims of third parties
equipment: goods used by a business in performing its function
equity: form of justice administered when there is no suitable remedy available in common law courts
escheat: passing of an intestate's property to the state because there are no close relatives
escrow: money or papers delivered to a third party to hold until certain conditions are fulfilled
estate: all the property owned by a decedent at death
ethical principles: basic conclusions about what is right and wrong
eviction: removal of the tenant from possession of all real property by action of the landlord
evidence: anything that provides information used to prove or disprove alleged facts
executed contract: contract that has been fully performed
execution: process by which a judgment for money is enforced by court order
executor or executrix: personal representative named by the testator to carry out the directions in the will
executory contract: contract that has not been fully performed
existing goods: goods that are physically in existence and are owned by the seller
expatriation: act of voluntarily giving up citizenship
extended term insurance: option that uses the cash value of the original policy to buy term insurance without further premiums
extortion: obtaining property wrongfully by force, fear, or the power of office
extraordinary bailment: bailment requiring an unusually high standard of care

F

face value: stated maximum amount to be paid in the event of the insured loss
false and misleading advertising: untrue claims of quality or effectiveness about goods or services offered for sale
false pretenses: obtaining property by lying
featherbedding: forcing an employer to pay for work not done or not to be done
felony: serious crime punishable by death or imprisonment for more than one year
fidelity bond: an insurance policy which pays the employer in case of theft by an employee
fiduciary duties: duties which require one to serve the best interests of another
finance charge: added cost for the payment in installments for goods or services
financing statement: brief, written notice of the existence of a security agreement
firm offer: a binding offer stating in writing how long it is to be held open
fixtures: personal property so closely associated with realty that it becomes part of the real estate
floater: insurance protection that follows the property
FOB: free on board
forbearance: refraining from doing what one has a right to do
foreign corporation: chartered in a state other than the one in which it is doing business
forgery: making or materially altering any writing, with intent to defraud
formal contract: written contract that must be in a special form to be enforceable
fraud: intentional misrepresentation of fact, relied upon by another to her or his injury
friendly fire: fire in its intended place
fringe benefits: special compensation paid in excess of wage or salary
full warranty: warranty that obligates a seller to repair or to replace a product without cost and within a reasonable time
fungible goods: goods of a homogeneous nature
future goods: goods that are either not existing or not identified

G

garnishment: court-granted right to intercept a debtor's wages for the purpose of paying a debt
general partnership: partnership in which all partners are fully liable; also, a partnership formed to conduct a general business
genuine assent: consent that is not negated by fraud, duress, undue influence, or mistake
gift: voluntary transfer of ownership without consideration
good faith: honesty in business conduct and transactions
goods: items of tangible, movable personal property
grand jury: group of citizens selected to hear evidence of alleged felonies
gratuitous agency: agency relationship in which the agent receives no consideration
gratuitous bailment: bailment which benefits only one party
group life insurance: insurance that covers all members of a group
guaranty: relationship in which a third party becomes secondarily liable for a debt upon default of the principal debtor
guardian: person who acts in place of parents
guardian ad litem: adult named to sue or defend on behalf of a minor
guest laws: claims which disallow suits based on ordinary negligence, brought by guests against drivers

H

heirs: those who receive the property of a person who dies without a valid will
holder: a party in possession of bearer paper or paper payable to the possessor's order

holder in due course (HDC): a holder who takes in good faith, for value, and without notice of defect or dishonor
holographic will: will written entirely in the testator's own handwriting
honor: to pay an instrument when due
hostile fire: fire started by accident, negligence, or arson; or friendly fire that becomes uncontrollable
hotelkeeper: one who furnishes rooms for transients
hung jury: jury unable to agree unanimously upon a verdict

I

identified goods: goods that are specifically selected as the subject matter of a particular contract
immunity: freedom from prosecution
incidental beneficiary: one who benefits from a contract but is not a party to it and cannot enforce it
incontestable clause: clause which disallows insurer's avoidance of a contract due to misrepresentations or concealment by the applicant
incorporators: persons who sign and submit the articles of incorporation
indemnify: to make good a loss
independent contractor: one retained to accomplish a specific result without supervision
indictment: accusation by a grand jury declaring there is reason to try a person for a crime
indorse: to sign on the reverse of the paper
infraction: minor misdemeanor punishable by a fine
inheritance tax: tax imposed on the right to receive property from a decedent at death
injunction: order of a court to do or not to do a specified thing
inside board: board of directors in which all the directors are officers
insurable interest: direct financial interest in the life of the insured or in the insured property
insurance: contract to pay for a specified loss if the loss occurs
intangible property: real value in rights to money, goods, or contractual performance
interstate commerce: commerce between two or more states which can be regulated by the federal government
intestate: one who dies without a valid will
intrastate commerce: commerce occurring within one state which cannot be regulated by the federal government
invasion of privacy: unlawful intrusion into another's private life causing mental or emotional injury
inventory: business goods that are intended for sale or lease

J

joint tenancy: co-ownership with the right of survivorship
joint venture: association of two or more firms or persons to do a single project
judgment: final result of a trial
justice: treating everyone fairly and impartially
juveniles: persons under the age of majority

L

labor union: organization of employees formed to negotiate with employers
land: surface of, matter beneath, and airspace above the earth, along with things permanently attached or embedded
landlord: person conveying possession of real property through a lease
lapse: to no longer be in effect
larceny: wrongful taking of money or other personal property
laws: rules of conduct made by the lawmaking authorities
lease: agreement in which possession of real property is exchanged for rent
legal rate of interest: rate of interest set by statute
legal tender: United States currency or coins
liability insurance: a type of casualty insurance protecting against claims arising from the insured's negligence
libel: written defamation
lien: a security interest giving the creditor the right to force the sale of the property to recover the debt amount
life insurance: insurance in which an insurer promises to pay a specified amount upon the death of a person
limited defenses: defenses good against all but an HDC or a holder through an HDC
limited partnership: partnership in which certain partners have limited liability
liquidated damages: amount agreed upon in advance of possible breach
liquidation: sale of corporate assets upon termination
litigate: to take a dispute to court
loan value: same as the cash surrender value; may be borrowed against the policy
lockout: shutdown of operations by an employer to bring pressure on employees
loss leaders: selected items sold at a loss to attract customers to buy costlier goods
lottery: gamble involving a payment to play, a winner determined by luck, and a prize to some participants

M

majority: age at which one is legally bound to contracts
maker: one who executes a promissory note or a certificate of deposit
material fact: fact which influences a decision
mediation: attempt by a neutral third party to achieve a compromise between two parties in a dispute
Medicaid: state-administered program for those without the income or resources to meet medical expenses
Medicare: governmental program to help pay hospital and other bills for eligible persons
merchant: one who regularly sells a particular kind of goods
merchantable: reasonably fit for normal use
merger: when one corporation absorbs another corporation; $A + B = A$ (or B)
minor: person who is under the age to have full adult rights and duties
misbranding: failure to state required facts on a label
misdemeanor: crime of a less serious nature punishable by fine and/or jail up to one year
mitigate: to reduce damages if reasonably possible
mixed board: board of directors composed of both officers and outsiders
mortgage: written document allowing the right of foreclosure

mutual-benefit bailment: bailment which benefits both bailor and bailee
mutual insurance company: insurance company owned by the insureds

N

naturalized persons: aliens who have become citizens
natural laws: laws which reflect ethical principles
natural rights: rights to which all persons are entitled because they are human beings
necessaries: goods and services essential to maintain one's lifestyle
negligence: causing injury by failing to act as a reasonable person
negotiability: quality of a properly transferred instrument which protects qualified transferees against certain defenses
negotiation: the proper transfer of a negotiable instrument
nominal partner: person who is held out as a partner but is not one
nonforfeiture options: ways of using the cash value if insurance policy lapses
nonprofit corporation: private corporation organized for a social, charitable, or educational purpose; does not return a financial profit to its members
no-par stock: share with no face value specified
novation: substitution of a party, creating a new contract
nuncupative will: oral will made during the testator's last illness

O

obligor: debtor
offer: proposal to enter into a legal agreement
omnibus clause: insurance clause which covers all drivers who are members of the insured's household and any person who is not a member but is permitted to drive the insured's car
open shop: establishment in which nonunion members do not pay union dues
option: underlying contract to keep an offer open
order paper: paper that is issued or indorsed to the order of a specified person
ordinance: statutory law created by a town, city, or county
outlawed debt: one that cannot be legally enforced because of the statute of limitations
outside board: board of directors with no corporate officers

P

pardon: release from all punishment
parity price ratio: balance between the prices farmers pay and receive
parole: early release of a prisoner with suspension of the remainder of the prisoner's sentence
parol evidence rule: rule that bars use of prior written or spoken words to alter a written contract which appears to be complete
participating policies: life insurance policies on which dividends are paid
participating stock: shares where after regular dividends are received, preferred stockholders share in further distribution of profits with common stockholders
partnership: association of two or more persons to carry on, as co-owners, a business for profit
par value: face value printed on a stock certificate
past consideration: value given before a contract is made
patent: government grant of exclusive right to make, use, and sell a product or process which is novel, non-obvious, and useful
pawn: pledge of tangible personal property
payee: one to whom commercial paper is payable
payment: buyer's delivery and seller's acceptance of the price
perfected security interest: protected interest resulting from the creditor's possession of collateral or the creditor's filing of a financing statement
performance: fulfillment of an agreement as promised
periodic tenancy: a lease for a renewable period with rent due at stated intervals
perjury: lying under oath
perpetual succession: power by which a corporation continues despite changes in its shareholder membership
personal property: tangible, movable property and intangible property
picket: walk with signs at employer's business to publicize dispute or influence opinion
plaintiff: one who brings a civil action
plea bargaining: pleading guilty to a less serious crime
pledge: situation in which personal property is given to a creditor as security
policy: written contract of insurance
postdated: dated later than the date of issuance
power of attorney: writing that appoints an agent
preemption: when federal law takes the place of conflicting state law
preemptive right: shareholder's right to buy a proportionate number of shares in a new issue of capital stock
preferred stock: shares with priority claims to dividends and liquidation funds; usually nonvoting
premium: consideration for an insurance contract
prescription: means of getting an easement to another's land by use without the owner's permission
price: consideration for a sale or a contract to sell
primary beneficiary: beneficiary designated to receive the policy proceeds if still alive at the time of death of the insured
primary boycott: boycott directed mainly against the struck employer
principal: one who authorizes an agent to make contracts
principal debtor: one who originally owes a debt in a three-party arrangement
private carrier: transporter of goods or members of its own organization only
private corporation: established by private citizens for a business or charitable purpose
privity of contract: relationship of persons who are parties to the same contract
probation: punishment allowing liberty under court-ordered supervision
procedural law: rules for enforcement of legal rights and duties
proceeds: money paid to the beneficiary of the policy
product liability: responsibility for injury caused by a defective product, based on warranty, fraud, negligence, or strict liability

profit: right to extract something from another's land
profit-making corporation: private corporation organized to produce a financial profit for its owners
promissory estoppel: when a promise is enforced even though no consideration is given for it
promissory note: unconditional written promise by one party to pay a certain sum of money to the order of another party on demand or at a definite time
promoters: persons who bring together interested persons and take preliminary steps to form a corporation
property: things and the corresponding group of legal rights and interests
prorate: to divide proportionately
prosecution: state as the party bringing a legal action against a person accused of a crime
proximate cause: reasonably foreseeable cause of injury
proxy: written authorization designating some person to vote in place of the signer in a corporate election
publication: act of informing attesting witnesses that the document being signed is the testator's will
public corporation: established for a governmental purpose
puffing: exaggerated sales talk
punishment: penalty imposed for committing a crime
punitive or exemplary damages: added damages intended to punish and make an example of the defendant

Q

qualified indorsement: an indorsement that eliminates an indorser's signature-based liability to later transferees
quasi contract: circumstances under which the parties are bound as in a valid contract to prevent unjust enrichment
quitclaim deed: deed which conveys the grantor's interest without warranties

R

ratification: approval of a voidable contract; also, approval of a previously unauthorized act
rationalization: using obviously invalid reasoning to justify an action or belief
real property: land and things permanently attached to the land
receipt of goods: buyer's taking of physical possession or control of goods
recognizance: promise of the accused person to appear in court, without posting bail
reinstate: to place an insurance policy back in force
remedy: means used to enforce a right or compensate for an injury
representations: statements of an applicant which are not part of the final insurance contract
rescission: return of parties to position before contract was made with no damages
restitution: restoring or making good a loss; repayment of money illegally obtained
restrictive indorsement: indorsement that indicates the use of the proceeds or imposes a condition on payment
revocation: withdrawal of an offer before acceptance
rider: attachment to a policy that alters the terms
right of foreclosure: right to have property that is subject to a mortgage sold to satisfy the debt
right of survivorship: right of one joint tenant to ownership of property when the other joint tenant dies
right-to-work-laws: state laws which ban both the union shop and the closed shop
risk: possible loss covered by an insurance contract
robbery: taking of property by force from the person or presence of another
Roman civil law: body of regulations imposed by emperors of ancient Rome

S

sale: contract in which ownership of goods passes immediately from the seller to the buyer for a price
sanctions: penalties for violations of legal orders
satisfaction: performance of a new contractual obligation
scofflaw: a person who does not respect nor comply with certain laws
scope of authority: within the range of authorized acts
secondary boycott: boycott directed mainly against third parties who deal with the struck employer
secret partner: partner who is not known to the public but is active in management
secured transaction: business deal in which a creditor gets a security interest in personal property
security interest: the creditor's right to enforce the debt against specific property of the debtor
selective perception: distortion of reality caused by attitudes or self-interest
self-defense: reasonable and lawful resistance to attack
settlement options: ways that the proceeds of a life insurance policy may be paid
shares of stock: units of ownership in a corporation
sight draft: draft payable on sight
silent partner: partner who may be known to the public but is not active in management
simple contract: contract that is not formal
slander: oral defamation
social insurance: indemnification from financial consequences of unemployment, retirement, and other social concerns
sole proprietorship: unincorporated business owned by one person
special indorsement: an indorsement that makes the paper payable to the order of a designated party
special partnership: formed to carry out a single transaction
specific performance: completion of an agreement as promised
standards: prescribed measures
stare decisis, doctrine of: the principle that new cases must be decided in ways consistent with prior case law
status offenses: acts which are wrongful because of the offender's age
statute: law enacted by a state or federal legislature
statute of frauds: law requiring certain contracts to be in writing and signed by the defendant in order to be enforceable
stock certificate: written evidence of ownership and rights in a corporation
stock insurance company: profit-making insurance company owned by shareholders
stop payment order: an order directing a bank not to pay on a check
strict liability: responsibility for injury regardless of negligence or intent

strike: concerted work stoppage by employees to bring pressure on the employer
Subchapter S corporation: small corporation taxed as a partnership
subletting: tenant's transferring part of interest to another
subpoena: written order commanding a person to appear in court as a witness
subrogation: assigned right, by operation of law, to recover damages
subsidy: financial assistance
substantial performance: incomplete but acceptable performance of contractual terms
substantive law: rules that define legal rights and duties
summons: court order directing the defendant to answer the plaintiff's complaint
suretyship: relationship in which a third party becomes primarily liable for a debt upon default of the principal debtor

T

tenancy: ownership interest in property
tender: offer to perform an obligation
termination statement: publicly filed acknowledgment that a secured debt has been paid off
testator or testatrix: a person who makes a will
third party beneficiary: one who is not a party to a contract but benefits from it and can enforce it
time draft: draft payable at a specified time or after a specified period
tort: an offense against an individual
trade fixtures: business appliances attached to rented real property used in a business
trademark: distinctive word, device, or symbol that identifies a product or service
trade secret: unpatented formula or process not known to others and which is valuable in business
trading partnership: formed to buy and to sell commercially
transcript: copy of the written record of a trial
trespass: wrongful interference with the use of another's property
trial court: court where a dispute is first heard
trust: a legal arrangement whereby one party holds title to property for the benefit of another

U

unconscionable contract: grossly unfair and oppressive agreement
undue influence: overpowering another's free will to take unfair advantage in a contract
unemployment compensation: governmental payment to lessen consequences of job loss
unfair labor practices: union or employer acts which violate the rights of employees with respect to union activity
unfair trade practice: dishonest or illegal method of business competition
unilateral contract: agreement in which only one of the parties makes a promise
unilateral mistake: important contractual mistake made by only one of the parties
union shop: establishment in which all workers must join the union within a prescribed period
universal defenses: defenses good against all obligees
unqualified indorser: an indorser with signature-based liability to later transferees
unsatisfied judgment funds: pools of money used to pay uncollectible judgments
unsecured debt: debt based only on a promise to pay
usury: charging a higher interest rate than that permitted by law

V

vendee: buyer
vendor: seller
verdict: decision of a jury
vicarious liability: responsibility of one person for the torts of another

W

waiver: voluntarily giving up a legal right
warehouser: one who stores goods for profit
warranty: a statement of product qualities which the seller assures is true; also, statement of an applicant that is part of the final insurance contract
white-collar crimes: nonviolent crimes committed by respected persons or corporations
will: legal expression of how a person's property is to be distributed after the person dies
winding-up period: time during which all business affairs of a partnership are concluded
witness: person who has personal knowledge of the facts
workers' compensation: laws creating an insurance program for injury to employees

Index

Italic page numbers are used to indicate the page(s) on which terms are defined.

D

E

F

G

Q

R

S